Malaŵi Cichlids
in their natural habitat
Fourth Edition

Malaŵi Cichlids
in their natural habitat
Fourth Edition

Ad Konings

Contents

Introduction 5
The lake 8
The cichlids, a species flock 13
Malaŵian cichlid taxonomy 24
The wave-washed upper rocky habitat 28
The sediment-free rocky habitat 48
The deep, sediment-rich rocky habitat 129
The intermediate habitat 172
The shallow intermediate habitat 264
Shallow sediment-rich bays 280
The sandy habitat 305
The unknown depths 388
References 412
Index 416

Photo cover: A male *Aulonocara gertrudae* in Chiofu Bay, Malaŵi.
Photo endpapers: Chiofu Bay.
Photo back-cover by Larry Johnson.

All photographs in this book by the author unless otherwise credited.

ISBN 978-1-932892-05-5

Copyright © 2007 by Cichlid Press
All rights reserved.
No part of this publication may be reproduced, stored in a retrieval system, or transmitted in any form or by any means — electronic (such as internet web sites), mechanical, photocopying, recording, or otherwise — without the prior permission of the author and publisher.

Cichlid Press, P.O. Box 13608, El Paso, TX 79913, USA
www.cichlidpress.com

Printed by Graspo CZ, a.s., Zlín, Czech Republic.

Dedication

This book is dedicated to Stuart M. Grant of Salima, Malaŵi, who for over 35 years introduced many new and exciting fishes into the aquarium hobby and delighted countless visiting aquarists with his very generous hospitality. His passing away on Oct 11th 2007 ended an important era in cichlid history. Malaŵi will never be the same again without him.

Introduction

No lake in the world contains such a diversified and distinct community of cichlid fishes as Lake Malaŵi. Over the years Malaŵi cichlids, which are among the most colorful freshwater fishes known, have become very popular among aquarists as they are easy to maintain and breed in captivity.

When the first edition of this book appeared in 1989, aquarists were for the first time provided with accurate first-hand information on the natural environment of their cichlids, enabling them to set up a Malaŵi aquarium suited to the specific requirements of its occupants. With the importation of ever-increasing numbers of species from the lake over the years, subsequent editions have continued to play an important role in encouraging the use of aquaria designed to simulate the natural habitats of the different groups. Not all Malaŵi cichlids require a tank full of rocks!

As in the previous editions, in this new book I have attempted to provide up-to-date information, chiefly about natural behavior, on every species that has been observed in the lake, with accounts of new species and of interesting and unusual behavior. In total 843 species—including all those that have been scientifically described—are mentioned, and most of these can be observed in the relatively shallow waters of the lake.

In addition, in recent years many new species have been discovered in the deeper layers of the lake, collected using gill nets, but for these virtually no behavioral data are as yet available. Although the main emphasis of this book is on natural behavior, these species are included for completeness and grouped together in the final chapter of the book, "The unknown depths", and because so little behavioral and environmental information on them are available, they are portrayed mainly by photographs, often of the preserved specimens. For those with a further interest in these species, the formal descriptions of about 40 taxa can be found in *The Cichlid Diversity of Lake Malaŵi/Nyasa/Niassa* edited by Jos Snoeks (2004), and an even larger number of undescribed species from deep waters are detailed by George Turner (1996) in his book *Offshore Cichlids of Lake Malaŵi*. Full details of both works will be found in the references at the end of this book.

The total number of cichlid species in the lake is now estimated at about 1000, which is about 200 species more than all the freshwater fish species of the North American Continent combined! And there is every indication that still more remain to be discovered.

This book represents the distillation of an extensive collection of data, photographs, observations, and ideas, and could never have come into being without the aid of a large number of friends. Without the very generous support of Stuart Grant, collector of tropical fishes in Salima, Malaŵi, it would have been impossible to make expeditions such as I have made along the shores of the lake. Jay Stauffer (Penn State University, Pennsylvania) has generously supported me on numerous expeditions and together we have collected tens of thousands of specimens for species descriptions for years to come. Many friends have accompanied and assisted me on various expeditions, and I would in particular like to thank Martin Geerts, Steve Somermeyer, and Lars Andersson.

It is with great appreciation that I thank Martin Geerts, Mary Bailey, Patrick Tawil, Jay Stauffer, George Turner, Martin Genner, and, in particular, the late Ethelwynn Trewavas, for sharing with me their vast knowledge of cichlids. A special word of thanks goes again to Mary Bailey as she has meticulously corrected and immensely improved the manuscript, and thus saved me from several blunders. Most of all I would like to thank my wife Gertrud for continuing to put up with her "cichlidiot" husband.

Ad Konings, Fall 2007

The lake and its habitats

When David Livingstone, on one of his many expeditions through Africa, stumbled upon Lake Malaŵi, he asked the natives the name of this impressive body of water. The fishermen told him "Nyassa", and Livingstone thus named it Lake Nyassa, unaware of the fact that *nyassa* itself means lake. Lake Malaŵi (its present name in Malaŵi) or Lake Nyasa, as it is known in Tanzania and Mozambique, is of great importance to Africans. Tens of thousands of tons of fish are harvested from the lake each year. Fish—mainly *utaka* (haplochromine cichlids), *chambo* (tilapiine cichlids), catfish, and *usipa* (lake sardines)—enrich the daily meal of *msima*, a type of corn flour, of the Africans living in the area.

The lake, the ninth largest in the world, is approximately 600 km long and, at some locations, 80 km wide. It has a maximum depth of 700 meters and its surface lies 472 meters above sea level. It covers an area of about 31,000 km² and is bordered by three countries. Most of the lake (the western and southern part) belongs to Malaŵi, the northeastern section to Tanzania, and a relatively large stretch of the eastern coast is under the jurisdiction of Mozambique. Two important islands, Likoma and Chizumulu, lie in Mozambique waters but belong to Malaŵi. Taiwanee Reef, a rocky reef about 7 km north of Chizumulu Island and previously known as Taiwan Reef, also lies in Mozambique waters, although only Malaŵian fishermen ply their nets there.

The lake's setting in the tropics prevents the surface waters from becoming much colder than the deeper layers, thus preventing any extensive vertical circulation of the water—although there is some. Only the upper 200 meters of the water column are sufficiently oxygenated to support life other than the anaerobic micro-organisms prevailing in the anoxic (and somewhat colder) layer below. The southeasterly wind (*mwera*)—most prevalent during the dry season from June to August—induces an upwelling of the somewhat colder layers in the most southerly parts of the lake, lowering the surface temperature in that region to 20 °C. In the rainy season (November to April), temperatures in sheltered bays may rise to above 30 °C. The average surface temperature, however, ranges from 23 to 28 °C.

The chemical composition of the water is rather uniform throughout the lake. Its pH, a measure of acidity/alkalinity, varies between 7.8 and 8.5. The difference between these two values is due mainly to the carbon dioxide (CO_2) content of the water. In the surf zone gas exchange is optimal, reducing the CO_2 content so that the pH is higher than in sheltered bays or deeper layers. The conductivity, a measure of the mineral content, ranges between 200 and 260 microSiemens, which is relatively low in comparison with the other lakes of the East African Rift Valley.

The seasonal variation in temperature and precipitation see a concomitant change in the visibility under water: this can change drastically from no visibility at all (less than a centimeter) on a hot day in February to more than 20 meters on a windless day in October. Areas with a rocky bottom support clearer water than those with a muddy substrate, but in general algae blooms account for the most important clouding of offshore waters. During the rainy season sediment-laden water from temporary rivers reduces visibility to zero for a few kilometers offshore.

The rains can be sufficiently heavy to cause the lake level to rise by more than a meter in a single month (e.g. in January 2003), and by the end of the rainy season (in May) it can be two meters higher than at the end of the dry (and windy) season (in November), as the only outlet from the lake is the Shiré river at its southern tip. Beside this annual fluctuation, the water level has changed visibly over longer periods of time. After reaching its highest recorded stand in August 1980 the water level dropped by several meters (!) during the years that followed.

During its history the lake level has dropped dramatically on several occasions. Scholz & Rosendahl (1988) found evidence that Lake Malaŵi was much smaller some 25,000 years ago as the water level reached a stand about 400 meters (!) below today's level. This low stand prevailed long enough to leave traces of a paleo-shoreline that can be detected by echo-sounding across the entire lake. The smaller paleo-lake was still a single lake and not divided into several lakes, as happened in Lake Tanganyika. Since that period the water level has increased as has the sediment on the bottom. It has been estimated that a layer of sediment about 40 meters deep has accumulated during the last 25,000 years. The total layer of sediment nowadays has a depth of four (!) kilometers, which points to an age of more than two million years for Lake Malaŵi. The latest estimates range between three and 20 million years.

It is generally accepted that such periods of low water level—examination of sediment layers suggests there have been several—were due to a hot, dry climate. Such dramatic fluctuations in the lake level will undoubtedly have been reflected in successive waves of speciation (and extinction) among the cichlids that inhabited the paleo-lake in its varying forms. In this book more than 800 species are mentioned, 600 of which are known only from relatively shallow water (most of the cichlids live along the coast while relatively few are further offshore). It is thought that at least another 100-200 species may be awaiting discovery in the deeper layers of the lake. The total of up to a thousand species thought to be present today is probably just a small fraction of the species that have lived in the lake at one time or another.

The shoreline of the lake falls into three main types. About a third is rocky while most of the remainder consists of sandy beaches. The third type—swampy areas with reeds—is found in the vicinity of river estuaries. Most cichlids occur in particular habitats and although none is totally restricted to its preferred environment, by far the majority are. The potential for geographical isolation due to the alternation of gently sloping sandy or swampy shores with steep rocky coasts has been, and still is, an important factor in the speciation of the cichlids. In addition, while most affluent watercourses are of a temporary nature, carrying water only during the rainy season, some larger, permanent, rivers have had, and still have, an impact on the distribution of rock-dwelling cichlids. These rivers often form the boundary between adjacent but morphologically different populations. Dividing the lake into habitats provides a convenient way to discuss the multitude of species to which it is home. Such a division is at least in part artificial, as many species move between habitats. In such cases the species concerned are discussed under the habitat in which they are most likely to be encountered.

The habitats recognized are as follows:

The wave-washed upper rocky habitat. The upper three to five meters of the rocky habitat, which consists of rocky outcrops, small islands, and steep rocky coasts, are usually characterized by clean but turbulent water. This zone always has a substrate free of sediment, and the algal mat (known as aufwuchs or biocover) covering the hard substrate contains many firmly attached algal strands.

The sediment-free rocky habitat. Sediment-free areas of rocky habitat are usually located on rather steep-sloping shores, and are normally populated by large numbers of cichlids. The size of the rocks may vary from football-size to huge boulders several tens of meters in diameter, with the latter supporting far fewer cichlids than the former. The rocks create many caves and crevices that are used by the smaller cichlids as spawning-sites. Food is available in abundance and competition is mainly for territories.

The deep, sediment-rich rocky habitat. The population density of cichlids in the sediment-rich and/or deep regions of the rocky habitat is much lower than in the upper regions. The probable reason is reduced availability of food: most rock-dwelling cichlids are dependent on

A

5. Minos Reef

2. Mphanga Rocks

6. Masimbwe, Likoma Island

3. Machili Island, Chizumulu

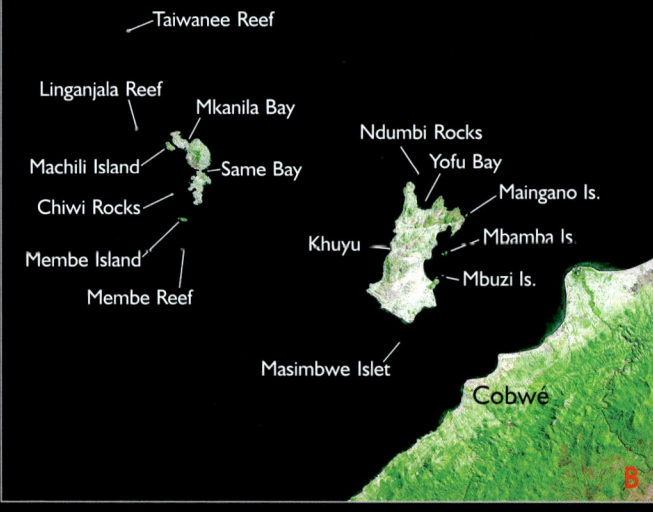

B

4. Ababi Island, Mbenji

1. Ndonga
2. Hongi Island
3. "Floating meadow", Kanchedza Island
5. Nankoma Island
7. Domwe Island

algae or on food items associated with the algal mat, and algal growth is in turn dependent on light intensity which is lower at depth. In addition, deposits of sediment may also impede algal growth.

The intermediate habitat (sand and rocks). This habitat represents the transition zone between the pure rocky habitats and the sandy (or muddy) lake floor, and comprises regions that include both rocks and sand. This type of habitat can occur at deep levels where it harbors an entirely different cichlid community to similar regions in shallow water (treated as a separate habitat—see below). The intermediate habitat harbors the most species-rich communities of the lake, but not necessarily the densest.

The shallow intermediate habitat. In many places the rocky coast is bordered by a shallow, gently sloping, shelf consisting of sand and rocks, before eventually dropping away at a much steeper angle, 20 to 50 meters from the shoreline. A number of species are restricted to this habitat, but many others are found there as well. This habitat is usually the best place for snorkelers to see a multitude of cichlids.

Sheltered bays with aquatic plants. This habitat is characterized by shallow water and muddy silt covering the sand and rocks on the bottom, and by beds of *Vallisneria spiralis*, the commonest of the handful of species of higher plants occurring in the lake. These beds of vegetation can be found at depths of up to six meters and provide cover and food for several cichlid species. The sediment-rich substrate provides ample nutrition for many organisms that are in turn consumed by cichlids.

The sandy habitat. Well over half of the shoreline of the lake consists of stretches of pure sand, which alternate with swampy and rocky shores. This open biotope offers little or no cover for small cichlids and hence most are found in large groups or shoals. A rock or tree trunk (washed down by floods) provides a reference point for several colony-breeding cichlids, and smaller species may find shelter there. Empty snail shells also perform a similar role for some species.

The unknown depths. The deep, offshore waters of the lake have not yet been visited by divers (or remote-operated video cameras) but hold a multitude of cichlid species that can be caught on hook and line and also with deep-reaching *chirimila* nets. Due to the lack of underwater observations no pertinent information about the structure of the bottom can be given or whether most of its inhabitants remain close to the substrate or live in the water column far above the bottom. It is, however, not unlikely that a large number of species live in contact with the bottom.

The cichlids, a species flock

A species flock is a group of closely related species inhabiting a geographically confined area (e.g. a lake) and endemic to this area (Greenwood, 1984). The cichlids of the great lakes of Africa provide prime examples of species flocks. Those of Lake Malaŵi can be divided into two groups: the haplochromine and the tilapiine cichlids. The haplochromines of the lake can in turn be divided into two main groups: the smaller, mostly rock-dwelling mbuna and the larger, mostly sand-dwelling "haps". The former is the name used for these small cichlids in Chi-Tonga, the language spoken in the northern part of Malaŵi, and they are also known as *chimbuzu* and, in Tanzania, *vidongo*.

It is probable that the haplochromine cichlids of the lake are descendants of fluviatile species which invaded the lake at an early stage in its history. Cichlids have many advantages when it comes to populating deep, static bodies of water, but tend to be fewer in numbers and less diverse in rivers. The rivers may "feed" the lake continuously with the ancestral species, at least in the early stages, but the reverse process of colonization of rivers by lacustrine species is unlikely. Over time some populations of the ancestral species may become isolated and diversify into new taxa within the lake, while others remain largely unchanged owing to free contact with fluviatile populations. Geophysical events—for example, extreme drought causing the drying up of the "feeder" rivers and loss of contact between fluviatile and lacustrine populations–may result in the lake residents evolving "beyond recognition" when contact is renewed hundreds or thousands of years later as the rivers become re-established. Such a repeated process of introduction, isolation, and speciation may have provided the basis for the species flock inhabiting the lake today. Two species, *Astatotilapia calliptera* and *Serranochromis robustus,* which are today found in both the lake and the surrounding rivers, may represent the primarily fluviatile descendants of forms that were ancestral to that species flock, although they are probably not themselves ancestral forms.

Feeding specializations

The cichlids are among the fishes best designed for life in a tropical lake, primarily because of their ability to adapt rapidly to new environments, and in particular to occupy the host of specialized feeding niches offered by the lacustrine environment. Their feeding equipment—maxillary and pharyngeal jaws and dentition—is able to evolve rapidly to cater for a particular new food source, and this gives them an advantage over other types of fishes that lack this dietary flexibility. Fryer & Iles (1972) coined the term "explosive radiation" to describe the evolution of the staggering number of variations in feeding strategies found in the cichlids of the great lakes of Africa. In Lake Malaŵi a huge range of feeding specializations can be seen in the haplochromine species flock: these cichlids feed on a wide range of items and include algae-feeders, macrophyte-feeders, piscivores, planktivores, snail-crushers, scale-eaters, and sand-sifters, as well as many other trophic groups (see Fryer & Iles, 1972; Ribbink *et al.*, 1983b). Nevertheless, astonishingly, many of these specialized species will readily eat other foods when available. During the plankton blooms that frequently occur in the lake, species with the most diverse feeding specializations congregate in the water column to feed on the plankton. Algae-feeding mbuna react eagerly to pounded fish-flesh bait. When the stomach contents of freshly-caught cichlids are analyzed there can be an astonishing similarity regardless of species and feeding specializations. These cichlids are extremely plastic when it comes to their feeding repertoire.

A possible explanation of the apparent discrepancy between the presence of these precise feeding adaptations on the one hand and the seemingly random feeding behavior of different species on the other is that these highly-de-

1. M.V. Sandra Lane, Tsano Rock

4

2. Lupingu

5. *Chaoborus edulis*

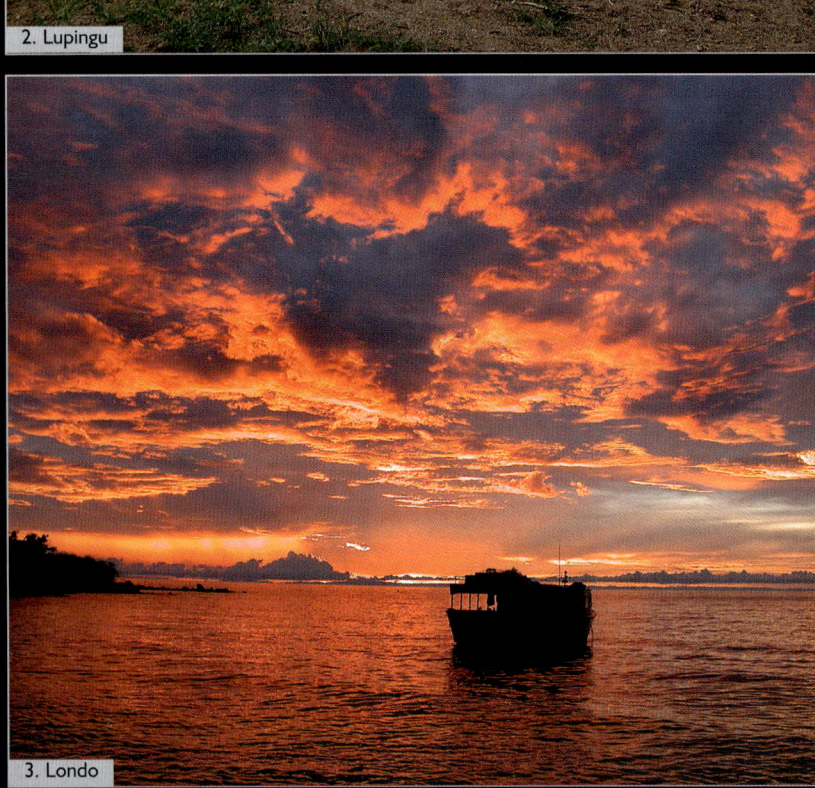
3. Londo

6

1. *Haliaeetus vocifer*, Mphanga Rocks

4. *Chamaeleo africanus*, Kambiri Point

5. *Loxodonta africana*, Shiré

2. Nakantenga Island, 11-Feb-2003

6. Nakantenga Island, 18-Nov-2004

3. M.S. Mtendere, Nkhata Bay

7. Adrian Mhone & *Bagrus meridionalis*

fined feeding specializations developed during periods when a severe paucity of food threatened the cichlids' survival (Pyke *et al.*, 1977). Although a few such specializations may be in the process of evolving at any time, it is, however, likely that the bulk of them occur after a major change in the environment has taken place and/or when food becomes scarce.

There is currently probably enough food available in Lake Malaŵi; it is a question of how efficiently a fish can harvest it without losing its territory or even its life. It is therefore mainly the composition of the local fish community (the type and degree of competition) that influences the survival rate of a particular species at a particular site.

The fishes are under continuous pressure from predators, competitors, and environmental factors, all of which inhibit their growth potential. In captivity, where fishes are usually fed on a protein-rich and easy digestible diet, many of the known species, in particular mbuna and *Aulonocara*, may grow to a size considerably larger than that observed in the wild. As well as the length, the body proportions may also change and the fins become proportionally enlarged as well.

Breeding

All Malaŵi cichlids, apart from one non-endemic species (*Tilapia rendalli*), are maternal mouthbrooders. This means that only the female takes care of eggs and fry. Males have no bond with their mates or offspring, and, freed from any need to participate in the three weeks of brood care (the average brooding period after which a female releases her fry), are thus able to fertilize the eggs of a succession of different females. The original colonizing cichlids were probably exclusively mouthbrooders, hence the absence of endemic substrate brooders.

The presence of sometimes more than 70 different species at a single locality might make it difficult for a female to find her correct mate. It is thought that, to counter this problem, most Malaŵian rock-dwelling cichlid species use colors and color patterns for identification, while many sand-dwelling species identify themselves by the type of spawning site they construct on the sand. The "sandcastles" constructed by many different species are often referred to as "nests" but they are not true nests in the sense of "a place where young are raised". They are often elaborate display sites that are analogous to those built by bowerbirds, and hence are referred to here as bowers, as suggested by McKaye *et al.*, 1990. Cichlids with nests are, however, found in other systems (e.g. Lake Tanganyika), as many substrate-brooding species do build nests, excavating holes and raising their fry in them.

In the lake males are rarely seen displaying to females of different species and it seems that not only females but also males are selective in choosing mates. In non-territorial species males court females upon encounter and here, in particular, specific recognition by the male plays an important role. Examples of such species are *Cyrtocara moorii*, *Labidochromis caeruleus*, and *Genyochromis mento*. In the case of *G. mento* the male and female may recognize each other by their specific shape (the strong, visibly protruding lower jaw), and characteristic behavior, but in the case of most non-territorial species they probably recognize each other primarily by color. When a male thinks he has found a mate he courts the female on the spot, simultaneously releasing a fluid that carries a species-specific scent (Plenderleith *et al.*, 2005). When the female is ready to spawn she can confirm the specific status of her prospective partner before she embarks on laying eggs.

A male of a territorial species exhibiting breeding colors is demonstrating to prospective mates that he has successfully secured a spawning site. In the case of some species this display is reinforced by the construction of a bower. Males of non-territorial species may exhibit their breeding colors at any time or place, but males of most species become territorial when reproductive competitors are in the area and become particularly motivated at the sight of other displaying conspecific males in their neighborhood. This mutual stimulation via display consumes a lot of energy and ensures that only the strongest males will be able to hold territory and eventually mate with several females. In addition, a group of territorial males is more conspicuous and hence more likely to attract females than each individual would be alone. This type of communal display, which is called arena-breeding or lek-breeding, is favorable for the survival of a strong and healthy population but imposes heavy demands on the males. This, however, is of minor importance when it comes to the overall well-being of a maternal mouthbrooding species.

Two different patterns of spawning are distinguished among the Malawi haplochromine cichlids: in the less-derived case the eggs are fertilized *outside* the female's mouth whereas in the more advanced species (the majority) the eggs are fertilized *inside* the mouth.

The courting and displaying male initiates the actual spawning. After he has secured and possibly constructed a spawning site he starts courting females. Once a female has decided to spawn with a male she stays in his territory; even when he is chasing intruders away from his domain, she remains in the territory patiently awaiting his return. In species where the eggs are fertilized outside the female's mouth the male takes the lead and tries to entice the female into circling around the spawning-site. After a few "dry runs" the female eventually slows down and deposits a few eggs, then turns around, followed by the male. The male discharges his sperm over the eggs while they are being picked up by the female, or, in some species, fertilizes them before the female starts to collect them (e.g. in *Cyrtocara moorii*). The pair continue circling in this way until they are disturbed or the female has expelled all her eggs. There is a tendency for females to pick up their eggs more quickly when the environment is crowded and predators are waiting to steal them before they can collect them.

In species where the eggs are fertilized inside the female's mouth the sequence is different. First the male leads the female to the actual spawning site and, once arrived, positions himself in front of and at right angles to her. He then lowers his body and presses his anal fin against the substrate. Quivering of the fins (especially the anal) accompanies this posture. While the male discharges sperm (which is sometimes visible) the female mouths his vibrating anal fin, thus picking up sperm before she has deposited a single egg. She also confirms by the male's scent that she has found her correct partner.

Next, the male starts circling around the female quivering his anal fin which is dragged over the spawning site. The female then follows the quivering anal fin and circles behind the male over the spawning site. After one or two rounds the female slows down and deposits some eggs. Without hesitation she quickly turns around and picks them up. The male stays alongside her, keeping the exposed eggs between her and himself (photo 2, page 18). He is not fertilizing them yet, and his position at this point may give protection to the vulnerable spawn. After the female has collected the small batch of eggs, the male repeats his quivering display and lets the female ingest his sperm again.

The advantage of such "internal" fertilization is the short exposure time of the eggs to the hostile environment. In crowded habitats many fishes are on the alert for pairs spawning, in the hope of a nutritious addition to their diet.

A female may spawn with several males and have her brood carry the genes of all her partners. After the female has had all her eggs fertilized she looks for a quiet refuge or joins a school of mouthbrooding females. During incubation the female does not eat for the first five to ten days. She may then start eating again, but very little and with great caution. Females of the larger piscivores that care for their fry after first release sometimes do not eat until all the fry have been abandoned (a month after first release). The incubation period averages 21 days but may, depending on temperature, range between 18 and 24 days.

Some species give postnatal protection to their offspring, but females of most species abandon them once they are released from the mouth. Some of the sand-dwelling species and several utaka release their offspring in schools of similar-sized juveniles. Often such schools are found in the very shallow vegetated areas but also over the nests of the catfish *Bagrus meridionalis*, locally known as *kampango* (see photo 3, page 242). In most species that do not practice lek-breeding females may protect their fry for up to six weeks before abandoning them. Such parental devotion is often abused by juveniles of other species which join these guarded broods (Ribbink *et al.*, 1980) (see photo 8, page 127). In the

1. *Copadichromis cyaneus* ♀♂ Otter Island

4. *Pseudotropheus* sp. 'elongatus ornatus' ♀ Ndumbi (Likoma)

5. *Pseudotropheus* sp. 'elongatus ornatus' ♀ Ndumbi (Likoma)

2. *Mylochromis lateristriga* ♂♀ Aquarium

6. *Tyrannochromis nigriventer* ♀ Chinyamwezi

3. *Copadichromis atripinnis* ♂ Thumbi West Island

1. *Genyochromis mento* OB ♀ Ndumbi (Likoma)
2. *Metriaclima zebra* OB ♂ Masinje 
3. *Metriaclima zebra* OB ♂ Linganjala Reef 
4. *Metriaclima zebra* OB ♀ Maleri Island 
5. *Tropheops tropheops* OB ♂ Zimbawe Rock
6. *Labeotropheus trewavasae* OB ♀ Ngwazi
7. *Labeotropheus trewavasae* OB ♂ Taiwanee Reef

aquarium females of some mbuna species release a few fry in different crevices of the tank's rockwork (Mary Bailey, pers. comm.).

Sometimes mouthbrooding females are seen defending a small site and exhibiting male coloration (e.g. in *Melanochromis auratus*, *Metriaclima lombardoi*, and *Pseudotropheus* sp. 'elongatus ornatus'). It is therefore possible that male breeding colors are in fact male aggression colors.

Orange and Orange-Blotch

Mate recognition in some widely distributed mbuna is based not only on male coloration but also on the characteristic shape and behavior of the male. It is only in these species that the so-called orange (O) and orange-blotch (OB) (Fryer, 1956a; Fryer & Iles, 1972) morphs are present. In these species a number of females are, instead of the usual beige, gray or brown, completely orange or orange with black speckles or blotches.

Because coloration is so important in mate selection (i.e. the female selecting her mate) in maternal mouthbrooders, the existence of these "deviant" O and OB color morphs in mbuna needs an explanation. I have argued (Konings, 2004) that the OB pattern is a combination of two types of color mutation, i.e. the orange coloration (a widespread and possibly ancestral feature of the cichlid family) and a second type that intersperses this orange background with black blotches. With the advent of a multitude of species in the lake all-orange individuals (the hypothetical ancestral form of the polymorphism) of various different species would look rather similar and species sorting would have been difficult. Hence the ancestral orange form could not be maintained, or perhaps just in a single species—*Melanochromis labrosus* (photo 5, page 214)? Now, the combination of these two patterns, i.e. black blotches and orange background, must have had some or other favorable effect because it has persisted in the approximately 20 polychromatic species known today. My speculation is that such a pattern afforded its bearer camouflage under certain circumstances. In some populations the blotched pattern matches the prevailing structure of the rocks of the environment (see photo 6, page 19). Such specific OB patterns are sometimes found in females of several different species at a single location, e.g. those of *Metriaclima zebra*, *Genyochromis mento*, and *Labeotropheus fuelleborni*.

The current orange morph, which is comparatively rare, is an OB pattern in which most of the black pigment is absent. The O morph has the disadvantage that it is more conspicuous than the normal morph, but this is probably an inevitable result of the nature of the OB pattern. In some populations of the Red Zebra (*Metriaclima estherae*) orange females are far more common than OB and normal colored ones, making it unlikely that such a pattern (O morph) has established itself for reasons of camouflage.

OB morphs seem to have evolved mainly in the older species with a wide distribution, perhaps because males of these species do not regard female color as a critical factor or they instinctively know that females can have several different color patterns. They even court such conspicuously colored females. One possibility is that the normal-colored females resemble those of a host of other (sympatric) species, and, since a male is better off courting only females of his own species, the OB trait may have evolved (or stabilized) in females in order to facilitate the *male's* choice (in my opinion sexual selection occurs in both directions, i.e. males too select their mates). Following this hypothesis, the frequency of OB females in a population may thus be dependent on the number of similar-looking females of other species at the same locality. OB females, of course, are not aware of their aberrant coloration, and breed with the same frequency as normal females. It is thus up to the male to decide whether to accept their advances or chase them from his territory.

OB males also exist and these interestingly colored males are called "marmalade cats" in the aquarium trade; a name possibly derived from the Chi-Tonga word *namakhati*, now used for all OB mbuna but originally only for OB male *L. fuelleborni*. On two different occasions I have witnessed an OB male *Metriaclima pyrsonotos* spawning with a normal-colored female and the male OB morph may thus possibly be more productive than I have previously anticipated (Konings, 2001).

Speciation

Speciation is the process whereby a single species splits into two or more taxa, and opinions are divided as to how it occurs. It is important to realize that while evolution can occur without speciation taking place, speciation cannot occur without evolution.

With the discovery that Lake Malaŵi has had periods of fluctuating water levels, the allopatric speciation theory has gained considerable credibility with regard to Malaŵian cichlids. According to this theory speciation takes place after a small number of individuals have become separated from a "mother" population and founded a new one. Little or no speciation will take place as long as sufficient individuals are present in the new, "daughter" population, because, given large numbers, there will be selection and hence stability. Meanwhile Van Oppen *et al.* (1997) have confirmed the older idea that many populations of rock-dwelling species are virtually isolated and that in principle thousands of genetically different populations can be distinguished (see also review in Markert *et al.*, 2001). This is not to say that these necessarily represent different species, because a degree of genetic variation between populations of a species can exist without speciation taking place. It does indicate, however, that populations separated by an inhospitable barrier of sometimes less than 500 meters have the potential to evolve into different species.

Most cichlids are bottom-oriented fishes and cannot normally cross deep open water to settle in another area. It can thus be accepted without much difficulty that a long tract of unsuitable habitat forms a similar barrier to the dispersal of certain species. If this were not the case, all rock-dwelling species would be found at each suitable area of rocky coast in the lake. Large parts of the lake's shoreline are separated from the opposite side of the lake by very deep water which cannot be crossed by cichlids. Thus if a cichlid from one side of the lake were to migrate to the opposite side, it would need to follow the contours of the shoreline, and hence the opposite side of a deep basin in the lake is often the most distant point in terms of cichlid dispersal. Nevertheless many species *are* found on both sides of the lake, without their range being continuous; they have dispersed to the other side of the lake but not along the *current* shoreline south or north of their restricted distribution.

Given that the lake level has fluctuated during the course of time, it is easy to envisage that these species were present in the much smaller prehistoric lake during a period of low water level. In this paleo-lake they were probably distributed along the entire shoreline, as the cichlid species of Lake Kivu are today (Snoeks, 1994). When the lake level rose they simply migrated upward and outward, remaining all the time at their preferred depth. Even though the populations on the eastern and western sides of the lake are now isolated, they are still the same species; at least there are no apparent differences to be found between them. (Genetically, however, they may be rather different.) The point is most convincingly illustrated by the discontinuous distribution of those species which are found on either side of the lake but not in suitable habitats north or south of their current range. These include *Aulonocara stuartgranti* (Usisya-Hongi, see page 247), *Copadichromis* sp. 'kawanga' (page 235), *Cynotilapia* sp. 'lion' (page 194), *Labeotropheus trewavasae* (Lundu-Lion's Cove; page 90), *Labidochromis caeruleus* (white form; page 139), and *Tropheops* sp. 'red fin' (page 199).

These species were probably present in the most recent such paleo-lake rather than having evolved after the lake had risen to its current level. One may, of course, argue that speciation usually takes much longer than the 25,000 to 50,000 years estimated as the time it took the lake to rise from its low level to its present position. But this is then at variance with the existence of more than 100 new species found around the islands of the lake, which could not have been there at the time of the low water level because that entire area was then dry land (see also Owen *et al.*, 1990)! These species must either be the sole remnants of paleo-lake species that have survived only in these new habitats, or have developed from species that dispersed from the paleo-lake populations into this area–which is, of course, the more likely explanation.

1. *Labidochromis caeruleus* Mbowe Island

2. *Nyassachromis prostoma* ♀♂ & *Otopharynx ovatus* Ntekete

1. *Protomelas* sp. 'steveni imperial' ♂ Yofu Bay (Likoma Island)

2. *Aulonocara baenschi* ♂ Nkhomo Reef

Malaŵian cichlid taxonomy

Since the publication of the third edition of this book in 2001 many newly discovered Malaŵi species have been scientifically described, as have a number of previously given "temporary" names. All these additions and changes have been included here, but despite these advances in taxonomy, many species discussed in this book remain undescribed and lack a scientific name. As in the past these have been given an interim name to facilitate identification and reference. Such names are always given in single quotation marks and preceded by "sp." (the abbreviation for species), for instance, *Aulonocara* sp. 'stuartgranti maleri'.

This new edition also encompasses changes in the taxonomy of the genera, and in particular in the precise application of the diagnoses of the genera *Metriaclima* and *Tropheops*. Konings & Stauffer (2006) published a revised diagnosis of *Metriaclima* and compared it with that of *Tropheops*. Apart from the characters that Stauffer *et al.* (1997) used to characterize their genus *Metriaclima*, several additional characters, behavioral as well as morphological, have been added in the revision. One of the main morphological characters defining a member of *Metriaclima* is the angle of the vomer (the "plowshare" bone in the "nose"). In the revised diagnosis the vomer in *Metriaclima* is moderately-sloped and forms an angle of 31-48° with the parasphenoid (n = 27 species) (see figure 1). *Tropheops* has a steeply-sloped vomer (71-96° with the parasphenoid; n = 20 species) (see figure 2) and lacks a swollen tip to the vomer. These characters can be seen in preserved museum specimens.

Another important diagnostic character, however, relates to the feeding behavior of these species and can, obviously, be recorded only when the fish is alive. Up to now I have found a 100% correlation between the way a *Metriaclima* or *Tropheops* species feeds and the angle of their respective vomers. Species of *Metriaclima* feed perpendicular to the substrate and are able to align the teeth of both upper and lower jaws in the same plane by opening the mouth until the jaws are at an angle of almost 180° to one another. The mouth is then pressed against the substrate and then closed, and in the process the teeth rake through the algae anchored to the substrate and collect so-called "loose aufwuchs" (Fryer, 1959). Numerous such bites at the substrate follow in rapid succession. During the process nothing is actually torn from the substrate; only diatoms and loose algal strands are harvested. In this respect, *Metriaclima* differs from *Tropheops* species which are unable to open their mouths to a 180° angle and do not rake loose algae from the substrate. Instead *Tropheops* feed by shearing algal strands from the substrate.

Both these genera were, of course, split off fairly recently from *Pseudotropheus*, whose type species, *P. williamsi* (see page 39), does not feed from the aufwuchs at all; moreover the angle of the vomer in two specimens I examined was 59 and 62° respectively, i.e. not within the range of either of the new genera. A large number of mbuna still grouped under *Pseudotropheus* are not closely related to *P. williamsi*, but since there is currently no better alternative they are retained in this genus for the time being.

In addition there is a group of small mbuna, currently assigned to *Metriaclima*, which may ultimately prove to belong elsewhere. This group includes, among others, *M. pulpican*, *M.* sp. 'lime', and *M.* sp. 'kingsizei lupingu'. It has been suggested that some of these species should be assigned to *Cynotilapia* (Tawil, 2002b), and *M. pulpican* was described in that genus, but as these small species have bicuspid dentition, and the current diagnosis of *Cynotilapia* specifies unicuspid teeth, a revision of that diagnosis would be required to accommodate them. However, I have been unable to formulate a diagnosis that would either include these small species in *Cynotilapia* or permit erection of a new genus for them.

The diagnoses of *Metriaclima* and *Tropheops* were revised in order to accommodate a number of species that at first glance might not appear to be members of those genera but are now thought to have a shared ancestry, which is the defining criterion of a genus. Apart from the small species mentioned above, a number of species that were previously included in the *Pseudotropheus elongatus* complex (Ribbink *et al.*, 1983b) are now also placed in *Metriaclima*, *Cynotilapia*, or *Tropheops*, while others remain in *Pseudotropheus*.

Returning to the genus *Tropheops*, here we find many different patterns, all based on vertical bars and two horizontal stripes. Based on pigmentation patterns I have distinguished six groups, each containing several species: the "sand type"—females exhibit broad vertical bars (see photo 7, page 195); the "black type"—females are dark, with vertical bars and a black band in the dorsal (photo 10, page 34); the "*romandi* type"—females have faint bars and a broad black band in the dorsal (photo 1, page 195); the "Chilumba type"—females have a single row of mid-lateral blotches, sometimes faint, and a thin black band in the dorsal (photo 7, page 86); the "mauve type"—females with faint vertical bars (photo 6, page 83); and the "double stripe type"—females have two horizontal rows of small spots, usually fused to form two horizontal stripes (photo 7, page 198). In addition to these groups two other groups are distinguished that differ morphologically from *T. tropheops*, the type species of the genus, i.e. the *lucerna* group (page 270) and the elongate group (page 87).

Hopefully these subdivisions will provide a clearer picture of the many different species, although it is important to realize that the cichlid species flock in Lake Malaŵi is one of the most complex assemblages of species in existence, and, since the majority of the species are still undescribed, it is often difficult to determine their phylogenetic relationships.

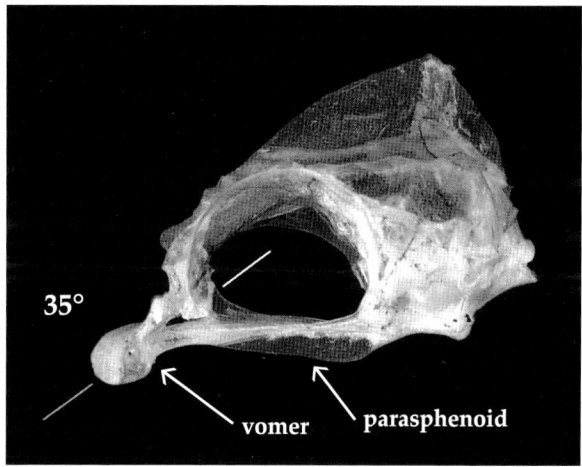

Fig. 1. Lateral view of the skull of *Metriaclima zebra* showing the moderately-sloped vomer, characteristic of all members of *Metriaclima*.

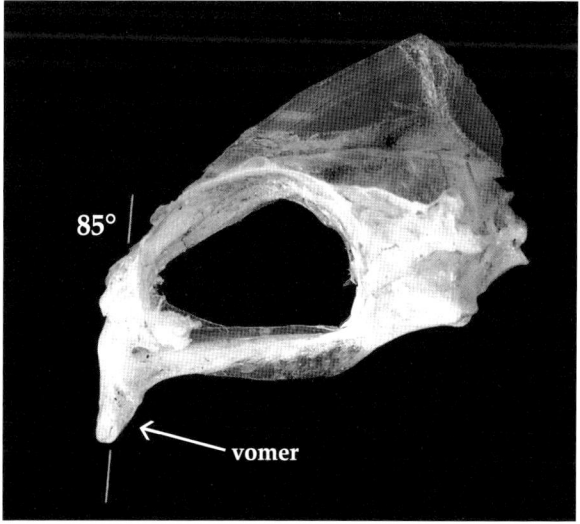

Fig. 2. Lateral view of the skull of *Tropheops* sp. 'maleri yellow' showing the steeply-sloped vomer, characteristic of all *Tropheops* species.

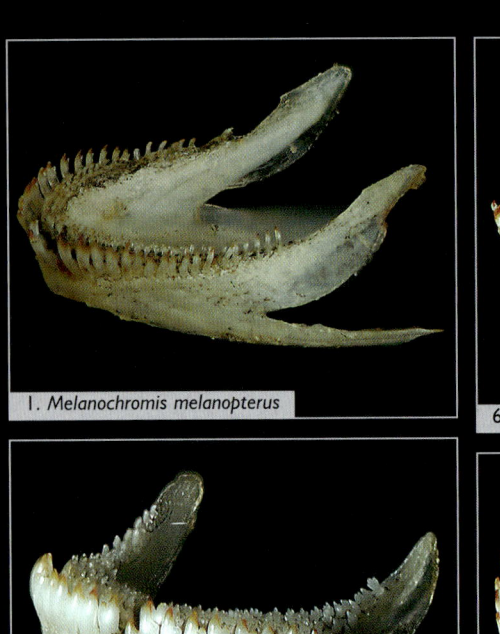

1. *Melanochromis melanopterus*

6. *Cyathochromis obliquidens*

10. *Iodotropheus sprengerae*

2. *Genyochromis mento*

7. *Metriaclima fainzilberi*

11. *Labidochromis gigas*

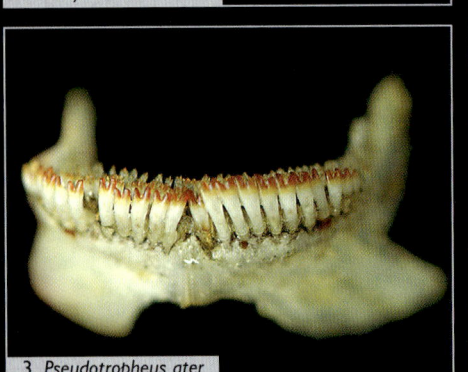

3. *Pseudotropheus ater*

8. *Petrotilapia* sp. 'yellow ventral'

12. *Gephyrochromis* sp. 'zebroides'

4. *Tropheops* sp. 'maleri yellow'

5. *Labeotropheus fuelleborni*

9. *Cynotilapia* sp. 'chinyankwazi'

1. *Tropheops tropheops* ♂ Makokola Reef

2. *Pseudotropheus* sp. 'tursiops chitande' ♂ Ngwazi

3. *Labidochromis heterodon* ♂ Boadzulu Island

4. *Sciaenochromis fryeri* ♂ Thumbi West Island

5. *Labeotropheus fuelleborni* ♂ Chinyamwezi Island

6. *Pseudotropheus* sp. 'elongatus aggressive' ♂ Zimbawe Rock

7. *Placidochromis milomo* ♂ Nakantenga Island

The wave-washed upper rocky habitat

The upper three to five meters of the rocky habitat of rocky outcrops, small islands, and steep rocky coasts are usually characterized by clean but turbulent water. These places all have a substrate free of sediment, and the algae mat covering the hard substrate (biocover) contains many firmly attached algal strands. When the rocks are small the power of the turbulent water is efficiently deadened by the many cracks and caves. The face of a large rock receives the full force of the waves and only a few species of mbuna are able to feed from such a surface during heavy swells. This habitat harbors only a handful of herbivorous cichlid species, all belonging to the mbuna group.

Labeotropheus

Labeotropheus fuelleborni has a clear preference for this kind of habitat and is found on any rocky coast throughout the lake. It is also found on small patches of rocks amidst sandy beaches, especially at wave-exposed sites. *L. fuelleborni* has two adaptations for living in the upper reaches of the rocky habitat. One of these features, which it shares with its congener *L. trewavasae*, is a broad underslung mouth coupled with a remarkable fleshy "nose". When the fish is held upside-down the mouth is seen to be a straight line across the full width of the head. Its ventral position allows *Labeotropheus* to feed in a position almost parallel to the rocks, its body making an angle of approximately 30° with the substrate. *Labeotropheus* thus remains in close contact with the substrate while cropping algae.

The fleshy nose, which overhangs the mouth, is even more remarkable. Both nose and chin are callused, probably as a result of continuous contact with rough substrates during feeding. The effect of the fish closing its mouth on the firmly attached filamentous algae is to pull it closer to the substrate, and the nose then functions as a fulcrum, allowing its owner to shear off the algae by leverage rather than energy-consuming jerking of the body. This not only saves energy but also allows *Labeotropheus* to remain in close contact with the rocks, thus reducing the risk of being swept away by the turbulent water. Moreover it allows greater quantities of, and more tightly attached, algae to be cropped using the three or more rows of tricuspid teeth in the outer jaws; this feeding method is so efficient that the algae are removed completely, leaving visible scrape marks in the biocover. The commonly observed large size of *L. fuelleborni* (max. total length approx. 18 cm) may be an indication of the beneficial effects of the nose.

In places where the turbulence of the surf is at its maximum the algae are very tightly anchored to the substrate, and harvesting them requires not only strong jaws but increased development of the fulcrum—*Labeotropheus* living in such areas have more prominent noses than individuals which feed from less tightly anchored biocover. The harder and more frequently the nose is pressed against the substrate, the larger it appears to grow. And the larger it grows, the smaller the "feeding angle" the fish can maintain with the substrate. Similar growth stimulations can be seen in cichlids with thickened lips, such as *Placidochromis milomo* and *Chilotilapia euchilus*.

The second feature that ensures *L. fuelleborni* a (physically) stable position in this habitat is its laterally compressed body. Together with the extended dorsal fin, which acts as a sail, it prevents the fish from wobbling. The laterally compressed *L. fuelleborni* is much better equipped for living in turbulent water than the cylindrically built *L. trewavasae* (see page 88).

Male *L. fuelleborni* defend their territories with great vigor, especially against conspecific males. Females and non-territorial males congregate in groups and feed from the upper parts of the habitat. *L. fuelleborni* does not penetrate deeper than about 35 meters (Ribbink *et al.*,

1983a). This means that the populations at rocky habitats separated by water deeper than this are virtually isolated. This may have led to the many color variants of this species. The coloration of the female does not vary much throughout the entire range of the species. Because of the distinctive shape, coloration may be of less importance than usual in mate recognition. This may also explain the orange (O) and the orange-blotched (OB) morphs present in males as well as in females. If a female can recognize a conspecific by its silhouette alone, spawning could in theory take place without the presence of nuptial coloration in the male. But another important function of bright colors is to advertise territoriality, i.e. the availability of a spawning site, and to display vitality, i.e. that the male carries so-called "good genes". Of course, spawning with uncolored males is far from the normal situation but it might explain the rare occurrence of OB males ("marmalade cats"). At some locations up to 50% of the females can be of the OB/O morph; typically, this occurs at places where *L. trewavasae* is not present, e.g. Mbenji and Chinyamwezi islands. At Mbenji the rare O morph of the male is occasionally seen. In such places *L. fuelleborni* also penetrates to the deeper regions usually inhabited by *L. trewavasae*. The orange-blotched form of the female may be an example of camouflage coloration, especially among rocks in the somewhat deeper areas. It is more often seen in *L. trewavasae,* which lives a more secretive life in such areas.

As regards breeding behavior, *Labeotropheus* is unusual among mbuna. The eggs are sometimes fertilized outside the female's mouth (Trewavas & Konings, 1992)! After the female has deposited a few eggs, the male, following behind her, fertilizes them on the substrate. The female, meanwhile, describes a large circle, and then collects the eggs on her next spawning pass, immediately before depositing the next batch. The fry, which are released for the first time after three weeks, find refuge inside the female's mouth for at least another week (Schönen, 1979). The egg-spots on the male's anal fin are proportionally the smallest (compared to the adult size of the fish) found in mbuna, whereas the eggs are among the largest!

In the northwestern part of the lake (north of Ruarwe) and at many sites on the eastern shoreline, a rusty colored variant of *L. trewavasae* shares the habitat with *L. fuelleborni*. This variant has anatomical features very similar to those of *L. fuelleborni* and has been observed feeding from the upper layers of the rocky biotope. At all such locations, however, it is also found at deeper levels where *L. fuelleborni* never ventures.

Tropheops

The genus *Tropheops* has several representatives inhabiting the turbulent areas of the rocky biotope. *Tropheops* sp. 'olive' is found in this habitat along the northwestern coast between Kande Island and Mdoka, and at the northeastern coast between Manda and Kirondo. Like most *Tropheops*, this species feeds from the biocover and tears off filamentous algae, usually with jerking twists of the body. Most *Tropheops* are sedentary, and this prevents the continual intermingling of genetic material between two neighboring populations that might otherwise be expected to occur. The lime-yellow color of the male varies slightly throughout the distribution of the species, but in general males at any single location look rather similar. Males at Kande Island are a less bright yellow than those at Chilumba. Territorial males on the eastern shores have dark ventral fins. Females of all known populations have a silvery-gray ground color with a very characteristic pattern of black bars and lines.

At several localities around the lake, e.g. Nkhata Bay and Lupingu, more than five different species of the genus are found sympatrically and each of them "interferes" in the specific color pattern of the others (to avoid interbreeding they have to be as diverse as possible). Male *T.* sp. 'olive' defend their territories—often the upper surfaces of large rocks—against all intruders. The result is that the algae, which are not entirely eaten by the resident male, grow to a thick layer. These so-called "algal gardens" can be readily seen as yellow-green patches on

1. *Labeotropheus fuelleborni* ♀ Chinyamwezi Island
2. *Labeotropheus fuelleborni* OB ♂ Maingano Island
3. *Tropheops* sp. 'olive' ♀ Magunga
4. *Labeotropheus fuelleborni* O ♀ Mbenji Island
5. *Labeotropheus fuelleborni* OB ♀ Nakantenga Island
6. *Tropheops* sp. 'olive' ♂ Ngwazi

the rocks. This may serve as an additional specific character to enable the female to recognize and locate her correct mate.

Tropheops sp. 'red cheek' is a popular mbuna of the wave-washed rocky biotope and often exported from Likoma and Chizumulu islands. It also occurs at Tsano Rock in the southeastern arm of the lake. Along the northeastern coast, between Ikombe and Cape Kaiser, a similar species inhabits the turbulent waters of the rocky shores: *Tropheops* sp. 'red cheek north'. Previously I regarded that form as constituting additional populations of *T.* sp. 'red cheek' but it is treated here as a separate taxon. The rocky coast south of Lumessi, Mozambique, drops at a steep angle. Here *Tropheops* sp. 'lumessi blue' inhabits the shallow, wave-washed part of the biotope. *T.* sp. 'lumessi blue' also resembles the "Red Cheek" in male as well as in female coloration and may therefore be another population of this species, but the "Lumessi Blue" is here considered a different species.

The geographical variation in the male coloration of these three species consists of the extent of the orange color on head and shoulders, *T.* sp. 'red cheek' being the most colorful. Females of *T.* sp. 'red cheek north' have a silvery-white ground color whereas females of the other two are yellowish-white or yellow. The "Red Cheek" is called "Big Eye" by Stuart Grant, exporter of Malaŵi cichlids, but is traded as "Macrophthalmus Red Cheek". The native name for this fish is *m'kokafodya,* which means "glowing fire" or "live coal", referring to the bright orange patches on the head and shoulders of the male.

Males defend territories on top of relatively large rocks with a diameter of one to two meters. Although the premises are guarded against all intruders with great zeal, the most aggression is directed towards conspecific males. Algal gardens are not found.

The discontinuous distribution of *T.* sp. 'red cheek' is surprising. The northern populations are separated from the southern—between Tsano Rock and Zambo Point—by a distance of more than 200 km. Although the rocky habitats between these two distribution areas have been visited, no other populations, apart from the very similar *T.* sp. 'lumessi blue' near Meponda, have been found. The two isolated populations evolving the same uncommon color pattern for both males and females seems improbable; therefore we may conclude that either the "Red Cheek" formerly had a much wider distribution along the eastern shoreline or that individuals from one of the northern populations were introduced at Tsano Rock—but there are no reports or rumors indicating such an event. If we assume the first hypothesis, the fact that only isolated populations still occur, may indicate that this is a relatively unsuccessful species. A factor that may influence the survival rate of the "Red Cheek" is its conspicuous male coloration. Birds may prey preferentially on dominant males as they are easily spotted from above.

Between Liutche and Londo on the central east coast of the lake, and also at Tumbi Point—all localities in Mozambique—a large member of the genus *Tropheops* inhabits the wave-washed rocky regions. This species, *Tropheops* sp. 'goldbreast', is not abundant and seems to prefer large rocks. The territory of the male usually includes a large rock but the spawning site lies in a cave beneath it, rarely on its top. The females are very dark and live solitary.

At Mbenji Island males of another member of the genus, *Tropheops* sp. 'mbenji blue', defend their territories above large rocks. The habitat of this species is not restricted to the surf zone, as in the previously discussed *Tropheops*, but includes the sediment-free rocky regions as well. In this respect it resembles *T.* sp. 'mauve' from the northwestern coast, which may be its closest relative (see page 81). The fact that the "Mbenji Blue" is found over a wider part of the rocky habitat is probably due to a lack of competing species of the same genus. Only one other species of *Tropheops* is found around Mbenji—*Tropheops* sp. 'mbenji yellow'—but in sediment-rich areas. The two species are easily distinguished, not by the male's overall coloration (which can be rather similar) but by the black submarginal band in the dorsal fin of the "Mbenji Yellow".

Five species of *Tropheops* are found around the Maleri Islands. Four of these can occasionally be observed in the extreme shallows of the rocky biotope, but two, *T.* sp. 'maleri blue' and *T.* sp. 'lilac', are predominantly found in this habitat. *Tropheops* sp. 'maleri blue' males defend territories on top of rocks that stand out from the rest of the rocky biotope. *T.* sp. 'maleri blue' is a rare species and is distinguished from another shallow water species, *T.* sp. 'maleri yellow' (see page 196), by the absence of yellow coloration on the body. *Tropheops* sp. 'lilac' lives among small rocks but is rare in the intermediate type of habitat. This species also occurs at several other islands in the southern part of the lake, i.e. Chidunga Rocks and Mumbo Island; at the latter it is found in the deeper regions of the sediment-free rocky habitats as well. Again, this is probably due to a lack of the competition that, at places with five or six sympatric members of the genus, would normally force each closely-related species to keep to its particular specialization or its preferred niche.

At Otter Island, *Tropheops* sp. 'gold otter' is again adapted to life in the turbulence of the upper region of the rocky habitat. As in most surge-inhabiting *Tropheops*, territories often include a large rock and spawning normally occurs alongside or beneath this feature.

Tropheops tropheops itself can frequently be observed in the shallow areas too, but holds territories at deeper levels, in the vicinity of shelter among smaller rocks.

To summarize: the species of the genus *Tropheops* inhabiting this biotope have a rather large average size (10 cm), defend their territories (males) with great zeal, and are generally very common. The territory encompasses the entire rock (1 to 2 meters in diameter) that the male chooses as his domain. All intruders are chased from the center of this territory and intruding conspecific males are chased beyond the boundaries as well.

Petrotilapia

Members of the genus *Petrotilapia* are characterized by broad, fleshy lips densely covered with slender flexible teeth with a tricuspid (three-pointed) crown. The teeth, many of them permanently exposed even when the mouth is closed, are excellent tools for combing loose aufwuchs. *Petrotilapia* feed at an almost perpendicular angle to the substrate and are able to align the teeth of both upper and lower jaws in the same plane by opening the jaws to a 180° gape. When the mouth is closed again the teeth comb through the algae anchored to the substrate and collect loose material. In comparison to *Metriaclima* bites at the substrate occur in slow succession. In contrast to *Labeotropheus* and *Tropheops*, *Petrotilapia* is not capable of scraping off or cutting filamentous algae from the substrate. *Petrotilapia* is ill at ease when dealing with thick layers of aufwuchs; it simply cannot cope with the abundant algae that become entangled between the teeth. Therefore these "tooth-covered" lips are usually seen combing the partially grazed-off biocover in the territories of other species or at places which are heavily visited by other mbuna.

Most of the species of this group are successful inhabitants of the rocky biotopes. Only males seem to be sedentary and occupy territories in the rocky regions. Non-territorial individuals are regularly observed singly, roaming through the habitat or congregating in schools to feed on algae or plankton.

Many rocky coasts harbor three different *Petrotilapia* species: *P. tridentiger* or similar species in the wave-washed rocky habitat, *P. genalutea* in the shallow intermediate biotopes, and *P. nigra* or similar species in the deeper rocky environments.

Petrotilapia tridentiger is found at every rocky shore on the western side of the lake; it is, however, absent from all islands and from the eastern coast between Cobwé and Makanjila Point. It is a well-established species, adapted to live in purely rocky environments, and rarely ventures into sandy areas.

Sexually active males have large territories (over 20 m²!) from which they chase only conspecific males. *P. tridentiger* has a maximum total length of almost 14 cm. Females usually lack any distinct pattern and are generally dark brown.

At some islands in the southern region, i.e. Maleris, Namalenje, and Mbenji, and also along the eastern coast between Makanjila and Tumbi

1. *Tropheops* sp. 'red cheek' ♂ Maingano Island

5. *Tropheops* sp. 'red cheek' ♀ Likoma Island

2. *Tropheops* sp. 'lumessi blue' ♂ Meponda

6. *Tropheops* sp. 'red cheek north' ♀ Lupingu

3. *Tropheops* sp. 'goldbreast' ♂ Londo

7. *Tropheops* sp. 'red cheek north' ♀ Matema

4. *Tropheops* sp. 'mbenji blue' ♂ Mbenji Island

8. *Tropheops* sp. 'lumessi blue' ♀ Meponda

9. *Tropheops* sp. 'goldbreast' ♀ Londo

10. *Tropheops* sp. 'mbenji blue' ♀ Mbenji Island

1. *Tropheops* sp. 'maleri blue' ♀ Nakantenga Island

7. *Tropheops* sp. 'maleri blue' ♂ Nakantenga Island

2. *Tropheops* sp. 'lilac' ♀ Mumbo Island

3. *Tropheops* sp. 'lilac' ♂ Nakantenga Island

8. *Tropheops* sp. 'lilac' ♂ Mumbo Island

4. *Tropheops* sp. 'gold otter' ♂ Otter Island

9. *Tropheops* sp. 'gold otter' ♀ Otter Island

5. *Petrotilapia* sp. 'yellow ventral' ♂ Chizumulu Island

6. *Petrotilapia tridentiger* ♀ Thumbi West Island

10. *Petrotilapia tridentiger* ♂ Boadzulu Island

Point (Mozambique), *P. tridentiger* is replaced by *P.* sp. 'yellow chin'. This mbuna is more commonly found in shallow intermediate habitats and will be discussed later (see page 265).

At Likoma the upper rocky biotope is inhabited by *Petrotilapia* sp. 'likoma barred', which is the largest mbuna known, sometimes attaining a maximum total length of 19 cm. It is also found at Taiwanee Reef. Non-territorial individuals frequently congregate in schools and feed on plankton, and when plankton is available the "Likoma Barred" may be encountered in other habitats as well. The coloration of males varies across several shades of blue but is characterized mainly by the heavily-barred pattern. Females have dark bodies with black bars.

At Chizumulu there are three species of *Petrotilapia* with overlapping habitat preferences. *Petrotilapia* sp. 'orange pelvic' is commonly encountered in the shallow wave-washed rocky areas free of sediment. It can attain a maximum total length of 15 cm. Females have a dark coloration with a distinct black submarginal band in the dorsal.

Pseudotropheus williamsi et al.

Pseudotropheus williamsi, named after its discoverer, Joseph Williams, is the type species of its genus. Although Regan noted the similarity of *Tropheops tropheops* (at that time in *Pseudotropheus*) to the *Tropheus* of Lake Tanganyika, he nevertheless incomprehensibly took *P. williamsi*, which does not resemble *Tropheus* at all, as the type species of his new genus *Pseudotropheus*. There are several species or variants assigned to the *P. williamsi* complex (Ribbink *et al.*, 1983b), but it is not clear whether or not these separate populations belong to a single species with a wide distribution. Until now no more than one variant has been seen at any one site, but since these cichlids live a very secretive life, more research needs to be done. Members of the *P. williamsi* complex can be very common in the turbulent habitat but difficult to observe owing to their shy behavior. At several localities, e.g. Chizumulu Island and Lumessi, *P. williamsi*-like cichlids occur in the shallow intermediate habitat but always in the neighborhood of large rocks. Large rocks also seem a prerequisite of the preferred habitat of other known populations. Rocky habitats with only football-sized rocks do not harbor *P. williamsi*-like cichlids.

The *P. williamsi* complex has a lake-wide distribution. These cichlids belong to the larger mbuna and males can attain a maximum total length of about 15 cm. At Likoma Island two different populations were recognized by Ribbink and coworkers (1983b). One, which they provisionally termed *P. williamsi* 'khuyu', inhabits the turbulent biotope on the southwestern side of the island and closely resembles the population at Same Bay, Chizumulu Island, termed *P. williamsi* 'chizumulu'. The other population at Likoma, termed *P. williamsi* 'maingano', is found along the northeastern coast. The type specimen of *P. williamsi* may have originated from the Chizumulu population. In my opinion all three populations belong to one species, *P. williamsi*.

At a number of locations on the Malaŵian mainland coast, from Nkhata Bay to Boadzulu Island on the western side and from Makonde to Makanjila Point on the eastern, populations of *williamsi*-like mbuna occur. The northwest and east coast "williamsi" lack the submarginal band in the unpaired fins seen in the Likoma and Chizumulu populations, at least in most cases. The species from the central eastern shore is named *Pseudotropheus* sp. 'williamsi makanjila'. The populations found at Makonde and Manda have a very attractive orange coloration, which is also seen, albeit to a lesser extent, in the population at Nkhata Bay. These populations are here referred to as *Pseudotropheus* sp. 'williamsi north'. The population in the southeastern arm of the lake is characterized by yellow-orange coloration on the head of territorial males and by a black submarginal band in the unpaired fins. This species is called *Pseudotropheus* sp. 'williamsi nkudzi' and is common around Boadzulu Island.

Ribbink *et al.* (1983b) mention *P. williamsi* 'namalenje', *P. williamsi* 'maleri', and *P. williamsi* 'mbenji' from Namalenje Island and the Maleri and Mbenji islands respectively. The first two forms are characterized by a red-colored dorsal fin in the male. Previously I regarded them as representatives of *P. galanos* (formerly *P.* sp. 'red dorsal'—see Konings, 2001), but here both populations are again regarded as *Pseudotropheus* sp. 'williamsi maleri' because I believe they have a closer relationship with *P. williamsi* than with *P. galanos*. The *P. williamsi*-like cichlid at Mbenji Island resembles *P.* sp. 'williamsi makanjila' and for the time being I regard them as a further population of that species.

Females of the *P. williamsi* complex, which look alike in all known populations, have two rows of black spots on the body, a character that is considered primitive (Eccles & Trewavas, 1989).

The slender teeth on the pharyngeal bones of the members of the complex indicate that only soft-bodied prey is taken. These fishes feed predominantly on insects and insect larvae, which are apparently located visually in open water rather than picked from rock crevices. Although this is a nutritious diet, large insects are not plentifully available, as other fishes, including those which are predominantly herbivorous, devour them as well. Members of the *P. williamsi* complex, however, will jump out of the water to get at insects! This is why they are normally found in areas where large rocks break the surface and form wind-still pockets in which large numbers of the lakefly (*Chaoborus edulis*) hover. The flies wait for calm moments to descend to the water's surface to deposit their eggs but are eaten while they hover near the surface. Not only the members of the *P. williamsi* complex snatch flying insects in mid-air, but *Melanochromis heterochromis* (see page 105) also occasionally breaches for a snack on the wing.

Males of the complex are territorial but defend their domains only against intruding conspecific males. Sexually active males each remain at a particular site and have to make do with the available food, as only the possession of a spawning site will attract a ripe female. Females and juveniles wander through the habitat, searching for food, and are rarely sedentary.

At Mbenji Island—in particular at Fuawe Rock—the turbulent regions of the rocky habitat are home to another mbuna that has features in common with the *P. williamsi* complex. The peculiarity of this species, *Pseudotropheus galanos* (previously *P.* sp. 'red dorsal'), is the fact that non-territorial individuals all dine on plankton from the water column (Ribbink *et al.*, 1983b) although it has a very steep snout—the vomer angle in one specimen was about 75°—which is a characteristic of mbuna that tear algae from rocks, such as *Tropheops*. *P. galanos* is common at Mbenji where it congregates in foraging schools. It is regularly caught, and traded under the name of "Red Top Brevis". It has proved to be an excellent resident for the mbuna community aquarium. This species differs from the *P. williamsi* complex by virtue of the vertical bars on the flanks in males and the dark-brown coloration of the females.

Superficially *Melanochromis brevis* resembles *P. williamsi*, but because of the slightly enlarged teeth on the pharyngeal bones it has been assigned to the genus *Melanochromis*. Although the enlarged teeth suggest a menu of invertebrates, mainly aufwuchs was found in the stomachs of the few individuals examined by Ribbink *et al.* (1983b). *Melanochromis brevis* is encountered in the southern part of the lake: Monkey Bay and the coast further south, Mumbo Island, Chinyamwezi and Chinyankwazi. The latter two islets harbor a race which is adorned with an orange-yellow chin and, sometimes, chest. Other populations are completely blue with two broken horizontal white stripes. The females are beige to light brown and have dark brown horizontal stripes (a pattern very similar to that of *P. galanos*).

The reverse coloration in the male is a known characteristic of *Melanochromis*. The current definition of this genus (Trewavas, 1984) excludes species with vertical barring, but nevertheless some species with such markings remain included pending formal revision. Ribbink *et al.* (1983b) place these species in a so-called "*Melanochromis* heterogeneous complex". *M. brevis* has some vertical barring and is thus assigned to this complex.

This species is specially adapted to a life in turbulent waters and, according to Ribbink *et al.*, (1983b), comes out of its shelter when the wave action becomes rough. Males are only

1. *Petrotilapia* sp. 'orange pelvic' ♂ Chizumulu Island

2. *Petrotilapia* sp. 'likoma barred' ♂ Likoma Island

3. *Melanochromis brevis* ♂ Chiinyankwazi Island

4. *Pseudotropheus galanos* ♂ Mbenji Island

5. *Petrotilapia* sp. 'orange pelvic' ♀ Chizumulu Island

6. *Petrotilapia* sp. 'likoma barred' ♀ Likoma Island

7. *Melanochromis brevis* ♀ Mumbo Island

8. *Melanochromis brevis* ♂ Mumbo Island

9. *Pseudotropheus galanos* ♀ Mbenji Island

1. *Pseudotropheus williamsi* ♀ Maingano Island

2. *Pseudotropheus* sp. 'williamsi north' ♂ Nkhata Bay

3. *Pseudotropheus* sp. 'williamsi north' ♀ Nkhata Bay

4. *Pseudotropheus* sp. 'williamsi makanjila' ♂ Mbenji Island

5. *Pseudotropheus* sp. 'williamsi maleri' ♀ Nakantenga Island

6. *Pseudotropheus* sp. 'williamsi nkhudzi' ♀ Boadzulu Island

7. *Pseudotropheus williamsi* ♂ Maingano Island

8. *Pseudotropheus* sp. 'williamsi north' ♂ Manda

9. *Pseudotropheus* sp. 'williamsi maleri' ♂ Nakantenga Island

10. *Pseudotropheus* sp. 'williamsi nkhudzi' ♂ Boadzulu Island

weakly territorial but chase conspecific males whenever they are encountered. Other species are tolerated within the boundaries of the male's territory. Small groups of females are usually found in the vicinity of a territorial male. This may result from the sedentary behavior of *M. brevis*: such small groups (including the male) may have been "born" at the same site and even originated from the same spawning. The secretive way of life is consistent with this idea.

Pseudotropheus demasoni

Pseudotropheus demasoni is endemic to small rocky reefs, Pombo Rocks and Ndumbi Rocks, south of the Ruhuhu River delta. It inhabits the upper three to four meters of the rocky habitat. It is seen regularly but almost all sightings involve solitary individuals. This species is evenly spread throughout the habitat, each individual having a feeding area about two meters in diameter. Such feeding areas normally include a large rock or the upper face of a boulder. *P. demasoni* is generally ignored by other species, but chased from some areas occupied by breeding males of more boisterous species. The occupation of such relatively large feeding areas may imply that suitable food is not abundant, and I would expect fierce competition to exist among conspecifics, resulting in aggressive behavior towards their own kind; but in actuality, where two or three individuals were found close together, I could see no hint of intraspecific aggression. In fact, in the lake, *P. demasoni* behaves remarkably peacefully towards all species, including its own.

P. demasoni feeds on algae attached to rocks. It bites the algal strands from the substrate, and feeding sites seem to be visually selected (as is the case with most herbivorous *Labidochromis*, see below). The relatively long gut (205% of standard length) in one investigated specimen suggests a high percentage of vegetable material in the diet.

P. demasoni matures at a very small size—at a total length of approximately 5 cm. Immatures with a length of 15 to 20 mm exhibit a color pattern indistinguishable from that of adults, according with the normal mbuna pattern of identical coloration in females and juveniles.

The pickers

Melanochromis joanjohnsonae and several cichlids of the genus *Labidochromis* represent another group of mbuna in the wave-washed rocky habitat. *M. joanjohnsonae*, which is found only in the upper four meters of the rocky habitat, is endemic to Likoma Island and is exported as the "Pearl of Likoma". It is caught mainly south of Makulawe Point on the western side of the island, although it occurs all around its coast.

M. joanjohnsonae has superficial affinities with *Labidochromis*, but is currently assigned to *Melanochromis*, in the heterogeneous group mentioned on page 105. This species has been the subject of much confusion in the taxonomic literature (Stock, 1976; Lewis, 1980). It was originally described as *Labidochromis joanjohnsonae* by Johnson (1974), then named *L. fryeri* by Oliver (1975), and *M. exasperatus* by Burgess (1976). Eventually Lewis (1982) reconciled this completely confused state of affairs and placed it in *Melanochromis*. The paratype from the type series of Johnson's *joanjohnsonae* was recognized as a completely different species and described as *L. textilis* by Oliver (1975). This species (see page 271) closely resembles *M. joanjohnsonae* but has unicuspid teeth in the outer jaws and a V-shaped dental arc, important characteristics of *Labidochromis*. On the other hand, in *joanjohnsonae* the bicuspid teeth in the outer jaws, and the structure of the jaws, are more typical of *Melanochromis*, although its narrow U-shaped dental arc is reminiscent of that of *Iodotropheus*. Its behavior, however, closely resembles that of insectivorous *Labidochromis*.

Like the latter, *M. joanjohnsonae* actively moves around its territory, screening the biocover for invertebrates. It halts regularly and focuses on a specific spot while hovering a few centimeters above the substrate. This behavior is often followed by a sudden dart forward and a bite into the biocover, in an attempt to dislodge the prey. Its food consists of nymphs and larvae of terrestrial and aquatic insects, small crustaceans, and the inevitable algae. It is interesting to note that nowhere else in such habitats is any small, insectivorous species recorded which does not belong to the genus *Labidochromis*. Of even more interest is the fact that all species of *Labidochromis* observed in the shallow waters at Likoma feed on algae! The carnivorous Pearl of Likoma appears to have found an otherwise unoccupied niche in this habitat. In fact, were it not for its bicuspid teeth and U-shaped dental arc it would be a worthy member of the genus *Labidochromis*. Moreover, the fact that females have been confused with those of *Labidochromis* spp. (even in the type series!) may indicate its close relationship with that genus. On the other hand, males and females are differently colored, and this is not very obvious in any of the described insectivorous *Labidochromis*. However, if it proves to be genuinely unrelated (genetically) then the similarity is a remarkable example of convergent evolution.

The Mozambique coast of the lake harbors several species of the genus *Labidochromis,* and two attractive species have found their niche in the wave-washed rocky habitat. Between Metangula and Thundu we find *Labidochromis* sp. 'textilis blue' and further south, between Lumessi and Meponda, *Labidochromis* sp. 'textilis cobalt'. These two species are closely related, but because the male coloration of the "Textilis Blue" does not change significantly along the 100 km of its range I regard those populations found south of the Lumessi River as belonging to the other species, *L.* sp. 'textilis cobalt'. The behavior of these two species does not differ greatly from that observed in *M. joanjohnsonae*. The females resemble those of the "Pearl of Likoma" in coloration.

Six different *Labidochromis* species inhabit the waters around Likoma Island. In the turbulent part of the rocky habitat we find *Labidochromis freibergi*, which has sometimes been exported as "Labidochromis Ewarti", and the closely related *Labidochromis zebroides*, which is restricted to the small Masimbwe islet. (In the Chi-Chewa language *masimbwe* means something slender and tall, and in the case of the islet it alludes to the almost vertical (underwater) slopes.) The maximum total length of both species is about 7 cm.

The upper rocky habitat around Chizumulu Island harbors another small mbuna of this genus: *Labidochromis strigatus*. Interestingly, all *Labidochromis* from Likoma and Chizumulu display territorial behavior. It seems that the *Labidochromis* from these islands have managed to find a niche among the herbivorous mbuna of the rocky habitat. The fact that they are restricted to the turbulent waters in areas with small rocks is probably their answer to the problem of competition for territory.

A similar situation is observed at the periphery of the distribution of the genus, i.e. in the far south of the lake. In earlier days herbivorous *Labidochromis* may have existed at other places as well, but better-adapted (more aggressive?) species have out-competed them. Herbivorous *Labidochromis* are still present at Likoma, Chizumulu, and south of Mbenji Island.

I think it possible (and if so, remarkable) that the insectivorous *Labidochromis* have evolved from aufwuchs-feeding ancestor species. The long slender teeth characteristic of this genus may initially have served to comb the filamentous algae in order to collect micro-organisms, or to extract aufwuchs from tiny pockets in the rocky substrate. This is probably still the case in a number of species, among them *Labidochromis heterodon*, which is endemic to Boadzulu Island. It suffers no competition from congeners and much less from other herbivorous mbuna than would be the case at the central rocky coasts of the lake. Only at the edge of its distribution is it confronted with *L. vellicans*, another herbivorous member of the genus.

L. heterodon has a vigorous growth of biocover all to itself. The numerous cormorants of this island stimulate the growth of algae with their droppings. The heavy load of nutrients also stimulates the growth of the snail population whose members may constitute part of *L. heterodon*'s diet. Stomach contents inventories have revealed chiefly algae, but the enlarged teeth on the pharyngeal bones may indicate that some harder material, such as crustaceans and maybe small snails, is eaten as well (Lewis, 1982). Unless *L. heterodon* finds itself compet-

1. *Pseudotropheus demasoni* ♂ Pombo Rocks

5. *Pseudotropheus demasoni* ♀ Pombo Rocks

2. *Melanochromis joanjohnsonae* ♂ Thumbi West Island

6. *Melanochromis joanjohnsonae* ♀ Maingano Island

3. *Labidochromis* sp. 'textilis cobalt' ♂ Chiloelo

7. *Labidochromis* sp. 'textilis cobalt' ♀ Lumessi

8. *Labidochromis* sp. 'textilis blue' ♀ Metangula

4. *Labidochromis* sp. 'textilis blue' ♂ Lumessi

9. *Labidochromis* sp. 'textilis blue' ♂ Chinuni

1. *Labidochromis zebroides* ♀ Masimbwe Island
2. *Labidochromis freibergi* ♀ Maingano Island
3. *Labidochromis strigatus* ♀ Machili Island
4. *Labidochromis strigatus* ♂ Membe Island
5. *Labidochromis heterodon* ♀ Boadzulu Island
6. *Labidochromis zebroides* ♂ Masimbwe Island
7. *Labidochromis freibergi* ♂ Maingano Island
8. *Labidochromis heterodon* ♂ Boadzulu Island

ing with congeners or similar species it is highly unlikely to evolve into a specialized mollusk-feeder or even into an insectivore.

Two further members of the genus *Labidochromis*, *Labidochromis vellicans* and *L. mylodon*, are present at Mumbo Island, where another cormorant colony fertilizes the algal layer on the rocks. The latter species, an insectivore, is discussed on page 140.

The herbivorous *Labidochromis* randomly nip at the aufwuchs and have to turn over much larger quantities than their insectivorous cousins to obtain a similar amount of nutritive foodstuff. They select small pockets and holes in the rocks that are overgrown with algae but inaccessible to most other herbivores. When I term a species herbivorous, this actually denotes that it feeds randomly from the biocover. The layer covering the substrate, however, contains a variable percentage of micro-organisms and small invertebrates as well as algal strands. In fact I should talk about omnivorous species instead. In practice I will, nevertheless, apply the term to those species (e.g. *Melanochromis melanopterus*) which feed from the aufwuchs as well as on invertebrates.

Labidochromis vellicans has spread mainly over the south of the lake; its northernmost localities being Senga Point on the west coast and Minos Reef on the eastern shore. The southernmost boundary of its distribution lies at Mpandi Island. It is, however, not found at Chinyamwezi Island. All in all *L. vellicans* has the widest distribution of the herbivorous species of the genus (the insectivorous *L. maculicauda* has a larger distribution in the north).

At Thumbi West Island *L. vellicans* shares the habitat with several introduced species of the genus. Ribbink *et al.* (1983b) do not believe in the purported introduction of *L. pallidus* at Thumbi as it is found all around the island. However, there is no doubt that *M. joanjohnsonae* has been introduced to this island, and this species is now found at the northwestern tip, far away from the site of its introduction. The other introduced species are found mainly at the site of their introduction, Mitande Rocks at the southeastern tip of the island. Many species from all over the lake have been released at this site and it is referred to as "The Aquarium" because most of the species have survived and small populations are still present. Other introduced *Labidochromis* species are *L. freibergi* and *L. gigas* (see page 101) from Likoma and *L. strigatus* from Chizumulu. They all belong to the herbivorous section of the genus and therefore suffer stronger competition from the indigenous *L. vellicans* and, of course, other herbivorous mbuna. This has undoubtedly hampered their dispersal along the shores of the island. Their territorial (sedentary) behavior is, however, probably the main reason for their slow progress in spreading. Another, undescribed, species, *Labidochromis* sp. 'blue bar', may also have been introduced at Mitande Rocks. This species is recorded from Namalenje Island where it is uncommon.

At Mbenji Island two species of *Labidochromis* are encountered: *Labidochromis mbenjii*, which is found in the upper rocky habitat, and *L. ianthinus*, which inhabits the calm waters of sediment-rich bays (see page 208). *L. mbenjii* feeds predominantly on biocover and on plankton when available.

Labidochromis maculicauda inhabits the surf biotope along the northwestern shores north of Kande Island on the west coast, and at all rocky shores north of Undu Point on the eastern shore. This small elongate species exhibits carnivorous feeding behavior and seems to be very successful as it is frequently seen in the preferred habitat of the genus. There are minor geographical differences between the many populations, and differences can also be detected between individuals of a single population. In contrast to other insectivorous *Labidochromis* there is sometimes a difference in coloration between male and female; although males do not appear to be territorial some can have a dark-blue cast on the body while others appear almost black.

All *Labidochromis* probably belong to the large group of mbuna whose eggs are fertilized inside the female's mouth. Interestingly the carnivorous species do not show any territorial behavior and in such species the sexes are usually almost identically colored. Male coloration might be important in mate recognition at a distance, a view supported by the fact that the territorial herbivorous *Labidochromis* from Likoma and Chizumulu have a more pronounced difference in coloration between the sexes. Females of the territorial species have to leave their feeding grounds to mate. They have to locate the right male which must therefore have a specific coloration. In the non-territorial carnivorous species breeding behavior is different: the male approaches the female and tries to coax her into mating. Spawning usually takes place inside a cave, but in captivity spawnings on the bare sand have been witnessed.

Non-mbuna

There is only one species group of non-mbuna found in the wave-washed upper habitat, consisting of four species which are all closely related and which show very similar behavior. They have a non-overlapping distribution throughout the lake and are common at steep rocky coasts.

The best-known species of this group is *Protomelas spilonotus*. This species is frequently collected at Mbenji Island and is known in the aquarium trade under the misleading name of "Haplochromis Ovatus". *Otopharynx ovatus* is in fact a different, egg-robbing species (see page 261). The type locality of *P. spilonotus* is at Chilumba. The populations at Chilumba and Ruarwe are indistinguishable from those at Mbenji Island and Eccles Reef (Malaŵi) and those at Minos Reef, Nkhungu Reef, Nkhungu Point, and Lumessi (Mozambique), and are likewise identical to those found at Magunga Reef, Tanzania. There is no doubt that we are dealing with the same species. However, in between these widely separated locations we find very similar but different species. In Tanzania *Protomelas* sp. 'spilonotus tanzania' occurs south of the Ruhuhu River and has been seen at Thumbi Point, and at Puulu, Hongi, Lundo, and Ngkuyo islands. At Undu Reef, Tanzania, and Wikihi and Londo, Mozambique, another species, *Protomelas* sp. 'spilonotus mozambique', occupies the same niche. Yet another species, *Protomelas* sp. 'spilonotus likoma', is found around Likoma and Chizumulu Islands, and also at Chilucha Reef near Metangula. The behavior of these four species and the niches they occupy in the biotope are so similar in each case that we cannot but conclude that they must be very closely related to each other.

Remarkably the gold-headed form of *P. spilonotus* (at Nakantenga Island the colored patch on the head is white-blue instead of sulfur-yellow) has two main areas of distribution which are more than 300 km apart and each of which has populations on opposite sides of the lake. Moreover the area in between these two main distribution regions harbors the very similar species mentioned above. This strongly indicates that *P. spilonotus* is the oldest species of the group and that the other three have evolved from this once more widespread species.

The species of the *P. spilonotus* group usually form small feeding schools and remain in midwater a few meters away from large boulders. They are carnivorous cichlids which feed on insects and other soft-bodied invertebrates that fall or are washed into the water. When plankton is available not only females but also males are found feeding on it. Male *spilonotus*-types normally defend territories in the open water and are much less aggressive in claiming their domain than, for example, *P. taeniolatus*. Territories are located in the upper five meters of the open water but spawning takes place in the caves of the rocky substrate. The maximum total length of *P. spilonotus* is around 25 cm (in males; females may reach a total length of about 16 cm). The other species in the *spilonotus* group remain about 5 cm smaller.

1. *Labidochromis vellicans* ♂ Thumbi East Island
2. *Labidochromis maculicauda* ♂ Lundo Island
3. *Labidochromis mbenjii* ♂ Mbenji Island
4. *Labidochromis vellicans* ♀ Thumbi West Island
5. *Labidochromis* sp. 'blue bar' ♂ Namalenje Island
6. *Labidochromis maculicauda* ♀ Ngwazi
7. *Labidochromis mbenjii* ♀ Mbenji Island

1. *Protomelas spilonotus* ♀ Thumbi West Island

2. *Protomelas spilonotus* ♂ Nakantenga Island

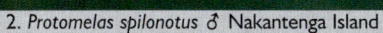
3. *Protomelas* sp. 'spilonotus likoma' ♀ Membe Point (Likoma)

4. *Protomelas* sp. 'spilonotus mozambique' ♀ Londo

5. *Protomelas* sp. 'spilonotus tanzania' ♀ Lundu

6. *Protomelas spilonotus* ♂ Chimwalani Reef

7. *Protomelas* sp. 'spilonotus likoma' ♂ Membe Island (Chizumulu)

8. *Protomelas* sp. 'spilonotus mozambique' ♂ Hai Reef

9. *Protomelas* sp. 'spilonotus tanzania' ♂ Puulu Island

The sediment-free rocky habitat

This habitat is normally populated by large numbers of mbuna. Food is available in abundance and thus competition is mainly for territories. The result is that every square meter has been claimed by one cichlid or another. The size of the rocks may vary from football-size to huge boulders several tens of meters in diameter. The sediment-free areas are usually located on rather steep sloping shores where the sediment accumulates at the base of the rocks (rather than on them), where the gradient changes to the slowly-sloping sand floor. The rocks are invariably covered with a layer of aufwuchs which contains more green algae in the shallow areas. The aufwuchs consists of a variety of algae: the tough strands of some filamentous algae (*Calothrix* and *Cladophora*) are attached to the rocks and form the matrix on which other algae, the so-called "loose aufwuchs", grow. The loose aufwuchs contains different types of algae strands, but the many unicellular algae (diatoms) also found on it may constitute its most nutritious part. No vertebrate animal is capable of digesting the outer wall of a plant cell without the help of micro-organisms. To be of nutritive value this wall has to be mechanically broken or crushed in order to expose the easily digestible contents of the cell. Diatoms have cell walls perforated by many pores and are therefore rapidly digested. It is, however, far from certain that the amounts of diatoms available are by themselves sufficient to support a healthy population of mbuna. The biocover contains not only algae and diatoms but, intermingled with the algae strands, there are enormous quantities of invertebrates, which, packed in a mass of algae, are an important source of proteins for the mbuna. Nevertheless, because algae dominate stomach contents in most species, we call these species herbivores.

Those mbuna that do approximate to true herbivores have numerous fine teeth on the pharyngeal bones. The upper and lower pharyngeal teeth are rubbed against each other and partially crush the algae cells between them. Nevertheless a lot remain intact and leave the body as a kind of indigestible fiber. To allow the digestive juices enough time to penetrate the broken algal cells, the intestine of herbivores is considerably longer than the fish itself (up to ten times longer). (In some piscivores the intestine may be only 30% of the fish's length.) The long gut in herbivores serves as a holding reservoir, as these species have a large intake of slowly digestible food. Typically, the lining of the body cavity in herbivores is pitch-black. Thus, without investigating the gut contents, we can tell immediately if the fish in question feeds on algae or has a carnivorous diet.

The rocks of this habitat create many caves and crevices that are used by mbuna as spawning-sites. Sometimes, in places with large boulders, the caves are deep and high. Such caves are preferred by some species of the genus *Cynotilapia*, many of the elongate species of *Pseudotropheus* and *Tropheops*, and a few larger non-mbuna. Many cave-dwelling mbuna of the sediment-free rocky habitat have a predominantly dark coloration.

The zebras

The sediment-free rocky habitat is home to the "zebra", *Metriaclima zebra*, and a number of other species in this genus collectively known as "zebra cichlids", which can be classified in three different groups.

The first group consists of the classic zebra complex: *M. zebra* plus *M. pyrsonotos, M. emmiltos, M. mbenjii, M. greshakei, M.* sp. 'zebra slim', and *M.* sp. 'red top londo'. Members of this group are found only in clear water at sediment-free rocky coasts and do not have a continuous distribution. Except at Mphanga Rocks and neighboring Luwino Reef, neither *M. zebra* nor any other member of this group occurs in the northwestern part of the lake (north of Mara

Rocks).

The second species group also has a wide distribution and consists of the "Cobalt Zebras": *M. callainos, M. estherae,* and *M.* sp. 'estherae blueface'. They are dealt with on page 56.

The third group, the "large zebras", also has a lake-wide, but patchy, distribution and are found mainly at extensive nutrient-rich rocky coasts. This group includes *M. fainzilberi, M. xanstomachus,* and *M.* sp. 'zebra chilumba'. This group is covered in detail on page 61.

At several localities members of all three groups occur sympatrically.

All the species in all of these groups exhibit polychromatism, i.e. their populations contain OB (orange blotch, i.e. orange with black blotches or spots) and O (orange) morphs (see page 20 for a general discussion of these morphs) as well as normally colored individuals. This is the main reason for grouping these fishes together as above.

The classic zebra complex

Metriaclima zebra, the classic "Zebra Cichlid", has black bars on a blue body, and is also called the "BB Zebra" (for the blue and black vertical barring (Fryer & Iles, 1972: 326)). It was among the first mbuna ever exported from the lake and was first collected for the aquarium trade around Cape Maclear in the southern part of the lake. *M. zebra* is one of the few species of mbuna that are found at many places around the lake. It occurs at sediment-free rocky coasts, and does not have a continuous distribution. It is found from Cape Manulo to Kande Island, around Namalenje Island, the Nankumba peninsula, Boadzulu Island, and from Makanjila Point to Mala Point, from Mbamba Bay to Lundu, and from Lumbila to Ikombe on the eastern shore. It is also found around Likoma and at Taiwanee Reef (previously known as Taiwan Reef). The holotype of *M. zebra* was collected by Woodward at Likoma Island (Barnes, 1933; Yarnton Mills, 1911) and the form at this island is characterized by a blue-black bar pattern and a blue dorsal fin.

The classic zebra complex contains various distinguishable forms that have a mostly patchy distribution. As well as the typical BB zebra there are non-barred populations found in areas with more sediment, the so-called "blue blaze" zebras, the red-top zebras, and a few species that do not seem to fit any of these four sub-groups.

While the BB zebra is a resident of sediment-free rocky coasts, *M. zebra*-like mbuna are also found at more sediment-rich areas where the rocks have become covered with sediment (over a period of time), and in these forms the bar pattern is not very distinct or completely lacking. Such populations are found mainly in between populations of *M. zebra* with distinctly barred individuals. For example, the BB populations at Kande Island and Namalenje Island are indistinguishable from each other but are separated by a large stretch of sandy shoreline, and the zebras present in between these two populations show only traces of vertical bars. Nevertheless, although genetic contact between the two populations of BB zebra (Kande Island and Namalenje) has been lost for thousands of years, we still regard them as belonging to one species, and likewise the unbarred zebras in between. However, mate-selection experiments (George Turner, pers. comm.) indicate that females of a northern population can distinguish between males of their own population and those of a southern, even when we cannot. Much additional research is required to resolve the situation.

Unbarred zebras are also found between Undu Reef and Londo, and between Lumbaulo and Mala Point on the east coast; at Jalo Reef; at Mbenji Island, at Maleri and Nankoma islands, at the southern part of Chizumulu Island, and at Makokola Reef in the southeastern arm of the lake. The populations at Mbenji Island and Makokola Reef are discussed on page 53.

The non-barred form at Maleri and Nankoma islands has been found to be morphologically indistinguishable from the nearest *M. zebra* population—the BB zebra at Namalenje Island—and is therefore regarded as another population of *M. zebra* (Konings & Stauffer, 2006). It is very common around two of the Maleri Islands (Maleri and Nankoma) and has a completely pale blue color without black bars.

1. *Metriaclima zebra* ♂ Same Bay (Chizumulu)

5. *Metriaclima* cf. *zebra* ♂ Lundo Island

2. *M. zebra* × *M. pyrsonotos* ♂ Makanjila Point

6. *Metriaclima zebra* ♂ Linganjala Reef

3. *Metriaclima zebra* ♂ Likoma

7. *Metriaclima zebra* ♀ Gome

4. *Metriaclima zebra* ♀ Boadzulu Island

8. *Metriaclima zebra* ♀ Lutara

The females are generally beige colored but a small part of the population is of the OB or the O morph. Interestingly this form is also found at Chidunga Rocks near Chipoka where it shares the habitat with *M. cyneusmarginatus*, a zebra of shallow intermediate biotopes. This is about six times as far from Maleri as nearby Nakantenga Island, where *M. zebra* is absent! At Nakantenga, however, *M. pyrsonotos* (see page 54) is the representative of the classic zebra complex that lives in this habitat. There is no deep trough between Maleri and Nakantenga but the rocks at the south side of Nakantenga lie deeper than those at Maleri and this may have led to the earlier settlement of Nakantenga as the lake level rose. The population of *M. zebra* at Maleri and Nankoma islands may be influenced by recurrent contact with some mainland populations (e.g. that at Chidunga Rocks). The rocks at Maleri have more sediment than those at Nakantenga and this may support the argument that the zebra here has "lost its bars" as is seen in other sediment-rich rocky biotopes (e.g. Jalo Reef and Membe Island). However, a reef a few hundred meters northeast of Nankoma Island is inhabited by *M. pyrsonotos* and no other zebra. The highest point of this reef is about 25 meters below the surface and the rocks are covered with a thick layer of sediment. (At the time of my visit (August, 1992) visibility in the water was extremely poor—less than one meter.) It thus seems that the timing of the first settlement of a rocky biotope, and its subsequent isolation from other such biotopes, may sometimes be the most important factor in the composition of the cichlid community (see page 20).

A further form of the classic zebra complex inhabits the rocky shores in the northeastern part of the lake. Males of these populations have a light blue blaze on the head—in fact it is the lack of the two black interorbital bars normally present in the classic zebra group that produces this pattern. Not only the color pattern but also the smaller size (compared to most other *M. zebra* populations) distinguishes these zebras from the others. In addition the "Blue Blaze Zebras" have a discontinuous distribution. They occur on the mainland coast between Kirondo and Manda, at Lundo Island, at Londo (Mozambique), and at the northern part of Chizumulu Island. The fact that these zebras are not found together with the blue-black or the non-barred zebras may indicate that they simply represent another geographical variant of *M. zebra,* and for the time being they are regarded as such. This view is supported by morphological comparisons between various Tanzanian populations of the blue blaze zebras and those of BB zebras from further south on the Mozambique mainland shore (Kristin Black, pers. comm.), which revealed that there was no significant distinction between any of the populations examined. In addition, Knight & Turner (2004) found no restrictions in mate recognition between the BB zebra population of Nkhata Bay and the blue-blaze form from Chizumulu Island.

The fourth form of the classic zebra complex, the so-called "Red-Top Zebras", is found at several locations around the lake. These mbuna have a similar color pattern to the BB zebra but in addition have an orange to red colored dorsal fin. Previously it was unclear whether these red-tops were a different species or a geographical variant, and there is no place where both the red-top and the BB zebra occur naturally together in the same habitat, a situation which, if it did occur, would indicate they were two different species. However, recent studies increasingly indicate that this is the case, and, indeed, that the red-top zebras may themselves constitute a species complex. A number of red-top zebras, found at geographically isolated areas in the lake, have already been described scientifically as distinct species, but not all of them are accepted as valid in this book. Konings & Stauffer (2006) compared the *M. zebra* at the Maleri and Namalenje islands and the ecologically equivalent red-top zebra at neighboring Nakantenga Island, described as *Metriaclima pyrsonotos,* and found convincing support for the hypothesis that *M. zebra* and *M. pyrsonotos* are two separate taxa. The distinct difference in coloration between *M. pyrsonotos* and both forms of *M. zebra* concurred with marked differences in morphometrics and they therefore concluded that these forms are heterospecific.

This is further corroborated by the presence of a small, introduced population of *M. pyrsonotos* at Maleri Island (Ribbink *et al.*, 1983b: 162), which, over two decades, has maintained its status (confirmed again in Oct. 2006) within the large population of *M. zebra* without visible hybridization and/or introgression.

Smith & Kornfield (2002) analyzed the genomes of four different red-top populations and found that the red-top population from Mphanga Rocks, described as *Metriaclima emmiltos*, is genetically distant from those in the southern part of the lake, but that the three populations in the south are genetically closely related. Accordingly, the red-top zebra found at Chimwalani (previously Eccles) Reef, described as *M. thapsinogen*, and the red-top that inhabits the shoreline at Nkhudzi and Mphande Island, described as *M. sandaracinos*, are in this book both regarded as populations, and hence junior synonyms, of *M. pyrsonotos*. These red-top populations are in relatively short range of each other, are genetically closely related (Smith & Kornfield, 2002), and, on the basis of coloration, there are no compelling arguments to regard each of them as a different species.

Research by George Turner and his colleagues at the University of Hull, UK, has also provided a lot of information regarding the relationships between the various zebras. The most revealing experiments performed were those where females of a single population were offered a choice of males derived from different populations. In the case of female *M. emmiltos* they were found to be true to their proper mates and were much less likely to mate with a regular BB zebra from Nkhata Bay (Knight & Turner, 2004). It is thus apparent that *M. emmiltos* should be regarded as a good species. Its distribution is restricted to Mphanga Rocks and Luwino Reef.

At Makanjila Point the zebra population consists of males that are variable in the coloration of the dorsal fin: some have a red-colored fin but in others it can be yellow or white. Smith *et al.* (2003) found, using DNA analysis, that this population consists of natural hybrids between the BB form of *M. zebra*—found north of Makanjila Point—and *M. pyrsonotos* from Chimwalani Reef.

For a long time it was thought that red-top zebras were not polymorphic, i.e. OB or O morphs were not found. However, a population of *M. pyrsonotos* with a high percentage of O morph individuals (including males) lives at a reef 500 meters south of Nakantenga Island. These orange-pink individuals are very conspicuous and seem to contradict the hypothesis that OB-morphs (and O-morphs) exist because their coloration blends in with the background (see page 20). A few so-called "marmalade cats" have also been seen at Nakantenga Island itself.

The populations of unbarred zebras with red dorsals found at Mbenji Island and Makokola Reef have been assigned to different species, *Metriaclima mbenjii* and *Metriaclima greshakei* respectively, a grouping that I will follow until a better understanding of their relationships with the other red-top zebra populations is achieved. The fact that they have a red-colored dorsal fin may indicate that, analogous to what is indicated by the red-top mate-selection experiments mentioned above, they are indeed different from *M. zebra*. In what respect they differ from *M. pyrsonotos*, apart from the obvious lack of vertical bars, remains to be investigated. Analogous to some of the unbarred forms of *M. zebra* (see above) the unbarred red-top zebras may equally be geographical variants of *M. pyrsonotos* that "lost" their bars as an adaptation to the increased sedimentation of their habitat.

M. mbenjii, regularly exported as the "Red-Top Cobalt", is endemic to the Mbenji islands and usually encountered in the clear waters around rocky outcrops. It has a remarkably high percentage of OB males (marmalade cats) and females. It is the only species of *Metriaclima* found in the sediment-free environment at Mbenji. Males stake out their territories in the sediment-free regions and display aggression mainly towards conspecifics, including marmalade cats!

Two further species that clearly belong to the classic zebra complex cannot be grouped in one of the four sub-groups mentioned above: *Metriaclima* sp. 'zebra slim' and *Metriaclima* sp.

1. *Metriaclima emmiltos* ♂ Mphanga Rocks

2. *Metriaclima pyrsonotos* ♂ Nakantenga Island

3. *Metriaclima pyrsonotos* ♂ Nkhudzi

4. *Metriaclima pyrsonotos* ♂ Chimwalani Reef

5. *Metriaclima emmiltos* ♀ Mphanga Rocks

6. *Metriaclima pyrsonotos* ♀ Nakantenga Island

7. *Metriaclima pyrsonotos* OB ♀ Nakantenga Island

8. *Metriaclima pyrsonotos* ♀ Nkhudzi

9. *Metriaclima pyrsonotos* ♀ Chimwalani Reef

1. *Metriaclima mbenjii* ♂ Mbenji Island

2. *Metriaclima mbenjii* OB ♀ Mbenji Island

3. *Metriaclima greshakei* ♀ Makokola Reef

4. *Metriaclima* sp. 'zebra slim' ♀ Higga Reef

5. *Metriaclima* sp. 'zebra slim' ♀ Ngkuyo Island

6. *Metriaclima* sp. 'red top londo' ♀ Londo

7. *Metriaclima mbenjii* ♂ Mbenji Island

8. *Metriaclima greshakei* ♂ Makokola Reef

9. *Metriaclima* sp. 'zebra slim' ♂ Ngkuyo Island

10. *Metriaclima* sp. 'red top londo' ♂ Londo

'red top londo'. *M.* sp. 'zebra slim' inhabits the rocky reef, known locally as Higga Reef, north of Ngkuyo Island (also known as Mbamba Bay Island), the island itself, and the rocky coast south of Mbamba Bay village, known as Chuwa. This species exhibits the same behavior as *M. zebra* at other localities and the distributions of these two species do not overlap. It is possible to argue that geographical variation between *M. zebra* populations is acceptable, and this may include variation in morphology, such that the "Zebra Slim" would become yet another geographical variant of *M. zebra*. But for the time being it is treated as a distinct species that is characterized by a slender body. It too exhibits polychromatism; OB females are very common at Higga Reef and even marmalade cats can be found there.

Recently I found a population of what I initially thought, based on coloration, was a variant of *Cynotilapia* sp. 'mbamba' (see page 71) at Londo, Mozambique. However, when I saw how they raked the algae from the rocks I anticipated that they would have bicuspid teeth in a configuration typical of *Metriaclima*. On examination this species did indeed turn out to be a member of *Metriaclima* and I have named it *M.* sp. 'red top londo'. The initial generic misidentification suggests that coloration is less likely to indicate to what genus a species belongs than is the particular feeding technique employed. Interestingly two different members of *Cynotilapia* are present at the same locality: *C. afra* and *C.* sp. 'mbamba'.

Regardless of their taxonomy, all species of the classic zebra complex have morphological and behavioral features in common. They feed in a position perpendicular to the substrate. The teeth in the outer row in each jaw have a double cusp and function as a comb. The teeth in the inner rows have three cusps and are movable. When the fish eats, the mouth is opened wide and the jaws are pressed against the substrate. As the mouth is closed, the teeth comb the so-called "loose aufwuchs" from the rocks. The filamentous algae remain fixed to the substrate. The zebras are specialized for this kind of browsing, but when plankton is available in sufficient quantities they usually feed from this source instead. Females do not have territories and congregate in large groups while feeding from the plankton in the water column. Males normally forage from the biocover within their territories, but when plankton is abundant they join the females and juveniles in the water column.

The zebras spawn in caves and the eggs are fertilized inside the female's mouth. The fry are guarded and take refuge inside the female's mouth for a few days after release. As discussed in a previous chapter (see page 17), females do not rely exclusively on male breeding coloration when choosing a mate (Plenderleith *et al.*, 2005), and this behavior would explain the presence of OB males. Mate recognition is dependent on several factors, of which color is just one. The courting behavior of the male, his territory, his contours, his scent, and the way he feeds from the substrate, are important features that the female evaluates during courtship. Furthermore, since zebras are sedentary and males have permanent territories, a female may remember where certain males in her neighborhood have their domains. All these factors may combine to produce an accurate species-recognition "picture" without male coloration being the sole trigger. Although male coloration may be the dominant factor for mate selection in most territorial mbuna, some territorial species (i.e. the classic zebras, *L. fuelleborni*, *L. trewavasae*, and a few species of *Tropheops*) seem nevertheless to have found (or retained?) additional ways of achieving partner recognition. This also means that males must recognize OB and O females in order to pass on the polymorphic genes. In October 2004 I witnessed an OB male of *M. pyrsonotos* at Nakantenga Island courting an O female and leading her into his cave. A few minutes later the same OB male led a normal-colored female into his cave where she proceeded to lay a single egg.

The second group: the cobalt zebras

Along the northwestern coast between Kande Island and Ngara, *Metriaclima callainos* occurs in three different populations which differ in coloration (Ribbink *et al.*, 1983b). The populations on the northeastern coast look alike and are distributed from Ikombe to Puulu.

The "Cobalt Zebra" form of *M. callainos* occurs from Kande Island to Mbowe Island and is one of the mainstays of the hobby. It is present in large numbers in its natural habitat. At Thumbi West Island and at Maleri Island, where it has been introduced, this form has established a healthy population. It was the "Cobalt Zebra" form which actually provided the type specimen of *M. callainos*.

A displaying cobalt male has a very light, brilliant blue coloration; females never attain a brilliant hue. A large part of the female population is blue, a feature it shares only with the females of *M.* sp. 'blue reef' and *M. lombardoi* (see page 185). The blue females are probably not quickly recognized as females by any other mbuna and thus avoid being courted by males of, for example, *M. zebra* (Holzberg, 1978). Since *M. zebra* has criteria other than male coloration by which the female selects her mate, a reliable segregation of the two species may also be possible on the basis of specific female coloration. If this is indeed the case then male behavior must play an important role in species recognition in *M. zebra*.

Some cobalt females, however, are white—the O morph equivalent in the blue form—while OB is expressed not as orange, but as pinkish-blue, with black blotches. These OB females are regularly caught for export. Pure white males are also seen; these are the equivalent of marmalade cats in this species. At Mara Rocks and Cape Manulo blue and white males have both been seen courting mainly blotched and white females.

The so-called "Pearl Zebra" belongs to the same species as the "Cobalt"—and is frequently observed along the west coast between Ruarwe and Ngara and the northeastern shore north of Puulu. As the name indicates, the color of the male "Pearl Zebra" is mother-of-pearl, while that of the female is more cream-like. Displaying males attain the whitest white possible in a cichlid. Blue males are seen occasionally in populations of the "Pearl Zebra" (e.g. at Katale and Chirwa islands, and at Makonde).

Chitande Island is home to the third color population of *M. callainos*. Males are indistinguishable from "Cobalt Zebra" males but females are white blotched.

Metriaclima estherae, the "Red Zebra", has much in common with *M. callainos* from the western coast, i.e. males are bright blue without barring. As is common in all members of the three zebra groups, polychromatism occurs in this species too. The normal color of females is beige to brown. The O females are, however, a deep red-orange color and are a very attractive addition to any aquarium. In the early 1970s exporters at Metangula selected these orange females—there are also OB females but it is not certain whether or not these were exported—for shipment with the blue males. The species was subsequently re-imported after a period of almost 20 years, but it had not vanished from the aquarium hobby. O morph males were also exported in the early 1970s together with normal-colored males. Marmalade cats of the OB morph are extremely rare. The O males (these have been seen only at Minos Reef) are a very light, white-pink color that becomes almost pure white when they are territorial. These O-morph marmalade cats have been used to produce a strain of orange-red males which is sometimes the most common variant of this species available from breeders. Orange-red males have not been seen in the wild, but as such males would be very difficult to distinguish among thousands of orange-red females it cannot be stated definitely that they do not exist. When a normal blue male is mated to an orange female, the fry can be sexed as soon as they appear from the female's mouth; males are beige-brown and females are orange.

In June 1994 I collected some specimens of these "Red Zebras" at Minos Reef (near Meluluca) in order to formally describe the species as *M. estherae*. During examination of these specimens I found that the blue females I had collected (I anticipated that the normal-colored females would be blue) did not have the same morphology as the red and blotched ones and were thus a different species. I found that there were two different kinds of males: one had yellow spots in the soft part of the dorsal fin and a broad mouth like the red females, while the

1. *Metriaclima callainos* ♂ Matema

6. *Metriaclima callainos* ♀ Matema

2. *Metriaclima callainos* ♂ Chitande Island

7. *Metriaclima callainos* ♀ Chitande Island

3. *Metriaclima callainos* ♂ Luwino Reef

8. *Metriaclima callainos* ♀ Luwino Reef

4. *Metriaclima callainos* ♂ Luwino Reef

9. *Metriaclima callainos* ♀ Luwino Reef

5. *Metriaclima callainos* ♂ Nkhata Bay

10. *Metriaclima callainos* ♂ Nkhata Bay

1. *Metriaclima estherae* O ♀ Minos Reef

2. *Metriaclima estherae* ♀ Chiloelo

3. *Metriaclima estherae* O ♀ Gome

4. *Metriaclima* sp. 'estherae blueface' ♀ Lumessi

5. *Metriaclima* sp. 'estherae blueface' OB ♀ Lumessi

6. *Metriaclima estherae* ♂ Chiloelo

7. *Metriaclima estherae* OB ♀ Minos Reef

8. *Metriaclima* sp. 'estherae blueface' ♂ Lumessi

other had tiny orange spots on the very edge of the dorsal and a narrower mouth. I thus discovered that at Minos Reef there are two species with almost identical males: *M. estherae* and *M.* sp. 'blue reef' (see page 177). Males of the "Blue Reef" court only blue females while *M. estherae* displays to just the red and OB females. The yellow spots in the dorsal of *M. estherae* are a helpful characteristic for differentiating those individuals that are found near *M. sp.* 'blue reef', which occurs in intermediate habitats at Minos Reef and at Nkhungu Reef, approximately 10 km south of Minos. Interestingly *M. estherae* males in populations north of Minos Reef lack the yellow spots. Such a shift in the morphology or behavior of one species with the presence or absence of a closely related form is not uncommon in the animal kingdom. If for example, females are keying in on the yellow spots in the dorsal fin then any female that selects a mate without these spots will fail to pass on her genes in the long term because she bred with the "wrong" species and hybrids resulted. In areas where the "Blue Reef" forms are not present there is no such penalty for breeding with males without the yellow spots. Thus there is no strong selection pressure for the yellow spots. Another remarkable observation is that at Minos Reef and at Nkhungu Reef all *M. estherae* females are either completely red or blotched (at least, I have never found other morphs). In other places the majority of *M. estherae* females are of "normal" coloration (beige or brown), although numerous red and OB individuals are seen as well.

The segregation of neighboring cichlid species in Lake Malaŵi is probably maintained by female selection of an appropriate mate. The differences in coloration between males of different species facilitate correct mate selection and thus a genetic segregation which keeps the species pure. In the case of *M. estherae* and the "Blue Reef", however, it is remarkable that the females of each species are able to recognize their true mates. On the other hand, they may rely heavily on the courting efforts of the male who is, without doubt, able to recognize the right female. At close quarters a female may confirm her initial mate recognition by the male's scent.

The distribution of *M. estherae* encompasses a much larger area than that of the "Blue Reef". It includes, as mentioned earlier, Chilucha Reef and also the southern tip of the Metangula peninsula. The latter locality may not be a natural habitat of *M. estherae* as it is the site where an exporter of ornamental fishes had his station. In November 1994 I discovered that the color of the females was not consistent as is the case in the other three known populations: some females were orange while others exhibited a bright red coloration, yet others had a few black blotches on the body (OB morph); plain beige-colored females were seen as well. North of the Nsinje River at Masinje, Malaŵi, and also a few kilometers north of Meponda, there are further populations of *M. estherae*. The blue males of *M. estherae* at Gome are very similar to those of *M. chrysomallos* (see page 177).

Between the population of *M. estherae* at Meponda and the one found at Nkhungu Point lies a 55 km long stretch of rocky coast not inhabited by this species. However, a zebra with a morphological resemblance to *M. estherae* (but different coloration) occurs in the sediment-free rocky habitat between these two localities (around Lumessi). On the basis of the similarity and geography I have named this mbuna *Metriaclima* sp. 'estherae blueface', the second name alluding to the dark blue color on the lower part of the male's head. Females are light brown, but orange and OB-females are also present. It is possible that *M. estherae* is strictly bound to sediment-free areas and that rocky shores with intermediate habitats or with a heavy load of sediment do not offer the proper environment. *M.* sp. 'estherae blueface' is possibly a geographical variant of *M. estherae*.

The third group: the large zebras

At Mphanga Rocks the most abundant zebra is *M. emmiltos*, which is observed in large schools foraging in the water column. The Pearl Zebra (*M. callainos*) is present and commonly observed in numbers, but *Metriaclima* sp. 'zebra chilumba"—the representative of this third, large zebra, group—is rather rare. A few kilometers south, at Luwino Reef, *M.* sp. 'zebra chilumba' is very common but *M. emmiltos* is much less common. A degree of habitat preference apparently exists among the zebras that live in the sediment-free habitat. The members of the classic zebra complex have a strong liking for a sediment-free environment and large rocks. The larger zebras, however, seem to have a degree of tolerance of sediment-covered habitats and are found mostly in the upper five meters of the rocky biotope consisting of medium-sized rocks.

M. sp. 'zebra chilumba' is caught (for export) at Luwino Reef where the distinctive yellow chin is most brightly colored. Its distribution stretches from Ngara to Chirwa Island, and although yellow-throated large zebras are found south of Chirwa Island as well I will regard these as belonging to another species, *M. fainzilberi*. The color pattern of *M.* sp. 'zebra chilumba' varies moderately from one population to another, but is rather constant in the populations between Ngara and Chirwa compared to that of the yellow-throated zebras found south of Chirwa Island. Solely for this reason I regard *M.* sp. 'zebra chilumba' as different from *M. fainzilberi*, but these two species are very closely related and could well be a single taxon.

As mentioned above, the large zebra forms found along the northwestern shore south of Chirwa Island are here referred to *Metriaclima fainzilberi*. These include the form at Mbowe Island, which bears a close resemblance to the "Chilumba Zebra"; and the form at Mara Rocks, which lacks any distinct vertical barring and thus resembles *M. xanstomachus* from the Maleri Islands. Both are here regarded as populations of *M. fainzilberi*. It is, however, almost impossible to find a good characteristic for differentiating between *M.* sp. 'zebra chilumba' and *M. fainzilberi*. Males of *M.* sp. 'zebra chilumba' do, however, lack the yellow patch at the base of the pectoral fins which is seen in almost all populations of *M. fainzilberi*. Moreover males of many populations of *M. fainzilberi* have a golden yellow color on the chest as well as on the throat. But not until all the forms involved have been carefully evaluated will it be possible to make any positive distinction between geographical variants and species.

M. fainzilberi was described from specimens collected near Makonde on the northeastern shore of the lake (Staeck, 1976) and has a wide distribution. It is found along the entire Tanzanian shore and into Mozambique waters as far south as Lumbaulo. In the southern part of Mozambique, at Lumessi, a yellow-breasted zebra occurs in the rocky habitat but this population is presently assigned to *M. zebra* (Kristin Black, pers. comm.). This just goes to show how complicated the mbuna community in Lake Malaŵi is, and I am talking here of only two or three species! Of course, I could just ignore such problems and assign each and every population to a different species, but this would still leave the problem of the intermediate forms, which are plentiful in the lake.

On the Malaŵi coast between Chirwa Island and Usisya the "Goldbreast Zebras", geographical variants of *M. fainzilberi*, are found. The golden color on the chest of territorial males is much brighter than that in the populations of *M.* sp. 'zebra chilumba'.

In Tanzania there are many localities where *M. fainzilberi* is sympatric with a member of the classic zebra complex; on the other side of the lake a large zebra is found sympatrically with a classic barred zebra only at Mphanga Rocks, Luwino Reef, and at Nakantenga Island, but in these cases the barred zebras have a red-colored dorsal fin. It is impossible to know at present whether all the barred zebras found in the southern half of the lake are derived from (or belong to) *M. zebra* or *M. fainzilberi*. I do not want to confuse matters further, but I would not be surprised if future research shows that these southern populations are in fact *M. fainzilberi* and not *M. zebra*. *M. fainzilberi* seems to have a higher tolerance of sediment-rich areas and may thus have a better chance of spreading itself around the lake and settling faster into new habitats.

In areas where the rocks are covered with a thick layer of sediment (e.g. Sani and Chidunga Rocks) a large zebra with a black stripe in the dorsal fin, *Metriaclima cyneusmarginatus*, is found. This zebra is closely related to *M.*

fainzilberi. An extensive distribution for *M. fainzilberi* would further explain the presence at the Maleri Islands of a large yellow-throated zebra which has been described as *Metriaclima xanstomachus* (Stauffer & Boltz, 1989). This population could have been founded by *M. fainzilberi* (or *M. cyneusmarginatus*) migrating along the mainland shores. But until the relationships between *M. fainzilberi* and the other large zebras are resolved, it is convenient to keep the names *M. cyneusmarginatus* and *M. xanstomachus*.

The large zebras prefer the upper regions of the biotope. The densest concentrations occur a few meters above the habitat of the somewhat deeper living classic zebras (at places where they are found side by side). The maps on pages 62 and 63 show the variation found in several large zebra populations and should help to illustrate the extent of the complexity encountered among these mbuna.

In all three zebra groups spawning takes place throughout the year. Sexually active males defend a cave in the rocky habitat from which all other fishes are chased. Ripe females are attracted to the male's cave where spawning takes place in seclusion. Mouthbrooding females hide among the rocks where they incubate the eggs and larvae for about three weeks. The juveniles are released among groups of similar-sized mbuna. The juveniles have the same coloration as the female unless she is of the OB or O morph, in which case the male juveniles exhibit the *normal* female coloration. The black blotches in OB juveniles do not appear until they are at least three months old.

More zebras

A few other species are grouped here because they have a similar coloration to members of the previous groups and are zebra-like in form. Although their direct relationship to the above-mentioned zebras is unclear, they are true members of the genus *Metriaclima*. The species of this "group" are *Metriaclima* sp. 'aggressive bars', *Metriaclima* sp. 'chinyankwazi', and *Metriaclima* sp. 'boadzulu'. Although the relationships between these species are also unclear they may in fact be conspecific or at least very closely related, but since they are nowhere very common (with the possible exception of the population at Chiloelo) different names have been given to the known populations. As well as having a similar color pattern—the black submarginal band in the dorsal is a very obvious shared character—they are usually found in the somewhat deeper rocky habitats. The zebras of this group are further characterized by the shape and structure of the oral teeth. The teeth in the outer rows are relatively large and spaced wider than in most other *Metriaclima*. In fact, these zebras may form a link between *Cynotilapia*—few, large teeth—and *Metriaclima*, characterized by its bicuspid teeth and its feeding behavior (see page 26). These mbuna are found south of the Rukuru River on the west coast and south of the Ruhuhu River on the eastern shore.

M. sp. 'chinyankwazi' occurs at Chinyankwazi and Chinyamwezi islands and *M.* sp. 'boadzulu' is found at Boadzulu Island and Makokola Reef. All other populations of similar-looking mbuna are assigned to *M.* sp. 'aggressive bars', which thus has a very extensive distribution: Thumbi Point and Puulu in Tanzania, Tumbi Point, Mbweca, Minos Reef, Nkhungu Reef, and Chiloelo in Mozambique, and Hora Mhango, Charo, Kakusa, Likoma, Chizumulu, and Taiwanee Reef in Malaŵi.

Females of all three forms are brown to dark-brown and exhibit little or no barring. Those of *M.* sp. 'chinyankwazi' were formerly considered a different species, *Melanochromis* 'brown' (Ribbink *et al.*, 1983b). This latter "species" was said to be restricted to Chinyamwezi Island, where underwater observations have now revealed that these brown mbuna are in fact females of *Metriaclima* sp. 'chinyankwazi', which is not common at this island.

The behavior of these three "species" does differ. The "Aggressive Bars" and "Boadzulu" live solitary and remain very close to the rocky substrate, often in large caves—they are shy mbuna—at depths of 10 meters or more. Females of *M.* sp. 'chinyankwazi' school in midwater and feed mostly on plankton. Males feed on the aufwuchs and on plankton when this is available in sufficient quantities. Males of all three species defend their spawning sites with great vigor.

Metriaclima sp. 'dolphin' has a very similar color pattern to the previous species but has a different behavior and habitat preference. It occurs along the northeastern shore between Ndonga and Puulu but seems to prefer the upper 5-7 meters of the rocky biotope. Male and female are indistinguishable, a further difference from the "Aggressive Bars'-like cichlids, and the species feeds predominantly from the aufwuchs, rarely on plankton. Females are bluebarred, and juveniles have a pretty blue coloration.

The elongate *Metriaclima*

On page 24 I have explained why and how in this book the catch-all genus *Pseudotropheus* has been split up according to the species" feeding behavior and the morphology of the skull. Because *Pseudotropheus* is at present polyphyletic (contains species which do not all share a common ancestor), at least one new genus will eventually have to be erected for most of the species it currently contains (those with no relationship to the type species, *P. williamsi*), but are still retained in *Pseudotropheus* in this book. In the case of some others, however, including some of the elongate species, a better generic placement is already available. After years of observation and video recording of most of the species previously and currently placed in *Pseudotropheus* I have found that only four different modes of feeding could be distinguished among all those species (see page 24). One of these modes appears identical to that displayed by species of *Metriaclima*. Konings & Stauffer (2006) have revised the diagnosis of the genus *Metriaclima* and made it feasible to include various elongate species previously placed in *Pseudotropheus*, which are much better grouped with *Metriaclima*. The fact that these species have an elongate body—the sole reason that most of them were grouped in the so-called *P. elongatus* complex (Ribbink *et al.* 1983b)—is, in my opinion, less important than the manner in which they feed from the aufwuchs. Apart from their feeding mechanism the elongate species of *Metriaclima* are characterized by a terminal mouth, somewhat thickened lips, and an angle of between 31 and 48° between the vomer and the horizontal axis of the fish.

The species of this group are not as abundant as the zebras discussed above. They have a similar color pattern to the classic zebras but are much more elongate in form. The slender body is an adaptation for life in caves and in small cracks among the rocks. They are often observed foraging from vertical substrates or from the ceilings of their caves. Elongate *Metriaclima* do not hold feeding territories.

Yellow-tailed elongate mbuna are known from several places around the lake and most of these belong to *Metriaclima* sp. 'elongatus yellow tail' (Zimbawe Rock and Mumbo Island), *Metriaclima* sp. 'elongatus linganjala' (Linganjala Reef and Chizumulu Island), *Metriaclima* sp. 'elongatus ngkuyo' (mainly from Ngkuyo Island but also found along the mainland shores between Njambe and Undu Point), and *Metriaclima* sp. 'elongatus mdoka' (Mdoka). *M.* sp. 'elongatus ngkuyo' was previously misidentified (Konings, 2001: 65) as *P. longior*. Most of the elongate *Metriaclima* of the sediment-free, shallow rocky habitat have yellow tails. The only clear exception to this rule seems to be represented by a blue-tailed form close to or conspecific with *M.* sp. 'elongatus yellow tail' and found at a tiny rocky outcrop southwest of Mumbo Island. For the time being I refer this population to *M.* sp. 'elongatus yellow tail'.

Females of these four species are beige brown, sometimes with a bluish cast, and all lack a black submarginal band in the dorsal and anal fins, a notable character of the male breeding dress.

Cynotilapia

The species of the genus *Cynotilapia* differ in one main anatomical characteristic from those of *Pseudotropheus*, *Metriaclima*, and *Tropheops*: they have widely spaced unicuspid (conical) teeth in the outer jaws while the other genera have bicuspid (two-pointed) teeth. The scientific name of this genus means "dog-tilapia" and alludes to the possession of these conical, ca-

1. *Metriaclima* sp. 'aggressive bars' ♂ Ndumbi Rocks (Likoma)

6. *Metriaclima* sp. 'aggressive bars' ♀ Ndumbi Rocks (Likoma)

2. *Metriaclima* sp. 'aggressive bars' ♂ Chiloelo

7. *Metriaclima* sp. 'aggressive bars' ♀ Chiloelo

3. *Metriaclima* sp. 'chinyankwazi' ♂ Chinyankwazi Island

8. *Metriaclima* sp. 'chinyankwazi' ♀ Chinyankwazi Island

4. *Metriaclima* sp. 'dolphin' Ndonga

9. *Metriaclima* sp. 'boadzulu' ♂ Boadzulu Island

10. *Metriaclima* sp. 'boadzulu' ♀ Boadzulu Island

5. *Metriaclima* sp. 'dolphin' ♂ Ndonga

11. *Metriaclima* sp. 'dolphin' ♀ Ndonga

1. *Metriaclima* sp. 'elongatus yellow tail' ♀ Zimbawe Rock

2. *Metriaclima* sp. 'elongatus yellow tail' ♂ Mumbo Island

3. *Metriaclima* sp. 'elongatus ngkuyo' ♀ Ngkuyo Island

4. *Metriaclima* sp. 'elongatus linganjala' ♀ Machili Island

5. *Metriaclima* sp. 'elongatus mdoka' ♀ Mdoka

6. *Metriaclima* sp. 'elongatus yellow tail' ♂ Zimbawe Rock

7. *Metriaclima* sp. 'elongatus ngkuyo' ♂ Higga Reef

8. *Metriaclima* sp. 'elongatus linganjala' ♂ Same Bay (Chizumulu)

9. *Metriaclima* sp. 'elongatus mdoka' ♂ Mdoka

nine teeth.

Cynotilapia are frequently encountered in the deeper regions of the sediment-free rocky habitat. Males are territorial and defend small caves as spawning sites. Several species prefer very dark, large caves. The peculiarity of *Cynotilapia* is that they feed predominantly on phytoplankton. Most mbuna feed on plankton when available but *Cynotilapia*, especially the non-territorial individuals, feed predominantly in the water column. Males, however, remain much closer to the substrate and sometimes feed from the biocover as well. Like the majority of the mbuna, they spawn in seclusion. The male has to combine his preference for plankton (feeding in mid-water) with the need for a suitably dark spawning site. These requirements are met in the large caves found among large boulders. Females and non-territorial males form large schools in the open water and feed on plankton. At dusk, when the plankton migrates to shallower water, *Cynotilapia* hide among the rocks, resuming their position in the water column at dawn.

The widely spaced, conical teeth of *Cynotilapia* are thought to be a relic of another feeding behavior (Fryer & Iles, 1972) and are thus not a specialized feature. Sharp, conical teeth appear to be present in large specimens of *M. zebra* (Trewavas, 1935) but I have never been able to find them in preserved specimens of any *Metriaclima*. Plankton can, in fact, be collected even without teeth, but males may need sharp teeth as persuading agents in their territorial defense! So, unicuspid teeth could equally have developed at a later stage in the evolution of these species.

If the feeding technique of *Cynotilapia* is compared with that of *Metriaclima* then it becomes apparent that the former is rather unspecialized when compared to other herbivorous mbuna. *Cynotilapia* sucks in plankton (mostly drifting diatoms, but also zooplankton) and does not need a specialized feeding apparatus or tooth structure to do so. When *Cynotilapia* feeds from the aufwuchs, as it sometimes does, it picks in a way similar to the pluckers of *Pseudotropheus*, never in the combing manner of *Metriaclima*.

There are several characteristics seen in *Cynotilapia* that I regard as primitive. *Cynotilapia* are commonly found in very deep water and are often one of the few species present on reefs deeper than 50 meters. It is often a characteristic of an old species that it is found all around the lake and/or at much deeper levels than those where most of the competition for food and space takes place. The species that have evolved special features to exploit a particular biotope often out-compete those that haven't, within the biotope in question. The trade-off is that the primitive species is more versatile and can survive, if not thrive, in more and less advantageous places.

At places where no member of *Metriaclima* is present, *Cynotilapia* can grow quite large, equaling in size the largest *Metriaclima* of the shallow waters. It is well-documented that when there is an algae bloom, most *Metriaclima* are found in the water column feeding from this source. This also confirms that the widely-spaced unicuspid teeth of *Cynotilapia* are not a pre-requisite for feeding on plankton. It has sometimes been suggested that the large unicuspid teeth may facilitate the retention of zooplankton once "inhaled' and that this was a specialization towards feeding on zooplankton, analogous to the unicuspid teeth of many utaka (mainly zooplankton-feeders). However, when Genner and coworkers (1999) compared the amount of zooplankton in the stomachs of *C. afra* and *M.* sp. 'zebra gold' living in the same area of the rocky habitat they found that the latter had eaten more. In other words, a species of *Metriaclima* with closely-set bicuspid teeth ate more zooplankton (percentage-wise) in the same foraging school than *C. afra* which purportedly has a more efficient feeding apparatus for this kind of food. The large unicuspid teeth may indeed be more effective in feeding on zooplankton, but *Cynotilapia* actually feeds mainly on the more abundant phytoplankton for which specialized teeth seem not to be necessary, and appears less adept than *Metriaclima* at feeding from the alternative food source. For these reasons I believe that *Metriaclima* is a more derived (highly evolved) group of mbuna than *Cynotilapia* and that they can be distinguished simply by the feeding method employed by members of either group.

Because *Cynotilapia* are found in open water and sometimes at relatively deep levels, it could be argued that these species are more easily able to spread to remote areas than other mbuna. However, this argument does not seem to hold for *Cynotilapia* sp. 'chinyankwazi' which is found around the two islets, Chinyankwazi and Chinyamwezi, in the southeastern arm of the lake, and also at a deep reef between Chinyamwezi and the mainland. These habitats are geographically isolated by deep (>100 meters) water, not only from the mainland but also from each other. Although several species of *Cynotilapia* exhibit dramatic geographical variation and even polychromatism (yellow or white dorsal fins) within some populations, the three populations of *C*. sp. 'chinyankwazi' are indistinguishable from one other. *C*. sp. 'chinyankwazi' probably populated these three habitats *before* they became geographically isolated from the mainland (i.e. when the lake level was much lower). At the moment these habitats are completely isolated, preventing a steady influx of individuals from neighboring populations. The populations at all three habitats are very large, guaranteeing a large gene pool and thus stabilizing the characteristics of this species.

Two species of *Cynotilapia*, *C. afra* and *C.* sp. 'mbamba', are often found sympatrically, but because of the enormous geographical variability of both species it is sometimes difficult to identify them with confidence. Although these species have different habitat preferences—*C.* sp. 'mbamba' occurs in more sediment-rich biotopes—they are often found side by side (syntopic).

C. afra has a very wide distribution along both sides of the lake. For a long time it was the only described species in this genus, and it also has the widest distribution. It is found at Likoma and Chizumulu and further north along the entire northwestern coast to Ngara, and on the eastern coast from Makanjila Point to Chuanga, at Tumbi Point, and from Lumbaulo to Ikombe. The populations at Jalo Reef and Mbenji Island, previously referred to as *C.* sp. 'yellow dorsal', are also now believed to belong to *C. afra*. The area in between Lumbaulo and Tumbi Point harbors at least three forms of *Cynotilapia* but at present these are difficult to classify. For instance *C. afra* at Mala Point is very elongate and resembles the population at Pombo Rocks almost 200 km further north, and that at Mara Rocks on the other side of the lake. In a neighboring population at Cobwé, 10 km north of Mala Point, *C. afra* has a very attractive but completely different color pattern—this variant has been exported under the trade name of "Afra Edwardi" or just "Edwardi" And at Mbweca, about 15 km south of Mala Point, two different species of *Cynotilapia* are found. One is *C. afra*, with a more "standard" color pattern, and the other is probably a variant of *C.* sp. 'mbamba'. The species previously referred to as *C.* sp. 'mbweca' has turned out to be a *Metriaclima* (see page 188). Between Wikihi (Mozambique) and Undu Reef (Tanzania) I have found a very small *Cynotilapia* that occurs in the intermediate and sediment-rich habitats. At Hai Reef and Chiwindi this form has a very attractive orange dorsal. These populations are assigned to *C. afra* for the time being.

The distribution pattern of *Cynotilapia* sp. 'mbamba' is similar to that of *C. afra* but is far from continuous. Along the northwestern coast it is sympatric with *C. afra* at most locations. In Tanzania, however, it has been seen only at Undu and Lundu, and in Mozambique south of Metangula as far as Malopa in Malaŵi. The populations in the southeastern part of the lake previously referred to *C.* sp. 'black eastern' are here regarded as belonging to *C.* sp. 'mbamba'. A species at the Mbenji islands, previously thought to be another member of *Cynotilapia* (*C.* sp. 'black dorsal"), now appears to be a *Metriaclima* (see page 176). However, *C.* sp. 'mbamba' is present at one of the islands (Penga Penga) at Mbenji.

C. afra has settled in virtually every rocky or intermediate habitat within its range, with males defending small caves among medium sized rocks. It has even established itself in sediment-rich habitats such as those at Hai Reef, Chiwindi, and Cobwé. The enormous variability in male coloration is remarkable, not only within the species as a whole but also within individual populations. Blue-barred males with

Cynotilapia afra

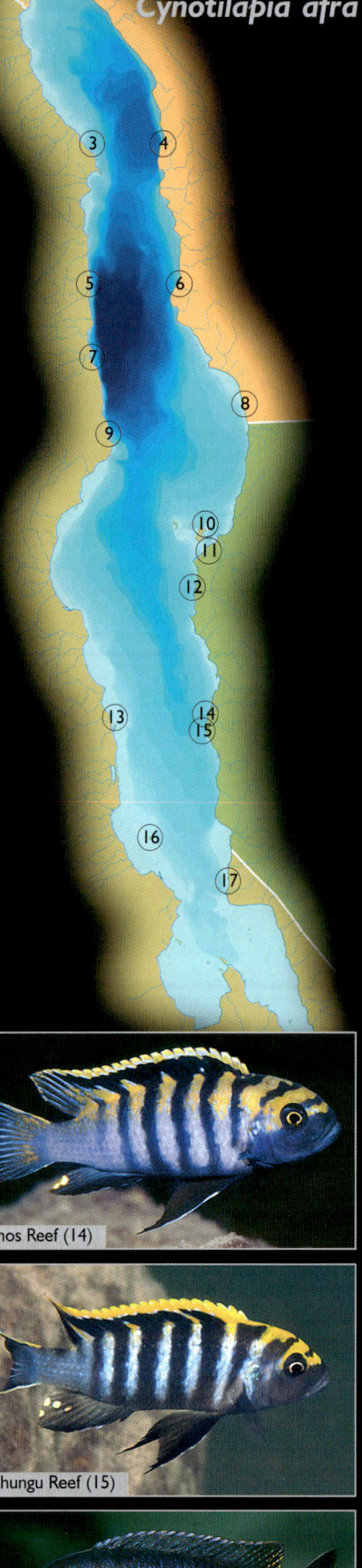

yellow, orange, white, or black dorsal fins are found only meters apart. Female coloration, however, does not seem to vary much throughout the entire distribution. Unlike those of *M. zebra*, females lack the vertical bar pattern almost completely and have a light blue-brown color overall. Females of *C.* sp. 'mbamba' have a silvery body, and in those populations where males have yellow dorsal fins the females also have yellowish dorsals.

Cynotilapia sp. 'ndumbi' is found at Likoma, Chizumulu (Linganjala Reef), Taiwanee Reef, Mphanga Rocks, Lupingu, and Magunga, at Higga, Chilucha and Makokola reefs, and at Narungu. It is a large mbuna, the males of which are dark blue-black with narrow blue bars. I have found them in large caves, where they stand out from the background by virtue of the white edges to their fins, and in schools at Linganjala Reef. It is not clear whether all these populations belong to the same species, but until a number of them have been collected and examined this is assumed to be the case. In anatomical characteristics male *C.* sp. 'ndumbi' resemble those of *Metriaclima* sp. 'aggressive bars' and can reliably be told apart only by examining the teeth, and both species can be found sympatrically (Ndumbi Rocks, Likoma). Females of both species are dark brown.

Two elongate species of *Cynotilapia* occur in the sediment-free rocky habitat, namely *Cynotilapia* sp. 'elongatus mbenji blue' (Mbenji Island) and *Cynotilapia* sp. 'elongatus taiwan' (Taiwanee Reef). Juveniles of these species are sometimes seen picking at the aufwuchs on the rocks but adults feed exclusively on plankton in the water column. These two species were previously placed in the *P. elongatus* complex (Ribbink *et al.* 1983b; see also page 24) but their unicuspid teeth and plankton-feeding behavior make them more probable members of *Cynotilapia*.

Petrotilapia

The general characteristics of species of *Petrotilapia* have been discussed on page 33. The members of this genus can be divided into three habitat-related groups, and many rocky shores harbor a species from each group. There is also a single locality where we find more than three species: Thumbi West Island.

The three groups are the *P. tridentiger* group, the *P. genalutea* group, and the *P. nigra* group. The members of the *P. tridentiger* group are found mainly in the wave-washed upper rocky habitat (see page 33) and include, as well as *P. tridentiger*, *P.* sp. 'likoma barred', *P.* sp. 'orange pelvic', and *P.* sp. 'yellow chin', The last-named species is frequently found in shallow intermediate habitats and will be discussed later (see page 265). *P. genalutea* is the most widespread member of *Petrotilapia* and lives in sediment-rich and intermediate habitats (see page 265). Only one other species is assigned to this group: *P.* sp. 'chitande'. The third group is by far the largest, containing more than a dozen species that are strictly bound to rocky environments. This could be the reason why there are so many species in this group: their preference for sediment-free rocky habitats isolates them geographically from neighboring populations. The three *Petrotilapia* groups can also be identified by female color pattern. The pattern in females of the *P. tridentiger* group consists of vertical bars—which are not, however, always in evidence—on a gray-brown to brown background. Females of the *P. genalutea* group are characterized by two rows of spots on the flank, the lower of which consists of a few large blotches. The background color is white or very light beige and the dorsal fin has a black submarginal band. Females of the *P. nigra* group often have a yellow or golden background color and a pattern consisting of two horizontal rows of spots, all more or less the same size (those of the midlateral row slightly larger). Often a pattern of vertical bars is superimposed on the two horizontal rows of spots and sometimes the spots merge to form solid horizontal lines.

Two species cannot be assigned to any of the three habitat groups: *P.* sp. 'mumbo blue' and *P.* sp. 'retrognathous'. The former occurs at Mumbo Island, Thumbi West, and, according to Ribbink *et al.* (1983b), Mbenji Island, but I have not yet been able to locate this species at the last of these. At Thumbi West Island it shares the rocky habitat with *P. tridentiger*, *P. nigra*, and

P. genalutea. Petrotilapia sp. 'mumbo blue' may be the "replacement" for *P. tridentiger* at Mumbo Island, where the latter is absent, but unlike that species both males and females have a dark submarginal band in the dorsal fin. The other species that cannot be placed in any of the three groups is *P.* sp. 'retrognathous', found at Chizumulu Island and Taiwanee Reef. It is a large mbuna (maximum total length approximately 18 cm), normally found in the shallow but not wave-washed habitat. Occasionally it is also found in intermediate habitats but it prefers clear water and avoids sediment-rich areas. Its presence at Taiwanee Reef may indicate that it is an "old" species which inhabited the lake when the water was at a much lower level several tens of thousands of years ago. It is easily identified by the downward-opening mouth, a character not found in any other *Petrotilapia*.

Petrotilapia nigra occurs in the south of the lake around the Nankumba peninsula, Thumbi West, and Domwe Island. Males are characterized by a dark blue color with prominent black barring.

The small islets of Chinyamwezi and Chinyankwazi in the south of the lake are the only two places known which are inhabited by only a single species of the genus *Petrotilapia*. This species, originally known as *P.* sp. 'gold', was described as *Petrotilapia chrysos* by Stauffer & Van Snik (1996); it was formerly collected for the aquarium trade but in 1986 these two islands became protected under the regulations of the Lake Malaŵi National Park and fishing is no longer allowed—officially. The forms previously called *P.* sp. 'gold eastern' and *P.* sp. 'nigra yellow dorsal', found between Chinyankwazi Island and Metangula, are here considered geographical variants of *P. chrysos*. Female *P. chrysos* in the populations south of Chiloelo are characterized by a golden yellow color with those at Gome having the brightest coloration. The females of the populations between Chiloelo and Metangula are light brown. Males of the populations south of Chiloelo are dark blue, a common male coloration among members of the *P. nigra* group; males at Chiloelo and further north have a yellow dorsal and a golden-yellow cast on the lower part of the body and head.

Because *P. chrysos* is the only representative of the genus at the two islets in the southeastern arm of the lake it does not have to share the habitat and is thus present in relatively large numbers. Females, non-territorial males, and juveniles are gregarious, with plankton constituting a major part of the diet. It is the only species of the *P. nigra* group in which females school together in large feeding groups—such collective feeding behavior is otherwise known only from *P. genalutea* (see page 265). Territorial males patrol large areas and feed only from the biocover. Even though the mouth of *Petrotilapia* is excellently equipped to comb fine, loose material from the rocks, the large size of these mbuna demands a high food intake. The preference of these species for relatively nutrient-poor areas leads to large territories being held by males and to the wandering behavior of non-territorial individuals.

Around the Maleri and Mbenji islands and around Jalo Reef the representative of the *P. nigra* group is *P.* sp. 'fuscous', a very dark species—the ground color is more brown than blue—with orange or rusty-colored patches on the lower head and chest. Males of this deeper dwelling species are perhaps less successful in obtaining a territory in the upper region of the habitat because they are less aggressive than other *Petrotilapia* in the same area. The deeper region is probably not the male's preferred habitat as females and other non-territorial individuals forage in the upper layer of the biotope.

Mumbo Island harbors *P.* sp. 'mumbo yellow', which may be the intermediate between *P. nigra* and *P.* sp. 'fuscous'. Although females of *P.* sp. 'mumbo yellow' have the characteristic pattern of the *P. nigra* group, the strong yellow color of the males is uncommon and otherwise found only in members of the *P. nigra* group in the northern half of the lake. *Petrotilapia* sp. 'mumbo yellow' is normally found at depths of more than seven meters.

Along the shores of Mozambique, at Tumbi Point, another member of the *P. nigra* group inhabits the sediment-free rocky habitat. This species, *P.* sp. 'nigra tumbi', is considered distinct from *P. chrysos* as it lacks the yellow color

1. *Petrotilapia* sp. 'retrognathous' ♂ Membe Island (Chizumulu)

5. *Petrotilapia* sp. 'retrognathous' ♀ Chizumulu Island

2. *Petrotilapia* sp. 'mumbo blue' ♂ Mumbo Island

6. *Petrotilapia* sp. 'mumbo blue' ♀ Mumbo Island

3. *Petrotilapia* sp. 'fuscous' ♂ Nakantenga Island

7. *Petrotilapia* sp. 'fuscous' ♀ Mbenji Island

4. *Petrotilapia* sp. 'mumbo yellow' ♂ Mumbo Island

8. *Petrotilapia* sp. 'fuscous' ♂ Mbenji Island

9. *Petrotilapia* sp. 'mumbo yellow' ♀ Mumbo Island

1. *Petrotilapia chrysos* ♂ Chinyamwezi Island

2. *Petrotilapia chrysos* ♀ Chiofu

3. *Petrotilapia nigra* ♀ Domwe Island

4. *Petrotilapia* sp. 'nigra tumbi' ♂ Tumbi Point

5. *Petrotilapia* sp. 'nigra tumbi' ♀ Tumbi Point

6. *Petrotilapia* sp. 'yellow ventral' ♀ Londo

7. *Petrotilapia chrysos* ♂ Nkhungu Reef

8. *Petrotilapia nigra* ♂ Thumbi West Island

9. *Petrotilapia* sp. 'yellow ventral' ♂ Londo

10. *Petrotilapia* sp. 'yellow ventral' ♂ Chiwi Rocks (Chizumulu)

in the dorsal fin and on the body. It is in fact very similar to *P. nigra* from the south, but should be regarded as a different species. It is rather different from the population of *P.* sp. 'yellow ventral"—another member of the *P. nigra* group—at nearby Mbweca.

Between Mbweca, Mozambique, and Undu Point, Tanzania, *Petrotilapia* sp. 'yellow ventral', again a species of the *P. nigra* group, occurs in a sediment-rich area. This stretch of shoreline does not have many steep rocky habitats; only at Lumbaulo and perhaps Liutche can the rocky habitat be termed sediment-free. Nevertheless two species of *Petrotilapia* are found here, namely *P. genalutea* and *P.* sp. 'yellow ventral'. There is no representative of the *P. tridentiger* group. *P.* sp. 'yellow ventral' is also found around Chizumulu Island. At Hai Reef, Undu Point, and at Ntumba males have an irregular pattern of blue and yellow all over their bodies. At most other localities the males are blue with a yellow area—varying in size according to the population involved—on the ventral region of the body and head. At Lumbaulo and at Cobwé males are entirely yellow, but those of a population between these two, at Ntumba, have a blue body with irregular yellow patches. Females of *P.* sp. 'yellow ventral' are light brown to silver-yellow and exhibit the pattern of rows of spots and indistinct vertical bars characteristic of the *P. nigra* group.

The nigra-type *Petrotilapia* at Likoma Island is called *Petrotilapia* sp. 'likoma variable' (Ribbink *et al.*, 1983b), and somewhat resembles *P.* sp. 'yellow ventral' in male breeding coloration. It received its name because of the variability of the blue body color, which ranges from sky to navy blue. All males, however, have a metallic sheen which may be the critical factor in mate recognition. Female *P.* sp. 'likoma variable' have light brown to dark brown bodies with a faint *nigra*-type pigmentation pattern.

From Mbamba Bay to Ikombe in the far north of the lake the *nigra*-type species, *Petrotilapia* sp. 'nigra tanzania', resembles the *P. nigra* of the Cape Maclear area, except in the case of the populations at two geographically isolated reefs, Magunga and Higga reefs, and the rocky shore just south of Mbamba Bay (Chuwa), where the *nigra*-type *Petrotilapia* has an overall ochre color. These three populations are all regarded as geographical variants of *P.* sp. 'nigra tanzania', even though they are very distinct from the others, because there is no discernible impassable barrier between these and neighboring populations. The Ruhuhu River, which forms a barrier in the distribution of many rock-dwelling species, does not seem to have had this effect on *P.* sp. 'nigra tanzania', as the male breeding coloration of populations north and south of the river is very similar. The female coloration is very similar in all populations, including the ochre-colored ones.

Along the north-western Malawîan shores, from Kande Island to Cape Manulo, males of *Petrotilapia microgalana* (previously *P.* sp. 'small blue') patrol territories at an average depth of 10-15 meters. Females, which are strikingly golden-yellow colored (north of Chirombo Point) are usually encountered in the upper regions.

The deeper rocky coasts from Mbowe Island to Mdoka provide territory for *Petrotilapia* sp. 'ruarwe'. Sexually active males are blue and found at an average depth of 15 meters in the southern part of the range and at about 10 meters in the northern. Females forage in the upper levels. This segregation of foraging and breeding sites is frequently seen in cichlids in which males are unable to establish territories successfully in the competitive upper region of the rocky habitat. In mbuna, however, this is rare. The juveniles of *P.* sp. 'ruarwe' are bright yellow in the southern part of the species" distribution, which could be an indication that this species is closely related to *P. microgalana*. The blue males have yellow-orange pelvic fins at Mbowe and Ruarwe, while these are blue in the northern populations. At Mbowe Island the males are a dark purple-blue color with a very bright orange chin and pelvic fins.

At Mphanga Rocks and Katale Island (and the reefs in between) a second species of the *P. nigra* group, *Petrotilapia* sp. 'black flank', occurs in the somewhat deeper rocky habitat. *P.* sp. 'black flank' is a very dark-colored mbuna, the females of which exhibit a similar melanin pattern as those of the sympatric *P.* sp. 'ruarwe' although the vertical bars are usually more prominent. *P.* sp. 'black flank' is most common at Mphanga Rocks where only a few individuals of *P.* sp. 'ruarwe' are found; at Katale Island the situation is reversed with *P.* sp. 'ruarwe' the more common of the two.

Tropheops

The genus *Tropheops* is well represented in the sediment-free rocky habitat. Together with the genus *Metriaclima* it is one of the most diversified species assemblies found in the lake. Owing to the apparently rapid generation of (geographically isolated) color variants and the existence of the mate-recognition process, many species of this genus can be observed living sympatrically. At Lupingu in Tanzania I have counted seven species of *Tropheops* within 25 meters of one other. The intermingling of previously isolated populations has possibly forced them either to interbreed or to differentiate into separate species. In such cases the species concerned share the available resources when food is plentiful, so male coloration (or other specific characteristics such as scent) needs to be as diverse as possible to guarantee genetic segregation. When genetic isolation has been established, each of the species may define a specific niche. As long as there is no problem in obtaining sufficient food, and as long as the environment does not change, there is no impetus to alter the composition of the community, which may thus remain as it was in the first days of its foundation. The process of differentiation may become activated when a limited food supply increases competition or when the environment changes so that highly-specialized species suddenly find themselves in a less than optimal situation.

Small isolated islands usually support only one or two species of a genus or species complex. This does not imply that competition is stronger at these places; usually it means that only one or two species have ever reached (or remained at) these remote habitats. In this respect we must not forget that the water level has fluctuated during the lake's history. When the level drops, the lake's perimeter becomes smaller, decreasing the amount of habitat, especially for rock-dwelling species. Some rocky islands may become dry land, and the shrinking lake margin may result in a rocky area becoming a sandy shoreline, which would drastically reduce the available habitat as far as most of the mbuna are concerned.

Ribbink and his co-workers (1983b) refrained from identifying any one of the variants of their *Pseudotropheus tropheops* complex (now the genus *Tropheops*) with the holotype of the nominal species. Although they chose *P. tropheops* "orange chest" for the drawing in their publication they did not suggest that this species is, as I believe to be the case, very probably identical to *P. tropheops* (now *T. tropheops)* as described by Regan in 1922. Wood, the collector of many Malaŵi cichlids, brought back two large specimens from the southern part of the lake: Regan's description mentions 116 and 122 mm total length. Moreover, the types have a prominent black submarginal band in the dorsal fin and some barring on the flanks. On the basis of length only three of the known species can be considered: *T.* sp. 'yellow chin' from Likoma, Chizumulu, and the central east coast (but which has no submarginal band in the dorsal), *T.* sp. 'dark', also from Likoma but lacking the barring on the body, and the "Orange Chest", which is one of the largest members of the complex and corresponds with all the other criteria mentioned by Regan. Trewavas (1935) mentioned that the types originated from the south, and this makes it obvious that the "Orange Chest" is the true *T. tropheops*.

I have given a classification of the genus *Tropheops* on page 25. The different species are grouped mainly according to the female pigmentation pattern, the exception being the elongate forms and the *lucerna* group which are grouped together on the basis of their shape. These groupings may, however, be artificial rather than phylogenetic. In many cases members of the same group establish themselves in similar habitats.

In the sediment-free rocky habitat we find species of *Tropheops* which are assigned to five different groups: the "black-type", the "chilumba-type", the "golden-type", the

1. *Petrotilapia* sp. 'likoma variable' ♂ Membe Point (Likoma)

2. *Petrotilapia* sp. 'ruarwe' ♂ Mbowe Island

3. *Petrotilapia microgalana* ♂ Lion's Cove (T'hoto)

4. *Petrotilapia* sp. 'nigra tanzania' ♂ Higga Reef

5. *Petrotilapia* sp. 'likoma variable' ♀ Maingano Island

6. *Petrotilapia* sp. 'ruarwe' ♀ Luwino Reef

7. *Petrotilapia* sp. 'ruarwe' ♂ Katale Island

8. *Petrotilapia microgalana* ♀ Nkhata Bay

9. *Petrotilapia* sp. 'nigra tanzania' ♀ Lupingu

10. *Petrotilapia* sp. 'nigra tanzania' ♂ Nkanda

1. *Petrotilapia* sp. 'black flank' ♀ Mphanga Rocks

2. *Tropheops tropheops* ♀ Thumbi West Island

3. *Tropheops* sp. 'chinyamwezi' ♀ Chinyamwezi Island

4. *Tropheops* sp. 'chinyankwazi' ♂ Chinyankwazi Island

5. *Tropheops* sp. 'chinyankwazi' ♀ Chinyankwazi Island

6. *Tropheops gracilior* ♀ Chitande Island

7. *Petrotilapia* sp. 'black flank' ♂ Mphanga Rocks

8. *Tropheops tropheops* ♂ Thumbi West Island

9. *Tropheops* sp. 'chinyamwezi' ♂ Chinyamwezi Island

10. *Tropheops gracilior* ♂ Lupingu

"mauve-type", and the "elongate-type".

The species of the black-type group are characterized by a black band in the dorsal and vertical barring on a dark background. Six species are placed in this group, which, taken as a whole, has an almost lake-wide distribution. It is the only group in which OB and O females have been found.

Tropheops tropheops, a member of the black-type group, occurs in the sediment-free rocky habitats around the Nankumba peninsula, all the islands around that peninsula, and at the Maleri islands. It is not, however, found at Mumbo Island. Besides the normal-colored females, OB females can be seen at almost all locations. *Tropheops* sp. 'chinyamwezi' is a very closely related species and may even be conspecific with *T. tropheops*. Chinyamwezi Reef, between the mainland and Chinyamwezi Island (the only place where *T.* sp. 'chinyamwezi' occurs), is also inhabited by a species resembling *T. tropheops*. At Chinyamwezi Island there is a relatively high percentage of OB and O females, probably because there is only one representative of *Tropheops* present at the island so mate color recognition is less critical. Interestingly Chinyankwazi Island is also inhabited by a single member of the genus, *Tropheops* sp. 'chinyankwazi', but one belonging to the chilumba-type group, and OB females have not yet been discovered.

The sediment-free rocky habitat along the northwestern and northeastern coast is inhabited by a species that was previously referred to as *T.* sp. 'black', but which is probably the true *Tropheops gracilior*. Jos Snoeks (pers. comm.) has noted that the six types of *T. gracilior* were from the northern part of the lake, not from the south. Ribbink *et al.* (1983b) tentatively referred to an elongate *Tropheops* found around the Nankumba Peninsula as *T. gracilior* but Snoeks found that the male as well as female types have a black submarginal band in the dorsal and, even after all the years in preservation, a generally dark color, including the females. The only northern species that matches the above description is the form formerly called *T.* sp. 'black'. To avoid confusion the latter name is retained for the black-type species group.

Tropheops gracilior is restricted to the rocky coasts north of Lundu on the eastern side of the lake and north of Mundola Point on the western side, and is limited to purely rocky areas where it is observed at rather deep levels. Males are territorial; females occur singly and behave pugnaciously towards conspecific females. As well as the dark coloration and submarginal band, the males of this widespread species show another (but not unique) characteristic of the black-type group, namely an orange or yellow patch on the lower parts of the head and body. Females have a very dark ground color and show some barring and a band in the dorsal fin.

Gallireya Reef, a reef in Youngs Bay, south of Chilumba near Hara Village, is inhabited by three different species of *Tropheops*, one of which is found only near larger accumulations of rocks (the other two are found in the intermediate zone, see page 200). This species is referred to as *Tropheops* sp. 'black hara' and alludes to the old name of *T. gracilior*; there is a strong resemblance between the females of the two species. Males lack any dark band in the dorsal and are mainly golden yellow. I nevertheless believe that this species is closely related to *T. gracilior*.

At Likoma Island we find another member of the black-type group: *Tropheops* sp. 'dark'. The name indicates that females are very dark, not unlike those of *T. gracilior*.

A further species in the black-type group, *Tropheops* sp. 'yellow gular', is found along the Mozambique and Malaŵi shorelines between Tumbi Point and Chimwalani Reef. Males have a blue body and yellow on the lower parts of the head and body. At Cobwé and Mala Point a species with a similar male breeding coloration inhabits the intermediate biotope. For the time being, however, this species is assigned to *T.* sp. 'yellow chin' (double-stripe type *Tropheops*, see page 196) for the following reasons. First of all, its habitat preference does not match that of the black-type species; and secondly, like *T.* sp. 'yellow chin' at Likoma and Chizumulu islands, males have a varying degree of yellow color on their bodies, and some are even completely yellow. However, the color pattern of the females at Mala Point does not match that of other *T.* sp. 'yellow chin' females: instead of two horizontal rows of black spots they have no black markings at all (a feature which corresponds better with the mauve-type species).

The *Tropheops* of the mauve-type group usually prefer clear water and a sediment-free habitat.

Tropheops sp. 'mauve' differs in color and size from *T. gracilior* with which it is found sympatrically for most of its range. *T.* sp. 'mauve' seems to be less restricted to purely rocky habitats and is also found in intermediate types of biotope, which must, however, be free of muddy sediment. *T.* sp. 'mauve' occurs from Ruarwe to Ngara on the west coast and has also been seen along the Tanzanian shore between Lupingu and Pombo Rocks. Male *T.* sp. 'mauve' are almost entirely light blue and lack a black band in the anal fin. Females are mainly yellow or yellow-white and have orange anal fins.

The females of the population at Magunga in Tanzania are not yellow even though yellow-colored female *Tropheops* occur there; these, however belong to a species which was previously thought to be a population of *T.* sp. 'mauve' but which appears to be a distinct species, *Tropheops* sp. 'mauve yellow'. After the discovery of entirely blue-colored *T.* sp. 'mauve' males at Magunga indicated that two species were involved, I found that the corresponding females are not yellow but silvery. They thus resemble those along the northwestern shore of the lake, but lack the orange color in the anal fin. Genner and coworkers (2004) found that there are likewise two similar species found sympatrically at Ruarwe on the western shore, both of which were referred to *T.* sp. 'mauve' (Ribbink *et al.*, 1983b). Between Ngara and Ruarwe male *T.* sp. 'mauve' are entirely blue, and between Ruarwe and Kande Island males of the other species are either entirely blue or blue with a yellow patch covering the head, breast, and shoulders (at Mara Rocks and Ruarwe). The yellow color may be restricted to the lower part of the head (at Mbowe Island, Mphandikucha, and Kande Island). In my opinion the second species at Ruarwe may be conspecific with *T.* sp. 'mauve yellow' from the eastern shore of the lake. Both forms are characterized by males with a black band in the anal fin and by yellow females. *T.* sp. 'mauve yellow' has a wide distribution and is further found from Makonde in Tanzania to Chiloelo in Mozambique. This species has previously been confused with *T. macrophthalmus*, males of which are distinguished by the lack of a black band in the anal fin, a distinctive character of male *T.* sp. 'mauve yellow', and by brown females. At Jalo Reef, north of Nkhotakota, there is a *Tropheops* closely resembling *T.* sp. 'mauve yellow', but for the time being this population is considered to be *T.* sp. 'mbenji blue' (see page 32).

Along the east coast, south of Lundu and north of Mbamba Bay, a very similar species, *Tropheops* sp. 'aurora', again belonging to the mauve group, inhabits the purely rocky habitats. This species is characterized by blue-yellow males with yellow dorsal fins and by females with a light brown color and which exhibit faint vertical bars. It is a very common species and certainly the most common *Tropheops* in this part of the lake.

Another interesting situation, further emphasizing the complexity of this group, is seen along the southeastern shore of the lake between Gome, Malaŵi, and N'kolongwe, Mozambique, where I have found two sympatric *Tropheops* species, the males of which are almost identical. These two species can be told apart mainly by the coloration of the females. One of the two species is the previously mentioned *T.* sp. 'yellow gular' and the other is *Tropheops* sp. 'gome yellow'. The females of the latter are yellow with a black submarginal band in the dorsal, at least in the southern populations; north of Meponda the female color fades to silver beige.

The golden-yellow *Tropheops macrophthalmus*, a widespread member of the golden-type group, is common along the northeastern corner of the lake but restricted to a few places elsewhere. Ahl described *T. macrophthalmus* in 1927 from a collection made by Fülleborn on the Tanzanian shore of the lake near Alt Langenburg, now known as Lumbila. The description includes two key definitions that have led me to conclude that the all-yellow *Tropheops* is the true

1. *Tropheops* sp. 'black hara' ♂ Gallireya Reef

5. *Tropheops* sp. 'black hara' ♀ Gallireya Reef

2. *Tropheops* sp. 'dark' ♂ Yofu Bay (Likoma)

6. *Tropheops* sp. 'dark' ♀ Yofu Bay

3. *Tropheops* sp. 'yellow gular' ♂ Chimwalani Reef

7. *Tropheops* sp. 'yellow gular' ♂ Nlhungu Reef

8. *Tropheops* sp. 'yellow gular' ♀ Chimwalani Reef

4. *Tropheops* sp. 'gome yellow' ♂ Gome

9. *Tropheops* sp. 'gome yellow' ♀ Chiofu

1. *Tropheops macrophthalmus* ♀ Matema

2. *Tropheops macrophthalmus* ♂ Kirondo

3. *Tropheops* sp. 'mauve yellow' ♀ Mbowe Island

4. *Tropheops* sp. 'mauve yellow' ♂ Mara Rocks

5. *Tropheops* sp. 'mauve' ♂ Chitande Island

6. *Tropheops* sp. 'mauve' ♀ Chitande Island

7. *Tropheops macrophthalmus* ♂ Matema

8. *Tropheops* sp. 'mauve yellow' ♂ Ngwazi

9. *Tropheops* sp. 'mauve yellow' ♂ Nkhata Bay

10. *Tropheops* sp. 'aurora' ♂ Ndonga

T. macrophthalmus (I have not re-examined the two types). Ahl noted that this species had no pigment in the fins and remarked that the head had a strongly convex, almost perpendicular, profile. Except for the all-yellow *Tropheops*, all species of the genus found north of the Ruhuhu River have markings in the fins; and the head of the golden species does have a very steep profile.

T. macrophthalmus occurs in the upper layers of the rocky habitat and is distributed along the northeastern shore from Matema to Kirondo in Tanzania. Males are not entirely golden yellow, but have light blue dorsal and anal fins. Females are brown and have no markings on body or fins. On the western shore the distribution of *T. macrophthalmus* is restricted to the northwestern coast between Mdoka and Chirwa Island. At Chizumulu Island (but not at Likoma) a golden *Tropheops*, formerly referred to as *Pseudotropheus tropheops* "gold" (Ribbink et al., 1983b), inhabits a similar habitat to that of *T. macrophthalmus* and is here regarded as a population of *T. macrophthalmus*. This view is supported by the existence of several other species with a discontinuous distribution. The females at Chizumulu Island are beige to brown like those of other populations. Previously I misidentified the populations of *T.* sp. 'mauve yellow' as *T. macrophthalmus*, but it is now evident that males of the former species are distinguished by a black band in the anal fin, and females are silvery-yellow to yellow, not brown as in *T. macrophthalmus*.

In Youngs and Chitimba bays there are other populations of golden yellow *Tropheops* which I previously referred to as *T.* sp. 'macrophthalmus chitimba', but I have subsequently realized that these in fact represent two distinct species (see page 200) and I no longer believe that they are closely related to *T. macrophthalmus*.

A species with a close resemblance to *T. macrophthalmus*, i.e. males are entirely yellow without black submarginal bands in the unpaired fins, occurs around Cape Maclear. Both male and female of this species, *Tropheops* sp. 'gold otter', are yellow.

The subgroup of *Tropheops* with the most species is without question the chilumba-type group. Members of this group seem to have a strong preference for sediment-free rocky habitats and are often found at islands and reefs. The distribution of the group as a whole does not encompass the entire shoreline of the lake and this is probably due to the fact that rocky sediment-free habitats are not found everywhere.

The name of the group is derived from *Tropheops* sp. 'chilumba', which is the best known species of this group and is frequently exported for the aquarium trade as the "Chilumba Macrophthalmus". It inhabits the rocky areas between Mdoka and Maison Reef in the northwestern part of the lake. Females are apricot-yellow, males dark blue with a red band below the black submarginal band in the dorsal fin.

Characteristic of the group are blue-barred males with a black submarginal band in the dorsal fin, and females which are either entirely yellow or have a mid-lateral row of gray blotches on a yellowish to gray body. The only exception to this rule is *Tropheops* sp. 'taiwan', whose females usually lack any markings on their silvery-beige bodies though some have broad bars reminiscent to those of the sand group of *Tropheops*. The fact that this species is the only representative of the complex at Taiwanee Reef may make a distinctive female pattern unnecessary; the color pattern of the male unquestionably fits the chilumba group. *T.* sp. 'taiwan' is a very large species with a somewhat elongate body, and resembles the large species found at Higga Reef and Ngkuyo Island, *Tropheops* sp. 'higga'. Female *T.* sp. 'higga' have a gray-yellow ground color and the characteristic mid-lateral row of gray blotches. Males closely resemble those of *T.* sp. 'chilumba'.

At Chiwindi, in a rather sediment-rich rocky area, and at Wikihi, I found a *Tropheops* which in color and size resembles *T.* sp. 'chilumba'. Males of this species, *T.* sp. 'chilumba type', are blue-barred, and females are yellow. I consider this a distinct species because it is the only member of the group found along an isolated stretch of shoreline with no large neighboring population inhabiting a purely rocky biotope.

Two species in the southeastern part of the lake live in purely rocky habitats: *Tropheops* sp. 'chinyankwazi' and *Tropheops* sp. 'black dorsal'. These two are very closely related, but since all the species of this group seem to have a restricted distribution, we can either regard them as populations of a single widespread species or, as I do here, consider each population a species in its own right until a better understanding of the situation has been achieved. Females of *T.* sp. 'black dorsal' are bright yellow all over, while those of *T.* sp. 'chinyankwazi' are a dull yellow color with a characteristic mid-lateral row of gray blotches. Sometimes large schools of foraging females migrate through the upper regions of the habitat.

The apparent liking of a species for a specific habitat is not always the result of a genuine preference but often just of a lack of the competitive strength needed to contend with the other species inhabiting more favorable sites. This is clearly demonstrated at (isolated) habitats where only one species of a certain group or complex is found. Such species usually inhabit the entire range of habitats occupied by other species of the same complex elsewhere. Examples are *T.* sp. 'chinyamwezi' and *T.* sp. 'chinyankwazi' both of which are endemic to their respective islands in the south of the lake. Both are found from the surface waters to depths below 25 meters. When a second species from the same complex is present then often a distinct division of the habitat occurs: one species specializes in the sediment-free upper region and the other in the sediment-rich area. Two species at Mumbo Island clearly demonstrate such a division: *T.* sp. 'lilac' (page 33), which lives in the rocky biotope, whereas *T.* sp. 'mumbo' (see page 196) inhabits the intermediate biotopes. The presence of a third and fourth species may narrow down the "preferred" habitat of each of the first two. When competition for food or breeding sites is less prevalent the partitioning of the available habitat is less distinct, but still present.

Species of the genus *Tropheops* feed from the same aufwuchs as many other mbuna. *Metriaclima zebra*, for instance, combs loose aufwuchs from the biocover and is very successful at it. *Tropheops* appears to spend more energy in obtaining enough food, as they tear off filamentous algal strands by vigorously shaking their bodies. This feeding method is, however, very efficient, so that the investment of energy is adequately rewarded. Most species of *Tropheops* feed at an angle of about 60° to the substrate. The species encountered in the surf zone, however, feed at a more acute angle, at about 45°.

The elongate *Tropheops*

The elongate species, formerly part of the *Pseudotropheus elongatus* complex of Ribbink *et al.* (1983b) but here assigned to the genus *Tropheops*, appear much less aggressive and less shy than those members of the complex retained in the genus *Pseudotropheus* (see page 85), and all have a vomer that lies at an angle of between 70 and 90° to the horizontal axis. In the sediment-free rocky habitat these elongate *Tropheops* appear to be restricted to the southern half of the lake.

The most common species is *Tropheops* sp. 'elongatus boadzulu', which is found from Domwe Island south along the eastern shore of the Nankumba Peninsula (including all its islands and reefs) to Chemwezi Rocks, the southernmost rocks in the lake. A second species, referred to as *Tropheops* sp. 'elongatus greenback', occurs at Mumbo and Otter islands. This name was coined by Reinthal (1990) for the population at Otter Island, which exhibits a greenish-blue color on the head and back. Both these species were previously regarded as one (as *T.* sp. 'elongatus greenback"; Konings, 2001) but since there is some difference in behavior I now prefer to regard them as distinct. *T.* sp. 'elongatus greenback' is characterized by the fact that, unlike other elongate types it "sticks" to the rocks and is normally found in an upside-down position. *T.* sp. 'elongatus boadzulu' is found around small and medium sized rocks and also in sediment-rich areas where it behaves like other members of *Tropheops*. Neither species is found around Thumbi West Island.

1. *Tropheops* sp. 'chilumba' ♂ Mphanga Rocks
6. *Tropheops* sp. 'chilumba' ♀ Mphanga Rocks

2. *Tropheops* sp. 'chilumba type' ♂ Chiwindi
7. *Tropheops* sp. 'chilumba type' ♀ Chiwindi

3. *Tropheops* sp. 'taiwan' ♂ Taiwanee Reef
8. *Tropheops* sp. 'taiwan' ♀ Taiwanee Reef

4. *Tropheops* sp. 'higga' ♂ Higga Reef
9. *Tropheops* sp. 'higga' ♀ Higga Reef

5. *Tropheops* sp. 'black dorsal' ♂ Luwala Reef
10. *Tropheops* sp. 'black dorsal' ♀ Chimwalani Reef

1. *Tropheops* sp. 'elongatus boadzulu' ♀ Mazinzi Reef

2. *Tropheops* sp. 'elongatus namalenje' ♂ Namalenje Island

3. *Tropheops* sp. 'elongatus namalenje' ♀ Namalenje Island

4. *Tropheops modestus* ♀ Maleri Island

5. *Tropheops* sp. 'elongatus mbako' ♀ Maingano Island

6. *Tropheops* sp. 'elongatus chisumulu' ♂ Chizumulu Island

7. *Tropheops* sp. 'elongatus boadzulu' ♂ Mazinzi Reef

8. *Tropheops* sp. 'elongatus greenback' ♂ Otter Island

9. *Tropheops modestus* ♂ Maleri Island

10. *Tropheops* sp. 'elongatus mbako' ♂ Yofu Bay (Likoma)

11. *Tropheops* sp. 'elongatus metangula' ♂ N'kolongwe

Two other elongate species of *Tropheops*, *Tropheops modestus* (described as *Pseudotropheus modestus* but prior to that known as *Ps.* sp. 'elongatus bar') and *Tropheops* sp. 'elongatus namalenje' are sometimes found in sediment-rich habitats and in this respect resemble *T.* sp. 'elongatus boadzulu'. The Maleri islands are home to *T. modestus*, and Namalenje Island harbors *T.* sp. 'elongatus namalenje', which is closely related. Namalenje Island is rather densely populated and the males of *T.* sp. 'elongatus namalenje' defend their domains with great vigor. This is in contrast to the elongate *Tropheops* found along the eastern shores of the lake which are only weakly territorial.

Tropheops sp. 'elongatus mbako' is rare at Makulawe Point, Likoma, but common at the northeastern end of the island. It is also found along the mainland shore between Undu Reef in Tanzania and Cobwé in Mozambique. The females of all populations are bluish brown.

At Chizumulu, about 10 km west of Likoma, *Tropheops* sp. 'elongatus chizumulu' is found in the sediment-free habitat. It closely resembles *T.* sp. 'elongatus mbako'. It has a very rounded head and feeds in a position almost parallel to the substrate. *T.* sp. 'elongatus chizumulu' is common around the island and surrounding reefs, and seems to experience little competition for territory and food. Males are weakly territorial.

Further south, along the eastern mainland coast, we encounter a similar species: *Tropheops* sp. 'elongatus metangula'. This is the only elongate type found on the east coast between Chuanga and Meponda and prefers small to medium-sized rocks. South of Meponda we find further similar species of the elongate group: *Tropheops* sp. 'elongatus reef' and *Tropheops* sp. 'elongatus reef east'. The former is a dark blue-black species and occurs in all rocky habitats between the Mozambique-Malaŵi border and the Nsinje River, and at Chimwalani and Luwala reefs further south. The rocky environments between the Nsinje River and Malopa are inhabited by *T.* sp. 'elongatus reef east', a tiny, mainly black, elongate species. This species is undoubtedly closely related to *T.* sp. 'elongatus reef' but its coloration is consistently different and it is sometimes found in large numbers while *T.* sp. 'elongatus reef' is a rather rare mbuna north of the Nsinje River.

Labeotropheus

Labeotropheus trewavasae is a rather common mbuna at many locations along the lake's rocky shores. It resembles its sibling species *L. fuelleborni* (see page 28) in almost every anatomical aspect, but has a slender body (in comparison with *L. fuelleborni* from the same locations) and prefers the somewhat deeper regions—most of them seen between five and 10 meters. Its elongate body enables it to penetrate small holes and cracks among the rocks. It is specialized in scraping and cropping algae from a sediment-free surface and it feeds predominantly from the vertical faces and undersides of rocks—the tops of most of the rocks in the available habitat are covered with a thin layer of sediment of low nutritional value. Its feeding technique and breeding procedure are similar to those described for *L. fuelleborni* (see page 28).

Interestingly, at submerged reefs only *L. trewavasae* is found. At these locations it has a deeper body than the individuals at adjoining rocky coasts where both species of the genus occur. Body depth can vary considerably in this species. At Chirwa Island near Chilumba, large orange specimens of *L. trewavasae* resemble *L. fuelleborni* in size and shape. Comparison with a few specimens of the latter species found at this location, which were extremely large and deep-bodied, revealed their true identity. *L. trewavasae* has a wider distribution than was originally believed. It is found on most rocky coasts except at Mbenji Island. It occurs at some places where *L. fuelleborni* is absent, i.e. Jalo Reef, and Taiwanee and Linganjala reefs, north and west of Chizumulu, respectively.

There are only a few places where males of both *L. fuelleborni* and *L. trewavasae* are entirely blue, for example, Mara Rocks and Nkhata Bay in Malaŵi, and Chilucha and Minos Reef in Mozambique. At most other locations either only one of the two species is present or the two are differently colored. There are three major color patterns known for both species and, in addition, each has a single pattern specific to the species in question. The most common coloration in *L. fuelleborni* is completely royal blue with distinct barring in territorial males. *L. trewavasae* also has completely blue races, but the variant at Nkhata Bay, for example, is cobalt blue and can thus be distinguished from the royal blue *L. fuelleborni* at the same location. At Minos Reef (Mozambique) the situation is reversed: here it is *L. fuelleborni* which is cobalt blue (see photo page 30).

The second color pattern seen in both species is a blue body with an orange or red dorsal fin ('red-top'). The third pattern consists of a yellow, orange, or rusty brown coloration on the flanks, belly and/or dorsal part of the body. Some populations of *L. fuelleborni* have a yellow or orange colored belly and/or flank. At the same location both species may have orange on the body. In *L. trewavasae* this is restricted to the upper half of the flank whereas in *L. fuelleborni* it is present on the lower half instead.

At Higga Reef, Ngkuyo Island, and the rocky coast south of Mbamba Bay, a unique color pattern occurs in *L. trewavasae*, consisting of a blue body and a broad black submarginal band in the dorsal and anal fins. This is not only unique to *L. trewavasae* but also restricted to these few populations near Mbamba Bay in Tanzania. Meanwhile, some *L. fuelleborni* males at Chinyankwazi Island in the southeastern arm of the lake have a black band in the dorsal but none in the anal fin.

The three main color patterns form part of the normal genetic variation of the two species. The basic color appears to be all blue as this is the form seen in almost all regions where only one of the two species is present. The presence of either one of the other two patterns seems to have originated in a random fashion. It may have helped to differentiate between the two species when they came into contact (or may have become the only way to differentiate). The chance expression of a pattern at each location, and the subsequent sexual selection, has developed into today's scattered distribution of the various color patterns.

The color pattern of *L. trewavasae* varies more abruptly between adjacent populations than does that of *L. fuelleborni*. *L. fuelleborni* is able to cross sandy areas in shallow water along the shoreline, while *L. trewavasae* is restricted to the deeper parts of the rocky habitat and may therefore never have genetic contact with nearby populations.

The *Pseudotropheus elongatus* complex

Ribbink *et al.* (1983b) grouped a number of elongate mbuna in the so-called *Pseudotropheus elongatus* complex. As I have explained earlier (see page 24), four different groups can be distinguished among these elongate species, three of them better placed in other existing genera, i.e. *Metriaclima*, *Tropheops*, and *Cynotilapia*. The elongate species that are here retained in the genus *Pseudotropheus* will eventually be placed in a new genus containing all the current members of the genus that are not related to *P. williamsi*, the type species of the genus.

The elongate species of *Pseudotropheus* are rather aggressive and many of the species maintain feeding territories (algal gardens). Apart from *Pseudotropheus* sp. 'elongatus aggressive' and *Pseudotropheus* sp. 'elongatus ndumbi' they are all small species with a standard length of less than 10 cm.

All elongate species of *Pseudotropheus* feed in an apparently less efficient manner than members of the genera *Metriaclima* and *Tropheops*. They neither comb with fully opened mouth like *Metriaclima*, nor tear off attached algae like *Tropheops*. They pick at the aufwuchs and mostly extract loose material. When feeding they angle their bodies at 30-60° to the substrate. The elongate species of *Tropheops* usually adopt a more acute angle to the substrate while feeding than do those of the *P. elongatus* complex but this is not a consistent character for distinguishing between these two groups. Elongate *Metriaclima* normally feed at a 90° angle. Most elongate members of *Pseudotropheus* defend a feeding area against all intruders and are probably trying to secure their existence by fierce defense of the foraging area. Females of, for example, *P.* sp. 'elongatus aggressive' are also

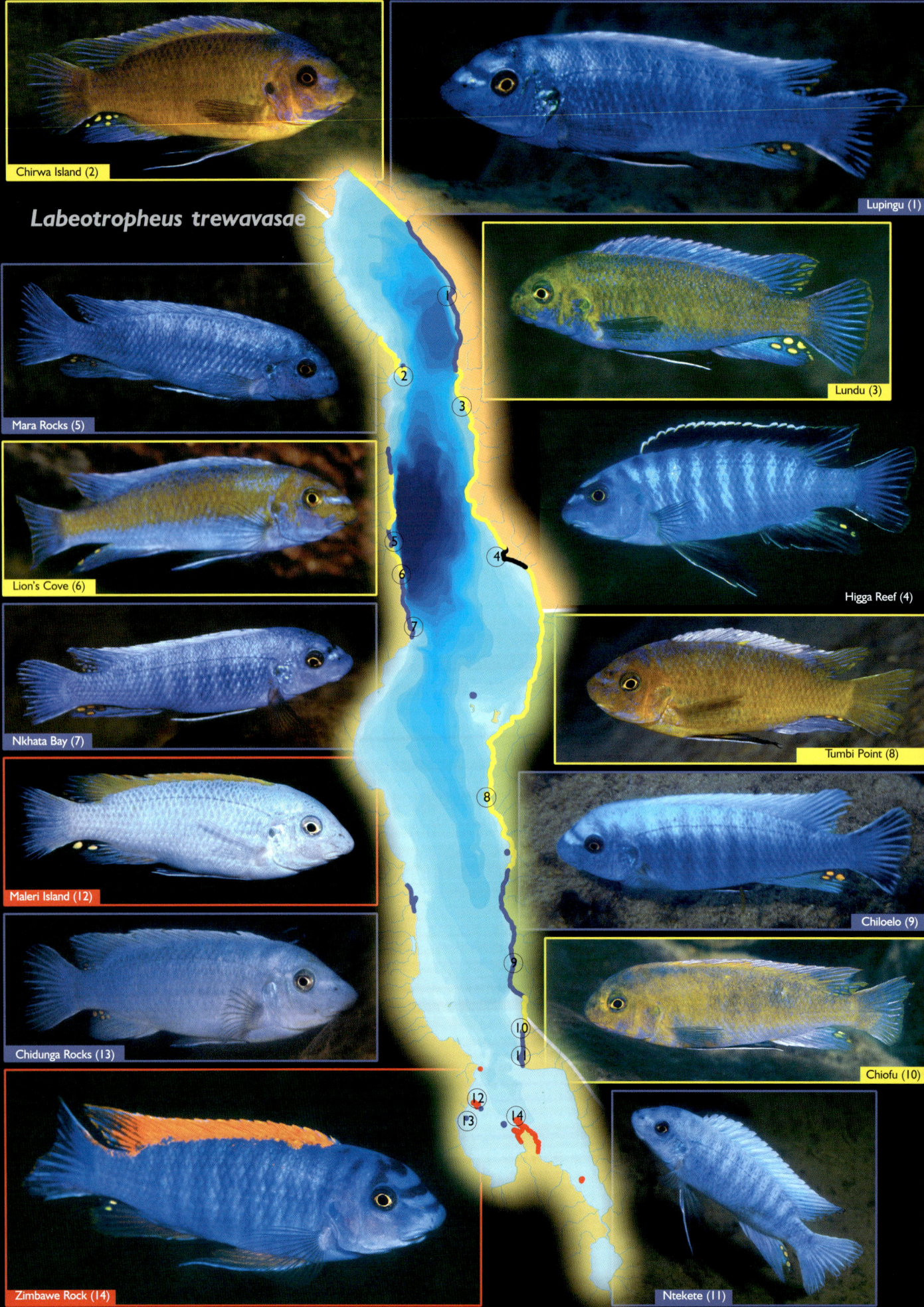

1. *Tropheops* sp. 'elongatus reef east' ♂ Ntekete

7. *Tropheops* sp. 'elongatus reef' ♂ Gome

2. *Pseudotropheus longior* ♀ Ndonga

8. *Pseudotropheus longior* ♂ Ngkuyo Island

3. *Pseudotropheus* sp. 'elongatus mphanga' ♀ Mphanga Rocks

9. *Pseudotropheus* sp. 'elongatus mphanga' ♂ Katale Island

4. *Pseudotropheus elongatus* ♂ Hongi Island

10. *Pseudotropheus* sp. 'elongatus masimbwe' ♂ Masimbwe Island

5. *Pseudotropheus* sp. 'elongatus nkhata blue' ♂ Kawanga

11. *Pseudotropheus* sp. 'elongatus ruarwe' ♂ Ruarwe

6. *Pseudotropheus* sp. 'elongatus spot' ♀ Puulu Island

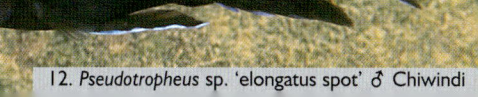
12. *Pseudotropheus* sp. 'elongatus spot' ♂ Chiwindi

involved in territorial defense, which clearly points to the fact that the species" food supply is limited.

Pseudotropheus elongatus was described by Geoffrey Fryer (1956a) from specimens collected in Mbamba Bay, Tanzania. The rocky shore near Mbamba Bay is inhabited by three elongate mbuna, one with a bright yellow tail (now assigned to *Metriaclima* as *M.* sp. 'elongatus ngkuyo', see page 65), another very dark blue with a dark blue tail, and a third also dark with prominent black submarginal bands in the unpaired fins. Seegers (1996) found that Fryer had described one of the dark forms as *P. elongatus* and he described the form with the black submarginal bands in the fins as *Pseudotropheus longior*. The elongate species found at Nkhata Bay, previously regarded as *P. elongatus* by Ribbink *et al.* (1983b), is now referred to as *P.* sp. 'elongatus nkhata blue'.

Pseudotropheus sp. 'elongatus mpanga' is common at reefs and islands between Mphanga Rocks and Maison Reef, and is characterized by a blue-black barred pattern and a yellow tail.

Pseudotropheus sp. 'elongatus masimbwe' lives at Likoma Island, mainly at the islet of Masimbwe but sporadically also at other locations around the island, and is again characterized by a blue-black barred pattern and a yellow tail. Although it has a rounded snout, suggesting that it may be a member of *Tropheops*, the angle of the vomer of a single specimen was found to be 57°, which would be too moderate for a member of that genus (see page 24). I have never seen it feeding like *Tropheops* but always found it picking at the aufwuchs the same way as other members of the *P. elongatus* complex.

Pseudotropheus sp. 'elongatus ruarwe' is an attractive and very elongate member of the mbuna community and is similar to *P.* sp. 'elongatus nkhata blue'. Although it occurs frequently in sediment-rich habitats, in areas where no other elongate mbuna is present, it lives in the sediment-free rocky biotope. On the coast between Ruarwe and Charo *P.* sp. 'elongatus ruarwe' is the only member of the *P. elongatus* complex present, and even along this small stretch it exhibits geographical variation. At Ruarwe males have light blue bars and a black belly whereas at Charo territorial males are almost entirely black, with a few light blue spots near the dorsal fin the only traces of the bars. The latter pattern also occurs in populations on the east coast, where a very similar species, *Pseudotropheus* sp. 'elongatus spot', is found from Cobwé in Mozambique to Liuli in Tanzania, and is also seen in sediment-rich rocky habitats.

North of the Ruhuhu River in Tanzania the *P. elongatus* complex is poorly represented, and I have seen only a few specimens of each of two species: one, *Pseudotropheus* sp. 'elongatus kirondo', at Kirondo, and another *Pseudotropheus* sp. 'elongatus makonde', at Makonde. The former has a very dark brown coloration and resembles *P. elongatus*. It lives in caves formed by large rocks. *P.* sp. 'elongatus makonde' was only observed feeding from plankton, something almost all mbuna do irrespective of their feeding specialization, and hence is only provisionally grouped in *Pseudotropheus*. Females are dark brown and have a black submarginal band in the dorsal; the latter is not a character found among the elongate members of *Metriaclima* present in the sediment-free rocky habitat (see page 67).

At Masimbwe Islet (Likoma) *Pseudotropheus* sp. 'elongatus ndumbi' is found sympatric with *P.* sp. 'elongatus masimbwe'. The dark-colored *P.* sp. 'elongatus ndumbi' lives in large caves and under overhanging rocks. Both male and female ferociously defend their foraging areas. In appearance this species resembles *Cynotilapia* sp. 'elongatus taiwan' (page 71), but I have not yet been able to compare its morphological features with latter species. Along the northern shores of Likoma *P.* sp. 'elongatus ndumbi' shares the habitat with an elongate mbuna now assigned to *Tropheops* as *T.* sp. 'elongatus mbako' and with *Pseudotropheus* sp. 'elongatus ornatus'. The latter, which enjoys considerable popularity among aquarists as "Pseudotropheus Ornatus", is restricted in its distribution to the rocks at Makulawe Point and Ndumbi Rocks. Around the shallow rocky reefs south of Mbamba Bay and along the rocky shores south of the reefs (Chuwa), a species with a male breeding coloration resembling that of *P.* sp.

'elongatus ornatus' occurs in the sediment-rich habitat. This species, *Pseudotropheus* sp. 'elongatus ornatus tanzania', has yellow or yellow-white colored females which differ from *P.* sp. 'elongatus ornatus' females by lacking the broad black submarginal band in the dorsal fin.

The two reefs south of Makanjila Point, Luwala Reef (previously West Reef) and Chimwalani Reef (previously Eccles Reef), are inhabited by two elongate mbuna: one as *T.* sp. 'elongatus reef' (see page 88) and *Pseudotropheus* sp. 'elongatus brown'. The latter closely resembles *P. longior* from the Mbamba Bay area in Tanzania.

Pseudotropheus ater, a completely black species of the *P. elongatus* complex, is encountered at Chinyankwazi and Chinyamwezi islands. It forages over large rocks and inhabits caves among the boulders. It resembles *P.* sp. 'elongatus aggressive' from Zimbawe Rock and *Pseudotropheus* sp. 'elongatus slab' from Maleri Island. It lives sympatrically with *Pseudotropheus flavus*—better known as "Dinghani"—at Chinyankwazi and with *Pseudotropheus cyaneus* at Chinyamwezi Island. The latter two species occur near small and medium-sized rocks in the somewhat deeper parts of the habitat. All these species aggressively defend their territories.

Pseudotropheus sp. 'elongatus slab' is common around Thumbi West, Mumbo and Otter islands, and is also found in the clearer waters around Nakantenga Island and along the southeastern shore of Maleri Island. Females as well as males are very aggressive in defense of their territories, which are almost always over large to very large rocks. Small cracks in these boulders usually serve as spawning sites.

Along the northeastern side of the Nankumba Peninsula a dark elongate species inhabits the shallow rocky habitat and these populations are referred to as *Pseudotropheus* sp. 'elongatus aggressive'. *P.* sp. 'elongatus aggressive' at Zimbawe Rock is larger than *P.* sp. 'elongatus slab' found around the Nankumba Peninsula and the distinction between these two species is questionable. According to Ribbink *et al.* (1983b) both species are sympatric around Nankumba but I have not been able to find both species at the same locality. There is another species, *P.* sp. 'aggressive brown' (see page 95), which may have confused their observations.

Mbuna with gardens

Besides the above-mentioned genera and the *P. elongatus* complex there is another group of mbuna living in the sediment-free rocky habitat. These species, all of which are undescribed scientifically, were grouped together by Ribbink *et al.* (1983b) as the *Pseudotropheus* "aggressive" species group. These aggressive mbuna have a specific behavioral characteristic in common: both male and female defend feeding territories. As mentioned previously, this behavior is usually seen in species that have to employ aggression in order to obtain sufficient food in the face of competition from mbuna with more efficient feeding specializations. Territoriality in females is probably governed by limitations in food supply. We encounter these aggressive species mainly in crowded habitats with numerous different species trying to make a living from the available resources.

There are three aggressive species in the sediment-free rocky habitat. Several more aggressive species are found elsewhere in the lake, but these will be discussed in the chapters dealing with their preferred habitats.

Two of these species, along with *Metriaclima* sp. 'aggressive zebra maleri' (page 264) were previously (Konings, 2001) considered representatives of a single species, i.e. *Pseudotropheus* sp. 'aggressive zebra' but are now regarded as three different entities. The first, *Pseudotropheus* sp. 'aggressive zebra mbenji' is found at the Mbenji islands, the Maleri islands, and at Nkudzi, and behaves much more aggressively than *M.* sp. 'aggressive zebra maleri', which is endemic to the Maleri islands and found in the shallow intermediate habitat. The second is *Pseudotropheus* sp. 'aggressive zebra likoma' and is endemic to the northern part of Likoma Island. *P.* sp. 'aggressive zebra mbenji' behaves like a deep-bodied form of the *P. elongatus* complex. Males have rusty brown to orange patches on the head, chest and shoulder. Females are dark brown and defend feeding territories.

1. *Pseudotropheus flavus* ♂ Chinyankwazi Island

2. *Pseudotropheus cyaneus* ♂ Chinyamwezi Island

3. *Pseudotropheus* sp. 'elongatus brown' ♂ Chimwalani Reef

4. *Pseudotropheus* sp. 'elongatus makonde' ♂ Makonde

5. *Pseudotropheus* sp. 'elongatus ornatus' ♂ Ndumbi Rocks (Likoma)

6. *Pseudotropheus* sp. 'elongatus ornatus tanzania' ♂ Chuwa

7. *Pseudotropheus flavus* ♀ Chinyankwazi Island

8. *Pseudotropheus cyaneus* ♀ Chinyamwezi Island

9. *Pseudotropheus* sp. 'elongatus brown' ♀ Chimwalani Reef

10. *Pseudotropheus* sp. 'elongatus kirondo' ♂ Kirondo

11. *Pseudotropheus* sp. 'elongatus makonde' ♀ Makonde

12. *Pseudotropheus* sp. 'elongatus ornatus' ♀ Ndumbi Rocks

13. *Pseudotropheus* sp. 'elongatus ornatus tanzania' ♀ Chuwa

1. *Pseudotropheus* sp. 'elongatus aggressive' ♀ Zimbawe Rock

8. *Pseudotropheus* sp. 'elongatus aggressive' ♂ Zimbawe Rock

2. *Pseudotropheus* sp. 'elongatus slab' ♀ Thumbi West Island

9. *Pseudotropheus* sp. 'elongatus slab' ♂ Thumbi West Island

3. *Pseudotropheus ater* ♀ Chinyamwezi Island

10. *Pseudotropheus ater* ♂ Chinyamwezi Island

4. *Pseudotropheus* sp. 'elongatus ndumbi' ♂ Ndumbi Rocks

11. *Pseudotropheus* sp. 'aggressive zebra likoma' ♂ Ndumbi Rocks

5. *Pseudotropheus* sp. 'elongatus ndumbi' ♀ Ndumbi Rocks

6. *P.* sp. 'aggressive zebra likoma' ♀ Ndumbi Rocks

12. *Pseudotropheus* sp. 'aggressive zebra mbenji' ♂ Mbenji Island

7. *P.* sp. 'aggressive brown' ♂ Thumbi West Island

Pseudotropheus sp. 'aggressive zebra likoma' often feeds on plankton in the water column. Females are dark brown and rather reclusive. Territorial males are very common at Ndumbi Rocks and chase all intruders from their domains, including females when they are not prepared to spawn. It is also found at Maingano Island but absent, or at least not common, at other places around Likoma.

Pseudotropheus sp. 'aggressive brown' inhabits the sediment-free rocky habitat around Thumbi West, Mumbo, and Harbour islands in the south of the lake. Both male and female are very dark with the male sometimes exhibiting a few blue bars. It is normally found in the very shallow rocky habitat of calm bays but not in surge zones. It is usually difficult to get a good look at this species as these cichlids come out of their hiding-places only to chase off intruders and to take a quick bite at the aufwuchs.

Unlike species of *Metriaclima*, the aggressive species pick and pluck the algae of the biocover, which is usually lush around their caves as they prevent other species from browsing it. Their teeth are stout and are closely set on the very edge of the jaws. As there is no tight fit between upper and lower teeth to grab hold of individual algal strands (as in *Tropheops*) there is enough hold, when the aufwuchs is luxuriant, to tear off chunks of the algal matrix.

A feature all these aggressive species have in common is that the visible territories of males are centered around a cave (into which the male hastily retreats as soon as he sees a diver approaching). Any intruder is fiercely repelled by a sudden dart out of this cave. Spawning in these species takes place inside the male's cave. Females therefore have temporarily to vacate their own quarters to enter those of the males. After spawning has taken place the females return to their own territories and release their fry in the guarded area.

Small but plucky

Along the northern coast of the lake several small species of the genus *Pseudotropheus* are found that belong to none of the groups discussed above. Males of these species aggressively patrol their territories. They have small mouths and nibble from the aufwuchs. The method of feeding is somewhat reminiscent of that of the herbivorous *Labidochromis*, but these species have bicuspid teeth set in a wide U-shaped jaw, which sets them apart from that genus.

As its name suggests, *P. minutus*, one such small and belligerent species, is one of the smallest mbuna. The maximum total length recorded is 66 mm. Nevertheless, males of this species effectively and actively defend their domains. In particular, they attack mbuna which enter their caves. Females, which are a brown color, are not territorial and occur singly or in small groups throughout the habitat. *Pseudotropheus minutus* is very common around Nkhata Bay and is found infrequently at northern locations as well, but not north of Lion's Cove. Ribbink *et al.* (1983b) reported its presence at Chitande Island, but I regard that small species as *P. perspicax* (see below).

There are several other small *Pseudotropheus* present in the rocky habitat along the northeastern shores and these are difficult to classify without giving each population a specific name. They are all similar in behavior but there are some differences in coloration. One group can be classified as the *minutus* group, members of which have a black submarginal band in the dorsal fin and show vertical barring on the side. The three *minutus*-type species are territorial and occupy tiny cracks and caves in and among the small rocks of the biotope.

Pseudotropheus sp. 'minutus tanzania' is similar to *P. minutus* in coloration. This species is distributed, in small numbers, between Matema and Ndonga. Males at Ikombe and Makonde lack most of the blue color and have an olive-colored upper body, and the vertical bars are hardly visible. They thus differ from the other populations where males all seem to have a blue-barred pattern.

Pseudotropheus sp. 'minutus mozambique' closely resembles *P.* sp. 'minutus tanzania' and lives in sediment-free rocky habitats on the Mozambique coast between Londo and Chiloelo. The observation that this species occurs in strictly sediment-free habitats may provide an explanation for its discontinuous distribution: it is found only in regions where the sediment-free rocky habitat encompasses a substantial area. It may therefore be conspecific with *P.* sp. 'minutus tanzania' because the large area in between the distribution of these two forms may just not contain suitable habitat. Such a scenario is, however, unlikely, as directly south of the southernmost population of *P.* sp. 'minutus tanzania' (Ndonga) *P.* sp. 'perspicax tanzania' (see below) appears to occupy the same niche at Njambe. *Pseudotropheus* sp. 'minutus mozambique' closely resembles *P.* sp. 'variable mozambique' (see below) but both species are sympatric at Chiloelo—and possibly at other sites as well—so that these must be two different species.

At Thumbi West Island a species similar to *P. minutus*, *Pseudotropheus* sp. 'tiny', occurs in the rocky and intermediate habitats. It is not found on nearby shores but is very common at Thumbi West. Females have similar markings to males but are dark brown instead of blue.

A second group of small mbuna consists of species that lack a black submarginal band in the dorsal. They are slightly more elongate than those of the *minutus* group and are also found in more sediment-rich areas. Ribbink *et al.* (1983b) found that one of the variants of this group could well be *Melanochromis perspicax* and reassigned this mbuna to the genus *Pseudotropheus*. Their argument that *Pseudotropheus* species are far more territorial than *Melanochromis* species, together with the fact that the single type specimen of *perspicax* lacks the color pattern of two horizontal bands found in most species of the latter genus, seems to justify their decision. I therefore believe it is appropriate to identify the small variable species found along the northwestern coast, between Ngara and Cape Manulo, as *Pseudotropheus perspicax*.

However, I have recently discovered a species near Hara Village at Gallireya Reef which has affinities with *P. perspicax sensu* Ribbink *et al.* in that its teeth are positioned on the very edge of the jaws. On the other hand, this species, which I have termed *Pseudotropheus* sp. 'perspicax hara', is larger than most of the other known forms in the *P. perspicax* group and has yellow-orange males and females that are dark brown with bold bars and an orange anal fin, as well as a black spot in the soft-rayed portion of the dorsal and light spots in the tail. Normally *P. perspicax* variants are small and very aggressive in their territorial defense but the species at Gallireya Reef appears to be non-territorial. Furthermore, a yellow male would also be unique in the *perspicax* group. All in all, it has a very unusual appearance and I am unsure in what "category' of mbuna it belongs. One possibility is that this species could in fact represent the true *P. perspicax*. *Melanochromis perspicax* was described from the Chilumba area and the single type had a total length of 81 mm (Trewavas, 1935), which is rather large for any of the known members of the *P. perspicax* group. But at least for the time being I will follow Ribbink *et al.* in regarding the smaller species as *P. perspicax*.

Pseudotropheus perspicax has such a variable coloration that it has appeared in the literature under three different names—the other two being *P. zebra* "ianth" and *P. elongatus* "mara" (Ribbink *et al.*, 1983b). At Ngara males are powder blue with a dark stripe beneath the eye (lachrymal stripe). About 10 km north of Chitande Island (Chesese), males are darker blue with vertical barring. At Chitande Island males are again blue but lack most of the vertical bars. This is perhaps the form that Ribbink and his co-workers (1983b) confused with *P. minutus*. At Chirwa Island, and south of Chilumba, males are powder-blue with a yellow patch on the lower part of the head. This is the population identified as *P. perspicax* by Ribbink *et al.* (1983b). Females at Chirwa Island have broad, brownish bars, which is the color pattern of males at Mphanga Rocks. Four kilometers south of the Rukuru River males are completely powder-blue again. At Chirkoole, north of Usisya, males are identical to those at Chirwa Island. At Mbowe Island males have numerous orange spots in the dorsal fin. The population at Mara Rocks has a similar pattern. Stressed males of these two populations can change color rapidly from powder-blue to the female pattern of broad vertical bars. At Cape

Manulo males are again completely powder-blue. The females of almost all of these variants exhibit broad vertical bars on a beige-colored body.

Unlike the females of *P. perspicax*, females of *P.* sp. 'polit' are light purple-brown without bars, supporting the view that it is another species. In the natural habitat some males have territories several meters (!) in diameter while females are non-territorial. An interesting feature of this cichlid is the male's ability to change color suddenly (like male *P. perspicax* from Mara Rocks and Mbowe Island). Sexually active and displaying males have light blue bodies and dark heads with two conspicuous white interorbital bars. In the event of fright or disturbance the specific male coloration disappears immediately and males become indistinguishable from females.

A species with some resemblance to *P.* sp. 'polit' seems to be restricted to Tumbi Point in Mozambique. This small cichlid, *Pseudotropheus* sp. 'polit tumbi', prefers dark caves at depths between 10 and 30 meters, and feeds by nipping aufwuchs from the rocks.

At Meponda in Mozambique and Gome in Malaŵi another small aggressive species inhabits the rocky biotope. This species, *Pseudotropheus* sp. 'variable eastern', lacks a black submarginal band in the dorsal. A further species, *Pseudotropheus* sp. 'variable mozambique', has a shape resembling that of *P.* sp. 'variable eastern' but differs in having a black submarginal band in the dorsal fin. The difference between *P.* sp. 'variable mozambique' and the sometimes sympatric *P.* sp. 'minutus mozambique' (to which it was previously assigned) is that the vertical bars, a prominent feature of the latter species, extend into the dorsal and blend with the submarginal band. This band appears isolated in the dorsal fins of *P.* sp. 'variable mozambique'. *Pseudotropheus* sp. 'variable mozambique' is found from Minos Reef to Chiloelo.

At Kande Island, *Pseudotropheus* sp. 'variable kande' inhabits the rocky habitat. This species too lacks a dark submarginal band in the dorsal. It is much more elongate than *P. minutus* and is certainly a different species, closely related to *P. perspicax*. Its distribution seems to be restricted to the island.

The various small mbuna found on the east coast of the lake, between Njambe and Undu Reef, are not easily assigned to either of the above-mentioned groups. The small mbuna found at all rocky habitats in this area has a body shape resembling that of *P. minutus* but with a color pattern more like that of *P. perspicax*. It lacks any black markings in the dorsal fin; females, though, are brown to dark brown without a trace of black markings and are much like those of *P. minutus*. The variant found at Undu Reef has a more elongate body and resembles *P. perspicax* more than any other population of this Tanzanian species. If the mbuna at Undu Reef is, as I believe, indeed part of this variable species, then the name *Pseudotropheus* sp. 'perspicax tanzania' would be the most appropriate, indicating that this species has closer ties with *P. perspicax* than with *P. minutus*.

At Pombo Rocks there are two small, territorially aggressive mbuna, either one of which may be a variant of *P.* sp. 'perspicax tanzania' but equally of *P. perspicax*. These two species closely resemble *P. perspicax*—in particular the yellow-snouted species has the same color pattern as *P. perspicax* at Chirwa Island, which is exactly opposite Pombo Rocks on the other side of the lake. The presence of two species with very similar females—brown with 9-10 narrow vertical bars—at the same locality cannot readily be explained at present. The situation at Pombo Rocks is further complicated by the presence of *P.* sp. 'minutus tanzania' and by *Labidochromis* sp. 'gigas pombo' both of which have females colored similarly to those of the former two species. The yellow-snouted species is termed *Pseudotropheus* sp. 'perspicax yellow breast' and the other, which has a rusty reddish patch on the head, is called *Pseudotropheus* sp. 'perspicax orange cap'. The geographical variant of the latter species at Ndumbi Reef has been named *Pseudotropheus* "Red Top Ndumbi" by Spreinat (1994). This form seems to lack any aggression. The yellow-snouted species behaves aggressively in defending its territory. The extent of the yellow color on the head and breast varies considerably but this color seems always to be present on the snout of male individuals.

Pseudotropheus saulosi, a beautiful species probably belonging to the small and belligerent mbuna, is endemic to Taiwanee Reef. The blue-barred males resemble male *P. minutus*, and even more so those of *P. demasoni* from Pombo Rocks, Tanzania. The females, however, are entirely orange-yellow. Males are territorial and remain in their domains at all times. Females formerly congregated in feeding schools consisting of more than 50 individuals, but the small size and attractive coloration of this species makes it a desirable aquarium resident and in the last few years the single population has been decimated by overzealous collectors so that schools of *P. saulosi* seem to be a feature of the past.

Labidochromis et al.

The genus *Labidochromis* is also represented in the deeper regions of the rocky biotope, although many species prefer the wave-washed upper parts while others search for insects in the sediment-rich areas.

At Likoma Island *Labidochromis gigas* is encountered in the sediment-free rocky habitat at deeper levels. Its maximum size of about 10 cm is noticeably larger than that of most other species in this genus. *L. gigas* is immediately recognizable underwater by its cobalt blue coloration and the black interorbital bar (males only). Females have an overall brown coloration. Young adult specimens are grayish. Its examination of the substrate during the search for food suggests a carnivorous diet, but stomach inventories have revealed a herbivorous menu (Lewis, 1982). This species picks out tiny pockets in the substrate, which are inaccessible to most other species and thus have a rich algal growth, albeit on a small scale. *L. gigas* jerks and nips at the aufwuchs, cutting off the algal strands. Females wander through the habitat and are frequently courted by males, which hold territories.

Distributed around the lake we find a handful of other *Labidochromis* that are large and have blue-colored males. I have placed these in the *gigas* group because of their large size and also because most of them are found in the sediment-free rocky habitat. Very small populations of a *gigas*-like *Labidochromis* occur at Cobwé, Mala Point, and Mbweca in Mozambique. The rocky habitats at the first two sites are mostly covered with sediment but, at least at Mala Point, there are sections relatively free. *Labidochromis* sp. 'gigas cobwe' prefers purely rocky areas but does not seem to be territorial; at least the few males I have observed were not. The reason may be that the number of sexually ripe males is so small that encounters are infrequent, and thus the drive to establish a territory is absent. On the other hand, *L.* sp. 'gigas cobwe' may feed only on invertebrates and thus needs to move through the biotope to obtain sufficient amounts of food. As mentioned before, the feeding behavior of *gigas*-like *Labidochromis* is like that of insectivorous species, but analyses indicate algae as the predominant item in the gut. I have not collected and examined *L.* sp. 'gigas cobwe' to obtain an indication of its diet, so, for the time being, I will regard this mbuna as distinct from *L. gigas*.

A similar in-limbo situation exists in other *gigas*-like species. Along the northwestern shores at Chirwa Island, Luwino Reef, Katale Island, and the coast between Chilumba harbor and Chirwa Island (the Luromo Peninsula), a blue-barred species, *Labidochromis* sp. 'gigas chilumba', inhabits the sediment-free rocky habitat. Territoriality was not seen in this species either. On the opposite side of the lake, at Pombo Rocks, a very similar species, *Labidochromis* sp. 'gigas pombo', prefers the purely rocky environments of the reef. Between Lupingu and Magunga I found a *gigas*-like species which closely resembles *L.* sp. 'gigas chilumba', but which is, for the time being, referred to as *Labidochromis* sp. 'gigas lupingu'. Again on the western coast, at Mara Rocks, a large, light blue species—*Labidochromis* sp. 'gigas mara"—frequents the rocky biotope. And finally, in the south at Chidunga Rocks, *Labidochromis* sp. 'gigas chidunga' is found on the rocky sections of the reef.

Females of all *gigas*-like *Labidochromis* have an overall brown color without black markings,

1. *Pseudotropheus* sp. 'variable eastern' ♂ Gome
2. *Pseudotropheus* sp. 'variable kande' ♂ Kande Island
3. *Pseudotropheus* sp. 'variable mozambique' ♂ Chiloelo
4. *Pseudotropheus saulosi* ♂ Taiwanee Reef
5. *Pseudotropheus saulosi* ♀♀♂ Taiwanee Reef
6. *Pseudotropheus* sp. 'variable eastern' ♀ Masinje
7. *Pseudotropheus* sp. 'variable kande' ♀ Kande Island
8. *Pseudotropheus* sp. 'variable mozambique' ♂ Minos Reef
9. *Pseudotropheus saulosi* ♀ Taiwanee Reef

1. *Labidochromis gigas* ♀ Thumbi West Island

2. *Labidochromis* sp. 'gigas cobwe' ♂ Mala Point

3. *Labidochromis* sp. 'gigas lupingu' ♂ Magunga

4. *Labidochromis* sp. 'gigas pombo' ♂ Pombo Rocks

5. *Labidochromis* sp. 'gigas chidunga' ♂ Chidunga Rocks

6. *Iodotropheus sprengerae* ♂ Chinyamwezi Island

7. *Labidochromis gigas* ♂ Machili Island

8. *Labidochromis* sp. 'gigas chilumba' ♂ Katale Island

9. *Labidochromis* sp. 'gigas mara' ♂ Mara Rocks

10. *Iodotropheus sprengerae* ♂ Boadzulu Island

and their fins are brown. Interestingly, all these large *Labidochromis* (except *L.* sp. 'gigas lupingu') are found at reefs and islands, i.e. geographically isolated places.

Iodotropheus sprengerae, thought to be an ancient species, is found in the southern part of the lake. It has a very limited distribution and is restricted to just three islands: Boadzulu, Chinyamwezi, and Chinyankwazi. Within its range this small cichlid can be seen anywhere rocks are present, including intermediate habitats.

The population at Boadzulu Island has been described as *I. declivitas* (Stauffer, 1994). Giving a population a specific name implies that a speciation event has occurred, but in this case I do not believe it has, and regard the Boadzulu population as *I. sprengerae*. The difference between these populations lies in morphological characters, e.g. the number of teeth on the lower pharyngeal bone—the individuals of the population at Boadzulu Island (*I. declivitas*) have more than those at Chinyankwazi and Chinyamwezi; and in the coloration of males—most males (not all) at Chinyamwezi and Chinyankwazi lack the bluish color seen in those from Boadzulu. Although descriptions of allopatric species (species not found at the same locality) are always a matter of the scientist's personal opinion, I do not agree with the splitting up of *I. sprengerae* solely because there is a measurable difference. I think that this genus is older than many others found in the lake. It is typical of old species among Malaŵi cichlids that they survive only in geographically isolated populations—not necessarily inhabiting the same areas over the years as the lake level fluctuates—and areas inhabited at present may have been dry land several hundreds of years ago (Owen *et al.*, 1990). In my opinion *I. sprengerae* would occur in similar habitats along the mainland shore if it was a newly radiating species. Old or less-specialized species are frequently found in geographically isolated areas that are relatively inaccessible to radiating, more specialized, or better equipped species.

The patchy distribution of *I. sprengerae* indicates it had a wider distribution in earlier days. Its habitat preferences and feeding technique rank this cichlid among the non-specialized mbuna. It feeds mainly from the aufwuchs on the rocks and does so by pushing itself against the substrate (using its pectoral fins) in order to get its teeth as deep as possible into the algal matrix. Ribbink *et al.* (1983b) found a large variety of foodstuffs in the stomachs of some individuals. On the basis of their data *I. sprengerae* can be regarded as an omnivore which nibbles from the biocover. At Chinyankwazi it apparently has competition from *L. vellicans* as it is seen much less often than at Chinyamwezi where *L. vellicans* is not found.

During the 1970s *I. sprengerae* was regularly exported as "*Melanochromis brevis*" and received trade names such as "Rusty Cichlid". It was among the very first cichlids ever exported from Lake Malaŵi. It is one of the few non-territorial mbuna and is, as such, a welcome addition to any community tank.

Iodotropheus sprengerae resembles many species of the genus *Labidochromis*, not only in the lack of territorial behavior but also in the color differences between the sexes. The coloration of females is basically identical to that of males but less intensely marked. Since a male has no permanent territory, he has, when sexually active, to indicate his intentions by means of behavioral gestures. When he encounters a female he displays in front of her, with fins extended, and it is then up to the female to respond to his invitation or resume her regular foraging activities. In most cichlid species that do not show a clear distinction between the color patterns of males and females, it is common for males not to hold courtship territories and for spawning to take place at any location in the habitat (not necessarily hidden from view). The drawback of such behavior is that the sexes have to meet at close quarters in order to establish their mutual states of ripeness. In most mbuna these somewhat elaborate encounters are made redundant by the specific colors of the male and his territorial behavior.

For some time the genus *Iodotropheus* was regarded as monotypic. However, another species has been recognized and described as *I. stuartgranti* (see page 273). A possible further species has been found along the central eastern shore of the lake between Londo and Msuli in Mozambique. No specimens were collected, so the assignment of *Iodotropheus* sp. 'londo' to this genus is still tentative. Male and female are dark brown with some dark-blue bars in the male. Territorial individuals have not yet been encountered, but *I.* sp. 'londo' was found to be very rare. The few individuals seen picked from the substrate, perhaps harvesting algae.

Melanochromis: mbuna with stripes

A genus that is well represented among the mbuna of the rocky habitat is *Melanochromis*. As originally defined, this genus included any mbuna with a number of enlarged teeth on the pharyngeals and bicuspid teeth in the outer jaws. Later Trewavas (1984) revised the definition to include only elongate species that possess horizontal stripes; Ribbink *et al.* (1983b) placed *M. joanjohnsonae, M. labrosus*, and *M. brevis* in a "heterogeneous" group, but I believe latter species clearly belongs to *Melanochromis*. About two thirds of the species currently in *Melanochromis* (and the type species *M. melanopterus*) exhibit the reversal type coloration, which means that in females the pattern consists of a light colored body with two dark horizontal stripes whereas in males these stripes are light blue or white while the body color is dark blue or black. The other species currently in this genus are not closely related to the members of the reversal group but retained here because placing them in *Pseudotropheus* as suggested by Tawil (2002a) is, in my opinion, no better alternative. There are, however, two species that clearly belong to the reversal group of *Melanochromis* but have a pigmentation pattern consisting of longitudinal stripes *and* vertical bars. These two are *Melanochromis baliodigma* (previously *M.* sp. 'blotch') and *Melanochromis* sp. 'robustus mbenji', and will be discussed in another chapter (see page 209).

Melanochromis parallelus and *Melanochromis heterochromis* (see page 273 for discussion on the status of this species and *M. vermivorus*, of which it was previously regarded as synonym) are both found in the sediment-free rocky habitat and show distinct sexual dichromatism.

These two species are omnivores which feed primarily on algae but pick at invertebrates as well. When plankton is abundant they also join with other mbuna in feeding in the water column. A diver may attract several of them when his fins stir up debris. Both species feed opportunistically, but I have observed another, most remarkable type of feeding behavior in *M. parallelus*. Eccles and Lewis (1976) describe the cleaning behavior of juvenile *Docimodus evelynae* which feed on the fungus and parasites attached to larger haplochromines (see page 168). After the rainy season, which is an important breeding period for many species, a number of larger haplochromines have damaged fins or scales, or have an anchor worm attached to the dorsal. The damaged areas are covered with fungus, preventing rapid healing. On several occasions I have observed adult females of *M. parallelus* picking fungus and anchor worms from larger haplochromines. In all instances the afflicted fish approached the "cleaner" and made clear, by lying on its side or hovering in a slanting, head-up position, that it would like to have a "treatment". In all cases the dorsal fin was presented first. The female *M. parallelus* then picked vigorously at the fungus or parasite and tore it off. Although this visibly hurt the "client' it remained in the typical position. When all its wounds were cleaned, which might take more than a minute, the larger haplochromine would resume its normal swimming position and disappear. Cleaning stations, as seen in marine fishes, were not observed: after the job was done the female *M. parallelus* would disappear from the scene as well. George Turner (pers. comm.) once found a juvenile *M. auratus* with a cleaning station based at a small rock at the edge of a breeding colony of a species of *Copadichromis*. Several utaka and rock-dwelling species were observed being cleaned, but in all instances these were large haps, never mbuna. Interestingly, *M. lepidiadaptes*, which received its name because the stomach contents of some specimens included scales (Ribbink *et al.*, 1983b), looks similar to *M. parallelus* and may have evolved its presumed scale-eating habit from cleaning other cichlids (see page 144 for further discussion).

1. *Iodotropheus sprengerae* ♂ Makokola Reef

5. *Iodotropheus sprengerae* ♀ Boadzulu Island

2. *Iodotropheus* sp. 'londo' ♂ Mesuli

6. *Iodotropheus* sp. 'londo' ♀ Londo

3. *Melanochromis parallelus* ♂ Thumbi West Island

7. *Melanochromis parallelus* ♀ Thumbi West Island

8. *Melanochromis parallelus* ♂ Linganjala Reef

4. *Melanochromis* sp. 'parallelus mbweca' ♂ Mbweca

9. *Melanochromis* sp. 'parallelus mbweca' ♀ Mbweca

1. *Melanochromis heterochromis* ♀ Jalo Reef

2. *Melanochromis heterochromis* ♀ Mbenji Island

3. *Melanochromis heterochromis* ♀ Chidunga Rocks

4. *Melanochromis heterochromis* ♀ Mumbo Island

5. *Melanochromis heterochromis* ♀ Chinyankwazi Island

6. *Melanochromis heterochromis* ♀ Chinyamwezi Island

7. *Melanochromis heterochromis* ♂ Jalo Reef

8. *Melanochromis heterochromis* ♂ Mbenji Island

9. *Melanochromis heterochromis* ♂ Chidunga Rocks

10. *Melanochromis heterochromis* ♂ Mumbo Island

11. *Melanochromis heterochromis* ♂ Chinyankwazi Island

12. *Melanochromis heterochromis* ♂ Chinyamwezi Island

M. parallelus has a wide distribution in the northern half of the lake and is found on the northwestern coast from Kande Island to Mphanga Rocks (not at Chitande Island and further north) and on the east side of the lake between Cobwé and Lutara Reef (north of Manda). It is also found around Likoma and Chizumulu Islands but not at Taiwanee Reef. It has further been introduced at Thumbi West Island.

A species with a resemblance to *M. parallelus* but with a slightly different morphology—it is smaller and the body is more slender—occurs between Mala Point and Mbweca in Mozambique. In this area I was unable to find *M. melanopterus* or a species with similar behavior (see page 144) and it seems like that the species present, *Melanochromis* sp. 'parallelus mbweca', occupies the ecological niches of both *M. parallelus* and *M. melanopterus*. Both these species are omnivores but *M. parallelus* tends more to a herbivorous lifestyle while *M. melanopterus* is more of a pursuit predator. *M.* sp. 'parallelus mbweca' could be an older and less specialized species, able to exploit a wider range of food sources because it has no competition from closely-related species.

Melanochromis heterochromis occurs at all sediment-free rocky habitats between Jalo Reef and Monkey Bay, including the Mbenji and Maleri islands, Chidunga Rocks, the area around the Nankumba Peninsula, as well as Chinyamwezi, Chinyankwazi, Chimwalani Reef, and Luwala Reef.

The pronounced difference in coloration between male and female *M. parallelus* and *M. heterochromis* suggests territorial behavior in the male. Territoriality is not, however, at all as clear-cut as might be expected. The reason may be the relatively low population density at most localities. At Chinyankwazi, Chinyamwezi, and Zimbawe Rock, however, the populations of *M. heterochromis* are dense and consequently the aggressive behavior and coloration of males are intensified. *M. heterochromis* at Mbenji and Maleri have increased competition from *M. melanopterus*, which may interfere with the population growth of the former. Some (but not all!) females at Mumbo Island have a yellowish background color instead of white. This may be caused by the type of food these individuals have been eating, but may equally be an indication that *M. heterochromis* is polymorphic, i.e. the yellowish individuals are analogous to the orange-blotch and orange forms found in some other mbuna.

The population of *M. heterochromis* at Chinyamwezi Island has in the past been called *M.* 'Chinyamwezi' (Ribbink et al., 1983b). Territorial males of this species are rare but have a very dark *heterochromis*-type coloration and are thus very different in color to females. Territories were found on top of large boulders where males defended cracks as spawning sites and chased away all intruders.

Melanochromis auratus is a popular species among aquarists, and was among the first cichlids exported from the lake. It is common throughout its distribution which lies along the western coast between Jalo Reef, near Nkhotakota, and Crocodile Rock at the southern tip of the lake. It is found at all rocky outcrops in the southern arm of the lake as well as at Chipoka, Rifu, Senga Point, and Nkhomo Reef. It is absent from Chinyankwazi and Chinyamwezi, and also from Zimbawe Rock. A few specimens of a species with a close resemblance to *M. auratus* were seen at Kande Island but these could be neither collected nor photographed.

Unlike the previous species, *M. auratus* is more inclined to feed from the aufwuchs and is less predatory. In spite of this *M. auratus* is a true omnivore. Its habitat preference is not well defined and it occurs in all rocky habitats including the intermediate zones. Males are weakly territorial, probably because population densities rarely attain competitive levels. Sexually active males, which are ready to spawn, defend a particular area when they are surrounded by ripe females but may vacate these sites when none of the females is interested. Since *M. auratus* (like most other species of this genus) is not very sedentary, virtually no geographical variants are discernible.

Along the Malaŵi east coast a similar species is found. Male and female coloration is clearly distinguishable from that of *M. auratus* (see photos). The maximum size of the latter ranges from 7.5 to 8.5 cm whereas *Melanochromis dialeptos* (formerly known as *M.* sp. 'auratus dwarf') never attains 7 cm (all measurements are taken from wild specimens and do not reflect the lengths many mbuna may grow to under artificial conditions). At Gome *M. auratus* is apparently "replaced" by two other species: the already mentioned *M. dialeptos*, and *M. simulans*. The latter is an elongate mbuna with carnivorous feeding habits, which occurs in the intermediate habitat (see page 208).

A similar splitting up of the habitat's resources is seen in Mozambique, where, at Chilucha Reef and in the rocky areas between Metangula and Nkhungu Reef, I found an elongate *auratus*-type which I call *Melanochromis* sp. 'auratus elongate'. The main anatomical difference between this species and *M. auratus* is the longer snout of *M.* sp. 'auratus elongate'. My reasons for regarding this species as different from *M. auratus* will be explained shortly. But first I would like to draw attention to the fact that 1 km south of Nkhungu Reef, the southernmost point in the distribution of *M.* sp. 'auratus elongate', the rocky habitat harbors two similar species, namely *M. dialeptos* and *M. simulans*. The niche occupied by *M.* sp. 'auratus elongate' north of Nkhungu Point, is here probably split into two niches, each occupied by a more specialized *Melanochromis*. *M. dialeptos* is more restricted to the purely rocky habitat and feeds predominantly on the algae of the biocover, while *M. simulans* inhabits the intermediate habitats and exhibits a more predatory behavior.

Melanochromis auratus, *M. heterochromis*, *M. dialeptos*, *M.* sp. 'auratus elongate', and probably *M. simulans* form a closely related group within the genus *Melanochromis*, and seem to influence each other's potential for specialization. The densest populations of *M. heterochromis* are found at Chinyankwazi, Chinyamwezi, and Zimbawe Rock, exactly the localities where *M. auratus* does not occur. At other locations where *M. auratus* is more prevalent, e.g. at Maleri and Mbenji islands, *M. heterochromis* is poorly represented. *M. heterochromis* and *M. auratus* are both omnivores but *M. auratus* is inclined to a herbivorous diet while *M. heterochromis* is more predatory. Within its area of distribution *M.* sp. 'auratus elongate' is the only member of this small group present in the rocky biotope and shows no obvious specialization for any particular type of food or habitat. It has a longer snout than *M. auratus*, which may be indicative of a more predatory nature (or which may allow the fish to reach deeper into the sediment accumulated at the base of rocks in the intermediate habitat). *M. simulans* has a longer snout than *M.* sp. 'auratus elongate' and prefers the intermediate habitat. It seems to be further specialized towards being a true predator, more so than *M. heterochromis*, although it still is an omnivore. By occupying this niche along the coast between Nkhungu and Makanjila Point it has "forced" *M. dialeptos* to specialize in a more vegetarian diet and a life in the purely rocky habitat. Of course, it is not just a case of the one species forcing the other; both influence each other. Because of the more generalized nature of *M.* sp. 'auratus elongate' I regard this species as different from *M. auratus*—in the same vein as I have separated *M.* sp. 'parallelus mbweca' from *M. parallelus* and *M. melanopterus* (see page 108).

There is another group of four species which have some anatomical resemblance to *M. auratus* but are not members of the reversal group. They have all been scientifically described: *Melanochromis johannii* is found on the east coast between Makanjila Point and Chuanga; *Melanochromis interruptus* originally occurred only around Chizumulu Island but was later introduced at Nkhata Bay, Likoma Island, and Thumbi West Island; *Melanochromis perileucos* is known only from the southern part of Likoma; and *Melanochromis cyaneorhabdos* only from the northern part of the same island.

Like *M. auratus* these species have a short snout and feed predominantly from the biocover. Apart from *M. cyaneorhabdos* they show a conspicuous color difference between the sexes. Males of all four species are mainly dark blue to black, while the females of three of them vary from orange-yellow (*M. johannii* and *M. interruptus*) to yellow-white (*M.*

1. *Melanochromis auratus* ♂ Nakantenga Island

6. *Melanochromis auratus* ♀ Mumbo Island

2. *Melanochromis auratus* ♂ Mbenji Island

7. *Melanochromis auratus* ♀ Mbenji Island

3. *Melanochromis* sp. 'auratus elongate' ♂ Minos Reef

8. *Melanochromis* sp. 'auratus elongate' ♀ N'kolongwe

4. *Melanochromis dialeptos* ♂ Gome

9. *Melanochromis dialeptos* ♂ Gome

5. *Melanochromis* sp. 'dialeptos blue' ♂ Lumessi

10. *Melanochromis* sp. 'dialeptos blue' ♀ Lumessi

1. *Melanochromis johannii* ♀ Gome
2. *Melanochromis johannii* ♂ Metangula
3. *Melanochromis interruptus* ♀ Membe island (Chizumulu)
4. *Melanochromis cyaneorhabdos* ♀ Maingano Island
5. *Melanochromis johannii* ♀♀ Chilucha reef
6. *Melanochromis johannii* ♂ Gome
7. *Melanochromis interruptus* ♂ Same Bay (Chizumulu)
8. *Melanochromis cyaneorhabdos* ♂ Maingano Island

perileucos). Females of *M. cyaneorhabdos* are identical to males. None of these species can be regarded as truly territorial, apart from defending a temporary spawning site. The difference in color between a male *M. johannii* and *M. cyaneorhabdos* is hardly discernible. Both species may be descendents of the same ancestor. At Maingano Island, off the northeastern coast of Likoma, there is *Metriaclima* sp. 'membe deep' and *Pseudotropheus* sp. 'ndumbi gold', females of which are yellow. Such conspicuous mbuna may be preferred by large predators. It may therefore have been beneficial for (the ancestors of) *M. cyaneorhabdos* to maintain or adopt a less conspicuous color on this coast and thus avoid much of the primed predation. An alternative explanation is that male *M. cyaneorhabdos* might court the wrong females or at least be confused by the presence in the biotope of a similarly-colored mbuna.

A female in male coloration is not an uncommon sight among *M. auratus*. Color switching in *M. heterochromis* (Mary Bailey, pers. comm.) and *M. johannii* has been observed in captivity too. In non-territorial species sexual dichromatism is more or less redundant, unless mate-recognition is a two-way process (male must recognize female and *vice versa*). The sex-linked color difference is present in *M. johannii*, but in the case of *M. cyaneorhabdos*, females with a male coloration could have been "promoted" by the environment.

Melanochromis interruptus, which is common only at the southwestern part of Chizumulu, inhabits the purely rocky habitat and has orange-yellow females. On the eastern side of Mbuzi Island (Likoma), at Thumbi West Island, and at the tip of the peninsula at Nkhata Bay, a small population of *M. interruptus* inhabits the rocky biotope. These populations were probably introduced by exporters of aquarium fishes (Tony Ribbink, pers. comm.). At Likoma it occurs sympatrically with *M. perileucos*.

The fin-biter

Genyochromis mento is a very common mbuna and the only one that is found in all habitats except the open water column, and at all locations around the lake. It has the nasty habit of feeding on the fins and scales of other cichlids. It shows a surprising agility and vigor in its attacks on other fishes. This mbuna does not seem to take a break during its 12-hour lunchtime! Small fishes, large fishes, anything that passes by is attacked, from below. The preferred sites of attack are the caudal peduncle and fins. Egg-spots are favored too, and many cichlids have notched anal and caudal fins, souvenirs of an encounter with *G. mento*. This predator utilizes the following technique: it remains in a particular, partially hidden, location and attacks, with lightning-fast sallies, as many fishes as possible. After a few minutes most of the sedentary mbuna will have noticed it and thereafter avoid passing by or chase it before it can attack. At this point *G. mento* moves to another site a meter away where it can again attack passing mbuna.

Adult *G. mento* seem to develop a liking for attacking fighting mbuna. Ribbink *et al.* (1983b) report that *G. mento* collects any scales that are dislodged from the combatants" flanks. It may also actively join in the combat and feed directly from the fins of the opponents, while they are concentrating on each other and hardly notice the stealthy approach of *G. mento*. Females are mutilated to a far lesser extent. The victims are usually mbuna, but larger haps are also attacked, especially those in rocky areas where *G. mento* can hide before it attacks. I have witnessed attacks launched from empty snail shells on a sandy bottom. The victims were sand-dwelling cichlids passing overhead. *G. mento* would quickly retreat into its shelter before any of the victims could retaliate.

Like most predatory fishes *G. mento* has a feeding territory, but in this instance the territory is an area with a radius of about 50 cm centered on the fish, and moves with it. Only conspecifics are chased from this territory. In captivity, this cichlid has to be kept by itself as it will start feeding from other inhabitants a few minutes after introduction. It will not, however, attack members of its own species.

The fin-biting habit may have evolved from the aggressive behavior known as tail chasing. Species of the genus *Melanochromis*—in both the reversal and the non-reversal group—are particularly inclined towards tail-chasing, which usually involves two males, or sometimes two females, simultaneously trying to bite each other's flank and at the same time avoid the other's attack. The result is a brisk circling by the two opponents without any actual injury to either of them. Somewhere in the development of *G. mento* this behavior may have escalated into feeding from the opponent's caudal peduncle and tail. The peduncle is also the preferred site of attack of other scale-eaters such as *Corematodus taeniatus* and *C. shiranus* (see page 385). It is, of course, also the site furthest away from the mouth of the victim, i.e. from possible retaliation.

G. mento seems to adopt a dark coloration when hunting in the rocky habitat so it blends in better with the background of nooks and crannies in the rocks. It is also found in sandy habitats where it seems to mimic the sandy-silvery coloration of most other species found there.

The fact that the type of color pattern is dependent on the type of habitat frequented indicates that the coloration of this species must have a camouflage effect. But *G. mento* goes even further. In order to enhance its "blending-in with the crowd" and be as casual as possible, it even mimics the coloration of some local species, usually members of the *P. elongatus* complex but also *Labeotropheus trewavasae* or *L. fuelleborni*. At several locations around the lake I have found *G. mento* mimicking local species: at Chinyankwazi Island, home of *Pseudotropheus flavus*, many *G. mento* have a yellow cast on their body. Potential victims passing by a fin-ripping and scale-stealing *G. mento* may thus be deceived into thinking they are passing by a *P. flavus*. This probably gives *G. mento* a few fractions of a second extra to complete its depredations. Interestingly, a solid black colored *elongatus*-type, *P. ater*, is found at the same island. And, as you may have guessed by now, there are also solid black colored *G. mento* around. However, I don't think that *G. mento*'s mimicry is intended to give it a better chance of feeding specifically on its model, but rather to deceive other species into thinking it a harmless herbivorous fellow-inhabitant of that particular area.

At some locations there are very conspicuous *G. mento* that seem to refute the ideas about camouflage put forward above. At Mphanga Rocks I have found several bright yellow *G. mento* and at most localities there are OB-morphs of this species. At first this seems to contradict the hypothesis that *G. mento* attempts to be as inconspicuous as possible, but closer examination of the situation in each individual habitat suggests an explanation. For instance, the OB individuals of *M. zebra* in the mbuna population near Gome have relatively large black blotches on an orange body. The rare OB *G. mento* found at Gome also has large black blotches. At Nkhata Bay the black blotches of OB Zebra females are smaller and the occasional OB *G. mento* found there likewise has smaller blotches. At Minos Reef in Mozambique I have seen a blotched *G. mento* with a bright orange body color, matching in every detail the coloration of the local OB morph of *M. estherae*. Furthermore, the yellow, non-blotched morph of *G. mento* found at Mphanga Rocks resembles the local yellow morph of *L. trewavasae*. So, again, we see that these conspicuous *G. mento* forms can prosper by virtue of the presence of similar forms of other, harmless, species. They merge into the particular crowd of which they form part and are not conspicuous at all from the viewpoint of their victims.

Mate recognition in *G. mento* takes place in a similar way to that described for other non-territorial species. Partners recognize each other by the peculiar shape (the strong, clearly protruding lower jaw), and characteristic behavior. Males court females on the spot and spawning takes place at any location in the rocky habitat.

The Stevenis

There are also cichlids other than mbuna in the sediment-free rocky habitat, and several of them have a lake-wide distribution. *Protomelas taeniolatus* is the most frequently encountered non-mbuna in this habitat and is also one of the most frequently exported haps from the

1. *Genyochromis mento* ♂ Higga Reef
2. *Genyochromis mento* ♂ Katale Island
3. *Genyochromis mento* Katale Island
4. *Genyochromis mento* Mumbo Island
5. *Genyochromis mento* ♂ Boadzulu Island
6. *Genyochromis mento* ♂ Chitimba Bay
7. *Genyochromis mento* Crocodile Rock
8. *Genyochromis mento* Chinyankwazi Island
9. *Genyochromis mento* ♀ Luwala Reef
10. *Genyochromis mento* OB ♀ Ndumbi Rocks

1. *Protomelas taeniolatus* ♂ Katale Island

8. *Protomelas taeniolatus* ♂ Lupingu

2. *Protomelas taeniolatus* ♀ Katale Island

6. *Protomelas taeniolatus* ♂ Nakantenga Island

9. *Protomelas taeniolatus* ♀ Lupingu

3. *Protomelas taeniolatus* ♂ Namalenje Island

10. *Protomelas taeniolatus* ♂ Gome

4. *Protomelas taeniolatus* ♀ Chimwalani Reef

7. *Protomelas taeniolatus* ♂ Chimwalani Reef

11. *Protomelas taeniolatus* ♀ Gome

5. *Protomelas taeniolatus* ♂ Boadzulu Island

12. *Protomelas taeniolatus* ♂ Chinyamwezi Island

lake. In the aquarium trade it is better known as "Haplochromis Steveni" (informally named after Stuart Grant's former head of the collecting teams, Steven Longwe). Many geographical races have evolved, as in the case of the rock-frequenting mbuna. Several localities are regularly fished for these variants which have all been given separate names. The aquarium favorites have received names such as "Steveni Tiger", "Red Empress". "Fire Blue", and "Haplochromis Hinderi", while others have been named after the locality where they were collected, e.g. "Steveni Mbenji", "Steveni Maleri", and "Steveni Eastern".

The fish collectors realized at an early stage that one location could harbor at least two varieties and these were both called "Stevenis", e.g. "Steveni Tiger" and "Steveni Thick Bars'. Although they have different habitat preferences, two Stevenis could be seen together in some places. The Steveni Thick Bars is in fact *P. fenestratus*, a species with a lake-wide distribution but remarkably little geographical variation, and is discussed in the chapter dealing with the intermediate habitat (see page 213).

Besides the thick-barred Stevenis there are other *Protomelas* also found sympatrically with *P. taeniolatus*. One of these has been given the name "Steveni Imperial" and was at one time considered a geographical variant of *P. fenestratus* (Konings 1989; Spreinat 1994) but this is probably incorrect. *Protomelas* sp. 'steveni imperial' is a distinct species found sympatrically with *P. taeniolatus* and *P. fenestratus* and seems to prefer the sediment-rich rocky habitat. In the absence of *P. taeniolatus*, however, it is also found in the upper rocky habitat. On the northwestern coast it is found (at Hora Mhango and Nkhata Bay) at the somewhat deeper levels of the rocky habitat, whereas on the Tanzanian coast (Nkanda, Kirondo, Makonde, and Lupingu) it occurs in the shallow, sediment-rich rocky habitat. The Tanzanian form is exported as "Imperial Tigress" and characterized by the yellow color on the shoulder. Males defend territories either on the sand under overhanging rocky ledges or on rocks. Spawning pits have not been seen. *P. fenestratus* males, by contrast, construct shallow spawning pits among the rubble on the sand floor and have an overall light blue coloration. Previously (Konings, 2001) this species was thought to perhaps be identical with *P. virgatus* (page 276) and referred to *P. cf. virgatus* pending confirmation of that assumption, but since *P. virgatus* has now been re-discovered and found to be different from the widespread "Steveni Imperial", the latter is now again termed *P.* sp. 'steveni imperial'.

Stauffer (1993) described the "Steveni Fire Blue" from Chinyankwazi and Chinyamwezi islands as *Protomelas dejunctus*. Although this form appeared different from the types of *P. taeniolatus,* a much larger sample of Stevenis from various localities around the lake should be compared to exclude (or not) *P. dejunctus* from being a geographical variant of *P. taeniolatus*. For the time being I regard the Fire Blue as just that—a geographical variant of *P. taeniolatus.*

P. sp. 'steveni imperial' is probably closely related to another attractive species, *Protomelas* sp. 'steveni taiwan', which is restricted to three isolated areas. The name is derived from Taiwanee (formerly Taiwan) Reef, a rocky reef north of Chizumulu Island, where the species was first discovered. Interestingly, almost identical populations, thought to be the same species, are found in Tanzania at Higga Reef and Ngkuyo (Mbamba Bay) Island and are known as "Chimoto Red" and "Chimoto Yellow" respectively. Territorial males of *P.* sp. 'steveni taiwan' defend territories on top of rocks at rather deep levels—most males are found at a depth of more than 15 meters. In contrast to *P.* sp. 'steveni imperial', which is often sympatric with other Stevenis, *P.* sp. 'steveni taiwan' is the only Steveni found in its area of distribution.

Given the distribution and habitat preference of *P.* sp. 'steveni taiwan' I conclude that this species is poorly specialized and old enough to have been present at low lake levels thousands of years ago. It may thus be impossible to unravel the ancestry of the Stevenis found on the eastern shores south of Mbamba Bay because they are probably more closely related to *P.* sp. 'steveni imperial' than to *P. taeniolatus*, formerly believed to be their closest relative. This would also explain the presence of two Stevenis at

Gome, because one of them is *P. taeniolatus* (previously referred to as *P.* sp. 'steveni blue black') and the other *P.* sp. 'steveni imperial' (known as "Steveni Eastern').

At several places along the northwestern shores between Kande Island and Mdoka another species of the Steveni group occurs in the rocky habitat. This species, *Protomelas* sp. 'steveni black belly', is rather rare at most localities but common at Kande and Mphandikucha Islands. It does not show much geographical variation throughout its range. It feeds from the biocover in a similar fashion to *P. taeniolatus* and *P.* sp. 'steveni imperial' but seems to wander through the habitat a lot more.

P. taeniolatus and *P.* sp. 'steveni imperial' occupy a special niche in the rocky habitat community. They are predominantly herbivorous cichlids which suck algae from small pockets in the rocks. In much the same way as *Labidochromis* and *Chilotilapia euchilus* (see page 213), the fish visually locates the site before "striking". When it strikes, the lips are pressed tightly against the substrate and the gill-covers closed to seal the buccal cavity, which is then expanded so that the resulting low pressure sucks the algal strands into the mouth. The bicuspid teeth in the upper jaw fit tightly over those of the lower, cutting off the strands. Such strikes occur in rapid succession and it may look as if the fish is feeding randomly from the aufwuchs. It is quite common for insect larvae to be collected in the same way, but the primary aim is to harvest algae. When plankton is abundant *P. taeniolatus* is seen feeding in the open water.

Males aggressively defend territories against all intruding species and algal gardens are frequently seen. Their territories are usually on top of large or medium-sized rocks. Ripe females approach the male's territory and spawning takes place immediately, on the top of a rock. Such a site is vulnerable to egg-robbing fishes, so rather a large territory is defended. The eggs are fertilized inside the female's mouth. After about three weeks incubation, the fry are released among the rocks but find refuge for another month inside the female's mouth.

A species that has confused me several times (in the taxonomic sense) is found at Likoma Island and at Nakantenga and Thumbi West islands in the south of the lake. I originally assigned this fish, here termed *Protomelas* sp. 'hertae', first (Konings, 1989) to *P. ornatus* and later (Konings, 1990) to *P. lobochilus*. After re-examination of the types of these two species, as well as that of *P. festivus,* I eventually came to the conclusion that the last two (*lobochilus* and *festivus*) are junior synonyms of *P. ornatus*. This means that the "Hertae", which is not *ornatus*, equally cannot be either of the other two.

The discontinuous distribution of *P.* sp. "hertae" is suggestive of an old species which had a wider distribution in earlier days. The species is characterized by moderately thickened lips that assist the fish in extracting invertebrates, such as insect larvae and nymphs, from tiny holes in the substrate. The soft tissue of the lips probably absorbs the shock when the fish sucks a prey item out of a narrow crack. *P.* sp. "hertae" sucks its prey out of the substrate instead of biting it free as in *Labidochromis*.

Males are territorial and chase all intruders from their premises. They defend special spawning sites that are constructed in the sand beneath rocks. In fact, during the breeding season the male occupies a large cave in which he builds a turret-like spawning cone on the sandy bottom (Horst Dieckhoff, pers. comm.). The fry are released after three weeks but usually find shelter inside the female's buccal cavity for another three.

The rock-breeding utaka

The utaka (the native name for the zooplankton-feeding haplochromines), are the most important and probably most successful group in the lake. As mentioned earlier, when dealing with *Cynotilapia*, feeding in the water column bestows one great advantage over all the bottom-dwelling cichlids, and that is the availability of space. A considerable drawback, however, is that these open water fishes are much more vulnerable to predation and also that for spawning purposes males of almost all species need to secure a territory in the overcrowded habitats near the bottom. This means that for-

1. *Protomelas* sp. 'steveni imperial' ♂ Nkhata Bay

8. *Protomelas* sp. 'steveni imperial' ♂ Makonde

2. *Protomelas* sp. 'steveni imperial' ♀ Nkhata Bay

6. *Protomelas* sp. 'steveni imperial' ♀ Lupingu

9. *Protomelas* sp. 'steveni imperial' ♂ Thumbi Tz

3. *Protomelas* sp. 'steveni imperial' ♂ Maingano Island

10. *Protomelas* sp. 'steveni imperial' ♂ Pombo Rocks

4. *Protomelas* sp. 'steveni imperial' ♀ Gome

7. *Protomelas* sp. 'steveni imperial' ♀ Tumbi Point

11. *Protomelas* sp. 'steveni imperial' ♀ Pombo

5. *Protomelas* sp. 'steveni imperial' ♂ Gome

12. *Protomelas* sp. 'steveni imperial' ♂ Chuanga

1. *Protomelas* sp. 'steveni taiwan' ♂ Higga Reef

2. *Protomelas* sp. 'steveni taiwan' ♀ Higga Reef

3. *Protomelas* sp. 'steveni black belly' ♀ Kande Island

4. *Protomelas* sp. 'hertae' ♂ Maingano Island

5. *Protomelas* sp. 'hertae' ♀ Linganjala Reef

6. *Protomelas* sp. 'hertae' ♀ Thumbi West Island

7. *Protomelas* sp. 'steveni taiwan' ♂ Taiwanee Reef

8. *Protomelas* sp. 'steveni taiwan' ♂ Ngkuyo Reef

9. *Protomelas* sp. 'steveni black belly' ♂ Kande Island

10. *Protomelas* sp. 'hertae' ♂ Nakantenga Island

aging takes place at a different location from spawning. In *Cynotilapia,* territorial males are normally separated from the females (as they have a continuous breeding season) and only during the actual spawning do females join the sexually active males.

Some utaka have a different strategy. Males and females forage together throughout the year and only during a short breeding period do they migrate *en masse* inshore to spawn. Zooplankton is not always plentiful in the lake and only at specific locations does a steady flow of fresh plankton supply the huge shoals of utaka, which know where to find these places. Local fishermen know these places as well and call them *chirundu* or *virundu* (plural). Characteristic of such places are rocks or reefs on the sandy bottom. These rocks cause turbulence in the current just "downstream" of them. It is here that large clouds of plankton can be found together with the foraging utaka.

There are several types of utaka. The natives use the name for any cichlid that can be caught with their special circular nets (*chirimila* nets) in the open water. This is not the definition applied by Bertram *et al.* (1942), who restricted the term utaka to those plankton-feeding haplochromines with strongly protrusible mouths. These species were subsequently assigned to the genus *Copadichromis* by Eccles & Trewavas (1989). I refer to utaka as the natives do and therefore include *Mchenga* and most *Nyassachromis* species as well.

Several breeding techniques have developed among the utaka. Some species (e.g. *Copadichromis quadrimaculatus*) breed in the rocky habitat without any demarcation of a spawning site, males of some other species (e.g. *Copadichromis likomae*) construct sand-castle bowers in the intermediate habitat, while yet others (e.g. *Mchenga* (formerly *Copadichromis*) *conophoros*) do so on the open sand. A fourth reproductive strategy is employed by *Copadichromis chrysonotus* (see page 124).

Copadichromis borleyi is readily recognized by the very elongate pelvic fins of the mature male, which probably act as a species-specific signal. This species appears to have no specific breeding season, and males in breeding dress are seen all year round. It grows to a maximum total length of approximately 16 cm. It is usually found at an average depth of 10 meters in the rocky habitat, where males defend territories alongside large boulders. It is nowhere seen in large numbers, and this is consistent with the sedentary behavior of the males at least, as zooplankton is not abundant at any one location the whole year around. *Copadichromis borleyi* is found at all the rocky shores I have visited except at Likoma Island. It is, however, present at Taiwanee Reef and Linganjala Reef.

Because of its sedentary behavior, *C. borleyi*, being restricted to rocky shores, has evolved many geographical races. The most obvious differences between these are in the male breeding colors, but the number of spots and the color of the fins in juveniles and adult females also differ from one locality to the next. Several populations in the southeastern arm of the lake lack spots on the flanks altogether while some others have only the first and third spots. Females of the most southerly populations have orange to deep red unpaired fins, while those along the eastern shores have yellow, and those of the northwestern populations colorless, fins.

Territorial males defend spawning sites alongside large boulders and spawning usually takes place against the vertical face. Sometimes they spawn upside-down under an overhanging rock. That geographical variation is not restricted to coloration alone is shown by the breeding behavior of *C. borleyi* from Kadango. This form has been observed breeding at different periods of the year and is no different to other *C. borleyi* populations in this respect. Its breeding behavior, however, as observed in captivity but also seen in the population at Crocodile Rocks, is rather atypical of utaka in that the male constructs a spawning platform of sand on the rocks. This behavior may have evolved as a result of the almost permanent turbidity of the water in its particular habitat, which consists of rocky reefs on a sandy floor in rather shallow water (no deeper than five meters). The lack of steep sloping rocky shores on the eastern coast near Kadango, and the abundance of plankton in that area, suggests a year-round low underwater visibility. Males build very shallow spawning platforms on top of rocks and it is possible that, owing to the turbidity of the water, this is to clearly demarcate the territory, making it stand out against the dark background. Males in more rocky environments normally have patches of algal growth marking their territories although at Lundu, Tanzania, and at Mbenji Island I observed males carrying sand to the top of a boulder, probably to mark their territories. Females are thus better informed as to the whereabouts of the breeding arenas of males. The ancestor of this species was probably not a bower builder from the sandy habitat, because the bower-construction of *C. borleyi* follows a different scheme to that commonly seen in sand-dwelling species. A typical sand-dweller starts digging from the center of its territory and deposits the scooped sand on the rim of its bower. When a reasonable pit has been formed, it starts taking sand from the surrounding area to complete the rim of the bower. Taking a mouthful of sand, it first swims to the center of the pit, and then spits out the sand while moving towards the bower perimeter. Herein lies the difference from *C. borleyi*, whose male cannot, of course, start from the center (solid rock!) but has to collect all his sand from the surrounding bottom. When he arrives at the site with a mouthful he does not move from the center to the rim, but instead sifts the sand through his gills while swimming over the rim of the bower. Only the very fine sand that has passed through the gills marks the spawning platform; coarser sand is spat out away from the site. Any coarse material is meticulously removed from the bower as the female may mistake this for eggs when she comes to pick up the real ones.

Copadichromis cyaneus is found all around the lake shore, as well as at Likoma and Chizumulu islands. It has not, however, been seen at Taiwanee Reef. It occupies a similar niche to *C. borleyi*, with which it is found sympatric at most places although it seems that *C. cyaneus* prefers cleaner water. Males defend sites on and alongside large boulders, but neither mark them with sand nor defend them so aggressively as to create visible algal growth. There is geographical variation in *C. cyaneus* as well. Male breeding coloration, which is completely blue in all known populations, is augmented in some populations by a yellow-orange edge to the anal fin (e.g. at Likoma and Chirwa islands) and/or by a light-blue blaze on head and nape (e.g. at Zimbawe Rock and Chirwa Island). Mature females of most populations have no markings or just a faint spot on the caudal peduncle. In almost all populations females have a yellow anal fin and the fry of several populations have yellow in all the fins except the pectorals. Juveniles often have a distinct spot on the caudal peduncle, but in most populations this fades when they grow older. In some southern populations, for example at Chinyankwazi Island, some females (not all) have two distinct spots. The local name at Monkey Bay is *mfufuma* (Jackson, 1961).

Copadichromis jacksoni, which has two small spots on the body, has a lake-wide distribution. It is one of the larger utaka with a maximum total length of about 20 cm. Males in breeding color, which are called *nguwa* by African fishermen, have a dark blue body with a white blaze on the head and nape. The breeding grounds of *C. jacksoni* are usually found along steep rocky shores where the water is clear. Breeding probably takes place throughout the year (Saulos Mwale, pers. comm.). Males, which are usually found in small breeding colonies, defend their territories on top of large boulders which usually protrude above the surrounding terrain so that the males are closer to the females in the open water. Territories are vigorously defended against all intruders and include thriving algal growth—this indicates that territorial defense takes place over a long period. Male *C. jacksoni* can count! At Likoma, where many different utaka inhabit the open water, sexually active males are surrounded by three-spotted, two-spotted, one-spotted, and plain silver utaka females. When I watched a small colony of territorial males in Mbako Bay, I noticed that only females with two spots provoked courtship displays by the males, although these females were sometimes *C. quadrimaculatus* or *C. diplostigma* rather than *C. jacksoni*. Females with three, one, or no spots at all were either chased from the spawning site,

1. *Copadichromis borleyi* ♂ Mdoka

6. *Copadichromis borleyi* ♂ Nkanda

2. *Copadichromis borleyi* ♂ Mphanga Rocks

7. *Copadichromis borleyi* ♂ Linganjala Reef

3. *Copadichromis borleyi* ♂ Nkhata Bay

8. *Copadichromis borleyi* ♂ Chimwalani Reef

4. *Copadichromis borleyi* ♂ Kande Island

9. *Copadichromis borleyi* ♂ Chinyamwezi Island

5. *Copadichromis borleyi* ♀ Nakantenga Island

10. *Copadichromis borleyi* ♂ Kadango

1. *Copadichromis cyaneus* ♀ Zimbawe Rock
2. *Copadichromis cyaneus* ♀ Minos Reef
3. *Copadichromis jacksoni* ♀ Maingano Island
4. *Copadichromis* sp. 'yellow jumbo' ♀ Chiofu
5. *Copadichromis borleyi* ♀ Chimwalani Reef
6. *Copadichromis cyaneus* ♂ Zimbawe Rock
7. *Copadichromis jacksoni* ♂ Matema
8. *Copadichromis* sp. 'yellow jumbo' ♂ Gome
9. *Copadichromis* sp. 'yellow jumbo' ♀ Chiofu

like any mbuna that tried to feed on the algae, or completely ignored.

An undescribed species, *Copadichromis* sp. 'yellow jumbo', breeds in a similar way to *C. jacksoni*. It is found at Chizumulu and Likoma islands and along the eastern shores from Makanjila Point to Nkanda. Females, which can attain a total length of about 13 cm, have light brown to silvery bodies and bright yellow fins. At Chizumulu these females have only a single small black spot, on the caudal peduncle, but in other populations females have three small spots along the flank and peduncle. Males are completely blue and attain a total length of more than 22 cm. They are extremely shy and their flight distance is about ten meters. They hold territories on the very edge of the rocky habitat where they occupy boulders that stand out from the surrounding terrain, but always in water with a depth of less than five meters. Females are occasionally seen guarding their offspring; this species, together with *C. trimaculatus*, is the only utaka to guard its fry after they have been released for the first time. A guarding female defends a nursery area about a meter in diameter, usually beneath an overhanging rock. The juveniles, who have very pretty yellow fins, feed from the aufwuchs, mainly on the vertical faces of rocks. Guarding females have been observed only in the rocky biotope. This species is probably a truly open water utaka which comes to shore only to breed. Brooding females have been seen in June (Chizumulu) and November (Nkanda, Tanzania and Gome, Malaŵi).

Copadichromis sp. 'mloto reef' has been found at several different localities: Mphanga Rocks and Maison Reef, both in Malaŵi, Higga Reef in Tanzania, and Minos Reef in Mozambique. The male's breeding color is blue, with a white blaze on the head and nape, and a yellow edge to the anal fin. Males thus resemble those of *C. cyaneus*. Female *C.* sp. 'mloto reef' are silvery with two spots (Higga Reef). Interestingly, breeding males station themselves in the open water column, at least two meters above or away from the rocky substrate, but defend a spawning site on top of a protruding rock. When disturbed a male will swim away for a long distance before hiding among the rocks. Despite its name, I believe that this species is not closely related to *C. mloto* (see page 313).

At Taiwanee Reef a yellow-finned species, *Copadichromis* sp. 'taiwan yellow', exhibits behavior uncommon in utaka. The few individuals observed were solitary and seemed to be feeding on something other than plankton. After I had observed a few of them I thought that they might be egg-robbers as they were fiercely chased by, for instance, males of *C.* cf. *nkatae* (page 153) as soon as they entered their territories in the caves. Such behavior of the resident male is commonly observed with known egg-robbers, such as *Protomelas insignis* and *Otopharynx ovatus*, i.e. they chase such robbers much further away than any other intruder. Later on I found some specimens of *C.* sp. 'taiwan yellow' in the catch of some fishermen, but examination of the stomach contents of a few of these proved nothing as they were empty. The mouth is not very protrusible and the maximum total length of the few specimens seen is estimated at about 12 cm.

The *Silibanga*

Copadichromis chrysonotus, locally known as the *silibanga*, is the only (known) utaka that spawns in the open water (Eccles & Lewis, 1981). It occurs throughout the lake but is nowhere present in large numbers (unlike *C. quadrimaculatus*, page 153). Due to its substrate-free spawning technique it is not restricted to a special breeding season, but breeding does, however, seem to cease during the rainy season (from December to April). Females and non-territorial males gather in schools composed of several species of utaka and feed on zooplankton. During the breeding season males stake out their three-dimensional territories in the upper three meters of the open water. They probably use rocks on the lake floor as reference points. Males on the outer edge of the school may relate their territorial boundaries to those of males further inshore. These territories are about three meters in diameter but may be smaller when more males are around. Males court females which enter their territories and lateral displays are commonly seen. Males have light-colored streaks and small spots on the anal fin, which are common in the anal fins of those utaka that breed in the rocky habitat. This suggests that *C. chrysonotus* may have evolved from a species which breeds in rocky habitats. Spawning takes place in mid-water (Eccles & Lewis, 1981). I have observed *C. chrysonotus* spawn several times and every time the pair behaved as if they were spawning on top of a rock. The technique is exactly as described on page 16. The eggs are immediately taken up by the female and fertilized when she mouths the anal fin of the displaying male. *Copadichromis chrysonotus* grows to a maximum total length of about 13 cm. Following the export of a few juveniles, it has become a relatively popular cichlid among hobbyists (Baasch, 1993).

The predatory haps

Three predatory species in particular are commonly found in the sediment-free rocky habitat, along with many piscivorous wanderers occasionally entering this biotope. These three piscivores are *Tyrannochromis nigriventer*, *Aristochromis christyi,* and *Exochochromis anagenys*.

Tyrannochromis nigriventer is one of the few predators that prey on adult mbuna, and can attain a total length of more than 30 cm. It has a lake-wide distribution, and occurs in some poorly-defined geographical variants that vary in their basic pigmentation pattern. The vertical elements in the pattern of the northern populations are stronger than in the southern variants. *Tyrannochromis nigriventer* is known in the aquarium hobby as "Haplochromis Macrostoma'. *T. macrostoma*, however, is a common cichlid of sediment-rich habitats (see page 253). The difference between these two species is readily discernible in the length of the premaxillary pedicel—the sliding element of the upper jaw—which can be seen as a small bulge on the snout of the fish. If this bulge is about halfway between the eye and the tip of the snout then we are dealing with *T. nigriventer*, but if it is closer to the eye than to the tip of the snout the fish is *T. macrostoma*.

T. nigriventer hunts by stealth, ambushing its prey from behind a rock. It moves slowly forward and suddenly opens its wide gape. Mbuna of up to 6 cm have been found in the stomach of this predator.

Male *Tyrannochromis* control territories only during the breeding season. I found small breeding colonies of *T. nigriventer* at Chitande Island at a depth of about 30 meters (Sept. 1992), at Hongi Island at a depth of about 15 meters (Nov. 1993), and at Thumbi West Island at a depth of about five meters (Aug. 2006). Each male had constructed a crater-shaped spawning pit, with a diameter of approximately one meter, against a large boulder. Several mouthbrooding females were seen near the territorial males but spawning was not observed. At other places I have seen single breeding males defending a site in the rocky habitat, but these had not constructed a spawning pit. Aquarium observations indicate that the eggs are fertilized inside the female's mouth. Interestingly, mouthbrooding females stay close to the male's territory and the fry are released among the rocks. Sometimes it seems as if the male is guarding the fry and the female. On numerous occasions, when a mouthbrooding or fry-guarding female was observed, a male in nuptial dress was seen too. The fry are guarded and taken back inside the huge mouth for as long as five or six weeks after first release. By this time the fry have reached about 3.5 cm in length. One would think that mbuna would have respect for a predator the size of *T. nigriventer*, but *Melanochromis melanopterus*, a notorious hunter of fry, is frequently observed shooting across the school of youngsters. Maybe it knows that the female does not eat during this period!

Aristochromis christyi is a peculiar and uncommon cichlid of the rocky habitat. Its size (maximum about 27 cm) and interesting "aristocratic" nose give it a distinctive appearance. It is not a swift swimmer, and has a characteristic manner of attacking prey. The characteristic feature of its hunting behavior is the tilted position of the body. The predator focuses just one eye on its prey and can tilt its body to either side. When it has "eyed up" its prey it slowly descends to approach the victim. Just before it

1. *Copadichromis* sp. 'mloto reef' ♂ Maison Reef

2. *Copadichromis* sp. 'taiwan yellow' ♂ Taiwanee Reef

3. *Copadichromis chrysonotus* ♂ Tsano Rock

4. *Copadichromis chrysonotus* ♂ ♀ Boadzulu Island

5. *Copadichromis* sp. 'mloto reef' ♀ Higga Reef

6. *Copadichromis chrysonotus* ♀ Boadzulu Island

7. Taiwanee Reef

1. *Exochochromis anagenys* ♀ Maison Reef

6. *Exochochromis anagenys* ♂ Boadzulu Island

2. *Exochochromis anagenys* ♀ Boadzulu Island

7. *Aristochromis christyi* ♂ Linganjala Reef

3. *Aristochromis christyi* ♀ Cobwé

4. *Tyrannochromis nigriventer* ♀ Mbenji Island

8. *Tyrannochromis nigriventer* ♀ Nkhata Bay

5. *Tyrannochromis nigriventer* ♂ Thumbi West Island

strikes it shakes its body as if it is a sick fish trying to regain normal position before falling to the bottom. When it comes within striking distance of the unwary prey a sudden stroke *sideways* with its head secures the victim between the jaws. *A. christyi* is specialized in hunting rather large prey, sometimes about a third its own length. The exceptionally strong jaws make sure that large prey will not get away once firmly seized.

In contrast to *T. nigriventer*, *A. christyi* moves through the habitat at a fairly constant speed. It also occurs over the sand-rock interface, and hunts predominantly the larger mbuna that live on the outer fringes of the rocky areas. Only once have I found a fry-guarding female *A. christyi*, at Cobwé. This particular female exhibited a color pattern different from the usual diagonal stripe although her offspring exhibited this marking. The female's pattern consisted of two horizontal stripes (see photo 3 page 127). This may be the breeding/brooding pattern in *A. christyi* or an abnormality. It could further indicate how the diagonal stripe pattern, unique to some Malaŵi haplochromines, may have evolved from a more basic (plesiomorphic) pattern of horizontal stripes and vertical bars.

An *Exochochromis anagenys* cruising through the rocky habitat is a striking sight. Unlike the other predators in this group it swims at high speed through the habitat, usually about a meter above the rocks. Every now and then it stops and tilts its body to hunt an mbuna. Maximum size is about 30 cm. Males have a blue breeding coloration; females and non-breeding males in the northern half of the lake are yellow with three spots on the body while those in the southern part are silvery. The mouth has a beak-like shape and is laterally compressed. Its shape is reminiscent of that of *A. christyi*. It enables the predator to get a better grip on its prey which is caught with a sideways stroke of the head. *Exochochromis anagenys* has a lake-wide distribution and is rarely seen over sandy areas.

Utaka youngsters are found regularly among the young of the piscivores *Tyrannochromis nigriventer* and *T. macrostoma*. The existence of such mixed species broods can be explained by the fact that juvenile haplochromine cichlids like to congregate. They are much safer in a school since a predator cannot concentrate easily on a single individual. When utaka fry are released and abandoned by the female they move in tight packs through the habitat as this gives them a feeling of security. The bigger the school, the safer the individual feels. This is the reason why we find youngsters (and adult fishes in hostile environments as well) joining other groups of young cichlids. They must all be of approximately the same size (otherwise the effect of blending into the crowd would be lost) and they also need to have the same swimming speed, but the kind of species is not important. The utaka regularly found among broods of large predators are of the same size as those of the foster-brood. In most cases they are much too large to fit inside the mouth of their own mother. When such a mixed brood is disturbed, the young of the guarding parent head for their mother's mouth followed by the "alien" young (see photo 8, page 127). Since the young utaka will probably never have taken refuge inside a female's mouth after their release, they usually stay outside and wait until the others reappear. Other, non-utaka species, which have mixed with such broods, may take refuge inside the predator's mouth. The female is not able to discriminate between the different broods in her care. The idea that the juveniles find their own way to the foster parent is supported by an observation made at Likoma Island. At Mbuzi Island, I found a female of an undescribed utaka (*Copadichromis* sp. 'yellow jumbo', see above) which, exceptionally for an utaka, cared for her youngsters. Among her own fry there were two alien youngsters, possibly *P. taeniolatus* (see photo in Konings, 1989: 36). Observations of mixed species broods have also been made in Lake Tanganyika (Konings & Dieckhoff, 1992).

The deep, sediment-rich rocky habitat

The deep rocky biotope—more than 15 meters deep—is usually, but not always, sediment-rich. The sediment consists of particulate matter that precipitates from higher levels, e.g. decaying micro-organisms, wastes, and stirred-up sand. A layer of such material covers the algal mat on the rocks and only certain algae are able to survive the reduced light conditions. Reduced light conditions are also found at deeper levels on rocky coasts that are largely sediment-free. Possibly the cichlids prevailing in the sediment-rich habitat have specialized in feeding on the type of algae which grow in poor light. The algal strands, growing through the sediment-rich coating, give the biocover a firm texture and may thus provide a habitat for many insect larvae and benthic crustaceans. The cichlids feed from the biocover by plucking, nipping, nibbling, jerking, and scraping it from the rocks. Many species present in this biotope are often seen crossing sandy patches between rocks (where they border the sand), but a distinction (artificial?) is made between the species of the intermediate habitat (page 172) and the species discussed here. The latter normally occur at deeper levels and are found predominantly among the rocks, whereas species from the intermediate habitat can also be encountered in shallow water and over the sand, which plays an important role in their behavior (e.g. foraging techniques and spawning sites).

Once again, the chief occupants of the deeper region of the rocky habitat are the mbuna. Many species have yellow as their main color. It is not clear whether this relates to the yellowish color of the aufwuchs (i.e. the fishes are better camouflaged) or is caused by elements in the aufwuchs that stimulate yellow pigment after digestion by the fish. While female mbuna from the upper layers of the habitat have a mainly gray-brown coloration (to make them inconspicuous), those in the sediment-rich region are predominantly yellow or yellowish.

The population density of mbuna in the deep rocky habitat is much lower than in the upper rocky habitats. The probable reason is availability of food, i.e. algae, which is less in deeper areas. This would further mean that most mbuna are dependent on the algae or on food items which in their turn are dependent on algal growth. If this is so then the view that the mbuna of this habitat are less specialized in feeding on algae than their cousins in the upper layers of the habitat seems to be justified. Better-adapted species would find a niche in an area with more food.

Golden zebras

Several species of the genus *Metriaclima* (the zebras) are encountered in the purely rocky habitat at deeper levels, with a few apparently restricted to levels below 10 meters. One of these is *Metriaclima* sp. 'zebra gold' which is better known under its trade name "Pseudotropheus Mustardi". It is found from Chirombo Point to Charo, but is caught for export mainly at a location just north of Nkhata Bay (Chadagha). *Metriaclima* sp. 'zebra gold' is frequently found at depths of more than 15 meters and also occurs over sandy patches between rocks.

Plankton is often abundant at a depth of 15 to 25 meters and many mbuna from these regions are regularly found dining on it. Territorial males of *M.* sp. 'zebra gold' forage more frequently from the biocover which, of course, is eaten by females as well. Aggression in sexually active males is directed only towards conspecifics. Females and non-territorial males occur singly or in small groups.

Some territorial males occupy areas on the sand next to rocks and dig their spawning cave beneath a rock. Such behavior is normally seen in areas where the rocks meet the sandy bottom at a depth of 10-20 meters. Spawning usually takes place in the privacy of caves among the rocks or an excavated spawning pit under a stone.

1. *Metriaclima* sp. 'zebra gold' ♂ Lion's Cove

2. *Metriaclima* sp. 'zebra gold' ♂ Charo

3. *Metriaclima* sp. 'zebra gold' ♂ Ruarwe

4. *Metriaclima* sp. 'zebra gold' OB ♂ Lion's Cove

5. *Metriaclima* sp. 'zebra gold' ♂ Nkhata Bay

6. *Metriaclima* sp. 'zebra gold' ♀ Charo

1. *Metriaclima* sp. 'zebra yellow tail' ♂ Manda

2. *Metriaclima* sp. 'zebra yellow tail' ♀ Lupingu

3. *Metriaclima* sp. 'black dorsal nkhungu' ♀ Nkhungu Point

5. *Metriaclima* sp. 'zebra yellow tail' ♂ Lupingu

6. *Metriaclima* sp. 'black dorsal nkhungu' ♂ Nkhungu Point

4. Lion's Cove

One would expect that species from deeper and/or sediment-rich areas would be better able to cross longer stretches of sand between two rocky habitats than the mbuna of the sediment-free habitats. If true, geographical variation among species of the sediment-rich rocky habitat would be less pronounced. This is in reality only partly correct, because many such habitats can support only a limited number of fishes and, as has been discussed before (see page 21), small founder populations are more likely to produce a geographical variant or new species. This seems to be the case with *M.* sp. 'zebra gold', which is known to occur in several different geographical variants. As usual this variation can be seen only in the male's territorial coloration. Normal female coloration is brown in all known populations. Polychromatism occurs, and although it is usually seen only in females it is also present in males—marmalade cats of *M.* sp. 'zebra gold' are among the most beautiful mbuna in the lake.

Many mbuna species found in the northern half of the lake occur on both eastern and western coasts. *M.* sp. 'zebra gold', however, has not been found on the east coast, but a similar species, possibly closely related, occurs in the deeper, sediment-rich rocky habitat between Lupingu and Manda. This mbuna, *Metriaclima* sp. 'zebra yellow tail', is characterized by an elongate body, not unlike that of *M.* sp. 'zebra gold', and both species may have affinities with the elongate cichlids in *Metriaclima*. Females are a rather dark color, like those of *M.* sp. 'zebra gold', and both male and female occur singly. Polychromatism has not (yet) been observed.

At Nkhungu, on the Mozambique shore of the lake, the deep rocky coast harbors a yellow species of *Metriaclima* which I have named *Metriaclima* sp. 'black dorsal nkhungu'. The color pattern of females suggests that this species has a closer relationship with the *M. flavifemina*-like mbuna (see page 173) than with the classic zebras (*M. zebra* and its close relatives). Females have a beige-colored body and a bright orange yellow anal fin. The dorsal and tail have yellow streaks. Males are completely yellow apart from a black submarginal band on the dorsal fin. Most individuals occur at a depth of 15-40 meters. This species has not been found at the rocky reef a few kilometers north of Nkhungu Point, or at rocky coasts south of it.

Elongate zebras

A number of elongate zebras are found in the deep rocky habitat. One of these species, *Metriaclima* sp. 'taiwan', was discovered only a few years ago at Taiwanee Reef. Although previously assigned to *Pseudotropheus* (Konings, 2001) it is now regarded as a member of the genus *Metriaclima*. It exhibits a feeding behavior similar to that of other members of its genus, but is not as slender as the species of the elongate group of *Metriaclima* found in the upper rocky habitat (see page 65).

Taiwanee Reef is one of the most interesting places to dive in Lake Malaŵi. It is completely isolated from the mainland and also from Chizumulu Island which lies about 7 km south of the reef and is separated from it by water deeper than 100 meters. One might therefore expect a number of endemic species at this reef. Interestingly it seems to be inhabited by only a few mbuna, with all the mbuna complexes mentioned in this book represented by just a single member apiece and *Labidochromis* not found at all (yet). *M.* sp. 'taiwan' is a rather rare species and only a few individuals have been seen thus far. Females are dark brown and are sometimes found in shallower water combing algae from the rocks. Males do not seem to be territorial. The few specimens observed were also attracted by debris (mainly droppings) whirled upwards by my fins. They also scrutinized the small amount of sediment on the rocks and picked out some bits and pieces to eat. The behavior of the deeper-living males resembles that of *Pseudotropheus crabro* (page 141) or *Melanochromis parallelus* (page 105).

Metriaclima sp. 'taiwan masimbwe' resembles the previous species and has been found only at the islet of Masimbwe, south of Likoma Island. Again it has an elongate body, but not as much so as the elongate *Metriaclima* of the upper rocky habitat. Males have a very dark blue-black coloration with narrow blue bars. Females are brown. I observed this species combing algae from rocks at a depth of about 30 meters and its feeding mechanism matched that of other members of *Metriaclima*—but no individuals were collected to verify their assignment to this genus.

A small, heavily barred, species, with a limited distribution directly north of Manda and at Pombo Rocks, is here only tentatively assigned to *Metriaclima* because I have not yet seen it feed from the aufwuchs. Females of this species, *Metriaclima* sp. 'cave manda', are very dark and also have a barred pattern. Very little is known of this species as most individuals were found inside caves, but although it has a rather elongate body it is, in my opinion, a member of *Metriaclima* rather than a member of the *Pseudotropheus elongatus* complex.

Many other species of *Metriaclima* also live in the sediment-rich region of the rocky biotope, but since most of these are more often found over sand they will be dealt with in the next chapter.

Cynotilapia

Species of the genus *Cynotilapia* are found primarily in the sediment-free rocky habitat, and most of them have been discussed earlier (see page 69). One species of this group, however, *Cynotilapia* sp. 'maleri', is found only in rocky areas deeper than 20 meters. At Maleri Island and at Nakantenga Island it occurs in the deeper rocky areas which are very sediment-rich at both locations. Interestingly, females are a silvery color and are found at the same depth as territorial males, which form breeding groups at depths ranging between 20 and 40 meters. Ribbink *et al.* (1983b) report that some males there have a yellow blaze, but I have been unable to find such polychromatism in the Nakantenga and Maleri populations. *C.* sp. 'maleri' seems to be closely related to *C.* sp. 'mbamba', in which polychromatism is common. Both female and male *C.* sp. 'maleri', including those defending territories, feed on plankton in mid-water in the fashion commonly observed in *Cynotilapia*.

A very large species of *Cynotilapia* occurs at a deep reef, Three Peaks Reef, between Mumbo Island and Zimbawe Rock. This rocky reef—which Howard Massey-Hicks (pers. comm.) discovered and named—is about 40 meters below the surface and only a few mbuna species live there. The most common is *Cynotilapia* sp. 'blue black', which forms large schools in the water column and feeds on the plankton. Male *C.* sp. 'blue black' are blue-black barred and resemble a very large black-top *C. afra*. The total length of males is estimated at about 13 cm.

As well as *C.* sp. 'chinyankwazi' (page 69), the two tiny islands of Chinyankwazi and Chinyamwezi, in the southeastern arm of the lake, harbor more species of this genus. *Cynotilapia* sp. 'lion chinyankwazi' occurs at a depth of more than 25 meters at both islands. It closely resembles *Metriaclima* sp. 'dumpy' (page 181) but has unicuspid rather than bicuspid teeth. Females are silvery-beige without a barring pattern.

At Chinyamwezi Island a third species of *Cynotilapia* inhabits the deep rocky habitat: *Cynotilapia* sp. 'flavus deep'. It has been found only at 35 meters or deeper. This species is also found at a deep reef near Chinyamwezi Island. The tops of the rocks of this reef are about 30 meters below the surface and *C.* sp. 'flavus deep' was seen at the upper surface of the reef. Were it not for its unicuspid teeth and shallow angle of the vomer (28°) this species would have been grouped with the *Pseudotropheus elongatus* complex (see page 85).

Gold and blue

Pseudotropheus sp. 'ndumbi gold' is an attractive species which is endemic to the rocky areas around Ndumbi Rocks, Makulawe Point, and Maingano, at Likoma Island. It was once thought that both male and female shared the conspicuous golden color (Ribbink *et al.*, 1983b), but Spreinat (1997) established that the blue mbuna known in the aquarium hobby as "M-12" and *P.* sp. 'ndumbi gold' were the male and female, respectively, of one and the same species. The adult male is blue and resembles a large individual of *P.* sp. 'elongatus ornatus'. *P.* sp. 'ndumbi gold' is an opportunistic feeder

1. *Metriaclima* sp. 'taiwan' ♂ Taiwanee Reef

2. *Metriaclima* sp. 'taiwan masimbwe' ♂ Masimbwe

3. *Metriaclima* sp. 'cave manda' ♂ Pombo Rocks

4. *Metriaclima* sp. 'taiwan masimbwe' ♀ Masimbwe

5. *Metriaclima* sp. 'cave manda' ♂ Manda

6. *Metriaclima* sp. 'cave manda' ♀ Manda

1. *Cynotilapia* sp. 'maleri' ♂ Nakantenga Island

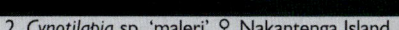

2. *Cynotilapia* sp. 'maleri' ♀ Nakantenga Island

3. *Cynotilapia* sp. 'lion chinyankwazi' ♀ Chinyankwazi Island

6. *Cynotilapia* sp. 'lion chinyankwazi' ♂ Chinyankwazi Island

4. *Cynotilapia* sp. 'flavus deep' ♀ Chinyamwezi Island

7. *Cynotilapia* sp. 'flavus deep' ♂ Chinyamwezi Island

5. *Pseudotropheus* sp. 'ndumbi gold' ♀ Ndumbi Rocks (Likoma)

8. *Pseudotropheus* sp. 'ndumbi gold' ♂ Ndumbi Rocks

which dines on anything available; aufwuchs, plankton, debris, and stirred-up particles are among the items on the menu. Both sexes are solitary. The very limited distribution and omnivorous feeding habits are indicative of an old, non-specialized species—not necessarily inhabiting the same areas over the years, as the lake level fluctuates and areas inhabited at present may have been dry land several hundreds of years ago (Owen *et al.*, 1990). *P.* sp. 'ndumbi gold' does not seem to be closely related to any other mbuna; at least there is no obvious candidate with matching behavioral and/or anatomical characteristics.

Mini mbuna

Pseudotropheus sp. 'dwarf nkhata' is a very small species which has been found only at Nkhata Bay, at a depth of about 20 meters. Its shape resembles that of an elongate miniature member of *Tropheops*. It may also have affinities with *P. perspicax,* found further to the north. However, no specimens have as yet been collected for more detailed examination. The species is not very aggressive although males are territorial. Both male and female regularly bite into the biocover on the rocks but it is not yet known whether they extract invertebrates or just browse the algae. Females are light beige with a barring pattern that is much less obvious in males. They are further distinguished by a black margin to the dorsal fin.

Another species in this informal group, *Pseudotropheus* sp. 'thin stripe', seems to be restricted to Likoma Island. This small cichlid prefers dark caves at depths between 10 and 30 meters, and feeds by nipping aufwuchs from the rocks. It appears to be related to *P. minutus* (see page 96) but lives in much deeper regions of the rocky habitat.

Another small species, found sympatrically at the islet of Masimbwe (Likoma) with *P.* sp. 'thin stripe', seems to be more closely related to *P. perspicax* and I have therefore named it *Pseudotropheus* sp. 'perspicax likoma'. Males lack a black submarginal band in the dorsal but have black pelvic fins and a conspicuous black band in the anal fin. Females are dark purplish-brown with an indistinct barring pattern. *P.* sp. 'perspicax likoma' feeds from the aufwuchs by nipping at spots that are free of sediment.

Two small members of the *P. elongatus* complex are restricted to the deep rocky habitat. *Pseudotropheus* sp. 'elongatus nkhata brown' has been recorded only from the Nkhata Bay area but probably has a wider distribution further north. Both males and females are very dark with a submarginal band in the dorsal, and live in rocky habitats deeper than 15 meters. Females are dark brown with the submarginal band in the dorsal slightly darker than the rest of the body. The species picks from the aufwuchs like other members of *Pseudotropheus*.

Pseudotropheus sp. 'elongatus thumbi' has been encountered only along the northwestern side of Thumbi West Island at a depth of more than 25 meters. As in *P.* sp. 'elongatus nkhata brown', both males and females have a black submarginal band in the dorsal but males are a lighter color—purplish-blue on the flanks and olive-green on the upper parts. Females are purplish-brown with a distinct black band in the dorsal and anal fins.

Both these elongate species appear less aggressive than similar-sized elongate cichlids in the upper rocky habitat. The same is true of a small species that I found at Three Peaks reef between Zimbawe Rock and Mumbo Island. The reef itself—is about 40 meters below the surface with three large boulders extending up to about 30 meters. Only a few mbuna call this place their home: *Cynotilapia* sp. 'blue black' (page 133), *Melanochromis heterochromis* (page 105), *Genyochromis mento* (page 112), and an endemic species, *Pseudotropheus* sp. 'three peaks'. This dwarf *Pseudotropheus* is rather uncommon at the reef and territorial males were not seen. All individuals observed so far fed from the plankton in the water column, with males remaining closer to the rocks than females.

Labidochromis—mostly insectivorous

The genus *Labidochromis* contains a group of species which have a very light and conspicuous coloration, but are nevertheless small and occur singly. All are insectivores that wander through the habitat, never lingering at any particular spot. They are tolerated in the territories of most other species and prefer dark caves, the ceilings of which are inspected for chance prey.

The best-known species of this group is *Labidochromis caeruleus*, which has a very large distribution in the northern half of the lake and occurs on both sides. In Malaŵi it is found between Chirombo Point and Charo. On the other side of the lake it has an even wider distribution: from Cape Kaiser in Tanzania to Londo in Mozambique. This large area contains a number of geographical variants and one of these, the so-called "Yellow Labidochromis" or "Electric Yellow", has become one of the most popular aquarium fishes from the lake. This bright orange-yellow morph is distributed between Charo and Lion's Cove and found at a depth of 20 meters. However, the yellow color variant is not present in all populations between Charo and Lion's Cove. The population of *L. caeruleus* at Nkhoso Point, the headland north of the bay at Ruarwe, is pure white. At Lion's Cove, a very narrow, deep bay about 25 km north of Nkhata Bay, there are two different populations: the one found along the northern part of the bay exhibits more yellow than that found along the southern side, which is yellow on the upper part of the body but white on the lower half. South of Kajizingi, a few kilometers south of Lion's Cove, all known populations are pure white.

In the early 1980s Pierre Brichard acquired some specimens of the yellow form in Sweden and bred them in Burundi. In 1986 he put them on the market as "Labidochromis Tanganicae", thereby causing immense confusion among hobbyists. Since then this mbuna has become a mainstay of the hobby and the numbers available to hobbyists are probably a hundred to a thousand times greater than the total population in the lake!

Some specimens of *L. caeruleus* have been caught that had enlarged pharyngeal teeth, and stomach contents analysis has revealed that these individuals had been feeding on snails. In his revision of *Labidochromis*, Lewis (1982) discusses the possibility of *L. caeruleus* existing in two sub-populations which could have become genetically isolated. One population might have remained in the rocky habitat, feeding on insects and other soft prey. The individuals of this population would have slender or little-enlarged teeth on the pharyngeal bones. The other population would probably live predominantly in beds of *Vallisneria* and feed on mollusks. Its members would have robust pharyngeal bones with enlarged molariform teeth.

Within a single population of *L. caeruleus* there may be some individuals with a black submarginal band in the dorsal and some that are entirely white. Such polymorphism should not be regarded as specific variation. There is a gradual change in the color pattern of the individuals of each neighboring population. In Tanzania the most northerly populations are entirely white; at Lundu males have a yellowish patch on the head; at Thumbi Point males have a blue hue all over the body; and at Liuli the population exhibits a degree of barring on a white body, a feature that is intensified in those at Hongi and Lundo Island. In Mozambique, at Liutche, these bars have almost disappeared, and at Londo *L. caeruleus* is white with a black band in the dorsal fin. Mixed populations (with or without a submarginal band in the dorsal) are also found at Nkhata Bay in Malaŵi.

A rare species at Jalo Reef near Nkhotakota, *Labidochromis* sp. 'caeruleus jalo', resembles the barred form of *L. caeruleus* but has a more pointed snout. It may also be closely related to *L. ianthinus* from the Mbenji islands and Nkhomo Reef (page 208) but that species appears much more robust and is more often found in intermediate habitats. *L.* sp. 'caeruleus jalo' feeds from the ceilings and walls of rocky caves and the few individuals seen were found at a depth of about 25 meters.

At Chizumulu Island *Labidochromis chisumulae* inhabits the sediment-rich rocky habitats and its behavior is identical to that of *L. caeruleus*. At Mbweca and Tumbi Point in Mozambique I have found a species which looks like a cross between *L. caeruleus* and *L. chisumulae*, which I have called *Labidochromis* sp. 'chisumulae mbweca'. The existence of these populations suggests that *L. chisumulae* and *L.*

1. *Pseudotropheus* sp. 'dwarf nkhata' ♂ Nkhata Bay

6. *Pseudotropheus* sp. 'dwarf nkhata' ♀ Nkhata Bay

2. *Pseudotropheus* sp. 'perspicax likoma' ♂ Masimbwe

7. *Pseudotropheus* sp. 'thin stripe' ♂ Masimbwe

3. *Pseudotropheus* sp. 'elongatus nkhata brown' ♂ Nkhata Bay

8. *Pseudotropheus* sp. 'perspicax likoma' ♀ Masimbwe

4. *Pseudotropheus* sp. 'elongatus thumbi' ♂ Thumbi West Island

9. *Pseudotropheus* sp. 'elongatus nkhata brown' ♀ Nkhata Bay

10. *Pseudotropheus* sp. 'elongatus thumbi' ♀ Thumbi West Island

5. *Pseudotropheus* sp. 'three peaks' ♂ Three Peaks Reef

11. *Labidochromis* sp. 'caeruleus jalo' ♂ Jalo Reef

Labidochromis caeruleus Kakusa (4)
Labidochromis caeruleus Cape Kaiser (1)
Labidochromis caeruleus Ruarwe (5)
Labidochromis caeruleus Chinyangi (2)
Labidochromis caeruleus Mbowe Island (6)
Labidochromis caeruleus Lundu (3)
Labidochromis caeruleus Lion's Cove (8)
Labidochromis caeruleus Lundo Island (7)
Labidochromis caeruleus Lion's Cove (8)
Labidochromis caeruleus Undu Point (9)
Labidochromis caeruleus Nkhata Bay (10)
Labidochromis caeruleus Londo (11)

caeruleus are very closely related.

The rocks at Chilucha Reef, offshore at Metangula, are free of sediment to a depth of at least 45 meters. The *Labidochromis* found here is closely related to *L. caeruleus*. Although *L. caeruleus* has a very extensive distribution, the closest known population to Chilucha is at Londo. In between, at Mbweca, a similar species, *L.* sp. 'chisumulae mbweca', frequents the intermediate habitat but resembles *L. chisumulae* more than *L. caeruleus*. For this reason, I regard the *Labidochromis* at Chilucha as distinct from *L. caeruleus*. *Labidochromis* sp. 'caeruleus chilucha' inhabits the deeper as well as the shallower parts of the reef which lies about five meters below the surface. Territoriality has not been observed and feeding behavior strongly indicates an insectivorous diet. *L.* sp. 'caeruleus chilucha' has also been seen at N'kolongwe and Nkhungu Point.

A very dark brown and secretive species of *Labidochromis* was encountered at Lupingu and at Magunga. The few individuals observed behaved like *L. caeruleus* while they were screening the ceilings of rocky caves for chance prey. One male was collected and although it appeared a mature individual it was completely dark-brown—a color normally expected in females—with a narrow orange margin to the dorsal. For the time being I refer to this cryptic species as *Labidochromis* sp. 'caeruleus brown'. It is probably not a geographical variant of *L. caeruleus* as a completely white variant of the latter was found sympatric with *L.* sp. 'caeruleus brown' at Magunga.

Along the eastern coast, at Higga Reef, a population of white *Labidochromis* inhabits the deep, rocky habitat. Although this is in the middle of the distribution of *L. caeruleus* this cichlid is regarded as a different species and has been given the name *Labidochromis* sp. 'perlmutt' (German for "mother-of-pearl"). *L.* sp. 'perlmutt' has also been seen at Ngkuyo Island, and along the coast south of Mbamba Bay (Chuwa) I found an adult *Labidochromis* with a yellow dorsal (a characteristic of the "Perlmutt") and also a white juvenile with a black band in the dorsal (a characteristic of *L. caeruleus*). A search for more specimens failed to answer the question whether I had found two different species or a single one "intermediate" between *L.* sp. 'perlmutt' and a white *L. caeruleus*. The latter would indicate that *L.* sp. 'perlmutt' is another geographical variant of *L. caeruleus*. For the time being, however, *L.* sp. 'perlmutt', a very attractive mbuna in itself, is regarded as different from *L. caeruleus*. At Higga Reef it is very rare and found only at depths of more than 30 meters. At Ngkuyo Island it is extremely rare (I have seen only two specimens) and also occurs at greater depths.

We find white *Labidochromis* in the southern part of the lake as well. The species at the Maleris and Thumbi West Island is named *Labidochromis pallidus* and that at Mumbo Island *Labidochromis mylodon*. These two species differ only in the size of the pharyngeal bone and it is doubtful whether more than one species will "survive" the next revision of the genus. Both *L. pallidus* and *L. mylodon* can be distinguished from *L. caeruleus* by the bicuspid teeth in the outer jaws. *L. caeruleus*, like most other *Labidochromis*, has conical teeth. *L. pallidus* is present around Thumbi West Island but it is uncertain whether it occurs there naturally or has been introduced. These two southern species do not differ in behavior from the other white *Labidochromis*.

At Likoma I have found a blue-gray *Labidochromis* with a great resemblance in behavior to the white species. It occurs at Maingano, Membe Point, Mbamba Island, and the islet of Masimbwe at a depth of more than 20 meters, and only solitary individuals have been found. This species, *Labidochromis* sp. 'likomae', apparently occupies the niche which is occupied by the white *Labidochromis* at other places. The obvious difference between *L.* sp. 'likomae' and *L. caeruleus* is that females of the former are differently colored—light-beige with brown bars—to males, which are light-blue without bars. The sexes in the *L. caeruleus*-like mbuna have identical or very similar coloration.

A species of *Labidochromis* from Tanzanian waters has a preference for deep, rocky habitats, although it appears to be herbivorous. *Labidochromis* sp. 'mbamba' is found at Ngkuyo Island and along the rocky coast south of

Mbamba Bay. Males are territorial—none of the insectivorous species is territorial—and defend their domain in a cave, usually at a depth of 15 meters or more. Females have rarely been seen and then always singly. Both sexes live a very secretive life, although the few females observed were continually on the move, swimming through the cracks and caves of the habitat looking for food. On a few occasions I have observed them feeding from the substrate, and it appeared that the same spot was sampled repeatedly. Such sites, however, were carefully selected, and this may indicate an insectivorous diet. On the other hand, *L. gigas* is similarly selective in choosing feeding sites but is herbivorous, as proven by examination of stomach contents. *L.* sp. 'mbamba' may therefore be a secretive member of the *L. gigas* species group discussed on page 101. It is clear that we need more information to determine whether or not this species is herbivorous.

Wasps without a sting

Pseudotropheus crabro is an interesting species originally assigned to *Melanochromis. Crabro* is the Latin word for hornet, a kind of wasp common in the western world, and aptly describes this mbuna's color pattern. It has been exported infrequently and given the trade name "Pseudotropheus Chameleo", owing to its ability quickly to change its characteristic color pattern of yellow with brown bars to a uniform dull brown. *P. crabro* has a symbiotic cleaner-fish relationship with the large catfish *Bagrus meridionalis,* and is thus normally found in the large caves in which the latter lurks during the day. It will sometimes follow a diver in a black wetsuit over long distances, presumably a case of mistaken identity! *P. crabro* picks the parasitic *Argulus africanus* (a fish-louse) from the catfish's skin. The parasites are firmly attached and are removed by a scraping action. The bicuspid teeth of *P. crabro*, reminiscent of those of *Metriaclima* but more pointed, are bent inwards and adapted to dislodge parasites from a smooth surface. The outer row is well separated from the second and third rows, enabling the teeth to lift the parasite from its position. The shape of the body, the coloration, the form of the snout, and the scraping movements of the mouth indicate that *P. crabro* has closer affinities with *Pseudotropheus* than with *Melanochromis*. Its development of a remarkable specialization that may have evolved during periods of severe competition for food, and the fact that it occurs over a large part of the lake, may indicate that *P. crabro* is an old species.

In my opinion the feeding behavior evolved during a time of food shortage at some time in the past; *P. crabro*, unable to compete with more aggressive and better adapted species, survived by taking advantage of an unusual food resource, the parasites on the skin of the *kampango* (the African name for the "client" catfish). Strong selection pressure thus led to a highly specialized species. At present food seems to be abundant because most species can generalize and "forget" their specializations. *P. crabro*, for example, also feeds on aufwuchs and plankton. Its specialization will never lead to large populations but may enable small numbers to survive during times of when alternative foods are in short supply.

Besides the beneficial effects of *P. crabro*'s attentions, the *kampango* is afflicted with a "treatment" of a more criminal nature. During the catfishes" breeding season *P. crabro*'s menu is greatly enriched by "caviar à la *kampango*". *P. crabro* has on several occasions been observed stealing eggs from beneath a guarding *kampango* pair. In the stomachs of three individuals of *P. crabro* (and another, unidentified mbuna) Ribbink and Lewis (1982) found 1068 eggs that had been stolen from a single pair of *kampango*! *P. crabro* and *B. meridionalis* live in a very peculiar symbiosis in which *P. crabro* acts as a beneficial vermin-killer one day and an egg-robber the next. Interestingly *P. crabro* does not eat *Argulus* from other fishes, as was demonstrated under artificial circumstances by Ribbink & Lewis (1982).

The cleaning behavior may have developed because *kampango*s lurk, during the daytime, in large caves, where they remain immobile so that even a diver can sometimes touch a catfish without scaring it away. *P. crabro* may have developed its cave-dwelling habit before it special-

1. *Labidochromis* sp. 'perlmutt' ♂ Higga Reef

2. *Labidochromis* sp. 'caeruleus chilucha' ♂ Chilucha Reef

5. *Labidochromis* sp. 'perlmutt' ♀ Higga Reef

3. *Labidochromis chisumulae* ♂ Same Bay

6. *Labidochromis* sp. 'caeruleus chilucha' ♀ Nkhungu Point

7. *Labidochromis chisumulae* ♀ Chiwi Rocks

4. *Labidochromis* sp. 'chisumulae mbweca' ♂ Mbweca

8. *Labidochromis* sp. 'caeruleus brown' ♂ Lupingu

1. *Labidochromis pallidus* ♂ Nakantenga Island

2. *Labidochromis pallidus* ♀ Maleri Island

6. *Labidochromis mylodon* ♂ Mumbo Island

3. *Labidochromis pallidus* ♀ Thumbi West Island

7. *Labidochromis* sp. 'likomae' ♂ Masimbwe

4. *Labidochromis* sp. 'likomae' ♀ Maingano Island

5. *Labidochromis* sp. 'mbamba' ♀ Ngkuyo Island

8. *Labidochromis* sp. 'mbamba' ♂ Ngkuyo Island

ized on the *kampango*'s parasites, and may thus have learned to "graze" on the *kampango*'s skin because these catfishes are present in almost every cave that is large enough to accommodate them. Tearing off tightly attached parasites may hurt a *kampango* but the catfishes have nevertheless come to accept a wasp-colored mbuna cleaning their skin. In fact, they may have become so used to *P. crabro* being around that their presence is ignored even during the breeding season. If *P. crabro* were openly to steal the catfishes' eggs, however, it would probably no longer be accepted as a cleaner. So it both conceals its identity and makes itself less conspicuous by quickly changing color to dull brown—this is also the male's breeding coloration—before darting under the guarding male to steal eggs (Saulos Mwale, pers. comm.).

P. crabro may have specialized initially in stealing eggs from the *kampango*, i.e. before evolving its cleaning behavior, but this seems unlikely as the catfish has a rather short breeding season (November to March). It is more likely, however, that it has simply learned to take advantage of the *kampango*'s acceptance of its presence (as cleaner), stealing eggs whenever the guarding male relaxes his vigilance. Breeding *kampango*s are usually surrounded by many small fishes including several *P. crabro*. McKaye (1986) discovered that female *kampango* release unfertilized eggs to feed their young. *P. crabro* may also feed on these eggs, and this would extend their egg-eating period considerably. However, since all cichlids are driven away from the centre of the brood by the catfish (Jay Stauffer, pers. comm.) this may not be the case.

Another mbuna with a similar color pattern, yellow with brown bars or blotches, is sometimes found near *kampango* nests as well. I have seen this species, *Melanochromis baliodigma* (page 211), feeding on *kampango* larvae, but rarely on eggs.

The distribution of *P. crabro* encompasses a large part of the lake, but it has never been encountered north of Hongi Island on the eastern side or north of Mara Rocks on the west coast. The *P. crabro* at Lion's Cove are more elongate than elsewhere, but I do not believe that they should be regarded as a different species.

Another species with a remarkably similar preference for caves and large catfishes (including divers that look like them!) has been observed at several localities north of *P. crabro*'s distribution. This species, called *Pseudotropheus* sp. 'crabro blue', has been found on the eastern as well as the western side of the lake and is very similar to *P. crabro* in its behavior and barring-pattern. However, males of *P.* sp. 'crabro blue' are, as the name indicates, blue-black while females are beige with brown bars. Like *P. crabro*, it is non-territorial. At Chewere, Malaŵi, I once observed two males and one female *P.* sp. 'crabro blue' feeding on *kampango* eggs after the guarding catfishes had been disturbed. From observations at other localities it seems that *P.* sp. 'crabro blue' resides in very large caves, near to the ceiling rather than the floor. The species is immediately attracted to large swimming "objects" in the water and is also attracted to debris stirred up by divers. In this respect it also closely resembles *P. crabro*. *P.* sp. 'crabro blue' has been recorded from Chewere, Chitande Island, Nkanda, and Magunga Reef. Spreinat (1994) records this species, under the name *P.* 'Broad Bar', from Lundu.

Blue and brown *Melanochromis*

The genus *Melanochromis* is represented mainly by *M. parallelus* in the northern half of the lake. This species, discussed in the previous chapter, is also common at deeper levels. Along the northern coastlines evolution and selection have taken place at a continuous pace since this area has never dried out during periods of low lake level. At such times species from all over the lake, predominantly from the southern half, either concentrated in the deep basin in the north or became extinct. The northern rocky coasts must have supported numerous species, most of them now extinct. *Melanochromis* is an old genus with many omnivorous species, and is poorly represented on this coast.

The type species of the genus, *Melanochromis melanopterus*, nominally has a lake-wide distribution apart from Chinyamwezi and Chinyankwazi islands (Ribbink *et al.*, 1983b), although I have not found it along the northwestern shore between Kande Island and Mdoka where another, but similar, species occupies the same niche. And along the eastern shore I have not seen *M. melanopterus* further north than Undu Point. It is a non-specialized, non-territorial cichlid which lives a predatory life but is also seen feeding on aufwuchs and plankton. Larger specimens (maximum total length lies around 13 cm) appear to be mainly piscivorous. The brown (female) to dark brown or blue-black (male) body coloration blends well with the recesses and caves of the rocky environment. Occasionally adult individuals are seen with a light brown ground color and black stripes. Adults are usually solitary but sub-adults are frequently seen in small "packs" of up to six individuals. Solitary adults usually station themselves under an overhanging rock or inside a cave and wait until small fishes come within reach. The species is not a true ambush hunter as it can frequently be observed chasing small mbuna, which are quicker and more agile than the predator. The small packs move quickly through the habitat and scavenge anything that seems to be worth eating. *M. melanopterus* can thus be regarded as a carnivore which will opportunistically prey on mbuna fry. Other items on its menu are crustaceans, insect larvae, and nymphs.

The name *M. melanopterus* is often erroneously used for other species of the same complex. *M. melanopterus* never exhibits the bright blue color seen in several other species of the "reverse coloration" group (see page 105). Males in breeding color are rare, and it is thus difficult to comment on geographical variation, but on the basis of the observations made we may assume that there is little, apart from the yellow-backed and blue-bodied variant found between Metangula and Minos Reef in Mozambique. Males of all populations have a yellowish patch on the nape and back but in most this is obscured by the generally brown-black ground color. *M. melanopterus* from the type locality, Monkey Bay, have more yellowish horizontal stripes compared to the light blue stripes in other populations.

The Mbenji and Maleri islands are home to a very similar mbuna (named *M.* 'slab' by Ribbink *et al.*, 1983b) that is here regarded as a localized population of *M. melanopterus*. The isolated position of these locations and the relative abundance of food have enabled *M. melanopterus* to populate the habitat in greater numbers than elsewhere. In consequence, some sexually active males of the Maleri and Mbenji populations do sometimes defend territories, even though the species is non-territorial at other locations, with males courting ripe females whenever they meet. This behavior can still be observed in the populations at Maleri and Mbenji where many individuals are not territorial at all. Even territorial males frequently court females "off the premises", whereas territorial males of other species usually remain within their private domains and attract females from a distance. Territoriality in the Maleri and Mbenji populations takes the form of bursts of aggression against conspecifics, but is of a temporary nature. Since competition among conspecifics increases with population density this is a natural variation in behavior. In less crowded populations, male *M. melanopterus* show aggression only when they meet. This has intensified into territorial behavior at the Maleri and Mbenji islands.

One large omnivorous species, which was named *Melanochromis* 'blue' by Ribbink *et al.* (1983b), is infrequently encountered on both sides of the northern half of the lake. This species was subsequently described by Johnson (1985) as *Melanochromis robustus*. It is supposedly found sympatric with *M. melanopterus*, and Ribbink and coworkers (1983b) report *M. robustus* from Likoma Island, but I have been unable to confirm this (I did find *M. melanopterus* at this island). *M. robustus* is usually encountered at depths of more than 20 meters, but north of Chitande Island it is also found in shallower water. *M. robustus* and *M. melanopterus* are distinguished by their basic color patterns. The latter has two horizontal stripes on the body whereas *M. robustus* has vertical bars in addition to these stripes. Territorial males of *M. robustus* are entirely blue whereas most *M. melanopterus* males are black with light-colored

1. *Pseudotropheus crabro* ♀ Chiofu 
2. *Pseudotropheus crabro* ♂ Lion's Cove
3. *Pseudotropheus* sp. 'crabro blue' ♂ Nkanda

4. *Melanochromis robustus* ♂ Chitande Island

5. *Pseudotropheus crabro* ♂ Chimwalani Reef

6. *Pseudotropheus crabro* Mbenji island

7. *Pseudotropheus* sp. 'crabro blue' ♀ Chitande Island

8. *Melanochromis robustus* ♂ Matema

9. *Melanochromis robustus* ♀ Chitande Island

1. *Melanochromis melanopterus* ♀ Nakantenga Island

2. *Melanochromis melanopterus* ♀ Mbenji Island

3. *Melanochromis melanopterus* ♀ Londo

4. *Melanochromis melanopterus* ♂ Mumbo Island

5. *Melanochromis melanopterus* ♂ Likoma Island

6. *Melanochromis* sp. 'robustus mbenji' ♀ Mbenji Island

7. *Melanochromis melanopterus* ♂ Nakantenga Island

8. *Melanochromis melanopterus* ♂ Thumbi East Island

9. *Melanochromis melanopterus* ♂ Minos Reef

10. *Melanochromis* sp. 'robustus mbenji' ♂ Mbenji Island

stripes. *M. robustus* occurs on the coast between Nkhata Bay and Mdoka in Malaŵi, and has been seen between Hongi Island and Ikombe in Tanzania.

At Mbenji Island I have found a rare species resembling *M. robustus* in several respects, but for the time being I have regarded it as distinct and called it *Melanochromis* sp. 'robustus mbenji'. Observation of the few individuals I have been able to find so far suggests that the species feeds on invertebrates which hide in the loose sediment that accumulates around the bases of rocks. On several occasions I have seen *M.* sp. 'robustus mbenji' plunge its head into this fluffy material and then sometimes swim away apparently chewing on prey. Breeding males have a coloration not unlike *M. melanopterus* from other localities than Mbenji and females show distinct barring. A territorial male I observed (Oct. 2006) had a spawning cave on the sand beneath a large boulder and would venture out only to court passing females.

At Chinyankwazi and Chinyamwezi Ribbink *et al.* (1983b) found an mbuna with an overall reddish-brown color and no distinction between the sexes (apart from some small eggspots on the male's anal fin). They called this species *Melanochromis* 'brown', even though it does not show any horizontal elements in the color pattern. I have been able to see some vertical barring in some individuals, but this was very indistinct. Since I have seen male *Metriaclima* sp. 'chinyankwazi' (see page 64) court such brown mbuna, I am convinced that *Melanochromis* 'brown' is in fact the female of *Metriaclima* sp. 'chinyankwazi'.

Utaka

A number of the plankton-feeding utaka are restricted to the deeper rocky habitat—at least that is the place they are encountered when diving. The so-called pure utaka (those without spots) are normally found in the open water but they come to shore to breed. The males then display their breeding colors and (in some cases) construct their bowers, and it becomes possible to distinguish the various species.

When Iles described *Copadichromis virginalis* in 1960 he pointed to the fact that the local fishermen distinguished between two forms which he regarded, at that time, as belonging to the same species. The fishermen called the two forms *kaduna* and *kajose*. The differences between the two forms are minimal. The *kaduna* has a smaller size, relatively larger eyes, and a deeper body and caudal peduncle than the *kajose*, and has little or no yellow pigment on the body (females and non-breeding males) and usually 16 spines in the dorsal fin. The *kajose* normally has 17 dorsal spines and a yellowish coloration.

Some years ago I suggested that these two forms represented two different species (Konings, 1991), with the *kaduna* being the true *C. virginalis* as the holotype of the species is a *kaduna*. The other species I termed *Copadichromis* sp. 'virginalis kajose'. I based my assumption that there were two species on the fact that at Gome, Malaŵi, two different forms of pure utaka occur, which clearly were different species—they were not found in exactly the same habitat. One of them, the cichlid known in the aquarium trade as the "Fire-Crest Mloto", corresponds well to the description of the *kaduna* and was at that time regarded as being conspecific with *C. virginalis* (but see below).

Further studies have revealed that the situation is much more complicated. The current situation is that we have six different species grouped in a *C. virginalis* complex, but which appear to breed in a different manner to *C. virginalis*. Only two of these, *C. virginalis* and *C.* sp. 'virginalis kajose', have a wide distribution, while the others have a very restricted range. It is almost impossible to differentiate these forms except on the basis of observations in the natural habitat.

Copadichromis virginalis does not construct any spawning site and males display on bare rocks as is also the case in *C. borleyi* and *C. cyaneus*. Along the northern section of coastline in Tanzania I have found large breeding schools of *C. virginalis* at Lupingu, Manda, and Higga Reef. At Lupingu breeding males defended rocks in the intermediate habitat at a depth of about 30 meters, but at Manda and Higga Reef I have seen spawning *C. virginalis* at a depth of sometimes less than 10 meters in the rocky habitat. Males defended spawning territories that were about 1 to 2 meters apart on top of large boulders and were visited by groups of females. This was in February, and I am thus certain that spawning in *C. virginalis* is restricted to a very specific time of the year as I have dived at these three localities before—at different times of the year—and failed to see even a single specimen of this species.

As mentioned above, for a long time I thought that what I now term *Copadichromis* sp. 'fire-crest mloto' was a geographical form of *C. virginalis*, and it was not until I found the latter species breeding that it became clear that two different species were involved, the reason being that male "Fire-Crest Mloto' construct bowers at rather deep levels. The "Fire-Crest Mloto" was formerly found at Gome, during the breeding period from August to November, at a depth of more than 30 meters. Unfortunately, this cichlid has never been seen after 1990 in the wild, but a small population is still being maintained by aquarists.

Copadichromis sp. 'virginalis kajose' seems to have a lake-wide distribution and is also present in Lake Malombe (Turner, 1996—as *C. virginalis*). This is the pure utaka that is most often collected by fishermen around the lake and is often misidentified as *C. mloto* or as *C. virginalis*. I have seen this form at several places around the lake; males build a bower against a rock while females forage in schools in the open water. The population in Lake Malombe must build bowers out of sand alone as there are no rocks in that lake. Breeding males usually occur at depths of more than 25 meters. Mouthbrooding females of *C.* sp. 'virginalis kajose' at Nkanda, Tanzania, have been observed simultaneously releasing their fry into an enormous school of utaka juveniles. This is probably the way new schools originate every year.

The second species at Gome, which was initially thought to be conspecific with *C.* sp. 'virginalis kajose', has been described (Konings, 1999) as *Copadichromis ilesi*. Snoeks and Hanssens (Snoeks, 2004) found that *C. ilesi* is very probably not a local form of *C.* sp. 'virginalis kajose' but a distinct species. As matters now stand, neither of the two pure utaka found at Gome (*C.* sp. 'fire-crest mloto' and *C. ilesi*) equates with the *kaduna* or the *kajose* form found at Nkhata Bay (the type locality of *C. virginalis*) but both are distinct species, each with a very restricted distribution, probably the most restricted of all known *Copadichromis*.

C. ilesi is larger, about 15 cm maximum total length, than the "Fire-Crest Mloto", which has a maximum size of about 12 cm. The females have a light, yellowish-brown coloration to the body and also differ in size from the smaller, silvery colored females of *C.* sp. 'fire-crest mloto'. The only noticeable difference between the males of the two species is the red band in the dorsal fin of *C.* sp. 'fire-crest mloto'. At a depth of 30 meters this red color appears as a black band and it may be that females distinguish the two males by the pattern in the dorsal. Mixed shoals of the females of both species have not been seen.

Breeding has been found to occur from May to December in *C. ilesi*. It is known that these cichlids migrate to inshore waters only to breed; outside this period they are not seen there at all. Breeding males are found mainly at depths of between 7 and 15 meters and build their cave-craters at a gently sloping area of the coast, whereas male *C.* sp. 'fire-crest mloto' construct similar bowers in steeper areas and at significantly deeper levels. These spawning sites consist of a crescent-shaped wall of sand located beneath a large overhanging rock. It is important that the rock forms the ceiling of the spawning site. Cave-craters of this type are constructed by all *Copadichromis* that have a black male breeding coloration with a light colored blaze on the head and dorsal.

I have not been able to relocate either of these two species in the last 10 years and this may be due to the time of year I have dived at Gome, usually between September and December and a few times in January. The fact that I saw *C. ilesi* breeding in November 1989 may be due to the long rainy season in that year. In my opinion *C. ilesi* and the "Fire-Crest Mloto" (and perhaps all *C. virginalis*-type cichlids) breed directly after the rainy season, usually March till June. In years with heavy and long-lasting rains the

1. *Copadichromis virginalis* ♂ Higga Reef

2. *Copadichromis* sp. 'virginalis kajose' ♂ Kirondo

4. *Copadichromis virginalis* ♂♀ Manda

3. *Copadichromis* sp. 'fire-crest mloto' ♂ Gome

5. *Copadichromis virginalis* ♀ Manda

6. *Copadichromis* sp. 'virginalis kajose' ♀ Thumbi West Island

1. *Copadichromis* sp. 'virginalis gold' ♂ Nkanda

2. *Copadichromis ilesi* ♂ Gome

5. *Copadichromis ilesi* ♂ Gome

3. *Copadichromis* sp. 'virginalis chitande' ♀ Chitande Island

6. *Copadichromis* sp. 'virginalis chitande' ♂ Chitande Island

4. *Copadichromis* sp. 'virginalis chitande' ♂ Chitande Island

6. *Copadichromis* sp. 'virginalis kajose' ♀♀ Nkanda

breeding period may be extended into November, and in years with hardly any rain at all they may start breeding as early as February.

The assignment of the two species at Gome to a *kajose*-like (*C. ilesi*) and a *kaduna*-like (*C.* sp. 'fire-crest mloto') is relatively simple; the situation may differ at places where only one *virginalis* type inhabits the biotope (or where only one type has so far been found). This may be the case at Chitande Island and Chewere on the northwestern shore. A population of a small *C. virginalis*-like cichlid inhabits a wide depth range along the rocky and intermediate coast. This species, *Copadichromis* sp. 'virginalis chitande', occurs at depths of between 5 and 30 meters. Males, with a maximum size of approximately 12 cm, have a dark blue breeding coloration with a light blue blaze on the head and upper part of the body. They construct bowers that consist of a crescent-shaped wall of sand against a rock, with an excavated spawning cavity beneath the rock. Females are silvery and found at rather deep levels (about 25 meters). The morphological features of *C.* sp. 'virginalis chitande' suggest that it is conspecific with *C. virginalis,* but now that we know the breeding technique of this species, the "Virginalis Chitande' must be either a population of *C.* sp. 'virginalis kajose' or a new species altogether. Moreover, the coloration and depth distribution does not agree with that of *C. virginalis* or *C.* sp. 'virginalis kajose'. More detailed study is needed before *C.* sp. 'virginalis chitande' can be assigned to *C.* sp. 'virginalis kajose' or described as a new species.

A different situation is found at Nkanda in Tanzania: there *C.* sp. 'virginalis kajose' shares the biotope with a smaller *C. virginalis*-like species, but the morphology of this smaller species cannot be matched with the description of *C. virginalis* by Iles (1960). Moreover males of this small species, called *Copadichromis* sp. 'virginalis gold', build cave-crater bowers similar to those of *C.* sp. 'virginalis kajose'. It is also found at a depth of more than 35 meters whereas *C.* sp. 'virginalis kajose' at the same locality is found defending bowers at about 25 meters. Males of *C.* sp. 'virginalis gold' have a broad blaze of gold on the head and in the dorsal fin, and a yellow tail. Probably because of their small size, several males were seen defending their bowers in a rather limited area. The distance between two males was sometimes as little as a meter. Male *C.* sp. 'virginalis kajose' usually maintain a distance of several meters. Breeding in *C.* sp. 'virginalis gold' was seen in September and November. I once visited Nkanda in February but failed to find a single individual.

Copadichromis geertsi (previously known as *C.* sp. 'virginalis blotch") is a large utaka, the males of which build cave-crater bowers usually at depths greater than 25 meters. The maximum total length of males is about 17 cm while females remain a few centimeters smaller. Mature females have sometimes one, but usually two, spots on the body. The spot on the flanks below the spinous part of the dorsal is large, but that on the caudal peduncle is absent from some individuals. Breeding males are dark blue, almost black, with a gold-colored blaze and very long pelvic fins. This species is one of the most beautiful utaka, but very difficult to collect when mature because of the depths at which both male and female occur. Mouthbrooding females swim to shallower water where they release their offspring among the schools of juvenile utaka commonly found above nests of the *kampango* (see also photo on page 242). *C. geertsi* is found along the eastern shores between Ntekete in Malaŵi and Thundu in Mozambique.

At Lupingu, Tanzania, at a depth of about 30 meters, an attractive utaka was seen breeding in February. This species somewhat resembles *C. geertsi* but its females have yellow fins. Males of this species, which I have named *Copadichromis* sp. 'yellow-black lupingu', were holding territories on top of medium-sized rocks. Cave-crater bowers were not seen but spawning was not observed either, so it is unclear whether or not it takes place on top of the male's rock. The rocks of some males were not very far apart and the distance between them was sometimes less than two meters. Most individuals had two spots on the body but some females had three.

Copadichromis trimaculatus is one of the larger

utaka; specimens from the Mbenji Islands can attain a total length of approximately 23 cm. It has a lake-wide distribution. This species, infrequently exported as "Haplochromis Borleyi Large" (from Mbenji), inhabits the open water over rocky biotopes. Males defend spawning sites near large boulders at an average depth of about 30 meters. Males in breeding color sometimes join the females in the open water and dine on plankton. *C. trimaculatus* is called *jakuta*, meaning "replete", by Malaŵians. It was given this name because most specimens caught in the lake look as if they are full of food. The stomach of this cichlid is usually crammed with phytoplankton. There are some other species that feed on phytoplankton, but *C. trimaculatus* and *C. pleurostigma* (page 237) are the only utaka that are apparently specialized on it. They have large pharyngeal bones with numerous short teeth, which grind the phytoplankton to render it digestible. The gut of *C. trimaculatus* is about five times the fish's standard length, i.e. about two to three times longer than in most other utaka.

C. trimaculatus probably breeds from August to December. Fry-guarding females have been seen at Jalo Reef in November at a depth of about 25 meters and at a depth of about 45 meters at Chiofu in October. It is virtually impossible to distinguish between female *C. trimaculatus* and those of the spotted variants of *C.* sp. 'yellow jumbo' (page 124). I have seen both these utaka fry-guarding at Chiofu; the latter in water as shallow as five meters and *C. trimaculatus* at 45 meters. It appears that females of *C. trimaculatus* have a slightly deeper body but that is not (yet) apparent in their fry. Males of the two species are easily told apart. It is interesting to note that these two species are the only known fry-guarding species of *Copadichromis*.

Copadichromis quadrimaculatus, called *mbarule* in Chi-Cheŵa, is one of the most economically important and abundant utaka in the lake. It is also one of the largest members of the group; adult males can attain a total length of about 23 cm. The type specimen of this species has four spots (hence its name), including the opercular spot. However, at Likoma and along Tanzanian shores *C. quadrimaculatus* has a variable number of spots. Females with two spots and no spots at all are rather common. It is probably the only truly pelagic *Copadichromis* (Fryer & Iles, 1972). After the juveniles (called *mbaba*) have spent two years in inshore waters, they migrate some kilometers offshore and join the shoals of adults. These adults, when they are at least three years old, leave the pelagic school in May and breed inshore until about August. The two-year-old individuals remain offshore. During the breeding season *C. quadrimaculatus* is caught for human consumption, by the millions! Breeding males hold territories on rocks at depths varying between 20 and 50 meters, and spawning sometimes takes place on an almost vertical substrate. Females, as in other seasonally breeding utaka, spawn only once during the breeding season, gathering in separate schools after spawning and moving closer inshore in the rocky habitat. The fry are released among rocks in very shallow water.

A species with a similar morphology to *C. quadrimaculatus* was caught by fishermen over an 80 meters-deep reef north of Chizumulu Island. The yellow dorsal, anal, and pelvic fins of the breeding male are clearly different from those of *C. quadrimaculatus*, which are blue or white-blue. I refer to this species as *Copadichromis* sp. 'quadrimaculatus yellow'.

Copadichromis nkatae was described from Nkhata Bay. It has never been exported as an aquarium fish. Iles (1960) reports that it is regularly caught on sandy shores from July to September, but the types were collected in a rocky habitat. *C. nkatae* has a maximum size of about 15 cm (Iles, 1960) and is characterized by three dark spots on the flanks. At Taiwanee Reef I have found a rather large utaka which I have previously termed *C.* sp. 'quadrimaculatus reef' (Konings, 1995b) but which may in fact represent a population of *C. nkatae* (Jos Snoeks, pers. comm.). Pending further study I refer to this species as *Copadichromis* sp. *cf. nkatae* as I have never been able to locate *C. nkatae* itself at its type locality, Nkhata Bay.

C. sp. *cf. nkatae* is easily recognized by its elongate shape and the three spots on the flanks, and resembles *C. quadrimaculatus* in size and

1. *Copadichromis geertsi* ♂ Chiofu

2. *Copadichromis quadrimaculatus* ♂ Tsano Rock

4. *Copadichromis geertsi* ♀ Chiofu

3. *Copadichromis trimaculatus* ♀ Ntekete

5. *Copadichromis quadrimaculatus* ♀ Jalo Reef

6. *Copadichromis trimaculatus* ♂ Gome

1. Lupingu

2. *Copadichromis* sp. *cf. nkatae* ♀ Taiwanee Reef

3. *Copadichromis* sp. 'yellow black lupingu' ♀ Lupingu

5. *Copadichromis* sp. 'quadrimaculatus yellow' ♂ Taiwan Reef

6. *Copadichromis* sp. *cf. nkatae* ♂ Taiwanee Reef

4. *Copadichromis* sp. 'yellow black lupingu' ♂ Lupingu

behavior. Males defend a spawning site inside a large cave or in a gap between large boulders. Males are blue with a white blaze and can attain a total length of about 20 cm. Females and non-territorial males gather in large schools with other species such as *C. trimaculatus* and *C. virginalis*.

C. nkatae and *C. chrysonotus* (page 124) may have a common ancestor, as is indicated by the fact that these two are the only known utaka to be parasitized by *Lernaea palati* (Fryer, 1956d; Fryer & Iles, 1972). If a parasite is selective in choosing its host it is likely that it has evolved together with that host. It follows that if the host species splits into two geographically separated populations the parasite will continue to affect both, even if they eventually evolve into distinct species. On the other hand, there is no obvious reason why such a parasite should suddenly select a completely different species as host.

Cave dwellers

There are two species of *Otopharynx* that share a preference for large caves and a mode of feeding which consists of scavenging material lying on the rocky substrate of their environment. This often includes the droppings of other fishes, probably those of herbivorous species, which have some residual nutritional value. One of these species, *Otopharynx lithobates*, is a well-known cichlid that enjoys a wide popularity in the aquarium hobby, even though all its populations reside within the boundaries of the National Park and hence are protected, so that aquarists are nowadays restricted to tank- or pond-raised specimens.

O. lithobates is found in the southern part of the lake where it occurs around the Nankumba peninsula and all its islands. It is seen infrequently at Chinyamwezi and Chinyankwazi islands as well. The maximum total length of this species is about 13 cm. It exhibits a high degree of geographic variation, with the sulfur-headed variant at Zimbawe Rock being the most attractive. The variant from Domwe Island was formerly exported under trade names such as "Aristochromis Lombardoi" and "Trematocranus Lombardoi". Males of this population have a blue body and an orange-red dorsal fin. The variant at the Maleri islands was described as *O. walteri* as it differed from *O. lithobates* from the type locality—Thumbi West Island—in having a shorter caudal peduncle and a larger mouth, but when it was compared with six other populations these differences fell within the variation now known to exist in *O. lithobates* (Rachel Cleaver & Jay Stauffer, pers. comm.).

Otopharynx sp. 'cave' is the second cave-dwelling scavenging species and has the widest distribution. It occurs on both sides of the northern two thirds of the lake and has also been found at Jalo Reef and Meponda. The "Cave" or "King-of-Cave" is larger than *O. lithobates*; adult males can attain a total length of about 20 cm. Apart from the smaller adult size and shallower body of *O. lithobates*, females of these two species are very difficult to tell apart.

As mentioned earlier, these two species are normally found in large caves and large catfishes frequently inhabit such caves as well. The cichlids may profit from the catfishes" presence, but in what manner remains as yet unclear. Nowhere are *O. lithobates* and *O.* sp. 'cave' found sympatric. The southernmost locality along the east coast where *O.* sp. 'cave' has been found is Gome. At this locality it shares the deep rocky habitat with another cave-dweller: *Stigmatochromis* sp. 'modestus eastern'.

This cave-dwelling cichlid may in fact belong to the genus *Otopharynx*, but because it has a coloration similar to that of *Stigmatochromis* and sparse, simple teeth, a diagnostic character of *Stigmatochromis*, it has been provisionally assigned to that genus. Territorial males are completely dark blue and live in caves. It has been found near Gome and Chiofu, and south of the Nsinje River near Malopa, but not yet along the shores of Mozambique. Males of the population near Malopa occur in shallower water (10-15 meters) than those of the population north of the Nsinje River where the species is encountered, but only rarely, at a depth of 30-40 meters. Because *S.* sp. 'modestus eastern' is so rare and secretive, not much is known about it except that it lives in caves most of the time.

I know even less about a species that I encountered just once at Membe Point, Likoma Island. A male of this species shot out of a cave, posed long enough for me to take a photo, and immediately disappeared into the cave again without returning into the open. The cave was at a depth of about 20 meters. Since the male was in full breeding color the basic melanin pattern was not discernible and it was therefore impossible unequivocally to assign it to a genus. Since its mouth resembled that of *Otopharynx ovatus*, I have named it *Otopharynx* sp. 'ovatus likoma'.

Rock-dwelling *Placidochromis*

Because there is at present no better alternative, several species of rock-dwelling cichlids are here assigned to the genus *Placidochromis* even though they are probably not closely related to the type species of the genus, *P. longimanus* (page 327). *Placidochromis* sp. 'blue otter' was originally termed *Otopharynx* sp. 'blue otter' (Konings, 1995b), but after I had seen more individuals, including females, at Otter Point and Tsano Rock, and when their scavenging behavior became evident, I decided this cichlid would be better placed in *Placidochromis*, at least for the time being.

Males of this species defend territories on top of large boulders at a depth of about 25 meters. Most are territorial only early in the morning, two to three hours after sunrise. Later in the day they join the foraging/scavenging groups common at depths of 25-40 meters. Females are silvery-yellow and lack any markings on the body; the juveniles are characterized by a yellow dorsal and exhibit a faint pattern of bars. Females and males occur in small foraging groups and feed from the sediment on rocks and sand. They are attracted to stirred-up debris, much as is *P. electra* in the north of the lake.

Placidochromis sp. 'jalo' appears to behave in a way similar to *P.* sp. 'blue otter'. It is endemic to Jalo Reef. Although males with breeding coloration are commonly found in the foraging groups with females, none of them appears to be territorial in this environment. It is not unlikely that they too exhibit reproductive territoriality during the first few hours of daylight.

A third species, *Placidochromis* sp. 'mbamba', may also belong to this small group of opportunistic feeders, but I have not yet seen this species in its natural habitat. It is reported as occurring in deep water at Mbamba Bay in Tanzania (Marc Danhieux, pers. comm.).

Yet another species, *Placidochromis* sp. 'chinyankwazi', is endemic to Chinyankwazi Island and behaves like the previous three species. These fishes seem to scavenge together in small groups but I have never seen large numbers—never more than three together. Males showing color are blue and yellow, with the latter on the lower part of the body. I have not yet seen territorial males, and even males showing color are very rare.

Rubber lips

There is a specific adaptation among cichlids which is seen in several species flocks, and which is anatomically characterized by thick, swollen lips. The function of these lips was originally attributed to prey location. They were thought to contain sensory tissue, with the lips being applied to the substrate and the mouth closed when they (the lips) had detected some prey item (Fryer & Iles, 1972). Histological investigations of the lip tissue did not, however, reveal any sensory structures at all—at least not until taste buds were discovered in the lips of the deep-living *Otopharynx pachycheilus* (Arnegard & Snoeks 2001; photo page 407)—and the feeding behavior of these fishes made this hypothesis seem unlikely.

The thick-lipped cichlids of the lake can be divided into two groups, one containing species with thickened lips which feed predominantly from cracks and slits between rocks (e.g. *Protomelas ornatus* and *Lichnochromis acuticeps*); and another consisting of species with very large, rubbery lips. The members of this second group likewise feed from the rocky substrate, from small pockets in the rocks rather than cracks and slits. Species of the first group usually align their bodies with the direction of the crack from which they want to feed. The

1. *Otopharynx lithobates* ♂ Zimbawe Rock

2. *Otopharynx lithobates* ♂ Domwe Island

6. *Otopharynx lithobates* ♂ Mumbo Island

3. *Otopharynx lithobates* ♂ Thumbi West Island

7. *Otopharynx lithobates* ♂ Chinyamwezi Island

4. *Otopharynx lithobates* ♂ Maleri Island

8. *Otopharynx lithobates* ♀ Thumbi West Island

5. *Otopharynx* sp. 'cave' ♂ Manda

9. *Otopharynx* sp. 'cave' ♀ Lundu

1. *Placidochromis* sp. 'blue otter' ♀ Otter Point

2. *Placidochromis* sp. 'mbamba' ♂ Mbamba Bay

3. *Placidochromis* sp. 'jalo' ♀ Jalo Reef

4. *Placidochromis* sp. 'chinyankwazi' ♀ Chinyankwazi Island

5. *Stigmatochromis* sp. 'modestus eastern' ♂ Nametumbwe

6. *Stigmatochromis* sp. 'modestus eastern' ♀ Gome

7. *Placidochromis* sp. 'blue otter' ♂ Tsano Rocks

8. *Placidochromis* sp. 'jalo' ♂ Jalo Reef

9. *Placidochromis* sp. 'chinyankwazi' ♂ Chinyankwazi Island

10. *Otopharynx* sp. 'ovatus likoma' ♂ Membe Point

rubber-lipped species do not. Small invertebrates, the main food source for rubber-lipped species, find shelter in the rough surface of the rocky substrate. The fish carefully selects the site of attack before striking the surface of the rock in order to extract the prey. If the site proves to be of nutritious value it will quickly "bite", thereby pressing its lips against the substrate in the process. When the sediment layer covering the aufwuchs is thick, a cloud of "dust" accompanies each bite.

The thick, soft lips have probably not developed to absorb the shock that occurs when the fish hits the rock, because when fish strikes the rock the lips are spread out and thus do not come between the fish and the rock. They may, however, perform that function in the thick-lipped species of the first group. (*Protomelas* sp. 'steveni imperial' (page 116) strikes the rock in a similar, rather violent fashion but lacks any fleshy thickening of the lips.) The lips of the species of the second group are very swollen and jellylike to the touch. When the fish strikes the substrate these lips are smashed against the rock and seal off the hole in which the prey has hidden itself (preventing it from escaping). When the buccal cavity is subsequently expanded the prey is neatly sucked out of its shelter. Growth of the lips appears to be somehow stimulated by the continuous abrasive action of the coarse rock surfaces since lip growth in tank-raised individuals is noticeably reduced. In captivity, even the swollen lips of wild-caught specimens seem to decrease in size.

Placidochromis milomo is a rubber-lipped species infrequently found in the deeper rocky habitats. It was originally introduced to aquarists as "Haplochromis Super VC 10", a name coined by Peter Davies (pers. comm.) to describe the swift way this cichlid makes its escape when fishermen approach with a net—the Super VC 10 was a type of plane that for a long period plied between Malaŵi and London. *P. milomo* has a lake-wide distribution and its maximum total length is about 20 cm. Its menu features items such as insect larvae, crustaceans, and, occasionally, mbuna fry. As is common practice in species with a very low population density, territorial behavior occurs only when several sexually active males meet at the same place. Only the sight of another male in breeding dress stimulates the male into defending a spawning site, so territoriality is usually not a common aspect of behavior in this species. Sexually active males instead swim up to females and court them. If the female is interested (and only those who are will come close to a sexually active male) she responds by spawning "on the spot". Females care for their offspring after first release.

Piscivores

Nimbochromis linni is specialized for snatching young mbuna out of cracks between rocks. Its characteristic behavior is not found in any other known predatory cichlid. The large size of *N. linni* (maximum 30 cm) prevents it from penetrating the hideaways of the small mbuna, but it has found another way to stalk them. Its mottled pattern blends well with the environment, as is the case with some orange-blotched mbuna females. It slowly cruises through the habitat and looks for a specific place to feed. It goes on the alert when it sees juvenile cichlids in or near a crevice. Having located such a site it slowly drops down onto a rock, with its characteristic downward-projecting snout at the edge of it, above the crevice. Then it remains motionless for several minutes while stealthily observing the small mbuna hiding in the crack. As soon as one of them comes within reach of the very protractile mouth it is sucked out of its shelter. When *N. linni* expands its buccal cavity its protruded mouth functions like the hose of a vacuum cleaner. Its sly and sedentary behavior is reminiscent of *N. livingstonii* (page 296) although it has a closer resemblance to *N. polystigma* (page 297) in appearance.

N. linni breeds in the deep rocky habitat and seems to have only a short breeding period every year. This does not fall in the same months for all individuals but depends on the sexual ripeness of the individual. These large predators refrain from feeding for the entire duration of the breeding period. Sexually active males can be seen throughout the year. Such males lose their camouflage coloration and are adorned with a dark blue all over the body. The anal fin has a black base but is red for the most part. The outer edge is yellow with a number of yellow-white egg-dummies. Outside the breeding season very large, orange spots are discernible on the center of the anal fin, but these disappear (in both sexes!) when the pair acquire their nuptial coloration. They cannot therefore function as egg-dummies! The coloration of the ripe female is not blue but gray-brown, and most of the mottled pattern disappears. Only during the breeding season does the male defend a territory. This is centered on a flat rock surrounded by some smaller rocks, or on the sand alongside a large rock. Sometimes a male patrols an area on the sand beneath an overhanging rock; sometimes he constructs a simple cave-crater bower. Almost all breeding males were seen in water deeper than 15 meters. Spawning takes place on a rock or on the sand close to rocks. The female picks up the eggs before the male can fertilize them (Peter Baasch, pers. comm.); the male then presents his anal fin and expels his sperm, which is sucked in by the female. In this respect the species differs from *N. livingstonii*, as eggs in that species are fertilized when they are still outside the female's mouth (Willemse, 1976). The anal fin spots, visible outside the breeding season, disappear in this species as well and are replaced by whitish streaks and spots bearing no particular resemblance to eggs.

Stigmatochromis modestus is known from many locations around the lake but is rarely seen. It is a very secretive piscivore but seems to be rather common on many stretches of coast. The color of females and non-breeding males, which is completely dark reddish brown, matches perfectly the shadows in recesses and caves between and underneath rocks. *S. modestus* commonly lurks in such caves and probably waits until its prey (juvenile mbuna) enters the hideaway. It can reach a maximum total length of about 16 cm and has a relatively large mouth. Breeding males appear to "cluster" in a small area of the rocky habitat, each defending his spawning-site, which is a cave or a place beneath an overhanging rock. During the breeding period the male refrains from feeding and stays at the entrance of his cave all the time. Spawning takes place on a rock inside the cave. I have never seen a fry-guarding female.

Snoeks & Hanssens (2004) have suggested that a species I have named *Stigmatochromis* sp. 'modestus makokola' could well be conspecific with *Otopharynx brooksi*. I had originally regarded this species as *O. brooksi* but was later of the opinion that its oral jaw teeth (numerous and unicuspid) did not accord with other species in *Otopharynx*. I have been able to examine a single specimen of *S.* sp. 'modestus makokola' and found that all measurements fell within the range given for *O. brooksi*. Although the types of *O. brooksi* are smaller than the norm for *S.* sp. 'modestus makokola', I now regard the two as conspecific.

As the name "Modestus Makokola" implies, *O. brooksi* is found at Makokola Reef in the southeastern arm of the lake, south of Boadzulu Island; it also occurs at other places around the Nankumba Peninsula, but always at a depth of more than 15 meters. The average size of adults ranges between 16 and 20 cm. *O. brooksi* has a deeper body than *S. modestus* and the three spots are more distinct. I have found *S. modestus* and *O. brooksi* together at Boadzulu Island and found a difference in their behavior; *S. modestus* lives in the rocky habitat where it usually hides in dark recesses. *O. brooksi* lives in the open rather than hiding among rocks. At Makokola Reef it seems to be more common near the intermediate habitat at a depth of about 35 meters. On a few occasions it has been seen cruising over the sand, probably hunting the small sand-dwelling cichlids that are abundant in that area. Males are territorial and defend a small spawning pit beneath a rock or sometimes between two rocks. Females guard their fry after they have been released for the first time.

Buccochromis heterotaenia is a very large piscivore frequently found in all kinds of habitats. Its maximum recorded standard length is 42 cm and that particular specimen (caught by Deon Haigh off Makanjila Point, pers. comm.) weighed 1.055 kilos. Sub-adults can be readily recognized by their characteristic color pattern consisting of a diagonal stripe and vertical bars.

1. *Placidochromis milomo* ♂ Nakantenga Island

2. *Placidochromis milomo* ♀ Chinyamwezi Island

1. *Placidochromis milomo* ♂ Chinyamwezi Island

2. *Otopharynx brooksi* ♀ Boadzulu Island

3. *Stigmatochromis modestus* ♂ Boadzulu Island

4. *Nimbochromis linni* Boadzulu Island

5. *Nimbochromis linni* ♀ Mbenji Island

6. *Otopharynx brooksi* ♂ Boadzulu Island

7. *Stigmatochromis modestus* ♂ Nakantenga Island

8. *Nimbochromis linni* ♂ Boadzulu Island

9. *Nimbochromis linni* ♂ Thumbi West Island

Males in breeding color are normally seen at great depths in the rocky habitat where they defend unmarked spawning sites on the rocks, but territorial males have also been seen on the open sand without a visible spawning site. The depth at which such males occur ranges from 30 to more than 80 meters—at least those are the depths at which the local fishermen catch them on hook and line. *B. heterotaenia* is not an obligate pursuit predator but is nevertheless frequently observed dashing after small mbuna or juvenile non-mbuna.

Rhamphochromis, collectively called *ncheni* in the native tongue, are known throughout the lake and several species are frequently caught together with their prey, *usipa* (the native name for the lake sardine). Some species range close to shore (e.g. *R. longiceps* (page 301) and *R. esox*) but most others are found a few hundred meters offshore. *Rhamphochromis* are elongate, usually silvery-colored, piscivores designed to swim swiftly in pursuit of prey. They normally swim in the open water, away from rocks, but one species can be regularly encountered in the deep rocky habitat: *R. esox*.

Rhamphochromis esox (*R. leptosoma* (Turner *et al.*, 2004) and *R. lucius* (Martin Genner, pers. comm.) are synonyms) has a silvery body with one or two horizontal, dark stripes on the flanks. It is the most streamlined species of *Rhamphochromis* and is probably frequently involved in lightning-fast pursuits of fast-moving prey. It attains a maximum standard length of 42 cm (Turner *et al.*, 2004). *R. esox* is the only *ncheni* that is encountered in rocky habitats; mouthbrooding females are not uncommon, but I have never seen a breeding male of this species.

Paedophages

The term paedophagy means "feeding on children" and is used to describe the feeding habits of a number of cichlid species that, in one way or another, are able to extract embryos or larvae from the oral cavity of a mouthbrooding female. Paedophagy was first described for a number of cichlids from Lake Victoria (Greenwood, 1959), some of which engulf the mouth of a female and suck out her brood (Wilhelm, 1980). Such behavior has not as yet been observed in the Malaŵi paedophages, where observation of the species involved points to head-ramming behavior in every case. This involves the predator approaching a mouthbrooding female from behind and impacting her buccal area from below. This may lead to the female expelling part of her brood which is immediately consumed by the paedophage. Although I have witnessed such attacks in Lake Malaŵi, I have never been able to actually see anything leave the female's mouth. Some of this feeding behavior may happen so fast that it is not registered by the naked eye.

Over the years I have collected various cichlids that, upon examination of their gut contents, have contained numerous cichlid embryos within their stomachs. Since all Malaŵi cichlids—apart from the substrate brooder *Tilapia rendalli* (page 304)—are maternal mouthbrooders, the only possible way these predators could have obtained this type of food was to extract it from mouthbrooding females. These paedophages include: *Caprichromis orthognathus* (page 345), *Hemitaeniochromis spilopterus* (page 344), *H.* sp. 'paedophage' (page 260), *H.* sp. 'spilopterus yellow' (page 344), and *H.* sp. 'spilopterus blue' (see below).

Almost all mouthbrooding cichlids are acutely aware of the danger posed by an approaching paedophage and will quickly avert an attack by turning away from the potential perpetrator. It is, understandably, not easy to extract part of a brood from a female's mouth, making paedophages relatively rare. Nevertheless, a number of species have evolved to feed exclusively on the broods of others. I have personally examined the guts of only the five species listed above, but from McKaye & Kocher (1983) we know that the stomachs of *Caprichromis liemi* (page 165) have also contained cichlid larvae and eggs.

Most cichlids enjoy a meal of eggs and will, because of their high nutritional value, immediately devour any available. But in the case of paedophages, eggs, embryos, and larvae represent their only source of nutrition. The hormonal changes that take place during breeding may put their taste for eggs "on ice", as is the case in all cichlids. Additionally, I have never witnessed a paedophage attacking a mouthbrooding member of its own species.

Hemitaeniochromis sp. 'spilopterus blue' is found throughout the lake and always in rocky habitats. It is easily recognized by the oblique mouth and heavy jaws (a characteristic of the genus), and by the two horizontal stripes on the body, the lower of which does not extend as far forward as the gill cover. This mid-lateral band does, by contrast, run the full length of the body in *H. spilopterus*, a species of sandy habitats (see page 344).

H. sp. 'spilopterus blue' is a predator but has not yet been observed chasing small fishes. Five specimens, among them four sexually active males, were the subjects of stomach contents analysis. The four sexually active males all had empty stomachs and a drastically reduced digestive system. The body cavities of these males were completely empty! The only organs showing normal dimensions were the gonads. The fifth specimen had several cichlid eggs, a number of catfish eggs, and catfish larvae in its stomach and gut! This could suggest that this species does not restrict itself to chasing mouthbrooding cichlids and that feeding takes place inside caves. Although I have observed this species on many occasions I have never noticed any indications of paedophagous behavior. It is therefore possible that *H.* sp. 'spilopterus blue' is just an opportunistic piscivore which seizes any chance to feed on delicacies such as cichlid eggs. Another possibility could be that it stalks mouthbrooding females in the dark recesses of rocky caves and may, therefore, primarily attack mbuna.

H. sp. 'spilopterus blue' is usually found in caves, and males even build their nests on the sandy bottoms of their caves. As mentioned earlier, stomach contents inventories indicate that sexually active males refrain from feeding. Breeding males have been found at different times of the year but it seems unlikely that a male is sexually active for more than two months at a time. Another possible scenario is that *H.* sp. 'spilopterus blue', having reached the adult stage, may put all its energy reserves into reproduction during the last phase of its life, which lasts until it dies of exhaustion.

Almost nothing is known about *Hemitaeniochromis* sp. 'spilopterus jalo', which was caught by Saulos Mwale in 1990 at Jalo Reef near Nkhotakota. It is quite a large species—approximately 15 to 20 cm total length—and characterized by strong jaws suggesting a predatory lifestyle.

A large (maximum total length 25 cm) predatory species, *Hemitaeniochromis* sp. 'insignis mumbo' (previously referred to as *H.* sp. 'urotaenia mumbo' (Konings, 1995b) and as *H. insignis* (Konings, 2001)), is found in the southern part of the lake. It occurs at depths of more than 25 meters. Territorial males build shallow sand-scrape pits among the rubble of the biotope. The species" feeding technique and its food preferences are unknown because all specimens brought to the surface had empty stomachs and feeding behavior has not yet been observed. The strong lower jaw is a character it shares with the other members of *Hemitaeniochromis* and it may therefore also be involved in stealing from the mouths of females. *H.* sp. 'insignis mumbo' has a deeper body than the similarly-sized *H. urotaenia* which is normally found in much shallower water.

Embryos or lice?

One of the most intriguing cases of paedophagy involves *Caprichromis liemi*, another species reported to steal embryos and larvae from mouthbrooding females (McKaye & Kocher, 1983). I have observed *C. liemi* at many different locations throughout the lake and it seems likely that their diet is not restricted to cichlid embryos and larvae. On several occasions I have witnessed *C. liemi* attack male cichlids, showing a preference for those with parasites—the fish louse *Argulus jollymani*—on their throat and breast. On one occasion I was SCUBA diving with a video camera and saw a *C. liemi* eyeing (or at least I thought so) a mouthbrooding *Copadichromis borleyi* several feet above it. I pointed my camera at the paedophage and started recording. However, before I could gauge the precise direction from which the *Caprichromis liemi* would attack, I recorded it

1. *Buccochromis heterotaenia* ♂ Tsano Rock

2. *Buccochromis heterotaenia* ♀ Otter Point

5. *Buccochromis heterotaenia* Hongi Island

3. *Rhamphochromis esox* ♂ Liuli

6. *Rhamphochromis esox* Londo

4. *Rhamphochromis esox* ♂ Narungu

1. *Hemitaeniochromis* sp. 'spilopterus blue' ♂ Tsano Rock

2. *Hemitaeniochromis* sp. 'spilopterus blue' ♀ Mesuli

3. *Hemitaeniochromis* sp. 'insignis mumbo' ♀ Boadzulu Island

4. *Hemitaeniochromis* sp. 'spilopterus jalo' ♂ Jalo Reef

5. *Caprichromis liemi* ♀ Luwala Reef

6. *Hemitaeniochromis* sp. 'insignis mumbo' ♂ Boadzulu Island

7. *Hemitaeniochromis* sp. 'insignis mumbo' ♀ Chinyamwezi Island

8. *Caprichromis liemi* ♀ Luwala Reef

striking the throat of a male *Labeotropheus fuelleborni*. Rather violently, it grabbed and twisted a louse from the mbuna's throat. The "victim' was shaken but no harm was done—on the contrary, it got rid of a blood-sucking parasite—and no retaliation was directed towards the vermin-killer. It is likely that *C. liemi* feeds partially, or even primarily, on these parasitic invertebrates, since fish with *Argulus* on their throats are very common.

The brutality with which *C. liemi* dislodges parasites from the throats of other cichlids makes it likely that when such behavior is directed towards a mouthbrooding female—they often have several lice attached to their throats—her brood is prone to be ejected. Once this more appetizing and easy-to-eat food appears, the hard-to-dislodge lice are no longer such an attractive menu option. Although it still obtains nutriment from fish lice, *C. liemi* seems to have learned over time that when you impact the throat of a mouthbrooding female, part of her brood becomes available for lunch.

Interestingly, the juveniles of various piscivores (paedophages are, of course, piscivorous) begin their lives as cleaner fishes (e.g., picking parasites and fungus from the fins of other fish). Juvenile *C. liemi* fit into this category, as do those of *Docimodus evelynae* (see below) and *Mylochromis melanonotus* (page 332). A cichlid distressed by parasites (e.g., anchor worms (*Lernaea lophiara*) that have attached themselves to the dorsal fin and caused infection) will gladly present its problem to these little predators, which then enthusiastically pick and tear at any parasites. In the case of *C. liemi*, adults may still favor parasites of other cichlids, male or female; the brood jettisoned by an attacked mouthbrooding female is just an "occupational benefit". Other paedophagous species may have abandoned the vermin-eradicating feeding strategy for the very specific diet of cichlid broods.

The fact that *C. liemi* is able to remain concealed and unnoticed in the rocky habitat prior to striking allows it accurately to target parasites on fish of both sexes rather than delivering a more random blow to the throat.

Catfish for dinner

In 1976 Eccles and Lewis published a very interesting paper on two predatory cichlids, *Docimodus johnstonii* and *Docimodus evelynae*, which have an interesting feeding behavior. One of these species, *D. evelynae*, was further investigated by Ribbink (1984), who described its life history, which is among the most remarkable observed in Malaŵi cichlids. Juvenile *D. evelynae* (total length between 40 and 75 mm) inhabit relatively shallow water and behave as cleaner fishes, screening client cichlids for parasites, usually anchor worms or patches of fungus. The client—only "haps" have been seen being cleaned by *D. evelynae*—initiates the procedure by presenting its dorsal fin (indicating it is not going to attack or run) to the cleaner, who then scrutinizes the client in search of irregularities that may be of nutritional value. Cleaning stations, such as are known to occur in marine environments, have not been observed. The contact between client and cleaner is probably made when the small and eager cleaner approaches the ailing fish to perform a "treatment".

When *D. evelynae* has grown to about 60 mm in length it gradually changes its teeth (!) and its feeding behavior. During this change it feeds from the aufwuchs or from the plankton, when available. By a size of about 10 cm, large conical teeth have replaced all the juvenile tricuspid ones, and at about the same time it starts to frequent much deeper regions, now feeding on scales from cichlids and barbs, and pieces of skin from catfishes! In particular, *Bagrus meridionalis*, the *kampango*, seems to be a victim of these nasty attacks, but attacks on clariid catfishes have also been seen. Furthermore, Ribbink (1984) observed *D. evelynae* following larger cichlids and biting off scales from the caudal peduncle. I have seen this behavior in *D. johnstonii* in the shallow sandy habitat at Cape Maclear where an individual with an approximate length of 12 cm attacked the caudal peduncle of a large *Taeniolethrinops praeorbitalis*. The difference in the size of *Docimodus* in the cleaning and predatory stages (<6 cm vs. >10 cm) is apparently sufficient for prospective clients (or victims!) to recognize the difference in its intentions and feeding behavior.

The fact that *D. johnstonii* exhibits similar predatory behavior to *D. evelynae* had previously been suggested by stomach inventories of adults, which revealed pieces of clariid catfish fins (Eccles & Lewis, 1976). Clariid catfishes are usually found over sandy and muddy substrates at deep levels and *D. johnstonii* may therefore be found more often in these habitats. Both species have a lake-wide distribution.

Territorial males of *D. johnstonii*, which have a very dark breeding color, were found at a depth of about 40 meters at Zimbawe Rock where they defended territories on top of large boulders. Fry-guarding females have not yet been seen. A territorial male *D. evelynae* has been seen defending a cave with a rocky bottom at a depth of 40 meters near Meponda. It actively chased and lured females into the cave.

1. *Docimodus evelynae* ♀ Maleri Island

2. *Docimodus evelynae* ♂ Meponda

4. *Docimodus evelynae* ♀ Chinyamwezi Island

5. *Docimodus evelynae* Londo

3. *Docimodus johnstonii* ♂ Jalo Reef

6. *Docimodus johnstonii* Senga Bay

1. *Metriaclima flavifemina* ♀ Thumbi West Island

2. *Metriaclima flavifemina* ♂ Thumbi West Island

3. *Metriaclima flavifemina* ♀ Maleri Island

4. Gallireya Reef

5. *Metriaclima flavifemina* ♂ Thumbi West Island

6. *Metriaclima flavifemina* ♂ Maleri Island

The intermediate habitat

The intermediate habitat includes those sections of the coast that have both rocks and sand. These regions form the transition zone between the pure rocky habitat and the sandy (or muddy) lake floor. The intermediate habitats can extend to very deep levels where they harbor an entirely different cichlid community to a similar region in shallow water.

The most common intermediate biotope is, however, usually no deeper than 25 meters. The quiet, shallow bays that have muddy bottoms and vegetated areas are not included here, nor are the extremely shallow intermediate habitats (no deeper than about three meters), which have a cichlid community of their own. Although some species dealt with in this chapter are also found around the small heaps of rocks in such areas, both the vegetated bays and the extremely shallow habitats are discussed in separate chapters (see pages 280 and 264 respectively). Each intermediate shore has its own mixture of cichlid species, and the mbuna in particular show extensive geographical variation.

Mbuna prefer pure rocky habitats where they find sufficient food and shelter. Some species, however, have a better-adapted feeding apparatus than others, enabling them to harvest more aufwuchs. A species which is able to collect food faster than others will grow more quickly and usually attain a larger adult size. Such species are normally found in the upper parts of the biotope, where greater light intensity produces a richer algal growth than at deeper levels. Although there is enough biocover to supply the needs of less well-adapted species as well, they have a reduced chance of securing a territory in the rich, upper regions unless they adopt an aggressive attitude, chasing all intruders from their feeding territories. Competition in today's lake is only partly related to the feeding specializations of individual species; obtaining a breeding territory in the preferred habitat is the important factor. A mbuna with a large size or aggressive territorial behavior is much more likely to secure a territory in its preferred habitat than is a small, peaceful species.

The zebras

The intermediate habitat in the southwestern part of the lake harbors a "zebra", *Metriaclima cyneusmarginatus*, which has been discussed earlier (page 64). This form may be the intermediate zone analogue of the classic zebra complex or of *M. fainzilberi*, all of which are normally found in rocky habitats. Apart from the blue-black barred *M. cyneusmarginatus*, males of which exhibit a particularly attractive color pattern in the population near Chia Lagoon (Sani), *Metriaclima* has many representatives that are found only in the intermediate habitat; so many that, for convenience, I have divided them into several groups: the "black-dorsal group", the "*aurora* group", and the "kingsizei group". This division has no phylogenetic basis but has been made chiefly according to male breeding coloration, even though the groups also have different distributions. The members of the black-dorsal and *aurora* groups are located mainly in the southern half of the lake, while the kingsizei-group mbuna are found chiefly in the north. The kingsizei group nevertheless has large areas of overlap with the other two groups. In addition there are several species that I have been unable to assign to any of the groups.

I have tried to define these groups so that each locality harbors only a single representative of each group—so we do not find, for example, two different members of the *aurora* group at one place—but this was not always possible.

The black-dorsal group

The name of this group is derived from the

unofficial name, "Zebra Black Dorsal", of *Metriaclima flavifemina*, a common mbuna found in the southwestern part of the lake. Males of *M. flavifemina* and those of most other members of the black-dorsal group have a black band in the dorsal fin. The females of *M. flavifemina* are completely yellow or beige-yellow while the color of the females of other members of the black-dorsal group varies from completely yellow to brown with only the tips of the unpaired fins yellow.

Metriaclima flavifemina was originally recorded from the Maleri islands and at Chidunga Rocks, near Chipoka, but Konings & Stauffer (2006) argue that the black-dorsal zebra at Thumbi West Island also belongs to *M. flavifemina*. This population, formerly termed *M.* sp. 'black dorsal heteropictus', has in the past repeatedly been mistaken for *Pseudotropheus heteropictus* (see page 201), a small mbuna from Chizumulu Island, but the latter exhibits a different feeding technique and has a rather different skull structure. There is some variation among male *M. flavifemina* at Thumbi West in the extent of the black band in the dorsal fin: some have a completely black dorsal while in others the band is restricted to the trailing part.

A single male *M. flavifemina* has also been caught at Namalenje Island and the species' distribution thus extends north of the Maleris.

At Thundu and at Chiloelo (both in Mozambique) the intermediate habitat is home to a single representative of the black-dorsal group at each locality: *Metriaclima* sp. 'black dorsal thundu' and *Metriaclima* sp. 'black dorsal chiloelo', respectively. Female *M.* sp. 'black dorsal thundu' are beige with yellow fins and are very common in shallow water. The females of *M.* sp. 'black dorsal chiloelo' are much darker and lack the yellow color altogether. The habitat at Chiloelo is very sediment-rich, at least at the places I have visited, so one would expect much yellower females, as is the case at many other localities with sediment-rich intermediate habitats. Most males of *M.* sp. 'black dorsal chiloelo' excavate holes under rocks, but some defend their territories among the small heaps of rocks present in the habitat.

Metriaclima sp. 'black dorsal nkolongwe', found at N'kolongwe, Mozambique, is one of the most attractive mbuna—at least in the case of males—found along the Mozambique shore of the lake; meanwhile females are dark brown with yellow-tipped unpaired fins. The territorial coloration of the black-barred males varies from cobalt blue to orange-yellow, while the ventral region and lower part of the head are orange-yellow. No two males look the same.

A very large and attractive mbuna, *Metriaclima phaeos*, has a rather wide distribution along the central east coast of the lake. It occurs in the intermediate habitat at Undu Point in Tanzania and along mainland shores to the south as far as Cobwé in Mozambique. It has not been found at Lumbaulo, where it appears to be replaced by a member of the *aurora* group, *M.* sp. 'aurora lumbaulo' (see page 177). *M. phaeos* is common throughout its range along the Mozambique and Tanzanian shores. Females at almost all localities are bright yellow, but at Londo, Mozambique, they are beige with yellow fins. The males at Londo have a slightly different pattern as well: the black bars on the bodies of most (but not all) individuals do not extend onto the dorsal fin and nape. *M. phaeos* is among the more popular mbuna exported regularly from the Tanzanian shores of the lake.

A mbuna with a black dorsal found at Lundo Island in Tanzania, *Metriaclima* sp. 'black dorsal lundo', has previously been regarded (Konings, 2001) as a further population of *M. phaeos*, and was thought to be closely related to a species at Likoma Island, formerly termed *M.* sp. 'black dorsal cobalt'. The latter now appears to belong to a different genus and is discussed later in this chapter as *Pseudotropheus* sp. 'sand cobalt' (page 208).

The situation at Lundo Island is complicated as two species that are members of the black-dorsal group can be found here. One of them is the already mentioned *M.* sp. 'black dorsal lundo' and the second a species that was previously placed in the so-called "Msobo Trio": *Metriaclima* sp. 'msobo heteropictus'. Both species are common at the island and both males and females of the two species are easily distinguishable. Female *M.* sp. 'msobo heteropictus' are white-yellow with a yellow anal fin

1. *Metriaclima* sp. 'black dorsal thundu' ♂ Thundu

5. *Metriaclima* sp. 'black dorsal thundu' ♀ Thundu

2. *Metriaclima* sp. 'black dorsal chiloelo' ♂ Chiloelo

6. *Metriaclima* sp. 'black dorsal chiloelo' ♀ Meponda

7. *Metriaclima* sp. 'black dorsal nkolongwe' ♀ N'kolongwe

3. *Metriaclima* sp. 'black dorsal nkolongwe' ♂ N'kolongwe

8. *Metriaclima phaeos* ♀ Londo

9. *Metriaclima phaeos* ♂ Chiwindi

4. *Metriaclima phaeos* ♂ Londo

10. *Metriaclima phaeos* ♀ Undu

1. *Metriaclima* sp. 'black dorsal lundo' ♀ Lundo Island

2. *Metriaclima* sp. 'msobo heteropictus' ♂ Lundo Island

3. *Metriaclima* sp. 'msobo heteropictus' ♀ Ndonga

4. *Metriaclima* sp. 'msobo' ♀ Ngwazi

6. *Metriaclima* sp. 'black dorsal lundo' ♂ Lundo Island

7. *Metriaclima* sp. 'msobo heteropictus' ♂ Ndonga

8. *Metriaclima* sp. 'msobo' ♂ Ngwazi

5. *Metriaclima* sp. 'msobo' ♂ Manda

while those of *M.* sp. 'black dorsal lundo' are beige-blue with a black band in the anal fin. Males of the latter species have a distinct pattern of vertical bars that extend into the dorsal while males of *M.* sp. 'msobo heteropictus' have a very variable pattern of vertical bars that never extend over the entire flank, leaving the upper part of the body light blue. *M.* sp. 'msobo heteropictus' is found between Njambe and Lundo Island.

The shores between Lundu and Njambe are sandy and this may act as a barrier in the distribution of both *M.* sp. 'msobo heteropictus' and *Metriaclima* sp. 'msobo', since intermediate forms have not been found. *M.* sp. 'msobo' is the ecological equivalent of *M.* sp. 'msobo heteropictus' north of Lundu. The northernmost point of its distribution is at Cape Kaiser, where I have found only a few females and no territorial male. It is fairly common at Ngwazi and was abundant at Magunga Reef before ornamental fish collectors almost completely eradicated it from this area—the species is very popular in the aquarium hobby. It is also found at Manda, as well as at Pombo Reef and Lundu. Females of all populations are bright orange-yellow. The coloration of males varies slightly from one end of the range to the other, but is generally blue-black with irregular light blue stripes and spots along the base of the dorsal fin and on the upper half of the body. Males of the populations south of the Ruhuhu River are generally much darker, almost completely lacking the light blue markings, but such males are sometimes also found in other populations.

The color pattern in some males suggests that its basic elements may in fact be two horizontal stripes instead of vertical bars, in which case a relationship to members of the genus *Melanochromis* needs to be considered. However, the feeding technique it employs to harvest algae from the rocks is unmistakably that of a *Metriaclima*. The lips are pressed tightly against the substrate and the algae are thus combed from the rock. *Melanochromis* species nip and bite at the aufwuchs but I have never seen them combing off algae.

A mbuna with a black dorsal at the Mbenji islands, *Metriaclima* sp. 'black dorsal mbenji', is assigned to the black-dorsal group of zebras but could be more closely related to the rock-dwelling *M.* sp. 'aggressive bars' than to *M. flavifemina*. The females of the former species are brown without any bar pattern while those of *M.* sp. 'black dorsal mbenji' do show barring on a blue-brown ground color, but lack the yellow coloration in the fins present in all other female members of the black-dorsal group. This species was previously regarded as a member of *Cynotilapia* (Ribbink *et al.*, 1983b: 222; photo captioned incorrectly as from Maleri Island) but its feeding technique and its bicuspid teeth are those of a true *Metriaclima*. There are two different species of *Cynotilapia* at the Mbenji islands (see page 69) and this may have started the confusion.

In general, the members of the black-dorsal group have a much milder temperament when defending territories than do the *Metriaclima* species of the purely rocky environments. This is possibly the result of the lower population densities found in the intermediate habitats, allowing males more space to stake out their territories. In the confines of the aquarium, however, most species can be as vigorous in territorial defense as any zebra of the rocky habitat.

The *aurora* group

The name of this group is derived from *Metriaclima aurora*, a very popular mbuna among aquarists. Like all members of this group it lacks a black band in the (yellow) dorsal fin. *M. aurora* inhabits the intermediate habitat and rarely ventures into deep regions. It has been regularly exported and was among the many species that were transplanted to Thumbi West Island by the first exporter of Malaŵi cichlids. The introduced population has become firmly established and is found at several places around the Nankumba Peninsula. The natural distribution of *M. aurora* includes Likoma Island; it is also quite common at Mala Point (formerly Mara Point), Mozambique, and a very attractive geographical race is found at Mbweca and Tumbi Point, both in Mozambique. Males of the latter variant exhibit broad brown bars superimposed on the usual color pattern. I have also seen *M. aurora* at N'kolongwe, but between this locality and Tumbi Point no *M. aurora*-type cichlid could be found.

Metriaclima sp. 'aurora bevous' is endemic to Chizumulu Island and is most common in sediment-rich intermediate habitats where males defend holes excavated under or between rocks. Females are gray-brown and live alone. It is usually found at depths below 10 meters. This species was initially thought to be a geographical variant of *Pseudotropheus* "zebra bevous" (Ribbink *et al.*, 1983b), but that species appears to be restricted to Likoma Island and is not a member of *Metriaclima* (Mary Bailey, pers. comm.; see page 207).

Metriaclima sp. 'aurora lumbaulo' is an *aurora* type similarly barred to the variant of *M. aurora* at Tumbi Point, Mozambique. It differs from *M. aurora* in having a deeper body and the fact that it occurs at deeper levels than is commonly observed in *M. aurora*. Territorial males of *M.* sp. 'aurora lumbaulo' are most common at a depth of about 15-25 meters whereas *M. aurora* is usually found at depths of 2-10 meters. *M.* sp. 'aurora lumbaulo' is found at Lumbaulo and Mesuli, Mozambique.

Metriaclima sp. 'aurora north'—a species previously referred to as *Pseudotropheus* sp. 'kingsizei north' but which, after a closer examination of the species, is now believed to be a member of the genus *Metriaclima* and the *aurora* group—has a wide distribution along the northeastern shore of the lake. It is found from Matema to a little north of Lupingu, and also from Ngwazi to Magunga, possibly to just north of Manda (Spreinat, 1994). Females of *M.* sp. 'aurora north' closely resemble those of *M. aurora* and *M.* sp. 'aurora blue' and the latter species may be its closest relative.

The intermediate habitat at Cobwé, between Lumbaulo and Mala Point, is home to another *aurora*-group species: *Metriaclima* sp. 'aurora blue'. Males are completely light blue, but recently a geographical variant of this species has been exported from Kanjindo Rocks in Mozambique (the precise location of this reef is not known but it is near Cobwé) and in this form, sometimes exported as "Pseudotropheus Flameback", males have an orange-yellow area on the upper part of the body and an orange-yellow snout. Females are indistinguishable from those of *M.* sp. 'aurora blue' at Cobwé.

Males of the Cobwé form resemble the Gome and Ntekete variants of *M. chrysomallos*, another member of the *aurora* group. There is a slight difference between these three forms in the extent of the yellow color on the lower part of the head and breast, in particular in that of the form at Gome. Males of the population at Ntekete in particular have an orange-yellow snout and breast. Females of all four forms have yellow-edged unpaired fins and can thus be distinguished from those of the Mumbo variant of *M. chrysomallos* which have beige-gray fins (and bodies). Nevertheless these two species look very much alike and may perhaps have formed a single population during an earlier stage of the lake's history.

Metriaclima chrysomallos, originally described from the population at Mumbo Island (Stauffer *et al.*, 1997), also occurs at Nakantenga Island and on the east coast between Makanjila Point and Meponda. It was previously known, depending on the population concerned, as *Pseudotropheus* sp. 'zebra masinje' and *P.* sp. 'zebra mozambique".

Metriaclima sp. 'blue reef' has been mentioned earlier (page 60) in association with *M. estherae*. Its behavior resembles that of *M. aurora*—and I believe it should be placed in that group—but females are light blue, quite a divergence from all other *aurora*-group cichlids. It has a rather limited distribution, although it can be found in huge plankton-feeding schools, and is found only at Minos and Nkhungu reefs.

A shallow reef in the southeastern arm of the lake, locally known as Mazinzi, harbors yet another *aurora*-group species, *Metriaclima benetos*. The females are brown with yellow-orange unpaired fins and thus fit the "diagnosis" for the *aurora* group. Males are light blue without bars and are characterized by a black interorbital bar. Some males have a yellow throat.

The Lumessi River in Mozambique is a permanent watercourse (i.e. one that does not dry up seasonally), but unlike most other rivers around the lake does not carry muddy or gritty

1. *Metriaclima* sp. 'black dorsal mbenji' ♂ Mbenji Island

2. *Metriaclima aurora* ♂ Thumbi West Island

3. *Metriaclima* sp. 'aurora bevous' ♂ Chizumulu Island

4. *Metriaclima* sp. 'aurora north' ♂ Magunga

5. *Metriaclima* sp. 'black dorsal mbenji' ♀ Mbenji Island

6. *Metriaclima aurora* ♂ Mbweca

7. *Metriaclima aurora* ♀ Yofu Bay (Likoma)

8. *Metriaclima* sp. 'aurora bevous' ♀ Chizumulu Island

9. *Metriaclima* sp. 'aurora lumbaulo' ♂ Lumbaulo

10. *Metriaclima* sp. 'aurora north' ♀ Magunga

1. *Metriaclima* sp. 'aurora blue' ♂ Cobwé
2. *Metriaclima* sp. 'aurora blue' ♀ Cobwé
8. *Metriaclima* sp. 'aurora blue' ♂ Kanjindo Rocks

3. *Metriaclima chrysomallos* ♂ Border
9. *Metriaclima chrysomallos* ♂ Mumbo Island

4. *Metriaclima chrysomallos* ♀ Ntekete
10. *Metriaclima chrysomallos* ♂ Nametumbwe

5. *Metriaclima chrysomallos* ♂ Gome
6. *Metriaclima* sp. 'blue reef' ♀ Nkhungu Reef
11. *Metriaclima* sp. 'blue reef' ♂ Nkhungu Reef

7. *Metriaclima benetos* ♀ Mazinzi Reef
12. *Metriaclima benetos* ♂ Mazinzi Reef

sediment in large enough quantities to form sandbanks at its mouth. The rocky coast north and south of the Lumessi is steep and the influence of the river water, which usually has a completely different chemistry to that of the lake, may therefore be restricted to a narrow section of coast. However, this river does appear to form a barrier in the distribution of certain cichlids, including two species of the *aurora* group: *Metriaclima* sp. 'aurora chinuni' and *Metriaclima* sp. 'aurora black tail'. The intermediate habitat along the shore immediately north of the river is home to *M.* sp. 'aurora chinuni' while the shore immediately south of it harbors *M.* sp. 'aurora black tail'. The coast south of the river is very rocky and steep, and only at a tiny (seasonal) river outlet a few kilometers south of the Lumessi do some intermediate habitats occur. Further to the north of Chinuni, a beautiful natural bay north of the Lumessi, we find another species of the *aurora* group: *Metriaclima* sp. 'aurora yellow'. Females of all three species are light brown with yellowish fins and are indistinguishable from each other when observed underwater.

Metriaclima hajomaylandi is endemic to Chizumulu Island and is popular among hobbyists. This species was formerly exported as "Pseudotropheus Greberi", named after one of exporter Davies's divers. It is seen more often among rocks and at deeper levels than those at which *M. aurora* is usually found. Females have bright yellow fins. Males of some populations have black markings in the dorsal fin, e.g. at Chiwi Rocks.

A species with a remarkable resemblance in size and coloration to *M. hajomaylandi* is found at Pombo Reef and Ndumbi Point in Tanzania. This species, *Metriaclima* sp. 'hajomaylandi pombo', inhabits the deepest parts of the rather shallow reefs between Lundu and the Ruhuhu River delta. These rocky reefs meet the sand at a depth of about seven meters and it is only in this restricted intermediate zone that *M.* sp. 'hajomaylandi pombo' makes its home. Females are brown-beige and lack the bright yellow in the fins seen in those of *M. hajomaylandi*, and resemble those of *M.* sp. 'black dorsal lundo' (see page 175) at Lundo Island.

Metriaclima barlowi is also assigned to the *aurora* group and has the widest distribution of all its members. It is found in the southern part of the lake at the Mbenji and Maleri islands, at Chidunga Rocks (Chipoka), around the Nankumba Peninsula (where it is relatively rare), and at Chimwalani and Luwala reefs. Ribbink and his co-workers (1983b) found a single individual of this species at Thumbi West Island, where the species may have been introduced by an exporter of aquarium fishes, but unable to establish itself. Another explanation could be that *M. barlowi* originally had a much wider distribution in the southern part of the lake, and that mainland (and near-mainland, such as Thumbi West) populations subsequently experienced heavier competition than those at isolated islands. *M. barlowi* is popular among aquarists and is sometimes known by the trade names "Pseudotropheus Fusco" and "Yellow Zebra". Males are rather aggressive in their territorial defense, especially at the Maleri and Mbenji islands where this species is very common and intraspecific encounters are frequently seen.

The kingsizei group

This group combines all the small species of zebra-like mbuna of the intermediate habitat that quite often feed on plankton as well as aufwuchs.

A few years ago Tawil (2002b) described the species from Likoma Island previously known as *Pseudotropheus* sp. 'kingsizei' as *Cynotilapia pulpican*, stating that he believed that *Cynotilapia* is a group that can contain, besides the *C. afra*-like cichlids, zebra-like cichlids as well. While I concur with him that the shape of teeth should not be the sole character on which the diagnosis of a genus is based, in my opinion the exact way a species feeds from the same or a very similar food source gives an indication of its relationship with other, closely-related species, much more so than coloration or tooth morphology. In analogy, a species' breeding behavior may likewise give clues to its descent. Accordingly, in my view this species should be assigned to *Metriaclima*, as although it often feeds from the plankton in the water column, at other times it feeds like a *Metriaclima*, raking the loose aufwuchs from the rocks.

Metriaclima pulpican is found along the east coast of Likoma Island, between Maingano and Mbuzi Island, and between Londo and Ntumba along the Mozambique shore. The latter populations were previously referred to as *Pseudotropheus* sp. 'kingsizei londo' but are now regarded as geographical variants of *M. pulpican*. Despite its trade name it has a maximum size of about 7.5 cm. Females are light brown and have yellowish fins.

Male *M. pulpican* aggressively defend their spawning sites, which are holes dug in the sand beneath a rock. Importantly, the male refrains from browsing the aufwuchs right above the entrance to this spawning cave. The intention appears to be to lure ripe females close to the male's den. The tenant male will allow a prospecting female to browse from the lush aufwuchs above his cave, but not for long. If she shows no interest in anything more than feeding from his rich table, the male will immediately chase her away.

The informal name "Kingsizei", used for this species before it was officially described, referred to the nickname, Kingsize, of a small but energetic diver working for one of the exporters. The name has also been used for another mbuna, *Cynotilapia axelrodi* (page 192), but confusion with this species is likely to be restricted to the name as the two can be easily told apart.

At the islet of Masimbwe, south of Likoma Island, a mbuna with a close affinity to *M. pulpican* occurs in the intermediate habitat. This species, *Metriaclima* sp. 'kingsizei masimbwe", is distinctly larger than *M. pulpican* and its females are rather dark blue-brown with a black band in the anal fin. *M.* sp. 'kingsizei masimbwe' appears to browse more often from the aufwuchs than *M. pulpican* at Maingano, but is still found feeding on plankton in the water column.

A kingsizei-like mbuna with a resemblance to the species found at Likoma is found along the Tanzanian shore between Lupingu and Cape Kaiser. This species, called *Metriaclima* sp. 'kingsizei lupingu', is rather common in its limited distribution. Between the range of *M.* sp. 'kingsizei lupingu' and that of the most northerly *Metriaclima* of the intermediate habitat, *M.* sp. 'aurora north' (page 177), lies a sandy bay, the northern bay of Lupingu. I have been unable to find *M.* sp. 'aurora north' anywhere in the distribution of *M.* sp. 'kingsizei lupingu', even though it occurs north of Lupingu along the entire northeastern shore to Matema and is also found south of Cape Kaiser as far as Manda. In the southern section of its distribution it is accompanied by a small species with close resemblance to *M.* sp. 'kingsizei lupingu' but which appears to be a member of *Cynotilapia*, *C.* sp. 'lion' (page 192). It is likely that *C.* sp. 'lion' and *M.* sp. 'kingsizei lupingu' are closely related—near Cape Kaiser the coloration of male *M.* sp. 'kingsizei lupingu' is indistinguishable from that of male *C.* sp. 'lion' further south; only the structure of their teeth can tell them apart. *M.* sp. 'kingsizei lupingu' could have switched to feeding on aufwuchs due to the absence of a more efficient aufwuchs comber, i.e. *M.* sp. 'aurora north' at Lupingu (Mary Bailey, pers. comm.).

The populations of *M.* sp. 'kingsizei lupingu' exhibit polymorphism in male breeding coloration. Some are light blue and others completely orange, with intermediates present as well. The orange males have been selectively collected and exported as "Pseudotropheus Solid Orange". At the head of the central bay at Lupingu most males are light blue and only a few orange-yellow individuals are seen, but between the southern bay and Cape Kaiser there are some populations with predominantly orange males and only small numbers of blue ones. At Cape Kaiser males have a light blue back and a yellow abdomen. Another interesting feature of this small mbuna is that most populations are very dense, with females and non-territorial males schooling in mid-water while feeding on plankton.

With its small and stocky shape, *Metriaclima* sp. 'dumpy' resembles *Cynotilapia* sp. 'lion', not only in color pattern but also in behavior. Ribbink *et al.* (1983b) found this small mbuna at Maleri and Nakantenga islands, at depths ranging between 13 and 28 meters. It lives in

1. *Metriaclima* sp. 'aurora blacktail' ♂ Chiloelo

6. *Metriaclima* sp. 'aurora chinuni' ♂ Chinuni

2. *Metriaclima* sp. 'aurora yellow' ♂ Lumessi

7. *Metriaclima* sp. 'aurora chinuni' ♀ Chinuni

3. *Metriaclima barlowi* ♂ Mbenji Island

8. *Metriaclima* sp. 'aurora blacktail' ♀ Chiloelo

4. *Metriaclima hajomaylandi* ♂ Chizumulu Island

9. *Metriaclima* sp. 'aurora yellow' ♀ Lumessi

10. *Metriaclima barlowi* ♀ Chimwalani Reef

11. *Metriaclima hajomaylandi* ♀ Chizumulu Island

5. *Metriaclima* sp. 'hajomaylandi pombo' ♂ Pombo Rocks

12. *Metriaclima* sp. 'hajomaylandi pombo' ♀ Pombo Rocks

1. *Metriaclima pulpican* ♀ Maingano Island

7. *Metriaclima pulpican* ♂ Maingano Island

2. *Metriaclima pulpican* ♂ Lumbaulo

3. *Metriaclima* sp. 'kingsizei masimbwe' ♀ Masimbwe

8. *Metriaclima* sp. 'kingsizei masimbwe' ♂ Masimbwe

4. *Metriaclima* sp. 'kingsizei lupingu' ♀ Lupingu

5. *Metriaclima* sp. 'kingsizei lupingu' ♂ Lupingu

9. *Metriaclima* sp. 'kingsizei lupingu' ♂ Lupingu

6. *Metriaclima* sp. 'kingsizei lupingu' ♂ Lupingu

10. *Metriaclima* sp. 'kingsizei lupingu' ♂ Lupingu

rather deep regions where the substrate (widely scattered small rocks on sand) is covered with a thick layer of muddy sediment. Males defend their territories—centered on a spawning cave, a tunnel dug under rocks—against all intruders. In most areas where we find *M.* sp. 'dumpy' we do not usually find many other mbuna species, so there is, in fact, not much competition for spawning sites. When the rocks in the habitat are completely covered with sediment *M.* sp. 'dumpy' feeds only from the plankton, but remains close to the substrate while doing so. A similar species—previously regarded as a population of *M.* sp. 'dumpy'—occurs along the southeastern shore of the lake between Makanjila Point and Meponda, but this form, *Cynotilapia* sp. 'lion ntekete', has unicuspid teeth (see discussion page 192).

It cannot be denied that *M.* sp. 'dumpy' closely resembles *C.* sp. 'lion ntekete' in shape and behavior. In analogy to the situation discussed on page 181 regarding *C.* sp. 'lion' and *M.* sp. 'kingsizei lupingu', *M.* sp. 'dumpy' may have developed its bicuspid teeth in response to the availability of aufwuchs and paucity of large algae browsers at the Maleri islands. Along the western side of the lake the shore drops to deeper levels rather gradually while this is not the case along the eastern side of the lake; here the shores are steep and water deeper than 100 meters is usually found within 500 meters of the shoreline. The visibility and light penetration is much greater along the eastern shore and one can expect more algal growth on rocks at depths beyond 15 meters. So the likelihood that a small, non-aggressive and deep-living mbuna will have to contend with competitors for food is greater along the eastern shore. There the aufwuchs on the rocks at a depth of 15-20 meters may be sufficient for a larger, more aggressive mbuna, e.g. *M. chrysomallos* (page 177), to survive. This may have prevented *C.* sp. 'lion ntekete' from competing with the other mbuna browsing from the aufwuchs on the rocks and restricting its diet to the plankton in the water column. By the same token the visibility around the Maleri islands is never very good and very few algae-raking mbuna are found deeper than 10 meters.

Thus a small, non-aggressive cichlid—*M.* sp. 'dumpy'—might be able to find enough nutriment from this food source due to a lack of competitors.

At several places in Tanzanian waters another very small mbuna inhabits the same biotope: *Metriaclima* sp. 'dumpy tanzania'. This species from the northern part of the lake exhibits similar behavior to that of *M.* sp. 'dumpy'. Because of the enormous distance between the ranges of these two forms I regard them as distinct species. *M.* sp. 'dumpy tanzania' occurs at Lupingu and Manda, both locations north of the Ruhuhu River, and has also been recorded from Puulu Island, near Liuli (as *Pseudotropheus* "Zebra Dwarf Tanzania"; Spreinat, 1994). The sandy intermediate habitats in Tanzania are not as sediment-rich as those on the Malaŵi side of the lake. *Metriaclima* sp. 'dumpy tanzania' is found near small heaps of stones lying scattered on the vast sandy bottom at depths of more than 25 meters. Some territorial males have been seen feeding from the biocover on the few rocks or even from the sand, but most individuals feed from the plankton, remaining within 30 cm of the bottom.

The northwestern coast harbors several species which I have assigned to the kingsizei group because they are small, elongate species preferring the more sediment-free and rocky parts of the intermediate habitat. One of them, *Metriaclima* sp. 'zebra ruarwe', is found from Mphanga Rocks to Ruarwe. Females are gray brown and have the same black markings in the fins as males.

Metriaclima sp. 'zebra mbowe', at one time considered a geographical variant of *M.* sp. 'zebra ruarwe' (Konings, 1990: 377), is here regarded as a distinct species of the kingsizei group, as I have been unable to find any population intermediate between the small, all-blue *M.* sp. 'zebra ruarwe' and the larger, yellow and blue *M.* sp. 'zebra mbowe'. There is no noticeable difference in behavior. A third species found on the northwestern coast, *Metriaclima* sp. 'zebra long pelvic', closely resembles *M.* sp. 'zebra mbowe', and in this case too I have been unable to locate any intermediate populations between the two species. *M.* sp. 'zebra long pelvic' occurs in the intermediate habitats at Ngara, Mdoka, and Chesese. Males of the Ngara population have a bright orange dorsal fin, whereas in those of the other two populations the fin is light blue. It is a very common mbuna within its range, but at Chewere, a few kilometers south of Chesese, its preferred niche seems to be occupied by *Metriaclima* sp. 'elongatus chewere' (see page 188), and *M.* sp. 'zebra long pelvic' (or a corresponding form) is completely absent.

Gallireya Reef in Youngs Bay is nowhere deeper than about 12 meters. The structure of the habitat is rather uncommon: strangely-formed rocks lie scattered on the lake bottom. It looks like they are of volcanic origin and are blocks of suddenly solidified lava. Almost all the rock-dwelling mbuna at this reef appear endemic to the area. One of them, exported as "Gallileo Red Top", behaves like a *Cynotilapia afra*, and for some time I was fairly certain that this was a local *afra* variant until I had a closer look at my photos. These revealed that the teeth of this attractive fish are bicuspid and for that reason it cannot be a member of *Cynotilapia*. I now believe it is a variant of *M.* sp. 'zebra long pelvic' or a closely related new species. *M.* sp. 'zebra long pelvic' is more elongate and has a whitish dorsal fin (apart from the Ngara population), while the form at Gallireya Reef is short and stocky with an orange dorsal—quite an attractive fish. For the time being I will call this mbuna *Metriaclima* sp. 'red top gallireya' (previously termed *M.* sp. 'zebra long pelvic hara') (Konings, 2004a)). Females of this species are dark brown-blue with a white submarginal band in the dorsal and orange tips to the lappets. *M.* sp. 'red top gallireya' is common in the rockier areas of the reef.

Odd-men-out

Five species cannot be convincingly grouped with any of the above and are discussed together here although they do not seem to be related to one other.

Metriaclima sp. 'patricki' is found along the southwestern shores of the lake. The species is named after the late Patrick Karonga, one of Stuart Grant's best fishermen. It occurs at Chidunga Rocks (Chipoka), the Maleri islands, Namalenje Island, the Mbenji islands, Nkhomo Reef, and Jalo Reef, near Nkhotakota. A few populations with a distinct coloration are known. That at the Mbenji islands is exploited for the aquarium trade. The "Patricki" may be an intermediate between a true sand-dwelling mbuna, such as *Pseudotropheus livingstonii* (formerly *Metriaclima*; page 305), and a rock-dwelling mbuna. An important difference from the sand-dwelling mbuna is its permanently territorial behavior, such as is common in most mbuna. Males in breeding dress are seen throughout the year and each excavates a hole beneath one of the scattered stones of the habitat. This is one of the few mbuna sometimes encountered over pure sand. It feeds from the aufwuchs on rocky and sandy substrates.

At Mbenji another species, *Metriaclima lombardoi*, is found together with *M.* sp. 'patricki' and *M. barlowi* in the sediment-rich and intermediate habitats. *M. lombardoi*, however, seems to be more restricted to the rocky part of the biotope, with its highest population density at a depth of approximately 10 meters.

M. lombardoi enjoys widespread popularity among aquarists and is one of the mbuna most frequently shipped from the lake. An unusual feature of this species is that males are yellow and females blue (barred). Blue females are found in some other species too (e.g. *M. callainos* ("Cobalt Zebra") and *M.* sp. 'blue reef' from Mozambique), but the combination of blue females and yellow males is unique to *M. lombardoi*. Before its formal description this mbuna was given several names in the aquarium hobby. The first was "Golden Zebra" followed in the USA by "Pseudotropheus Kenyi" and in Europe by "P. Lilancinius". Its distribution is not restricted to Mbenji alone, as it is encountered at Nkhomo Reef as well. According to Stuart Grant (pers. comm.) this latter population has a somewhat less intense coloration after it has been captured. Underwater observations, however, reveal no difference between the two populations. The reversed coloration can be regarded as unusual for mbuna, and furthermore, in captivity, it frequently hap-

1. *Metriaclima* sp. 'dumpy' ♂ Maleri Island

2. *Metriaclima* sp. 'zebra ruarwe' ♂ Hora Mhango

3. *Metriaclima* sp. 'zebra long pelvic' ♂ Mdoka

4. *Metriaclima* sp. 'zebra mbowe' ♂ Mbowe Island

5. *Metriaclima* sp. 'dumpy tanzania' ♂ Manda

6. *Metriaclima* sp. 'dumpy' ♀ Maleri Island

7. *Metriaclima* sp. 'zebra ruarwe' Ruarwe

8. *Metriaclima* sp. 'zebra ruarwe' ♂ Ruarwe

9. *Metriaclima* sp. 'zebra long pelvic' ♀ Mdoka

10. *Metriaclima* sp. 'zebra mbowe' ♀ Mbowe Island

1. *Metriaclima* sp. 'red top gallireya' ♂ Gallireya Reef (Hara)

2. *Metriaclima* sp. 'red top gallireya' ♀ Gallireya Reef

3. *Metriaclima* sp. 'patricki' ♀ Mbenji Island

4. *Metriaclima* sp. 'patricki' ♂ Jalo Reef

5. *Metriaclima lombardoi* ♀ Mbenji Island

6. *Metriaclima* sp. 'patricki' ♂ Chidunga Rocks

7. *Metriaclima lombardoi* ♂ Mbenji Island

pens that the offspring of normally colored parents include females that are initially blue but develop yellow coloration, and these are fertile (pers. obs.; Mary Bailey, pers. comm.). Occasionally, mouthbrooding females are observed in the wild which have (partly) adopted male territorial coloration (i.e. yellow). This apparently signals to other fishes the aggressive nature of their brood-defending behavior.

Another "odd-man-out", *Metriaclima* sp. 'aggressive grey head' (previously assigned to *Pseudotropheus*) occurs in large numbers around the three Maleri islands. Males and females have more or less the same color pattern. I have been unable to assign this species to any of the many mbuna groups within *Metriaclima*. The yellow color on the head varies within the population and appears to be most prominent in individuals from sediment-rich environments.

At Likoma Island several species of *Metriaclima* inhabit the intermediate habitat, and it would appear that this island harbors some older species, some of which have a very restricted distribution. One of these species, *Metriaclima* sp. 'membe deep', is small with unusually colored males (resembling those of an unrelated species, *Pseudotropheus* sp. 'polit'; see page 100) and dark yellow females. Its distribution is restricted to the northeastern coast of Likoma Island, between Membe Point and Maingano, where it occurs in the sediment-rich intermediate habitat at depths between 15 and 30 meters. Males of this attractive species feed predominantly from the aufwuchs while females feed on plankton as well. As in *P.* sp. 'polit' at Lion's Cove (see photo page 99), males can rapidly change their black and light blue coloration to a drab gray-blue. Although *M.* sp. 'membe deep' is an attractive species it has never been exported in numbers. The reason is probably twofold: a low population density and the depth at which it lives.

The fifth species is *Metriaclima* sp. 'mbweca'. This species occurs in the intermediate habitats at Mbweca, Mala Point, and Cobwé—all three localities in Mozambique—at a depth of approximately 10-25 meters. It was previously thought that this species was a member of *Cynotilapia*, but since I have seen it browsing the aufwuchs in the way zebras do, and since it has bicuspid teeth, it is now placed in *Metriaclima*. Male *M.* sp. 'mbweca' hover about 50 cm above their spawning cave while feeding on plankton. Females gather in schools of up to 50 individuals and remain very close to the territorial males. The color pattern of males is very dark and shows few markings apart from a copper to gold patch on the head behind the eyes. Females are also very dark but lack the golden color.

The elongate *Metriaclima*

The various species discussed in this section were previously assigned to the *Pseudotropheus elongatus* complex (Ribbink et al., 1983b). This group has, however, now been in part split up (Konings & Stauffer, 2006; see page 24) and a number of the species placed in *Metriaclima* because of their skull morphology and feeding technique.

Near the small fishing village of Chewere (Malaŵi), at a small reef no larger than a soccer field, there is a dense population of *Metriaclima* sp. 'elongatus chewere'. Females and non-territorial males gather in large foraging schools in mid-water about one to four meters above the substrate. The highest population density is found at the transition zone between rocks and sand at a depth of about 16 meters. Territorial males defend their spawning holes, some of them only about 50 cm apart, against all intruders. Most holes are dug beneath a rock or are sited on the sand between two adjacent rocks.

M sp. 'elongatus chewere' is rather different in appearance to the yellow-black barred *Metriaclima* sp. 'elongatus chailosi' at Chitande Island, only 10 km further south. I have been unable to find similar habitats between these two localities that could possibly harbor intermediate forms. These two species are apparently so restricted to their particular localities that 10 km of open sand is sufficient to maintain such a profound difference between them.

Metriaclima sp. 'elongatus bee' resembles *M.*

sp. 'elongatus chailosi' more than it does *M.* sp. 'elongatus chewere', but nevertheless I regard this species as equally distinct. Its distribution extends from Chilumba to the southern tip of Chirwa Island and is separated from that of *M.* sp. 'elongatus chailosi' by Chilumba Bay. *M.* sp. 'elongatus bee' has a deeper body than the preceding two species, and to some extent resembles *Cynotilapia* sp. 'lion' (see page 192) in both shape and coloration.

A yellow-brown elongate mbuna, *Metriaclima* sp. 'elongatus usisya', is found at Usisya and Mara Rocks. Even though it occurs in a sediment-rich environment, it feeds from the sediment-free biocover beneath or on the vertical sides of large rocks. Stomach contents inventories have revealed a predominance of loose aufwuchs, but plankton is also consumed in large quantities (Ribbink *et al.*, 1983b). Females are dark brown with a thin blue stripe between the eyes.

The sediment-rich intermediate biotopes around Likoma and Chizumulu Islands are inhabited by *Metriaclima* sp. 'elongatus gold bar'. Males of this attractive species defend small territories, normally in shallow water. The variant at Chizumulu Island is darker and exhibits less golden yellow than the variant found on the west coast of Likoma. This species has not been exported in large numbers but its small size (maximum about 10 cm TL) and attractive coloration would make it a good aquarium resident.

At Chidunga Rocks near Chipoka, in the southern part of the lake, *Metriaclima* sp. 'elongatus chidunga' occupies a niche which it would probably decline given the option of living in a rockier environment. *M.* sp. 'elongatus chidunga' feeds from the aufwuchs on the rocks. Territorial males dig tunnels under or between rocks and remain very close to the substrate.

The lime group

The intermediate habitat along the northeastern shores of the lake also harbors elongate species but these are placed another group, the *Metriaclima* sp. 'lime' group. The members of this group have bicuspid teeth, but a morphology and behavior similar to the conical-toothed *Cynotilapia axelrodi* and *C.* sp. 'lion'. The morphology of the skull and the bicuspid teeth make these species members of *Metriaclima* although they are not closely related to the zebras that were originally the only members of this genus. One of these, *Metriaclima* sp. 'daktari', became a popular aquarium fish as soon as it was exported from Tanzanian waters. *M.* sp. 'daktari' is closely related to *Metriaclima* sp. 'lime' and *Metriaclima* sp. 'lime nkhomo'. Males of all three species have similar color patterns and two geographical races of each species are known.

M. sp. 'daktari' occurs at Undu and Hai reefs in Tanzania and at Chiwindi and Liutche in Mozambique. The populations in Tanzania are indistinguishable, with males being completely yellow. In Mozambique males have a blue sheen on a light yellow body. At Membe Point, Likoma Island, males of *M.* sp. 'lime' are almost indistinguishable from those of the Tanzanian "Daktari", but at Mbamba Island, a few kilometers south of Membe Point, males are light blue. The females of *M.* sp. 'lime' are silvery beige with a yellow dorsal fin. Female *M.* sp. 'daktari' are beige in Tanzania and yellowish in Mozambique. Both the "Lime" and the "Daktari" live at depths ranging between five and 15 meters.

At Nkhomo Reef, near Benga, *M.* sp. 'lime nkhomo' inhabits the sandy intermediate habitat at somewhat deeper levels (15-25 meters) than the previous two species. It is also found at the Mbenji islands where males are a brighter yellow.

A species with a slightly different color pattern inhabits the intermediate habitat at Jalo Reef. Males of this species, *Metriaclima* sp. 'lime jalo', have very little yellow and are light blue-gray with a dark-colored tail. Females have a similar pattern but are a lighter color. Males behave aggressively towards conspecifics, but I haven't seen one with a spawning cave. The species is quite rare and most individuals are solitary.

1. *Metriaclima* sp. 'aggressive greyhead' ♂ Nakantenga Island

2. *Metriaclima* sp. 'membe deep' ♂ Maingano Island

3. *Metriaclima* sp. 'mbweca' ♂ Mbweca

4. *Metriaclima* sp. 'elongatus chailosi' ♂ Chitande Island

5. *Metriaclima* sp. 'elongatus bee' ♂ Katale Island

6. *Metriaclima* sp. 'aggressive greyhead' ♀ Nakantenga Island

7. *Metriaclima* sp. 'membe deep' ♀ Membe Point (Likoma)

8. *Metriaclima* sp. 'mbweca' ♀ Mbweca

9. *Metriaclima* sp. 'elongatus chewere' ♀ Chitande Island

10. *Metriaclima* sp. 'elongatus chewere' ♂ Chitande Island

11. *Metriaclima* sp. 'elongatus chailosi' ♀ Chitande Island

12. *Metriaclima* sp. 'elongatus bee' ♀ Katale Island

1. *Metriaclima* sp. 'elongatus usisya' ♀ Mara Rocks

2. *Metriaclima* sp. 'elongatus chidunga' ♂ Chidunga Rocks

3. *Metriaclima* sp. 'elongatus goldbar' ♀ Same (Chizumulu)

4. *Metriaclima* sp. 'lime' ♀ Membe Point (Likoma)

5. *Metriaclima* sp. 'lime' ♂ Mbamba Island (Likoma)

6. *Metriaclima* sp. 'lime jalo' ♂ Jalo Reef

7. *Metriaclima* sp. 'daktari' ♂ Undu

8. *Metriaclima* sp. 'elongatus usisya' ♂ Tchinga Reef

9. *Metriaclima* sp. 'elongatus goldbar' ♂ Same (Chizumulu)

10. *Metriaclima* sp. 'lime' ♂ Membe Point (Likoma)

11. *Metriaclima* sp. 'lime nkhomo' ♂ Mbenji Island

12. *Metriaclima* sp. 'daktari' ♂ Chiwindi

Cynotilapia

Cynotilapia axelrodi is found from Lion's Cove to Mundola Point, south of Nkhata Bay. It has been regularly exported from Nkhata Bay under the trade name "Pseudotropheus Kingsizei", not to be confused with *Metriaclima pulpican*, the "Kingsizei" from Likoma Island (see page 183). Although it is found sympatrically with *C.* sp. 'lion' it is more frequently seen over sand away from rocks (Ribbink *et al.*, 1983b).

Cynotilapia sp. 'lion' has a widespread distribution and is also found along the eastern shores of the lake between Ngwazi and Lundu. Along the western shore it occurs between Mara Rocks and Chadagha. Males at Sanga have a golden yellow ground color while those at most other localities are blue on the upper body. The populations of *C.* sp. 'lion' along the Tanzanian shore are rather homogeneous in male coloration, and show little geographical variation throughout this part of the range.

Male *C.* sp. 'lion' stake out their territories on the open sand (or mud) floor. The center of each male's domain is a group of two to five small rocks under which he digs his spawning cave. Most of the time the resident male hovers about 30 cm above his territory while feeding on plankton. Individuals in the populations along the eastern shores seem to prefer a rockier habitat to those of the western. The fact that all habitats on the northeastern shores are far less sediment-rich than those on the western side may obscure the true preference of this species.

Cynotilapia sp. 'lion' and *C. axelrodi* have unicuspid (conical) teeth in the outer row of the jaws and are thus assigned to *Cynotilapia*. In behavior and habitat preference they are similar to several other species from the sandy intermediate habitat, and differ in these respects from other *Cynotilapia*. Some species with bicuspid teeth (e.g. *Metriaclima* sp. 'elongatus bee') are strikingly similar to these *Cynotilapia*, but unicuspid teeth are rare among mbuna, so the obvious course, given our present knowledge, is to assign these two species to *Cynotilapia*.

Cynotilapia sp. 'lion ntekete' is another small mbuna with a resemblance to *C.* sp. 'lion'. Some populations of this species, those near Ntekete, were previously regarded as a population of *Metriaclima* sp. 'dumpy' (Konings, 2001: 167, as *Pseudotropheus* sp. 'dumpy'), while a small population consisting of all-yellow males at Liwani was previously considered a separate species: *Pseudotropheus* sp. 'dwarf gold' (Konings, 2001: 162). *C.* sp. 'lion ntekete' occurs from Meponda to Makanjila Point and the male's coloration seems to vary with each population. It inhabits the deeper regions of the intermediate habitat and is rarely found in water shallower than 10 meters. Females are light brown and exhibit some faint vertical barring.

In Chitimba Bay, at a very sandy intermediate habitat (with too few rocks to justify the name of reef) at a depth of approximately 22 meters, I found an attractive elongate mbuna: *Cynotilapia* sp. 'elongatus chitimba', which was previously grouped in the *Pseudotropheus elongatus* complex but turns out to possess unicuspid teeth. The habitat is about 3 km offshore and isolated from nearby rocky shores by open sand. Such isolated intermediate habitats may form sanctuaries for any species that chance to arrive (or have survived) there.

One of the more common mbuna present at Gallireya Reef is *Cynotilapia* sp. 'hara'. Males as well as females are bright blue. Territorial males have a pattern of black bars, some of which sometimes extend into the dorsal fin. Bars extending into the dorsal is a character often found in *Cynotilapia afra* and this is probably the reason that this species has received the trade name of "Gallileo (=Gallireya) Blue Afra". The teeth of this species are unicuspid and it is clearly a member of *Cynotilapia*. Usually I am able to distinguish *afra*-like species by their behavior in the wild. *Cynotilapia* feed from the plankton in the water column and in addition males hover above their spawning caves picking at particles in the water. *C.* sp. 'hara' does not exhibit this kind of behavior. Both male and female remain near the substrate, even when they are picking at particles in the water column. I believe this species is not closely related to *C. afra* although most populations of the latter species also have blue-colored females. Another character that is unlike *C. afra* is the long pelvic fins of males. This is a very attractive fish with cobalt-blue colored juveniles.

Petrotilapia

In Chitimba Bay, south of Chilumba, at a depth of about 22 meters, there is a meager array of flat stones widely scattered on the sandy bottom. This provides habitat for just a few mbuna species, among them *Petrotilapia* sp. 'chitimba'. *Petrotilapia* can readily be classified into three different groups: the *tridentiger* group, the *nigra* group, and the *genalutea* group (see page 33). On the basis of its markings (no black band in the dorsal) it might be thought that *P.* sp. 'chitimba' probably belongs to the *tridentiger* group, but I believe that it has affinities with *P.* sp. 'ruarwe' (page 76). The population at Chitimba Reef is rather small and only small numbers have been used to establish an aquarium population. Females and juveniles have a very attractive pattern consisting of a few broad black bars. Territorial males are blue with yellow fins.

The *Petrotilapia* at Gallireya Reef is rather different from, but I believe closely related to, *P.* sp. 'chitimba'. Adult males are entirely yellow while females have a light brown background color with somewhat darker bars; these are clearly visible only when the female is mouthbrooding or in aggressive mood, otherwise the entire body is light brown. For the time being I regard this all-yellow *Petrotilapia* as a different species and refer to it as *Petrotilapia* sp. 'hara'.

Tropheops

The genus *Tropheops* is represented in the intermediate habitat by several species. As in most mbuna of this habitat, males excavate tunnels beneath rocks when their territories are situated on the sand. The growth of aufwuchs in the sediment-rich and intermediate biotopes is rather limited, and feeding cichlids cannot easily separate the indigestible detritus from the nutritious part of the biocover. *Tropheops* search for relatively sediment-free patches of biocover on the rocks.

In one species of this genus, *Tropheops romandi* (previously known as *Pseudotropheus* sp 'tropheops intermediate'), it is mainly territorial males that are found in the intermediate habitat. Females and juveniles, which are completely yellow, wander through all kinds of habitats and feed from the sediment-free algal mat (Ribbink *et al.*, 1983b).

Other species of *Tropheops* likewise occur in the intermediate zone—for example, *T.* sp. 'gracilior nankumba', *T. microstoma* at Cape Maclear (Otter Point to Masasa Reef), *T.* sp. 'boadzulu' (Boadzulu Island and Makokola Reef), and *T.* sp. 'mumbo' (endemic to Mumbo Island)—and most are regularly found in water deeper than 10 meters.

These species can be assigned to groups within the *Tropheops* genus, as discussed on page 25. *T. romandi*, *T.* sp. 'gracilior nankumba', and *T.* sp. 'mumbo' belong to the *romandi* group, whose members are characterized by a black band in the dorsal and narrow bars in females. *T. microstoma* and *T.* sp. 'boadzulu' are assigned to the so-called sand group, which includes those species with a pattern of broad vertical bars and found in sediment-rich sandy or intermediate habitats.

Tropheops romandi was described from Thumbi West Island, but is also found along the eastern side of the Nankumba Peninsula from Domwe Island to Nkhudzi, including the various reefs in between. DNA from specimens from Mazinzi Reef has been compared with that of Thumbi West Island individuals and found to be nearly identical (Michael Kidd, pers. comm.).

T. romandi closely resembles *Tropheops* sp. 'gracilior nankumba' (previously thought to be *T. gracilior*, a northern species of rocky environments (page 80)), but can be distinguished by female coloration. Females of *T. romandi* are yellow and those of *T.* sp. 'gracilior nankumba' are light beige with an orange-yellow anal fin. Males of some populations are much more difficult to tell apart. At Thumbi West and Mazinzi Reef male *T. romandi* have an overall dark blue coloration, while at the first of these localities male *T.* sp. 'gracilior nankumba' are blue-brown with a rusty orange color concentrated on the

1. *Cynotilapia* sp. 'lion' ♂ Lutara

7. *Cynotilapia* sp. 'lion ntekete' ♂ Liwani

2. *Cynotilapia* sp. 'lion' ♂ Sanga

6. *Cynotilapia* sp. 'lion' ♂ Lion's Cove

8. *Cynotilapia* sp. 'lion ntekete' ♂ Malopa

3. *Cynotilapia* sp. 'hara' ♂ Gallireya Reef (Hara)

9. *Cynotilapia axelrodi* ♂ Nkhata Bay

10. *Cynotilapia* sp. 'hara' ♀ Gallireya Reef

4. *Cynotilapia* sp. 'elongatus chitimba' ♂ Chitimba Bay

11. *Petrotilapia* sp. 'hara' ♂ Gallireya Reef

5. *Petrotilapia* sp. 'chitimba' ♂ Chitimba Bay

12. *Petrotilapia* sp. 'chitimba' ♀ Chitimba Bay

1. *Tropheops romandi* ♀ Thumbi West Island

2. *Tropheops romandi* ♂ Thumbi West Island

3. *Tropheops romandi* ♀ Nkhudzi

4. *Tropheops* sp. 'gracilior nankumba' ♀ Nkhudzi

5. *Tropheops microstoma* ♀ Masasa Reef

6. *Tropheops* sp. 'mumbo' ♀ Mumbo Island

7. *Tropheops* sp. 'boadzulu' ♀ Boadzulu Island

8. *Tropheops romandi* ♂ Mazinzi Reef

9. *Tropheops* sp. 'gracilior nankumba' ♂ Domwe Island

10. *Tropheops microstoma* ♂ Masasa Reef

11. *Tropheops* sp. 'mumbo' ♂ Mumbo Island

12. *Tropheops* sp. 'boadzulu' ♂ Boadzulu Island

shoulders but in some males extending onto the rest of the body. *T.* sp. 'gracilior nankumba' has a slightly wider distribution—from Otter Point to Nkhudzi—but has not been found at Mazinzi Reef or any other reef deeper than five meters around Nankumba. At Tsano and Nkhudzi males of the two species are almost impossible to distinguish. Male *T. romandi* are normally found at deeper levels and are a very dark blue-brown; males of *T.* sp. 'gracilior nankumba' are also dark but have a little of the rusty orange color on the shoulders. Ribbink *et al.* (1983b) and all subsequent authors have been confused by the similarity of these two species and have stated that females of *T.* sp. 'gracilior nankumba' at the same locality may have two different color patterns, either gray-white or yellow. I have seen a yellow female of a *romandi*-type member of *Tropheops* at Mumbo Island, but I have never found a possible *T. romandi*-like male. The common *romandi*-type *Tropheops* at Mumbo Island, *Tropheops* sp. 'mumbo', is closely related to *T.* sp. 'gracilior nankumba'.

Tropheops sp. 'broad mouth' (double stripe group) occurs in the southern part of the lake. Its extensive distribution stretches from the southern tip of the lake to Minos Reef on the eastern shore and to Chia Lagoon on the western side of the lake, and it is also found around Mumbo Island. It is found mainly in shallow, sediment-rich environments, usually no deeper than 10 meters, but is nevertheless present at Mazinzi Reef. Males prefer to defend territories on a horizontal rocky surface but are found patrolling over sand as well. Spawning takes place, as usual, inside small caves, the availability of which is a prerequisite for the occupation of an area. This species is found primarily at places where the rocks are not heavily covered with thick layers of sediment. At sites where sediment does coat the biocover even females are found occupying feeding territories, presumably to ensure they get enough to eat. *T.* sp. 'broad mouth' is one of the most widely distributed species of the genus, possibly due to its habitat preference (or indifference). Males are distinguished from those of *Tropheops novemfasciatus* (also double stripe group), which is found sympatric in the southeastern arm of the lake, by having black bars on nape and shoulder, lacking in *T. novemfasciatus*. Females are much more difficult to tell apart as both have two horizontal rows of spots on the flanks, but those of *T. novemfasciatus* tend to blend more into lines than those of *T.* sp. 'broad mouth', which appear more as distinct dots.

Tropheops sp. 'yellow chin' (double stripe group) is a very common mbuna of the intermediate habitats at Likoma and Chizumulu Islands. At Likoma it is a species of shallow water, while at the southern part of Chizumulu it is frequently seen in the sediment-rich rocky biotope at greater depths as well. The range of *T.* sp. 'yellow chin' extends far beyond these two islands: the most northerly point of its distribution is Njambe in Tanzania and the most southerly Ntumba in Mozambique, possibly even as far south as Mala Point. Population densities vary considerably throughout this range, as does male breeding coloration. Females of almost all populations have a basic pigmentation pattern consisting of two horizontal rows of spots and no black band in the dorsal.

The status of the *Tropheops* at Cobwé and Mala Point is currently unclear, and it is here only tentatively assigned to *T.* sp. 'yellow chin'. The coloration of males agrees with that of the other members of the double stripe group but females lack the double row of spots and are very dark gray-brown, sometimes with a bar pattern visible. Male coloration within a single population varies from light blue with a yellow chin to completely yellow. Completely yellow males are more common in sediment-rich habitats.

As is commonly the case where sediment-free algae are not abundant, males of *T.* sp. 'yellow chin' defend their territories aggressively against all intruders. Females, however, are not territorial and forage alone.

Tropheops sp. 'mbenji yellow' and *Tropheops* sp. 'maleri yellow' are both members of the double stripe group and found in the intermediate habitat. *T.* sp. 'mbenji yellow' is endemic to the Mbenji islands while *T.* sp. 'maleri yellow' occurs around all three Maleri islands as well as at Namalenje Island, where it is the only representative of *Tropheops*. It is usually the case in areas with a paucity of species that the few present are found in a wider variety of habitats than at places with many species, especially those where there are more species of the same genus (or complex) present. For this reason it comes as no surprise that at Namalenje *T.* sp. 'maleri yellow' is found at all levels (from the surface, in the rocky habitat, to the deepest regions where rocks meet sand at a depth of about 12 meters), while it is restricted to the upper intermediate habitat around the Maleri islands, where four other species of *Tropheops* have been recorded.

At Mbenji there are two species of *Tropheops*, with *T.* sp. 'mbenji yellow' most frequently found in sediment-rich habitats while *T.* sp. 'mbenji blue' (see page 32) appears to prefer sediment-free, rocky environments.

A species with a very wide distribution, on both sides of the lake, is *Tropheops* sp. 'red fin' (*romandi* group). On the northwestern shore it occurs from Hora Mhango to Mara Rocks, and on the eastern coast from the Ruhuhu River in Tanzania to Lumbaulo in Mozambique. Although it is quite common at most localities within its distribution, it is never found in schools or large groups. Adult males are an overall orange-yellow to deep orange color; females and juveniles have a different but again very attractive coloration. The orange anal fin is responsible for the name, given to this species by Ribbink *et al.* (1983b). Male *T.* sp. 'red fin' are territorial but not very aggressive. Sometimes males defend spawning sites on the sand between rocks, and sometimes a shallow crater is dug alongside and/or under a rock (Knabe, 1994). *T.* sp. 'red fin' is a species of the deeper areas and rarely found in water shallower than 10 meters.

Around Likoma Island, and along the Mozambique coast between Mala Point and Tumbi Point, *Tropheops* sp. 'membe' (*romandi* group) occupies the same niche as *T.* sp. 'red fin' elsewhere. Females of the two species look very much alike except that those of *T.* sp. 'membe' lack a black submarginal band in the dorsal fin. Males at Mbweca (Mozambique) have a bright orange dorsal fin, but those at Tumbi Point are almost indistinguishable from those at Likoma. In all aspects of behavior *T.* sp. 'membe' resembles *T.* sp. 'red fin' from the more northerly regions of the lake. The population density of *T.* sp. 'membe' is higher than that of any known population of *T.* sp. 'red fin' and territorial males also occur at shallower levels—up to a depth of three meters at Likoma (Ribbink *et al.*, 1983b). *Tropheops* sp. 'membe' also occurs along the southeastern point of Thumbi West Island where it was introduced in the 1970s.

At Nkhata Bay *Tropheops* sp. 'deep' (sand group) shares the sediment-rich intermediate habitat with *Tropheops* sp. 'rust' (double stripe group). *T.* sp. 'deep' seems to be restricted to the rockier part of the habitat at a depth of 15 meters or more, while *T.* sp. 'rust' is also found in shallower water up to a depth of about five meters. Both species display territoriality but only towards conspecific males. Like all species of this genus they feed from the biocover by nibbling and jerking algae from the rocks, using characteristic twisting jerks of the body in order to dislodge filamentous algae.

The distribution of *T.* sp. 'rust' and *T.* sp. 'deep' includes the rocky shores between Nkhata Bay and Cape Manulo in Malaŵi. *Tropheops* sp. 'lucerna north' (page 269) has previously been confused with *T.* sp. 'rust' (Konings, 2001). These two species do resemble each other morphologically but not in feeding behavior and habitat preference. The former is found in very shallow water where it aggressively defends feeding territories.

Genner *et al.* (2004) first reported on *Tropheops* sp. 'orange head', a member of the sand group, found at Mphanga Rocks. It also occurs at Luwino and Maison reefs as well as around Katale Island. Most individuals occur in the deep intermediate habitat (deeper than 25 meters) at Mphanga Rocks and Maison Reef but occur in shallower water at Luwino and Katale. Females were frequently seen feeding from the sandy patches between rocks but several males were observed holding territories in the rocky habitat, jerking algae off the rock in a typical *Tropheops* fashion.

When I first visited Chitimba Reef I found

1. *Tropheops* sp. 'broadmouth' ♂ Mumbo Island

6. *Tropheops* sp. 'broadmouth' ♂ Minos Reef

7. *Tropheops* sp. 'broadmouth' ♀ Harbour Island

2. *Tropheops novemfasciatus* ♂ Mvunguti

8. *Tropheops novemfasciatus* ♀ Kanchedza Island

9. *Tropheops* sp. 'yellow chin' ♀ Londo

3. *Tropheops* sp. 'yellow chin' ♂ Londo

10. *Tropheops* sp. 'yellow chin' ♂ Linganjala Reef

4. *Tropheops* sp. 'mbenji yellow' ♂ Mbenji Island

11. *Tropheops* sp. 'mbenji yellow' ♀ Mbenji Island

5. *Tropheops* sp. 'maleri yellow' ♂ Maleri Island

12. *Tropheops* sp. 'maleri yellow' ♀ Nakantenga Island

1. *Tropheops* sp. 'red fin' ♂ Hora Mhango

2. *Tropheops* sp. 'red fin' ♀ Londo

3. *Tropheops* sp. 'membe' ♂ Yofu Bay (Likoma)

4. *Tropheops* sp. 'membe' ♀ Yofu Bay (Likoma)

5. *Tropheops* sp. 'deep' ♀ Nkhata Bay

6. *Tropheops* sp. 'rust' ♀ Lion's Cove

7. *Tropheops* sp. 'orange head' ♀ Maison Reef

8. *Tropheops* sp. 'red fin' ♂ Mesuli

9. *Tropheops* sp. 'membe' ♂ Mbweca

10. *Tropheops* sp. 'deep' ♂ Nkhata Bay

11. *Tropheops* sp. 'rust' ♂ Lion's Cove

12. *Tropheops* sp. 'orange head' ♂ Mphanga Reef

what I thought were two different members of the genus *Tropheops*. I noticed yellow, mouth-brooding females and yellow, territorial males, and territorial males that were partly yellow (on the head) but with a blue body. I was unable to discern a female partner for the latter and I regarded this male as a geographical variant of *Tropheops* sp. 'weed' (Konings, 1995b). The yellow form I called *T.* sp. 'macrophthalmus chitimba'. When I visited Chitimba Reef again I established that blue-yellow *Tropheops* courted yellow females. I couldn't see any difference between these females and those of the all-yellow males and thought that the blue-yellow males were more mature males of the same species. The blue-yellow males behaved more aggressively, it seemed, but there were less of them than the all-yellow males, which were territorial as well. So I regarded the blue-yellow males as also being *T.* sp. 'macrophthalmus chitimba' (Konings, 2001).

When I examined the fish community at Gallireya Reef (the reef nearest to that in Chitimba Bay) I again found an all-yellow male *Tropheops* courting yellow females. However, there is also another common *Tropheops* at this site, in which the females are a gray color. The male of this latter species is again bright yellow, like those of the other *Tropheops*. There is a small difference between these males and those of the yellow male/yellow female form: the latter are entirely yellow (apart from a bluish anal fin), and the former (with gray females) have a narrow black submarginal band in the ventral fins and a dark edge to the anal fin. Not a very prominent difference, but a difference nonetheless. Close examination of these two species revealed that the form with a gray female has a slightly shallower body and a less acute snout than that where the female is yellow.

I now realized that there are also two species involved at the other reef (Chitimba), but there it is the females that look identical and the blue-yellow male is not, after all, a mature male of the all-yellow form. It might be assumed that these two species were conspecific with the pair at Gallireya Reef but close examination of freshly-caught specimens showed that the morphological differences present between the Gallireya species were not present between the two forms at Chitimba, and the latter were morphometrically similar to the yellow-female form at Gallireya. I nevertheless regard the Chitimba form with blue males as a distinct, third species. The form with yellow males and females (both reefs) now retains the name originally given to its Chitimba population, *T.* sp. 'macrophthalmus chitimba', the Chitimba species with the blue males is termed *T.* sp. 'macrophthalmus chitimba blue', and the gray-female Gallireya form is *T.* sp. 'macrophthalmus gallireya'. Needless to say, DNA study will be necessary to determine the status of these forms unequivocally, and fin clips were taken for the purpose in January 2007.

Elongate *Pseudotropheus*

Two elongate species with a generally brown coloration inhabit the intermediate habitat. *Pseudotropheus* sp. 'elongatus mozambique brown' is observed infrequently in the deeper regions of the rocky coasts between Londo and Tumbi Point (Mozambique). It lives in shallow areas as well, and is characterized by broad black bands on all the fins except for the pectorals. These bands are so wide that the whole of the dorsal, ventral, and anal fins seems black while the tail has broad upper and lower bands. In the light-colored females and juveniles this produces an attractive pattern, whereas the black markings are hardly noticeable in the chocolate brown males. Males at Mbweca are light to yellow-brown and resemble *Metriaclima* sp. 'elongatus usisya' in their coloration.

Pseudotropheus sp. 'elongatus mbenji brown' occurs in sediment-rich but shallow rocky areas. It is found around the Mbenji islands as well as at Nkhomo Reef and the intermediate habitats along the shore near Sani. Females are very dark brown, quite the opposite of those of *P.* sp. 'elongatus mozambique brown'.

Small *Pseudotropheus*

Likoma and Chizumulu islands harbor a large variety of mbuna with a preference for intermediate habitats. At Likoma, which is the larger of the two and has alternating sandy and rocky coasts, several of these species have a localized distribution. At Chizumulu, by contrast, the different species are usually dispersed along the entire coast in their preferred habitats.

Pseudotropheus heteropictus is a small mbuna from Chizumulu Island that has been exported as "Pseudotropheus Newsi" and achieved a degree of popularity among hobbyists under this trade name. The scientific name *P. heteropictus* has in the past erroneously been applied to a large species from Thumbi West Island, subsequently known as *Metriaclima* sp. 'black dorsal heteropictus' when the error was recognized but now formally described as *M. flavifemina*. The main defining character of *Metriaclima* is its skull morphology, and *P. heteropictus* does not conform in respect of this character and this is further reflected in the different feeding techniques of the two species. *Metriaclima* feed from the aufwuchs by raking loose algae (mainly diatoms) from the algal strands that are firmly anchored to the rocky substrate. The teeth of the upper jaw do not fit precisely onto those of the lower and thus when the fish closes its mouth it cannot actually grab hold of the algae. The situation is quite different in *P. heteropictus*. The teeth in the upper and lower jaws fit together precisely to grasp attached aufwuchs and tear it from the rocks, rather than raking loose algae.

P. heteropictus lives all around Chizumulu Island in intermediate habitats. It prefers areas with little sediment on the rocks, but is sometimes to be found in sediment-rich areas as well. Most individuals occur at a depth of between three and 10 meters, though some populations occur on reefs at depths of 18 meters or more. Males are territorial and defend small holes between rocks that serve as their spawning sites, sometimes digging a small burrow beneath one of the rocks.

The coloration of male *P. heteropictus* normally resembles that of *P. socolofi* (page 204), and in particular those populations of the latter that lack a black submarginal band in the dorsal fin. However, the population of *P. heteropictus* at a reef south of Chizumulu Island has very attractively-colored males and females, both exhibiting a wide black submarginal band in the dorsal fin (in addition to the black bands in the anal and pelvic fins). The reef population shows quite a bit of variability in the banding pattern; some individuals exhibit a very broad band in the dorsal, covering almost the entire fin, while others have only a narrow submarginal band. This is true for both males and females. Some females have a black band only in the dorsal, lacking such bands in other fins, while others have black bands in the dorsal, anal, and pelvic fins. Another difference between the reef and island populations is that I failed to find any females with egg-spots in the anal fin, a common trait in specimens from the island.

A tiny mbuna, endemic to the rocky coast of Tumbi Point in Mozambique, has a preference for a sediment-free intermediate habitat. The coast at Tumbi Point is very steep and a sediment-free type of intermediate habitat is found even at depths of more than 20 meters. *Pseudotropheus* sp. 'kingsizei tumbi' is found at depths of between 15 and 25 meters, where males defend small territories centered on small holes excavated under or between rocks. Females are characterized by a few broad, but tapering, brown bars on a beige body, with the widest parts of the bars near the dorsal fin.

The intermediate habitat in Chitimba Bay consists of a few large slabs of sandstone and a few heaps of rocks set on a flat sand floor. Here too there is a small cichlid, *Pseudotropheus* sp. 'dumpy chitimba', which somewhat resembles *Metriaclima* sp. 'dumpy' from the Maleri islands but is not a member of *Metriaclima*. Only a few males have been seen so far, and even though they exhibited breeding coloration they didn't seem to be territorial.

The burrower and the pindani

A small, cobalt blue mbuna, *Pseudotropheus* sp. 'burrower', inhabits the transition zone between sand and rock at the Maleri islands and at Chidunga Rocks near Chipoka. Males dig tunnels beneath rocks and the heap of sand at the entrance of the tunnel easily identifies territories. Females, which are brown, are solitary

1. *Tropheops* sp. 'macrophthalmus chitimba' ♂ Gallireya Reef (Hara)

2. *Tropheops* sp. 'macrophthalmus chitimba blue' ♂ Chitimba Bay

3. *Tropheops* sp. 'macrophthalmus gallireya' ♂ Gallireya Reef

4. *Pseudotropheus* sp. 'elongatus mozambique brown' ♂ Mbweca

5. *Tropheops* sp. 'macrophthalmus chitimba' ♀ Gallireya Reef

6. *Tropheops* sp. 'macrophthalmus chitimba' ♂ Chitimba Bay

7. *Tropheops* sp. 'macrophthalmus gallireya' ♀ Gallireya Reef

8. *Tropheops* sp. 'macrophthalmus chitimba' ♂ Gallireya Reef

9. *Pseudotropheus* sp. 'elongatus mozambique brown' ♀ Londo

1. *Pseudotropheus* sp. 'elongatus mbenji brown' ♀ Mbenji

7. *Pseudotropheus* sp. 'elongatus mbenji brown' ♂ Mbenji

2. *Pseudotropheus heteropictus* ♂ Membe Island (Chizumulu)

3. *Pseudotropheus heteropictus* ♀ Same Bay (Chizumulu)

8. *Pseudotropheus heteropictus* ♂ Membe Reef

4. *Pseudotropheus heteropictus* ♀ Membe Reef (Chizumulu)

5. *Pseudotropheus* sp. 'kingsizei tumbi' ♀ Tumbi Point

9. *Pseudotropheus* sp. 'kingsizei tumbi' ♂ Tumbi Point

6. *Pseudotropheus* sp. 'dumpy chitimba' ♂ Chitimba Bay

and, like males, feed from the aufwuchs on the rocks.

The distribution of *Pseudotropheus socolofi*, named after Florida's pioneer fish-farmer Ross Socolof, is along the Mozambique shores of the lake and extends from Tumbi Point to Cobwé. The individuals of the populations at Cobwé and Mbweca lack the black submarginal band in the dorsal seen in those at Mala Point and Tumbi Point. Some female *P. socolofi* lack distinct egg-spots in the anal fin but females are otherwise indistinguishable from males.

Prior to its formal description, *P. socolofi* was exported for years as "Pseudotropheus Pindani" (and is still sometimes traded under that name), named after James Pindani, the dive-team leader of exporter Peter Davies, and subsequently constructor of Stuart Grant's fish-house complex. It resembles *P.* sp. 'burrower' in coloration (males only) and habitat preference. *P. socolofi* picks its food from the biocover on the rocks. Its picking technique does not appear to be very advanced: the fish merely picks among the short algae strands without shearing them off or thoroughly combing them. The mouth seems never to touch the rock.

In the early 1970s *P. socolofi* was introduced at Thumbi West and Otter islands, but the introduced fish failed to thrive and may even have become extinct. According to Ribbink *et al.* (1983b), males (at Thumbi West) are territorial, which is unusual for an mbuna that lacks sexual dichromatism. Territoriality in the populations along the Mozambique shores is only weakly expressed, with males wandering through the habitat in a manner similar to that of females. Nowadays most captive specimens are tank-raised. It is sometimes astonishing to see the size attained in captivity—16 cm or more! In the lake this species grows barely larger than 7 cm.

Interestingly a *P. socolofi*-like cichlid, currently regarded as a distinct species (page 273), is found in a different habitat (very shallow water) at N'kolongwe, also home to *Metriaclima aurora*—or a visually indistinguishable species. *P. socolofi* and *M. aurora* are found together at Mala Point and Tumbi Point, but neither occurs in the area between Tumbi and N'kolongwe.

Gephyrochromis

The members of *Gephyrochromis* have bicuspid teeth in the outer rows of the jaws. There is a difference from those of *Pseudotropheus* though: the teeth are very slender and long, and bent inward to form a kind of "scoop". In addition, the two cusps of each tooth are not equal in size—one is much larger than the other. In older specimens the teeth of the outer rows tend to lose the second cusp and become unicuspid (photo 12, page 26).

Some *Gephyrochromis* live on the open sand floor (see page 309), as do several species of mbuna belonging to different genera, but others are found in the intermediate habitat. *Gephyrochromis* scoop algae (including diatoms) from the sand/mud substrate. And now it becomes clear why the teeth are long, slender, and bent inward: when a mouthful of substrate is scooped up most fine-grained material falls through the teeth back to the bottom while algal strands and other light material are retained on top of the tips of the teeth. When stomachs of *Gephyrochromis* are examined they are stuffed with sand grains; the scoop may not work all that efficiently but is effective enough to extract food from a substrate where other mbuna find nothing to eat.

It is this habit of scooping up small quantities of sand from the top layer of the sand/mud substrate that unites the members of *Gephyrochromis*—other mbuna don't feed in this way. In my opinion feeding behavior is a more important character, albeit more difficult to define, than the structure of the teeth.

Gephyrochromis sp. 'zebroides' occurs on both sides of the lake and has been found at Ruarwe, Hora Mhango, Metangula, Lumessi, Chiloelo, and Gome. The population at Metangula lacks the black submarginal band in the dorsal seen in the other populations, but otherwise all have a similar coloration, with vertical bars the most prominent feature. The zebra-like pattern is that most commonly encountered, but males in breeding coloration and mouthbrooding females normally lack the barred pattern. Males are very dark gray to coppery-blue while mouthbrooding females are light gray. I have not seen territorial males and it seems that they don't need to be territorial to spawn. The depth preference of *G*. sp. 'zebroides' varies between seven and 25 meters.

In 1995 I named some sand-dwelling mbuna from Tanzania *Pseudotropheus* sp. 'tropheops sand' and *P*. sp. 'tropheops sand blackfin' as I thought that they belonged to the species group that has subsequently become the large genus *Tropheops*. However, I was recently able to examine some preserved specimens and found that their tooth structure resembled that of *Gephyrochromis*. Subsequent observations of their feeding behavior have made it clear that they are members of this genus. In breeding behavior they seem to be similar to what I have seen of *G*. sp. 'zebroides"; males in breeding color are quite attractive but do not behave territorially. Females and non-breeding males are characterized by a barred pattern. *Gephyrochromis* sp. 'sand blackfin', distinguished by the black band in the anal fin, occurs along the northeastern shores, north of Lundu, while *Gephyrochromis* sp. 'sand' is found south of Liuli, at least as far as Londo in Mozambique. Recently I found a population of this species at Membe Point on Likoma Island. Breeding males are quite colorful and would be a peaceful addition to a Malaŵi aquarium. The population at Likoma occurs in quite deep water—about 30 meters—but along the Mozambique and Tanzanian shores both species can be found in water as shallow as five meters.

Years ago I found a species similar to *G*. sp. 'sand' at Minos Reef in Mozambique and named it *Metriaclima* sp. 'patricki minos' because the coloration and bar pattern resembled that of *M*. sp. 'patricki' (page 187), an algae-raker of similar habitats in the southern part of the lake. During a subsequent visit to Minos Reef I noticed that the species scoops sand from the soft bottom and although I have not yet examined specimens I believe that this species too is a member of *Gephyrochromis* and now refer to it as *Gephyrochromis* sp. 'patricki minos'.

A species I previously named *Metriaclima* sp. 'zebra mbamba' (Konings, 2001) now appears not to be a member of *Metriaclima* after all. This species—for years known only from a photograph of a male and another of a female—occurs around the two small Mbamba islands at Likoma. Recently I have able to observe it in its natural setting and saw that it scoops mud and sand from the bottom. I anticipated that it would be another species of *Gephyrochromis* and a quick examination of the teeth seemed to confirm this surmise. There are a few discrepancies though; along the southern side of the two islands there are many territorial males in rather shallow water. Males burrow beneath flat rocks and have a blue breeding color—both characters are absent in all other known members of *Gephyrochromis*. A closer examination of the teeth revealed that they are not exactly like those of *Gephyrochromis*. In the latter the outer teeth become unicuspid with age while all the inner rows of teeth are tricuspid. In the species from the Mbamba islands the outer teeth, although bent inward to form a scoop, are distinctly bicuspid with equal-sized cusps while those of the inner rows are unicuspid, a feature otherwise known among the mbuna only from *Cynotilapia*. This observation, together with the territorial males and their blue breeding coloration, suggests that the species is probably not a *Gephyrochromis*. Hence, for the time being, I assign this species to *Pseudotropheus*, even though it does not even appear to be a typical member of that genus, because there is no better alternative. I believe that it is perhaps related to the smaller species of that genus but has evolved (or is evolving) a method of collecting algae from the soft muddy substrate, paralleling the behavior of *Gephyrochromis*.

The "Zebra Mbamba" appears to be identical to a species Ribbink *et al*. (1983b) referred to as *P*. 'zebra bevous', although they used this name for two different species. The one from Chizumulu Island is now termed *Metriaclima* sp. 'aurora bevous' (see page 177) and the one from Likoma Island, "our" blue, sand-scooping mbuna, I have called *Metriaclima* sp. 'black dorsal cobalt' (Konings, 2001). Now that I have observed other populations of this species—all around Likoma Island and none at Chizumulu—it is clear that its color pattern varies between individuals of the same population: some individuals lack the vertical bars that are

1. *Pseudotropheus* sp. 'burrower' ♂ Chidunga Rocks

2. *Pseudotropheus socolofi* ♂ Tumbi Point

3. *Gephyrochromis* sp. 'zebroides' ♂ Ntekete

4. *Gephyrochromis* sp. 'zebroides' Malopa

5. *Pseudotropheus* sp. 'burrower' ♀ Maleri Island

6. *Pseudotropheus socolofi* ♂ Mbweca

7. *Pseudotropheus socolofi* ♀ Tumbi Point

8. *Gephyrochromis* sp. 'zebroides' ♀ Narungu

9. *Gephyrochromis* sp. 'zebroides' ♀ Chiloelo

1. *Gephyrochromis* sp. 'sand' ♀ Hongi Island

2. *Gephyrochromis* sp. 'sand' ♂ Membe Point (Likoma)

3. *Gephyrochromis* sp. 'sand blackfin' ♀ Lundu

4. *Gephyrochromis* sp. 'patricki minos' ♀ Minos Reef

5. *Pseudotropheus* sp. 'sand cobalt' ♂ Mbamba (Likoma)

6. *Pseudotropheus* sp. 'sand cobalt' ♀ Mbamba (Likoma)

7. *Gephyrochromis* sp. 'sand' ♂ Londo

8. *Gephyrochromis* sp. 'sand blackfin' ♂ Makonde

9. *Gephyrochromis* sp. 'patricki minos' ♂ Minos Reef

10. *Pseudotropheus* sp. 'sand cobalt' ♂ Mbamba (Likoma)

prominent in others. I suggest calling this blue mbuna from Likoma *Pseudotropheus* sp. 'sand cobalt'.

Labidochromis

Three small species of *Labidochromis* inhabit the somewhat deeper intermediate habitats of the lake. A very popular species among aquarists is *Labidochromis* sp. 'hongi' which was originally collected at Hongi Island in Tanzania. The species also occurs at Lundo Island and the rocky reefs in between these two localities. A few specimens have been seen at Liuli, and Spreinat (1994) records this species from Ngkuyo Island and Undu Point as well. The population at Undu Point consists of dark blue males with a rust-colored patch on the nape and light brown females. By far the most attractive populations are found at Hongi and Lundo islands. Males of other populations have a much less conspicuous color pattern. Although *L.* sp. 'hongi' appears to search for particular feeding sites, observations of its feeding technique indicate that we are dealing with a herbivore. Males are strongly territorial at Hongi Island and are also very common there.

Labidochromis ianthinus lives around the Mbenji islands and is also found at Nkhomo and Jalo reefs. It is an insectivore, and males, as in most insectivorous mbuna, are not territorial. Male and female have almost the same coloration, but males have a mauve sheen on the body and on the cheeks.

On the east coast of the lake, between Lumessi, Mozambique, and Masinje, Malaŵi, a scientifically undescribed species of *Labidochromis* lives at rather deep levels (about 15 meters) in the intermediate habitat but also occupies caves in shallower water. Its color pattern is rather atypical for *Labidochromis* and the species may be derived from the herbivorous *L. lividus*-like species found in shallow intermediate habitats. Females of this species, *Labidochromis* sp. 'zebra eastern', have the same color pattern as males but the bars blend into the darker background color to a greater extent. Judging by its feeding behavior, it seems likely that *L.* sp. 'zebra eastern' is an insectivore, but stomach contents analysis is required to confirm this.

Attractive *Melanochromis*

The species currently assigned to *Melanochromis* include some of the less specialized mbuna. They are omnivorous, but more predatory than herbivorous, leaving most of the algae in the biocover to the species with specialized feeding techniques. They could, of course, survive by feeding on algae, but their relatively primitive collecting technique (nipping and plucking) leaves most of it for the combers, scrapers, and shearers.

Melanochromis chipokae is uncommon and endemic to the shallow rocks at Chidunga Rocks near Chipoka. Its color pattern resembles that of *M. parallelus* and *M. heterochromis*, but females are much yellower. It is probably the largest species of the genus, with a maximum total length of approximately 17 cm (in the aquarium). Males as well as females are seen cruising through the habitat. Males are weakly territorial and are aggressive only in the defense of their spawning sites. *M. chipokae* is regularly exported and enjoys wide popularity among hobbyists.

Melanochromis simulans is found at Gome and further north along the shores of Mozambique, up to Nkhungu. It resembles *M. auratus* (see page 110) to some extent, but has a more elongate shape and a longer snout. In the rockier habitats throughout most of its range there is a similar member of the genus, *Melanochromis dialeptos* (formerly *M.* sp. 'auratus dwarf'). On page 109 I have explained the possible relationship of *M. simulans* and *M. dialeptos* with another *Melanochromis*, *M.* sp. 'auratus elongate', which has a distribution north of that of the other two species. *M. simulans* is less common than *M. dialeptos*; males in breeding coloration are rarely seen, and when they are, they do not appear to be territorial. *M. simulans* occurs chiefly in the shallow intermediate habitat, but is occasionally seen at depths of more than 20 meters.

Along the northeastern Tanzanian shores of the lake a large, all-blue (males) *Melanochromis*, with a resemblance to *M. simulans* and *M. chipokae*, inhabits the intermediate habitat: *Melanochromis* sp. 'northern blue'. Females of this attractive species are characterized by an orange-yellow anal fin. The species attains a rather large size; males with a total length of about 16 cm have been seen. *M.* sp. 'northern blue' is more common in the mbuna populations north of Lupingu—it is found as far north as Nkanda—than in those between Lupingu and Lundu, the southernmost point of its range. *M.* sp. 'northern blue' does not show much territoriality. It wanders through the habitat hunting small mbuna, but is also attracted to stirred-up debris.

Melanochromis lepidiadaptes (previously known as *M.* sp. 'lepidophage') appears to be endemic to shallow reefs near Makanjila Point where it is rather common. The name *lepidiadaptes* alludes to the scales found in the stomachs of several specimens examined by Ribbink et al. (1983b). Other specimens had empty stomachs, which led to the conclusion that this mbuna is most likely a specialized scale-eater. In captivity, however, *M. lepidiadaptes* can be kept with other mbuna without fear of it "descaling" them, in contrast to *Genyochromis mento* (page 112), which will immediately feed on the fins and scales of tankmates. The natural prey of *M. lepidiadaptes* seems to be a non-mbuna. Scale eating in the aquarium (an attack by a group of *M. lepidiadaptes* on *Nimbochromis venustus*) has been reported by René Krüter (pers. comm., see Konings, 1989: 163), and Denis Belloy (pers. comm.) has also observed this species attacking a *Nimbochromis* in the aquarium. Belloy has suggested that *M. lepidiadaptes* may resort to scale eating and attacking larger non-mbuna only when they (the *M. lepidiadaptes*) are in a large group, preferably containing more than 30 individuals. In all cases (three attacks have been observed so far) the *Nimbochromis* was stripped clean five minutes after the attack began!

In its natural habitat the species is most frequently seen hunting in groups, feeding on anything palatable, not necessarily the scales of other cichlids. Having failed to observe scale-eating behavior in the wild population, I collected six specimens which all seemed to have eaten shortly before being captured, judging by the shape of the abdomen. During stomach analysis of these six individuals I found that just one, a male, had eaten three small scales, along with a quantity of less identifiable material. The scales were most likely of cichlid origin. Three of the other five individuals had dined on *kampango* (*Bagrus meridionalis*) eggs, another on *kampango* larvae, and the sixth, a ripe female, had less identifiable contents.

In my opinion *M. lepidiadaptes* is not a habitual scale-eater, but may occasionally rip scales from the flanks of diseased fishes or those trapped in fishermen's nets, which form easy prey for predators such as this species. This scenario offers a plausible explanation for the presence of scales in their stomachs. The fact that stomach contents analysis revealed other items as well points more to a scavenger-type of feeding behavior, correlating with that actually observed in the lake.

The species formerly known as *M.* sp. 'blotch' has a widespread distribution along the eastern shores of the lake, from Tumbi Point in Mozambique to Makanjila Point in Malaŵi. It is also found around Chizumulu Island. However, the form seen at Membe Island (Chizumulu) has a somewhat different pattern to that of the mainland forms. This difference was regarded as a significantly differentiating character when the two forms, the mainland and the Chizumulu, were described as *Melanochromis baliodigma* and *Melanochromis xanthodigma* respectively (Bowers & Stauffer, 1997). In practice, however, the differences are far from clear-cut. Individuals of the mainland populations have a pattern of broad, irregular bars and two horizontal stripes, but patterns with narrow bars are also present. Furthermore, while most individuals at Membe Island have narrow, regular bars, individuals with wider bars, resembling those of the common pattern seen in mainland populations, have been seen as well. The purported difference in the number of egg-spots in the anal fin, namely two to four in *M. baliodigma* and five to seven in *M. xanthodigma*, has not been substantiated during my examination of the various populations along the

1. *Labidochromis* sp. 'hongi' ♂ Hongi Island

2. *Labidochromis* sp. 'zebra eastern' ♂ Chiofu

3. *Labidochromis ianthinus* ♂ Mbenji Island

4. *Melanochromis chipokae* ♂ Chidunga Rocks

5. *Labidochromis* sp. 'hongi' ♀ Lundo Island

6. *Labidochromis* sp. 'zebra eastern' ♂ Gome

7. *Labidochromis ianthinus* ♀ Mbenji Island

8. *Melanochromis chipokae* ♀ Chidunga Rocks

1. *Melanochromis simulans* ♀ Masinje

2. *Melanochromis* sp. 'northern blue' ♀ Manda

3. *Melanochromis lepidiadaptes* ♀ Aquarium

4. *Melanochromis baliodigma* ♀ Membe Island (Chizumulu)

5. *Melanochromis baliodigma* Gome

6. *Melanochromis baliodigma* ♂ Lumessi

7. *Melanochromis simulans* ♂ Ntekete

8. *Melanochromis* sp. 'northern blue' ♂ Manda

9. *Melanochromis lepidiadaptes* ♂ Makanjila Point

10. *Melanochromis baliodigma* ♂ Narungu

Mozambique shore. In fact, males of almost all populations rarely have more than four egg-spots. Ripe males are rarely seen, but in all populations where they have been observed breeding coloration is a gray-blue body with the non-breeding pattern no longer present. Although each population differs slightly from the next, I believe that all of the mainland populations, along with that at Chizumulu, belong to a single species, *M. baliodigma*, which is closely related to *M. robustus* (formerly *M.* sp. 'blue'). *M. xanthodigma* is thus regarded as a synonym of *M. baliodigma*.

The diet of *M. baliodigma* consists mainly of invertebrates, but Ribbink and his co-workers (1983b) report that the species also attacks fishes trapped in nets. This species also feeds on the larvae and fry of the *kampango*, *Bagrus meridionalis*, and is often seen near the breeding caves of these catfish.

Melanochromis perileucos (formerly *M.* sp. 'black-white johannii') is one of the more peaceful members of the genus and is common along the southeastern shores of Likoma Island. Females are whitish-yellow and have a broad black band in the dorsal and an orange-yellow anal fin. Males are almost completely blue-black with a light blue wedge on the caudal peduncle and the posterior part of the body. In contrast to species of the genus *Pseudotropheus*, where such pronounced sexual dichromatism often coincides with strong territorial behavior in males, those of *M. perileucos* are only weakly territorial. In captivity spawning can take place on the open sand, but males excavate spawning sites beneath rocks in the wild. Only at specific locations, where the population of males is denser, can territorial defense be observed. Mouthbrooding females are frequently seen and do not seem to hide as much as most other brooding mbuna.

It is possible that *Melanochromis labrosus* may not in fact belong to this genus, but it is definitely a mbuna (Lewis, in Ribbink *et al.*, 1983b; David Eccles, pers. comm.) and not a 'hap'. At Chitande Island I once found an orange *M. labrosus* (see photo 5, page 214), evidence of polychromatism in this normally brown colored species. Polychromatism occurs in mbuna but has not yet been found in the haps of Lake Malaŵi.

M. labrosus is seen sporadically all around the lake but is found most frequently at islands and along the northeastern shores, north of the Ruhuhu River. This distribution pattern is characteristic of an old species with a narrowly defined specialization. The pointed, fleshy, and recurved lips are the main feature of this mbuna. Both sexes are dark brown, but males may have a reddish sheen overlaying the brown ground color. Another characteristic, not seen in any other mbuna, is the strongly laterally compressed body. As in the similarly compressed *Altolamprologus compressiceps* of Lake Tanganyika, this adaptation enables the fish to penetrate into narrow slits and cracks between the rocks. The soft, fleshy lips are used to seal off the crack while the prey is sucked out of its shelter. Like other laterally compressed cichlids with swollen lips (e.g. *Lichnochromis acuticeps*, *Protomelas ornatus*), it feeds primarily from horizontal cracks and slits inside caves. In order to penetrate such cracks it turns on its side just before entering. *M. labrosus* moves in and out of caves searching for small mbuna and crustaceans. Males do not defend a spawning site, but when two conspecifics meet both male and female display aggressive behavior (defense of the feeding site).

Haps with thick lips

The haps, the non-mbuna, are well represented in the intermediate habitat. It is in fact the "meeting place" of the two groups. The interaction is usually to the benefit of the larger haplochromines as many of them eat mbuna juveniles.

Protomelas sp. 'mbenji thick lip' is endemic to the Mbenji Islands. It resembles *P. ornatus*, a species of shallow intermediate habitats (see page 273) and not present at Mbenji, but is normally found at deeper levels, below 10 meters. *P.* sp. 'mbenji thick lip' is frequently exported under the trade name "Haplochromis Labrosus". It is laterally compressed but not as much so as *P. ornatus*, and the thickening of its lips resembles that of *Placidochromis milomo* (which I have never seen at Mbenji) rather than that of *Protomelas ornatus*. Sub-adult individuals, characterized by a dark *Protomelas*-type pattern with a dark lower half to the body, are commonly seen around the island. With the recent increase in ornamental fish collectors in the area *P.* sp. 'mbenji thick lip' is one of the species that seems to have suffered from increased fishing pressure. Males exhibiting breeding coloration are territorial, defending a large cave in the intermediate habitat, but are rarely seen. Like *P. ornatus,* this thick-lipped species grows to a considerable size (a total length of about 25 cm) and feeds on invertebrates and small fishes.

Chilotilapia euchilus is another hap with noticeably "overdeveloped" lips. Unlike the previous species it feeds primarily on invertebrates. *C. euchilus* is usually observed over sandy sections of the intermediate habitat, but feeds from the rocks that are scattered on the sand. Sometimes *C. euchilus* is caught in beach seine nets over purely sandy bottoms. Interestingly, such individuals lack the swollen lips, suggesting that feeding from rocky substrates stimulates the growth of the latter. Juveniles are frequently found in shallow areas where mud and rocks meet. The species is easily distinguished from the broad-barred *Placidochromis milomo* by the two horizontal stripes on the silvery-yellow body. *C. euchilus* rarely ventures into the deeper regions of the habitat and is observed mostly in water less than 10 meters deep. Sexually active males are completely steel blue but are not always territorial. Frequently a non-spawning adult pair can be found together and it seems that some kind of ritual precedes the spawning, which takes place in the rocky part of the biotope. *C. euchilus* is probably descended from a different ancestor to the other thick-lipped species, and may have evolved from sand-dwelling cichlids characterized by longitudinal striping. On the other hand its characteristic pattern may be an adaptation for living on the sand, where it blends in with the ubiquitous diagonally-striped haplochromines (e.g. *Mylochromis* spp.).

Lichnochromis acuticeps has somewhat thickened lips and a lake-wide distribution. It is sometimes exported under the trade name "Malaŵi Gar". It seems to be more of a sand-dwelling cichlid that feeds from scattered rocks in relatively shallow water, at depths of between five and 15 meters. It behaves like a large *Melanochromis labrosus*, but does not live a secretive life. *L. acuticeps* covers large distances, moving at a fairly steady pace and pausing only when prey is detected. One of its main characteristics is the strongly laterally compressed body; the head in particular is very narrow when viewed from above. The snout is very pointed, and the fleshy lips appear almost to form no part of it—at first glance they seem to start where one would expect the snout of a fish to finish. Like other laterally compressed species it turns its body through 90° to permit access into narrow horizontal slits between rocks and sand. When it strikes it propels itself with much force and wedges its head in the narrow crack between small rocks. In the case of *L. acuticeps* the thick lips may have more of a shock-absorbing than a sealing function. From stomach contents analysis it appears that its primary aim is to collect insect larvae and small mbuna. Ripe males don a blue and yellow breeding dress and court females whenever they are encountered. Spawning has not yet been observed in the wild, but in captivity takes place on the sandy bottom near or between rocks.

Sand-blowers and pebble-pushers

The intermediate habitat also provides a specific habitat for a number of other non-mbuna. Species of the genus *Protomelas* are the most widespread non-mbuna in rocky habitats, and the intermediate areas are no exception.

Superficially *Protomelas fenestratus* looks like a geographical variant of *P. taeniolatus* (see page 115), but in behavior it is quite different. *P. fenestratus* is known in the hobby as "Steveni Thick Bars" and is collected regularly at Likoma and Chizumulu islands. It is less common than *P. taeniolatus,* which is found almost exclusively in sediment-free rocky habitats, but like the latter has a lake-wide distribution. *P. fenestratus* has the peculiar habit of blowing away the sedi-

1. *Melanochromis perileucos* ♂ Masimbwe

4. *Melanochromis perileucos* ♀ Masimbwe

2. *Melanochromis labrosus* ♂ Chiloelo

5. *Melanochromis labrosus* O ♀ Chitande Island

6. *Melanochromis labrosus* ♀ Chiloelo

3. *Protomelas* sp. 'mbenji thick-lip' ♂ Mbenji Island

1. *Chilotilapia euchilus* ♀ Lupingu

2. *Protomelas fenestratus* ♀ Chiofu

3. *Protomelas fenestratus* ♂ Chiofu

4. *Protomelas* sp. 'mbenji thick-lip' ♀ Mbenji Island

6. *Chilotilapia euchilus* ♂ Pombo Rocks

7. *Protomelas fenestratus* ♂ Chiofu

8. *Protomelas* sp. 'mbenji thick-lip' ♀ Mbenji Island

5. *Lichnochromis acuticeps* Gome

ment covering the biocover on rocks and sand to reveal its prey, which consists mostly of insect larvae and crustaceans. In contrast, *P. taeniolatus* is a herbivore which feeds on algae. It is fun to observe *P. fenestratus* "blowing" their way through the habitat revealing prey, and also attracting juveniles of sand-dwelling cichlids wanting to pick their share from the stirred-up sediment. Ripe males excavate shallow spawning pits in the sand between small stones and rocks in the habitat. Territorial males have a light blue color which completely obscures the neutral-mood pattern of broad bars seen in females and juveniles. In general *P. fenestratus* females are characterized by a melanin pattern consisting of vertical bars and thin horizontal lines, a coloration which varies throughout the species' range. At most localities, however, the pattern is dominated by heavy bars and very faint horizontal stripes. As in *P. taeniolatus*, female *P. fenestratus* continue to guard their offspring after they have been released.

Some areas of the intermediate habitat consist of extensive beds of small pebbles which may be remnants of river-beds that carried water when the lake level was lower. There are two species found in such areas, *Protomelas* sp. 'johnstoni solo' and *Mylochromis labidodon*, and both are found all round the lake. *P.* sp. 'johnstoni solo' feeds on invertebrates and algae which it picks from the pebbles and occasional rocks of the habitat, covering large distances while foraging. This species was previously placed in *Placidochromis* as it bears some resemblance to *P. johnstoni*, but I believe that both species would be better placed in *Protomelas* (together with *Placidochromis milomo*). Work is in fact in progress to confirm this reclassification, but because *P. johnstoni* and *P. milomo* are both commonly kept cichlids and have long been known to aquarists as *Placidochromis* I have refrained from reclassifying them here. The name "solo" alludes to the fact that this species is always found alone. At Makonde in Tanzania it is more common, but even there does not form feeding groups. Although several populations have been located there is no obvious geographical variation. Males in breeding coloration are very rare; the few I have seen did not defend a spawning site, but in captivity males do show some aggression in territorial defense.

Protomelas sp. 'virgatus luwala' is a virtually unknown cichlid that was seen once at a depth of about 20 meters at Luwala Reef and never seen again. Although males and females were seen picking at the sand no interactions between the sexes or even males in breeding color were seen. The basic melanin pattern suggests that it is a member of *Protomelas*.

Mylochromis labidodon can be regarded as the *Labidochromis* analogue among the haps. Its teeth are pointed and considerably larger at the center (front) of the jaws. It is common over pebble beds where it turns over any small stone it can grasp with its mouth! When it finds something palatable beneath the stone, it quickly dives into the rubble to seize it. *M. labidodon* has been exported for the aquarium trade on several occasions, and the specimens concerned were caught in Senga Bay with beach seine nets dragged over pure sand. The species has a very silvery body with broad vertical bars and a very thin red edge to the dorsal fin. There is some geographical variation that seems to be restricted to the normal pigmentation pattern. Members of the genus *Mylochromis* are characterized by a diagonal stripe on the flanks but such a stripe is rarely seen in *M. labidodon*; only the northern populations have a diagonal stripe but this is hardly ever a continuous line from the nape to the caudal peduncle. The southern populations have a very pronounced pattern of vertical bars. The juveniles of such barred individuals, however, have an incomplete diagonal line.

Haps with a diagonal line

The genus *Mylochromis* consists of species characterized by a diagonal line on the body. Many are found in the pure sandy habitat but a few occur in the intermediate zone as well.

Mylochromis epichorialis has a lake-wide distribution but is a rare sight at any location. Its strong pharyngeal plates with large molariform teeth indicate a menu of hard-shelled invertebrates. At many different locations I have observed this cichlid attacking and eating a crab (*Potamonautes orbitospinus*) and it is likely that *M. epichorialis*, at least as far as adult specimens are concerned, has specialized in feeding on these large crustaceans. Males in breeding color are rare but when encountered are always in shallow water and also in the water column. I have never seen a spawning site but it is possible that they breed inside caves which they quickly abandon when approached by a diver. Although it is not a rare species I have never encountered a fry-guarding or even mouthbrooding female.

Mylochromis sp. 'lateristriga makanjila' is better known by the trade names of "Makanjila Longnose", "Pointed Nose", and "Makanjila Mola", and has been exported from the Malaŵian east coast since the mid 1980s. Its range encompasses the entire east coast of the lake from Ikombe in the north to Makanjila Point in the south. Even though this area is very large, there are no geographical color variants known. The populations found north of the Ruhuhu River in Tanzania, however, consist of individuals with thicker lips than those elsewhere. In addition, females have a darker coloration. This variant is known as "Mylochromis Mchuse" (Spreinat, 1994). I don't believe this form represents a different species.

The diagonal line is blotchy in most individuals, but some have a complete diagonal line extending from the nape to the caudal peduncle, while in others the line starts after the third vertical bar. This type of variation can also be seen in aquarium specimens originating from the same locality, suggesting that it may be dependent on the fish's mood. By contrast, in *M. lateristriga* (see page 292), a much larger member of the genus restricted to the southern shores of the lake, the diagonal line is solid and regular, and extends from the nape to the caudal peduncle.

The maximum length of *M.* sp. 'lateristriga makanjila' is approximately 16 cm in males and about 11 cm in females (*M. lateristriga* can reach a total length of about 22 cm). The diet of *M.* sp. 'lateristriga makanjila' consists of soft-bodied invertebrates found in the sand. The thick lips of this species absorb the shock when the fish plunges its head into the bottom in search of food. Males in breeding coloration are found throughout the year but mainly during the period between August and January. Territorial males construct small semicircular sand-scrape pits against rocks or small cave-crater spawning sites in the intermediate habitat at depths varying between three and 15 meters.

Along the western coast, at Nkhata Bay, Lion's Cove, Ruarwe, and Hora Mhango, a similar species occurs in the intermediate habitat. Although it is likely that this species is closely related to—and may even be conspecific with—*M.* sp. 'lateristriga makanjila', for the time being I will refer to it as *Mylochromis* sp. 'lateristriga nkhata'. It seems to have a relatively shorter snout than *M.* sp. 'lateristriga makanjila'. Females of both species guard their young after they have been released for the first time.

For a long time I confused a species from Likoma Island with *Mylochromis mollis*, because when I examined a specimen of the Likoma fish, exported as "Haplochromis Margrette Diagonal Stripe", it was not yet known that the haps in Lake Malaŵi had also undergone extensive speciation and many species were simply not known to science. The most prominent difference between the holotype of *M. mollis* and "Margrette Diagonal Stripe" is the thin lips of the former that barely protrude at all from the profile of the snout. In some individuals the lower jaw is slightly shorter than the upper but this is true for both species. The lips of *Mylochromis* sp. 'mollis likoma', as I now refer to "Margrette Diagonal Stripe", are more developed and in some individuals even form a kind of pointed snout. Adult *M. mollis* are generally a few centimeters longer than adult *M.* sp. 'mollis likoma' and usually have a rounder snout profile. The upper snout profile of *M.* sp. 'mollis likoma' is often straight and the snout is more pointed, reminiscent of that of *M.* sp. 'lateristriga makanjila', to which it may be more closely related than to *M. mollis*.

There are other differences, mainly in behavior (see below), but morphologically the two species, which can be found sympatrically at Likoma Island, are very similar. *M.* sp. 'mollis

1. *Protomelas* sp. 'johnstoni solo' ♂ Aquarium

5. *Protomelas* sp. 'johnstoni solo' ♀ Matema

2. *Mylochromis labidodon* ♂ Mbenji Island

6. *Protomelas* sp. 'johnstoni solo' ♀ Matema

7. *Mylochromis labidodon* ♀ Mumbo Island

3. *Mylochromis epichorialis* ♀ Boadzulu Island

8. *Protomelas* sp. 'virgatus luwala' Luwala Reef

4. *Mylochromis epichorialis* ♂ Maingano Island

9. *Mylochromis epichorialis* Likoma Island

1. *Mylochromis* sp. 'lateristriga makanjila' ♀ Gome

2. *Mylochromis* sp. 'lateristriga makanjila' ♀ Lupingu

3. *Mylochromis* sp. 'lateristriga nkhata' ♀ Nkhata Bay

4. *Mylochromis* sp. 'mollis likoma' ♀ Masimbwe

5. *Mylochromis mollis* ♀ Gome

6. *Mylochromis mollis* ♂ Chimwalani Reef

7. *Mylochromis* sp. 'lateristriga makanjila' ♂ Chiofu

8. *Mylochromis* sp. 'lateristriga makanjila' ♂ Lupingu

9. *Mylochromis* sp. 'lateristriga nkhata' ♂ Nkhata Bay

10. *Mylochromis* sp. 'mollis likoma' ♂ Maingano

likoma' has been found only at (and all around) Likoma Island but not (yet?) at Chizumulu Island or at Cobwé. I have seen *M. mollis* at Likoma, Cobwé, and Gome, at Luwala and Chimwalani reefs, and at Thumbi West Island.

While I have not yet been able to examine stomach contents of *M.* sp. 'mollis likoma', its behavior suggests that it feeds on insect larvae and crustaceans picked from debris-laden creases in rocks or from the band of accumulated organic debris that usually forms at the base of rocks where they contact the sand. Sometimes foraging individuals visually inspect the terrain in a manner reminiscent of *Labidochromis*. The feeding technique of *M. mollis* is much more like that seen in *Lethrinops*: small amounts of sediment are scooped up, chewed, and screened for anything edible. Both species are, unfortunately, rarely seen feeding. The reason for this is unclear. *M. mollis* appears very shy and is often seen only in retreat from the observer. Breeding individuals of both species are much less shy but usually do not eat during the breeding period.

M. sp. 'mollis likoma' breeds in shallow water, forming leks consisting of about 25 breeding males, each with a bower about two meters away from neighboring males. The bower consists of a tiny sandy dish with a diameter about the length of the male himself, and is sometimes demarcated by small stones. Because the bottom is usually covered in small stones and pebbles with no open spaces of bower-size in between, the male has to cover some of them with sand to create an even dish. I have not seen males carrying or pushing stones to create a spawning dish although the appearance of some bowers does almost suggest this (see photo 10, page 219). Once I found a male that had chosen a small spot at the edge of the pebbly area, but instead of using the sand of the bower's surrounding, he was displaying over a small sandy dish, demarcated from the adjoining sand by three small stones. It almost looked as if human intervention had helped this male create his bower—a unique spawning site among Malaŵi cichlids.

Breeding males of *M. mollis* have been seen only sporadically, and where spawning sites were seen these were rudimentary—cleaned sand adjacent to rocks, although the rocks were not part of the "construct".

Displaying males of *M.* sp. 'mollis likoma' remain very close to the spawning dish, almost sitting on it, while male *M. mollis* station themselves over the site more or less level with the tops of the surrounding stones and rocks. I do not think this position is "prescribed" for each species but a result of the surroundings: open sand with pebbles does not block a male *M.* sp. 'mollis likoma' from view while ripe females wouldn't easily see a territorial male *M. mollis* if he remained near the bottom among the rocks.

In the past I have also confused other species with *M. mollis*. One of these is the *Mylochromis* at Hora Mhango, Kakusa, and Katale Island, which is now referred to as *Mylochromis* sp. 'mollis north'. Males of the latter species again have a yellow breast and a solid diagonal stripe. They feed from the sandy substrate, like *M. mollis*, but males construct cave-crater bowers. The diagonal stripe, a prominent feature of the female melanin pattern, is blotchy and irregular when compared to the uniform diagonal stripe in *M. mollis*. The blotchy diagonal line of *M.* sp. 'mollis north' also distinguishes it from yet another *mollis*-like species, found at Gallireya Reef, *Mylochromis* sp. 'mollis gallireya'. The diagonal band in the latter species is very narrow and never continuous. Breeding males of *M.* sp. 'mollis gallireya' have a black breast and black pelvic fins, and again construct cave-crater bowers. They feed from the sandy substrate between the rocks, just like *M.* sp. 'mollis north'.

Mylochromis sp. 'mollis chitande', found between Mdoka and Maison Reef, has a more pointed snout than the previous two species and may not be closely related to *M. mollis*. It is more often found in the rocky part of the intermediate habitat where it appears to pick its food—invertebrates—more from rocky than from sandy substrates. The diagonal stripe is broad, blotchy, and irregular. Males in breeding color have been seen foraging but not (yet) defending a spawning site. This is not a very common cichlid.

In the southern part of the lake a similar species, *Mylochromis* sp. 'incola mumbo', occurs in the intermediate habitats. It was first recognized at Mumbo Island, where some individuals roll over small pebbles in the same fashion as *M. labidodon* (page 216), and later at most other locations south of Senga Point, where it is quite often found in pure rocky habitats such as Chinyankwazi Island and Zimbawe Rock. Most individuals behave as opportunistic scavengers that are also attracted to stirred-up material. Breeding males have been encountered only at Boadzulu Island, where they defended small sand-scrape bowers at a depth of about 20 to 25 meters. Mouthbrooding females were seen at the same depths and were solitary.

A single individual with a resemblance to *M.* sp. 'mollis gallireya' was found at Ikombe, Tanzania. It is distinguished from the latter by a smaller mouth and a solid diagonal stripe. For the time being I refer to it as *Mylochromis* sp. 'ikombe' until more information becomes available.

Mylochromis sp. 'guentheri mbenji' occurs at the Mbenji and Maleri islands, and is easily recognized by its large size (usually more than 18 cm) and very strong lips. It rams its snout with great vigor into the coarse gravel of its preferred habitat. No other species can repeatedly "jackhammer" itself with such force into the gravel although there are other species that obtain their food in a similar manner in coarse substrates, e.g. *Protomelas* sp. 'oxyrhynchus mix' (page 288) and *Lethrinops macrochir* (page 376). Neither breeding males nor mouthbrooding females have as yet been spotted.

There are other species with a diagonal stripe on the flanks in the intermediate habitat but not all are members of *Mylochromis*. One of them, *Tramitichromis brevis*, is rather common in the intermediate habitat but will be discussed in detail in the chapter on sand-dwellers, which deals with the other members of this genus (page 364).

The vacuum cleaner

The sediment-covered substrate of the intermediate habitat is rich in micro-organisms and debris which are eaten by small crustaceans. *Ctenopharynx pictus*, a peculiar cichlid, is specialized in feeding on these small invertebrates. This three-spotted species has a lake-wide distribution but is restricted to feeding from the rocks. It has a very protrusible mouth which opens downward. The extended gape, which makes a 45° angle to the body, is held a few millimeters above the substrate and the buccal cavity is then expanded by opening the gill covers wide. As a result a stream of water is sucked into the mouth. Largely because of the wide gape, only the small and free-moving invertebrates are sucked into the mouth, while most of the actual sediment remains on the rocks. *C. pictus* literally vacuum-cleans the algal carpet. To prevent the food-particles thus collected from escaping via the gills, the anterior gill arches bear a set of no less than 35 rakers!

Only during the breeding season does the male *C. pictus* don a light blue nuptial color. Territoriality is weak and directed only against conspecific males. Males select spawning sites on top of rocks near sand in the intermediate habitat and often carry sand up the rock to make a bower. Most breeding activity seems to take place during the rainy season or shortly thereafter. Outside this period males have a similar color pattern to females, i.e. three large dark blotches on the flanks. Females guard their offspring, which show the characteristic three blotches as soon as they are "born" from the female's mouth, for three to four weeks after first release. When the female can not hold all of her fry in her mouth any longer she often releases them near the nest of a *kampango* (*Bagrus meridionalis*).

In its normal dress *C. pictus* resembles *C. intermedius*, which is found over sandy bottoms (see page 337). These two species can be distinguished by the fact that the premaxillary pedicel (the sliding part of the upper jaw) in *C. pictus* is much longer than in *C. intermedius* and extends to above the eyes. With a maximum total length of about 14 cm, *C. pictus* is also visibly smaller than *C. intermedius*, which has a maximum total length of 20 cm.

1. *Mylochromis* sp. 'mollis north' ♂ Katale Island

2. *Mylochromis* sp. 'mollis north' ♂ Hora Mhango

3. *Mylochromis* sp. 'mollis gallireya' ♂ Gallireya Reef

4. *Mylochromis* sp. 'mollis chitande' ♂ Masimbwe

5. *Mylochromis* sp. 'mollis north' ♀ Katale Island

6. *Mylochromis* sp. 'mollis north' ♂ Katale Island

7. *Mylochromis* sp. 'mollis gallireya' ♀ Gallireya Reef

8. *Mylochromis* sp. 'mollis chitande' ♀ Chitande Island

9. *Mylochromis* sp. 'mollis chitande' ♂ Maison Reef

1. *Mylochromis* sp. 'incola mumbo' ♂ Boadzulu Island

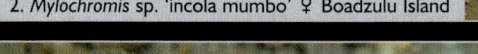

2. *Mylochromis* sp. 'incola mumbo' ♀ Boadzulu Island

3. *Mylochromis* sp. 'incola mumbo' ♀ Mumbo Island

4. *Mylochromis* sp. 'ikombe' Ikombe

5. *Ctenopharynx pictus* ♀ Chiofu

6. *Mylochromis* sp. 'guentheri mbenji' ♀ Mbenji Island

7. *Ctenopharynx pictus* ♂ Mbenji Island

8. *Ctenopharynx pictus* ♂ Liwani

Spotted cichlids

At Likoma a cichlid known in the trade as "Haplochromis Margaretae", "Haplochromis Margrette", or "Haplochromis Big Blotch" is frequently seen at the boundary of sand and rocks. This popular cichlid, *Otopharynx* sp. 'auromarginatus margrette', is undescribed, although some specimens were included in the type series of *O. auromarginatus,* a large cichlid of sandy habitats (see page 336). The "Margrette" can attain a maximum total length of about 18 cm. The population around Likoma is the only one known and is frequently exploited for the aquarium trade. Females and juveniles are characterized by a large spot on the middle of the flank and one or two smaller spots on the caudal peduncle. This species normally feeds from sandy substrates where it scoops up the muddy layer covering the sand. Females and non-territorial males, however, often congregate in schools to feed on plankton. The gut is about four times the length of the fish, indicating a herbivorous diet. Territorial males defend caves at the level of the lake floor, usually choosing a large overhanging rock from beneath which they chase away all intruders. Spawning takes place inside the cave.

Males of *Otopharynx* sp. 'auromarginatus mara' station themselves alongside a rock, apparently defending a spawning site, but bower construction has not yet been observed. This species occurs at Mala Point and Cobwé and is usually found at a depth of about 10 meters. Females, characterized by three large blotches on the flanks and caudal peduncle, forage on the sand, but also feed on plankton in the open water. At Mala Point *O.* sp. 'auromarginatus mara' is a common species, whereas only a few individuals have been seen at Cobwé.

At N'kolongwe, and at Minos and Nkhungu reefs (all in Mozambique), I have found a three-spotted cichlid that probably belongs to the *auromarginatus* group. There is a possibility that this cichlid may be a variant of *Otopharynx heterodon* (see page 224), but I have named it *Otopharynx* sp. 'auromarginatus goldhead', assigning it to this group of larger species because it has a larger adult size than any known *O. heterodon*. Again, females are characterized by three large blotches on the flanks and caudal peduncle. The breeding coloration of the male differs from the normal pattern: the head is golden yellow and the body purplish blue. Both males and females feed from the sediment on the rocks or from the sand, at a depth varying between 10 and 20 meters. The male constructs a small semi-circular spawning dish against the base of a slanted rock, beneath the overhanging part. Females are led from afar to the male's abode (sometimes from further away than 10 meters) and courted all the way.

The fourth species of the *auromarginatus* group occurs in the south of the lake, around the Nankumba peninsula. This species, *Otopharynx* sp. 'heterodon nankumba', may likewise be a large representative of *O. heterodon,* but again I here include it in the group containing the larger cichlids. Breeding males at Thumbi West Island defend shallow sand-scrape spawning sites situated between rocks, or sometimes inside a cave. Females and non-territorial males forage on the sand at a depth ranging from two to 15 meters. They often plunge their snouts into the loose material that collects at the base of rocks, probably searching for invertebrates.

Otopharynx heterodon, already mentioned above, is a small, three-spotted, cichlid exported infrequently as "Haplochromis Royal Blue", and only from Chizumulu Island, although it has a lake-wide distribution. This deep-bodied cichlid is usually seen over sand and mud between rocks, but is also found in the deeper, sediment-rich, rocky habitat. Males in breeding coloration are frequently seen, but rarely defend a territory. Spawning takes place on the sand between a few small rocks or sometimes on top of some small stones. When stones or rocks abound the male clears a small horizontal spawning site on the sand between them. Male breeding coloration varies mainly in the relative amounts of blue and yellow on the flanks, each population having its own characteristic pattern. The *O. heterodon* found along the northeastern shores of the lake is sometimes called "Big Spot Tanzania" and characterized by large spots, whereas in most other populations these are small. There is no real borderline north of which the spots are much larger. In my opinion all these populations belong to the same species, *O. heterodon*.

The lectotype of *O. heterodon* (caught in Monkey Bay) has a black blotch right in front of the dorsal, a feature only known from *Otopharynx* sp. 'heterodon nankumba' and never seen in the forms here referred to as *O. heterodon*. It is thus possible proper examination of the type material (I have only a photo of the lectotype) and comparison with fresh material from the type locality will indicate that *O.* sp. 'heterodon nankumba' is actually *O. heterodon*. In that case a new name will be required for the other species, assuming it proves to be distinct.

At Lundo and Hongi Islands, and along the shores around Liuli and Thumbi Point (all locations in Tanzania), the intermediate biotope harbors another three-spotted cichlid with a close resemblance to *O. heterodon*, namely *Otopharynx* sp. 'heterodon longnose'. Its snout is much longer than that of *O. heterodon*, but these two species are clearly closely related—and the two do not occur sympatrically. *O.* sp. 'heterodon longnose' is rather common in shallow water, with territorial males defending their domains at deeper levels (between seven and 15 meters). The (for *Otopharynx*) unusually long snout has confused dealers and aquarists who have given this species the trade name of "Maravichromis Three Spot". Although it exhibits differences in male color pattern that are usually taken as an indication of geographical variation, a difference in morphology could equally be regarded as such, so *O.* sp. 'heterodon longnose' may be a geographical variant of *O. heterodon*. But until this view is supported by other (morphological or behavioral) data, it is regarded as a distinct species.

At the extreme northern end of the lake, near Ikombe, a small male cichlid with a resemblance to *O. heterodon* was encountered in the intermediate habitat. Only a single male was seen, and this had three small spots on the body. The nearest known population of *O. heterodon*, at Lumbila, has large blotches, and hence I refer to the form at Ikombe as *Otopharynx* sp. 'heterodon ikombe'.

At a depth of about 35 meters at Boadzulu Island I have found male *Otopharynx* sp. 'heterodon boadzulu' defending territories in the sandy part of the intermediate habitat. I was unable to find spawning sites on the sand—the males were instead defending the upper surfaces of low rocks. The breeding colors of the male are very attractive, with an orange hue on most of the flanks and a blue head. This would be a beautiful addition to any Malaŵi aquarium were it not restricted to Boadzulu Island, which is part of the National Park and off-limits to fish collectors. The maximum total length of males is estimated at about 17 cm; females are much smaller and have a maximum total length of about 13 cm.

Spots or no spots

The sand and rubble of the intermediate zone at Nkhomo Reef and the rocky shores south of Chia Lagoon are inhabited by an undescribed species, *Otopharynx* sp. 'spots', characterized by the peculiar position of a number of spots on its body: It is assigned to *Otopharynx* not without hesitation, because it could equally be a member of *Mylochromis* or *Protomelas*. Juveniles, however, exhibit the characteristic spotted pattern of adults as soon as a pigmentation pattern is visible (Gary Kratochvil, pers. comm.). Juveniles of *Mylochromis* exhibit a diagonal stripe. Males in breeding dress are frequently seen wandering through the habitat and do not appear to be restricted to a territory. The species behaves like an opportunistic feeder as it is easily attracted to stirred-up material. Males and females usually form small schools while foraging from the sand. Near Chia Lagoon the species occurs in very shallow water, at depths of less than five meters; at Nkhomo Reef, however, it is seen at depths of about 20 meters. In the wild it attains a total length of approximately 9 cm, but in captivity the attractively colored males can grow to a length of 17 cm.

The rocky shores at the northeastern end of the lake, between Lumbila and Ikombe, are inhabited by a small species (maximum size about 10 cm) at depths ranging between 10 and 25 meters. At first glance this species, *Otopharynx*

1. *Otopharynx* sp. 'auromarginatus margrette' ♂ Mbamba Island (Likoma)

2. *Otopharynx* sp. 'auromarginatus mara' ♂ Mala Point

3. *Otopharynx* sp. 'auromarginatus goldhead' ♂ N'kolongwe

4. *Otopharynx* sp. 'heterodon nankumba' ♂ Otter Island

5. *Otopharynx* sp. 'auromarginatus margrette' ♀ Maingano

6. *Otopharynx* sp. 'auromarginatus mara' ♀ Mala Point

7. *Otopharynx* sp. 'heterodon ikombe' ♂ Matema

8. *Otopharynx* sp. 'spots' ♂ Chia

9. *Otopharynx* sp. 'auromarginatus goldhead' ♀ N'kolongwe

10. *Otopharynx* sp. 'heterodon nankumba' ♀ Thumbi West Island

1. *Otopharynx heterodon* ♀ Maleri Island

2. *Otopharynx heterodon* ♂ Katale Island

3. *Otopharynx heterodon* ♀ Katale Island

4. *Otopharynx heterodon* ♀ Lupingu

5. *Otopharynx heterodon* ♂ Gome

6. *Otopharynx* sp. 'heterodon longnose' ♀ Hongi Island

7. *Otopharynx* sp. 'heterodon boadzulu' ♀ Boadzulu Island

8. *Otopharynx heterodon* ♂ Maleri Island

9. *Otopharynx heterodon* ♂ Chizumulu Island

10. *Otopharynx heterodon* ♂ Lupingu

11. *Otopharynx* sp. 'heterodon longnose' ♂ Lundo Island

12. *Otopharynx* sp. 'heterodon boadzulu' ♂ Boadzulu Island

sp. 'golden blueface', looks like a member of the genus *Aulonocara*, yet when its feeding technique is observed—it picks items from the substrate—it is clear that it cannot be assigned to this genus of "sonar-feeding" cichlids (see page 240). It is also unlikely that this species belongs to the genus *Copadichromis*, as members of that genus forage in mid water and form large schools. Its present assignment to the genus *Otopharynx* is equally questionable. The majority of females do not exhibit the three spots characteristic of the genus; just a few juveniles were seen with such spots. But even though the spots are an important characteristic of *Otopharynx*, several species suppress their expression in the adult stage. Such spots are usually exhibited at night or when the fish is distressed. Furthermore, males of the "Golden Blueface" defend a small patch of sand between rocks as their territory—the construction of a sand-scrape spawning pit has not been observed. By contrast, all the species of *Copadichromis* known so far that breed in the sand of the intermediate habitat, e.g. *C. azureus*, *C. mbenjii*, *C.* sp. 'kawanga', do construct bowers. Even so, *O.* sp. 'golden blueface' most closely resembles *C.* sp. 'kawanga' (see page 233), but its behavior correlates more with that of the members of the genus *Otopharynx*.

Utaka

The *Copadichromis mbenjii* group (see page 120) contains species that breed throughout most of the year in intermediate habitats, and males of all these species construct spawning sites of sand. In all the species known thus far a rock is a feature of the spawning site (bower) and most often a rock is integrated in the rim of the spawning dish.

Many of the utaka species available in the trade are members of the *C. mbenjii* group and all of them are favorites in the hobby. Interestingly, none of the dozen species known in this group was scientifically described before 1990. This is probably because foraging individuals of species of this group do not feed in the open waters of the lake where they might be caught in fishermen's nets. They feed in the water column but never far from rocks or more than a couple of feet off the bottom. In the past almost all fishes described from the lake were collected from fishermen's catches, including those of young boys fishing with hook and line while standing on the rocks of the shoreline. It was only after SCUBA divers searched for species to collect for the ornamental fish trade that many new species were discovered.

Within the *C. mbenjii* group there are two subgroups that are characterized by the shape of the bower. Males of one group use much more sand (if available at the particular locality), constructing a bower mainly of sand with a small rock in the rim or wall of the sand-castle. Males of the other group dig beneath a larger, flat rock and spawning takes place in a much more secluded manner. The spawning site of the latter group has a larger rock than sand component. At many places representatives of both subgroups (burrow and sand-castle spawner) can be found in the same area. At Mbenji Island both *C. azureus* (burrow spawner) and *C. mbenjii* (sand-castle spawner) can be found side by side and this seems to be true for most localities: Chizumulu and Likoma islands have *C. chizumuluensis* and *C. diplostigma* respectively, both sand-castle spawners, while *C. trewavasae*, a burrow spawner, occurs at both islands in similar habitats. At Gome you can find *C. verduyni* (burrow spawner) and *C. atripinnis* (sand-castle spawner) within a few feet of each other. By contrast, between the Chiloelo and Lumessi rivers along the Mozambique shore I have found both *C. parvus* and *C. cyanocephalus* in the same habitat, and both these species are burrow spawners. Females of the two species cannot be told apart. In some areas of the southern part of the lake there is only a single species of the *C. mbenjii* group present. At Chinyankwazi and Chinyamwezi islands we find only *C. insularis*, a burrow spawner, and at Thumbi West and Mumbo islands males of *C. atripinnis* build their characteristic sand-castle bowers.

There are also other characters that distinguish the two subgroups: males of the burrow-spawning group usually have a much darker breeding color than those of the sand-castle spawners, which are often light blue.

Copadichromis mbenjii is endemic to Mbenji Island in the southern portion of the lake. It occurs at the sand/rock interface at depths of 7-20 meters with most individuals in the shallower parts of the range. Territorial males build a sand-castle bower, normally adjacent to a rock. The diameter of the spawning "dish" ranges between 20 and 40 cm and the rim is 4-7 cm high. The rock used for the bower varies between fist-size and slightly larger than the dish itself. The rim normally describes more than half a circle and the center of the dish is often located just beneath the rock. The small cave created under the rock is used as the spawning site. Breeding is seen throughout the year.

Females occur in schools numbering up to 50 individuals and remain within two meters of the bottom. Males and females feed on plankton in the water column and on benthic invertebrates. Females and non-breeding males have colorless fins and three spots on the body. *C. mbenjii* has a clearly rounded head, a feature which distinguishes it from *C. borleyi*.

Copadichromis azureus is also found at Mbenji Island as well as at Nkhomo Reef. This species has been sold as "Haplochromis Chrysonotus" and is very popular among aquarists. Most territorial males defend their bowers at a depth of 20-25 meters. The dish in front of the spawning cave occupies about half a circle or less and is composed of the sand that was excavated from underneath the rock. Males have never been observed carrying sand from the surrounding area to enhance the bower, a behavioral trait that is commonly observed in *C. mbenjii*. The entrance to the spawning cave has a height of 3-7 cm and the bower has a diameter of 20-35 cm. Individual bowers are 3-10 meters apart. Females gather in small groups or are solitary, and feed from the plankton and benthic invertebrates near the bottom. Maximum total length is about 16 cm for males and 11 cm for females, with the population at Mbenji Island containing the largest individuals.

Copadichromis sp. 'azureus jalo' resembles *C. azureus* from Mbenji but has only two spots on the body, instead of three. It is endemic to Jalo Reef near Nkhotakota. Males construct large burrows beneath large rocks, usually at depths of 20-25 meters. Females occur in small groups or even singly in shallower water, but still deeper than 10 meters, where they feed from plankton in the water column over rocks.

Copadichromis verduyni occurs along the eastern shores of the lake between Chimwalani Reef (Eccles Reef) and Gome village. Male *C. verduyni* defend the least visible spawning site of any member of the *C. mbenjii* group. Sometimes the spawning caves have a rocky bottom and lack a sand-dish entrance entirely. In many cases, however, small amounts of sand are moved from the bottom of the little caves in which spawning takes place and used to form a bower. In the northern part of its distribution this species shares the sand/rock habitat with *C. atripinnis*, but the latter is almost always found at deeper levels than *C. verduyni* and in more open habitat. Most male *C. verduyni* defend spawning sites at depths of 9-15 meters. Females and non-territorial males feed from the plankton in the water column 1-3 meters off the bottom and on benthic invertebrates. The species is very closely related to *C. insularis* but can be distinguished by a supra-anal spot that is separate from the upper lateral line (vs. in contact with it in *C. insularis*).

Copadichromis insularis (burrow spawner) inhabits the intermediate habitat of the Maleri islands at depths of 13-18 meters, and is found over sandy patches around Chinyankwazi and Chinyamwezi islands at similar depths. A very similar and probably conspecific form has also been seen at Tsano Rock but no specimens were collected to verify their identity. Females and non-territorial males gather in small schools (up to 10 individuals) and feed on plankton in the water column 1-3 meters above the bottom. Territorial males usually excavate their spawning dish partly underneath flat rocks that are normally larger than the diameter of the dish. The diameter of the dish is 20-35 cm and the height of the spawning cave 3-10 cm. The dish in front of the rock spans roughly a half circle or a little less. Spawning takes place underneath the rock.

The distribution of the recently described

1. *Otopharynx* sp. 'golden blueface' ♂ Ikombe
2. *Copadichromis azureus* ♂ Mbenji Island
3. *Copadichromis mbenjii* ♂ Mbenji Island
4. *Otopharynx* sp. 'golden blueface' ♀ Ikombe
5. *Copadichromis azureus* ♀ Mbenji Island
6. *Copadichromis mbenjii* ♀ Mbenji Island
7. *Copadichromis mbenjii* ♂ Mbenji Island

1. *Copadichromis* sp. 'azureus jalo' ♀ Jalo Reef

2. *Copadichromis insularis* ♀ Chinyankwazi Island

3. *Copadichromis verduyni* ♀ Ntekete

5. *Copadichromis* sp. 'azureus jalo' ♂ Jalo Reef

6. *Copadichromis insularis* ♂ Chinyamwezi Island

4. *Copadichromis verduyni* ♂ Border

Copadichromis cyanocephalus, formerly known as *C.* sp. 'verduyni blueface', includes the rocky shores from a few kilometers north of Meponda to the Lumessi River. Territorial males defend bowers at depths of 15-22 meters. The spawning site is partly underneath a rocky ledge from beneath which the sand has been excavated and deposited in front of the cavity's opening. There is rarely any sign of a dish with a rim; the sand is just carried away from the spawning cave. The rock used in such constructions is almost always larger than the spawning dish's diameter, which is 18-30 cm. The entrance to the spawning cavity is 4-5 cm high. Females live in small groups and are normally found within a meter of the bottom.

Copadichromis parvus, another recently described burrow spawner, previously known as *C.* sp. 'verduyni dwarf', is one of the most widely distributed species of this group. The southernmost point of its range lies just north of the Chiloelo River, where it shares the habitat with *C. cyanocephalus*, and its distribution extends to the bay north of Metangula, entirely in Mozambique. Territorial males occur at depths ranging between 10 and 25 meters and construct bowers by excavating sand from beneath rocks. The spawning dishes have a diameter of 15-22 cm and the entrance to the cavity has a height of 3-6 cm. Most frequently the rock used in the construction is larger than the spawning dish's diameter and spawning takes place inside the cavity. On sandy bottoms there is a shallow dish-like "frontage" to the cavity but on softer substrates no such "vestibule" to the spawning cavity is present. Foraging females and non-territorial males feed in the open water column 1-3 meters off the bottom and on benthic invertebrates. Mouthbrooding females are solitary and remain close to the substrate.

Copadichromis atripinnis—a sand-castle spawner previously known as *C.* sp. 'eastern three-spot'—occurs along the rocky shores of the Nankumba Peninsula and at Domwe, Thumbi West, Mumbo, and the Maleri islands, at Chidunga Rocks, and along the shores between Chimwalani Reef and Gome village on the Malaŵi east coast. It inhabits the intermediate habitat at depths of 12-25 meters. Territorial males construct bowers on sand slopes near rocky areas, with distances between bowers 2-7 meters. The spawning dish has a diameter of 25-40 cm and the rim is 3-9 cm off the bottom. The rock used in the construction is small and rarely wider than a third of the dish's diameter. Excavations from beneath the rock have not been observed. The spawning dish is inclined towards the rock and often spans more than three-quarters of a circle. Females gather in large schools, sometimes numbering more than a hundred individuals. Foraging schools swim about 2-3 meters off the bottom and feed on plankton in the water column and on benthic invertebrates. Mouthbrooding females are found close to the bottom.

Copadichromis trewavasae (formerly known as *C.* sp. 'mloto likoma') is a well-known burrow spawner and a very popular cichlid among aquarists. The populations around Likoma and Chizumulu Islands have both been exploited for the aquarium trade. The species' distribution is not limited to these two islands: it is regularly seen along the Tanzanian shore from Makonde to Manda, and a small population occurs at Cobwé, Mozambique, as well. The northernmost population, at Makonde, is characterized by males having orange-red spots in the dorsal fin, but this, and the extent of the white to mother-of-pearl color on the body, is about as far as geographical variation goes in this species. *C. trewavasae* inhabits the sand/rock interface at depths of 15-25 meters. Territorial males construct a bower by excavating sand or mud from beneath a rock and depositing it in front of the spawning cave to form a semi-circular elevated entrance. The slightly elevated rim of the bower gives only a vague impression of a dish. Spawning takes place underneath the rock. Females normally occur in small groups, rarely numbering more than 10 individuals, and remain close to the bottom. Both males and females feed on plankton in the water column near the bottom, and on benthic invertebrates.

The recently described *Copadichromis melas*, formerly known as *C.* sp. 'midnight mloto', occurs at the sand/rock interface along the Mozambique shore of the lake between Tumbi

Point and Cobwé. At the latter locality it can be found together with *C. trewavasae*, another burrow spawner. Territorial males build their bowers at depths of 10-15 meters. These bowers are excavated under rocks that are often larger than the spawning dish's diameter. They have elevated rims which are normally much higher at the point of contact with the rock than at the center of the rim. The width of the spawning cave beneath the rock is 7-25 cm and the entrance height 3-7 cm. Females are commonly solitary or found in small groups of a few individuals. Both males and females feed on plankton near the bottom and on benthic invertebrates.

Copadichromis chizumuluensis (a sand-castle spawner) is endemic to Chizumulu Island and was previously known as *C.* sp. 'chizumulu blue'. Males build bowers in the intermediate habitat at depths ranging between 12 and 20 meters. The spawning dish is not always beneath a rock and may also be alongside one. On sandy bottoms a male can bank sand up to 30 cm high. Such a bower looks more like a sand turret than a dish, and spawning takes place between the rock and the mound of sand. On muddy substrates males often excavate beneath a rock and have much shallower bowers. Spawning dishes have a diameter of 25-40 cm and the entrance to the spawning cave beneath the rock, if present, can be up to 10 cm high. Females occur in small groups and, like males, feed on plankton in the water column and on benthic invertebrates.

Copadichromis diplostigma, a recently described sand-castle spawner previously termed *C.* sp. 'likoma blue', appears to be endemic to Likoma Island. Territorial male *C. diplostigma* construct bowers at the sand/rock interface at depths of 12-18 meters. On bottoms with fine sand the bower consists of a sand mound with a high wall opposite the rock and a slanted spawning dish. Males carry sand from the environment to build their bowers because the shape demands much more material than can be obtained from beneath the rock. On muddy bottoms, or those with coarse substrates, males defend much shallower bowers. On average a spawning dish has a diameter of approximately 20 cm and the height of the outer rim varies between 3 and 10 cm. Females and immature males occur in small groups and feed on plankton in the water column.

Copadichromis sp. 'chizumuluensis londo' occurs along the eastern shores between Undu in Tanzania and Tumbi Point in Mozambique, and is a sand-castle spawner. It resembles and may even be conspecific with *C. chizumuluensis*. Males build bowers in the intermediate habitat at depths ranging between 10 and 15 meters. The spawning site is almost always a very open spawning dish with a small rock in the rim. In areas with fine-grained sand a lot of this material is used to build a large slanted spawning platform, but in areas with coarse sand or small pebbles the spawning dish is little more than a shallow "scrape" in front of a small rock. Females occur in small groups or are solitary and, like males, feed on plankton in the water column over sandy substrates.

Copadichromis sp. 'chitimba' resembles *C.* sp. 'chizumuluensis londo' but is found along the western shore in two sandy bays south of Chilumba: Youngs Bay and Chitimba Bay. In the former it occurs at a depth of about 10 meters while in Chitimba Bay it is found at a depth of 22 meters. Males construct a sand-castle type bower in which a relatively small rock sits in the rim of the spawning dish. Females in Chitimba Bay lack spots on the flank but juveniles do exhibit them. Females in Youngs Bay have three small spots on the flank.

The member of the *C. mbenjii* group with the widest distribution is unquestionably *Copadichromis* sp. 'kawanga', commonly known as the "Kawanga Borleyi". It was given this name because it was first collected near Kawanga, a small village 15 km north of Nkhata Bay.

C. sp. 'kawanga' occurs along the eastern shores of the lake between Kirondo and Mbamba Bay, including all islands, and along the western shores between Mdoka and Nkhata Bay. Geographical variation is virtually absent on the west coast but evident in the northernmost populations of the eastern shore; those at Kirondo and Makonde differ considerably from all other known populations as regards male breeding coloration. The most prominent dif-

1. *Copadichromis atripinnis* ♂ Chiofu

5. *Copadichromis atripinnis* ♀ Thumbi West Island

6. *Copadichromis cyanocephalus* ♀ Chiloelo

2. *Copadichromis cyanocephalus* ♂ Chiloelo

7. *Copadichromis melas* ♂ Mala Point

3. *Copadichromis parvus* ♂ Nkhungu Reef

8. *Copadichromis melas* ♀ Mala Point

9. *Copadichromis parvus* ♀ Nkhungu Reef

4. *Copadichromis trewavasae* ♂ Lupingu

10. *Copadichromis trewavasae* ♀ Yofu Bay (Likoma)

1. *Copadichromis chizumuluensis* ♀ Chizumulu Island

2. *Copadichromis* sp. 'chizumuluensis londo' ♀ Londo

3. *Copadichromis diplostigma* ♂ Likoma Island

4. *Copadichromis diplostigma* ♀ Yofu Bay (Likoma)

5. *Copadichromis* sp. 'chitimba' ♀ Gallireya Reef

6. *Copadichromis* sp. 'kawanga' ♀ Ndonga

7. *Copadichromis* sp. 'kawanga' ♂ Makonde

8. *Copadichromis chizumuluensis* ♂ Chizumulu Island

9. *Copadichromis* sp. 'chizumuluensis londo' ♂ Londo

10. *Copadichromis* sp. 'chitimba' ♂ Gallireya Reef

11. *Copadichromis* sp. 'kawanga' ♂ Ndonga

ference is the white blaze on the head, which is seen only in the populations north of Lupingu. This geographical variant lives at the outer fringe of the species' distribution. All other populations on the east coast resemble those on the western side of the lake. Although there are minor differences between the remaining populations none is as significant as that mentioned.

At Makonde, Tanzania, *C.* sp. 'kawanga' occurs at a depth of about five meters whereas at Chitande Island, Malaŵi, it occurs down to a depth of about 35 meters. In general it lives at depths of between 10 and 20 meters, usually at the edge of the rocky habitat. The species is a burrow spawner and breeding males, which are found all year round, remain close to the substrate where they build cave-crater type spawning sites. Territorial males are found in breeding colonies where the distance separating individual males varies between one and two meters. Spawning takes place as deep as possible "inside" the bower. The rock under and beside which the spawning pit is excavated protects the spawning pair from egg-robbers. Egg-robbing cichlids are so common in the breeding colonies of other species that any type of protection against these predators is a great advantage. Females and non-breeding males feed on plankton in mid-water above the sand.

Another burrow spawner with a close resemblance to *C.* sp. 'kawanga'—it may actually be a geographical variant of this species—occurs along the shores between Undu in Tanzania and Lumbaulo in Mozambique. It is called *Copadichromis* sp. 'kawanga no spot' because mature females do not exhibit spots on the flanks—although juveniles do. Interestingly this species (or variant) looks like *C. cyanocephalus*, which is found in the south of Mozambique. Like the latter it seems to have a closer association with rocks than the "Kawanga", although there is very little difference in behavior. Most breeding males are found below 15 meters of depth, with the densest concentration at about 20 meters, where breeding leks sometimes occur. Females normally occur in small groups feeding from plankton in the water column a little off the bottom. Maximum total length is about 14 cm.

Little is known about *Copadichromis* sp. 'mloto undu' as I have observed only a single territorial male. In behavior it resembled the burrow spawner *C.* sp. 'kawanga' and the male had constructed a similar spawning pit beneath a rock. However, its color pattern—white blaze on a dark blue body—does not resemble that of males of the neighboring (Mbamba Bay) population of *C.* sp. 'kawanga'.

Copadichromis sp. 'lupingu blue', found only near Lupingu, Tanzania, is the exception to the "rule" that the sand-castle spawners have a light, less intense coloration. Males exhibit a very dark blue breeding dress but construct spawning sites that contain very open, shallow dishes in the sand with a small rock in the rim. This species is found with another, but dark-colored, member of the *C. mbenjii* group, *C. trewavasae*, in the same habitat. Female *C.* sp. 'lupingu blue' lack spots on the flank and have yellow anal and ventral fins. I have not seen juveniles to check whether spots are present at an earlier stage in life, but stressed females do not exhibit spots.

In all these species breeding takes place in the intermediate habitat. Mouthbrooding females gather in schools and move closer inshore. The fry are released in very shallow water near plants or among the rubble of the rocky shore. They are abandoned almost immediately after first release and school together in enormous shoals, and constitute food for the numerous predators of these shallow areas.

A two-spotted utaka at Makanjila Point in the southern part of the lake may also belong to the *C. mbenjii* group, but breeding males have not yet been seen to confirm this. The species, provisionally referred to as *Copadichromis* sp. 'makanjila', resembles *C. likomae* (see page 237) but is smaller and has a somewhat different shape. Males have a white blaze on the head and nape but have not yet been seen defending a territory. Females are brown-silvery and have two distinct round spots on the flank, and some individuals have a third faint spot in between.

Males of a few utaka species of the intermediate habitat do not construct a spawning site (and are thus not members of the *C. mbenjii* group) but defend the upper surface of a rock instead. At the Mbenji islands, *Copadichromis* sp. 'mbenji blue' is a rather common species at the shallow rock-sand interface. Like several other utaka at the islands this species too has three spots on the flanks, making identification difficult. It has a deeper body than the other three-spotted species, and males defend spawning sites on top of rocks in the intermediate habitat. Males closely resemble those of *Copadichromis* sp. 'pictus maleri' but have a yellow breast and pelvic fins while the breast in males of the latter species is blue and their pelvic fins are black. Female *C.* sp. 'pictus maleri' have a row of several large black blotches while those of *C.* sp. 'mbenji blue' have three spots. Territorial male *C.* sp. 'pictus maleri' defend a spawning site on top of a large boulder on the sand. Males hover about a meter over the sand next to their rock. *C.* sp. 'pictus maleri' has been found only at the Maleri islands.

A small species, here termed *Copadichromis* sp. 'maison', is found at Maison Reef, south of Chirwa Island in the northern section of the lake. It is not certain whether it belongs to *Copadichromis* because only a few breeding individuals have been found and it could equally be a member of *Otopharynx*. However, the male defends his territory on top of a large rock and would be the first known *Otopharynx* species to do so. The female has three spots on the flank but none of them is distinct. The estimated maximum total length is about 12 cm. A breeding group was seen at a depth of about 25 meters.

The following species of utaka cannot be grouped into any of the three divisions in *Copadichromis*. *Copadichromis likomae* resembles *C. quadrimaculatus* in its morphology, but is distinguished by its smaller size (maximum about 15 cm) and by having only two spots on the flanks. Both species have only sporadically been exported as aquarium fishes, the reason being their total lack of color outside the breeding season. *C. likomae* was described from Likoma Island but is found all around the lake. It is the only known species of spotted *Copadichromis* in which males build large sand-castle bowers in the intermediate habitat but do not use any rock(s) in the construction. These bowers measure about 75 cm in diameter. The breeding period probably extends from June to November. The fry are released in very shallow water among rocks and plants.

A very similar species, *Copadichromis* sp. 'likomae masinje', is found in water deeper than 25 meters between Makanjila Point and Gome along the Malaŵi east coast. Some males at Gome construct bowers in which they include a small rock, while others of the same population defend a prominent flat rock as their spawning site. These rocks are prepared with a covering of fine sand from which all larger grains have been removed. Males in a population near Narungu were found to have constructed sand-castle bowers without any rock in the construction even though they were only meters away from rocks. *C. likomae* occurs in the same area but in shallower water, but the two species have an approximately similar size and morphology. Males of *C.* sp. 'likomae masinje' can easily be told apart from those of *C. likomae* by their steel blue color, yellow anal, and yellow trailing part of the dorsal fin. Females have only a single spot, on the caudal peduncle, and the anal fin is yellow with large yellow spots on its edge. All unpaired fins in juveniles are yellow.

Copadichromis pleurostigma is known only from the northern half of the lake and is closely related to *C. trimaculatus*, or may even be conspecific (Jos Snoeks, pers. comm.). It is normally found over sand in the intermediate or sandy habitat. At Msuli Point mouthbrooding females have been observed (in November) releasing their fry among the small schools of other utaka juveniles that are usually found above nests of the *kampango* (*Bagrus meridionalis*). It thus appears they do not guard their offspring after release, but rely on the catfish to protect the brood along with its own young. Juveniles are bright yellow all over but lose the yellow color on their flanks as they mature. Breeding males have not yet been found.

Copadichromis pleurostigmoides is distinguished from *C. pleurostigma* by the more pointed head and the fact that it is normally found over more rocky substrates. Male *C.*

1. *Copadichromis* sp. 'kawanga no-spot' ♂ Londo

2. *Copadichromis* sp. 'mloto undu' ♂ Undu

3. *Copadichromis* sp. 'lupingu blue' ♂ Lupingu

4. *Copadichromis* sp. 'mbenji blue' ♂ Mbenji Island

5. *Copadichromis* sp. 'kawanga no-spot' ♀ Londo

6. *Copadichromis* sp. 'mloto undu' ♂ Undu

7. *Copadichromis* sp. 'makanjila' ♂ Makanjila Point

8. *Copadichromis* sp. 'makanjila' ♀ Makanjila Point

9. *Copadichromis* sp. 'lupingu blue' ♀ Lupingu

10. *Copadichromis* sp. 'mbenji blue' ♀ Mbenji Island

1. *Copadichromis* sp. 'pictus maleri' ♀ Nakantenga Island

2. *Copadichromis likomae* ♀♀ Chinuni

3. *Copadichromis* sp. 'maisoni' ♂ Maison Reef

4. *Copadichromis* sp. 'maisoni' ♀ Maison Reef

5. *Copadichromis* sp. 'likoma masinje' ♀ Gome

6. *Copadichromis pleurostigma* ♂ Aquarium

7. *Copadichromis* sp. 'pictus maleri' ♂ Nakantenga Island

8. *Copadichromis likomae* ♂ Chiofu

9. *Copadichromis* sp. 'likoma masinje' ♂ Narungu

10. *Copadichromis pleurostigma* ♀ Msuli Point

pleurostigmoides develop a dark blue nuptial color with a distinct whitish blaze on the head and nape. Females have yellow fins and three black spots, though in some females the middle spot is absent. This species' breeding season is from April to August (Iles, 1960). Males defend spawning sites on top of flat rocks at depths of between 20 and 40 meters in sediment-rich intermediate habitats.

Copadichromis sp. 'tumbi two spot' occurs at Tumbi Point in Mozambique, and resembles *C. quadrimaculatus*. Male *C.* sp. 'tumbi two spot' construct a kind of spawning platform of sand on top of a large boulder, not unlike those of *Mchenga conophoros* at Cape Maclear or *M. thinos* at Mdoka (see page 314). Mature females have three spots, but the middle one is very faint in most individuals so that they appear to have only two. *Copadichromis* sp. 'tumbi two spot' occurs at an average depth of 15 meters.

Copadichromis sp. 'flavimanus lundu', which has been given the trade name of "Copadichromis Chingata", is found at Lundu (Tanzania). A single specimen has been examined and was found to be different from the types of *Mchenga flavimanus*. In November large schools of juveniles inhabit the deeper levels (average depth 25 meters) of the rocky and intermediate habitats at Lundu, but adult individuals have not been seen at that time. The breeding period seems to be from May to July. Males build cave-craters in the intermediate habitat at a depth of 25 to 35 meters (Annette Bentler, pers. comm.).

In Liuli Bay, Tanzania, I once photographed, at a depth of about 15 meters, a male of *Copadichromis* sp. 'mloto liuli', a *mloto*-like cichlid that defended its territory on top of a large boulder. In shape and coloration it resembled *C. mloto* (page 315), but since it did not have a spawning site, its assignment to that species would be questionable. Females were not observed, and to the best of my knowledge the species has never been exported.

A few undescribed utaka species were characterized by Chisambo & Snoeks (2004) in a key to the spotted utaka, but I could not find a match for two of their species in the lake: *Copadichromis* sp. 'grey' and *Copadichromis* sp. 'stigma'. The latter species was collected at Ndumbi Rocks near Likoma and is characterized by a large supra-pectoral spot, four scales wide. *C.* sp. 'grey' is morphologically similar to *C. quadrimaculatus* (page 154) and was collected near Nkhata Bay and Chinteche. Color patterns of live or freshly-caught specimens were not given.

Sonar feeders

A totally different group of cichlids, popularly known as peacock cichlids, have their special niche in the transition zone where sand and rocks meet. Almost all of them belong to the genus *Aulonocara* and every rocky coast has its own set of representatives of this genus. Molecular investigations by Moran *et al.* (1994) have suggested that *Aulonocara*, together with the genera *Lethrinops* and *Alticorpus*, belongs to the mbuna, but it is more plausible that these three genera form a separate coherent group, distinct from the mbuna as well as from other Malaŵian haplochromines (Geerts, 1995).

Spawning in rock-associated *Aulonocara* takes place in caves, as is the case in almost all rock-dwelling haplochromines. Furthermore, breeding occurs throughout the year and males in breeding dress can be seen at any time and at any location within their range. The maximum size of the rock-dwelling species known in the aquarium hobby never exceeds 13 cm for wild specimens. In captivity, where fishes are fed on a protein-rich and easily digestible diet, many of the known species may grow to a considerably larger size.

All members of *Aulonocara* are characterized by an enlarged lateral line system (the sensory system, comparable to our ears), in particular on the head. This extension of the "ears", which makes them much more perception-sensitive, is clearly visible externally as pits and grooves, especially on the lower part of the head. There are other Malaŵian genera containing species with similar pressure-wave-sensitive organs, e.g. *Alticorpus* (page 400) and *Trematocranus* (page 353), and in Lake Tanganyika several cichlid genera, e.g. *Trematocara* and *Aulonocranus*, have developed similar sensory pits. All cichlids equipped with such "sonar" use these organs as sensitive food-detectors, not for detecting predators.

The natural behavior of *Aulonocara* provides the vital clue to the purpose of the enhancement of the sensory system on the head. Territorial males as well as females and juveniles all hover about a centimeter above the sandy substrate. Each of them barely moves a fin! It looks as if they are all asleep. Every now and then, a sudden dive by an individual into the sand interrupts the "trance" in which these foraging cichlids remain stationary over their feeding grounds. Now it becomes clear why most of the sensory pits are located on the lower part of the head. They register, with high sensitivity, the minute movements of crustaceans, snails, and other invertebrates hidden (!) in the sand. As soon as a moving prey item is detected a quick bite in the sand secures it inside the predator's mouth. By "chewing" the fish separates the prey from the mouthful of sand and either expels the latter through the gills or spits it out. *Aulonocara* are not built to sift and filter sand continuously, like *Lethrinops* (page 361) and possibly *Alticorpus* (page 400), but the three genera probably share a common ancestor and may represent intermediates between the larger haplochromines and the mbuna. Most *Aulonocara* forage on the sand outside their caves, and feeding takes place during the day. At night they retreat into their shelters. Some species, which are seen only in caves and which were previously assigned to *Trematocranus*, forage from the sandy or muddy bottom of their homes.

The genus *Aulonocara* is large and contains two different assemblages of species. The aquaristically well-known group comprises small cichlids with a preference for the intermediate habitat, which are known as the rock-dwelling *Aulonocara*. The other group consists of mainly sand-dwelling cichlids recognizable by the very large sensory pores in the enlarged infra-orbital bones (the bones partially surrounding the lower part of the eyes). This group undoubtedly has a closer relationship to *Lethrinops* than does the group of rock-dwellers (see page 356 for further discussion of the sand-dwelling group and *Trematocranus*). The *Aulonocara* that live in the intermediate habitat can be divided into five different groups: the *jacobfreibergi* types (cave dwellers), the *stuartgranti* types, the chitande types, the *maylandi* types, and the non-territorial *A. saulosi*.

The *jacobfreibergi* types

Some species of *Aulonocara* are normally found in caves. These species, originally assigned to *Trematocranus* and still sometimes seen under that name in the hobby, are commonly known as "Malaŵi Butterflies" or by a host of other trade names. The sensory pits in cave-dwelling *Aulonocara* (e.g. *A. jacobfreibergi*) are less enlarged than those of the other members of the genus. If the pits in the heads of *Aulonocara* had been developed to sense better in the dark, then one would expect the cave-dwelling members of this genus to have even larger pits—but they don't. The cave-dwelling species may therefore represent an older branch of the genus, from which other species, the ones with more sensitive sonars, are derived.

The first specimens of this sub-group were caught at Otter Point in the south of the lake and exported as "Trematocranus Trevori". Owing to the sparkling colors displayed by males of this species it quickly received the trade name "Malaŵi Butterfly" in some countries. This species was subsequently scientifically named *Trematocranus jacobfreibergi*, but is now assigned to *Aulonocara*. Several geographical variants have since been discovered around Cape Maclear and given fancy trade names such as "Trematocranus Catherinae", "T. Carolae", "T. Saulosi", "T. Vanessae", and "T. Reginae". They are all merely geographical variants of *A. jacobfreibergi*, which has a widespread distribution along the western shores of the lake. On the eastern coast it occurs at Lupingu, north of the Ruhuhu River, and along the shore south of this river between Pombo Rocks and Undu Reef. Each population has its own particular male breeding coloration; the ones found in the northern part of the lake have a generally yellow-based coloration whereas southern populations are more orange-blue. In recent years the so-called "Mamelela", the variant at Undu

1. *Copadichromis* sp. 'tumbi two-spot' ♂ Tumbi Point
2. *Copadichromis pleurostigmoides* ♂ Nkhata Bay
3. *Bagrus meridionalis* ♂ Chiofu
4. *Copadichromis* sp. 'flavimanus lundu' ♂ Aquarium
5. *Copadichromis* sp. 'flavimanus lundu' ♀ Ndumbi Point
6. *Copadichromis pleurostigmoides* ♀ Nkhata Bay
7. *Copadichromis* sp. 'mloto liuli' ♂ Liuli

1. *Aulonocara jacobfreibergi* ♂ Cape Kaiser (Aquarium)

2. *Aulonocara jacobfreibergi* ♂ Hongi Island

3. *Aulonocara jacobfreibergi* ♂ Tchinga Reef

4. *Aulonocara jacobfreibergi* ♂ Mumbo Island

5. *Aulonocara jacobfreibergi* ♂ Domwe Island

6. *Aulonocara jacobfreibergi* ♀ Otter Island

7. *Aulonocara jacobfreibergi* ♂ Chitande Island

8. *Aulonocara jacobfreibergi* ♂ Undu

9. *Aulonocara jacobfreibergi* ♂ Otter Island

10. *Aulonocara jacobfreibergi* ♂ Boadzulu Island

Reef, has become very popular among aquarists.

Stuart Grant's fishermen discovered a second cave-dwelling *Aulonocara* at Membe Point, Likoma Island, and named it "Trematocranus Walteri". This species, which is a much darker color than *A. jacobfreibergi*, has been found at other sites around the island and occurs at Chizumulu as well. *Aulonocara* sp. 'walteri' is closely related to, and perhaps conspecific with, a species found on the southeastern coast of the lake, between Meponda and Ntekete. This species, *Aulonocara* sp. 'trematocranus masinje', better known as just "Trematocranus Masinje", is normally found at depths exceeding 20 meters. At Likoma *A.* sp. 'walteri' occurs in very shallow water, sometimes no deeper than three meters. Male coloration, however, is similar in both species (forms), except for the iridescent blue on the snout and lower part of the head in *A.* sp. 'walteri', which is absent in the deep-dwelling *A.* sp. 'trematocranus masinje'.

A third form of dark-colored *Aulonocara* is found at Hai Reef in Tanzania and along the coast near Chiwindi in Mozambique: *Aulonocara* sp. 'lwanda'. This very attractive species, with trade names such as "Aulonocara Lwanda" and "Aulonocara Red Dorsal", lives in shallow, intermediate habitats at depths ranging from three to 10 meters.

Ripe males of *A. jacobfreibergi* and other cave-dwelling members of the genus invariably defend territories inside caves, with several males sometimes found inside a single large cave. Males do not construct anything resembling a spawning crater. The spawning site is frequently located in cracks in the walls of the cave, sometimes in gaps close to the ceiling, but also on the sandy floor. Females usually forage on the bottom of the cave or outside, near the entrance. They are rarely found on the open sand among other *Aulonocara* species.

Besides these relatively well-known species there is one other *Aulonocara* found in the caves of the intermediate habitat: *Aulonocara* sp. 'jalo'. This interesting species lives around the rocks of Jalo Reef, near Nkhotakota. The color pattern of breeding males resembles that of the yellow form of *A. stuartgranti* (see page 247).

The mouth, however, is rather large, and the sensory pores on the head are less enlarged than in other species of the genus. Large specimens of *A.* sp. 'trematocranus masinje' have a similarly large mouth. There is no reason, based on anatomical features, to exclude *A.* sp. 'jalo' from *Aulonocara*. Its behavior, however, deviates from the general pattern observed in members of this genus. Neither males nor females have been seen hovering over sandy substrates in search of food. *Aulonocara* sp. 'jalo' lives in caves and is a rare sight anywhere around the reef. It feeds on invertebrates which it probably finds in the cave. Males defend territories but wandering males in breeding dress are sometimes seen outside caves as well. The color pattern of males, however, has a striking resemblance to that of some *Aulonocara* and this species undoubtedly belongs to that genus.

Aulonocara trematocephalum is known only from the holotype, which was collected by Moore at the end of the 19th century. Its locality was mislabeled as the north end of Lake Tanganyika and it was first described as *Tilapia trematocephala*. Later, Poll (1987) suggested that this species belonged to the Malaŵian fauna and assigned it to *Trematocranus*. Eccles & Trewavas (1989) further investigated the small (7.5 cm SL) holotype and came to the same conclusion about its origin. *A. trematocephalum* may be one of or closely related to the group of cave-dwelling *Aulonocara*. We will probably never know with which of the known species it is conspecific.

The *stuartgranti* types

Most species of this group of the genus *Aulonocara* inhabit the boundary between rocks and sand at depths ranging between five and 15 meters. All forms of the *stuartgranti* group behave in a similar manner. They are rather common in the intermediate habitat where females and juveniles are found in small groups (or singly) feeding from the sandy patches between the rocks. They are most numerous on gently sloping coasts where many rocks lie scattered on the sandy floor. Males excavate holes between rocks and territories are marked with a shallow rim of sand at the entrance of the spawning cave. Digging is rarely observed in *Aulonocara,* although males of several species have tunnels beneath stones. The small caves that are used for shelter are at the same level as the sand floor. When foraging *Aulonocara* of this group are disturbed they immediately seek shelter between and under the rocks.

Along the entire northwestern coast, and on the eastern shores south of the Ruhuhu River, this niche is occupied by *Aulonocara stuartgranti*. This species occurs in many different geographical variants (see page 247). It has been in the aquarium hobby for many years and was formerly exported under the trade names "Aulonocara Chilumba" for the blue variant from Chilumba and "Aulonocara Usisya" or "Flavescent Peacock" for the yellow variant from Usisya. *A. stuartgranti* has also been exported from Tanzania, and these forms are known in the trade as "Aulonocara Yellow Tanzania" and "Aulonocara Blue Neon".

On the northwestern coast *A. stuartgranti* occurs at every locality between Kande Island and Ngara where the intermediate habitat is no deeper than 25 meters. Between Charo and Mara Rocks the male breeding coloration of the different populations of *A. stuartgranti* varies from all blue to blue-yellow to completely yellow, and then back again to all-blue. The stretch of coast along which these various populations are found is no longer than about 40 km (in a straight line). There are behavioral differences between the various populations, but these are caused by differences in the environment, and can in no instance be correlated with the variations in male breeding color. *A. stuartgranti* from Usisya has a larger adult size than all other known races along this coast. This is probably due to the higher percentage of digestible food present in the sand around Usisya. *Protomelas fenestratus* found in the same area are on average 3 cm longer than those at neighboring locations (Mara Rocks and Mbowe Island).

The geographical variation of *A. stuartgranti* further south along the western coast is likewise rather pronounced. For example, there are two populations in Chitimba Bay, separated from each other by about 2 km of sand. One population, which was discovered by Alfred Maulana (one of Stuart Grant's dive-team leaders), inhabits the shallow intermediate area at a depth of about five meters, while the other is found at a deeper locality in the same bay, about 2.5 km offshore, where the biotope consists of sheets of sandstone. The *A. stuartgranti* found at this second site has an overall blue color and orange ventral fins—the golden band behind the head seen in the shallow-water population is completely absent. Besides the difference in coloration there is also one in body length. *A. stuartgranti* "Maulana" (the trade name of the shallow-water form) is, with a maximum length of 9-10 cm, much smaller than the deeper water variant (trade name "Aulonocara Maisoni") which is estimated to have a maximum size of about 13 cm.

In Tanzania the distribution of *A. stuartgranti* is bounded by the Ruhuhu River, north of which it is absent. South of the river, along the entire coastline of Tanzania and Mozambique and into Malaŵi territory, *A. stuartgranti* populates almost all shallow intermediate habitats. The first specimens are seen at Ndumbi Point, but dense populations are not found until south of Liuli, especially at Hongi and Lundo islands. Although I have not found this species at Ngkuyo (Mbamba Bay) Island and Higga Reef, almost all other suitable biotopes between the Ruhuhu and the border with Mozambique are inhabited by *A. stuartgranti*. Interestingly, along a rather long stretch of coastline, from the Ruhuhu delta to Chuwa (the rocky area south of Mbamba Bay), there is no noticeable geographical variation among the populations. And even further south, at Undu and Hai reefs, which are separated from the rocky area at Mbamba Bay by at least 20 km of sandy shores, the male breeding coloration of this form, known as *A. stuartgranti* "Blue Neon" is very similar to that of the other Tanzanian populations.

The "Blue Neon", characterized by a yellow body and "neon blue" fins, also occurs in the northern part of Mozambique, at Chiwindi, Wikihi, and Londo. Males of the population at Chiwindi show the brightest yellow. At Lumbaulo, and even more so at Ntumba, males are

1. *Aulonocara* sp. 'walteri' ♂ Chizumulu Island

2. *Aulonocara* sp. 'Iwanda' ♂ Chiwindi

3. *Aulonocara* sp. 'trematocranus masinje' ♂ Gome

4. *Aulonocara* sp. 'jalo' ♂ Jalo Reef

5. *Aulonocara* sp. 'walteri' ♀ Likoma Island

6. *Aulonocara* sp. 'walteri' ♂ Likoma Island

7. *Aulonocara* sp. 'Iwanda' ♀ Hai Reef

8. *Aulonocara* sp. 'trematocranus masinje' ♀ Gome

9. *Aulonocara* sp. 'jalo' ♀ Jalo Reef

10. *Aulonocara trematocephalum* holotype

almost blue with only the breast and pelvic fins dark orange-yellow. At Cobwé the males are blue with bright orange-red pelvic fins. Peter Davies, who exported this form as "Aulonocara nyassae" and transplanted it to Cape Maclear — where it still thrives — exploited this population in the early 1970s. This form has more recently been exported again as "Aulonocara Cobwe". Continuing further south along the shores of Mozambique, the dominant color of the males remains blue but at some locations, e.g. Metangula and south of Chiloelo, they have an orange-red band on the shoulder, varying in width depending not only on the particular population but also on the individual. On the Malaŵi east coast, south of the Mozambique border, the distribution of *A. stuartgranti* continues as far south as Luwala Reef. The Malaŵian population, which bears the trade name of "Aulonocara Red Flush", has been described as *A. hansbaenschi*, but this name should be regarded as a synonym of *A. stuartgranti*.

There has been some confusion about the identity of the so-called "Usisya Aulonocara", which is in fact a yellow variant of *A. stuartgranti*, but sometimes referred to as *A. steveni* (a junior synonym). Although on the face of it there is no reason why the "Usisya Aulonocara" should not be assigned to a different species — the male breeding coloration is quite different to that of the blue-colored holotype of *A. stuartgranti* — there are data pointing clearly to the conspecificity of these two populations. In the early 1980s we knew only those variants that were exported from Malaŵi, among them the all-blue variant from Chilumba and the yellow *Aulonocara* from Usisya ("Flavescent Peacock"). At that time most of us believed that these two were different species. Later, when I visited many localities between these two populations, I found that there is no clearly defined border between the all-blue and the all-yellow populations. There is a gradual change from one extreme (all-blue) to the other (all-yellow), and although males of any given population show a more or less constant coloration; the color changes with the population, not within a population. From these observations I have come to the conclusion that both the "Usisya Aulonocara" and that from Chilumba are one and the same species.

There are several species of strictly rock-dwelling cichlids found on opposite coasts of the lake. Some of these species are known to occur in several geographical variants and some of these are also found on both sides of the lake (see page 21). This fact makes it logical to assign the Tanzanian peacocks to *A. stuartgranti* as well. Interestingly, the "hot spot" for *A. stuartgranti* on the Tanzanian coast is at Hongi Island and that for the similar looking variant on the west coast is at Usisya. These two localities are directly opposite each other (see map page 6). And since there is again a gradual change in male breeding coloration from one population to the next, all forms found along the Mozambique and eastern Malaŵi shores should be assigned to *A. stuartgranti* as well. I have been unable to find two adjacent populations where the males of one population had a color pattern noticeably different from that of the males of the other.

The *Aulonocara* at Mbenji, the so-called "Blue Regal", is in many respects similar to the Chilumba form of *A. stuartgranti* and was previously termed *A.* sp. 'stuartgranti mbenji'. There is, however, a clear distinction between these two species: females and non-territorial males of the "Blue Regal" are characterized by broad bars and, superimposed on these, large elongate spots on the flanks. Egg-spots, which are visible in all northern races of *A. stuartgranti*, are not present on the anal fin of the "Blue Regal", but are also absent in the southern variants of *A. stuartgranti* along the Mozambique shores. The "Blue Regal" could be regarded as a population of *A. stuartgranti*, but since the females exhibit an appreciable difference from those of *A. stuartgranti* it has recently been described as *Aulonocara koningsi*.

The peacock found at the Maleri Islands is known in the hobby as the "Yellow Regal", while the form at Chidunga Rocks near Chipoka is exported as the "Sunshine Peacock" or "Orange Peacock". These are both populations of *Aulonocara* sp. 'stuartgranti maleri', which is also found at Mumbo and Namalenje Islands. Largely because intermediate populations do not exist between Mbenji and Namalenje or between Mumbo and Ntekete, *A.* sp. 'stuartgranti maleri' is considered different from *A. koningsi* or *A. stuartgranti*.

Aulonocara baenschi was described from Nkhomo Reef, near Benga, and is frequently exported as the "Benga Aulonocara". It is characterized by a convex snout profile; this feature is straight in the preceding three species. In this respect it looks more like the species of the chitande type group of *Aulonocara*. It also occurs at a greater depth than any of the three preceding species. Females of this species can readily be distinguished from those of *A. koningsi*, which lends credibility to its being regarded as a different species.

Aulonocara korneliae, which is endemic to Chizumulu Island, and *Aulonocara hueseri*, endemic to Likoma Island, both belong to the *stuartgranti* group. Males never dig but occupy a cave between rocks on the sand. Females are regularly seen in large schools foraging from the sand. *A. korneliae* is exported as "Aulonocara Blue Gold" while *A. hueseri* has received trade names such as "Night Aulonocara" and "Aulonocara White Top".

The chitande types

The species of the third group, which are known as chitande type *Aulonocara*, are characterized by anatomical as well as behavioral features. The former include a more or less convex snout profile and a ventrally-positioned mouth. The egg-spots are very conspicuous in males, and females have in general a more silvery color than those of other groups, perhaps with the exception of *A. kandeense*. The chitande types are found in the intermediate habitat, yet females and juveniles group together in schools and forage on the sand, sometimes meters away from the rocks. Schools numbering more than a hundred individuals are not uncommon. Although females are found in shallow water (at a depth of about three meters), breeding males prefer deeper regions, most being found at a depth of about 25 meters, rarely shallower than 15 meters. Interestingly, most territorial males of these species have their domains far away from most of the females. Only ripe females will approach a territorial male and deposit their eggs in his spawning pit. In the deep regions, where other species of the rock-dwelling *Aulonocara* are absent, the spawning site may be a small cave; in the presence of other rock-dwelling *Aulonocara*, however, it is no more than a very shallow dip in the sand, usually excavated alongside a small stone. Mouthbrooding females either congregate in separate schools (when the population is dense) or seek a more private retreat. Once the fry have been released they are guarded for only one or two days. Juveniles are very secretive and remain among the rocks until they have reached a size of about 3 cm.

Only one species of this group has been described: *Aulonocara ethelwynnae*. It occurs between Chilumba and Mdoka at deep levels, the population at Chitande Island being the densest. It is known among hobbyists as the "Northern Aulonocara" or "Chitande Aulonocara". Most males have their territories centered on small caves.

The deeper intermediate biotope at Likoma and Chizumulu islands, at Mala Point in Mozambique, and along the western shores between Hora Mhango, Mbowe Island, and Nkhata Bay, is inhabited by *Aulonocara* sp. 'chitande type north'. On the western coast this species occurs at depths ranging between 25 and 40 meters. The males of these populations are normally found in caves. At the first two islands and at Mala Point males are rarely seen in caves: they usually defend small pits in the sand, but this defense consists merely of raising the dorsal fin when another male in breeding color approaches. The "Chitande Type North" is distinguished from *A.* sp. 'chitande type mozambique', *A.* sp. 'chitande type masinje', and *A.* sp. 'chitande type nkhomo' by the black marginal band in the dorsal, which is white in these species. *Aulonocara* sp. 'chitande type mozambique' lives at depths varying between 10 and 25 meters between Hai Reef and Lumbaulo. It resembles *Aulonocara* sp. 'chitande type masinje', a species from the southern part of the lake. The latter occurs on the east coast between Ntekete in Malaŵi and Chiloelo in

1. *Aulonocara* sp. 'stuartgranti maleri' ♂ Chidunga Rocks

2. *Aulonocara baenschi* ♂ Nkhomo Reef

4. *Aulonocara* sp. 'stuartgranti maleri' ♀ Maleri Island

5. *Aulonocara* sp. 'stuartgranti maleri' ♀ Nankoma Island

3. *Aulonocara koningsi* ♂ Mbenji Island

6. *Aulonocara baenschi* ♀ Nkhomo Reef

7. *Aulonocara koningsi* ♀ Mbenji Island

1. *Aulonocara korneliae* ♀ Chizumulu Island

6. *Aulonocara korneliae* ♂ Chizumulu Island

2. *Aulonocara hueseri* ♀ Yofu Bay (Likoma)

3. *Aulonocara ethelwynnae* ♀ Chitande Island

7. *Aulonocara hueseri* ♂ Likoma Island

4. *Aulonocara* sp. 'chitande type north' ♂♀ Masimbwe

8. *Aulonocara* sp. 'chitande type north' ♂ Hora Mhango

5. *Aulonocara ethelwynnae* ♂ Chitande Island

Mozambique.

At Kande Island another dark chitande type occurs in the intermediate habitat, albeit together with two other rock-dwelling *Aulonocara*, *A. stuartgranti* (yellow form) and *A. kandeense*. Males of *Aulonocara* sp. 'chitande type kande', which seems endemic to the island, defend shallow pits in the sand among the rubble on the sandy floor. The immense numbers of *Aulonocara* at Kande pose the question whether or not the sand holds sufficient food for all these "sonar-feeders".

At Nkhomo Reef, almost 200 km further south, we encounter a more elongate member of the chitande type group: *Aulonocara* sp. 'chitande type nkhomo', which also has a localized distribution. As almost all the rocks at this reef lie at a depth of about 22 meters, both the *Aulonocara* found here—*A. baenschi* also occurs at this site—are necessarily found at this depth. Closer to shore there is a reef at a depth of about seven meters but neither *A. baenschi* nor *A.* sp. 'chitande type nkhomo' could be found here.

Aulonocara sp. 'yellow collar', a member of the chitande types, is distributed around the Nankumba peninsula (but not at Thumbi West and Mumbo islands) and at Chemwezi Rocks. It exhibits some geographical variation, with the northern populations the brightest in color. The southern ones are darker and have less blue on the head.

The *maylandi* types

At Kande Island *A. stuartgranti* and *A.* sp. 'chitande type kande' share the habitat with another member of the genus, namely *Aulonocara kandeense*. Although there is a slight difference in the habitat preferences of these species, they are all three seen side by side (literally). Unfortunately a recent increase in fishing pressure from the ornamental fish trade has had a profound impact on the population density of *A. kandeense*; a visit in October 2006 revealed that this species had been almost extirpated from the island.

Not only is there a conspicuous difference in male coloration, but, in addition, the pharyngeal dentition of *A. kandeense* differs from that of the other two species, possibly indicating a different dietary preference. The pharyngeal teeth of *A. stuartgranti* and *A.* sp. 'chitande type kande' are all very slender, suggesting a diet of soft-bodied invertebrates. Those of *A. kandeense*, however, are greatly enlarged (at least in the few specimens examined by Meyer *et al.*, 1987) and are probably used to crush small snails, remains of which have been found in the stomachs of preserved specimens. To the best of my knowledge, Kande Island is the only location where more than two rock-dwelling *Aulonocara* share the same habitat. Females of *A. kandeense*, which is better known as the "Blue Orchid Aulonocara", forage further away from rocks than those of *A. stuartgranti*. The number of "Chitande Type Kande" individuals is much smaller than that of either *A. kandeense* or *A. stuartgranti*. *A. kandeense* females have a more silvery color than those of *A. stuartgranti* and can be distinguished from those of *A.* sp. 'chitande type kande' by a deeper body and the lack of a yellow margin to the dorsal.

Aulonocara maylandi resembles *A. kandeense* in male color pattern (but not color itself) and the two species are probably closely related. *A. maylandi* is found on submerged reefs (Chimwalani and Luwala reefs) south of Makanjila Point and shares the habitat with the "Aulonocara Red Flush" form of *A. stuartgranti*. It is also known by the trade name of "Sulfurhead Aulonocara". Both *A. maylandi* and *A. kandeense* are characterized by the fact that broods consist of numerous (sometimes more than 100) very small fry.

Aulonocara saulosi

Aulonocara saulosi was described from a population on the eastern shore in Malaŵi. Other populations of this species have been located at Tsano Rock at the Nankumba Peninsula, around Likoma Island, at Londo in Mozambique, and at Undu and Hai reefs in Tanzania. It is exported as "Aulonocara Special", "Aulonocara Greenface", and "Aulonocara Green Metallic". Although males and females have a generally dark coloration, they are often found on the sand and feed in exactly the same way as described earlier. However, *A. saulosi* has one behavioral characteristic that is not seen in any other *Aulonocara*. When frightened it does not seek shelter in a cave, because it has none! This species roams through the intermediate habitat and "samples" sandy patches between rocks. Males in breeding dress behave in a similar way. When two males meet there is a short display, but both individuals continue on their way soon after the encounter. Although I have observed many males in breeding dress, none of them showed any territoriality. Probably only during the actual spawning is a site defended.

Piscivores

Besides the predators that feed mainly on invertebrates, there are other, piscivorous, predators present in the intermediate habitat.

Tyrannochromis macrostoma, a very common piscivore of the intermediate habitat, is characterized by a black belly and peculiar hunting behavior. This large cichlid shows a remarkable degree of morphological variation, even within a single population. This confused taxonomists for a long time, with separate names being given to what subsequently proved to be merely forms of one species—*T. maculiceps* and *T. polyodon* are both synonyms of *T. macrostoma*. After collecting 72 specimens at more than 20 localities around the lake I have been able to demonstrate that we are dealing with a single species with a high degree of anatomical variation. Another member of the genus, *T. nigriventer* (see page 125), is distinguished by a shorter premaxillary pedicel (the sliding element of the upper jaw); in *T. macrostoma* the tip of the pedicel reaches almost to between the eyes whereas in *T. nigriventer* it remains in front of them.

Snoeks & Hanssens (2004) report a species of *Tyrannochromis* that has a melanin pattern resembling that of *T. macrostoma* but which has a short premaxillary pedicel. The single specimen found is referred to as *Tyrannochromis* sp. 'macrostoma short pedicel'.

The peculiar hunting technique mentioned above involves a head-down position of the body (angled at about 45°) which is also tilted to one side. This posture is adopted after the prey has been located and allows the fish to focus on the victim which is then suddenly snatched from its hideout. A similar feeding technique is observed in *Exochochromis anagenys* and *Aristochromis christyi* as well (see page 125).

A sexually active male *T. macrostoma* constructs a semi-circular sand wall against a rock, usually in the intermediate habitat. This spawning dish, which has an approximate diameter of 50 cm, is much smaller than that built by *T. nigriventer*, which can be more than a meter in diameter. I have never seen more than one male in breeding colors in a particular area.

Sciaenochromis fryeri is a piscivorous cichlid that enjoys widespread popularity among hobbyists and is exported frequently. This species, which has been confused with *S. ahli* in almost all the aquaristic literature, was described from the population at Mbenji Island, but its distribution encompasses the whole lake, including isolated reefs and islands. Likoma is the place where most of the "Electric Blues"—the trade name of *S. fryeri*—are now caught for export, although the first specimens shipped out of Malaŵi were caught at Maleri Island and around Cape Maclear. These were labeled "Haplochromis Electric Blue" or "Haplochromis jacksoni". These individuals, like most other *S. fryeri*, had a total length of about 12 to 14 cm. Males of the southern populations have, in addition to the overall electric blue coloration, a whitish blaze on the head, extending from the tip of the upper lip to the dorsal fin. Most males from Likoma lack this white blaze on the head and have a more reddish-colored anal fin, but a white blaze is present in very large specimens. Females of all populations are dark brown and very secretive. At first, when exports of this species had just started, only about five females were caught every year (Grant, pers. comm.), but when it was discovered that *S. fryeri* specifically hunts the utaka juveniles in the "clouds" above *kampango* nests (see page 258), it became more frequently seen in shipments from Malaŵi.

S. fryeri is occasionally seen roaming through

1. *Aulonocara* sp. 'chitande type mozambique' ♂ Londo

2. *Aulonocara* sp. 'chitande type kande' ♂ Kande Island

3. *Aulonocara* sp. 'chitande type nkhomo' ♂ Nkhomo Reef

4. *Aulonocara* sp. 'chitande type masinje' ♂ Nametumbwe

5. *Aulonocara* sp. 'chitande type mozambique' ♀ Londo

6. *Aulonocara* sp. 'chitande type mozambique' ♂ Wikihi

7. *Aulonocara* sp. 'chitande type nkhomo' ♀ Nkhomo Reef

8. *Aulonocara* sp. 'chitande type masinje' ♀ Gome

9. *Aulonocara* sp. 'chitande type masinje' ♀ ♂ Gome

1. *Aulonocara* sp. 'yellow collar' ♀ Thumbi East Island

2. *Aulonocara* sp. 'yellow collar' ♂ Otter Island

3. *Aulonocara kandeense* ♀ Kande Island

4. *Aulonocara maylandi* ♀ Luwala Reef

5. *Aulonocara saulosi* ♀ Harbour Island

6. *Aulonocara saulosi* ♂ Border

7. *Aulonocara* sp. 'yellow collar' ♂ Mazinzi Reef

8. *Aulonocara kandeense* ♂ Kande Island

9. *Aulonocara maylandi* ♂ Luwala Reef

10. *Aulonocara saulosi* ♂ Membe Point (Likoma)

the habitat in search of food. Most of the sightings are of males in breeding dress moving in and out of caves in the rocky habitat. *S. fryeri* dines on small fishes and is specialized on juveniles of non-mbuna. Most often it is seen stalking juveniles of *Protomelas taeniolatus* or other silvery-colored non-mbuna. Typically *S. fryeri* swims at a steady pace over the substrate, either pure rocks or rocks and sand, and halts at strategic points when it notices one or more inch-long juveniles of *P. taeniolatus* or similar. Instead of immediately pursuing the small fish it tries, little by little, to get closer to the prey without alarming it. It probably knows from experience that an immediate attack from a distance will have the prospective prey disappearing between the rocks before jaws can be closed around it, and that it needs to close in to have any chance of success. Now comes the most interesting part, because *S. fryeri* starts rocking back and forth like a herbivorous mbuna feeding from the aufwuchs! It swims about 8 cm above the substrate, dips its head down, almost touching the rock, then swings back into its normal, horizontal, position. Each dip, during which the body is at an angle of about 45° to the substrate, lasts approximately a second. Two to ten dips follow each other in a rhythmic fashion, with *S. fryeri* all the time watching its prey closely, and with each dip moving a little bit closer to the prey. It doesn't head directly for the victim but appears to be passing by at a short distance, occupied with its own business rather than interested in the prey. Unsuspecting, the victim remains where it is, and when *S. fryeri* has closed in far enough, with luck a sudden sideways strike will secure the prey between the jaws of the cunning predator. This ingenious hunting behavior was first videoed by Larry Johnson at Thumbi West Island, and I have observed it about 15 times, mostly around Thumbi West and Maleri islands, and once each at Chitande Island and Chinyankwazi Island.

S. fryeri has a second feeding specialization: as mentioned earlier it hunts the juvenile fishes that hover over nests of the catfish *Bagrus meridionalis* (*kampango*). Almost every *kampango* nest has a school of juvenile non-mbuna hovering over the catfish pair. The catfish babies wriggling on the bottom of the nest are protected by the smaller male, who hovers a few inches above them. The female hovers over the male (but is easily scared when approached by a diver). This very large catfish forms a formidable barrier for cichlid predators wanting to eat the catfish young and few of these cichlids dare to approach within reach of the catfish parents. The nest of the *kampango* is thus such a sheltered (from predators) place that mouthbrooding cichlids—usually *Copadichromis* females but also those of *Ctenopharynx pictus* and even *Rhamphochromis esox*—regularly abuse the *kampango*'s defensive efforts and release their offspring near such nests. The freshly-released juveniles immediately group together and join the cloud of other juveniles already hovering over the nest. Some *kampango* nests have more than a thousand juvenile cichlids over them.

Most predatory cichlids have only a fleeting interest in hunting these juveniles as the catfish foster-parents are too close for comfort, but not so in the case of *S. fryeri*, which seems to "understand" that the catfish parents are not defending the cichlid juveniles hovering over the nest and specifically targets them. Although *S. fryeri* is more often encountered in rocky habitats I have seen them around *kampango* nests on the sand 10 meters or more away from the rocky habitat. *S. fryeri* is so common around *kampango* nests that even females and immatures can be seen there while normally they live such a secluded life in the rocky habitat that a diver would never see them. At the periphery of one *kampango* nest at Thumbi West Island I once witnessed seven hunting *S. fryeri*, of which three were females, at the same time.

Although I have also observed the "feedingmbuna" ploy at the edge of *kampango* nests, most *S. fryeri* simply station themselves at the periphery of the nest and try to single out a small utaka for a lightning-fast dart to secure it between the jaws. The success rate of *S. fryeri* is rather high for a predator and in the course of an hour up to five successful attacks per individual may be achieved.

In captivity males show their breeding colors throughout the year and it seems that this is the case in the lake as well. A non-mbuna permanently in breeding dress is very uncommon in the lake. Territoriality is very rare in *S. fryeri* and I have observed it only twice, at Lupingu and at Liuli, Tanzania, where a group of males had gathered in a small area and each one of them had constructed a so-called cave-crater spawning dish. Apart from hunting at *kampango* nests, this type of "open-air" spawning is the only occasion that females can be seen outside the protection of rocky crevices. Males may dig large craters in the aquarium but in the wild this behavior is rare. Spawning normally takes place in seclusion, usually beneath rocks under which the male has constructed a spawning area by turning his body in the sand.

S. fryeri is probably an old species, not only because of its sparse but lake-wide distribution, but also because of its breeding technique: the eggs are fertilized outside the female's mouth. The male sheds his sperm over the newly laid eggs while the female collects them. Mouthbrooding females probably hide among rocks, at least I have never seen a mouthbrooding female (apart from those directly involved in spawning) in the lake, and release their fry after three weeks of incubation (on the basis of aquarium observations).

At various localities in the southern half of the lake I have found a species that resembles *S. fryeri* in shape, and which I refer to as *Sciaenochromis* sp. 'nyassae'. *S.* sp. 'nyassae' is rare and only once have I seen two individuals at the same locality. A male seen in breeding colors at Chidunga Rocks exhibited no territoriality and wandered through the habitat like other, non-breeding, individuals. This species hunts juvenile cichlids, and once it has spotted a likely victim it almost "explodes" forwards, sometimes bouncing off rocks, to snatch the prey. So although no specimens have been collected for examination of the stomach contents its behavior is indicative of a piscivore. The basic melanin pattern of *S.* sp. 'nyassae' resembles that of *S. benthicola* (page 354) but it is generally larger and deeper-bodied than the latter.

A predatory species found in the northern half of the lake, including Likoma Island, feeds in a similar manner to *S.* sp. 'nyassae' but is encountered even less frequently. Its melanin pattern consists of two elements, a horizontal stripe composed of three elongate spots merging into one another; and a diagonal stripe running from the front of the dorsal to the mid-flank, where it merges with the horizontal stripe to create a large, elongate blotch. This is quite different from the bar pattern in *S.* sp. 'nyassae' and so for the time being I regard the northern form as a different species, *Sciaenochromis* sp. 'stripe tanzania'.

Sciaenochromis ahli was described from a population near Lumbila, in the northern part of the lake belonging to Tanzania (Ahl, 1927). The maximum length of this predator is about 20 cm. It has been sporadically exported from the Tanzanian coast as "Haplochromis Big Eye". Its distribution appears to be restricted to the northern end of the lake where it occurs on the west as well as the east coast. In Malaŵi its range is limited to the coast north of Chitande Island, plus Likoma Island and Taiwanee Reef. In Tanzania it is found between the mouth of the Ruhuhu River and Nkanda, and is fairly common at Makonde and Kirondo. *S. ahli* hunts over the sand but is evidently bound to rocky shores—otherwise one would expect it to have a lake-wide distribution. Males in breeding color have been caught at Mdoka at a depth of about 20 meters, which is also the depth at which females are seen. Territorial males have been observed at the islet of Masimbwe, just south of Likoma. At a depth of about 35 meters, and in an area about 20 meters square, five males were each defending a shallow spawning pit built against a medium-sized rock. About 20 females, some of them already mouthbrooding, were in the immediate area and apparently wanting to spawn with the males. Fry-guarding females and juveniles have not yet been found.

At Mbenji Island, in the intermediate habitat at a depth of about 12 meters, I on one occasion encountered two large (approximately 20 cm TL) blue males of an unknown species that were chasing each other. It appeared that these were breeding individuals that were defending some sort of spawning area in the large caves of the

1. *Sciaenochromis fryeri* ♂ Chinyamwezi Island

2. *Sciaenochromis fryeri* ♂ Thumbi West Island

3. *Sciaenochromis* sp. 'nyassae' ♂ Chidunga Rocks

4. *Sciaenochromis* sp. 'stripe tanzania' ♂ Lundu

5. *Sciaenochromis fryeri* ♀ Chimwalani Reef

6. *Sciaenochromis fryeri* ♀ ♂ Liuli

7. *Sciaenochromis* sp. 'nyassae' ♀ Maleri Island

8. *Sciaenochromis* sp. 'stripe tanzania' ♀ Cobwé

1. *Sciaenochromis ahli* ♀ Masimbwe

6. *Sciaenochromis ahli* ♂ Masimbwe

2. *Tyrannochromis macrostoma* ♂ Higga Reef

7. *Tyrannochromis macrostoma* ♂ Gome

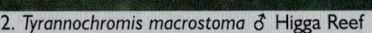
3. *Tyrannochromis macrostoma* ♂ Mbenji Island

4. *Tyrannochromis* sp. 'macrostoma short pedicel' Ifungu

8. *Tyrannochromis macrostoma* ♀ Nakantenga Island

5. *Tyrannochromis macrostoma* ♀ Gome

habitat (no actual spawning sites were found). Evaluating the two photographs I was able to take—one male had three spots on the body—I tentatively place this rare species in the genus *Stigmatochromis*. In the same area there were also *S. modestus* but they are much smaller and have a shallower body than the new species. I suggest the name *Stigmatochromis* sp. 'modestus mbenji' for the big blue males; I have not yet been able to relocate the species or find females.

Thick-chinned predators

The "Haplochromis Jack Dempsey" gained its trade name from its prominent, thick, lower jaw and wide mouth. It is exported infrequently from Chizumulu Island, but has a lake-wide distribution. The scientific name for this fish is *Naevochromis chrysogaster*. Its peculiar mouth bears some resemblance to that of the paedophage *Caprichromis orthognathus* (see page 345) and to that of *Hemitaeniochromis spilopterus* (see page 344). The teeth are completely embedded in the gums, perhaps implying that prey is obtained by suction and that this species takes soft-structured food. However, although it can be regularly seen in the intermediate habitat I have never seen it feeding. On several occasions I have seen it follow (chase?) mouthbrooding females—often dark-colored mbuna females—but I have never seen it attack one. In most cases, however, the brooding female was very wary of her stalker and tried energetically to get out of harm's way. So there is as yet no concrete evidence that this species robs mouthbrooding females of their broods.

On one occasion I observed a male scooping up sand, but this was not feeding behavior as he used the material for constructing a kind of spawning pit, situated on top of some rubble beneath an overhanging rock. Bower building in *N. chrysogaster* is rudimentary and usually the small spawning pit is hardly noticeable among the rubble of the environment. Territorial males do not eat during the breeding period.

There is some geographical variation in the various populations known. In most populations *N. chrysogaster* has three (sometimes elongate) spots on the flanks; but most—not all—of the individuals along the west coast south of Nkhotakota, and along the east coast south of the Nsinje River, lack the middle one. In some individuals of all known populations the mid-lateral spot is more elongate and appears to be superimposed onto a diagonal line. Breeding individuals most often exhibit such a diagonal line, but at the moment of spawning all black markings disappear in both male and female. Females and juvenile males at some localities, e.g., Katale Island, have a brassy-yellow ground color. Male breeding coloration appears to be similar in all known populations.

On the northwestern coast and around Chizumulu and Likoma Islands I have observed the behavior of an undescribed brood-robbing species, *Hemitaeniochromis* sp. 'paedophage'. This cichlid, which has a maximum total length of about 20 cm, is sometimes seen among schools of mouthbrooding utaka. In contrast to the other paedophages whose behavior has been recorded, this predator attacks mouthbrooding females from above. Such attacks are sometimes initiated several meters above the victim. It is thought that the mouthbrooding female may release some or all of her brood at the moment the paedophage hits her head. In most observed instances the females were aware of the approaching thief and chased it away. The diagonal position of the mouth may be an adaptation to this hunting technique since, coming from above, it will be in a straight line with the fry when these are expelled.

Hemitaeniochromis sp. 'urotaenia tanzania' is a rare cichlid which I have seen only at Kirondo and Makonde in Tanzania. Snoeks & Hanssens (2004) record this species from the northern end of the lake and a single specimen from Domira Bay. They also suggest that this species is closely related to *Otopharynx brooksi* and name it *O.* sp. 'brooksi striped'. However, its main characteristics are a prominent chin and a pigmentation pattern of two interrupted horizontal stripes, corresponding to the pattern found in the other members of *Hemitaeniochromis*. The few individuals seen exhibited predatory behavior, hunting small fishes. Territorial males or males in breeding coloration have not yet been found.

A few specimens have been caught and exported to the USA, but the species has not yet become established in the aquarium hobby.

Eggs for dinner

Egg-robbing is another specialization, exploiting the eggs frequently available in large arenas of breeding cichlids. Such breeding areas are visited by a few species that steal the eggs as soon as they have been deposited. Before the female can turn around and pick up the eggs, an egg-robber can be on the spawning site and snatch the spawn. It is thus important for the breeding species that the eggs are fertilized inside the female's mouth or else there is a high risk of their being eaten by one of these egg-robbers.

Two such egg-robbers have been identified: *Protomelas insignis* (formerly referred to as *P.* sp. 'insignis small') and *Otopharynx ovatus*. Both species hold feeding territories above leks. Males of *O. ovatus* have a completely blue breeding dress. Females and non-territorial males of *O. ovatus* are beige-silvery and have three small spots on the body. They are sometimes seen over breeding arenas along sandy shores. Fry seen being guarded by a female at Nkhata Bay already exhibited the three-spot pattern. The name *ovatus* (egg-like) refers to their oval shape, not to their egg-robbing behavior.

Protomelas insignis is characterized by two horizontal stripes, the mid-lateral beginning 5 or 6 scales behind the gill cover and the dorso-lateral stopping halfway along the flank. Breeding males are entirely blue and defend cave-craters in the intermediate habitat. Ripe females of both *P. insignis* and *O. ovatus* can be recognized by their very dark (almost black) color. Maximum total length of both species is about 18 cm.

Both egg-robbing cichlids recognize other species in the process of spawning and wait at a fair distance from the spawning pair—usually more than a meter away—till the right moment to strike. Just after the female has laid one or more eggs the egg-robber accelerates at an incredible rate, darting forward and snatching the egg(s) before the female has a chance to take them into her mouth (see photo 2, page 22). These lightning-fast sallies must have quite an impact on the egg-robber's lips when they collide with the sand of the spawning site, and that may be the reason that they are thick and strong in these two species.

Mylochromis obtusus grows a little larger than the previous two species but may be involved in similar activities, as has been indicated by observations in the aquarium (Peter Baasch, pers. comm.). It is characterized by an oblique stripe and belongs to the large group of mainly sand-dwelling species with such stripes. Breeding males acquire a blue color on the silvery body and aquarium observations suggest that they make a spawning site on the sand.

1. *Stigmatochromis* sp. 'modestus mbenji' ♂ Mbenji Island
2. *Naevochromis chrysogaster* ♂ Chizumulu Island
3. *Naevochromis chrysogaster* ♂ Mbenji Island
4. *Naevochromis chrysogaster* ♂ Membe Island (Chizumulu)
5. *Naevochromis chrysogaster* ♀ ♂ Mbenji Island
6. *Naevochromis chrysogaster* ♀ ♂ Mbenji Island

1. *Otopharynx ovatus* ♀ Chinyamwezi Island

6. *Otopharynx ovatus* ♂ Boadzulu Island

2. *Protomelas insignis* ♀ Nkanda

7. *Protomelas insignis* ♂ Mbweca

3. *Hemitaeniochromis* sp. 'paedophage' Mdoka

4. *Hemitaeniochromis* sp. 'urotaenia tanzania' Makonde

8. *Mylochromis obtusus* ♂ Aquarium

5. Maleri Island

The shallow intermediate habitat

The shallow intermediate habitat is not an artificial sub-division of the transition zone between rocks and sand, dealt with in the previous chapter, but a distinct habitat frequently found on rocky coasts. At many places the rocky coast has a shallow, gradually shelving edge consisting of sand and rocks before it eventually drops away at a much steeper angle, 20 to 50 meters away from the shoreline. I have not included this biotope in the intermediate habitat chapter as there is a small group of cichlids restricted to this type of habitat. Of course, other cichlid species are found in this habitat as well, but they have already been discussed in the preceding chapter.

A single zebra

Possibly owing to the large number of algae-combing species at the Maleri islands, *Metriaclima* sp. 'aggressive zebra maleri' is found mainly in the very shallow part of the intermediate habitat. It rakes loose aufwuchs from the rocks and is not very aggressive, despite its name. It has previously been confused with a different species, an aggressive algae-picker which is now referred to as *P.* sp. 'aggressive zebra mbenji' (page 93).

Dolphin mbuna

The "Dolphin Mbuna" are herbivorous species that bite and comb loose algae from the biocover. The pointed snout enables them to reach into cracks that are inaccessible to most other species of similar size. When feeding the dolphin mbuna usually wedge their snout as deep as possible inside a crack and try to bite off as much as possible from the algae that thrive beyond the reach of most other mbuna. This niche, feeding from the lush growth within cracks, is occupied by similarly-shaped mbuna all over the lake.

In *Metriaclima*, which harvest algae by combing the biocover, the mouth is widened in order to accommodate as many teeth as possible to rake the aufwuchs. In dolphin mbuna the mouth is not broad but long and V-shaped, probably for the same reason: to enlarge the algae-browsing apparatus. These V-shaped jaws are set with large bicuspid teeth that enable the owner to collect algae using the sides of its mouth (the arms of the V). When one of these mbuna feeds from the vertical sides of a rock it strikes it with one side of the jaw or the other.

The name of the group is derived from *Pseudotropheus tursiops* from Chizumulu. Burgess and Axelrod, the describers (1975) of *P. tursiops*, considered that their new species bore some resemblance to the bottle-nosed dolphin (*Tursiops truncatus*), and gave the cichlid the dolphin's name. *P. tursiops* and two closely related species, *Pseudotropheus* sp. 'tursiops mbenji' (Mbenji Islands) and *Pseudotropheus* sp. 'tursiops chitande' (from Chirwa Island to Ngara on the west coast and from Manda to Nkanda on the northeastern shores), are restricted to the very shallow intermediate habitat. All three species share the rare feature of an elongated, beak-like snout. The characteristic color pattern of *P.* sp. 'tursiops chitande' is reminiscent of that of *P. williamsi* and also of *Melanochromis brevis,* and may be indicative of an ancient species.

Males of *P. tursiops* and *P.* sp. 'tursiops mbenji' defend their territories with great vigor. They chase any intruders from their domain and algal gardens often indicate the precise location of their territories. Such gardens can be more than a meter in diameter and usually extend over the horizontal surfaces of several rocks. Males of *P.* sp. 'tursiops chitande' appear less aggressive towards other species.

Pseudotropheus fuscus is a very common mbuna of the shallow intermediate habitat, found on the northwestern coast between Kande Island and Chilumba. Both male and female defend a feeding territory. Fryer (1956a) found that at Nkhata Bay a very similar, but different, species lived sympatric with *P. fuscus* and named this species *Pseudotropheus fuscoides*. He found that the latter fed predominantly on insect larvae while *P. fuscus* fed primarily on loose aufwuchs. Ribbink *et al.* (1983b) suggest that *P. fuscoides* may be young specimens of *P. fuscus* living at a somewhat deeper level than their stronger elders. When they are strong enough to defend a territory they move to the upper regions of the habitat. When they become territorial they may have to change their food source in the process. *P. fuscoides* is here likewise regarded as synonymous with *P. fuscus*.

An aggressive species with a close resemblance to *P. fuscus,* and a superficial resemblance to *P. tursiops,* occurs around Likoma Island. This species, *Pseudotropheus* sp. 'aggressive grey', is very common and occupies large sections of the upper three meters of the intermediate habitat. Females are dark brown and lack the light blue seen in the male's dorsal fin.

Pseudotropheus purpuratus is found at Maleri, Nankoma, and Thumbi West islands; along the shores of the Nankumba peninsula north of Monkey Bay; and across the lake along the eastern shore, where I have found it at Gome and as far north as Thumbi Point in Tanzania. In behavior and morphology it closely resembles *P. tursiops*, the only difference being the vertical barring in females; female *P. tursiops* have two horizontal lines. Female *P. purpuratus* are brown and, like males, defend feeding territories.

The males of all dolphin mbuna reside in caves where spawning takes place. The dolphin mbuna live secretive lives, but territories are nevertheless aggressively patrolled, even by females. In contrast to the schooling behavior seen in other mbuna, females react aggressively towards conspecific females and also successfully defend their domains against males. The reason can only be competition for food, and the area they defend aggressively is thus called a feeding territory.

Petrotilapia

Petrotilapia genalutea is among the most widely distributed mbuna of the lake and there are only a few places known which are not inhabited by this species: Likoma, Chizumulu, Chinyankwazi, Chinyamwezi, and the western coast north of the South Rukuru River. The last of these is inhabited by a species with a similar habitat preference and behavior—*Petrotilapia* sp. 'chitande'. *P. genalutea* can cross sandy plains in shallow water and has thus populated several remote and/or isolated rocky areas. It is found at Senga Point and at Rifu, which are rather inhospitable places for mbuna. Furthermore it is encountered at all the islands in the western half of the lake. It is easily recognized in the lake by the black submarginal band in the dorsal fin and by the two rows of blotches on the flanks.

P. genalutea is a very successful species and is common throughout its range, forming large feeding groups when food is hard to come by. Such feeding groups have been observed at several different places and seem to be characteristic of this species. *P. genalutea* is less aggressive than some other rock-dwelling cichlids. Only a small fraction of the male population is territorial. A few sexually active males have large breeding territories (over 20 m2!) from which they chase conspecific males only, but most males join with the females in the foraging schools. Schooling is probably more energy-effective than single-handedly securing a feeding territory. A foraging school of *Petrotilapia* cannot possibly be "seen off" by any single mbuna, and so each individual in the group gets food which would be difficult to obtain if it were to forage on its own.

P. genalutea has frequently been exported from the lake as "Petrotilapia Tridentiger".

Petrotilapia sp. 'yellow chin' is closely related to *P. tridentiger*, which lives in the surf zone of the purely rocky habitat (page 33). Nowhere are these two species found sympatric. *P.* sp. 'yellow chin', a popular cichlid among aquarists, occurs at islands in the southern part of the lake, i.e. Mbenji, Namalenje, and all three Maleri islands, and along the eastern shores from

6. *Metriaclima* sp. 'aggressive zebra maleri' ♀ Nakantenga Island

7. *Pseudotropheus tursiops* ♀ Chizumulu Island

1. *Metriaclima* sp. 'aggressive zebra maleri' ♂ Nakantenga Island

2. *Pseudotropheus tursiops* ♂ Chizumulu Island

8. *Pseudotropheus tursiops* ♂ Chizumulu Island

3. *Pseudotropheus* sp. 'tursiops mbenji' ♂ Mbenji Island

9. *Pseudotropheus* sp. 'tursiops mbenji' ♀ Mbenji Island

10. *Pseudotropheus* sp. 'tursiops chitande' ♀ Matema

4. *Pseudotropheus* sp. 'tursiops chitande' ♂ Ngwazi

5. *Pseudotropheus fuscus* ♂ Nkhata Bay

11. *Pseudotropheus fuscus* ♀ Nkhata Bay

1. *Pseudotropheus purpuratus* ♀ Mumbo Island

2. *Pseudotropheus* sp. 'aggressive grey' ♀ Masimbwe

3. *Petrotilapia* sp. 'chitande' ♂ Luwino Reef

4. *Petrotilapia genalutea* ♂ Ngwazi

5. *Petrotilapia genalutea* ♀ Thumbi West Island

6. *Petrotilapia* sp. 'yellow chin' ♂ Mbweca

7. *Petrotilapia* sp. 'yellow chin' ♀ Chiofu

8. *Pseudotropheus purpuratus* ♂ Thumbi Point

9. *Pseudotropheus* sp. 'aggressive grey' ♂ Maingano Island

10. *Petrotilapia genalutea* ♂ Boadzulu Island

11. *Petrotilapia* sp. 'yellow chin' ♂ Nakantenga Island

Makanjila to Chuanga, to the north of Metangula in Mozambique waters. There is not much geographical variation between the known populations; a single slight difference in male coloration is found in the population at Makanjila, where the yellow patch on the chin is smaller and blends with the light blue body color. Males are territorial, defending caves in the heaps of large rocks sometimes found in the shallow intermediate habitat. Females, which are brown, forage on their own, and are ardently courted by males who may follow ripe females for several meters in their courtship fervor.

The *lucerna* group

The species of the so-called *lucerna* group are the most characteristic inhabitants of the shallow intermediate biotope and are not found anywhere else. They are placed in the genus *Tropheops* because one of the main characters given in the diagnosis of this genus is the possession of a lower jaw that is shorter than the upper. But although all members of the *lucerna* group fulfill this requirement, they do not feed by twisting off algae. But since they are much more closely related to the other members of *Tropheops* than to the type species of *Pseudotropheus* they are retained in the former genus.

Tropheops lucerna was described from the population at Chilumba (Trewavas, 1935) and previously erroneously identified as a different species (*T.* sp. 'lucerna blue aggressive'— (see Konings, 2001), but similar species are found all around the lake. Several different populations or species were discovered and catalogued by Ribbink *et al.* (1983b).

The general characteristics of the *lucerna* group are an average-shaped body, a convex upper head profile, and a ventrally positioned mouth (but not as underslung as in *T. tropheops* and its closest relatives). Males of all known species defend their domains with great zeal. The center of each territory is often a small hole excavated beneath small rocks. All members of the *lucerna* group pick from the algae of the biocover on the rocks. Because very little is known about these fishes from aquarium observations (only one of the nine species now recognized, *T.* sp. 'lucerna blue cobalt', has been exported, and then only sporadically) I prefer to regard as a separate species each population with noticeably differently colored males, at least for the time being.

Tropheops sp. 'lucerna nkhata', which has a wide distribution along the northwestern shores, was previously misidentified as *T. lucerna*. A similar population occurs at Londo in Mozambique and for the time being I will assign this form to *T.* sp. 'lucerna nkhata' as well.

Ribbink *et al.* (1983b) reported on *Tropheops* sp. 'lucerna brown', which occurs along the rocky shores south of Monkey Bay but not at Monkey Bay itself. I have found this species in the very shallow intermediate habitat at Mphandi Island and along the shore of Nkhudzi. *Tropheops* sp. 'lucerna brown chia' lives in the shallow intermediate habitat near Chia Lagoon and may have a wider distribution. Another member of the group is found at Likoma Island. Ribbink and his colleagues named this species *Pseudotropheus* 'fin spot', but in order to indicate its relationship to *T. lucerna* it is here referred to as *Tropheops* sp. 'lucerna fin spot'. The name alludes to black spots in the trailing portion of the soft-rayed dorsal fin, a feature in fact found in almost all members of the *lucerna* group.

Chizumulu Island is almost completely surrounded by rocky habitats and most of the inshore waters are of the shallow intermediate type. A very aggressive member of the *lucerna* group, *Tropheops* sp. 'lucerna blue cobalt', is rather common around the island. This species has been exported as "Pseudotropheus Jacksoni".

Along the eastern shores of the lake I have found three other members of the *lucerna* group. In Tanzania at Njambe and Puulu, and in Mozambique at Chiwindi, the shallow intermediate biotope harbors an attractive member of the group: *Tropheops* sp. 'lucerna blue tanzania'. Males are characterized by a blue body and a large orange patch on the breast and lower half of the head. This species is also known as "Pseudotropheus Aggressive Puulu" (Spreinat,

1994). Another species of the group, *Tropheops* sp. 'lucerna blue mozambique', is found at Chuanga and Metangula. Males are completely blue and defend their territories aggressively. Females are bluish brown and solitary.

Tropheops sp. 'lucerna north', a common species of the shallow intermediate habitat along the northern shores of Tanzania, north of the Ruhuhu River, was previously thought to be a local form of *Tropheops* sp. 'rust' (see Konings, 2001). *T.* sp. 'lucerna north' may in fact be an intermediate between *Tropheops* (in the strict sense) and the *lucerna* group. It is the only species of the latter group that lacks the black spots in the trailing part of the dorsal. It is, however, very aggressive and defends feeding territories. None of the individuals observed have been seen to jerk algae from the rocks in the manner typical of *Tropheops*. It is commonly found between Lupingu and the Ruhuhu River.

All *lucerna*-type cichlids are very difficult to observe or photograph because they are very cautious, and, having fled to shelter, remain hidden for 10 to 15 minutes or more before resuming their normal activities. This may be because they are within reach of fishing birds that are especially attracted to active, colorful fishes.

Band or no band

As well as the *Tropheops lucerna* group there are several other representatives of *Tropheops* in the shallow intermediate habitat. Most of these, such as *T.* sp. 'maleri yellow' and *T.* sp. 'yellow chin', which are frequently found in the upper regions of the intermediate habitat, have been dealt with earlier (see page 196).

In the shallow transition zone at Nkhata Bay, Ribbink *et al.* (1983b) distinguished two almost identical species which they named: *Pseudotropheus* 'tropheops band' and *P.* 'tropheops no band'. The sole difference in coloration between these two forms is the black submarginal band in the dorsal of the former. Females of the two forms, however, are indistinguishable, being gray with light yellowish-gray fins. Ribbink and his co-workers found that territorial males of the form with a band were on average a centimeter longer than males of the other type. In any competition for territory between two such similar species larger individuals are likely to have the advantage, and this may be the reason why the smaller form is much less common than the larger. If these two forms prove to be separate species then this will represent the smallest known interspecific color difference found in any two sympatric cichlids in the lake. However, I regard both forms as belonging to a single species, *Tropheops* sp. 'band', and believe that "no band" individuals are just young *T.* sp. 'band'.

A species similar to *T.* sp. 'band', *Tropheops* sp. 'chitimba', is found in the shallows of Chitimba Bay, where males defend holes in the very large sandstone slabs found in this habitat. This species is much smaller than *T.* sp. 'band' and has an estimated maximum total length of about 8 cm, whereas that of *T.* sp. 'band' is estimated at about 12 cm. Females of *T.* sp. 'chitimba' are characterized by a bright yellow anal fin and faint beige bars on a very light body, and thus resemble those of *T.* sp. 'mauve' (page 81). *T.* sp. 'chitimba' could indeed be a geographical variant of *T.* sp. 'mauve' but "normal" colored individuals of the latter are found north and south of Chitimba Bay in similar habitats.

Small pickers

A number of small species of *Labidochromis* inhabit the shallow intermediate habitats in the central and southern part of the lake. Only one of them, *Labidochromis flavigulis*, which occurs in shallow water at Likoma and Chizumulu islands, is territorial; the others wander through the habitat feeding from rocky substrates. Male *L. flavigulis* dig spawning holes in the sand. Their territories are characterized by a heap of sand piled up in front of the entrance to each cave. The population density of *L. flavigulis* is high in some places, and here males defend their domains with great vigor. Females wander through the habitat, sometimes in small groups, but most of the time singly. The food consists of algae which are harvested from the biocover on the rocks (Ribbink *et al.*, 1983b).

1. *Tropheops lucerna* ♂ Chewere

5. *Tropheops* sp. 'lucerna blue mozambique' ♂ Metangula

6. *Tropheops* sp. 'lucerna fin spot' ♂ Likoma Island

7. *Tropheops* sp. 'lucerna fin spot' ♀ Likoma Island

8. *Tropheops* sp. 'lucerna blue cobalt' ♀ Same Bay

2. *Tropheops* sp. 'lucerna blue cobalt' ♂ Same Bay (Chizumulu)

9. *Tropheops* sp. 'lucerna brown' ♀ Nkhudzi

10. *Tropheops* sp. 'lucerna nkhata' ♀ Nkhata Bay

3. *Tropheops* sp. 'lucerna brown' ♂ Mphandi Island

4. *Tropheops* sp. 'lucerna nkhata' ♂ Nkhata Bay

11. *Tropheops* sp. 'lucerna blue tanzania' ♂ Undu

1. *Tropheops* sp. 'lucerna brown chia' ♂ Chia

2. *Tropheops* sp. 'lucerna north' ♀ Magunga

3. *Tropheops* sp. 'chitimba' ♂ Chitimba Bay

4. *Tropheops* sp. 'chitimba' ♀ Chitimba Bay

5. *Labidochromis flavigulis* ♀ Machili Island (Chizumulu)

7. *Tropheops* sp. 'lucerna north' ♂ Magunga

8. *Tropheops* sp. 'band' ♂ Nkhata Bay

9. *Labidochromis textilis* ♂ Hai Reef

6. *Labidochromis flavigulis* ♂ Machili Island

In this respect this species differs from *Labidochromis textilis*, a small *Labidochromis* from the Tanzanian and Mozambique shores, which probably feeds on insects and crustaceans judging by its foraging behavior. *L. textilis* was described from an aquarium specimen with a total length of about 9 cm, a size never seen in wild specimens. In Lake Malaŵi, individuals larger than 6 cm are very rare—at least I have never seen one. *L. textilis* is very common in the shallow intermediate habitat and has a wide distribution ranging from Undu Reef in Tanzania to Metangula in Mozambique. Males are not territorial and have a color pattern not much different to that of females. The main difference is the size of the egg-spot(s) on the anal fin; these are, of course, larger in the male. Ripe males have a light bluish sheen over the normal pattern of narrow bars and orange streaks resulting from the orange scalloped marking on each scale. The main differences between *L. textilis* and *L. flavigulis* are the shorter jaw and the protruding teeth in the latter. The oral teeth are not visible in *L. textilis* when the mouth is closed (Lewis, 1982).

I have also found an insectivorous *Labidochromis* species at Mala (previously Mara) Point and Mbweca in Mozambique. The male coloration of this species, *Labidochromis* sp. 'mara', differs from that of *L.* sp. 'likomae' (page 140) by the black submarginal band in the dorsal fin. In fact this species more closely resembles *L. maculicauda* (see page 44), which occurs along the northern shores of the lake. At Mala Point *L.* sp. 'mara' occurs in the shallow but sediment-rich rocky habitat and may represent a population (the southernmost) of *L. maculicauda*, but in the "wrong" habitat.

The *Labidochromis* with the southernmost distribution, *Labidochromis shiranus*, is a herbivore and is even found in the Shiré River at Mangochi (Lewis, 1982). The northernmost part of its range is at Makanjila Point, and it is also found along the eastern shores of the southeastern arm of the lake. Males are not territorial; they are distinguished from females by the orange egg-spot, which is either very small or absent in females. *L. shiranus* is often found in very turbid and sediment-rich environments.

Labidochromis lividus is found on the western and northern shores of Likoma Island, where several other herbivorous *Labidochromis* are also present. Most of the latter live in the purely rocky habitat while *L. lividus* inhabits the small caves of the shallow transition zone between sand and rocks. It is a very secretive species, normally feeding from the algae at the entrances of crevices and caves. Sediment-free patches on rocks are especially attractive to this algae-picker.

A similar species, but with a more elongate body, occurs along the Mozambique shores. This algae-picker, *Labidochromis* sp. 'lividus mozambique', is found at Londo, Cobwé, Metangula, and Chilucha Reef (where it occurs in the upper part of the rocky habitat). South of Metangula, at N'kolongwe and Nkhungu Point, a *Labidochromis* with a similarly elongate body, but lacking the blue bars, occupies the same niche. The females of this mbuna, *Labidochromis* sp. 'lividus nkhungu', likewise lack such bars and are completely brown, while those of *L. lividus* and *L.* sp. 'lividus mozambique' are light brown with gray-brown bars.

A *lividus*-like cichlid also occurs in the shallow intermediate habitat along the western shore, between Hora Mhango and Mbowe Island. Males of this species, *Labidochromis* sp. 'hora', are blue-black barred and have an attractive yellow edge to the tail.

Labidochromis sp. 'lundu blue' is found at Lundu, in Tanzania, in the very shallow (maximum depth about two meters) intermediate habitat. This species is assigned only tentatively to this genus, and may in fact be the local variant of a small, territorial species, *Pseudotropheus* sp. 'minutus tanzania' (page 96). The latter is present at all shores north of Lundu (north of the Ruhuhu River) but has not been found at Lundu itself, while no mbuna similar to *L.* sp. 'lundu blue' is found to the north or south of that location. The pointed snout of *L.* sp. 'lundu blue', however, differs from the blunt nose of *P.* sp. 'minutus tanzania'. Unfortunately no specimens of *L.* sp. 'lundu blue' have been caught for examination, so for the time being any decision has to be based on superficial characteristics. The fact that *L.* sp. 'lundu blue' does not employ aggressive territorial defense of the kind seen in *P.* sp. 'minutus tanzania' lends credibility to its current assignment to *Labidochromis*.

A small species with some resemblance to the sympatric *P.* sp. 'minutus mozambique' (see page 97) is seen in the very shallow intermediate habitats at Londo in Mozambique. This small species is named *Pseudotropheus* sp. 'fuscus dwarf'. Both males and females are plucky in their territorial defense: although maximum total length is estimated at about 6 cm they chase away intruders twice their size.

Iodotropheus stuartgranti is found in the shallow intermediate habitat between the Nsinje River (Malaŵi) and Chiloelo in Mozambique. In behavior this species resembles *Labidochromis*. Territorial males have not yet been seen. Females have a color pattern very similar to that of the sympatric *L. vellicans* and are thus difficult to distinguish from that species under water. These two species differ in the structure of the outer teeth, which are conical in *Labidochromis* and bicuspid in *Iodotropheus*.

Other mbuna

A few other mbuna species are restricted to the shallow intermediate habitat. *Pseudotropheus* sp. 'aggressive yellow fin' is found around Chizumulu Island. It is deep-bodied, unlike other aggressive species, and characterized by a cobalt blue body lacking any black markings. Females are dark brown, a color that seems to be common to all territory-defending females. Its aggressive behavior is reminiscent of the small *P. perspicax* from the northwestern shores of the lake.

At Chiloelo, Mozambique, I have photographed a species that initially appeared to be an oddly colored *Labeotropheus trewavasae*. However, I subsequently found several individuals of the same species, and these appeared different to *L. trewavasae*. Both *L. trewavasae* and *L. fuelleborni* were present in the same area so the new form was probably not a variant of either. Unfortunately none were caught for further examination, and the only information I can provide is that this species is found primarily over sand in the shallow intermediate habitat.

I have not been able to observe it feeding but the underslung mouth suggests that it scrapes algae from rocks. I provisionally refer to this species as *Labeotropheus* sp. 'trewavasae chiloelo'. A possible explanation of the rarity of this species—I have not seen it since—was suggested by Mary Bailey (pers. comm.) who found that this form resembles hybrids she had seen in the aquarium between *Labeotropheus* and mbuna from other genera.

The shallow intermediate habitat at N'kolongwe harbors a small blue mbuna bearing a resemblance to *P. socolofi* (see page 204), but for the time being this cichlid is referred to as *Pseudotropheus* sp. 'socolofi nkolongwe'. Females are blue but duller than males. Males are territorial and defend holes, dug under and between rocks, against conspecifics. The species has been found only in very shallow water, no deeper than about three meters.

Melanochromis vermivorus is a rare occurrence in the shallow intermediate habitat at Nkhudzi, Mphande and Boadzulu islands, but also at deeper levels at Makokola Reef. It is attracted to stirred-up sediment and appears to have a mostly opportunistic feeding behavior. Its distribution lies south of Kanchedza Island in the southeastern arm of the lake. It has never been found sympatric with either *M. heterochromis* (page 105) or *M. melanopterus* (page 144). It is distinguished from *M. heterochromis*, which was previously regarded as *M. vermivorus* (see Konings, 2001), by a longer lower jaw and a darker female coloration, and from *M. melanopterus* by a deeper body (Gertrud Konings, pers. comm.). In analogy to the suggested niche-segregation by some other *Melanochromis* species (see pages 109 and 208), it is possible that *M. vermivorus* occupies the combined ecological niches of *M. heterochromis* and *M. melanopterus*. Territorial males have not yet been encountered although males in breeding colors roam through the habitat, attracted to any form of food.

Protomelas

Protomelas ornatus has a lake-wide distribution, but is not found at Mbenji Island or at

1. *Labidochromis* sp. 'mara' ♂ Mbweca

2. *Labidochromis shiranus* ♂ Kanchedza Island

3. *Labidochromis lividus* ♂ Likoma Island

4. *Labidochromis* sp. 'hora' ♂ Mbowe Island

5. *Labidochromis* sp. 'lundu blue' ♂ Lundu

6. *Labidochromis* sp. 'mara' ♀ Mala Point

7. *Labidochromis shiranus* ♀ Nkhudzi

8. *Labidochromis* sp. 'lividus mozambique' ♂ Cobwé

9. *Labidochromis* sp. 'lividus mozambique' ♀ Cobwé

10. *Labidochromis* sp. 'lividus nkhungu' ♂ N'kolongwe

11. *Labidochromis* sp. 'lividus nkhungu' ♀ Nkhungu Point

1. *Pseudotropheus* sp. 'fuscus dwarf' ♀ Londo

2. *Iodotropheus stuartgranti* ♀ Meponda

3. *Pseudotropheus* sp. 'aggressive yellow fin' ♀ Chizumulu

4. *Pseudotropheus* sp. 'socolofi nkolongwe' ♂ N'kolongwe

5. *Pseudotropheus* sp. 'socolofi nkolongwe' ♂ N'kolongwe

6. *Melanochromis vermivorus* ♀ Boadzulu Island

7. *Pseudotropheus* sp. 'fuscus dwarf' ♂ Londo

8. *Iodotropheus stuartgranti* ♂ Chiofu

9. *Pseudotropheus* sp. 'aggressive yellow fin' ♂ Chizumulu

10. *Labeotropheus* sp. 'trewavasae chiloelo' ♂ Chiloelo

11. *Melanochromis vermivorus* ♂ Nkhudzi

purely rocky habitats such as small islands and reefs. Unlike *Placidochromis milomo* (see page 160), *Protomelas ornatus* occurs in rather shallow water where juveniles and females are seen frequently in small groups. Its lips are enlarged and approach the condition seen in *Placidochromis milomo*. However, in *P. milomo* the lips are recurved and swollen in all directions, while those of *Protomelas ornatus* are pointed and laterally compressed. *P. ornatus* itself is laterally compressed and can be regarded morphologically as a larger version of *Melanochromis labrosus*.

P. ornatus is well known among hobbyists as "Haplochromis Flavimanus", under which trade name it is exported from the lake. Unfortunately that is also the original scientific name of a utaka species, now *Mchenga flavimanus* (page 313), and many utaka are still labeled "Haplochromis" in the aquarium trade. Ribbink et al. (1983b) refer to *P. ornatus* as *Cyrtocara* 'maleri thick lip'. Because of its lake-wide distribution several marginally recognizable, geographical variants can be distinguished and two of these have been scientifically described, as separate species, i.e. *Haplochromis lobochilus* and *H. festivus*, but these are now regarded as synonyms.

The diet of *P. ornatus* consists chiefly of small fishes, mostly mbuna, but it dines on larger invertebrates as well. This predator cruises through the habitat and every now and then presses its lips into cracks and grooves. As seems to be typical of laterally compressed piscivores hunting in rocky habitats, it turns its body through 90° before striking. The reason is obvious: the prey seeks shelter beneath overhanging rocks. While the swollen lips of *Placidochromis milomo* and *Chilotilapia euchilus* (page 213) are designed to seal off a more-or-less round or wide hole in the rocks, those of *Protomelas ornatus* are specialized to seal off grooves or slits in which prey has hidden. This has the effect of creating two different niches, allowing *P. ornatus* and *C. euchilus* to share the same habitat without competing with each other for food. *P. ornatus* seems to have obtained the better deal in this resource sharing, as it is seen much more frequently than *C. euchilus*. The coloration of *P. ornatus* males appears to be rather constant throughout the species' range, with only small variations in the proportion of yellow on the lower part of the body and head. Males are territorial during the breeding period and build semicircular spawning sites of sand against the sides of large boulders. Like all known members of *Protomelas*, female *P. ornatus* guard their offspring after first release.

In 2003 I re-discovered *Protomelas virgatus* very near its type locality, Monkey Bay in the southern part of the lake. *P. virgatus*, which I had previously confused with another "Steveni-type" (see page 115), was seen at Harbour Island, which is less than a kilometer south of Monkey Bay, in a shallow intermediate type of habitat. *P. taeniolatus* and *P. fenestratus* were present around this small island as well.

Males form breeding leks although only a few territorial males are involved. Each male defends a spawning platform, with a diameter of about 50 cm, on top of a rock. These platforms are very shallow and consist of nothing more than a thin layer of sand spread out over the rock. The rocks are not prominent and certainly not the highest around. Females, characterized by two rows of spots on the flanks, occur singly and spend most of the time picking at the biocover on the rocks. Sometimes they are courted by the males, but most of the time the males are busy contesting the boundaries of their territories with neighboring males.

Protomelas virgatus is not restricted to the Monkey Bay area as I have also seen them at Namalenje and Kanchedza islands, Sani Hill (south of Nkhotakota), Chidunga Rocks, Tsano Rock, and Nkhudzi. The species thus seems restricted to shallow intermediate habitats in the southern section of the lake. It has been exported from Namalenje Island as "Steveni Green".

According to Eccles & Trewavas (1989), *P. virgatus* is diagnosed as possessing a peculiar shape to the jaws, which are narrow anteriorly but wider at the posterior ends. It seems to pick, rather than suck (as is the case in *P. taeniolatus*), algae from the substrate. It is quite common for insect larvae to be collected in the same way, but the primary aim is to harvest algae.

Mylochromis

The genus *Mylochromis* is characterized by having a diagonal black line, either solid or composed of spots, on the upper body. In a future revision of the genus the solid-line species may need to be assigned to a separate genus as the type species of *Mylochromis* is *M. ericotaenia*, a blotched-line species.

Mylochromis subocularis is a small sand-dwelling species, common at most locations around the lake, which was formerly assigned to the genus *Placidochromis* on the basis that specimens of some populations exhibit distinct vertical bars. But the diagonal line is, as mentioned above, a very characteristic feature of *Mylochromis*, especially when, as in this case, it is broken up into several spots. I have therefore re-assigned this species to *Mylochromis* (Konings, 1995b). *M. subocularis* is distinguished from the other species of the genus by 6 to 8 prominent spots arranged in a diagonal line; this often consists of two partly overlapping lines, a feature seen in other species as well (e.g. in some species of *Lethrinops*). *M. subocularis* males form small breeding colonies in the shallow intermediate habitat and construct shallow spawning pits. Territorial males can be found as close as a meter apart. A population with distinct vertical bars has become established in the aquarium hobby. This population originates from Lake Malombe and has very large molariform teeth in the pharyngeal jaws. This suggests that *M. subocularis* (or the Lake Malombe population at least) feeds primarily on hard-shelled invertebrates and small snails, which it finds in the sand.

Sungwa

Sungwa is the local name for *Serranochromis robustus*, a non-endemic piscivorous cichlid that can also be found in the rivers flowing into the lake. This large (maximum total length about 50 cm) predator is usually seen in very shallow water where it hunts mbuna and small sand-dwelling cichlids. It is common near river estuaries, but rare on long, uninterrupted, stretches of rocky coast. Mouthbrooding females are rarely seen, but the few I have seen were hiding in caves. Fry-guarding females—broods can contain more than 500 fry—are usually found in the shallow intermediate habitat.

The genus *Serranochromis* comprises about 20 species found in various parts of southern and central Africa, where they form a common part of the local ichthyofauna. *S. robustus* or one of its precursors may therefore have been among the first species to colonize the lake, and it has been suggested (Eccles & Trewavas, 1989) that it may even have been the ancestor of some endemic Malaŵi cichlid species. Although some authors do not agree with such an evolutionary scheme (Greenwood, 1993) there are some endemic Malaŵian cichlids that exhibit some similarity to *S. robustus*. In my opinion *Nimbochromis* and *Tyrannochromis* are obvious candidates when considering which genera might be descended from *Serranochromis*-like ancestors. *N. fuscotaeniatus* (see page 297) in particular may have links with the non-endemic *S. robustus*.

1. *Protomelas ornatus* ♂ Ntekete

2. *Protomelas ornatus* ♀ Ntekete

5. *Protomelas ornatus* ♂ Gome

3. *Protomelas virgatus* ♂ Kanchedza Island

6. *Protomelas virgatus* ♂ Harbour Island

7. *Protomelas virgatus* ♀ Harbour Island

4. *Mylochromis subocularis* ♂ Thumbi West Island

8. *Mylochromis subocularis* ♀ Malopa

1. *Serranochromis robustus* ♂ Chiofu

2. *Serranochromis robustus* ♂ Minos Reef

4. *Serranochromis robustus* ♂ Otter Island

3. Chiofu Bay

Shallow sediment-rich bays

Sheltered bays are characterized by muddy sediment covering the sand and rocks on the bottom. In some bays the sediment forms just a thin coating of silt but in very shallow areas a thick layer of sediment covers the sand. This muddy substrate provides ample nutrition for many organisms. The muddy layer is scored by the tracks of numerous snails, mainly members of the two genera *Lanistes* and *Melanoides*. The latter comprises small snails, characterized by cylindrically coiled shells, which are seen most frequently in the muddy regions. *Lanistes nyassanus* also occurs in areas of pure sand and sometimes on sediment-covered rocks in the intermediate habitat. The ooze consists mainly of dead plankton and soil that has been washed into the lake, and is recycled by bacteria, snails, and aquatic plants. Five species of higher plants are common in the lake itself: *Vallisneria spiralis*, *Potamogeton pectinatus*, *P. schweinfurthii*, *Myriophyllum spicatum*, and *Ceratophyllum demersum*. The first of these is the most common and beds of this plant can be found at depths of up to six meters, providing shelter and food for several cichlid species. The micro-organisms that which recycle the sediment provide food for dense clouds of zooplankton which is consumed by shoals of juvenile utaka—sometimes numbering hundreds of thousands—that have been released in such bays for just this purpose. The small utaka are in turn eaten by sub-adult predators. As they mature the juvenile utaka descend to deeper levels where they are hunted by "grown-on" juvenile predators that have migrated with them.

Mbuna

In these shallow bays, with their usually rich cover of sediment, beds of plants provide food and shelter for some specialized mbuna. In such habitats rocks are rare or scattered; where they do occur they provide shelter for the mbuna. The most common species in such environments is *Cyathochromis obliquidens*, which is found throughout the lake but is absent at Chinyankwazi and Chinyamwezi, which are purely rocky islets. Male coloration varies slightly along the entire coastline, while juveniles of all populations are greenish-brown and have bars on the body. Males are quite aggressive in their territorial defense; females and juveniles occur singly or in very small groups. Spawning holes are sometimes excavated under a rock but spawning sites are frequently found in *Vallisneria* beds as well.

The leaves of the higher plants in the lake provide an anchoring substrate for algae. *C. obliquidens* is one of a group of fishes (which also includes *Tropheops novemfasciatus* and *Hemitilapia oxyrhynchus*) which feed from this aufwuchs. It is assigned to a separate genus because of its distinctive teeth (whose oblique tips give the fish its name), which are used to brush and cut algae from *Vallisneria* leaves, and sometimes from rocks as well. Its feeding technique resembles that of *Metriaclima*, none of which has, however, ever been observed feeding from plant leaves.

The genus *Tropheops* includes a few species that nibble and snatch at the aufwuchs on plants. *Tropheops* sp. 'broad mouth' (page 196) has a wide distribution because of its tolerance of a wide variety of food and habitat conditions. It is among the least specialized members of the genus and can therefore be encountered in all kinds of biotopes, including plant beds. Another poorly-specialized species of *Tropheops* is *Tropheops novemfasciatus*, which is usually seen among beds of *Vallisneria* close to rocks and is common in the shallow, calm waters along the shoreline south of Monkey Bay. It is one of the very few mbuna in which males excavate a saucer-shaped spawning site in the muddy bottom between aquatic plants. Territorial males chase all intruders from the premises and court females, which live in small schools of up to 15 individuals. This species feeds from plant leaves and rocks; its diet consists primarily of algae.

Tropheops sp. 'weed' occurs in sediment-rich habitats and has a discontinuous distribution. On the northwestern coast it is found from Usisya to Ngara, and on the eastern shoreline it inhabits the vegetated biotopes between the Ruhuhu River in Tanzania and Mbweca in Mozambique. It feeds in the typical *Tropheops* fashion, tearing algal strands from the substrate; in this case plant leaves as well as rocks. Male *T.* sp. 'weed' defend their territories among sediment-covered rocks in the vicinity of plants. *T.* sp. 'weed' resembles *T. novemfasciatus,* and this may have been the reason for the misidentification of specimens in Christy's collection, which were erroneously assigned to *T. novemfasciatus* (Trewavas, 1935). Even though the range of *T.* sp. 'weed' is rather extensive, geographical variation is minimal.

The prototype

Astatotilapia calliptera is one of the few species in the lake that is also found in the surrounding rivers. It is common in shallow water, particularly where the bottom is covered with a patchwork of *Vallisneria* beds or where dense stands of reeds provide shelter. It is sometimes seen in the shallow intermediate habitat as well. It is one of the few cichlids found in but not endemic to the lake, and it has been suggested that it may be related to the ancestor of at least part of the Lake Malaŵi species flock (Fryer & Iles, 1972: 478). However, Lippitsch (1993) has shown that a particular granulation of the scales of the river-dwelling (fluviatile) species of *Astatotilapia* (including that of *A. calliptera*) is unique to this group and not found in any of the Malaŵi cichlids examined. The anal fin of male *A. calliptera* bears egg-spots, a feature shared with almost all mbuna, but at present there is no species in this large group that is morphologically similar.

It is the ability of *A. calliptera* to tolerate large variations in water chemistry that has allowed it to occupy not only the rivers flowing into the lake, but the lake itself, whose waters are a hundred to a thousand times more alkaline. This remarkable difference may be the factor that prevents many endemic haplochromines from spreading past the boundaries of the lake, but the turbidity and difference in temperature of river water may be a more important barrier to such an exodus.

The populations of *A. calliptera* in the surrounding rivers probably act as a "buffer" against any speciation of the lacustrine population. This is the only plausible explanation of why there is no clearly visible difference between the two groups—but there may be differences in their feeding regimes (see below). A regular exchange of genetic material between the lacustrine and fluviatile populations prevents any segregation. I have observed mouthbrooding females of *A. calliptera* at Mbenji—this island is at least 10 km away from any mainland river—which implies that a significant migration must occur between the mainland and island populations to prevent speciation in the latter group. *A. calliptera* is also a common inhabitant of so-called floating islands which are washed out from river mouths during the rainy season (Oliver & McKaye, 1982; see photo 3 page 11).

It appears that at least the lake-dwelling forms of *A. calliptera* (I have not examined any riverine form) are specialized in feeding on snails. The pharyngeal jaws of three separate populations (Mbenji Island, Chembe Beach, and Thumbi East Island) are very heavy and set with very large, molariform teeth. Females and non-territorial males forage in groups of up to 30 individuals. When hunting, these fishes position themselves head-down among the *Vallisneria* and wait until a snail reveals its position by moving. Shells of relatively small snails are crushed between the pharyngeal jaws and the prey swallowed.

Males of *A. calliptera* dig tunnels beneath rocks or sometimes among the roots of *Vallisneria*. Spawning takes place on the sand in the male's hole. The eggs are fertilized mostly outside the female's mouth (just before she picks them up) and are incubated for about two weeks (not three as is common in mbuna) before the fry are released. The fry are cared for by the female for about a week after release.

The *Astatotilapia* that occurs at Chizumulu

1. *Cyathochromis obliquidens* ♂ Maingano Island

4. *Cyathochromis obliquidens* ♀ Thumbi East Island

2. *Cyathochromis obliquidens* Otter Island

5. *Cyathochromis obliquidens*

3. *Ceratophyllum demersum* Chiofu Bay

1. *Astatotilapia calliptera* ♂ Thumbi East Island

2. *Astatotilapia calliptera* ♂ Chembe

6. *Astatotilapia calliptera* ♀ Mbenji Island

3. *Astatotilapia* sp. 'calliptera chizumulu' ♀ Chizumulu Island

7. *Astatotilapia* sp. 'calliptera chizumulu' ♂ Chizumulu Island

4. *Tropheops* sp. 'weed' ♂ Mbweca

5. *Tropheops* sp. 'weed' ♀ Mbweca

8. *Tropheops* sp. 'weed' ♂ Chewere

Island differs substantially in coloration from the known southern populations and is here regarded as a different species, *Astatotilapia* sp. 'calliptera chizumulu'. In addition to the difference in male coloration, the teeth on the lower pharyngeal jaw of *A.* sp. 'calliptera chizumulu' are not very much enlarged, at least not in the same fashion as in *A. calliptera*.

Kambuzi

Kambuzi is the name used collectively by African fishermen for a group of species that includes *Protomelas similis*, *P. kirkii*, *P. labridens*, and *P. pleurotaenia*. They are characterized by one, sometimes two, horizontal stripes on a silvery body.

Protomelas similis is the most common member of this group and is locally known by the names *namdyatsini* and *chidyabango* (Jackson, 1961). It is often confused with the other members of the group, and *P. kirkii*, *P. pleurotaenia*, and *P. labridens* are all exported as *P. similis*. There are, of course, differences in morphology and coloration, but there are also differences in their behavior and habitat preference. All four species occur in vegetated areas, and by virtue of that fact are rarely found deeper than 10 meters, but there are noticeable differences in the preferred habitat of each species in such areas. *Protomelas kirkii* is found in the shallowest parts of plant beds and rarely occurs in water deeper than three meters. On exposed shores aquatic plants occur—if at all—at deeper levels than in sheltered bays and *P. kirkii* seems to be restricted to shallow bays of this type where it occurs in the inshore, shallow-water margins of the plant beds. *Protomelas labridens*, however, seems to occur more frequently in the deeper sectors of the plant beds, whereas *P. similis* occurs mainly in areas close to rocks—either a few single rocks or the margin of a full-scale rocky habitat. *Protomelas pleurotaenia* occurs in the deeper parts of the plant beds but may also venture out over sand or nearby rocks.

P. similis and *P. kirkii* have a larger mouth than *P. labridens* and *P. pleurotaenia*. The latter has a more elongate body than *P. labridens* and an even smaller mouth. The mid-lateral stripe in *P. pleurotaenia* is often absolutely straight, while in the other members of the group it is curved. *P. kirkii* has a deeper body and a longer snout than *P. similis*. Freshly caught females of the latter species can be recognized by the yellow color of their pelvic fins.

Breeding males of *P. similis* are bright blue with a reddish patch behind the gill cover. The anal fin is dark, sprinkled with light spots, and has an orange edge. Males of *P. labridens* are a lighter blue-green color, with the upper part of the body, along the base of the dorsal fin, olive green. The anal fin is usually very dark with an orange edge, and lacks the spots seen in *P. similis* and *P. kirkii*. Sometimes dark red spots can be distinguished on the male's anal fin when the light is from behind. Males of *P. kirkii* are turquoise and have an orange-brown anal fin bearing many light spots. Males of *P. pleurotaenia* are entirely blue in the northern section of the lake and multi-colored in the south, specifically a blue head with a yellowish body and blue and yellow fins with red spots. The anal fin of male *P. pleurotaenia* is similar to that of *P. labridens*.

P. similis is frequently seen foraging in aquatic plant beds, usually accompanied by several other species: groups of feeding *P. similis* are often joined by small bands of *Astatotilapia calliptera*, solitary *Placidochromis johnstoni*, and individuals of *P. labridens*. To the best of my knowledge *P. similis* is the only species regularly exported from the lake that eats higher plants. It bites pieces out of the leaves although it appears to be interested primarily in the algae which are firmly attached to them. The only way to obtain these algae is to pluck them off the plant and often pieces of leaf are eaten as well. The outer teeth in the jaws are very sharp and are close-packed near to the edge of the jawbone. The pharyngeal teeth are sharp and strong, and macerate the torn-off tufts of algae and pieces of plant leaves before they are swallowed.

Breeding males defend a small area which they have previously cleared in a *Vallisneria* bed. These small circular spawning sites are about 20 to 40 cm in diameter and the sand is clearly visible. Sometimes sand from nearby areas is used to enhance the spawning site, resulting in a slanted sand-cone.

P. kirkii inhabits the very shallow waters of calm bays and feeds primarily on small mollusks and other hard invertebrates, picking this prey from the bottom or from plant leaves. Owing to the very intense fishing pressure in Lake Malaŵi this species has dwindled in numbers because it easily falls prey to beach seines. At the same time most of the plant beds in shallow water have disappeared, as the nets, which are continually dragged over the bottom, have uprooted and thus destroyed the plants. Breeding male *P. kirkii* build small spawning cones on the sand or in plant beds, where still present. A small area is cleared and sand is heaped to indicate the location of the spawning site to females. Females often forage in small groups on the sand in the very shallow water or singly in the plant beds.

The invertebrate feeder *P. labridens* is less common than *P. similis* and *P. kirkii*, and normally accompanies foraging groups of these two species. It picks invertebrates from plant leaves—often small snails such as *Bulinus succinoides*, only a few millimeters in diameter. *P. labridens* is most common at depths of five meters or more and almost all the spawning sites along the deeper edge of a plant bed belong to breeding males of this species.

In appearance *P. pleurotaenia* resembles *P. labridens,* but can immediately be distinguished by its behavior. *P. pleurotaenia* blows in the sediment covering the sand and in particular that covering the bases of plants. In this layer of mud and debris it finds insect larvae and soft-bodied crustaceans. It shares this particular feeding technique with *P. fenestratus,* which is found in rockier environments. Females and non-territorial males are further characterized by distinct red lappets in the dorsal fin. The dorsal fins of the other species mentioned here may sometimes exhibit a very narrow red margin, but this is not as obvious as in *P. pleurotaenia*.

These four *kambuzi* have a lake-wide distribution. However, there are one or two (maybe) additional species that are local in their occurrence. One specimen among the *P. pleurotaenia* collected by Moore at the end of the nineteenth century has very large pharyngeal teeth and has been assigned, together with another specimen from Nkhotakota, to a distinct species: *Protomelas macrodon* (Eccles in Eccles & Trewavas, 1989). Since it is now known that the structure of the pharyngeal teeth can vary from individual to individual within a single population it is unclear whether *P. macrodon* is in fact a distinct species or a local variant of *P. pleurotaenia* or even a polymorphic form of it. Observations in the wild, combined with the study of additional preserved material, may provide an answer this question.

The vegetated areas in the shallow water around Mumbo Island harbor a medium-sized cichlid which is difficult to classify. I believe that this species belongs to *Protomelas* even though the mid-lateral line is broken into three large, elongate blotches suggesting a relationship with *Otopharynx*. A second horizontal line, again broken up into spots, completes the pigmentation pattern of this species, which I provisionally call *Protomelas* sp. 'virgatus mumbo'.

Masimbwe

In the shallow bays larger haplochromines are usually present in greater numbers than mbuna. One of the most common haps of the lake is *Hemitilapia oxyrhynchus*, called *masimbwe* in the Chi-Tonga language. It has a lake-wide distribution and is always found in or near beds of *Vallisneria* or other higher plants. It is specialized in scraping aufwuchs from *Vallisneria* leaves, but is seen feeding from *Potamogeton* as well. It does not eat the leaves, but just "cleans" them of attached algae and invertebrates. Its feeding technique is very characteristic and can be readily appreciated when observing these cichlids in the lake. The leaves are scraped from bottom to top and the fish turns on its side before grasping the base of a leaf. It then slides the leaf through its mouth by jerking three or four times. When the leaves are thickly covered with aufwuchs *H. oxyrhynchus* can also be observed slowly nibbling its way to the top of the leaf. The teeth of the outer jaws are situated deep inside the mouth, especially along the sides. As the leaves are scraped clean the aufwuchs accumulates in the space between the

1. *Protomelas similis* ♂ Thumbi West Island

5. *Protomelas similis* ♀ Thumbi West Island

2. *Protomelas kirkii* ♂ Mvunguti

6. *Protomelas kirkii* ♀ Border

3. *Protomelas labridens* ♂ Chiofu

7. *Protomelas labridens* ♀ Likoma Island

8. *Protomelas labridens* ♂ Likoma Island

4. *Protomelas pleurotaenia* ♂ Otter Island

9. *Protomelas pleurotaenia* ♀ Harbour Island

1. *Hemitilapia oxyrhynchus* ♂ Chiofu

2. *Hemitilapia oxyrhynchus* ♂ Chiofu

5. *Hemitilapia oxyrhynchus* ♀ Maleri Island

3. *Hemitilapia oxyrhynchus* ♀ Cobwé

4. *Protomelas macrodon* type

6. *Protomelas* sp. 'virgatus mumbo' ♀ Mumbo Island

teeth and the lips. The fish may turn onto either its right or its left side before it strips a leaf. When observed in this position from above, the silvery body reflects the light and small *H. oxyrhynchus* are thus vulnerable to predation by birds. This cichlid is rather shy, and when approached usually disappears from the plant beds to deeper water.

George Turner and Rosanna Robinson (pers. comm.) have observed a marked diurnal rhythm in the behavior of this cichlid. At Chembe Beach small numbers ascend from deeper water around midday and by the afternoon they are present in huge crowds. They appear to move to deeper water at night. Spawning takes place in a "scrape" cleared by the male in a *Vallisneria* bed. Males in breeding dress are frequently seen among the females foraging in the plant beds.

There is a difficult to classify, medium-sized cichlid, with an apparently limited distribution, that inhabits vegetated areas in shallow water around the islands of Maleri, Mumbo, and Thumbi West. I believe it to be a species of *Protomelas* even though the midlateral line is broken into three large elongate blotches suggesting a relationship with *Otopharynx*. A second horizontal line, again broken up into spots, completes the pigmentation pattern of this species, which I provisionally call *Protomelas* sp. 'oxyrhynchus mix'. It is a rather rare cichlid which has a body shape very similar to that of *Hemitilapia oxyrhynchus* and, interestingly, it joins foraging groups of the latter species in search of food. In contrast to the leaf-stripping behavior of *H. oxyrhynchus*, however, *P.* sp. 'oxyrhynchus mix' is not a herbivore. Because of its size and shape it is very difficult to distinguish this species in a school of *H. oxyrhynchus*, but when a group of the latter descends on a patch of *Vallisneria P.* sp. 'oxyrhynchus mix' displays a rather different feeding pattern. Even though it remains close to the foraging herbivores it starts ramming its head into the bottom searching for prey. It appears very particular as to the location where the head is forced into the sand and it may swim several meters away from "its" school of *H. oxyrhynchus* to find suitable sites. When an interesting site is found the fish positions itself head-down in a vertical position before an "attack" is launched. It is currently unknown what type of prey it is seeking, but it may well be dragonfly larvae, which are often found among the roots of aquatic plants. The lips of *P.* sp. 'oxyrhynchus mix' are thick and strong, which is probably necessary to cushion the force with which its head is rammed into the bottom. Another interesting fact is that when the host group of *H. oxyrhynchus* moves on to another section of the *Vallisneria* bed, *P.* sp. 'oxyrhynchus mix' stops its search and rejoins the ranks of the school. It is not entirely clear what the advantages are to *P.* sp. 'oxyrhynchus mix' of adhering to schools of *H. oxyrhynchus*, other than protection (safety in numbers, blending into the crowd) from large predators such as otters and cormorants. Since it is a rare cichlid I have not yet seen two individuals of *P.* sp. 'oxyrhynchus mix' together, although once I observed a male in breeding coloration at Thumbi West Island, feeding without the presence of *H. oxyrhynchus*; it was not territorial and females were not found in its immediate surroundings.

Snoeks & Hanssens (2004) report on a species resembling *Fossorochromis* in melanin pattern with the dentition of *Hemitilapia*. They refer to this species as *Fossorochromis* sp. 'oblique teeth' and it may be conspecific with *P.* sp. 'oxyrhynchus mix'.

Placidochromis johnstoni is a widespread and common species of shallow bays, in particular in association with plants. It is not restricted to muddy environments but is seen over sand in intermediate habitats as well. It is frequently exported, sometimes under its indigenous name of *kachimanga*. Like *H. oxyrhynchus* it is also given the name *masimbwe*, which is applied to both these fishes and the plant *Vallisneria spiralis*! *P. johnstoni* usually forages in mixed species groups, but may form bands of more than 50 of its own kind, with only a single male exhibiting breeding coloration. In addition, it sometimes joins packs of *Nimbochromis polystigma* to hunt fry. Males have never been seen defending spawning sites. They probably lead females from the school and spawn at any spot they choose. This relatively small species (16 cm maximum total length) is not a colony breeder. Males lack the distinct egg-spots usually seen in species that construct bowers on the sand, so they may just clear a spawning-site in a *Vallisneria* bed, as do most other species that forage in these beds.

P. johnstoni feed by blowing away the top layer of the muddy sediment at the bases of aquatic plants or rocks. They plunge their heads deep down among the plants and snap their mouths shut. The small amount of sediment covering the bases of the leaves is thus squirted away, probably exposing invertebrates that then try to escape to another hiding place. The predator, alert for any movement, quickly snatches them up.

As mentioned earlier (page 216) I believe that *P. johnstoni* would perhaps be better placed in the genus *Protomelas*. In some individuals one can see the typical melanin pattern of that genus, consisting of two horizontal stripes and vertical bars. In the case of *Placidochromis johnstoni* (and *P. milomo*) the vertical bars of the pattern are simply much more pronounced than the horizontal elements. Also, in terms of its behavior, *P. johnstoni* seems to be more closely related to, for example, the *kambuzi* of the lake than to *P. longimanus* (page 327), the type species of *Placidochromis*.

Protomelas triaenodon is a common species in the southern part of the lake and attains a maximum total length of about 18 cm. I have also seen it in the bay at Liuli in Tanzania, so it may have a much wider distribution than previously believed. The peculiarity of this species is the fact that the outer teeth in the jaws are tricuspid. Those in the pharyngeal jaws are fine and numerous. It is thus unlikely that *P. triaenodon* filters sand because those species that do so usually have a few enlarged teeth on the pharyngeal jaws and never tricuspid teeth in the jaws. The teeth point to a diet of algae, possibly scraped from small rocks in the habitat, but although I have encountered this species at various places I have never been able to witness it feeding. Some specimens, caught in Senga Bay, have been exported (Stuart Grant, pers. comm.) but reports of its behavior in the aquarium are not at present available.

Snails for lunch

Chilotilapia rhoadesii is found throughout the lake and is seen predominantly over muddy bottoms, where it finds the food for which it is specialized: mollusks. Small snails are cracked between the pharyngeal jaws but larger ones are tackled with the mouth. Both sets of teeth, i.e. those in the outer jaws and those on the pharyngeal bones, are stout and blunt and designed to withstand the forces developed during the crushing of a shell. The head of this cichlid is very compressed laterally and allows maximum force in a vertical direction. *C. rhoadesii* crushes snails mainly with the mouth. The snail *Melanoides tuberculata* is one of its favorites; only the wide end of the shell is bitten off, and the soft animal inside thus extracted. Another favorite, the much larger *Lanistes nyassanus*, is sucked out of its shell. This feeding technique can be observed in the aquarium when large snails are offered as food: they are sucked out of their shells in a matter of seconds.

C. rhoadesii can sometimes be seen in large schools of up to a few hundred individuals. Only a single male in breeding dress is present in such groups; other males have a coloration similar to females. Each group seems to have a large feeding territory. They move in formation through the biotope while foraging, but the same group will still be found in the same area many days later. A similar observation has been made regarding groups of *Fossorochromis rostratus* (see page 320).

Ribbink *et al.* (1983b: 246) report that at Chemwezi Rocks males defend territories over rocks. I have noticed, however, that males at this location have their territories, which are in fact on the sand, marked with empty *Lanistes* shells. These shells are not carried in by the tenant male but are "unearthed" by the removal of sand in that particular area. Long disused snail shells, which are white in color, are rather abundant in some areas and the male has only to remove the sediment and sand to expose them. As with several other cichlid species, *C. rhoadesii* may become territorial when more than one ripe male is present in a small area. Mouthbrooding females remain within the for-

1. *Protomelas* sp. 'oxyrhynchus mix' ♂ Thumbi West Island

4. *Protomelas* sp. 'oxyrhynchus mix' ♀ Thumbi West Island

5. *Protomelas* sp. 'oxyrhynchus mix' ♀ Thumbi West Island

2. *Placidochromis johnstonii* ♂ Likoma Island

6. *Placidochromis johnstonii* ♀ Ntekete

3. *Placidochromis johnstonii* ♂♀♀ Likoma Island

1. *Protomelas triaenodon* ♀ Kande Island
2. *Mylochromis incola* ♀ Mbenji Island
3. *Chilotilapia rhoadesii* ♀ Cobwé
4. *Chilotilapia rhoadesii* ♂ Chembe
5. *Protomelas triaenodon* ♂ Liuli
6. *Mylochromis incola* ♂ Nankoma Island

aging school.

C. rhoadesii is normally found in water deeper than five meters, and can penetrate to very deep levels (up to 100 meters; Eccles & Trewavas, 1989). Specimens caught at such depths are very large, with a maximum total length of more than 30 cm, and probably occur in small groups or singly.

Mylochromis

Mylochromis incola is an invertebrate feeder with a lake-wide distribution, and found mainly among *Vallisneria* beds. This cichlid, with an average size of 15 cm, picks insects and crustaceans from among the plants. The pharyngeal bones are set with stout blunt teeth. Specimens from Nankoma Island have been exported as "Haplochromis Golden Mola". When breeding males and females seem to move to the intermediate habitat, and it is there that males in breeding dress are seen most frequently. Bower building has been observed in the population at Nankoma Island; males construct a spawning pit beneath a small, overhanging rock. Geographical variation in male breeding coloration is not apparent.

Mylochromis mola is frequently seen at many different locations around the lake, in the northern as well as the southern part. A silvery-white body, a diagonal row of large black blotches, and, in the northern populations, orange anal and pelvic fins, characterize this common species. The orange color is weak in the southern populations and all the fins are hyaline. The species is easily distinguished from the very similar *M. sphaerodon* (page 328) by the form of the diagonal line: in *M. mola* this consists of several large blotches which never form a continuous, solid line. In *M. sphaerodon* the diagonal line is thin and solid and lies on the upper lateral line, while in *M. mola* the diagonal line is fragmented and runs below the upper lateral line on the posterior half of the body.

M. mola has large, rounded pharyngeal teeth and dines on small snails and crustaceans. The breeding color of males is blue, and the diagonal line disappears. Territorial males of *M. mola* defend a small area in the rubble of the intermediate habitat. A bower is not constructed but a small spawning patch is cleared of irregularities.

The range of *Mylochromis plagiotaenia* seems to be restricted to the southern and southeastern shores of the lake. It has an oblique black stripe, which may occasionally be broken up into about ten small spots, extending from the nape to the base of the tail. Its maximum total length does not usually exceed 12 cm. Breeding males have been observed in November and December but may be present all year round. Territorial males clear a small area, with a diameter of about 10 cm, in plant beds, in such a way that the underlying sand is visible from above as a light spot. Such spawning sites are more conspicuous than the sand-turrets built by other species. In other places males clear a small area (with a diameter of about 20-30 cm) on the sand next to a small object—a small rock, a piece of wood, or rubbish that has been washed into the lake. Mouthbrooding females group together over the sand.

Mylochromis lateristriga grows to a maximum length of about 23 cm and is encountered infrequently in the southern part of the lake. It digs into the sand and filters any palatable items (mainly crustaceans and insect larvae) from it. At Cape Maclear it is sometimes followed by *Cyrtocara moorii* (Kocher & McKaye, 1983). *M. lateristriga* has been exported as "Giant Flame Oxyrhynchus" and is often found among groups of the leaf-cleaning *Hemitilapia*. The only locality where it has been caught regularly is at Maleri Island—before the National Park regulations were brought into force. A *M. lateristriga* male secures a breeding territory shortly before spawning and seduces a ripe female into following him to his spawning site, usually a shallow saucer-shaped pit dug in the sand, although a flat stone may be chosen instead. During spawning the eggs are immediately collected by the female before being fertilized inside her mouth.

M. lateristriga appears to be restricted to areas with vegetation as it was almost extirpated from the Maleri islands through the extensive use of beach seines, which uprooted and removed almost all the aquatic plants around the islands. Recently the area has come under the protection of a private group overseeing the activities around the islands, and the plants and the cichlids seem to be slowly returning to their original state.

Mylochromis balteatus is an enigmatic species. It was described from a few specimens caught at the north end of the lake. As well as the diagonal stripe, it is characterized by stout teeth on the pharyngeal jaws and strong lips (not unlike *M. melanotaenia*; see page 330). Over the years I have photographed single individuals at various places around the lake and logged them as *M. balteatus*. However, comparing these populations I believe that they represent at least three different species. The form most closely resembling the type of the species is that I have found in the vegetated areas of the southern part of the lake. It is a robust species with thick lips and a diagonal stripe that seems to be draped over the nape. In the type the diagonal stripe has a similar appearance and this has given the species its name: balteatus meaning girdled. Another species, previously (Konings, 2001) referred to as *M. balteatus*, has been found at Londo and at Tumbi Point (both in Mozambique). Although I have seen males in breeding colors courting females, spawning sites were not found. For the time being I will refer to this form as *Mylochromis* sp. 'balteatus mozambique'. The third form, which I found in the beach seines of fishermen at Karonga, probably represents *Mylochromis guentheri* (see page 328).

An extremely rare species, *Mylochromis* sp. 'torpedo elongate', was once collected by fishermen in the very shallow water near Kambiri Point (in 1989). I have never seen this exceptionally elongate species in its habitat. It is further characterized by a tiny mouth and a lachrymal stripe between eye and lip.

Other plant-dwellers

Two other species are found among beds of *Vallisneria* and *Ceratophyllum*, especially in the southern section of the lake. *Otopharynx tetrastigma* and *O. tetraspilus* are found mainly in the southern part of the lake and in the Shiré River as well.

Otopharynx tetrastigma scoops up and filters muddy sediment, retaining anything palatable such as insect larvae and small crustaceans. It also feeds on zooplankton that approaches the substrate. Territorial males have been observed in both August and December, so the breeding season may extend over the entire year. Males, whose breeding coloration is dark blue-brown but nevertheless attractive, defend a cleared patch among the plants or establish a breeding territory on the muddy sand near plants. The spawning site consists of a "scrape" with a diameter of approximately 50 cm, with a large heap of sand right next to it. The actual spawning dish is fashioned alongside the heap of sand (see photo 9 page 295). These spawning dishes, including those among aquatic plants, have a diameter of about 10 cm. Ripe females are enticed from the foraging groups and led to the spawning dish. Maximum total length in this species is about 14 cm.

Otopharynx tetraspilus grows to a length of approximately 16 cm. Stomach contents analysis has revealed algae, pieces of higher plants, and small crustaceans (Eccles & Trewavas, 1989).

In the early 1980s a cichlid with the trade names of "Haplochromis Yellow Fin Mloto" and "Yellow Princess" was exported from the south of the lake. The low number of gill-rakers in this species (14 on the lower arch in one specimen) probably excludes it from the plankton-feeder group (utaka). Young aquarium specimens of this species resemble *O. tetraspilus* to a certain extent, but in my view this alone is not enough for it to be regarded as conspecific with *O. tetraspilus*, even though its meristic data correspond to those of that species. However, large specimens of the "Yellow Fin Mloto" do resemble the preserved type specimens of *O. tetraspilus*, so I suggest that it should after all be assigned to that taxon.

Snoeks & Hanssens (2004) report on *O.* sp. 'tetraspilus molariform', which is in most anatomical characters identical to *O. tetraspilus* but which has molariform teeth on the pharyngeal jaws while those of *O. tetraspilus* are fine and pointed.

1. *Mylochromis mola* ♂ Chizumulu Island

5. *Mylochromis mola* ♀ Maleri Island

2. *Mylochromis lateristriga* ♂ Maleri Island

6. *Mylochromis lateristriga* ♀ Maleri Island

7. *Mylochromis balteatus* ♂ Aquarium

3. *Mylochromis balteatus* ♀ Mvunguti

8. *Mylochromis plagiotaenia* ♀ Mvunguti

4. *Mylochromis plagiotaenia* ♂ Mvunguti

1. *Mylochromis* sp. 'balteatus mozambique' ♀ Tumbi Point

2. *Otopharynx tetrastigma* ♀ Thumbi East Island

3. *Otopharynx tetraspilus* ♂ Maleri Island

4. *Otopharynx tetraspilus* ♀ Aquarium

5. *Otopharynx* sp. 'tetraspilus molariform' Chipoka

7. *Mylochromis* sp. 'balteatus mozambique' ♂ Tumbi Point

8. *Otopharynx tetrastigma* ♂ Thumbi East Island

9. *Otopharynx tetrastigma* ♂ Kanchedza Island

6. *Mylochromis* sp. 'torpedo elongate' Kambiri Point

Martin Geerts

Tramitichromis

The genus *Tramitichromis* is characterized by the peculiar shape of the lower pharyngeal bone of its members. The teeth on this bone are all slender and long; those situated at the front are the longest—an unusual feature. These long anterior teeth are further characterized by their long tips, which are bent backwards. In most other species the anterior pharyngeal teeth are small and their tips point forward. The reason for this particular development in *Tramitichromis* is not clear, but most likely its origin lies in the feeding behavior or the type of food. Another feature of *Tramitichromis* is the downward projecting anterior blade of the pharyngeal bone. Most species of this genus are found in the sandy type habitat (page 364) but a single species, *Tramitichromis intermedius* occurs in the shallow vegetated areas.

T. intermedius is a small species—maximum total length about 14 cm—which was assigned to the genus by Eccles & Trewavas (1989), though this classification is questionable. The three spots on the flank do not correspond with the pigmentation pattern (a diagonal stripe on the flank) seen in the type species of the genus, *T. brevis*. Moreover, the lower jaw of *T. intermedius* has large sensory pores, much larger than in any other species of *Tramitichromis*. This feature and, in particular, its pigmentation pattern, correspond more with the definition of the genus *Trematocranus*.

T. intermedius is normally found singly or in small groups foraging over sediment-covered sand in the shallow water of muddy bays. It feeds on insect larvae and other soft invertebrates. *T. intermedius* has a lake-wide distribution. Breeding males defend small pits in the mud or sand as territory, usually near reed stands.

Kaligonos, the "sleeping" predators

The range of *Nimbochromis livingstonii* encompasses the entire lake but it is most often seen in the southern half. It is common in the shallow muddy habitat. Its characteristic behavior, responsible for its Chi-Chewa name *kaligono*—meaning "sleeper"—can also be observed in captivity. *N. livingstonii* is a piscivore which has developed a remarkable ambush-hunting technique. When not breeding, both male and female exhibit several characteristic liver-colored patches on a whitish body, a color pattern unique among Malaŵi cichlids. The *kaligono* feeds on small, inexperienced cichlids but never pursues its prey. It has developed another technique to obtain its daily meal, wherein its unique coloration plays the key role. A white-colored object is very attractive to any cichlid and *msima* (white, boiled maize flour) is widely used as bait by young fishermen angling for *kambuzi* from the shore. But although the white color may attract small fishes, they would never approach within striking distance of a recognizable *kaligono*. It has therefore developed several procedures to prevent its prey from recognizing it as a piscivore. One of these is employed when the bottom is covered with a layer of mud a few centimeters thick: the predator lies down on its side and wriggles itself into the sediment, remaining in that position without moving a fin. If the bottom is sandy it may stir up some sand as it lies down on its side. It can also drop on one side on a rock. The result of all these techniques is that the outline of the fish is partially camouflaged, and while it lies on one side it is not directly recognized as a threat by small cichlids—in other words, they no longer recognize it as a fish.

A *kaligono* shamming death presents a very realistic picture of a decaying fish but, as George Turner (pers. comm.) has pointed out, it is not imitating one. Dead fishes are rarely seen in the lake (I have seen only three or four in more than 1500 hours of diving). *N. livingstonii* may lie motionless for at least three minutes before it moves to another site. The sand and debris that it occasionally stirs up (as it lies down) may attract all kinds of small fishes, but often the predator just waits until a small cichlid inspects this very interesting white-colored "thing" that is lying on the bottom. The "sleeping" predator does not appear to be recognized as such by them. Larger fishes are sometimes attracted too, but in this case the sleeper avoids contact by "waking up." When the small fishes are within striking distance, the *kaligono* quickly awakens and attacks with a sideways stroke.

A similar hunting technique, in which the hunter relies on its cryptic coloration and motionless posture, is found in *N. venustus* (see page 352) and in *N. polystigma* (see below) as well. Such cryptically-colored predators are also known from other parts of Africa. The Lake Tanganyika cichlid *Lepidiolamprologus lemairei* has been observed hunting in this way (Konings, 1998) and the characteristic coloration of *Serranochromis longimanus* from the Okavango Delta suggests similar behavior.

McKaye (1981) found that every adult *N. livingstonii* has its own feeding territory of about 40 meters of shoreline. Neighboring individuals contest territorial boundaries with a short display, and then return to their own feeding grounds. At Chizumulu, where most *N. livingstonii* are caught for export, sometimes up to 30 sub-adult specimens can be seen within an area about 25 meters in diameter. Adults, however, seem to have large private feeding areas.

Breeding males of *N. livingstonii* are a dark sky-blue which completely obscures the blotched pattern. Neighboring individuals probably recognize each other, and females in adjacent territories notice the sexual ripeness of the male. It is not uncommon to find a few breeding males forming a lek but such groups usually do not contain more than a handful of males. However, at Makokola Reef, in the southeastern arm of the lake, I found a large group of breeding males at the edge of the rocky reef at a depth of about 30 meters. Some females (in captivity) have been observed cleaning (!) the stone on which they subsequently deposit their eggs (Willemse, 1976). This behavior is reminiscent of substrate brooders. Spawning usually takes place at the edge of the rocky biotope, where the male will have dug a shallow saucer-shaped spawning site beside a large rock. The male fertilizes the eggs while they are still on the spawning substrate. Both male and female circle around each other, the female depositing a batch of eggs and then moving forward to make room for the male, who fertilizes them. On the next pass the female picks up the fertilized eggs and then deposits a new batch. Mouthbrooding females normally remain solitary and guard their free-swimming offspring for several weeks after they have been released for the first time.

Nimbochromis polystigma is rather common in shallow vegetated and intermediate habitats and can sometimes be found in groups of 20 to 500 (sub-)adult individuals. Such groups cruise through the habitat like packs of hungry wolves, devouring any small fishes they come across. The specific color pattern serves as camouflage when they roam through the biotope singly. When on their own they swim at a slower pace and behave like a *kaligono*—the vernacular name is also applied to this species, and to *N. venustus* as well. When ambushing prey *N. polystigma* remains motionless on the sand but does not lie on its side like *N. livingstonii*.

Sexually active males assume a sky-blue color that completely overlays the spotted pattern. Spawning takes place in the intermediate habitat, where males dig large but shallow saucer-shaped spawning pits beside large rocks, sometimes creating a cave-crater bower. Breeding males refrain from feeding during the breeding period (as they have lost their camouflage) and defend their territory mainly against conspecifics. They appear to feel vulnerable in breeding colors and flee quickly when approached by a diver. The spawning behavior of *N. polystigma* resembles that of *N. livingstonii*, i.e. the eggs are fertilized outside the female's mouth. After first release the fry are taken back into the mouth for at least another four weeks.

Predators that don't sleep

Nimbochromis fuscotaeniatus is assigned to *Nimbochromis* (Eccles & Trewavas, 1989), but in view of its strong resemblance to *Tyrannochromis nigriventer* it might be better placed in that genus. Its color pattern, while reminiscent of *Nimbochromis*, is probably an adaptation to environment rather than signifying any relationship to that genus. *N. fuscotaeniatus* is a well-known predator regularly encountered in shallow water. It is endemic to the southern and western parts of the lake—it has been seen at

1. *Tramitichromis intermedius* ♂ Gallireya Reef
2. *Nimbochromis livingstonii* ♀ Lutara
3. *Nimbochromis livingstonii* ♂ Cobwé 
4. *Nimbochromis livingstonii* Lupingu
5. *Tramitichromis intermedius* ♀ Tumbi Point
6. *Nimbochromis livingstonii* ♀ Cobwé

1. *Nimbochromis polystigma* ♂ Chembe

2. *Nimbochromis polystigma* Maleri Island

5. *Nimbochromis polystigma* ♀ Mvunguti

3. *Nimbochromis polystigma* ♂ Mazinzi Reef

6. *Nimbochromis fuscotaeniatus* ♀ Mazinzi Reef

4. *Nimbochromis fuscotaeniatus* ♀ Mazinzi Reef

7. *Nimbochromis fuscotaeniatus* ♂ Kanchedza Island

Kande Island on the western shore but no further north than Chimwalani Reef along the eastern side of the lake—and has been found in Lake Malombe as well. With a maximum total length of more than 25 cm, it is a redoubtable predator. It is never seen lying on its side but its pattern of brown blotches on a light body may provide the camouflage needed to ambush small prey. *N. fuscotaeniatus* breeds in a similar fashion to most other haplochromines, i.e. the eggs are fertilized inside the female's mouth (Dorenstouter, 1982).

The Chi-Tonga name for *Champsochromis spilorhynchus* is *njeruwa*, and it has been given several other native names such as *tabwa* and *damphila*; it has been exported as "Haplochromis Mbwanae". It has a lake-wide distribution. Its maximum total length can be more than 35 cm and it is a formidable piscivore, following its prey over long distances (rather than ambushing it like the previous three species). Its main characteristic is the black lachrymal stripe between the eye and the corner of the mouth. Because of over-fishing with beach seines in shallow, vegetated areas the once common *C. spilorhynchus* has been brought to the brink of extinction and is now very rarely encountered—in hundreds of hours of diving only a few juveniles have been seen in plant beds in very shallow water.

Dimidiochromis compressiceps is particularly associated with higher plants, and is rarely encountered in the rocky habitat—apart from the rocky reefs at Chizumulu Island. This species, locally known as *chimpeni* (meaning "big knife"), is very well known to aquarists and is regularly exported. There is a geographical variant in which non-territorial individuals are a golden yellow color instead of the normal silver. This yellow *D. compressiceps* is found at Chizumulu Island and at Cobwé in Mozambique. *D. compressiceps* was once regarded as a trophic specialist, feeding on eyes (Wickler, 1966)—hence its popular name of "Malaŵi Eyebiter"—but such behavior has never been observed in the lake. *D. compressiceps* is in fact a piscivore and is specially designed to conceal itself among reed stands and in beds of *Vallisneria*. Its silvery body is extremely laterally compressed and its back bears a dark stripe. When lying in ambush, it positions itself head-down among the reeds or *Vallisneria*, and waits motionless for small fishes to pass by. Prey is quickly seized and sucked inside the protrusible mouth. Unlike other laterally-compressed predators, *D. compressiceps* locates its prey with both eyes and seizes it with a thrust of the body. It starts its piscivorous life at a size of about 4 cm; smaller juveniles feed mainly on plankton. Predators like *D. compressiceps* are particularly abundant at locations where many utaka release their fry, i.e. in very shallow water among reed stands. During the breeding season males develop a metallic blue hue over the entire body and stake out a temporary spawning site. A kind of bower is constructed in the sand, sometimes resembling a shallow saucer, usually in plant beds but sometimes also in the shallow intermediate habitat. Ripe females in the surrounding area are enticed to the site. There is little aggression among conspecifics, and small groups of this piscivore may occasionally be seen cooperating to decimate a large school of juvenile utaka.

Dimidiochromis strigatus has a lake-wide distribution but is infrequently caught. Reports on its feeding behavior describe it variously as a predator hunting fishes and feeding on invertebrates, or a herbivore feeding on aquatic plants (Eccles & Trewavas, 1989). However, the size of its oblique mouth, together with aquarium observations, suggests that it is an ambush predator, preferring live food to plants. *D. strigatus* is irregularly exported as "Haplochromis Sunset".

Morphologically this species resembles *D. compressiceps*, although its body is deeper and less compressed. The lower jaw is longer than the upper. The horizontal mid-lateral stripe on the body is a characteristic of all species of *Dimidiochromis*. The largest specimen recorded measured about 25 cm in total length. Males defend territories in which they dig a crater in the sand, with a diameter of about 50 cm and a depth of about 5 to 10 cm, usually between clumps of *Vallisneria* but not in the denser beds. Before their numbers were decimated by overfishing it was not uncommon to see a dozen territorial males in a relatively small area, defending spawning sites around a reed stand. The distance between males varies between two and three meters. Mouthbrooding females often hide deep in the reed stands and are often found solitary. The number of eggs per brood can be staggering: in captivity a female once released 230 fry at the end of the incubation period (Baasch, 1992a).

Dimidiochromis dimidiatus seems to be more common in the northern than in the southern part of the lake. It is infrequently taken by seine nets at Kambiri in the south, but most records are from the north (Eccles & Trewavas, 1989). It resembles *Rhamphochromis* (see below) in its shape and silvery color, but, unlike members of that genus, is probably restricted to the shallow inshore waters. I have observed this species only near Kambiri Point in the southern part of the lake, in water no deeper than about three meters. Although males in breeding attire were seen on occasion, none of them behaved territorially. Females and non-breeding males cruise over the sandy substrate in search of food, which consists of small fishes and larger invertebrates. The fishermen employed by exporter Stuart Grant seem to be most successful catching this species using termites as bait. Underwater, *D. dimidiatus* is a very shy species and trying to catch one with a barrier net is a real challenge. Although the species has been bred in captivity little information is available as to whether males build bowers or spawn at any given site. *D. dimidiatus* is the smallest member of the genus and the largest males seen were about 20 cm total length.

Ncheni

The genus *Rhamphochromis*—all species are known locally as *ncheni*—consists of mainly very large piscivores that hunt in the very deep open waters of the lake. A few species, however, are commonly found in shallow water and the type species of the genus, *R. longiceps*, is most often found in the shallow vegetated areas of the lake—at least in the case of females and subadult males. It grows to an average total length of 24 cm and has the smallest teeth of the group. It can further be recognized by its small mouth, elongate body, and the lack of a horizontal stripe in adult specimens. I have seen it prey on very small fishes in the shallow vegetated areas. Martin Genner (pers. comm.) found mostly *usipa* in the stomachs of adults.

According to Genner *et al.* (2007b) there are two other *ncheni* that closely resemble *Rhamphochromis longiceps*, namely *R.* sp. 'longiceps greyback' and *R.* sp. 'longiceps yellow belly', but these are found in the deep open water (page 393). *R. longiceps* is distinguished from these species by a blue-green sheen on the back and by the lack of dark striations on the dorsal part of the body, a feature present in the other two. In the aquarium *R. longiceps* often displays a horizontal stripe (Martin Genner, pers. comm.) but this is not obvious in the lake. Males have bright yellow anal and ventral fins while those of females are colorless. Maximum size is about 27 cm.

Another interesting observation by Martin Genner (pers. comm.) is that he found females of *R. longiceps* migrating into lagoons at various places around the lake. These females were caught with gill nets set across the channel or river connecting the lagoon with the lake. All the adult fish collected were females, either brooding or recently spawned, but there was never a single adult male among the hundreds of individuals collected. Juveniles were also very common. He suggested the likelihood that females migrate into the lagoons to brood and release their young. Over time some of these lagoons have apparently become isolated from the lake, an example being Lake Chilingali, a shallow lagoon near Nkhotakota. Interestingly, Genner *et al.* (2007b) discovered a small species of *Rhamphochromis*, with a very modest maximum total length of about 12 cm, in this lagoon. It is thought that in the case of Lake Chilingali some *R. longiceps* had been trapped in the lagoon, and this isolated population had eventually evolved into a new species. The new taxon is referred to as *Rhamphochromis* sp. 'chilingali'.

Tilapias

Oreochromis shiranus is a tilapiine cichlid, and

1. *Champsochromis spilorhynchus* ♂ Aquarium

5. *Champsochromis spilorhynchus* Harbour Island

2. *Champsochromis spilorhynchus* Mazinzi Reef

3. *Dimidiochromis compressiceps* Chiofu

6. *Dimidiochromis compressiceps* Thumbi East Island

4. *Dimidiochromis compressiceps* ♂ Masinje

7. *Dimidiochromis compressiceps* ♀ Chizumulu

1. *Dimidiochromis strigatus* ♀ Kambiri Point
2. *Dimidiochromis dimidiatus* Kambiri Point 
3. *Rhamphochromis longiceps* ♂ Otter Island 
4. *Rhamphochromis longiceps* Lundu
5. Lake Chilingali 

6. *Dimidiochromis strigatus* ♂ Kambiri Point
7. *Dimidiochromis dimidiatus* ♂ Senga Bay (Aquarium) 
8. *Rhamphochromis longiceps* ♀ Kambiri Point
9. *Rhamphochromis* sp. 'chilingali' ♂ Lake Chilingali

is found in very shallow bays, especially among reeds. It is not endemic to the lake, but is encountered in the surrounding rivers as well. It is restricted to shallow water and has never been found far from the shoreline, although it is found around the Maleri Islands and Thumbi West as well as at Chizumulu Island, indicating either that the species is able to cross open water or that these populations are relics of periods of lower lake levels (Turner, 1996). A few specimens at Chizumulu Island were found to have black head markings not seen in any other population. This may indeed point to a relict population that is no longer in contact with the mainland populations.

Like the other three species of this genus found in the lake, *O. shiranus* feeds on algae and phytoplankton. Non-breeding fishes are golden yellow, in particular on the anal fin, with black horizontal stripes and sometimes iridescent blue spots. Sexually active males dig craters in the sand in very shallow, secluded areas and are jet black, sometimes with white spots on the scales. They can be distinguished from other male *Oreochromis* in the lake by a bright red dorsal-fin margin and by the absence of a genital tassel. This species also differs from the other three in that spawning is not restricted to a specific season and a female may raise six to eight broods each year (Fryer & Iles, 1972). Moreover, *O. shiranus* differs morphologically from all other cichlids in the lake by normally having four anal fin spines as opposed to three (Turner, 1996). Males can attain a maximum total length of about 37 cm.

Oreochromis karongae has an average total length of 29 cm, lives close to the shore, and is frequently observed among plants in shallow bays and lagoons (Lowe, 1953). It feeds on diatoms and debris that it collects from the bottom, rocks, and aquatic plants. During the breeding season (ranging from August to March, depending on the area), the black males dig their characteristic pits, with spawning cones, in the sand, sometimes among *Vallisneria* beds. Such bowers are typical of this group of tilapias (*O. karongae*, *O. squamipinnis*, and *O. lidole*) and have never been found in any haplochromine. After the females have laid their eggs they retreat to very shallow areas and spend the incubation period among the plants, where the fry are released. There they find enough food and shelter to grow to *kasawala*, as juveniles are called in the native tongue. George Turner (pers. comm.), who has extensively studied the tilapias in the southern part of the lake, discovered that there are two morphs of *O. karongae* present around Cape Maclear. One has only three to six rows of teeth in the lower jaw and is found predominantly in open water and over sand. The other, which he calls "multitooth," is found mainly in the rocky area, and is characterized by very broad bands of teeth in the jaws. This morph feeds on the aufwuchs on rocks and rakes the loose algae in a manner very similar to that of *Metriaclima*. Turner did not find any clear segregation between the two morphs during breeding, suggesting that they are conspecific. Non-breeding individuals are distinguished from those of *O. lidole* and *O. squamipinnis* by the bright yellow lappets in the dorsal fin (Turner, 1996).

Tilapia rendalli is the only substrate-brooding cichlid in the lake, and is not endemic. This vegetarian is common throughout the southern part of Africa and is regularly found in isolated pools surrounding the lake. In the lake itself it is seen infrequently among reed stands. A pair bond is formed between male and female and several broods per year are raised. The pair prepares for spawning by clearing a site in a plant bed or in the shallow intermediate habitat. The eggs are deposited on the vertical surface of a rock and guarded by both parents. Usually several holes/tunnels are dug in the bottom in the breeding territory, sometimes ending in an underground chamber, in which the wrigglers are kept. The free-swimming fry are led through the habitat where they feed on plankton and detritus. Both parents defend the fry, but most fall prey to cichlids such as *Dimidiochromis compressiceps* and the other piscivores mentioned above.

The sandy habitat

More than half of the lake's shoreline consists of pure sand, which alternates with swampy and rocky shores. This open biotope offers little or no protection to small cichlids and most of them are thus found in large groups or shoals. A single rock or tree trunk provides a reference point for several lek-breeding cichlids, while smaller species may find shelter there. The sandy biotope is inhabited by one of the lake's most successful cichlid genera: *Lethrinops*. The species of this genus are gregarious bottom grubbers. Their schools are often encountered in somewhat deeper regions where the sandy plain is uninterrupted by rocks or plants. In the shallower areas (usually no deeper than 15 meters) there may be some rocks on the sand, called *virundu* by the natives, and large shoals of haplochromines from other genera are frequently seen there.

Mbuna

Even some mbuna species occur regularly over the sand, and one of these, *Pseudotropheus livingstonii,* is a true sand-dwelling cichlid.

Jay Stauffer (pers. comm.) has recently examined the type material of this species, previously thought to be a *Metriaclima*, and discovered that another taxon, *P. elegans*, is in fact a junior synonym of *P. livingstonii*, a name which it now also turns out has been incorrectly used for decades, by aquarists and scientists alike, for *Metriaclima lanisticola*, a look-alike species that lives in and around empty shells (see below). I in turn have found that on both morphological and behavioral grounds *P. livingstonii* does not belong to *Metriaclima* at all and is better re-assigned to *Pseudotropheus*. The species occasionally seen in the aquarium hobby as *P. elegans* is thus the true *P. livingstonii*, and the hobby *livingstonii* is correctly *M. lanisticola*.

Around Likoma Island, along the northern shores of Mozambique, and south of Monkey Bay, *P. livingstonii* is found in shallow water (two to 15 meters). In these areas *P. livingstonii* is common to abundant and regularly forms schools. At Chembe Beach and Likoma small individuals have been observed using empty shells of *Lanistes nyassanus* as shelter, but the maximum size of this species (about 15 cm in the aquarium) precludes the use of these empty shells as shelter by adult specimens. Those too large to fit into a shell group together, sometimes forming large schools. Mouthbrooding females are frequently seen in such schools. Ribbink *et al.* (1983b) found this species inhabiting the rocky biotope at Chemwezi in the deep south of the lake. Rocks give better protection to the individual than that found in a school over the sand, and may in fact be their true preferred habitat; competition from more aggressive rock-dwellers may have driven them out onto the sand in other areas. The population of *P. livingstonii* near Usisya has bright yellow fins, making it the most attractive geographical variant. Males and females in all populations are difficult to tell apart; usually males have a somewhat brighter, more contrasting coloration than females.

The graceful movements of *P. livingstonii* while foraging on the sandy bottom are accentuated by the black band in the anal fin of both male and female. The soft-rayed parts of the anal and dorsal fins are greatly extended and undulate behind the moving fish.

P. livingstonii feeds by picking or scooping algae from the sand or from objects on the sand. *Metriaclima* feed by raking the loose algae from the aufwuchs on rocks (or other hard objects). The angle of the vomer in a single specimen of *P. livingstonii* was 62°, well outside the range found in *Metriaclima* (35-50°). There are also other morphological differences between *P. livingstonii* and *Metriaclima* species: the latter rarely have more than four rows of teeth in the oral jaws while *P. livingstonii* usually has five or six rows. The teeth of the inner rows in *Metriaclima* are widely spaced whereas they are

1. *Oreochromis shiranus* ♂ Chizumulu Island

5. *Oreochromis shiranus* ♀ Chitande Island

2. *Oreochromis karongae* ♂ Otter Island

6. *Oreochromis karongae* ♀ Thumbi West Island

3. *Oreochromis karongae* ♂ Otter Island

7. *Tilapia rendalli* Thumbi West Island

4. *Tilapia rendalli* ♀ Ndonga

8. *Tilapia rendalli* Chembe

9. *Tilapia rendalli* ♀ Chiloelo

1. *Lethrinops* spp. N'kolongwe

2. *Pseudotropheus livingstonii* ♀ Maingano Island

3. *Pseudotropheus livingstonii* ♂ Liuli

4. *Pseudotropheus livingstonii* ♂ Luwala Reef

5. *Pseudotropheus livingstonii* ♂ Tchinga Reef

6. *Pseudotropheus livingstonii* ♀ Chembe

close-packed in *P. livingstonii*. The holotype of *livingstonii* has six rows of close-packed teeth.

A number of other mbuna with a similar appearance to *P. livingstonii* likewise occur over pure sandy bottoms. The best-known of these is *Metriaclima lanisticola*, which is commonly found over sandy bottoms where empty shells of *Lanistes nyassanus* or similar hiding-places are available.

As far as is known both *P. livingstonii* and *M. lanisticola* have an almost lake-wide distribution, but *M. lanisticola* has not yet been seen along the eastern shore north of Makanjila Point. It is in fact difficult to tell the two species apart, in particular in isolated populations. I have found that *M. lanisticola* of all known populations are characterized by a caudal fin that has a pattern consisting of irregular yellow and blue stripes. The caudal fin of *P. livingstonii*, however, is clear and usually has a black upper and lower edge. In addition, *M. lanisticola* feeds on algae which are raked from shells, shell fragments, or small pebbles lying on the sand. Their feeding technique is thus that of a true member of the genus and differs from the picking technique displayed by *P. livingstonii*.

The maximum total length of *M. lanisticola* in most populations is a mere 6 cm and these small individuals have a strong association with empty *Lanistes* shells. They are almost always found in or near such shells. Because their habitat is restricted to areas with such shells and because breeding in several populations takes place in the rocky habitat, several geographical variants have developed along the lake's shores. This variation is most prominent in the fin coloration of both male and female; there is no variation in behavior.

On the west coast all the populations north of Monkey Bay consist of small adults which are almost always found in empty shells at a depth varying between 10 and 30 meters. In some southern populations a maximum size of more than 6 cm prevents adults from entering empty *Lanistes* shells. In the southern half of the southeastern arm of the lake these large adults are often seen foraging over sand. Large *M. lanisticola* are also found in Lake Malombe.

A shell-dwelling mbuna found between Chitimba Bay and Kaporo closely resembles *M. lanisticola* but both males and females have a distinct black submarginal band in the dorsal fin, a feature not found in other known populations of *M. lanisticola*. For the time being I refer to these northern populations as *Metriaclima* sp. 'lanisticola north'.

The population of *M. lanisticola* at Kanchedza Island (south of Monkey Bay) was described as *Pseudotropheus pursus* (now *Metriaclima pursus*) by Stauffer (1991). Some individuals of this population are found in the intermediate habitat where they sometimes clean the fins of other cichlids (Stauffer, 1991). This population is, however, an intermediate between the small shell-dwelling species found in deeper water north of Monkey Bay and the group-forming, larger specimens common south of Crocodile Rock, so in my opinion there is no reason to single it out as a separate species. The change from the small shell-dwelling forms to the large group-forming populations is gradual. Stauffer (1991) mentions that *M. pursus* is not associated with empty *Lanistes* shells, but at Mazinzi Reef (locally known as Mwala wa Kweenie) and Nkhudzi I have seen subadult specimens using such shells as shelter. Hence, because *M. pursus* is similar to *M. lanisticola* in morphology and habitat preference, and because cleaning behavior has also been observed in various other species, I regard *M. pursus* as a junior synonym of *M. lanisticola*

At Mazinzi Reef I have myself observed *M. lanisticola* cleaning the fins of other cichlids. The fungus that often grows around infected wounds—caused by predators, competitors, or parasites such as the common anchor worm—may encourage *M. lanisticola* to clean the fins of any non-mbuna presenting them. The wounded client normally lies on the bottom and extends the problem area, usually the dorsal fin, for closer inspection.

According to Van Duinen (1978), who has bred *M. lanisticola* several times, the incubation period of the eggs inside the female's mouth is no longer than 16 days, i.e. about five days shorter than in any other known endemic cichlid of the lake. This could be an adaptation towards the shell-dwelling habits of this mbuna. Since the juveniles are well protected by the shell there is probably no longer any need to release larger fry after 21 days.

In nature, male *M. lanisticola*—and probably females as well—defend their shells and regard them as territory. Large individuals are sometimes found in the deeper rocky habitats (e.g. at Mbenji Island), suggesting that *M. lanisticola* may have separate foraging and breeding grounds.

Pseudotropheus sp. 'acei', an mbuna known in several distinct geographical variants, bears a close resemblance to *Gephyrochromis moorii* and has a lake-wide distribution. It is often found near (branches of) trees that have been washed into the lake. It feeds from the aufwuchs covering the waterlogged wood. It is also seen over pure sand where there is nothing to provide it with shelter or food, but here it is rare. Both males and females of the population between Nkhata Bay and Bandawe are blue with yellow fins. This is the variant that was first exported some years ago. The individuals seen at Bandawe and at Luwala Reef have a similar coloration. The population between Ngara and Karonga is somewhat similar except that the fins are white instead of yellow and the body darker. The trade name for this population is "White-Tail Acei". The neighboring population at Chitande Island is quite different from the one at Ngara, with both male and female sporting a gray-blue body and a yellowish dorsal. This color pattern resembles that of the population found in Senga Bay, and that of *G. moorii*—but both these "Acei" forms have the bicuspid teeth characteristic of *Pseudotropheus*.

In captivity *P.* sp. 'acei' breeds throughout the year. In the aquarium males excavate pits between rocks and are territorial. In the lake males in breeding coloration are not territorial and do not seem to build a spawning pit. Interestingly, at Ngara thousands (!) of individuals of the "White-Tail Acei" have been seen to form massive schools near a single tree-trunk.

The main feature that separates *Gephyrochromis* species from the other mbuna is the special shape of the teeth. The jaws are set with a dense row of very long thin bicuspid teeth. The row in the upper jaw is bent inward but that in the lower jaw protrudes forward. In addition, the two cusps of each tooth are not equal in size—one is much larger than the other. In older specimens the teeth of the outer rows tend to lose the second cusp and become unicuspid. Protruding teeth in the lower jaw are a characteristic of sand-dwelling cichlids in general, found in all *Lethrinops* and some *Mylochromis* species, and also seen in some cichlids from Lake Tanganyika, e.g. *Xenotilapia*.

Gephyrochromis moorii lives over the bare lake bottom and is rarely seen near rocky outcrops. I have seen it only once, in rather deep water off Msuli Point near Nkhata Bay. *Gephyrochromis lawsi* is also rather rarely encountered though I have seen it more often. It seems to enter shallower water more frequently and is sometimes seen near rocky shores. A good place to find *G. lawsi* is at Ruarwe at a depth of about 20 meters or across the lake at Chiwindi in Mozambique in much shallower water (7-10 meters). Fryer (1957) reports that *G. lawsi* was most commonly seen over pebble/shingle substrates near Chilumba. Both species seem to have a northerly distribution as they have never been encountered or captured in the southern half of the lake.

Protomelas

Although *Protomelas marginatus* is purported to be a common cichlid (Eccles & Trewavas, 1989), I have seen only a few populations at various places around the lake. The species has a lake-wide distribution and can be distinguished from other species of the *kambuzi* group (page 284) by its relatively large mouth and eyes. Two subspecies have been described: *P. marginatus marginatus* and *P. marginatus vuae*. The former is found at the southern end of the lake and the latter at the northern. The two forms may represent the extremes of a single, widely distributed species, but not until specimens from locations between the two have been examined can anything meaningful be said about their relationship. It is worth noting that I have found a population consisting of slender individuals (at Tchinga Reef near Usisya);

1. *Metriaclima lanisticola* ♂ Dwangwa
2. *Metriaclima lanisticola* ♂ Mbenji Island
3. *Metriaclima lanisticola* ♂ Senga Bay
4. *Metriaclima* sp. 'lanisticola north' ♂ Gallireya Reef
5. *Metriaclima lanisticola* ♂ Chembe
6. *Metriaclima lanisticola* ♂ Crocodile Rock
7. *Metriaclima* sp. 'lanisticola north' ♀ Chitimba Bay

1. *Pseudotropheus* sp. 'acei' ♀ Ngara

2. *Pseudotropheus* sp. 'acei' ♂ Chitande Island

3. *Gephyrochromis moorii* ♂ Msuli Point

4. *Gephyrochromis moorii* ♀ Aquarium

5. *Gephyrochromis lawsi* ♀ Chiwindi

6. *Protomelas marginatus* ♀ Chizumulu Island

6. *Pseudotropheus* sp. 'acei' ♂ Aquarium (Ngara)

7. *Pseudotropheus* sp. 'acei' ♂ Dwangwa

8. *Pseudotropheus* sp. 'acei' ♀ Chimwalani Reef

9. *Gephyrochromis lawsi* ♂ Nkhata Bay

10. *Protomelas marginatus* ♂ Chizumulu Island

for the time being this form is regarded as conspecific with *P. marginatus* although it may represent a separate species.

Eccles & Trewavas (1989) report that stomach contents analysis revealed algae and plant debris, suggesting that *P. marginatus* feeds from and on plant leaves. Males defend breeding territories in the shallow intermediate habitat and construct a very shallow spawning dish next to a rock that is smaller than the diameter of the dish. Males on a lek in Mkanila Bay (Chizumulu Island) were stationed two to five meters apart.

Mchenga and *mloto*

The silvery, nondescript utaka which are sometimes found in huge schools over sandy bottoms in shallow water have recently been grouped into a new genus, *Mchenga*, which comprises a series of small, slender cichlid species frequenting shallow habitats—between three and 25 meters deep (Stauffer & Konings, 2006). The name of the genus means "sand" in Chi-Chewa. The low number of gill rakers (10-18), a protrusible mouth that can form a sucking tube, and the lack of spots or stripes on the body distinguish *Mchenga* from all other Malaŵi genera except *Copadichromis*, the genus to which all the *Mchenga* species listed below were previously assigned. Male *Mchenga* have small bicuspid teeth in the outer row of the upper and lower oral jaws while male *Copadichromis* have enlarged unicuspid teeth in the outer row of both jaws.

Male *Mchenga*, at least in the case of those species that have been observed in the lake, build bowers on the bottom in sandy habitats. In extensive leks, with many males holding a territory, some males may build a spawning site on top of large boulders in the vicinity of the lek. But the boulders are used merely as a foundation for the structure, and there is no rock incorporated in the rim of the bower in these species, a feature that distinguishes them from those members of *Copadichromis* that build bowers, i.e. all members of the *C. mbenjii* group (page 228).

Two species, *Mchenga eucinostomus* and *Mchenga inornata*, are known only from the type specimens and their breeding biology is unknown. They were placed in *Mchenga* based on the presence of small bicuspid teeth on the outer jaws of adult males.

M. inornata is known only from two museum specimens with a total length of about 9 cm, which could in fact be juveniles. The collection site is not known and it is therefore unlikely that this species will ever be specifically identified in the field.

The specific name *eucinostomus* has been used for a group of elongate utaka which are found mainly in the shallow water over a sandy substrate. The lectotype of *M. eucinostomus* is a small mature male and was probably collected in the southern part of the lake. Stauffer *et al.* (1993) described three new species allied to *eucinostomus* but failed to relocate the population from which the types of the latter were taken. The most important character they chose to distinguish between their three new species, *Mchenga conophoros*, *Mchenga cyclicos*, and *Mchenga thinos*, was the size and shape of the mound and spawning dish of the bower.

M. thinos is the smallest of the three, but appears to be sufficiently different from the lectotype of *C. eucinostomus* (which is a similar size to adult *C. thinos*) to be regarded as a different species. There is a difference in the number of gill rakers, which is 11 to 13 in *M. thinos* and 17 in the two types of *M. eucinostomus*. *M. thinos* is further characterized by females that have yellow spots in the anal fin. However, females of all *Mchenga* species are nondescript and have a silvery body, and cannot be differentiated in the field. At present I also find it impossible to distinguish between males of *M. cyclicos*, *M. thinos*, and *M. conophoros* on the basis of coloration.

M. thinos was described from the population at Mazinzi Reef, but since it is the smallest of the trio and similar in size to the *eucinostomus*-like species found throughout the lake I have assigned almost all populations of the latter to this species. It thus has a lake-wide distribution and represents the common *Mchenga* that is most often referred to as *M. eucinostomus*.. At some places it has been found sympatric with *M. cyclicos* (e.g. at Masasa Reef). Males defend small spawning sites on the sand and females gather in large schools a few meters above the bottom. Only males of the populations in shallow water around the Nankumba Peninsula have been seen constructing tall spawning cones, a character of *M. conophoros*, and they are therefore assigned to that species.

Territorial males of *M. conophoros* and *M. cyclicos* are found throughout the year but there are seasonal peaks of reproductive activity. They are rather small cichlids with a maximum total length of about 14 cm. Non-breeding individuals never stray far from the breeding arenas and thus do not have to undertake a yearly migration from foraging to breeding grounds.

Breeding males of all three *Mchenga* and those of *Nyassachromis prostoma* (see below) can be very common at certain sites, although *N. prostoma* prefers very shallow water and is rarely seen in large numbers at depths of more than 10 meters. However, the *Mchenga* males can be distinguished from *N. prostoma* by the lack of the large yellow-orange patch on the nape which is prominent in the latter. Moreover territorial males of the *Mchenga* remain closer to their bowers than do those of *N. prostoma*. The bowers of *M. thinos* and *N. prostoma* can be found side by side; those of *M. thinos* are usually taller than those of *N. prostoma* at the same site, but identically shaped bowers have been found side by side as well.

Populations of these *Mchenga* can be very dense, with males building their bowers in large arenas. Heavy competition for spawning sites prevents a male from vacating his bower while courting females. Every morning the territorial landscape is set anew because males at the periphery of the colony leave their bowers at night (Jay Stauffer, pers. comm.). At Cape Maclear and Mdoka these *Mchenga* are seen in the rocky habitat as well, although most males are found over sand. Some males (which probably could not find a place in the colony on the sandy bottom) carry sand high up onto the rocks and build their spawning sites on top of them (!), i.e. kilos of sand are transported up the rocks in order to construct a real sand-castle! Competition among males, however, seemed much greater on the sand than on the rocks, although the latter group of males was apparently closer to the females. An investigation as to whether rock-breeding males are more successful than sand-breeding individuals would be worthwhile.

Another member of the genus, *Mchenga flavimanus*, lacks any markings on the body and is largely unknown to the hobbyist. Subadults of *M. flavimanus*, or a species with a close resemblance to it, have been found in very shallow water in the intermediate habitat at Chitande Island. It has also been seen at Mbowe and Kande Island. *M. flavimanus* (the specific name means "yellow hand") can be distinguished from other nondescript utaka by the yellow anal and pelvic fins. It attains a total length of approximately 12 cm (Iles, 1960).

The name *mloto* has been used in the trade for a wide variety of species, but the true *Copadichromis mloto* has never been exported for the aquarium hobby. The confusion started with the erroneous identification as *mloto* of a species common in the southeastern arm of the lake, which was in fact *C. virginalis* or a very closely related species. Specimens of this *virginalis*-type are also labeled *mloto* in some museum collections. The type of *C. mloto*, however, is a very elongate fish and rather different from the deep-bodied *C. virginalis*; in fact this elongate body shape may indicate that *C. mloto*, and a number of other elongate species currently assigned to *Copadichromis*, belong to a different, as yet undescribed, genus. The high number of gill rakers (21-24) and the tiny unicuspid teeth in the oral jaws preclude it from being a member of *Mchenga*, which is characterized by a relatively low number of gill rakers (10-18) and bicuspid teeth.

I have found *C. mloto* breeding at Otter Point and have seen mouthbrooding females at Luwala and Chimwalani reefs. The male, which is black with a white or yellowish blaze on the head and nape, defends a shallow spawning dish in the sandy part of the intermediate habitat. At Otter Point I have found territorial males at a depth of about 23 meters. Females are found in large schools but mouthbrooding females seem to stay closer to the bottom in small groups.

1. *Mchenga conophoros* Chembe

2. *Copadichromis mloto* ♂ Otter Island

3. *Copadichromis mloto* ♀ Luwala Reef

4. *Mchenga flavimanus* Kande Island

5. *Copadichromis mloto* ♂ Otter Island

6. *Copadichromis* sp. 'mloto goldcrest' ♂ Chitimba Bay

Some years ago a species with a close resemblance to *C. mloto* was collected at Nkanda in Tanzania (DeMason, 1993) and given the trade name "Nyassachromis Goldcrest". Examination of a single male has revealed that this species is very closely related to *C. mloto*, the only difference being the length of the caudal peduncle. Another difference is seen in the type of bower each species constructs. Males of *C. mloto* excavate very shallow saucer-shaped depressions in the intermediate habitat while "Nyassachromis Goldcrest" males build large sand-castle bowers on the open sand floor. For the time being this species is referred to as *Copadichromis* sp. 'mloto goldcrest'; like *C. mloto*, it may belong to a different genus. Males of the population at Makonde, Tanzania, construct their large bowers on the sand at a depth of about 20 meters although some males are found as shallow as seven meters. Females have not been seen near the breeding arenas (October, 1996), but a small school was found at the edge of the rocky habitat at a depth of about seven meters. Other populations of *C.* sp. 'mloto goldcrest' have been found near Chilumba and in Chitimba Bay; males of these populations again defended their bowers at a depth of about 20 meters.

Silvery sand-dwellers

Since the revision of the larger Malawîan haplochromines by Eccles & Trewavas (1989), it has become apparent that the basic color pattern (preferably of juvenile fishes) provides a clue to the correct generic assignment of any particular species. If the color pattern of a particular group goes hand in hand with its other characteristics, such as breeding behavior, then obviously the species with such shared characteristics belong to the same group.

Members of the genus *Nyassachromis* are characterized by a relatively small head, a slender body, and a usually distinct mid-lateral stripe on the body. The basic pigmentation pattern of *Nyassachromis prostoma* and *Nyassachromis boadzulu*—two species that previously were placed in *Copadichromis*—suggests that they do indeed belong to *Nyassachromis* rather than *Copadichromis*, since all utaka in *Copadichromis* have a pattern of spots or lack any pattern (the pure utaka). This view is supported by the shape and position (on the open sand) of their sand-castle bowers. Such bowers are also built by *Mchenga* species but none of the latter have a mid-lateral stripe. *N. prostoma* and *N. boadzulu* clearly do not belong in *Copadichromis* even though their mouth is protrusible (one of the characters of *Copadichromis* as defined by Eccles & Trewavas).

The name *boadzulu* has been frequently but erroneously used for *Protomelas taeniolatus* from Namalenje Island, a very popular species among aquarists. The true *N. boadzulu* is a rare cichlid, small populations of which inhabit sandy regions in the southeastern arm of the lake. Breeding males have been observed at Kanchedza Island where they defended cave-crater bowers in the intermediate habitat. In this respect they differ from most other members of *Nyassachromis*—but not from *N. breviceps*, the type species of the genus—in using rocks in the construction of the spawning site. In captivity males construct spawning cones with a height of about 25 cm on the sand (Peter Baasch, pers. comm.).

N. boadzulu belongs to the utaka group and feeds on plankton in the open water. Its basic pigmentation pattern shows some vertical barring but this is seen mainly in breeding males. Its main characteristic is a horizontal midlateral line which runs from the second vertical bar to the caudal peduncle. A second horizontal (dorsolateral) stripe, which is characteristic of *P. taeniolatus*, is entirely lacking. Fully colored males have a whitish-blue blaze on the head, and this continues as a white marginal band in the dorsal fin.

N. prostoma is often found together with *Mchenga thinos* in shallow water. Non-breeding males and adult females are difficult to distinguish from those of *Nyassachromis breviceps* when only shape and pigmentation pattern are considered. *N. breviceps*, however, lacks the protrusible mouth of *N. prostoma*, which is the larger of the two and may attain a total length of about 16 cm, whereas *N. breviceps* grows to only about 14 cm. Both species breed more or less at the same time (from August to December) but territorial males are easily told apart. Not only the breeding coloration but also the bower construction and preferred depth are different. *N. prostoma* is found in very shallow water and constructs bowers on the sand. The bower of *N. breviceps*, however, is a cave-crater similar to those seen in some *Copadichromis* of the *C. mbenjii* group. The male digs a semicircular crater below or against a small to medium-sized rock. Males lead females from mid-water to the spawning site. Spawning takes place under the partly excavated rock. Apart from *N. boadzulu*, none of the other species currently in *Nyassachromis* utilizes a spawning site of this type. It is possible that the low population density is a factor in the construction of the cave-crater bower as opposed to the more open sand-castle bower. Spawnings in a small breeding group are more likely to be affected by egg predators than are those on large breeding leks. I have found *N. breviceps* only at Nkhomo Reef, at a depth of 22 meters.

Nyassachromis sp. 'interruptus' has a characteristic pigmentation pattern consisting of a horizontal stripe which is faintly visible but not continuous as in most other members of the genus. This stripe consists of two elongate horizontal blotches and a faint spot on the caudal peduncle. This species has been encountered along the northwestern shores (for instance in Ruarwe Bay), and at Chizumulu and Likoma islands. Territorial males construct turret-like bowers on the open sand in rather shallow water. Females and non-territorial males gather in large schools, foraging on plankton in midwater. Maximum total length is about 14 cm.

Nyassachromis sp. 'mphanga' has been found only at Mphanga Rocks in the northern part of the lake, at a depth of about 36 meters. Territorial males build tall turrets that have a slightly slanted spawning dish on top. *N.* sp. 'mphanga' is probably the smallest species of *Nyassachromis* as breeding males have a maximum total length of about 10 cm.

The largest species of the genus, by contrast, is probably *Nyassachromis nigritaeniatus*, males of which build enormous mounds of sand with horizontal spawning platforms on top. Such bowers have been seen at Ntekete on the Malaŵian east coast, but *N. nigritaeniatus* has a wider distribution in the southern part of the lake. Maximum total length is about 22 cm. Mature females are characterized by a prominent horizontal stripe on the flanks.

Another large species, *Nyassachromis serenus*, is found mainly in the northern part of the lake although I have seen it at Mbenji Island as well. Males can attain a total length of about 21 cm. They construct rather shallow bowers (at in least the population at Mbenji Island) in water no deeper than about 10 meters. At Mbenji Island I have seen a few males which had made a bower of sorts against a small rock on the muddy bottom. The substrate was obviously too soft to use for the construction of a bower, but equally I have not seen males at other places around Mbenji building regular sand-turrets. I have not seen territorial males underwater at Likoma Island, but Saulos Mwale (pers. comm.), who caught one, noticed that males there do construct bowers.

Males of both *Nyassachromis purpurans* and *Nyassachromis microcephalus* build sand-turrets on the open sand floor. The bower of *N. microcephalus* is characterized by a slanted spawning dish on top. *N. purpurans* can grow to a length of about 18 cm while the maximum total length of *N. microcephalus* is about 14 cm. The latter species has a lake-wide distribution and is rather common in shallow water along steeply sloping sandy shores. *N. purpurans* seems to be restricted to the northern half of the lake where it occurs over gradually sloping sandy bottoms. A breeding lek seen at Chitande Island contained 20 to 30 males that were several meters apart. Most of their bowers were at a depth of three to six meters. The bowers of *N. purpurans* are similar in shape to those of *N. microcephalus*, but larger (as the species is larger) and not as slanted as is usual in the latter species.

Nyassachromis leuciscus is a small sand-dwelling cichlid which is common in shallow water at depths of seven to 25 meters. Unusually for a *Nyassachromis*, it does not exhibit a stripe on the body when seen alive in the lake, but preserved specimens do display a faint mid-lateral

1. *Nyassachromis prostoma* ♂ Nkhudzi

4. *Nyassachromis prostoma* ♀ Nkhudzi

5. *Nyassachromis boadzulu* ♂ Kanchedza Island

2. *Nyassachromis breviceps* ♂ Nkhomo Reef

6. *Nyassachromis boadzulu* ♀ Crocodile Rock

3. *Nyassachromis boadzulu* ♂ Kanchedza Island

1. *Nyassachromis* sp. 'interruptus' ♀ Tchinga Reef

2. *Nyassachromis microcephalus* ♀ Thumbi West Island

3. *Nyassachromis nigritaeniatus* ♂ Ntekete

4. *Nyassachromis purpurans* ♀ Chitande Island

5. *Nyassachromis* sp. 'mphanga' ♂ Mphanga Rocks

6. *Nyassachromis serenus* ♂ Mbenji Island

7. *Nyassachromis* sp. 'interruptus' ♂ Tchinga Reef

8. *Nyassachromis microcephalus* ♂ Ntekete

9. *Nyassachromis microcephalus* ♂ Chiofu

10. *Nyassachromis purpurans* ♂ Chitande Island

11. *Nyassachromis leuciscus* ♂ Thumbi West Island

stripe. *N. leuciscus* occurs in areas that are not too exposed to wave action and is frequently found among rubble and small stones on the sand. Its maximum length is about 10 cm. It feeds on the layer of silt lying on the sand and is also seen feeding on plankton. Breeding males have beautiful colors. The head and the dorsal part of the body are deep blue. The anal and pelvic fins are black. I have seen breeding males defending sand bowers at a depth of about 15 meters at Domwe Island. Individual males were about two meters apart. I have also seen males at Otter Point that had spawning sites on rocks which were almost entirely covered by sand.

At Otter Point and at Domwe Island, in the southern part of the lake, I have found a species that was initially difficult to assign to a genus. The distinct horizontal stripe on the flank and the protrusible mouth were suggestive of a *Nyassachromis*, but on the other hand, the first males that I saw had built their bowers on top of large boulders even though sufficient open space on the sand appeared available. The latter indicated that a placement in *Protomelas* was an alternative possibility as several species of that genus spawn on top of rocks. However, I later found some males with a more conventional (for a *Nyassachromis*) sand-castle bower on the open sand and hence I believe the species to be a member of that genus. Males of this species, *Nyassachromis* sp. 'otter', carry several kilos of coarse sand to a strategic position on top of a large boulder where they fashion a relatively small sand-castle with a horizontal spawning dish. This is meticulously cleaned of any coarse sand, making it immediately stand out against the wall of coarse sand and gravel. Mouthbrooding females gather in groups (uncommon in *Protomelas*) and station themselves in the open water alongside the boulders (mouthbrooding *Protomelas* normally hide among rocks or plants).

Chimbenje: the sly fox

The sandy areas devoid of plants are the habitat mainly of carnivorous cichlids. Most of the larger haplochromines dine on invertebrates but many piscivores are present too. One of the largest cichlids to feed on invertebrates, which it sifts from the sand, is *Fossorochromis rostratus*. This peculiar fish has a lake-wide distribution and is frequently seen in shallow water. Males of this species are among the most striking cichlids in the lake in terms of color contrast. A group of these large bottom feeders, which may consist of up to 50 individuals, occupies a large feeding territory, with usually only a single male exhibiting breeding coloration. His colors and sexual activity intensify in the early morning. Later in the day he mainly feeds. When plankton is abundant these large cichlids (maximum length about 35 cm) dine on these tiny organisms, but the food extracted from the sand consists mainly of chironomid (midge) larvae.

When more than one ripe male is present then they usually construct large craters in the sand, normally at depths of just one or two meters! A ripe male courts females and leads them back to his spawning site, and never behaves aggressively towards other species. The male lacks egg-spots in the anal fin, which is very rare for a haplochromine cichlid with a sand bower. The eggs are fertilized inside the female's mouth. Mouthbrooding females stay with the group, but when the fry are released they are guarded for several weeks at a protected site in the intermediate habitat. Juvenile *F. rostratus* congregate into schools and forage at the very shallow (30 cm deep) edge of the sandy shore or in the rocky habitat. Subadult specimens are occasionally seen in the rocky habitat as well.

Africans call this fish *chimbenje*, and at Nkhata Bay it is also called *chigumbuli*, with both names meaning "a sly person". The same words are used in daily conversation. *F. rostratus* has been afforded this distinction because it is able to avoid the seine nets of the local fishermen by burying itself in the sand. Juveniles use this tactic in order to escape predators and the behavior is retained in adults when threatened with capture. Similar dives into the sand can be observed when we try to net it out of a tank; it completely disappears into the sand (or at least tries to).

The blue followers

Along the coast from Nkhata Bay to Chilumba *Fossorochromis rostratus* has been seen in association with *Cyrtocara moorii* and *Protomelas annectens* (Jackson 1961). These two species profit from the extensive digging performed by *F. rostratus*, but more so from that of species of *Taeniolethrinops*. These foot-long cichlids filter large amounts of sand through their gills and a lot of detritus is stirred up during the process. This attracts a number of cichlids, among them *C. moorii* and *P. annectens*, which pick palatable items from the freshly exposed sand. *C. moorii*, probably an old species, is the best adapted of the group and feeds exclusively in this manner. *P. annectens* utilizes other resources as well and is more commonly an inhabitant of the deeper sandy areas. *C. moorii* has a lake-wide distribution and has several native names — one of them, *gunda mwala* (Ambali *et al.*, 2001), means "collided with rock"! Its maximum size can be more than 20 cm, but such large specimens are rare and caught mainly in Lake Malombe where it is present as well.

One or more individuals of *C. moorii* (or any of the other "blue follower" species) closely follow a large host (usually *Taeniolethrinops praeorbitalis*). The host does not seem to be bothered by these "freeloaders", which swim behind it like dogs at heel. Kocher and McKaye (1983) have studied this unusual behavior in *C. moorii* and *P. annectens* in the south of the lake and found that *C. moorii* defends the host as its mobile feeding territory. A *C. moorii* that had "latched on" to a host would chase conspecifics as well as *P. annectens* away from the host. When more than one individual followed a large host there was a clear difference in their size. Since these followers regard the host as their territory they assume a dominant, territorial coloration. *C. moorii*, when not following a host or when subordinate, exhibits a color pattern of three dark blotches on a light gray-blue background, but when it gains a dominant position behind a host it turns dark royal blue. The same is true of *P. annectens*. A host is not followed forever but changes occur infrequently. *C. moorii* is always dominant over *P. annectens* and will not allow the latter near its host. The reverse has never been observed.

A cichlid that I once collected from a beach seine resembled *Placidochromis electra* (see below) in appearance but had teeth on the outside of the jaws, similar to *C. moorii*. I have never observed this species underwater and, lacking any behavioral information, I refer to it as *Cyrtocara* sp. 'kaporo' since I collected it near Kaporo in the north of the lake.

Placidochromis electra, which occurs in several different geographical populations, has been collected for export mainly at Likoma Island. The other known populations are found along the Mozambique shore from Chiwindi to Lumbaulo, at Mala Point, and from Lumessi to the Malaŵian border and further south to Ntekete in Malaŵi. The population at Chiwindi is almost identical to that found around Likoma; the other populations differ slightly in the black markings on the cheeks and flanks. Males of *P. electra*, originally imported as the "Deep Water Hap" or "Haplochromis Jahni", defend territories between rocks in the intermediate habitat (Ribbink *et al.*, 1983b). Males in breeding coloration, however, are frequently seen over the open sand. Like the previous two species *P. electra* is attracted to stirred-up debris, and like them sometimes follows *Taeniolethrinops praeorbitalis*. Its niche is not restricted to deep water, as was formerly assumed, but it is commonly encountered at levels deeper than seven meters. *P. electra* does not dig in the sand; instead food is picked from its surface. It is frequently found among schools of *Lethrinops* and seems to profit from the continuous digging activities of these grubbers. It is an opportunistic feeder that rushes from one "dust-cloud" to the next.

From Ikombe (in the far north of Tanzania) to the Ruhuhu River *Placidochromis* sp. 'electra blackfin' occupies the same niche as *P. electra* at other localities. Females and non-territorial males are characterized by black anal and pelvic fins. At Hongi and Lundo Islands, and along the coast south to Mbamba Bay, a similar species is found, namely *Placidochromis* sp. 'electra blue'. This form may be just another geographical variant of *P. electra*, but until intermediate

1. *Nyassachromis* sp. 'otter' ♂ Otter Island
2. *Fossorochromis rostratus* ♀ Nkhata Bay
3. *Fossorochromis rostratus* ♂ Otter Point

4. *Nyassachromis* sp. 'otter' ♂ Otter Island 
5. *Nyassachromis* sp. 'otter' ♀ Otter Point
6. *Fossorochromis rostratus* ♂ Otter Point

1. *Cyrtocara moorii* ♀ Chembe

2. *Cyrtocara* sp. 'kaporo' ♂ Kaporo

3. *Protomelas annectens* ♀ Chizumulu Island

4. *Protomelas annectens* ♂ Chizumulu Island

5. *Placidochromis electra* ♀ Chiofu

6. *Placidochromis electra* ♂ Londo

7. *Cyrtocara moorii* ♂ Chembe

8. *Protomelas annectens* ♂ Chizumulu Island

9. *Protomelas annectens* ♂ Malopa

10. *Placidochromis electra* ♂ Liwani

populations are discovered it is best to regard these two forms as different species. *P.* sp. 'electra blue' completely lacks the broad, black lachrymal stripe that sometimes covers the entire cheek in *P. electra*.

At various places around the lake further *electra*-like cichlids occur over sandy substrates. None of these species has ever been seen following large sand-grubbing cichlids but all of them are attracted to stirred-up sediment. One of them, *Placidochromis* sp. 'electra mozambique', has been found at Lumessi and in Chiofu Bay, at a depth of about 25 meters. It feeds by dipping its snout into the soft substrate and extracting invertebrates from the material thus collected. Mouthbrooding females occur in the same areas as those where males in breeding coloration and non-brooding females forage. Males are not territorial but courting can often be witnessed.

At Boadzulu Island I have found another blue *electra*-type cichlid which behaves like an opportunistic feeder. It wanders through the habitat and has also been seen near rocks. None of the individuals observed stayed at any particular site longer than a minute. Male *Placidochromis* sp. 'electra boadzulu' are completely blue while females are gray-yellow and display up to 12 very narrow bars. It is probably conspecific with Turner's (1996) *Placidochromis* 'longimanus Chirombo', although that species was collected at depths ranging between 20 and 50 meters while *P.* sp. 'electra boadzulu' has rarely been found deeper than 10 meters.

In contrast to the previous two species, which are easily differentiated, *Placidochromis* sp. 'electra type' may in fact be a group of look-alikes. It occurs at various places in the southern half of the lake: Mala Point, Mozambique, and Luwala and Nkhomo Reef in Malaŵi. It is often seen near sand-grubbing *Taeniolethrinops* but has never been seen following them around. It has a very light blue coloration, and in this species the sexes seem to be similar in color. *Placidochromis* 'longimanus Maleri' (Turner, 1996) may be conspecific with (one of the forms of) *P.* sp. 'electra type'.

Placidochromis phenochilus, which seems to be closely related to *P. electra*, occurs in the northern part of the lake, where I have found it near Mdoka, Chesese, and Chirwa Island. It is characterized by white lips and a blue body, and at Mdoka even juvenile *P. phenochilus*, 6 cm in length, have the typical dark blue coloration of adults.

The form from Tanzania, previously included in *P. phenochilus*, is now regarded as a distinct species and referred to as *Placidochromis* sp. 'phenochilus tanzania'. It occurs along the eastern coast between Makonde and Lupingu, and also at Kasinda, on the opposite shore in Malaŵi. Females and juveniles of *P.* sp. 'phenochilus tanzania' exhibit a pattern of broad black bars. Adult males are blue with a spangling of light blue and white spots and are among the most attractive cichlids from the lake. In the aquarium older females can also assume an all-blue color.

The inclusion of these two taxa in *Placidochromis* is based on their close resemblance to *P. electra*, their opportunistic feeding behavior, and the vertical barring sometimes displayed by territorial males.

Carsten Gissel (pers. comm.) discovered that along the Malaŵi east coast between Gome and Ntekete there is another *phenochilus*-like species, which I term *Placidochromis* sp. 'phenochilus gissel', which shares the habitat with *P. electra*. It is very similar to the latter but can be distinguished by the fact that its fins do not have a yellow margin as in *P. electra*. This is readily apparent in juvenile and female individuals but some male *P. electra* are virtually identical to those of *P.* sp. 'phenochilus gissel'.

A dark-colored sand-dwelling haplochromine, *Otopharynx selenurus*, is infrequently exported from Kambiri Point as "Haplochromis Nussae", but is found at many other locations around the lake. It is a very rare cichlid which seems to be seen more often in the southern half of the lake. It feeds by filtering crustaceans from the sand. Males and females are barely distinguishable and their colors are not unlike those of *C. moorii*. This species has been bred in captivity (Peter Baasch, pers. comm.) but details of the spawning sequence are not available. Juveniles exhibit the genus-typical blotch pattern until they reach a length of approximately 7 cm.

Interestingly these "follower" species have a very conspicuous coloration whereas most other sand-dwelling cichlids are silvery or beige. In particular *P. phenochilus, O. selenurus,* and to a somewhat lesser extent *C. moorii,* always show a distinct blue coloration. These three species seem to be mostly dependent on a large, sand-sifting host, while the *electra* types and *Protomelas annectens* are also found foraging on their own. It is possible that the conspicuous colors of the former group may warn off other followers from trying to join their host. In sandy regions cichlids commonly occur in groups or schools, often consisting of mixed species, and it would thus be normal for an individual to try to join such a group. The amount of food exposed by the "plowing" activities of a large digger may not be sufficient for more than one adult follower, and if the latter is highly dependent on the host, it may signal its "ownership" to other species by taking on territorial coloration. In particular individuals of the same species are wary of approaching an "occupied" host.

The differences seen not only in their basic melanin patterns but also in their breeding behavior point to different ancestral origins for these genera of sand-dwelling cichlids. Breeding in *C. moorii* is primitive compared to many other Malaŵian cichlids. A male in blue breeding dress courts a female and spawning occurs, wherever they happen to be. The eggs are normally fertilized outside the female's mouth (Stein 1976; Menger 1986), but sometimes inside (DeLanghe 1982). Juveniles spend the first year of their lives in the very shallow water at the edge of the lake and feed primarily on plankton. *Protomelas annectens* is also primitive in that the eggs are fertilized outside the female's mouth, but in contrast to the previous species it digs a spawning pit (at least in captivity) and defends it aggressively (Drummond, 1976). *Placidochromis electra* has a more advanced spawning routine than that of *Protomelas annectens,* i.e. the eggs are fertilized inside the female's mouth.

Other *Placidochromis*

Much less is known about the following *Placidochromis* because only a handful of individuals have been seen.

Placidochromis longimanus is endemic to the southern part of the lake and, according to Eccles & Trewavas (1989), found mainly among unrooted plants (*Ceratophyllum*) at a depth of about 10 meters. I found a species that is very probably conspecific with *P. longimanus* at Thumbi East Island at a depth of about 20 meters, but it was not seen in shallow water among aquatic plants. In addition, Turner (1996) views the information in Eccles & Trewavas with some caution. The species at Thumbi East Island did not behave like *P. electra,* i.e. it was not attracted to stirred-up debris or and did not follow large sand-grubbing cichlids. Males, which are a slightly bluish color, defended a muddy area between a few large boulders and courted females (which are silver). I have not observed them feeding and they may have gathered near the rocks for breeding purposes. One of the main characters of *P. longimanus* is the very long pectoral fin that reaches to almost halfway along the anal-fin base.

Placidochromis sp. 'longimanus mumbo' occurs at Mumbo Island, where it is found in a vegetated area. It belongs to a group of similar-looking species that are closely related to *P. longimanus.* Turner (1996) mentions the existence of several of this group, and some of the species may in reality be geographical variants of others. I have photographed two members of this group, but in both cases I saw only a single male that disappeared as soon as I took its picture. *Placidochromis* sp. 'longimanus thumbi' somewhat resembles Turner's *P.* 'longimanus Maleri' but lacks the yellow margin to the dorsal. According to Turner *Placidochromis* sp. 'longimanus namiasi' occurs at Namiasi Bay and south of Boadzulu Island. I have photographed a male at a depth of about 30 meters at Boadzulu Island.

Diagonal lines

Members of the genus *Mylochromis* are char-

1. *Placidochromis* sp. 'electra blackfin' ♂ Magunga

2. *Placidochromis* sp. 'electra blue' ♂ Hongi Island

3. *Placidochromis* sp. 'electra boadzulu' ♂ Boadzulu Island

4. *Placidochromis* sp. 'electra mozambique' ♂ Chiofu

5. *Placidochromis* sp. 'electra blackfin' ♀ Makonde

6. *Placidochromis* sp. 'electra type' ♂ Nkhomo Reef

7. *Placidochromis* sp. 'electra boadzulu' ♀ Boadzulu Island

8. *Otopharynx selenurus* ♂ Aquarium

9. *Placidochromis* sp. 'electra mozambique' ♀ Lumessi

10. *Placidochromis* sp. 'longimanus namiasi' ♂ Boadzulu Island

1. *Placidochromis phenochilus* ♂ Mdoka

2. *Placidochromis* sp. 'phenochilus tanzania' ♀ Makonde

3. *Placidochromis* sp. 'phenochilus gissel' ♀ Border

4. *Placidochromis* sp. 'longimanus thumbi' ♂ Thumbi West

5. *Placidochromis* sp. 'longimanus mumbo' ♂ Mumbo Island

6. *Placidochromis longimanus* ♀ Thumbi East Island

7. *Placidochromis* sp. 'phenochilus tanzania' ♂ Makonde

8. *Placidochromis* sp. 'phenochilus gissel' ♂ Border

9. *Placidochromis longimanus* ♂ Thumbi East Island

acterized by a diagonal stripe on the flanks which in some species consists of a row of spots. Most *Mylochromis* species occur in the sandy habitat.

Mylochromis melanotaenia has been found in the south and along the eastern shores, and also at Makonde in the northern section of the lake. It continually digs and filters the sand for anything palatable; it is characterized by stout teeth on the pharyngeals and thick stout lips, which suggests that it may suck snails out of their shells. It is generally found on muddy bottoms near river outlets at depths varying between 15 and 40 meters. Breeding males of *M. melanotaenia* are mainly steel blue, with a yellowish tail, and they appear not to be territorial.

Mylochromis anaphyrmus, which superficially resembles *Mylochromis sphaerodon* (see below), is a snail-crusher endemic to the southern and western parts of the lake. It is frequently seen at Cape Maclear, foraging on the sandy bottom. It is more robust and seems to be more restricted to deeper regions of the shoreline than *M. sphaerodon*, females of which are characterized by orange-colored anal and pelvic fins while those of *M. anaphyrmus* have colorless fins except for the tail, which is yellowish. Breeding males of this species are completely blue and the diagonal stripe may disappear completely. There are prominent dark vertical bars on the flanks of territorial males, which defend sand-castle bowers on the open sand floor and attract females to these structures with a quivering display.

A species with a similar morphology but a larger eye, and found at depths between 25 and 45 meters, was collected by Turner (1996) near the Maleri islands and in Domira Bay. He named this species *Mylochromis* sp. 'deep' and recorded maximum total length as 18 cm.

M. sphaerodon resembles *M. anaphyrmus* and *M. mola* (page 292) and is encountered only in the shallow waters of the southern part of the lake. It has a much smaller mouth than *M. anaphyrmus* and a narrower, more solid diagonal stripe than that of *M. mola*, which consists of a few large blotches. *M. sphaerodon* is again a snail eater, with these and other invertebrates being crushed using the powerful teeth on the pharyngeal jaws.

A species found at Nkhomo Reef resembles *M. sphaerodon* in having a solid, narrow, diagonal stripe and a yellow anal fin, but the snout is shorter and the mouth larger. I refer to this attractive sand-dweller as *Mylochromis* sp. 'sphaerodon nkhomo'. No stomach contents were examined so at present it is unknown what type of food it searches for in the sand bottom.

Another species with a narrow diagonal stripe, and which again resembles *M. sphaerodon*, has been described as *Mylochromis chekopae* by Turner & Howarth (2002), and occurs in the southern part of the lake. Turner (1996) found that this species, which he then termed *Mylochromis* 'chekopae', feeds on planktonic invertebrates and algae, and that it apparently feeds from the water column as no sand grains were found in stomach inventories. The few individuals I have found at Chimwalani Reef were never seen to scoop up sand but were foraging close to the bottom. They sometimes picked something from the surface of the sand. Breeding males have not yet been observed in the lake but a male in breeding colors was obtained from a fisherman at Maleri Island.

Mylochromis guentheri is another sand-dwelling cichlid with a diagonal line. It is characterized by the fact that the lower jaw is shorter than the upper. The species appears to have a lake-wide distribution (Eccles & Trewavas, 1989) but is nowhere common. A breeding colony was observed in January, during the rainy season, at Chitande Island at a depth of about eight meters. Males had built bowers using a rock as part of the construction and were between five and 10 meters apart. Mouthbrooding females were solitary and often rested on the sand of the intermediate habitat. The fishes I observed did not feed; they had probably congregated in the intermediate habitat to breed. The small teeth on the pharyngeal jaws and the procumbent (forward-pointing) teeth in the lower oral jaw suggest that the species skims the surface of the sand, possibly collecting detritus.

Mylochromis sp. 'liemi small-mouth' has been found only once, at Luwala Reef, where it was found together with *Caprichromis liemi* (page

165). Little is known about it other than that it picks invertebrates from the surface of the sand.

Mylochromis ericotaenia is found in the shallow sandy habitat all around the lake. It is rare in most places, but common at Hai Reef in Tanzania and at Chiwindi in Mozambique. Non-breeding individuals are characterized by a pigmentation pattern consisting of four to eight broad vertical bars, some or all of which are accentuated as dark blotches in a diagonal series. Rarely—and then only in juveniles—the spots may form an almost solid line. The vertical bars are so prominent (but not black) that when the first specimens were exported for the aquarium trade they were classified as members of the genus *Placidochromis* (Marc Danhieux, pers. comm.). Large males (maximum total length is about 20 cm) acquire a slight nuchal hump and a somewhat longer snout. Breeding males are blue but territorial males have not been seen (yet?).

The species known to aquarists as "Haplochromis Yellow-Black Line" is regularly exported and is commonly seen around Namalenje Island and Luwala Reef. It has a lake-wide distribution but its occurrence is irregular. Its bright yellow color is unusual for a sand-dwelling cichlid and renders it conspicuous among the other fishes of this habitat. One population of these cichlids, at Luwala Reef (where a breeding group was seen in both December 1989 and October 1998), has been found to include individuals with differences in the structure of the lower jaw. I have found that some aquarium individuals, usually males, of the "Yellow Black Line" have a very flat lower jaw while others exhibit a more "normal" profile. Old specimens that have been raised in the aquarium have a flat lower jaw, though not to the same degree as is seen in wild-caught individuals.

Historically, these two forms have been regarded as distinct species by some authors. The individuals with a flattening of the lower jaw were originally assigned to *Haplochromis melanonotus* by Regan (1922), and, because of the very peculiar shape of this jaw, Eccles & Trewavas (1989) erected a new genus, *Platygnathochromis*, to accommodate this species. The individuals with a normal-shaped lower jaw were described as *Haplochromis semipalatus* by Trewavas (1935), and this species was later included in *Mylochromis*.

I regard *Mylochromis semipalatus* as a junior synonym of *Platygnathochromis melanonotus* on the basis that individuals with differences in the lower jaw structure have been found in a single breeding community (pers. obs.). The only difference between the two is the structure of the lower jaw. *M semipalatus* has the same yellow coloration and the same morphological characteristics as *P. melanonotus.*

The flattening of the lower jaw may be a phenotypic adaptation to the type of habitat in which the fish lives or to the type of food it eats. Swollen lips, found in some other species, are generally recognized as phenotypic adaptations to feeding from rocky substrates. The same species usually do not develop such swollen lips in captivity and such lips are likewise not found in individuals caught over sandy substrates. The extreme flattening of the lower jaw in the "Yellow Black Line" may be an adaptation to the way this species feeds. I have observed several times that it scoops its prey, probably small fishes or similarly-sized invertebrates, from the sand. Small specimens have been seen cleaning the fins of other cichlids of fungus and parasites! The "Yellow Black Line", which has a lower pharyngeal jaw set with fine teeth, has probably not developed a technique for sifting sand like many other species—sand-filtering species normally have thickened teeth on the lower pharyngeal jaw. Moreover, the behavior of this cichlid in its natural habitat seems to be that of a piscivore rather than a sand-sifting predator. A flattened lower jaw neatly separates the intended prey from the substrate and thus avoids the intake of sand. However, there may be individuals which prefer to stalk their prey in rockier or perhaps muddy biotopes. If we accept the hypothesis presented above, these would not need to develop a flat lower jaw. I am therefore of the opinion that *Platygnathochromis melanonotus* is better accommodated in the genus *Mylochromis* and that there is no need to retain a separate genus for it.

With regard to the feeding behavior of *Mylochromis melanonotus,* I have observed that

1. *Mylochromis melanotaenia* ♂ Lumessi

5. *Mylochromis melanotaenia* ♀ Gome

6. *Mylochromis anaphyrmus* ♀ Thumbi East Island

2. *Mylochromis anaphyrmus* ♂ Thumbi East Island

7. *Mylochromis* sp. 'deep' ♂ Maleri Island

8. *Mylochromis sphaerodon* ♂ Senga Bay

3. *Mylochromis sphaerodon* ♂ Senga Bay

9. *Mylochromis chekopae* ♀ Chimwalani Reef

4. *Mylochromis* sp. 'sphaerodon nkhomo' Nkhomo Reef

10. *Mylochromis chekopae* ♂ Nakantenga Island

1. *Mylochromis ericotaenia* ♀ Ntekete
2. *Mylochromis* sp. 'liemi small-mouth' Luwala Reef
3. *Mylochromis guentheri* ♀ Chitande Island
4. *Mylochromis melanonotus* ♂ Luwala Reef
5. *Mylochromis melanonotus* Chiofu
6. *Mylochromis ericotaenia* ♂ Magunga
7. *Mylochromis guentheri* ♂ Chitande Island
8. *Mylochromis melanonotus* ♀ Londo

occasionally this species is attracted to large black catfishes (or to myself, wearing a black diving suit!). I once observed several individuals attacking a breeding pair of the catfish *Bagrus meridionalis* (*kampango*) and trying to snatch fry out of the nest.

Breeding male *M. melanonotus* are completely blue and lack the diagonal stripe. Eight to nine vertical bars are present on the flanks of territorial males, which defend spawning sites between rocks in the intermediate habitat or may defend craters in the sand. The eggs are fertilized inside the female's mouth. On one occasion I witnessed the moment a female released her youngsters in front of a *kampango* nest, i.e. like many utaka species she was apparently relying on the presence of the large catfish to protect her young from predators.

An extremely elongate *Mylochromis* with a solid diagonal stripe occurs over sandy bottoms in the southern part of the lake. This species, described as *Mylochromis ensatus* by Turner & Howarth (2002), feeds on invertebrates that it finds on the sand. It never scoops up sand but quickly screens the bottom for anything edible and moves rather quickly through the habitat. I have seen this species at a depth of about 10-15 meters at Chembe and at a depth of about 20 meters at Masasa Reef, south of Monkey Bay. Breeding individuals have not been seen underwater but the photo of a freshly-caught individual in Turner (1996) indicates that *M. ensatus* would be a popular aquarium fish—but unfortunately they are rather rare.

The elongate-blotch group

The members of this group, tentatively assigned to *Otopharynx*, have three elongate spots that are arranged in a more or less diagonal line, a feature that led me previously to refer them to *Mylochromis*.

Otopharynx sp. 'silver torpedo', a very elongate cichlid found in shallow muddy habitats, was previously thought to be a member of *Mylochromis* (Konings, 1995b), but underwater observation of a small number of individuals at Liuli and in Senga Bay has revealed that it has three obscure blotches on the flanks, not unlike those found in *O. argyrosoma*. The relatively small mouth suggests that its food is also small. Its habitat, the muddy (extreme) shallows at Kambiri Point on the southwestern shore of the lake, teems with tiny sand-dwelling cichlids, which may well be the food of this cylindrical predator. Its elongate shape probably allows it to penetrate water just a few centimeters deep: the area with the highest density of juvenile cichlids. Breeding males of *O.* sp. 'silver torpedo' are yellow-blue with a metallic blue head and have egg-spots on the anal fin. This species, which has a maximum total length of about 18 cm, may, like other sand/mud-dwelling species with egg-spots, construct a bower, but no such edifice has as yet been found. Snoeks & Hanssens (2004) record this species as *O.* sp. 'productus sharp snout'.

Another torpedo-shaped species of *Otopharynx* with elongate blotches in a diagonal line, *Otopharynx* sp. 'torpedo blue', has been found over sand at various places around the lake, i.e., Ntekete, Chiloelo, Mdoka, and Nkhudzi. It has also been exported, for the aquarium hobby, from Tanzania, and Turner (1996) lists this species from the southeastern arm of the lake, where the blotch pattern is much less obvious in live individuals, as *O.* 'productus'. This species is much smaller than *O.* sp. 'silver torpedo', with a maximum total length of approximately 12 cm. Males in breeding coloration are occasionally seen but are apparently never territorial. Mouthbrooding females occur singly and move about over the open sand.

Otopharynx argyrosoma bears some similarity to *Nyassachromis leuciscus* (page 319), but occurs at somewhat shallower levels than the latter, grows to a larger size (maximum about 15 cm), and has a more elongate body. Non-breeding individuals are silvery and have a rather high dorsal fin which has a faint mother-of-pearl coloration. When the dorsal is erected, the clear pearly sheen may make the fish more visible in murky water and thus function as a signal to keep the school together. In the breeding season the spots in the anal fin become obscured and only a bright orange marginal band is visible, while breeding males of *N. leuciscus* have distinct egg-spots in the anal fin. Like *N. leuciscus* this species has a lake-wide distribution and is frequently caught in beach seine nets. It has been assigned to *Otopharynx* because it sometimes exhibits three spots but the spots are so faint and irregular that it is unlikely to be closely related to *O. auromarginatus*, the type species of *Otopharynx*. *O. argyrosoma* feeds predominantly on benthic crustaceans, which are collected from the sand. Territorial males construct small sand-castles on the open sand. *O. argyrosoma* has been exported as "Haplochromis Longimanus" and "Haplochromis Eucinostomus" and is referred to as *O.* sp. 'argyrosoma red' by Turner (1996).

The fourth species of the elongate-blotch group of *Otopharynx*, *Otopharynx decorus*, has been found at various places around the lake (e.g. at Mdoka and Masinje) and may have a lake-wide distribution. This species was originally (Konings, 1995b) referred to as *Mylochromis* sp. 'double spot', but Turner (1996) compared it with the types of *O. decorus* and came to the conclusion that they are conspecific. The species I formerly called *O. decorus* turns out to be undescribed and is now referred to as *O.* sp. 'decorus jumbo' (see below).

Otopharynx decorus is a rather small, sand-dwelling cichlid, whose maximum size is known to be less than 14 cm (total length). It is characterized by a diagonal row of three double spots. In some specimens the spots are so large that they form a broad, almost solid, black band. This species prefers the open sandy regions and is usually found at depths between five and 30 meters. Most individuals forage on their own; rarely two or three individuals are seen together. A rather dense population, whose members, however, have never been seen to forage in groups or schools, inhabits the coast near Ntekete. At the other locations where I have seen *O. decorus* only single individuals were found. The individuals of the east coast population have a yellow coloration on the body and especially on the fins, whereas specimens from other locations are more silvery and have colorless fins.

The mouth of *O. decorus* is very small and is utilized to pick small invertebrates from the sand, which is scrutinized for anything palatable. The characteristic posture of this cichlid is poised over the sand, visually screening the area in front of the head with its large movable eyes. The fish swims from one place to the next, each time halting and scrutinizing the sand. In this respect *O. decorus* resembles *O.* sp. 'decorus jumbo', which, however, usually forages in small groups.

The specialized feeding behavior of *O. decorus* may also be used for cleaning parasites and fungus from the bodies and fins of afflicted fishes. I once observed a female *Nyassachromis prostoma* (see page 318), with visible fungus on the dorsal fin, apparently present the affected fin for "treatment" by lying down on the sand in front of a foraging *O. decorus*. At the same moment a *Mylochromis labidodon* disturbed the scene, so I was unable to see whether the *decorus* actually cleaned the *prostoma*'s fin or not. It is, however, quite possible that such behavior does occur. The specific color pattern of *O. decorus* is unique among the haplochromines of the lake and may function as a signal to other species that it is a cleaner.

Males of *O. decorus* gather in breeding colonies and build sand-castle bowers three to five meters apart. These bowers have a base diameter of about 60 cm and are about 10 cm high. The characteristic blotches are obscured completely by the male's breeding coloration.

Otopharynx sp. 'decorus jumbo' is a medium-sized cichlid which is found primarily over the open sandy bottoms of the lake. Its distribution probably encompasses the southern part of the lake but I have seen it only in Senga Bay and at Dwangwa. The maximum size of *O.* sp. 'decorus jumbo' is about 18 cm (total length); females are only slightly smaller than males. It lives in small groups, usually numbering no more than six. Solitary individuals are frequently observed as well. Territorial males have not been seen.

The feeding behavior of *O.* sp. 'decorus jumbo' is rather characteristic of an insectivorous cichlid. It carefully screens the sand with its large eyes, biting into the substrate only after it has located something interesting. Its food consists mainly of invertebrates hidden in the

1. *Mylochromis ensatus* ♀ Masasa Reef

2. *Mylochromis ensatus* ♂ Monkey Bay

5. *Otopharynx* sp. 'silver torpedo' ♂ Senga Bay

3. *Otopharynx* sp. 'silver torpedo' ♂ Aquarium

6. *Otopharynx* sp. 'silver torpedo' ♀ Aquarium

7. *Otopharynx* sp. 'torpedo blue' ♀ Ntekete

4. *Otopharynx* sp. 'torpedo blue' ♂ Ntekete

8. *Otopharynx* sp. 'torpedo blue' ♀ Nkhudzi

1. *Otopharynx decorus* ♂ Mbuyu

2. *Otopharynx decorus* ♀ Mbuyu

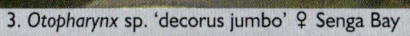
3. *Otopharynx* sp. 'decorus jumbo' ♀ Senga Bay

4. *Otopharynx* sp. 'argyrosoma deep' ♂ Monkey Bay

5. *Otopharynx argyrosoma* ♀ Chidunga Rocks

6. *Otopharynx* sp. 'decorus featherfin' ♂ Kande Island

7. *Otopharynx* sp. 'decorus jumbo' ♂ Senga Bay

8. *Otopharynx argyrosoma* ♂ Harbour Island

sand. The teeth on the lower pharyngeal bone are somewhat enlarged in the center, a common feature in cichlids which feed on crustaceans and insects. The feeding behavior closely resembles that of *O. decorus*, with which it is found sympatrical.

The basic melanin pattern consists of three rather large blotches on the flank. These blotches are not always distinct. The species is easily recognized among the sand-dwelling cichlids of the lake by the combination of its small mouth and overall size. Identification of aquarium or preserved specimens is simplified by the fact that *O.* sp. 'decorus jumbo' has 13 or 14 soft rays in the dorsal fin (an unusually high number) whereas most other haplochromines, except *O. decorus*, have fewer than 12. Snoeks & Hanssens (2004) refer to this species as *O.* sp. 'productus' (not to be confused (!) with Turner's (1996) usage of this name for the species here termed *O.* sp. 'torpedo blue').

Turner (1996) reports on a deep-bodied species which he named *O.* sp. 'argyrosoma deep' and which, with a maximum total length of about 16 cm, is larger than *O. argyrosoma*. He further reports that the species is common at a depth of 30-50 meters in the southeastern arm of the lake between Monkey Bay and Boadzulu Island.

Cichlids with spots

The genus *Otopharynx* is characterized by the three spots found on the flanks of all its members. Many of the species in the genus *Copadichromis* likewise have three spots on the body but are distinguished by very protrusible jaws and their feeding behavior, i.e. taking plankton from the water column. *Otopharynx* are normally found close to the substrate and lack the protrusible jaws. In many species the three spots are large, but in none do they contact the dorsal fin (as in *Trematocranus* and *Hemitilapia*). The best way to determine whether or not a species belongs to *Otopharynx* is to examine the color pattern of very young juveniles. If they have distinct, round to slightly elongate, blotches they can be regarded as members of this genus. In cases where juvenile patterns are unknown we can only assume a particular generic assignment.

Otopharynx auromarginatus is a large cichlid which can attain a total length of 25 cm. Sometimes schools of this species can be seen feeding on the sediment lying on the sand. It has a lake-wide distribution, but most specimens have been collected in the southern part of the lake. Breeding males are completely blue and have bright yellow edges to the anal and dorsal fins; these are the reason for its scientific name—*auromarginatus* means gold-edged. Males are territorial when breeding and construct large—approximately a meter in diameter—spawning pits. If there are rocks in the vicinity these are integrated into the structure, which is shallow and consists merely of a rim raised about 10 cm above the sand floor (see photo 9, page 338). I have seen such bowers at depths varying between 10 and 25 meters. Although several breeding males can be found in the same area they probably do not breed in leks as the spawning sites are spaced at least eight to ten meters apart.

A similar species occurs on the eastern side of the lake. At Chizumulu Island this species, *Otopharynx* sp. 'auromarginatus jakuta', occurs in the sandy habitat, although males need a small rock next to which to construct a spawning site and are therefore regularly found in the intermediate habitat. A form with identical breeding behavior has been found at Ntekete and Gome on the Malaŵi east coast and is regarded as conspecific. The spawning sites in this population are similar to those found at Chizumulu and consist of a 30-40 cm high sand-castle which is piled alongside a small rock. The sand-castle is slanted at an angle of 30-40° to the horizontal. The actual spawning dish is close to the rock.

The word *jakuta* means replete in Chi-Cheŵa and this is what the fish is called by natives. Females and non-breeding males often have very full stomachs, filled with debris and plankton collected just above the sand. The pigmentation pattern of the *jakuta* differs from that typical of *O. auromarginatus*, consisting of a large elongate blotch (which seems almost to be composed of two parallel, contiguous, horizontal stripes) and two or three additional spots which are much smaller. In size, shape, and feeding behavior it resembles *O. auromarginatus* and is probably closely related to this species. The *jakuta* found at Gome and Ntekete differs from that at Chizumulu by a slightly smaller eye and larger cheek. The species referred to by Snoeks & Hanssens (2004) as *O.* sp. 'tetraspilus elongate spot' is possibly conspecific with the *jakuta*.

Otopharynx sp. 'auromarginatus stripe' attains a maximum total length of about 18 cm and is locally abundant in the southernmost part of the lake (Turner, 1996). It has a large supra-pectoral spot and an elongate supra-anal spot that sometimes unites with the caudal spot to form a short horizontal band. I have not seen this species in the lake although it is found in relatively shallow (5-30 meters) water.

Fryer (1956b) mentions a cichlid, erroneously identified by him as *O. heterodon*, at Likoma, males of which construct bowers on the sand—*O. heterodon* does not construct bowers. This lek-breeder is an undescribed species, *Otopharynx* sp. 'heterodon likoma', which is found sympatric with *O. heterodon* (see page 224) at Ndomo Point, Likoma. It grows to a considerably larger size and has a more elongate body than *O. heterodon*. There are many overlapping morphological characters but it nevertheless differs from the type specimens of *O. heterodon*. Like *O. auromarginatus,* this species has three spots on the side of the body. The largest, below the dorsal, is elongate. In *O. heterodon* the spots are much smaller and the vertical bars more prominent. *O.* sp. 'heterodon likoma' attains a maximum total length of about 20 cm and exhibits similar feeding behavior to *O.* sp. 'auromarginatus jakuta', with which it is likewise found sympatric.

The members of *Ctenopharynx* are also characterized by three spots, but these spots are very large, with the supra-pectoral lying on the upper lateral line.

Ctenopharynx nitidus is a rather common sand-dwelling cichlid which is found throughout the lake. Maximum total length is around 17 cm for males; females remain considerably smaller and have not been seen larger than 12 cm. The preferred habitat is the open sand at depths below 15 meters. *C. nitidus* is easily recognized by its three large blotches, the yellow coloration on the lower part of the body and on the head, and the very large mouth, which is designed to scoop up large amounts of the silty sediment that lies on the sand. This is filtered for anything edible, mainly invertebrates. In some areas large schools forage over the sand, but small groups of about five individuals are more common. Males in breeding color are sometimes territorial, but are also seen in the company of foraging females. Territorial males construct large sand-castles at least a meter in diameter and about 50 cm high. Male *C. nitidus* pursue females over a relatively large distance.

Ctenopharynx intermedius closely resembles *C. pictus* from the sediment-rich rocky habitat (see page 221) but attains a much larger maximum size (22 versus 14 cm total length). The three spots are smaller in *C. intermedius* but are nevertheless very prominent features of its melanin pattern. Breeding males are an overall powder blue color and lack the conspicuous spots. They closely resemble males of *C. pictus* but can be distinguished by the much smaller eye of *C. intermedius* as well as the difference in total length. Like *C. pictus* this species feeds on small invertebrates which are scooped from the sand and mud, but the mouth of *C. intermedius* does not point downwards when extended as it does in *C. pictus*, which "vacuum-cleans" the aufwuchs in a peculiar manner. The species has a lake-wide distribution.

Spotted piscivores

It is difficult to define the habitat of many predators as they often move around from biotope to biotope. Some of the larger predators mentioned in the discussion of other habitats are frequently observed over the open sand as well.

Stigmatochromis woodi is a rather common sight in the intermediate as well as in the sandy habitat. Small specimens hide under overhanging rocks but subadult and fully-grown individuals are frequently seen over the open sand. They prey on small fishes which are caught with a sudden dart from the normal stationary posi-

1. *Otopharynx* sp. 'auromarginatus jakuta' ♂ Malopa

2. *Otopharynx* sp. 'auromarginatus jakuta' ♂ Malopa

3. *Otopharynx* sp. 'auromarginatus jakuta' ♂ Chizumulu

4. *Otopharynx auromarginatus* ♂ N'kolongwe

5. *Otopharynx* sp. 'heterodon likoma' ♂ Likoma

6. *Otopharynx* sp. 'heterodon likoma' ♀ Likoma

7. *Otopharynx* sp. 'auromarginatus jakuta' ♀♀ Malopa

8. *Otopharynx* sp. 'auromarginatus stripe' Monkey Bay

9. *Otopharynx auromarginatus* ♂ Chembe

10. *Otopharynx auromarginatus* ♀ Thumbi West Island

1. *Ctenopharynx nitidus* ♂ Mbuyu

2. *Ctenopharynx nitidus* ♀ Dwangwa

3. *Ctenopharynx nitidus* Gallireya Reef

4. *Ctenopharynx nitidus* ♀ Otter Point

5. *Ctenopharynx intermedius* ♀ Makokola Reef

6. Malopa

7. *Ctenopharynx nitidus* ♂ Liuli

7. *Ctenopharynx intermedius* ♂ Makokola Reef

tion. When hunting these fishes remain very close to the substrate while searching for prey. Breeding *S. woodi* are found at deeper levels (between 20 and 40 meters), with sexually active males donning a very dark blue to black dress and constructing large but shallow spawning pits in the sand floor. The eggs are fertilized inside the female's mouth. Mouthbrooding females ascend to shallower water and release their fry in the intermediate zone. The species can attain a total length of a little over 25 cm.

Morphologically *Stigmatochromis* sp. 'tolae' is very similar to *S. woodi*, but males do not appear to construct bowers on the sand. *S.* sp. 'tolae' occurs at Mbenji Island and at Chimwalani Reef, and probably has a wider distribution in the southern part of the lake. The two species occur sympatrically. *S.* sp. 'tolae' can be distinguished from *S. woodi* by the smaller mouth, not almost in line with the horizontal as is the case in *S. woodi*, and by a deeper body.

Stigmatochromis pholidophorus has been recorded from many places around the lake, in particular from the eastern shores. It is a predator that is characterized by the rounded profile of the snout and by its peculiar hunting technique. It is normally encountered poised in midwater, approximately a meter above the substrate (usually sand), waiting for potential prey to come within reach, then darting to the bottom to seize it. Apparently juvenile sand-dwelling cichlids expect piscivore attacks only at more or less their own level, otherwise it is difficult to explain how *S. pholidophorus* can be successful at hunting fishes that are at least a meter away when it lunges! This species has been exported, albeit infrequently, as the "Torpedo" (in reference to its hunting technique) or "Kambiri Torpedo", but has not become established in the aquarium hobby.

An undescribed, ventrally flattened cichlid, *Stigmatochromis* sp. 'spilostichus type', is known from Likoma Island and along the shores of Mozambique and the southeastern arm of the lake. The trade names of this species are "Haplochromis Spilostichus Type" and "Haplochromis Epichorialis". The shape of the head resembles that of *S. woodi* but maximum total length is no more than 20 cm. *S.* sp. 'spilostichus type' occurs sympatrically with *S. woodi*. Juveniles of *S. woodi* have three distinct spots on the flank, but in older specimens additional spots may give the row of spots the appearance of a diagonal line. The same is true of *S.* sp. 'tolae'. In *S.* sp. 'spilostichus type', however, juveniles lack the distinct spots and instead exhibit vertical bars which are accentuated in three places by dark spots. The pigmentation pattern in adults resembles that of *S. woodi* and in my opinion these three species belong to the same genus. *Stigmatochromis* sp. 'spilostichus longsnout' is probably conspecific with this species (Snoeks & Hanssens, 2004).

Turner (1996) reports on a small species of *Stigmatochromis*, with a resemblance to *S. woodi*, which he calls *S.* 'guttatus'. Its maximum total length is 16 cm and it is common in deeper water in the southeastern arm of the lake. Turner also mentions that ripe males have prominent dark vertical bars. *Stigmatochromis* sp. 'guttatus' has also been collected in Tanzanian waters and some have been exported.

At Mdoka I found a colony of a large predator (maximum total length estimated at about 20 cm) breeding on the sand adjacent to the reef at a depth of about 25 meters. At first this species appeared to be very similar to *Mylochromis gracilis* (see below), but when females were "matched" to the breeding males—the breeding colors of the male completely hide the basic melanin pattern—it turned out to be a member of *Stigmatochromis*. The pigmentation pattern consists of two small and three large spots, which is common in *Stigmatochromis* species. This type of pattern appears to consist of two horizontal lines which are broken into a small number of spots: the upper line has only two spots and the lower has three spots which are usually much larger (see photos on pages 342 and 343). Initially I thought that this species was *S. pleurospilus* but Snoeks & Hanssens (2004) have rediscovered that species (see below) and it has a much smaller adult size than the Mdoka species. They also report on a species they named *Sciaenochromis* sp. 'spot bicuspid' which is possibly conspecific with the species at Mdoka, but pending further study the latter is here referred to as *Stigmatochromis* sp. 'pleurospilus mdoka' as I do not share their opinion that a species with such distinct spots can be a member of *Sciaenochromis*.

Stigmatochromis sp. 'pleurospilus mdoka' is a lek breeder, and the colony at Mdoka consisted of 21 territorial males (November 2000), each defending a large bower, with a diameter of about 100-150 cm, on the sand. These bowers were not complete circles but had a wall about three quarters of the way around the spawning area. The position of the gap in the wall was different in each bower. Brooding females remained over the sand but retreated closer to the rocks of the reef. I have not yet seen this species hunting so nothing can be said about that aspect of its behavior.

Stigmatochromis pleurospilus was until recently known only from the type, a single juvenile (?) specimen of 40 mm standard length from Christy's collection made at Lupembe in the far north of the lake about a hundred years ago. Interestingly, although Christy also collected similar-sized *S. woodi* at the same time and locality, the type of *S. pleurospilus* was sufficiently different to be considered distinct. The drawing of *S. pleurospilus* published in Eccles & Trewavas (1989) (who postulate that the type might be a juvenile of another species) lent credence to my initial view that *S.* sp. 'pleurospilus mdoka' was conspecific with *S. pleurospilus*, because the three spots on the flank of the juvenile are round and closely match those of the Mdoka species. Snoeks & Hanssens (2004) found two more specimens of *S. pleurospilus* that were nearly adult but no more than 9 cm standard length. These two specimens were collected at Ifungu (Kirondo) in Tanzania.

Striped piscivores

A number of predatory *Mylochromis* are also found in the sandy habitats. The genus *Mylochromis* contains an array of very different species, some of them plump and slow-moving while others are torpedo-shaped pursuit predators, but all share a common pigmentation pattern consisting of a diagonal line.

Mylochromis formosus is one of the elongate predators of this large genus and has been exported irregularly. It is sometimes caught in beach seine nets that are dragged over the sand. Underwater observations indicate that most juvenile individuals live in the intermediate habitat where they hunt for small fishes. The species occurs in shallow water, usually no deeper than 15 meters. In *M. formosus* the diagonal line is usually continuous but sometimes partially broken up into spots. The most characteristic feature of this species is the presence of a black lachrymal stripe which it shares only with the much more robust *Champsochromis spilorhynchus* (page 300). Maximum total length is about 15 cm. Breeding has not been witnessed in the wild, but in the aquarium ripe males are territorial and dig spawning pits (Peter Baasch, pers. comm.).

Mylochromis gracilis—some authors place this species in *Sciaenochromis*—was described from three specimens in the Christy collection. Single specimens have been imported alive under trade names such as "Torpedo" or "Dark Line Torpedo". The distribution of this rare species seems to be restricted to the southern part of the lake. The narrowly pointed head with its slightly downward-curving upper profile is a striking feature, reminiscent of *Nimbochromis linni*. Its large mouth, its teeth, and its shape all suggest a predatory lifestyle. On two occasions (both in Senga Bay) I have seen it hunting the shell-dwelling *Metriaclima lanisticola*, during which the mouth was "fired" into the shell (to no avail).

Sexually active males defend a territory and construct a sand-castle bower with a diameter of about 50 cm. The eggs are very small and are fertilized inside the female's mouth (Baasch, 1991). Juveniles are very small and slim in comparison to those of other predators of similar adult size. *M. gracilis* grows to a maximum size of about 25 cm. Snoeks & Hanssens (2004) report on a species they identify as *gracilis* (they actually place it in *Sciaenochromis*) but which is not conspecific with the species I have described above. Their species has a deeper body and a less regular, blotchy diagonal stripe than the lectotype—collected at Monkey Bay—or the forms I have identified as *M. gracilis*. Their spe-

1. *Stigmatochromis woodi* ♂ Masasa Reef

5. *Stigmatochromis woodi* ♀ Luwala Reef

6. *Stigmatochromis* sp. 'tolae' ♀ Mazinzi Reef

2. *Stigmatochromis* sp. 'tolae' ♂ Mazinzi Reef

7. *Stigmatochromis pholidophorus* ♂ Aquarium

3. *Stigmatochromis pholidophorus* ♂ Chiofu

8. *Stigmatochromis pholidophorus* Meponda

9. *Stigmatochromis pleurospilus* Ifungu

4. *Stigmatochromis* sp. 'spilostichus type' ♂ Aquarium

10. *Stigmatochromis* sp. 'spilostichus type' ♀ Mala Point

1. *Stigmatochromis* sp. 'guttatus' ♂ Mumbo Island

2. *Stigmatochromis* sp. 'pleurospilus mdoka' ♂ Mdoka

3. *Stigmatochromis* sp. 'pleurospilus mdoka' ♀ Mdoka

4. *Mylochromis formosus* ♀ Mvunguti

5. *Mylochromis gracilis* ♀ Chembe

6. *Mylochromis spilostichus* ♀ Luwala Reef

7. *Stigmatochromis* sp. 'guttatus' ♂ Aquarium

8. *Stigmatochromis* sp. 'pleurospilus mdoka' ♂ Mdoka

9. *Mylochromis formosus* ♂ Aquarium

10. *Mylochromis gracilis* ♂ Aquarium

11. *Mylochromis spilostichus* ♂ Makokola Reef

cies was collected in Chilola Bay, Mozambique, and I believe it is conspecific with *Mylochromis spilostichus*.

The spots on the flanks of *Mylochromis spilostichus* are arranged in a distinct diagonal line, although they are not always the same size. This very elongate predator resembles *M. gracilis*, which exhibits a diagonal line consisting of similarly-sized spots, which in *M. spilostichus* are less regular. *M. spilostichus* has been seen at Makokola and Luwala reefs, where it hunts small fishes over the sand at a depth of about 35 meters. Territorial males defend small shallow spawning pits in the sand near rocks. Mouthbrooding females move about over the sand. The species has also been found at Mbenji Island but not observed underwater. The total length of *M. spilostichus* is about 25 cm. The species Snoeks & Hanssens (2004) identify as *Sciaenochromis spilostichus* is, in my opinion, an undescribed species from deep water (see page 403) that does not resemble the holotype collected at Monkey Bay.

An elongate species with some resemblance to *M. gracilis* and to members of the genus *Buccochromis* (see below) occurs at Kande Island and has been named *Mylochromis* sp. 'kande'. Breeding males are light blue dorsally and have a yellow chin and chest. Territorial males defend a small (about 10 cm in diameter) cleared site among the rubble on the bottom, usually against a small rock or other suitable object. Females, which have a distinct and continuous diagonal stripe, are found in the vicinity of such males. The lower lobe of the tail in females and non-breeding males is yellow, a feature which it shares with several species of the genus *Buccochromis*. Several breeding males are found within a small area but the species does not seem to be a lek-breeder. Maximum size is about 20 cm.

At Mdoka a species with a shape very similar to that of *Naevochromis chrysogaster* (page 262) has been found at a depth of about 15 meters over sand near a rocky reef. I have also seen this species at Luwala Reef in the southern part of the lake, but I find it difficult to speculate on its relationship to *N. chrysogaster*. Remarkably these individuals had a diagonal line rather than three spots on the flanks, and for this reason, and in order to conform to the pigmentation-pattern-based classification of other Malaŵi haplochromines, I have classified this species as *Mylochromis* sp. 'chrysogaster line'. The thick chin suggests that this species may also be a paedophage, but feeding behavior has not been observed.

Two further thick-chinned species, *Hemitaeniochromis urotaenia* and *Hemitaeniochromis spilopterus* (some authors place the latter in *Protomelas*), are known under the trade name of "Gaisi". The genus *Hemitaeniochromis* was originally regarded as monotypic, with *H. urotaenia* the sole species (Eccles & Trewavas, 1989), but in my opinion *H. spilopterus* belongs to this genus as it shares all its morphological characteristics. The only discrepancy is that the mid-lateral stripe is continuous in most specimens (see also below); some individuals (e.g. at Ntekete), however, do not exhibit a lateral stripe at all. A few other thick-chinned species with a *Protomelas*-type pigmentation pattern (or derivatives thereof) have been discovered, and probably also belong to this genus, which would thus currently include *H. urotaenia*, *H.* sp. 'urotaenia tanzania' (page 260), *H.* sp. 'paedophage' (page 260), *H. spilopterus*, *H.* sp. 'spilopterus blue' (see page 165), *H.* sp. 'spilopterus yellow', *H.* sp. 'spilopterus kande'" and *H.* sp. 'spilopterus jalo' (see page 165).

One of the "Gaisi" species, *H. urotaenia*, has been exported in the past as "*Haplochromis* Kachimanga", *kachimanga* being the vernacular name given to it (as well as to *Placidochromis johnstoni*) by natives in the Monkey Bay area. It is easily distinguished from *H. spilopterus* by the longer snout and the interrupted horizontal lines on the flanks, consisting of a few elongated spots extending from halfway along the body to the tail. The horizontal stripe in *H. spilopterus* is continuous and begins at the gill-cover. Both species have a large oblique mouth, but that of *H. spilopterus* is more steeply angled.

Territorial males of *H. urotaenia* are metallic blue and excavate very shallow spawning pits in the sand, often using a small stone in the construction but also without any object marking the spawning dish. Their maximum total length can be more than 25 cm.

H. spilopterus has been given several native names: *kamwena, mbaba,* and *kadyapola* (Jackson, 1961). Eccles & Trewavas (1989) suspected that *H. spilopterus* is a paedophage, i.e. that it steals broods from mouthbrooding females. They based this assumption on a publication by McKaye & Kocher (1983) in which the latter describe the behavior of three paedophagous cichlids, only two of which were identified, while the third, according to Eccles & Trewavas, may have been *H. spilopterus*. However, the peculiar hunting technique of *H.* sp. 'paedophage' (see page 260) corresponds much more closely to that described by McKaye & Kocher for the third species. Nevertheless I too believe that *H. spilopterus* is a paedophagous cichlid, although I have never observed it attacking mouthbrooding cichlids or any other fishes. Stomach contents analysis of two specimens revealed soft egg-colored material but recognizable cichlid eggs were not found. Whole cichlid eggs and larvae (still with a large yolk sac) were found in the stomachs of *H.* sp. 'spilopterus blue', *H.* sp. 'paedophage' and *H.* sp. 'spilopterus yellow' which suggests that these species, and maybe other members of *Hemitaeniochromis*, are paedophagous. I have not yet observed the feeding techniques of thick-chinned species other than *H.* sp. 'paedophage' and *H. urotaenia* (which is a piscivore).

Breeding male *H. spilopterus*, which attain a maximum total length of about 21 cm, construct spawning pits in the intermediate habitat. These spawning sites are never seen on bare sand and always include small rocks. The male breeding color of *H. spilopterus* in the southern part of the lake is metallic green while that of northern populations is blue. At most locations it occurs sympatrically with *H.* sp. 'spilopterus yellow', from which it can be distinguished, by the relatively larger eye in *H. spilopterus* as well as the yellow color of the "Spilopterus Yellow", which is often seen in females of that species as well.

H. spilopterus and *H. urotaenia* have a lake-wide distribution. *H.* sp. 'spilopterus yellow' also has a lake-wide distribution but is nowhere found in numbers—usually one to three individuals are encountered and breeding leks have not been seen. Territorial males of *H.* sp. 'spilopterus yellow' defend the upper surface of a large rock in the intermediate habitat but station themselves about a meter above the rock. Females are courted in mid-water and followed far away from the spawning site.

Caprichromis orthognathus is usually encountered in the sandy habitat where it stalks the larger sand-dwelling cichlids, in particular *Fossorochromis rostratus*. It is interested only in the eggs and larvae in the mouths of brooding females: it is a specialized paedophage. Mouthbrooding females are attacked from below, the predator butting its head against the buccal pouch holding the brood. Although I have seen the hunting behavior of *C. orthognathus* on several occasions I was unable to see if it actually ate the brood. Stomach contents analyses, however, reveal that its diet consists exclusively of cichlid eggs and larvae. Males in breeding colors defend large bowers that are usually built alongside a large rock. It is not known whether mouthbrooding females are attacked by their own species. *C. orthognathus* has a lake-wide distribution and attains a maximum total length of about 20 cm.

At Mdoka I have seen and collected *H. urotaenia, H. spilopterus, H.* sp. 'spilopterus yellow', *H.* sp. 'spilopterus blue', and *Caprichromis orthognathus*. At least three of these species have been proven to eat cichlid eggs, and all may turn out to be paedophages. This may give us an indication of the predatory pressure to which mouthbrooding females in general are subject.

Taeniochromis holotaenia is characterized by a horizontal band connecting the eye with the caudal peduncle. An additional bar between the eyes gives the impression that the fish is completely circumscribed by a black line—*holotaenia* means complete stripe. Depending on the fish's mood, vertical bars may be present as well. This unique and remarkable pattern was the reason for this species being placed in a genus of its own, *Taeniochromis*, although it bears some resemblance to species of the genus *Dimidiochromis*.

T. holotaenia, which can grow to a length of about 22 cm, has a lake-wide distribution. It is

1. *Mylochromis* sp. 'kande' ♂ Kande Island

5. *Mylochromis* sp. 'kande' ♀ Kande Island

6. *Mylochromis* sp. 'kande' ♂ Kande Island

2. *Hemitaeniochromis urotaenia* ♂ Otter Point

7. *Mylochromis* sp. 'chrysogaster line' Luwala Reef

8. *Hemitaeniochromis urotaenia* ♀ Otter Point

3. *Hemitaeniochromis spilopterus* ♂ Mdoka

9. *Hemitaeniochromis spilopterus* ♀ Mdoka

4. *Hemitaeniochromis spilopterus* ♂ Mazinzi Reef

10. *Hemitaeniochromis spilopterus* ♀ Mazinzi Reef

1. *Hemitaeniochromis* sp. 'spilopterus yellow' ♀ Tsano Rock
2. *Hemitaeniochromis* sp. 'spilopterus kande' ♀ Kande Island
3. *Caprichromis orthognathus* ♀ Mdoka
4. *Taeniochromis holotaenia* ♂♂ Lupingu
5. *Hemitaeniochromis* sp. 'spilopterus yellow' ♂ Masasa Reef
6. *Caprichromis orthognathus* ♂ Tsano Rock
7. *Taeniochromis holotaenia* ♀ Chimwalani Reef

seen over sand and in the intermediate habitat at a depth ranging between 10 and 20 meters. *T. holotaenia* is a pursuit predator and usually hunts in packs—sometimes consisting of more than a hundred individuals and sometimes together with other species such as *Nimbochromis polystigma*. The male excavates a very shallow dip in the sand as a spawning site, usually near a rock (sometimes even under one). Male *T. holotaenia* have a blue breeding coloration with yellowish fins. Mouthbrooding females remain over the sand and are sometimes found in small groups.

Buccochromis nototaenia can attain a total length of well over 35 cm. This large piscivore has a lake-wide distribution and is called *mbowe* by the locals, a name under which it is sometimes exported. It is regularly seen in the sandy habitat but sometimes ventures into intermediate zones as well. It preys on juvenile haplochromine cichlids, in particular those living over the sand. A male *B. nototaenia* in nuptial dress is a splendid sight to behold. Sometimes a male constructs his bower among rocks but normally it is found on the sand (Saulos Mwale, pers. comm.). Females guard their offspring in the intermediate habitat. The female cares for the fry for at least four weeks after release. Female coloration consists of a silvery body, a distinct solid diagonal stripe, and yellow on the snout, the ventral and anal fins, and the lower lobe of the tail.

Buccochromis rhoadesii is distinguished from *B. nototaenia* by a shallower body. Both species have yellow heads and ventral fins and in practice the two species are almost impossible to distinguish unless fully adult individuals are compared. I have usually found *B. rhoadesii* at deeper levels. A diagonal line is rarely visible in *B. rhoadesii* from Likoma and Chizumulu islands but in southern populations it is often as distinct as that in *B. nototaenia* and *Buccochromis lepturus* (see below). In the lake small groups of adult individuals of *B. rhoadesii* can sometimes be found at a depth of 15 to 30 meters. Usually there is only a single sexually active male in such groups. Juveniles are found in large numbers in the very shallow sandy habitat and are often caught in beach seines. At Mdoka I found (October, 2005) a small breeding colony of *B. rhoadesii* consisting of four territorial males. Each male—they were more than five meters apart—had constructed a large heap of sand with a slanted spawning surface. The bowers were about 60-70 cm high but did not have a raised wall around the spawning area.

B. rhoadesii is sometimes exported as "Haplochromis Lepturus" or "Yellow Lepturus" but *B. lepturus* is a different species, also found in the sandy habitat. The two species are easily distinguished by the yellow color in *rhoadesii* which is absent in *lepturus*, which has been given the trade name "Lepturus Green". Territorial males of *B. lepturus* have not been seen, and they do not excavate spawning pits in the aquarium.

Buccochromis spectabilis is often regarded as a synonym of *B. lepturus*, but a form has been caught in Tanzanian waters that has a different coloration to the latter. Snoeks & Hanssens (2004) collected similar individuals and identified them as *B. spectabilis*, which they regard as a valid species. The difference between *B. spectabilis* and *B. lepturus* is that the former attains a much smaller adult size of about 20 cm versus about 40 cm for *B. lepturus*. Breeding male *B. spectabilis* resemble those of *B. rhoadesii* (in coloration) but can be distinguished by the elongated pelvic fins which in *B. rhoadesii* do not extend beyond the anal pore while in *B. spectabilis* they can reach as far as halfway along the anal-fin base.

Two smaller species of *Buccochromis*, *B. oculatus* and *B. atritaeniatus*, each with a maximum total length of around 25 cm, have been reported (Eccles & Trewavas, 1989) as occurring in the southern half of the lake but both Turner (1996) and Snoeks & Hanssens (2004) doubt the validity of these two species. Both may in fact be conspecific with (and thus synonyms of) *B. nototaenia*. The male in breeding colors I previously identified as *B. atritaeniatus* (Konings, 2001: 273) is now referred to *B. nototaenia*.

Snoeks & Hanssens (2004) discovered a single specimen of a species of *Buccochromis* at Nkhotakota that did not correspond to any of the described species, and named it *Buccochromis* sp. 'large mouth'. It is characterized by a relatively large mouth and a very distinct but narrow diagonal stripe.

Shallow-water predators

Two shallow-water species behave in a similar way to *Rhamphochromis* (page 388). That with the closest resemblance to the silvery predators is *Champsochromis caeruleus*, which also sometimes feeds on *usipa* (lake sardines). Its close resemblance to *Rhamphochromis* has probably led to the erroneous identification of this species as *Rhamphochromis ferox* (e.g. by Lienard, 1983). But in contrast to the short and sometimes stubby fins of *Rhamphochromis*, *C. caeruleus* has beautifully elongated fins with the soft-rayed portion of the dorsal and anal sometimes extending halfway along the tail in fully adult males. *C. caeruleus* is well known among aquarists and is irregularly exported under a variety of names. The first specimens were called "Haplochromis Thola", but at present it is generally known as the "Trout Cichlid". Natives call this cichlid *mbuchi* (Ambali *et al.*, 2001) and it is occasionally caught by hook and line. Infrequently small schools of juveniles are seen, but the species usually occurs singly once it attains a size of about 10 cm.

Breeding in *C. caeruleus* takes place on the sand in the intermediate habitat. Males in a breeding colony in Same Bay, Chizumulu, observed in October (1999), had constructed bowers consisting of a rampart in the shape of an oxbow and hence open on one side. These bowers had a diameter of about 100-140 cm and the wall was about 20-30 cm high. This breeding arena was at a depth of about 12 meters. In the aquarium the male clears a small pit by circling around over the spawning site, and then courts a ripe female (Peter Baasch, pers. comm.). If the female is willing to spawn, the pair descend to the bottom and start spawning. The eggs are fertilized inside the female's mouth. Maximum total length can be more than 25 cm. This species is most closely related to *C. spilorhynchus* (see page 300).

Dimidiochromis kiwinge is a gregarious predator with an average adult size of about 30 cm, and is called *binga* or *liyani* in Chi-Cheŵa. These fishes not only prey on small cichlids but dash frantically after anything edible that they come across on their "raiding forays" through the habitats. As in *Nimbochromis. polystigma*, adult individuals group together and feed in a frenzied manner, gobbling up anything in sight. When the *usipa* are inshore they are one of the best indicators that *D. kiwinge* are around, because in their attempts to escape these voracious predators they jump out of the water, sometimes hundreds at a time. In this respect *D. kiwinge* resemble hunting packs of *Lepidiolamprologus elongatus* in Lake Tanganyika, whereas *N. polystigma* hunt closer to the substrate and thus resemble (in behavior) the Tanganyika species '*Lamprologus*' *callipterus* (see Konings, 1998).

Breeding in *D. kiwinge* usually takes place on sand near rocks in the intermediate habitat, but at Otter Point and Likoma Island many males can be seen defending spawning sites in the sediment-free rocky habitat. Males of this lek-breeding species normally construct raised craters. The eggs are fertilized inside the female's mouth (Peter Baasch, pers. comm.) and the fry are cared for after they have been released for the first time. The female *D. kiwinge* usually releases her fry in the water column where they feed on plankton.

A wolf in sheep's clothing

All the sand-dwelling species with the characteristic diagonal stripe are attacked by the scale-eater *Corematodus taeniatus*. Like its victims, *C. taeniatus* has a diagonal stripe on its body, which it has evolved as camouflage to render it inconspicuous among the schools of sand-dwelling cichlids. *C. taeniatus* feeds mainly from the caudal peduncle of its prey and frequently scrapes and bites off the small scales covering this vulnerable part of its victims. The numerous teeth in its jaws are positioned in wide bands and feel like sandpaper to the touch (see photo 2, page 351). It enjoys a lake-wide distribution and is rather common among schools of sand-dwellers. Breeding takes place on rocks and many breeding individuals are observed at rocky islands adjacent to large

1. *Buccochromis nototaenia* ♂ Mazinzi Reef

2. *Buccochromis rhoadesi* ♂ Mdoka

3. *Buccochromis lepturus* ♂ Aquarium

4. *Buccochromis spectabilis* ♂ Aquarium

5. *Buccochromis nototaenia* ♀ Mazinzi Reef

6. *Buccochromis rhoadesi* ♂ Aquarium

7. *Buccochromis rhoadesi* Chembe

8. *Buccochromis lepturus* Chembe

9. *Buccochromis* sp. 'large mouth' Nkhotakota

10. *Buccochromis spectabilis* ♀ Aquarium

1. *Champsochromis caeruleus* ♂ Chizumulu Island

2. *Corematodus taeniatus* ♀ Chiofu

3. *Corematodus taeniatus* ♀ Mdoka

4. *Dimidiochromis kiwinge* ♂ Chiofu

5. *Dimidiochromis kiwinge* ♀ Mdoka

6. *Champsochromis caeruleus* ♂ Chizumulu Island

7. *Champsochromis caeruleus* ♀ Chizumulu Island

8. *Corematodus taeniatus* ♂ Londo

9. *Dimidiochromis kiwinge* ♂ Mumbo Island

stretches of sand. Males hold territories on top of rocks and lead ripe females to their spawning sites. This cichlid has been exported as "Haplochromis Jacksoni". Its true identity explains the "aggression" of this cichlid in hobbyists' tanks....

Sciaenochromis

Sciaenochromis psammophilus is better known as the "Electric Blue Kande" and is seen mostly at a depth of between five and 30 meters. It is uncommon at most locations as it is a solitary hunter of sandy habitats; only at places where males have gathered for breeding purposes can larger numbers be encountered. Around Kande Island and at Mazinzi and Masasa reefs breeding individuals are common throughout the year. *S. psammophilus* (or at least a cichlid with a close resemblance to this species) has also been observed at Likoma Island, Masinje, Senga Bay, and Mdoka. Except when breeding, *S. psammophilus* is a solitary hunter which swims about 30 cm above the sand searching for small, sand-dwelling prey. It has been observed hunting small cichlids, but invertebrates are taken as well.

Breeding males are territorial and defend an area about two meters in diameter. The center of the territory is a spawning pit excavated in the sand, partly under a rock, creating a cave-crater. When more breeding males are present than suitable rocks, bowers are also constructed on the open sand. These are very shallow and probably used only to bridge a period of temporary shortage of more amenable spawning sites. Males guarding such sites do not seem to have the same intense breeding colors as males defending cave-craters. The breeding coloration of males in the southeastern arm of the lake is more of a metallic green than the blue of those found in more northerly locations.

Sciaenochromis benthicola is a deep-water species which also breeds at deep levels. The males have distinct egg-spots in the anal fin. The species probably has a lake-wide distribution as it has been collected at Mdoka, Ntekete, and in the southeastern arm of the lake. A few specimens have been collected in Tanzanian waters and are being bred in the aquarium (Mark Danhieux, pers. comm.).

Another sleeper

Nimbochromis venustus is known from many locations around the lake but prefers deeper regions—usually deeper than 15 meters—than its close relative *N. livingstonii*. It has adopted a somewhat similar hunting tactic to *N. livingstonii*, but is, however, never seen lying on its side; instead it remains motionless after "plowing" slightly into the sandy bottom after spotting potential prey—small fishes. It stays in this position for a long time, waiting for the prey to come within reach. The yellow coloration may function as an attractant for juvenile cichlids. Because of its behavior, *N. venustus* has, like its congener, been given the native name *kaligono*, meaning "sleeper". *N. venustus* also feeds on invertebrates and preys on small fishes in a more normal manner. It uses its special hunting technique only when a group of tiny cichlids is encountered. Small individuals are sometimes encountered in rocky habitats.

Trematocranus

The enlarged sensory pores on the head of *Trematocranus* (see page 240 for the function of these organs) are able to register the movements of snails and possibly other invertebrates, even when the fish is at some distance from the bottom. In establishing a new genus, *Alticorpus*, in which some species with such extended sensory organs are included, Stauffer & McKaye (1988) pointed to the fact that this specialization is certainly not monophyletic (originating from one ancestral species). As discussed earlier, this specialization is observed in cichlids from other lakes as well. The potential for developing such extensions of the lateral line organ is probably present in many African cichlids, and occasionally it is expressed when cichlids are competing for food. It therefore should not surprise us that the development of these organs has taken place in several lineages of Malaŵian cichlids.

Trematocranus placodon is well known to

aquarists and adults are frequently exported. It has small teeth and weak jaws reminiscent of species of the genus *Lethrinops,* and this "equipment" certainly does not suggest a habitual snail-crusher, which it is—*T. placodon* feeds on thin-shelled snails (Turner, 1996). Just as *Aulonocara* species hover a few millimeters above the sand, *T. placodon* remains motionless at a distance of about 30-50 cm above the substrate. Snails are constantly moving through the top layer of the muddy sediment on the sand and such movements can be registered visually as well as sensed with the pores on the lower part of the fish's head—*T. placodon* just waits patiently until something edible moves within its sensory radius. Two species of snails are eaten, *Bulinus nyassanus* and *Melanoides turberculata,* with the former the favorite. During the breeding season (from July to September, but breeding males can be encountered throughout the year), a ripe male assumes his nuptial dress and constructs a bower, with a diameter of about 70 cm, on the lake floor. Most of these bowers are located in the somewhat muddy part of the biotope at a depth of about 5-15 meters. When a territorial male spots a female, he swims several meters from his bower to display in front of her, and subsequently tries to lead her back to his spawning site. Mouthbrooding females remain over the sand but may release their offspring in the rocky or vegetated habitat. The maximum total length of males is about 23 cm.

Snoeks & Hanssens (2004) report on a *placodon*-like cichlid from 10-13 meters depth near Cobwé, Mozambique. They found that, as its name implies, *Trematocranus* sp. 'thick-lip bicuspid' has thick lips and closely-set bicuspid teeth in the oral jaws. I have not recognized this species underwater.

Trematocranus microstoma is again characterized by enlarged sensory pores on the lower half of the head. It is closely related to *T. placodon* and like it has three spots on a silvery body. Maximum total length ranges between 20 and 25 cm. The diet consists of crustaceans and small snails which are located with the aid of the sensory pores. According to Jackson (1961), *T. microstoma* is restricted to the northern half of the lake. It is, however, regularly caught in beach seine nets in the south (David Eccles, pers. comm.; Stuart Grant, pers. comm.). I have observed *T. microstoma* at Chembe Beach and at Kambiri Point, where it was very common in July and August before over-fishing wiped out most of these populations. *T. microstoma* probably acquired a reputation for rarity because it is difficult to distinguish from *T. placodon*. It has six to eight rows of conical teeth in the outer jaws whereas *T. placodon* has only four. The three spots in *T. microstoma* are usually in contact with the dorsal and the mid-lateral spot lies almost entirely above the upper lateral line; and sometimes all three spots are invisible. The spots in *T. placodon* are always visible (except when the male breeding colors obscure them) and the mid-lateral spot almost always straddles the upper lateral line.

Cichlids with "big ears"

Aulonocara includes several species that are encountered over sandy and muddy bottoms. These species vary between 11 and 20 cm in maximum total length. Eccles, in Eccles & Trewavas (1989: 138), defines *Aulonocara* as having the infra-orbital bones so expanded that they exclude scales from most, or all, of the cheek area. In the currently accepted concept of the genus, however, this applies only to the sand-dwelling species. The rock-dwelling species (see page 240) also have enlarged sensory pores in the skull, but in some cases the degree of expansion allows for two to four rows of scales on the cheek (e.g. in *A. jacobfreibergi*). Other rock-dwelling species have just a single row of scales on the cheek (e.g. *A. stuartgranti*) and share this character with most sand-dwelling *Aulonocara*.

Aulonocara can be better characterized by their foraging behavior, which has been described earlier (see page 240). This behavior, termed "sonar-feeding", is seen in all the species of *Aulonocara* that have been observed in their natural environment. It involves hovering motionless about 5-10 mm above the sandy substrate and making an occasional dive with the snout into the sand. While the fish is hover-

1. *Sciaenochromis psammophilus* ♂ Kande Island

2. *Sciaenochromis psammophilus* ♂ Kande Island

4. *Sciaenochromis psammophilus* ♀ Masasa Reef

5. *Sciaenochromis benthicola* ♀ Aquarium

6. *Sciaenochromis benthicola* ♀ ♂ Aquarium

3. *Nimbochromis venustus* ♂ Chembe

7. *Nimbochromis venustus* ♀ Chembe

1. *Trematocranus microstoma* ♂ Chembe

2. *Trematocranus microstoma* ♀ Chembe

3. *Trematocranus* sp. 'thicklip bicuspid' ♂ Cobwé

4. *Trematocranus placodon* ♀ Chembe

5. *Trematocranus placodon* ♀ ♂ Chembe

6. *Trematocranus placodon* ♂ Mvunguti

ing its enhanced sensory system registers any movement in the sand, and the prey, once located, is captured during the dive. This behavior is very characteristic of *Aulonocara*.

As mentioned above, the sand-dwelling species are characterized by greatly enlarged pores in the bones of the skull. A similar situation is found in the rock-dwelling members of the genus, but in most species the enlargement of the infra-orbitals is less. There is no clear distinction between the rock- and sand-dwelling *Aulonocara* other than the observation that the sand-dwellers normally forage and breed in open habitats. They do not seem to be restricted to a specific area of (rocky) coast and usually have a wide distribution.

In 1935 Trewavas described two large *Aulonocara* which differed from each other in the length of the pectoral fin, the size of the eye, and the depth of the body. She named them *Aulonocara rostratum* and *A. macrochir*. The latter was described from a single specimen with a standard length of 149 mm. Later it was found that individuals within a single breeding colony exhibited a large variation in morphology (Konings, 1990), with characters overlapping those of the two described species, and that similar variation existed in two different colonies. I therefore regard *A. macrochir* as synonymous with *A. rostratum*. Turner (1996), however, records another species with a considerable resemblance to *A. rostratum*, which he refers to as *Aulonocara cf. macrochir*. This species occurs in large numbers at a depth of about 50 meters near Boadzulu Island.

Aulonocara rostratum has a lake-wide distribution and has been observed in its natural habitat at Mdoka, Msuli Point, Kande Island, and Luwala and Chimwalani reefs in Malaŵi, and at Hongi Island in Tanzania. *A. rostratum* is regularly seen over open sandy substrates at depths varying from 15 to 30 meters. True geographical races are not known but males in the northern population appear to be a deeper blue. Males in territorial (breeding) coloration group into breeding colonies. Territorial males are found throughout the year; each digs a spawning crater in the sand and defends it against all intruders. These spawning sites are located about two meters apart and lack the rim usually seen in other bowers in the lake. Females normally forage in separate groups or are solitary, and apparently visit the otherwise exclusively male breeding colonies only when ready to spawn. Spawning has not been observed in the wild. In the aquarium broods can be as large as 150 fry (Reitz, 1992).

Eccles & Trewavas (1989) discuss the relationships of three other species which have been assigned to *Aulonocara* but whose status within the genus is unclear. One of these is *Aulonocara auditor*, whose holotype, a mature female with a standard length of 77.5 mm, was caught near Vua in the north of the lake. *A. auditor* does not share the characteristics of the sand-dwelling group, i.e. the bones below the eye are not so enlarged that the cheeks are scaleless or have only a single row of scales. It has three rows of scales on the cheek and in addition exhibits an indistinct pattern of three series of spots on the flank and at the base of the dorsal. This pigmentation pattern is reminiscent of *Protomelas* rather than *Aulonocara*. Not until more (live) specimens have been examined can this species be assigned with certainty to *Aulonocara*.

The holotype of *Aulonocara nyassae*, the type species of the genus, is from an unknown locality and was collected by Wood at the beginning of the 20th century; Eccles collected this species south of Boadzulu Island. Mazinzi Bay, where I have studied and photographed it, is also situated in the southeastern arm of the lake.

A. nyassae of the population in Mazinzi Bay are found in the sandy habitat where small groups of 10 to 25 individuals were seen foraging from the substrate. *A. nyassae* is seen only at depths of more than 15 meters. Small groups usually contain a single male exhibiting territorial (breeding) coloration. When the group is not feeding there seems to be some territorial activity on the part of this male but no spawning site is constructed. This may suggest that spawning takes place at any random site, but since mouthbrooding females have not yet been seen it is not clear whether or not the individuals observed so far were sexually active.

The name *Aulonocara nyassae* has been incorrectly applied to many different species, mainly members of the rock-dwelling group, by the aquarium trade. The confusion has not been restricted to the aquarium hobby, either. Eccles (in Eccles & Trewavas, 1989) found that the three specimens Regan used in 1922 for the description of *A. nyassae* in fact included two different species. As Regan did not designate a holotype, Eccles had to select a lectotype from the three specimens to serve as the definitive specimen for *A. nyassae*. He chose the specimen from which the drawing in Regan's description was made; the other species he described as *Aulonocara guentheri*. Eccles recognized *A. nyassae* in a population south of Boadzulu Island and gave a detailed description of its live coloration, which agrees with that of the fishes from Mazinzi Bay.

A. guentheri is common in the southeastern arm of the lake and is occasionally caught in beach seines in Senga Bay. I have observed this species in Monkey Bay, near Kadango, and near Makanjila Point. Before the onslaught by beach-seine fishermen *A. guentheri* was a common cichlid of shallow sandy habitats where it was normally seen foraging in small groups of about 10 individuals. Males and females, which both have yellow on the lower part of the head, are found in the same group, and such groups frequently mingle with parties of other sand-dwelling species. Males with territorial (breeding) coloration have not been observed underwater, but some have been found in the beach seines of local fishermen in November and December. This may suggest a restricted breeding season, but further observations are needed before a clear picture can be obtained.

Another species, *Aulonocara* sp. 'nyassae mumbo', was originally erroneously identified as a population of *A. nyassae* (Konings, 1990), but lacks the much enlarged infra-orbital bones of the latter. Moreover, the thick lips and stouter appearance suggest a generic placement other than in *Aulonocara*. Nevertheless, it remains in this genus as more research is required before it can be properly classified. *A.* sp. 'nyassae mumbo' lives at depths of between 30 and 45 meters (and probably deeper) at Mumbo Island. Males in breeding dress are seen amidst other foraging members of the group. They do not seem to be territorial.

Aulonocara gertrudae has a very wide distribution and is found on the western as well as the eastern shores of the lake. The northernmost population was found at Ikombe, Tanzania, in the extreme north of the lake, while the southernmost population is that at the type locality near Masinje, Malaŵi, on the east coast. It has been observed along the entire shoreline of Tanzania, and at Mdoka, Msuli, and Cape Manulo in Malaŵi, and also at Lumessi and Mala Point in Mozambique.

A. gertrudae appears to forage mainly in the somewhat muddy sediment on sandy bottoms near river mouths. It is usually found at depths of more than 15 meters, but north of the Ruhuhu River in Tanzania it seems to exploit the intermediate habitat (Konings, 1995a). Males of the northern populations have a bright orange patch on the shoulder which is absent in the southern populations, i.e. at Lundu and further south. *A. gertrudae* may be the sand-dwelling species most closely related to the rock-dwelling members of the genus.

Territorial males dig craters in the sand or defend a rocky cave (north of the Ruhuhu) or may dig a spawning pit against a rock. Spawning pits can be up to 50 cm deep where the composition of the substrate can accommodate such deep excavations. Females, which can easily be recognized by the yellow spots in the anal fin, forage in small groups in the neighborhood of the territorial males. Males in nuptial colors have been observed at all times of the year.

The fact that *A. gertrudae* of the populations north of the Ruhuhu River exhibit a different coloration and behavior to that of the other known populations could be interpreted as suggesting that they represent another species. However, the general morphology and the basic color pattern of male as well as female—the distinctive yellow spots in the anal fin in combination with the yellow ventral fins of the female are useful characteristics for distinguishing it *in vivo* from other *Aulonocara*—permits the grouping of all populations into a single species. The difference in spawning site preference in northern males may well be influenced by the lack of rock-dwelling *Aulonocara* north of

1. *Aulonocara rostratum* ♂ Chimwalani Reef
2. *Aulonocara rostratum* ♂ Kande Island
3. *Aulonocara rostratum* ♀ Luwala Reef
4. *Aulonocara nyassae* ♂ Masasa Reef
5. *Aulonocara* cf. *macrochir* ♂ Monkey Bay
6. *Aulonocara auditor* holotype
7. *Aulonocara* sp. 'nyassae mumbo' ♂ Mumbo Island
8. *Aulonocara nyassae* ♀ Masasa Reef

1. *Aulonocara gertrudae* ♂ Chiofu

2. *Aulonocara gertrudae* ♂ Chiofu

3. *Aulonocara gertrudae* ♀ Makonde

4. *Aulonocara guentheri* ♀ Thumbi East Island

5. *Aulonocara gertrudae* ♂ Lupingu

6. *Aulonocara guentheri* ♂ Thumbi East Island

the Ruhuhu River.

Aulonocara brevinidus is also known as "Aulonocara Blue Gold Sand". The northernmost localities where *A. brevinidus* has been observed are at Lupingu and Manda, Tanzania, while the southernmost population known is at Ntekete and Nkhomo Reef, Malaŵi. In Mozambique it has been found at Wikihi, Mala Point, and at Chiloelo. Males of the northern and southern populations do not differ significantly in their territorial (breeding) coloration. At all known localities *A. brevinidus* has been found at a depth of about 20 meters. Males are territorial and defend a very shallow spawning pit no deeper than 2-3 cm with a diameter of about 15-20 cm. Sometimes a male defends a sandy patch between small stones. Territorial males station themselves about two meters from each other in the Masinje population. Only a few territorial males of the other populations have been observed and these were more than five meters apart. The gut of the single specimen examined for stomach contents contained sand grains, tiny snails, and rather large (1.5-2 cm) shrimp-like crustaceans.

Aulonocara aquilonium was described in 1995 from a population at Mdoka in Malaŵi. It had been exported previously as "Aulonocara Auditor". In November and December *A. aquilonium* is abundant at the rock-sand interfaces near Mdoka and this is the period during which territorial males are observed; in June foraging individuals are seen but in much smaller numbers. Territorial males defend a very shallow depression in the sand against conspecific males only, and are found at a depth of approximately 20 meters. Foraging females and non-territorial males congregate in large schools and are found over the sand between and near rocks, at depths varying from 12 to 25 meters.

According to George Turner (pers. comm.) a species which I previously placed in *Lethrinops* (as *L.* sp. 'maylandi mix') is probably conspecific with a species he terms *Aulonocara* sp. 'pyramid' (Turner, 1996). *A.* sp. 'pyramid' has a small size—about 10 cm maximum. It has been found at two localities: Kande Island and Luwala Reef. I named this species "Maylandi Mix" because at both locations it was found mingling with schools of other *Aulonocara*—*A. kandeense* at Kande Island and *A. maylandi* at Luwala Reef. Males (apparently in breeding color but not territorial) as well as females were seen in these schools but I could not find out on what or how they feed. The most interesting feature of this species is that it occurs sympatrically with two different but closely related *Aulonocara* species which live at two isolated localities in the lake, about 220 km apart! Turner (1996) collected this species between Monkey Bay and Boadzulu Island in the southeastern arm of the lake, at a depth between 30 and 72 meters.

Lethrinops

Species of the genus *Lethrinops* are among the most successful cichlids of the lake. These cichlids have occupied the largest habitat—the vast stretches of sandy and muddy bottoms in the lake, about 95% of the total available living space for bottom-dwelling fishes—and one which provides them with ample space and food. They are probably equaled in their success only by the utaka.

All members of *Lethrinops* have a silvery body when not breeding and most species gather in large schools when foraging. The generally small size of most *Lethrinops* dictates gregarious behavior, as many predators are confused when they have to deal with an abundance of prey. They cannot focus on a particular individual and hence find it more difficult to seize a victim. Only when a member of the school behaves differently, or when it has a distinct color pattern, is it immediately singled out by predators as a target. This is probably the reason why most sand-dwelling species look rather similar. We may also invert this statement and argue that a sand-dwelling cichlid can normally be successful only if it looks like the others. The same is true of species that feed in the open water (utaka, *Rhamphochromis*, and *Diplotaxodon*).

The silvery bodies of *Lethrinops* reflect the sunlight and so they also appear to blend with the background—the sand. Before over-fishing in the southern part of the lake took its toll

Lethrinops was one of the most important catches for commercial trawlers.

Most species of the genus appear to have a specific breeding season; for most of the year, however, they merely forage in the sand or mud. Breeding takes place in a group (in those species that are gregarious) and males usually construct bowers on the sand. All breeding males have a specific coloration and distinct egg-spots in their anal fins, and are thus able to attract females (by flaunting these spots) and lead them to their spawning sites. Except for a few species that do not construct a bower (see page 369), all *Lethrinops* (as far as has been ascertained) construct sand-castles on the open sand. Males defend their bowers with vigor, and never leave them unguarded during the day. This is important as competing conspecific males have their territories nearby and many ripe, but non-territorial males, will be waiting for a male to vacate his site. At the end of the day some males, in particular those at the periphery of the colony, leave their territories and join the females in a school for the night. Males with prime positions in the center of the arena remain there during the night (Jay Stauffer, pers. comm.). Every territorial male improves on the construction of the spawning site and the strongest (largest) males usually have (or acquire) the biggest and tallest bowers.

Common *Lethrinops*

A number of species that live in the shallows are sometimes exported as aquarium fishes, normally when they are exhibiting their breeding colors.

Lethrinops microstoma has been given the trade name "Lethrinops auritus" but this name belongs to another species (see page 369). Another trade name is "Lethrinops Yellow-Black Dorsal". It has a lake-wide distribution and builds its bowers in the intermediate habitat. Its sand-castle bowers are enormously high for what is a relatively small cichlid (maximum total length about 15 cm). During the breeding season (from August to December) this species is the most frequently seen member of its genus, and the moonscaped sand often betrays its presence. *L. microstoma* feeds predominantly on zooplankton and other small invertebrates which it finds just above the sand. Sometimes it feeds more than a meter off the bottom, which is remarkable for a *Lethrinops*. The fact that this species gathers at places where plankton is abundant may indicate a feeding behavior reminiscent of that of the utaka.

Lethrinops parvidens (*L.* sp. 'microstoma gold' (Konings, 2001) has now been identified as this species) occurs along the Malaŵi east coast near Ntekete and in the southeastern arm of the lake. In morphology and size it is very similar to *L. microstoma*, with which it occurs sympatrically. At N'kolongwe, Mozambique, I have found it together with *L. microstoma* over pure sand and males had built bowers on the sand. These were identical to those of *L. microstoma* and females could probably distinguish between the two species only by the male breeding colors. Male *L. parvidens* have a golden yellow blaze on the head, which is not seen in *L. microstoma*.

Lethrinops lethrinus, the type species of the genus, is another species that is regularly encountered. It has a lake-wide distribution and is one of the few Malaŵian cichlids that can occasionally be found upstream of river mouths. Its maximum standard length is recorded as 16 cm (Eccles & Trewavas, 1989). Its food consists of small crustaceans and insect larvae which it finds in soft substrates consisting of a mixture of sand and mud. *L. lethrinus* can be distinguished from other *Lethrinops* by the two spotted horizontal lines on the flank. Males in breeding color are turquoise blue. The pigmentation pattern resembles that of several *Protomelas* species and *L. lethrinus* is sometimes difficult to identify among *P. kirkii* (see page 286). Breeding males are found mainly from June to August. They make very large bowers that consist of a large horizontal circular "courtyard" surrounded by several (three to seven) large turrets of sand/mud. At the base of one of these turrets a small spawning pit is excavated. Probably because the substrate the males use is very loose their bowers often look sloppy. Near Otter Point most breeding males build their edifices at a depth of about seven meters.

The classification of Malaŵi cichlids is based

1. *Aulonocara aquilonium* ♂ Mdoka

2. *Aulonocara* sp. 'pyramid' ♂ Kande Island

4. *Aulonocara aquilonium* ♂ Mdoka

5. *Aulonocara aquilonium* ♀ Mdoka

3. *Aulonocara brevinidus* ♂ ♀ Liwani

1. *Lethrinops microstoma* ♂ Aquarium

2. *Lethrinops microstoma* ♂ N'kolongwe

3. *Lethrinops parvidens* ♂ Aquarium

primarily on the basic pigmentation pattern, and this has led to two new genera, i.e. *Taeniolethrinops* and *Tramitichromis*, being created for species that were previously assigned to *Lethrinops*. Following this principle we ought to assign *L. lethrinus* to the group of species that contains *Protomelas*, but since *lethrinus* is the type species of *Lethrinops* all species currently in *Protomelas* would then have to be assigned to *Lethrinops*, while all other *Lethrinops* species would then have to be assigned to a new genus. The confusion this would cause is probably not worth the effort of proving *L. lethrinus* closely related to *Protomelas*-like cichlids.

Lethrinops furcifer is the largest of the commonly-seen *Lethrinops* and its maximum total length can slightly exceed 20 cm. It is regularly caught in beach seines. Breeding males are blue with a beautiful metallic green head, and are sometimes exported as "Green Face Lethrinops". They construct enormous bowers and during the breeding season large numbers of these edifices moonscape the shallow water along sandy shores. Breeding has been observed from May to November. These cichlids feed on plankton and soft benthic invertebrates such as insect larvae.

Tramitichromis

The genus *Tramitichromis* is characterized by the peculiar shape of the lower pharyngeal bone of its members. The teeth on this bone are all slender and long; those situated at the front are the longest—an unusual feature. These long anterior teeth are further characterized by their long tips, which are bent backwards. In most other Malaŵi species the anterior pharyngeal teeth are small and their tips point forward. Another feature of *Tramitichromis* is the downward projecting anterior blade of the pharyngeal bone. The upper edge of this blade runs horizontally in most cichlids but in *Tramitichromis* it projects downwards (at more than 50° to the horizontal in *T. variabilis*). The reasons for these particular developments in *Tramitichromis* are unclear, but most likely their origin lies in their feeding behavior or the type of food.

The lower gill-rakers in *Tramitichromis* are squat and strong, as in most sand-sifting *Lethrinops*. The first two rakers are usually no more than small knobs on the gill arches. The central three to five rakers on the lower arches are wide and much larger. The tips of these broad rakers combine to form an almost horizontal grid at the bottom of the buccal cavity and this may be used to separate the heavier material from the lighter when a mouthful of sand and sediment is taken into the mouth. The heavier sand drops through the rakers and is carried to the outside via the gill slit, while the lighter material, including invertebrates and algae, remains inside the mouth. The strength of the rakers is probably needed to withstand the abrasive action of the sand. The need to keep the tips of the pharyngeal teeth in the same plane as the gill-rakers may have led to the situation seen in *Tramitichromis* (anterior teeth relatively longer than in other cichlids). The anterior pharyngeal teeth of *Lethrinops leptodon*, for example, are short and lie below the level of the raker-tips.

Five species of *Tramitichromis* have been described: *T. brevis*, *T. variabilis*, *T. lituris*, *T. intermedius* (see page 296), and *T. trilineatus*. I have never been able to examine specimens of *T. trilineatus*.

Tramitichromis brevis has been exported as "*Lethrinops variabilis*" and "*Lethrinops* Chizumulu" and is easily recognized by its small adult size (about 14 cm total length) and by the prominent diagonal stripe on its flank. It is a common cichlid which is found all around the lake. It has a preference for muddy bottoms between rocks where it feeds on worms and other soft invertebrates that live in the sediment on the bottom. At Likoma *T. brevis* is called *kambuzi wa chigongo*. It is possible that *T. brevis* breeds all the year round since males in breeding colors have been seen at different times of the year. The main feature of the male's bower is a small stone around which a semicircular rim of sand (oxbow) is deposited (see photo 7, page 366). The female lays her eggs as far as possible beneath the small stone.

At Magunga, Tanzania, I found a species of *Tramitichromis* that resembles *T. brevis* in melanin pattern but males construct a completely different bower. Instead of a sand-castle with a rock in its rim, males at Magunga defended a loose array of heaps of sand in the middle of which they had cleared a small patch as a spawning site. I refer to this species as *Tramitichromis* sp. 'brevis magunga'.

Tramitichromis sp. 'brevis two' differs from *T. brevis* by having an elongate toothed area on the lower pharyngeal bone (Ngatunga & Snoeks, 2004). I have not knowingly seen this species underwater.

In my opinion the type material of *Tramitichromis variabilis* consists of at least two different species; Matt Lisy (pers. comm.) has confirmed this and has a description for the second species in preparation. He found that all the specimens of the type series that are conspecific with the lectotype he has chosen for *T. variabilis* were collected in the southern part of the lake. The second species he found among the *T. variabilis* type material appears to have representatives in the northern as well as in the southern part of the lake and is characterized by a diagonal band of spots.

Cichlids that may be conspecific with *T. variabilis* are collected in Senga Bay and exported as "Lethrinops Red Flush". This cichlid has only vague markings on the body. In the aquarium the "Red Flush" male does not build a spawning pit; spawning takes place on the "virgin" sand (Peter Baasch, pers. comm.).

A species from Likoma Island, which I previously regarded as a form of *T. variabilis*, is now regarded as a different entity and referred to as *Tramitichromis* sp. 'variabilis likoma'. It lacks the diagonal band characteristic of the second (to be described) species from the type material of *T. variabilis*, but the anterior blade of the lower pharyngeal is steeply inclined.

A form Jay Stauffer and I collected at N'kolongwe exhibits a diagonal band but has a shallower body than *T. brevis*. It may be conspecific with a form Ngatunga & Snoeks (2004) refer to as *Tramitichromis* sp. 'maculae'. The latter also report a further species, termed *Tramitichromis* sp. 'variabilis deep', with a diagonal band of blotches; I have not seen this species underwater or in fishermen's nets.

Like *T. variabilis*, *Tramitichromis lituris*, as previously understood, has turned out to be polytypic. Lisy (pers. comm.) has found that the type material represents two species, one from the northern and one from the southern part of the lake, and designated a specimen from the northern part of the lake as lectotype of *T. lituris*. In addition he has a description for the southern species in preparation.

T. lituris has only recently been exported for the hobby for the first time. I have observed a breeding colony of this species near Mdoka (in November and December; it is unlikely that the species breeds throughout the year as it was not seen at the same location in May 1989), where most members of the school were found at a depth of seven to 15 meters. Some territorial males constructed a cave-crater type spawning site, but those on the open sand, where no rocks were available, constructed sand-castle bowers.

This breeding colony of *T. lituris* at Mdoka was mixed with a breeding colony of *Mchenga thinos*, males of which build shallow bowers in the sand when breeding at deeper (than seven meters) levels, though some males instead defend a spawning site on top of a rock. But not only the *Mchenga* but also some *T. lituris* males had constructed their bowers on top of rocks! In utaka such unusual behavior can be explained by the observation that females feed from the plankton in open water and males are thus closer to the females (even if they have to carry the sand up the rock!). *Tramitichromis*, by contrast, forage on the sand, so one would expect that males that built spawning sites on top of rocks would reduce their chances of mating. At Mdoka, however, I found females about a meter above the substrate. Initially I assumed that these had been attracted there by the males with territories on rocks, but when I later examined a few preserved specimens I found their long guts (2.5 times standard length) completely filled with phytoplankton. It is thus possible that the males in the rocky area have adapted their choice of spawning site to take advantage of the fact that females feed in the open water column at times of a plankton bloom.

The lower pharyngeal jaw of *T. lituris* from Mdoka has the typical shape of that of a *Tramitichromis* and this begs the question what

1. *Lethrinops lethrinus* ♂ Otter Point

5. *Lethrinops lethrinus* ♀ Mazinzi Reef

2. *Lethrinops lethrinus* ♂ Otter Point

6. *Lethrinops furcifer* ♀ Tchinga Reef

3. *Lethrinops furcifer* ♂ Chizumulu Island

7. *Tramitichromis brevis* ♂ Chizumulu Island

4. *Tramitichromis brevis* ♂ Mala Point

8. *Tramitichromis brevis* ♀ Hai Reef

1. *Tramitichromis* sp. 'brevis magunga' ♀ Magunga
7. *Tramitichromis* sp. 'brevis magunga' ♂ Magunga

2. *Tramitichromis* sp. 'brevis magunga' ♂ Magunga
3. *Tramitichromis trilineatus* Chembe
8. *Tramitichromis variabilis* ♂ Aquarium

4. *Tramitichromis* sp. 'variabilis likoma' ♂ Likoma
5. *Tramitichromis lituris* ♂ Mdoka
6. *Tramitichromis lituris* ♀ Mdoka
9. *Tramitichromis* sp. 'maculae' ♂ N'kolongwe
10. *Tramitichromis lituris* ♂ Mdoka

its function is in this (sometimes) plankton-feeding species. It is thus possible that the peculiar shape of the lower pharyngeal is a no longer functional, inherited, trait rather than an adaptation to current feeding behavior (in other *Tramitichromis* species as well), in which case the particular structure of this bone can indeed be used to define lineages among some Lake Malaŵi cichlids.

Be that as it may, it is remarkable that a bottom-feeding species, which apparently needs the protection (during spawning) of a cave-crater nest, can switch to an open type of bower a few meters above the lake floor. And the strategy is apparently successful, as I have observed females accepting this alternative type of bower and spawning with the owner.

A species which I have named *Tramitichromis* sp. 'lituris yellow' was exported on one occasion from Senga Bay but has never been seen again. The exported specimens had an average total length of about 12 cm. The species is readily recognizable by its yellow anal and pelvic fins. The throat and breast have a yellow cast as well. A species Turner (1996) refers to as *T. lituris*, collected in the southeastern arm of the lake, may be conspecific with *T.* sp. 'lituris yellow', but is more likely another species altogether, possibly the new southern species mentioned above, as Turner doesn't mention yellow pelvic fins. Nor does Lisy (pers. comm.) with regard to the new species. I therefore believe there may be at least three species in what I will term the *T. lituris* group and Turner's species from the south is for the time being termed *Tramitichromis* sp. 'false lituris'.

In addition to the new species already mentioned, the genus *Tramitichromis* encompasses many more species than previously thought. Along the four kilometers of shoreline at Chembe at Cape Maclear at least six (!) different species of this genus have been distinguished. Four of them breed at the same time of year and their breeding arenas are only a few hundred meters apart. To make matters worse all these species have very similar male breeding coloration but they differ in bower construction and depth of breeding. Although at least four of these forms have been collected and have been proven to be genetically distinct (Kidd *et al.*, 2006) many more species abound in the shallow waters of the lake.

The species catalogued below were observed underwater, males in breeding colors were photographed, and the shape of the bower and depth recorded. Females of most of these species all look alike and cannot be distinguished morphologically. I have not used any of the names Kidd *et al.* published to designate these species as there is no published record of male breeding color and so I cannot definitely match them to the forms I have seen in the field.

In August 2006 I found a breeding arena consisting of 50-100 males at Chembe, near Fat Monkeys campsite, at a depth of between four and seven meters. The site was dived in the morning and in the afternoon, but females were very rare and may visit only when ready to spawn. The construction of the bower was peculiar: most were a perfect volcano-shape with a horizontal spawning platform. The base of each "volcano" was surrounded and demarcated by a shallow ditch, a perfect circle, from which the male had taken the material to construct his bower. This species, here referred to as *Tramitichromis* sp. 'chembe circle', probably has a wider distribution than Cape Maclear, and I have also seen (deserted) bowers of this particular type at Kanchedza Island.

Another species, *Tramitichromis* sp. 'chembe shallow', was found at the same location along Chembe Beach but in water just one to two meters deep. In August 2006 males were rare and it was apparently not their breeding season. A few males weakly defended a tall volcano-like sand-castle with a horizontal spawning platform surrounded by a rim that had a raised lip on one side (Kidd *et al.* (2006) have coined the term "backsplash" (= splash-back in some countries) for this feature). These bowers did not show any circular demarcation at the base. This species may be conspecific with *Tramitichromis* sp. 'lituris yellow gular' (Kidd *et al.*, 2006).

At Liwani, just south of the Nsinje River on the Malaŵi eastern shore, I found yet another *Tramitichromis*, males of which construct small to medium-sized bowers with a typical horizontal spawning platform surrounded by a rim. Since this bower is different from that of other species of the extreme shallow water (1-2 meters) I regard this a distinct species and refer to it as *Tramitichromis* sp. 'east-coast shallow'.

At Mvunguti a slender-bodied species, *Tramitichromis* sp. 'mvunguti', occurs in the shallow (3-5 meters) water. Males construct medium-sized bowers with a horizontal spawning platform surrounded by a rim that is irregular or has two opposing back-splashes.

Further south, at Songwe Hill, males of a small species, *Tramitichromis* sp. 'red gular', defend very shallow bowers in two to three meters of water. The bower seems to consist of just the back splash and is barely raised above the surrounding sand. Breeding males are characterized by a deep orange-red throat.

A bower similar to that built by *T.* sp. 'red gular' is constructed by *Tramitichromis* sp. 'kande' at Kande Island on the central western shore of the lake, but males of the latter species have a very distinct gold-orange patch on head and nape. *T.* sp. 'kande' was found breeding at a depth of about eight meters.

Small *Lethrinops*

Lethrinops auritus is the smallest *Lethrinops* that has been described, growing to a total length of a mere 8 cm. As far as I know it has never been exported as an aquarium fish but it would surely make a good resident, even in small tanks. I have observed this little *Lethrinops* at (among other places) Otter Point where males construct their very elaborate spawning sites in the muddy sediment on the bottom. During the breeding season, which is from June to September, breeding *L. auritus* are rather common in the southeastern arm of the lake. Most of the territorial males are found at a depth of about seven meters but they are also common at Masasa Reef at a depth of about 16 meters. The bower consists of a circle of 2-25 mud cones with an overall diameter of approximately a meter. In the center of the circle the male makes another cone, usually of sand, alongside which he digs a spawning pit with a diameter of about 10-20 cm. The movement of the water frequently destroys the mud-cones so that males have continually to repair their "courtyards". *L. auritus* is a deep-bodied cichlid with a rather large mouth. It dines on all kinds of small organisms such as invertebrates and occasionally diatoms, sifting the sediment and the sand-mud mixture of its habitat.

In May 1995 I found another small *Lethrinops*, dubbed *Lethrinops* sp. 'auritus lion', in the narrow bay at Lion's Cove, locally known as T'hoto. Unfortunately I saw only a single male who had established his territory on the sand at a depth of about 25 meters. The bower consisted of several heaps of sand which were, however, not placed in a circle. The heaps were about 15 cm tall and sited 50 to 80 cm apart. As is common among *Lethrinops* the females were silvery without markings.

There are several other species that resemble *L. auritus* in color and shape, but all of these build different types of spawning sites. At Selewa I found a breeding colony of an undescribed species, *Lethrinops* sp. 'auritus selewa', males of which construct spawning sites against large rocks in the intermediate habitat. This species too is not much longer than 10 cm and would be a good aquarium resident.

An undescribed cichlid that resembles the rock-frequenting *Aulonocara* species is seen at many locations around the lake, but is in fact a small *Lethrinops* which grows no larger than 10 cm. I have named it *Lethrinops* sp. 'nyassae' to indicate that it occurs all around the lake. This sand-grubbing cichlid is normally found in shallow water; it prefers sandy substrates near rocks and, unusually for *Lethrinops*, seeks shelter among rocks when threatened. Territorial males are found throughout the year but do not construct a spawning edifice themselves, although they do sometimes defend large craters that are the remains of the spawning sites of other species; otherwise they simply defend a shallow irregular pit in the sand. Females are led to the spawning site. This species is often found in small groups. Small rocky areas bordering a long stretch of sand sometimes harbor more than a hundred individuals.

A deep-dwelling species with a close resem-

1. *Tramitichromis* sp. 'lituris yellow' Aquarium

6. *Tramitichromis* sp. 'false lituris' ♂ Monkey Bay

2. *Tramitichromis* sp. 'chembe circle' ♂ Chembe

7. *Tramitichromis* sp. 'chembe circle' ♂ Chembe

3. *Tramitichromis* sp. 'chembe shallow' ♂ Chembe

8. *Tramitichromis* sp. 'chembe circle' ♀ Chembe

4. *Tramitichromis* sp. 'east-coast shallow' ♂ Liwani

9. *Tramitichromis* sp. 'chembe shallow' ♂ Chembe

5. *Tramitichromis* sp. 'east-coast shallow' ♀ Liwani

10. *Tramitichromis* sp. 'east-coast shallow' ♂ Liwani

1. *Tramitichromis* sp. 'mvunguti' ♂ Mvunguti

2. *Tramitichromis* sp. 'red gular' ♂ Songwe Hill

3. *Tramitichromis* sp. 'red gular' ♀ Songwe Hill

4. *Tramitichromis* sp. 'kande' ♂ Kande Island

5. *Lethrinops auritus* ♂ Masasa Reef

6. *Lethrinops* sp. 'auritus selewa' ♂ Selewa

7. *Tramitichromis* sp. 'mvunguti' ♂ Mvunguti

8. *Tramitichromis* sp. 'red gular' ♂ Songwe Hill

9. *Tramitichromis* sp. 'kande' ♂ Kande Island

10. *Lethrinops auritus* ♂ Otter Point

11. *Lethrinops* sp. 'auritus lion' ♂ Lion's Cove

blance to *L.* sp. 'nyassae' and to members of the genus *Aulonocara* (so much so that Ribbink and his co-workers (1983b) named it *Aulonocara* 'yellow collar') occurs at Thumbi West Island, at the islet of Masimbwe south of Likoma, at Masinje, and at Chiloelo, Mozambique. At Thumbi West it lives at a depth of about 35-50 meters while at Masimbwe a breeding colony has been found at 53 meters. Males of this species, *Lethrinops* sp. 'yellow collar', do build bowers of their own. These are about a meter in diameter and saucer-shaped, and often excavated alongside a large rock. In the center of the edifice the male constructs a small spawning platform. Spawning has not been observed. Males of the populations at Chiloelo and Masinje build bowers on the open sand but the construction resembles that of the Masimbwe population, albeit without rock. The bower resembles an oxbow (back splash), with a shallow heap of sand, the spawning cone, at its center (see photo 6, page 374).

Lethrinops sp. 'mdoka red', a species that does not construct a bower, occurs at Mdoka, where it is found together with *L.* sp. 'nyassae'. In this case females have to rely on the specific coloration of the males (which is different but not very conspicuous) and/or their scent when choosing a spawning partner, as neither of the two species builds a characteristic bower by which the correct male could be identified. Male *L.* sp. 'mdoka red' have a reddish blotch behind the gill cover and male *L.* sp. 'nyassae' have a prominent golden-yellow blaze on head and nape.

A small *Aulonocara*-like *Lethrinops* from Tanzania, *Lethrinops* sp. 'aulonocara type', was introduced into the hobby some years ago. Male breeding coloration resembles that of an *Aulonocara* but the species lacks the large sensory pores on the head, characteristic of members of that genus.

Recently a number of additional small *Lethrinops* have been exported from the Tanzanian part of the lake but I have not yet been able to observe these underwater. One of them, *Lethrinops* sp. 'red cap', is rather popular and characterized by an orange-red patch on head and nape. Purportedly it was collected near Itungi. This species may in fact belong to *Tramitichromis*. The same generic question mark applies to *Lethrinops* sp. 'mbasi', sometimes termed the "Mbasi Rainbow". Yet another species from an unknown location in Tanzania exhibits narrow red bars on a rather dark body. I refer to this form as *Lethrinops* sp. 'red bar'.

Carsten Gissel (pers. comm.) collected another red-capped *Lethrinops* at Tsano Rock in the southeastern arm of the lake. He caught a few specimens of *Lethrinops* sp. 'red cap tsano' at a depth of 4-5 meters on the sand, but not far from rocks. He did not see any bowers and males never built spawning sites in his aquaria either. He further found that females do not mouthbrood for longer than about 10 days while similar-sized *Lethrinops* usually carry their brood for about three weeks. The largest number of fry per brood was recorded at 30.

Lethrinops macrophthalmus has been found only near Nkhotakota, at Jalo Reef. It is rather small, attaining a maximum total length of about 11 cm. It has not yet been exported and very little is known about it. It feeds on a wide variety of foods including insect larvae, diatoms, and plant roots (Trewavas, 1931).

A few small elongate species are regularly caught in beach seine nets off sandy shores in quiet bays. The bottom is usually overlain with a layer of sediment which supports the invertebrates that are sifted out by these cichlids. One of them, *Lethrinops albus*, is an attractive and relatively small species (maximum total length approximately 13 cm), characterized by a very rounded head and almost vertical snout. At Kande Island territorial males do not construct a spawning edifice but defend a spawning site close to rocks. At Mphandikucha Island males defend a small heap of sand that serves as a back-splash in the very shallow water. The sandy bottom here is rippled by wave action and males use the troughs of these ripples as spawning sites (see photo 2, page 375). Females are courted all over the surrounding area and led to the spawning sites on the sand. Breeding has been observed in May, June, and October.

A species similar to *L. albus,* but with a number of enlarged teeth on the pharyngeals, is infrequently caught at Kambiri Point. It is sometimes exported, when in full breeding color, as "Lethrinops Rounded Head". The classification of *Lethrinops*-like cichlids is so complicated that the species cannot be confidently assigned without detailed investigation, but according to Ben Ngatunga (pers. comm.), who has examined this cichlid, it is probably *Lethrinops marginatus*. Ngatunga & Snoeks (2004) synonymized *L. oculatus* with *L. marginatus*.

A *Lethrinops* in Liuli Bay has also been considered a candidate for *L. marginatus* (Konings 2001: 292), but in the light of Ngatunga's identification of the Kambiri Point form is now regarded as a separate species, *Lethrinops* sp. 'marginatus liuli'. It was found in rather shallow water, at a depth of about five meters, where males defended small bowers with a diameter of about 25 cm.

Lethrinops sp. 'longimanus likoma' is a small species (maximum total length about 10 cm) found at Likoma Island and at Mala Point, Mozambique. A large breeding colony was observed at Mala Point (in November), with hundreds of females and non-territorial males gathered into a large school. A few males were territorial and had made large circular constructions, sometimes against a large rock, at depths varying between 15 and 30 meters. The edge of the bower was marked by 3-9 mud cones but there was no central spawning cone; spawning takes place on the sand at the center of the ring of cones. Feeding has not been observed and it may be that these individuals were gathered there for breeding purposes only. I have named this species "Longimanus Likoma" because in shape and in the structure of the mouth it resembles the larger *L. longimanus* (see page 394).

Lethrinops sp. 'micrentodon makokola' is found around Makokola Reef in the southeastern arm of the lake. Males stake out territories between small rocks in the intermediate zone and construct a shallow saucer-shaped spawning site. Small rocks are normally included in the construction. The spawning site is a small heap of sand piled in the center of the bower (Baasch, 1992b). Maximum total length is about 13 cm for males, while females, which produce 50-60 fry per brood, can attain a maximum length of approximately 10 cm.

In Lake Malombe *Lethrinops turneri* is the most important commercial species with 2,500 metric tons seined each year (Turner, 1996). It also occurs in Lake Malaŵi where it is restricted to the southeastern arm of the lake. I have seen it at a depth of about 10 meters at Mazinzi Reef. *L. turneri* feeds by scooping up the upper layer of silt/mud from the sand and sifting it for anything edible. Turner found mostly copepods and insect larvae in stomach analyses.

At Boadzulu Island I have encountered a small species of *Lethrinops* characterized by bright yellow pectoral fins. It was seen in the intermediate habitat over sand and only a few individuals were observed. It is possible that this a much more common species at deeper levels over open sand but at the island I found only solitary individuals at a depth of about 30 meters. I refer to this species as *Lethrinops* sp. 'boadzulu'.

Large *Lethrinops*

There are a number of *Lethrinops* that are larger than the species of the previous group and even more difficult to assign to described species. I have examined several of these species and could assign only some of them with "certainty" to a scientifically known species. Even then such identifications tend to hold good only until a similar form is found which fits the scientific description even better! Describing Malaŵi cichlids is extremely difficult, at least if we want to avoid creating synonyms, and next to impossible in the case of *Lethrinops* unless the particular form has been observed in its natural environment. The following species have been kept in the aquarium but very few differences in behavior have been found. The identification of some of them is thus questionable.

One species that may not be that difficult to identify underwater is *Lethrinops macrochir*. It is characterized by a deep body, a yellowish snout, and yellow ventral and anal fins, the latter with yellow egg-spots. The body has an overall light golden sheen. The breeding color of males is dark blue-brown. On the flanks there are two diagonal lines which overlap beneath

1. *Lethrinops* sp. 'nyassae' ♂ Mdoka

2. *Lethrinops* sp. 'yellow collar' ♂ Masimbwe (Likoma)

3. *Lethrinops* sp. 'mdoka red' ♂ Mdoka

4. *Lethrinops* sp. 'red cap' ♂ Aquarium

5. *Lethrinops* sp. 'red cap tsano' ♂ Aquarium

6. *Lethrinops* sp. 'yellow collar' ♂ Masinje

7. *Lethrinops* sp. 'yellow collar' ♀ Masinje

8. *Lethrinops* sp. 'aulonocara type' ♂ Aquarium

9. *Lethrinops* sp. 'aulonocara type' ♀ Aquarium

10. *Lethrinops* sp. 'red bar' ♂ Aquarium

11. *Lethrinops* sp. 'red cap tsano' ♀ Aquarium

1. *Lethrinops macrophthalmus* ♂ Jalo Reef

2. *Lethrinops albus* ♂ Mphandikucha Island

3. *Lethrinops albus* ♀ Kande Island

4. *Lethrinops* sp. 'longimanus likoma' ♂ Mala Point

5. *Lethrinops marginatus* ♂ Senga Bay

6. *Lethrinops* sp. 'marginatus liuli' ♂ Liuli

7. *Lethrinops* sp. 'boadzulu' Boadzulu Island

8. *Lethrinops* sp. 'mbasi' ♂ Aquarium

9. *Lethrinops albus* ♂ Kande Island

10. *Lethrinops* sp. 'longimanus likoma' ♂ Cobwé

11. *Lethrinops* sp. 'micrentodon makokola' ♂ Makokola Reef

12. *Lethrinops turneri* ♂ Mazinzi Reef

the spinous part of the dorsal, a feature also seen in *Lethrinops leptodon* (see below) and *L. marginatus*, and forming a dusky blotch. The last-named two species, however, do not have red lappets in the dorsal and lack the yellow color on the snout and fins. Turner (1996) reports on *L. macrochir* from Lake Malombe, where breeding males lack the red marginal band in the dorsal, which is yellow instead. The simplest way to identify *L. macrochir*, however, is the manner in which it rams its head into very coarse sand or gravel in search of insect larvae. *L. macrochir* is found almost exclusively over gravelly bottoms, but before beach seining was banned it showed up regularly in the nets of fishermen in Senga Bay where the bottom is pure sand without gravel. Breeding males even use the coarse sand/gravel to construct their bowers; and only the spawning dish inside the volcano is meticulously cleaned of coarse material so that the fine-grained sand clearly demarcates the spawning surface. *L. macrochir* grows to an average size of 15 cm and is rather common at depths between 10 and 40 meters (Eccles & Lewis, 1978).

Males of a species that resembles *L. macrochir* were found at Nkhudzi at a depth of about 12 meters. Only two males in breeding color were seen and they were not territorial. *Lethrinops* sp. 'macrochir nkhudzi' appears to be several centimeters smaller than *L. macrochir* and is further distinguished by an orange patch on head and nape.

At Mumbo Island I encountered a small breeding group of *Lethrinops* at a depth of about eight meters. Feeding behavior has not been observed but the few males seen had constructed their bowers using gravel, in a way reminiscent of *L. macrochir*. This species, *Lethrinops* sp. 'macrochir mumbo', is here regarded different because females are silvery without any yellow on the lower part of the body.

Lethrinops lunaris grows to a maximum total length of about 16 cm and is closely related to *L. leptodon*. Trewavas (1931), however, described *L. lunaris* as having only two rows of teeth in the lower jaw whereas *L. leptodon* has three to four. The specimens infrequently collected for the hobby in Senga Bay have two rows of teeth in the lower jaw, and on this feeble basis I have identified them as *L. lunaris*. According to Ngatunga & Snoeks (2004) *Lethrinops lunaris* is characterized by an elongate dark spot on the lateral line between the 4th and 12th dorsal spines and by a shorter head than *L. leptodon* and *L. lethrinus*. It usually also has more soft dorsal-fin rays (11-13) than the latter two species, which both have 9-11 dorsal rays.

According to Eccles & Lewis (1978), *Lethrinops leptodon* appears to be restricted to the northern part of the lake where it is caught regularly in beach seines. On two occasions, however, I have received and examined specimens purporting to be this species from Senga Bay in the south of the lake. Both specimens had enlarged teeth on the lower pharyngeal bone, and one of them even had several molariform teeth. This is not in agreement with the type specimens of either *L. leptodon* or *L. lunaris*, but, since little is known about the variability of this character, these southern forms are here regarded as conspecific with *L. leptodon*. The food of this elongate *Lethrinops* ranges from insect larvae and crustaceans to zooplankton.

Lethrinops altus is found mainly over soft substrates such as mud or diatomaceous ooze in relatively shallow waters, while a similar species, *L. longipinnis*, occurs over similar substrates at deep levels (page 396). *L. altus* may have a lake-wide distribution. It has been seen at Thumbi East Island in the southern part at a depth of about three to 15 meters, but most specimens collected by trawlers were caught at depths ranging between 20 and 60 meters. *L. altus* attains an average total length of about 16 cm. Its food consists of insect larvae and other soft-structured invertebrates which are obtained by plunging its head, and often its entire body, into the very soft substrate. When *L. altus* is observed feeding it appears that it does not randomly plunge its head into the bottom but rather examines the surface before it dives quickly into the ooze.

Lethrinops sp. 'longipinnis ntekete' has been found in small numbers in shallow water only on the east coast near the village of Ntekete. Males, which have a maximum total length of approximately 19 cm, construct a type of bower that is unique among Malaŵian haplochromines. It consists of a large crater dug in the sandy bottom, bounded by a ring of five to eight large turrets, each about 30 cm high and about 50 cm wide at the base. The diameter of the complete structure is about two meters! Several of these constructions have been seen in two to three meters of water. Breeding males have been observed defending these peculiar spawning sites in November. Females are solitary and forage on the sand.

Four other *Lethrinops* species build turrets around the spawning site: *L. auritus* (see page 371), *L.* sp. 'auritus lion' (see page 369), *L.* sp. 'longimanus likoma' (see page 375), and *L. lethrinus* (see page 366). None of them digs a crater, but they instead construct turrets in a circle.

L. sp. 'longipinnis ntekete' resembles *L. longipinnis* in appearance but has a longer snout, a shallower body, and shorter pectoral fins than that species, which is known only from the southern part of the lake. Females have a mid-lateral stripe, not unlike that seen in most *Protomelas* species.

A species I previously (and erroneously) assigned to *L. oculatus* (now regarded a junior synonym of *L. marginatus*; see page 373) has proved to be yet another undescribed *Lethrinops* from shallow water and is now referred to as *Lethrinops* sp. 'yellow chest'. It was collected in Senga Bay by seining fishermen.

A rare and intriguing species has been photographed at Mbenji Island by Larry Johnson. It is characterized by a very rounded head and steeply inclined snout, weak jaws, and a very broad black diagonal stripe. These characters suggest that it might belong to *Mylochromis* (diagonal stripe), *Tramitichromis* (diagonal stripe and weak jaws), or *Lethrinops* (weak jaws and general morphology). Not until specimens can be examined with regard to jaw morphology can anything meaningful be said about the systematic placement of this species, but in the *interim* I refer to this cichlid as *Lethrinops* sp. 'mbenji roundhead'.

Taeniolethrinops

The genus *Taeniolethrinops* was erected by Eccles & Trewavas (1989) for the very large *Lethrinops*-like cichlids of the shallow sandy habitats of Lake Malaŵi. For some years it was thought to comprise just two species, *Taeniolethrinops praeorbitalis* and *Taeniolethrinops furcicauda*, until Turner (1996) examined the various sand-dwelling cichlids and suggested that there were at least three, perhaps four, of these large sand-grubbers.

One of the two diagnostic characters of the genus is a dark diagonal stripe from nape to caudal base, which, incidentally, is now known to be absent in adult individuals of the type species, *T. praeorbitalis*. Eccles & Trewavas (1989) suggested that *Taeniolethrinops laticeps* (which does exhibit a diagonal stripe) was perhaps not distinct from *T. praeorbitalis*, but Turner (1996) found that the former species is distinct and often found sympatric with the latter. Trewavas (1931) synonymized *Lethrinops macrorhynchus* Regan, 1922 with *praeorbitalis* but Turner (1996) re-examined the type of *macrorhynchus* and noted that while it resembled *praeorbitalis* morphologically it also exhibited a very prominent diagonal stripe. He further noted that some small specimens collected near Nkhata Bay resembled *macrorhynchus*.

Taeniolethrinops macrorhynchus is distinguished from *T. laticeps* by having a noticeably longer snout; in fact the snout is about as long as that of *T. praeorbitalis,* but, as mentioned earlier, the latter species lacks a diagonal band on the flank. Non-breeding individuals of the fourth species, *T. furcicauda*, are easily recognized by the yellow coloration on the lower half of the body and fins, and by the distinct diagonal stripe. There are more differences between these species which will be discussed below. I have been fortunate enough to observe three of these species breed in the lake and here too they show differences. All four species are sympatric at Luwala and Chimwalani reefs in the southeastern arm of the lake.

The largest species of the genus, *T. praeorbitalis*, is found at depths of between five and 40 meters. It attains a maximum total length of

1. *Lethrinops macrochir* ♂ Otter Point

5. *Lethrinops macrochir* ♀ Boadzulu Island

2. *Lethrinops* sp. 'macrochir nkhudzi' ♂ Nkhudzi

6. *Lethrinops macrochir* ♂ Otter Point

3. *Lethrinops lunaris* ♂ Senga Bay

7. *Lethrinops lunaris* ♂ Aquarium

8. *Lethrinops* sp. 'macrochir mumbo' ♂ Mumbo Island

4. *Lethrinops* sp. 'macrochir mumbo' ♂ Mumbo Island

9. *Lethrinops* sp. 'macrochir mumbo' ♀ Mumbo Island

1. *Lethrinops leptodon* ♀ Chembe

5. *Lethrinops leptodon* ♂ Chiloelo

2. *Lethrinops altus* Harbour Island

6. *Lethrinops altus* Harbour Island

3. *Lethrinops* sp. 'longipinnis ntekete' ♂ Ntekete

7. *Lethrinops* sp. 'longipinnis ntekete' ♂ Ntekete

4. *Lethrinops* sp. 'yellow chest' ♂ Senga Bay

8. *Lethrinops* sp. 'mbenji roundhead' Mbenji Island

about 30 cm and I have seen it only in the southern part of the lake, south of Nkhotakota. I have previously reported (Konings, 2001) that the species occurs throughout the lake but I was confused by other, look-alike species.

T. praeorbitalis is found over purely sandy areas as well as in the vicinity of rocks. It is very common at Chembe Beach (Cape Maclear) where it is found plunging its head into the mud-sand substrate and scooping up large quantities of material which are sifted through the gills. The long snout allows for sifting through a deeper layer of the substrate than most other species. While most sand-grubbing species sift through the upper 1-2 cm of the bottom, *T. praeorbitalis* "dives" as deep as 10 cm and creates quite large pits in the process. Digging individuals are often accompanied by *Cyrtocara moorii* or *Protomelas annectens* who scrutinize the material expelled from the sifter's gills for edible morsels. The food *T. praeorbitalis* extracts from the sand consists mostly of chironomid midge larvae but Turner (1996) reports that, large amounts of sand and detritus are ingested as well, along with diatomaceous material. Juvenile *T. praeorbitalis* also sometimes follow an older individual and feed on the invertebrates exposed by the digging of the larger fish.

Breeding males of *T. praeorbitalis* have been observed in July and August at Cape Maclear. They construct gigantic sandcastle bowers that can have a diameter of more than 2.5 meters! These large structures are surrounded by a ring of small pits where the male has removed sand to build the enormous wall of his spawning site. Most bowers were found at a depth of about 7-10 meters and the distance between bowers is usually more than five meters, with an estimated average of 8-10 meters. Male interaction was rarely seen—perhaps because of the distance between neighboring males—and most energy was spent in improving the bower and chasing away heterospecific intruders seeking to examine the freshly-exposed sand of the construct. I have not witnessed spawning, but males become wildly active when a ripe, prospecting female comes close to their domains. I have not yet observed fry-guarding females but would expect them to guard their offspring as *T. laticeps* and *T. furcicauda* do.

The species is distinguished from the other three species by the lack of a diagonal band and in addition from *T. laticeps* and *T. furcicauda* by a longer snout. In the aquarium *T. praeorbitalis* sometimes exhibits a diagonal band, depending on its mood (Peter Baasch, pers. comm.), but subadults in the lake (recognizable by the long yellow snout) lack the diagonal band. The snout in juveniles is not as long (relatively) as that of adult individuals.

Taeniolethrinops macrorhynchus was long synonymized with *T. praeorbitalis* and, as mentioned earlier, Turner (1996) was the first to cast doubt on this assumption. A long time ago I photographed some large sand-sifters in the northern part of the lake, identifying them as *T. praeorbitalis* although they showed a distinct diagonal band. These banded individuals also had a yellow snout but this was too long for them to be classified as *T. furcicauda*. Initially I thought that these were northern variants of *T. praeorbitalis* that did exhibit a diagonal band but later I found long-snouted *Taeniolethrinops* both with and without diagonal bands at Luwala Reef and these appeared to represent two different species. One of them was undoubtedly *T. praeorbitalis*, because that is the only species in this group without a diagonal band, and I think the other, banded, species could well have been *T. macrorhynchus* as it had a long snout and a slightly larger mouth. Instead of giving each population a different name, I prefer to group all the long-snouted forms with a distinct diagonal band together as *T. macrorhynchus*, including those along the northwestern shores of the lake which show yellow coloration on the snout and lower part of the body. I also include a form which has been imported as "Lethrinops Laticeps Itungi" (and sometimes as "Aulonocara Rostratum"). I have never seen breeding males of this species but a group of mouthbrooding females was encountered at a depth of about 20 meters at Luwala Reef, Malaŵi. *T. macrorhynchus* is distinguished from *T. laticeps* and *T. furcicauda* by having a long snout.

Taeniolethrinops laticeps is distinguished from *T. praeorbitalis* by a deeper and more robust body, a shorter caudal peduncle, lack of yellow coloration, a distinct black diagonal band, and a larger mouth. It is distinguished from *T. furcicauda* by a longer snout and lack of yellow coloration, and from *T. macrorhynchus* by a deeper and more robust body, a deeper head, and a shorter caudal peduncle.

T. laticeps is frequently encountered at depths of 20 meters and more when not breeding. It appears more common in the southern part of the lake but has also been found at Chizumulu Island and at Liuli in Tanzania. It seems to prefer a more sandy type of bottom to the shallow mud-sand mixture favored by *T. praeorbitalis*. Its diet is similar to that of the latter species (midge larvae) with lots of sand grains and sediment ingested as well.

The only breeding males that I have encountered excavated a deep crater (about 1.5 meters in diameter and about 60 cm deep) as a spawning dish. At both localities (Mumbo Island and Tsano Rock) these bowers were at a depth of 30 to 35 meters. On one occasion a male was seen to follow and court a ripe female for more than an hour, and at the time was in shallow water, far away from his bower; but early in the morning (before 08:00 hours) males seem to stay at their bowers and court females in the vicinity. Mouthbrooding females are normally found in the shallow intermediate habitat.

Taeniolethrinops furcicauda — at least the form I regard as representative of this species — is an elongate cichlid with a moderately rounded head and can be nearly as large as *T. praeorbitalis*, but appears more robust, similar to *T. laticeps*. Trewavas (1931) described *T. furcicauda* as having "an oblique dark band from nape to caudal" and the types I have seen still exhibited a distinct diagonal band. The form Turner (1996) regards as *T. furcicauda* lacks such a diagonal band. Needless to say, there are many more large sand-sifters in the lake and more work needs to be done to sort all of them out. I have seen "my" *T. furcicauda* only along the eastern shores of the lake, more specifically between central Mozambique and Luwala Reef in Malaŵi, but it may have a lake-wide distribution. A breeding group was observed at Lumessi in Mozambique, where, at a depth of about 35 meters, males had constructed enormous bowers with a diameter of at least 3 meters! Neighboring bowers were sometimes less than a meter away. Another breeding lek was observed at Liwani, just south of the Nsinje River on the Malaŵi east coast. Males here seemed more robust than those in the population at Lumessi and had enormous bowers in very shallow water, not much deeper than five meters. Females at both localities were indistinguishable. The silvery body has a dark diagonal stripe from the nape to the base of the tail. This stripe runs across the upper flanks, close to the base of the dorsal fin. The snout, lower parts of the body, anal fin, and lower lobe of the caudal are yellow. Some foraging individuals were found in the shallow sandy and intermediate habitat but these may have been ripe females searching for territorial males with whom to spawn. The normal foraging areas may be in much deeper regions as mouthbrooding females seem to be more common in shallow water than non-brooding individuals.

Taeniolethrinops sp. 'furcicauda ntekete' has been found near Ntekete on the eastern shores of Malaŵi. Breeding males construct large — approximately a meter in diameter — sand-castles on the sand. Several such bowers have been seen in November at a depth of about 15 meters. Females are found solitary, foraging on the sand in the vicinity of the males' bowers. *Taeniolethrinops* sp. 'furcicauda ntekete' bears some similarity to *T. furcicauda*, from which it differs by having a shorter snout and a larger eye. It grows to a total length of about 20 cm.

A smaller species, *Taeniolethrinops* sp. 'furcicauda liuli', has been found at a depth of about 15 meters in the bay at Liuli, Tanzania. Males construct very large bowers with a height of about 40-50 cm and a spawning dish with a diameter of about 75 cm. Such bowers have a diameter of more than a meter at the base. Females are characterized by a diagonal stripe on a silvery body and mouthbrooding individuals have been found over the sand surrounding the various bowers. The maximum total length of this species is estimated at about 16 cm.

Taeniolethrinops cyrtonotus was described

1. *Taeniolethrinops praeorbitalis* ♂ Chembe

2. *Taeniolethrinops praeorbitalis* ♀ Chembe

4. *Taeniolethrinops praeorbitalis* ♂ Chembe

5. *Taeniolethrinops macrorhynchus* Matema

3. *Taeniolethrinops macrorhynchus* ♀ Chimwalani Reef

6. *Taeniolethrinops macrorhynchus* ♂ Itungi

1. *Taeniolethrinops laticeps* ♀ Thumbi West Island

5. *Taeniolethrinops laticeps* ♂ Tsano Rock

2. *Taeniolethrinops* sp. 'furcicauda ntekete' ♂ Ntekete

6. *Taeniolethrinops furcicauda* ♀ Malopa

3. *Taeniolethrinops furcicauda* ♂ Liwani

4. *Taeniolethrinops furcicauda* ♂ Liwani

from a single specimen measuring 11 cm in length. It is a deep-bodied cichlid with a peculiarly rounded back, the highest point of which is at the center of the spinous part of the dorsal, after which it curves sharply down. There is a black line just below the base of the dorsal. The shape is reminiscent of that of the Volkswagen "Beetle". Before *T. cyrtonotus* was caught again (Ngatunga & Snoeks, 2004) it was thought that the type specimen might be an aberrant individual of a *Mylochromis* species (Eccles & Trewavas, 1989). Apparently the curiously curved back of *T. cyrtonotos*—the specific name means "arched back"—is also not a deformity as more than five individuals were collected that exhibited the same profile.

Chambos and their "boss"

The tilapiine cichlids in the lake form a completely separate group which includes three distinct lineages. We have already discussed *Oreochromis shiranus*, *O. karongae*, and *Tilapia rendalli*, all three prevalent in shallow, inshore areas (see page 304). An economically important lineage contains three species, *Oreochromis karongae*, *Oreochromis lidole*, and *Oreochromis squamipinnis*, which are all endemic to the lake and never found upstream in affluent rivers. These species closely resemble each other and probably have a recent common ancestor.

These tilapias are very important food fish and all are generally known as *chambo*. *Chambo* tops every menu in Malaŵi. Together with *ncheni* (*Rhamphochromis*) and *kampango* (*Bagrus meridionalis*) it is a highly recommended dish if you visit the lake.

It is barely possible to distinguish these three *chambos* just by looking at them. During the breeding period males (and sometimes females of *O. karongae*) assume a different coloration. *O. karongae* and *O. lidole* males become sooty black whereas *O. squamipinnis* males have a blue, white, or green blaze on the head, a dark gray chin, and a silvery body (Turner & Robinson, 1991).

The timing and place of breeding in the three species is important. *O. karongae* breeds from August to March in shallow (2-15 meters) water (Lowe, 1953; Turner & Robinson, 1991) whereas *O. lidole* breeds during the same period on steep rocky-sandy shores at a depth of about 15 to 30 meters. *O. squamipinnis* males breed from November to March at a depth of about four to 15 meters in intermediate or rocky habitats (Lowe, 1953).

O. lidole females are barred whereas breeding *O. karongae* females are yellowish-brown with only very faint barring. It is thus possible that segregation of the two species is guaranteed by males courting only the correct females. It is rather unusual for male cichlids to be able to make such a distinction, but this would explain why the females of the two species have distinctive color patterns.

O. lidole, with an average length of 33 cm, lives mostly offshore and congregates in large schools. Its food consists predominantly of phytoplankton. Males construct their large bowers on the sand near rocks. The bower is not simply an excavated crater but has an additional spawning-cone in the center. The diameter of such craters can exceed 2.5 meters! During the breeding season females swim in close formation in circles above the breeding arenas of the males. When a spawning site becomes available a ripe female descends to the bower and lays the only batch of eggs she will produce that breeding season. Mouthbrooding females withdraw among the plants or rocks in very shallow areas. After release, the fry slowly migrate to deeper levels as they mature. On attaining a length of about 15 cm they venture into the open water. Throughout their entire lives they remain together in groups, and before the large-scale fishing operations decimated most populations of this species, schools of more than 300 adult individuals could frequently be observed, especially in the south.

O. squamipinnis males also construct spawning cones in their bowers. Like *O. karongae* this species feeds on diatoms and detritus, and like it is found closer to shore than the far-ranging *O. lidole*. Adult *O. squamipinnis* have an average size of 26 cm and may shoal or form small foraging groups (George Turner, pers. comm.).

Males of all three species develop a genital tassel just behind the genital aperture during the breeding season. This consists of a mass of soft tissue a few centimeters long and resembles the shape and configuration of a clutch of eggs. After a female has deposited some eggs, she immediately collects them in her mouth. The male then drags his tassel over the spawning site, meanwhile discharging his sperm; the female tries to collect these "eggs" and sucks the sperm into her mouth so that the real eggs are fertilized. After the breeding season this tassel is re-absorbed by the male's body. These three species are the only cichlids in Lake Malaŵi with three-dimensional egg-dummies, comparable to the lappets on the pelvic fins of *Ophthalmotilapia* in Lake Tanganyika (Konings, 1998). Females guard their free-swimming fry among the plants or sometimes also among rocks until they are too big to fit inside the female's mouth.

Corematodus shiranus is a cichlid of haplochromine lineage whose size, coloration, and behavior mimic those of the *chambos*. Like the latter it has an average length of 27 cm and gray-yellow body coloration with some black barring on the dorsal part of the flanks. Like them it swims in the open, and single individuals join schools of foraging tilapias. The reason for this perfect mimicry is that *C. shiranus* feeds on the small scales on the caudal peduncle and tail of *Oreochromis*! The *chambos* are unable to distinguish between conspecifics and the predator. The large mouth of the latter is the only obvious feature that reveals its true identity. The evolution from a "normal" haplochromine to one that closely resembles a tilapiine cichlid must have taken a long time. *C. shiranus* is known only from the southern half of the lake and is named *yinga* or *nandere* by natives, meaning something like "boss" of the school (Jackson, 1961). The broad bands of teeth in the mouth of *Corematodus* scrape off the scales in a manner which is (presumably) painful, as the *Oreochromis* attempt to avoid such attacks. Nothing is known about the breeding activities of *C. shiranus*.

1. *Taeniolethrinops* sp. 'furcicauda liuli' ♂ Liuli

5. *Taeniolethrinops* sp. 'furcicauda liuli' ♀ Liuli

2. *Oreochromis lidole* ♂ Chinyamwezi Island

6. *Taeniolethrinops* sp. 'furcicauda liuli' ♂ Liuli

3. *Oreochromis squamipinnis* ♂ Lupingu

7. *Taeniolethrinops cyrtonotus* holotype

8. *Oreochromis lidole* ♀ Gome

4. *Oreochromis* sp. ♂ Chiloelo

9. *Oreochromis squamipinnis* ♀ Likoma

10. *Corematodus shiranus* ♀ Nkopola

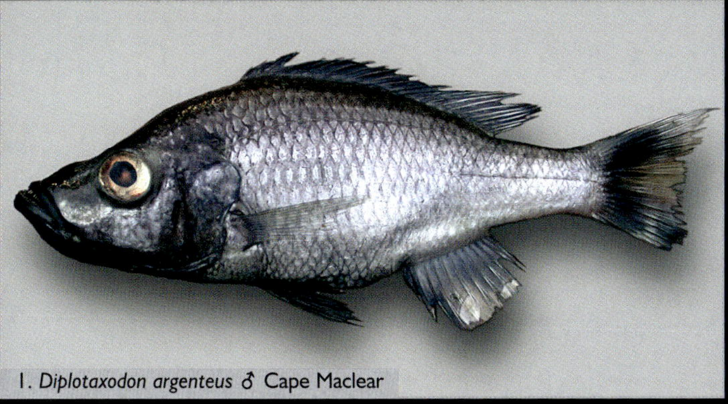

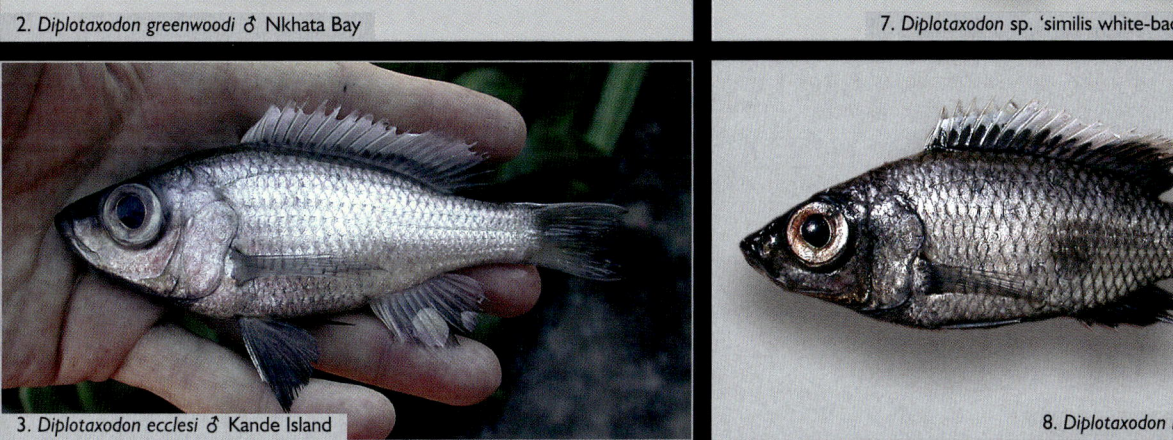

1. *Diplotaxodon argenteus* ♂ Cape Maclear

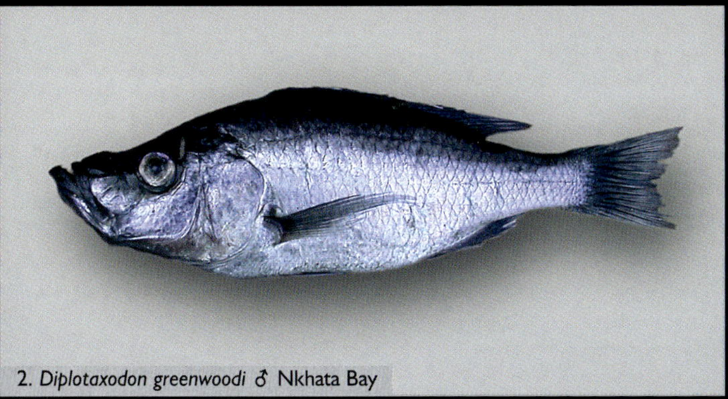

2. *Diplotaxodon greenwoodi* ♂ Nkhata Bay

3. *Diplotaxodon ecclesi* ♂ Kande Island

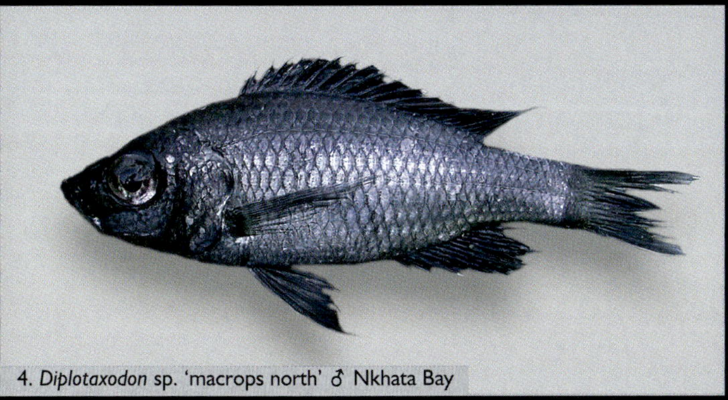

4. *Diplotaxodon* sp. 'macrops north' ♂ Nkhata Bay

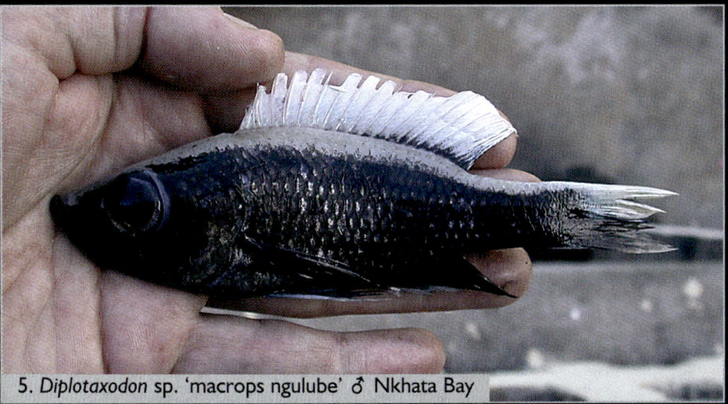

5. *Diplotaxodon* sp. 'macrops ngulube' ♂ Nkhata Bay

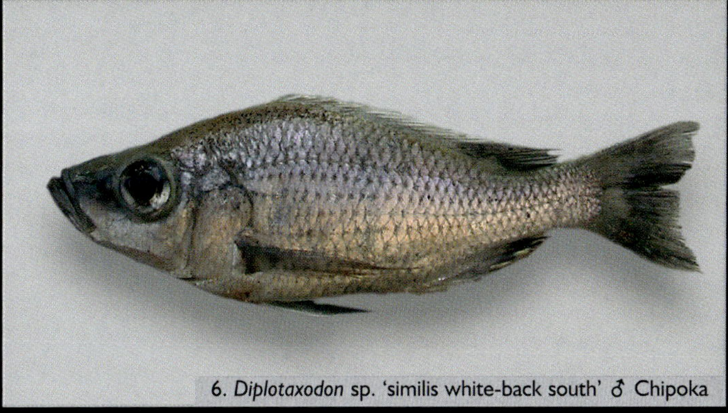

Martin Genner

6. *Diplotaxodon* sp. 'similis white-back south' ♂ Chipoka

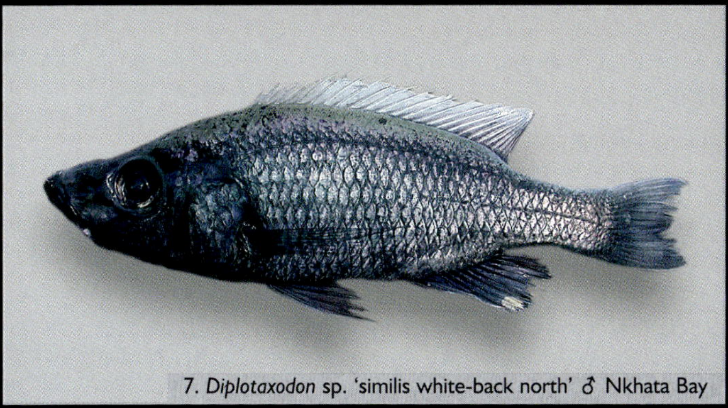

Martin Genner

7. *Diplotaxodon* sp. 'similis white-back north' ♂ Nkhata Bay

Martin Genner

8. *Diplotaxodon macrops* ♂ Monkey Bay

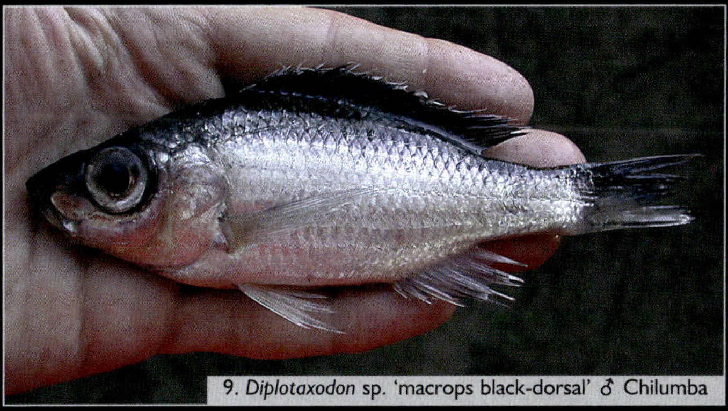

Martin Genner

9. *Diplotaxodon* sp. 'macrops black-dorsal' ♂ Chilumba

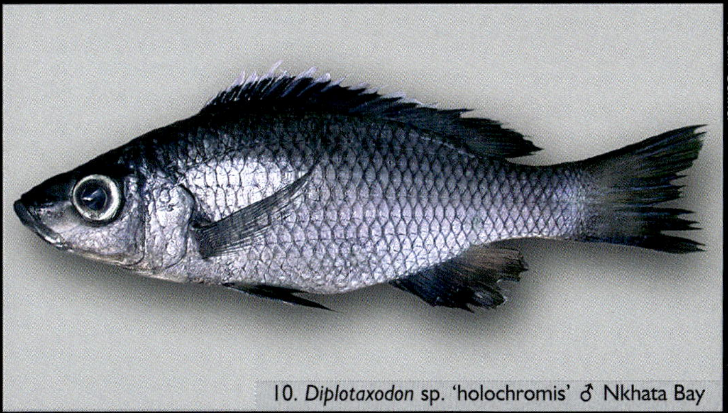

Martin Genner

10. *Diplotaxodon* sp. 'holochromis' ♂ Nkhata Bay

The unknown depths

Since the early days of exploration of Lake Malaŵi it has become apparent that its deep waters hold a multitude of cichlid species that can be caught on hook and line and also with deep-reaching *chirimila* nets. None of the species mentioned in this chapter have been observed in their natural habitat and thus no pertinent information about their feeding and breeding behavior can be given. Some species shown in this chapter may even be found in shallow water but data on the depth from which they were collected was not available. A few species have been exported alive and some behavioral information has been gained from aquarists keeping these denizens of the deep.

Open-water predators

Cichlids are primarily bottom-dwellers, and it is a testament to their great adaptability that a number of them have developed into truly open-water species. Two different genera of predatory cichlids, *Rhamphochromis* and *Diplotaxodon*, hunt in mid-water and at least some of them breed there as well. They feed primarily on crustaceans and *usipa* (the lake sardine).

Adult *usipa* feed on plankton close to the shore and are highly valued as food fishes—on many sandy shores they are caught with seine nets. They taste very good, and presumably to predatory fishes as well as to humans! They are also used as bait for line fishing. Adult lake sardines (maximum size about 12 cm) breed in the open water offshore and the shoaling juveniles are pelagic, i.e. they are found in open water in the middle of the lake. Here they constitute prey for at least 15 species of *Diplotaxodon* (Turner *et al.*, 2004; Martin Genner, pers. comm.). When the lake sardine matures it often migrates inshore and forages over the sandy bottom in very shallow water where it forms prey for other predators, such as *Dimidiochromis* and *Champsochromis*.

Rhamphochromis feed on juvenile utaka and other small cichlids as well as lake sardines, and are sometimes found near the shore when they follow the shoals of *usipa*. By contrast, *Diplotaxodon* rarely move inshore and remain at a depth of at least 30 meters in the open water of the lake (Fryer & Iles, 1972). Males of some species of this genus have very large, distinct egg-spots and may breed under the worst light conditions where such spots are still perceived by females. Other species, however, lack any trace of egg-spots in the anal fin. Some may have developed an open-water breeding technique—mid-water spawning has been recorded in a species of *Rhamphochromis* (Spreinat, 1991). In water deeper than 150 meters the oxygen content is very low or even non-existent and the water column above may be too turbid to permit light penetration to the bottom. If it transpires that mid-water spawning is more widespread among these cichlids then it may have evolved because of the unavailability of suitable substrates, either because these were fully occupied by better-adapted (more aggressive) species or because they were out of reach.

Ndunduma

The local name for all species of *Diplotaxodon* is *ndunduma*, and they are also known as *masahunju* or *jamisoni*. The genus contains seven scientifically described species: *D. argenteus, D. ecclesi, D. greenwoodi, D. aeneus, D. apogon, D. macrops,* and *D. limnothrissa*, though *D. apogon* may be a junior synonym of *D. ecclesi* (Martin Genner, pers. comm.). Turner *et al.* (2004) list 18 additional undescribed species. Many of these were caught together at the same spot on the same day, which suggests that some of them at least school together and feed from the same source, i.e. *usipa* and plankton. By contrast Martin Genner (pers. comm., who has kindly provided the unpublished field data used in this chapter except where otherwise indicated) has extensively researched the deep-water cichlids of the lake and found only nine undescribed species of *Diplotaxodon* besides the described taxa. He regards some of the undescribed species reported by Turner *et al.* (2004) as (possibly) conspecific with other known taxa: *D.* sp. 'offshore' may be conspecific with *D. ecclesi*, *D.* sp. 'similis' may well be conspecific with *D. argenteus*, and *D.* sp. 'brevimaxillaris' is probably conspecific with *D. greenwoodi*. He classifies the various species in three main groups: the *D. macrops* group, the *D. limnothrissa* group, and the *D. argenteus* group.

The *macrops* group, characterized by a relatively small size and large eye, includes the described taxa *D. macrops*, *D. ecclesi*, and *D. aeneus*, and three undescribed species, *D.* sp. 'macrops black-dorsal', *D.* sp. 'macrops north', and *D.* sp. 'macrops ngulube'. *D. ecclesi* has a lake-wide distribution, while all three undescribed species are restricted to the northern half of the lake, north of Nkhata Bay, and *D. macrops* occurs only in the southern part of the lake and has never been found north of Tukombo. Genner has not yet encountered *D. aeneus*. The members of the *macrops* group are small species and may be specialized in feeding on plankton rather than *usipa* (Turner & Stauffer, 1998).

The *limnothrissa* group, characterized by a very slender body, contains *D. limnothrissa*, which has a lake-wide distribution, and the following undescribed species: *Diplotaxodon* sp. 'limnothrissa black-dorsal' (with a lake-wide distribution), *Diplotaxodon* sp. 'limnothrissa black-pelvic' (as yet found only north of Nkhata Bay), and *Diplotaxodon* sp. 'limnothrissa msaka' (to date collected only in the southwestern arm of the lake at Msaka). *D. limnothrissa* has an elongate body and resembles the lake sardine. Its maximum total length is about 16 cm. According to Turner (1994a) this species feeds on zooplankton and sometimes on *usipa*; females guard their young after first release; and it is probably a mid-water spawner. The *Diplotaxodon* I have previously termed *D.* sp. 'white spot' (Konings, 2001: 337) is conspecific with *D. limnothrissa*.

The *argenteus* group, characterized by a relatively large size and a "standard" body, includes *D. argenteus* (with a lake-wide distribution) plus the undescribed taxa *Diplotaxodon* sp. 'holochromis' (with a lake-wide distribution), *Diplotaxodon* sp. 'similis white-back north' (as yet found only north of Nkhata Bay), and *Diplotaxodon* sp. 'similis white-back south' (which Genner found near Chipoka and in the southeastern arm of the lake). Based on preserved material, Turner *et al.* (2004) record three more forms, *D.* sp. 'deep', *D.* sp. 'large black', and *D.* sp. 'black argenteus', all three similar in shape to *D. argenteus*. The *Diplotaxodon* I previously termed *D.* sp. 'macrostoma' (Konings, 2001: 337) is possibly conspecific with *D.* sp. 'holochromis'.

D. greenwoodi does not seem to belong to any of these groups. It is a paedophage which steals fry from the mouths of brooding females (Stauffer & McKaye, 1986). It has a characteristic oblique mouth with a protruding lower jaw. When the mouth is closed there is still a small round opening between the jaws. This species is occasionally caught by hook and line, which may indicate that it is not restricted to its feeding specialization. It has been found all over the lake.

The different species of *Diplotaxodon* show considerable variation in the shape and structure of the body and mouth. There are also notable differences in length. *D. greenwoodi* can attain a total length of at least 25 cm whereas some other species never grow larger than 12 cm.

Although many species of *Diplotaxodon* may be found in mixed schools, it seems that each has its own specialization. Specialization is normally unnecessary when food is abundant. *Usipa*, the primary food for *Diplotaxodon* species, occurs in all stages from larvae to adults in the open water. Several species of *Diplotaxodon* could thus feed on the different stages of *usipa* and on plankton without competing with each other. Given the probably long-term relationship between the food in the open water and *Diplotaxodon* (and *Rhamphochromis*) it is possible that this genus of cichlids is not monophyletic at all, i.e. it did not originate from a single ancestral species. At some time in the past different species may have taken to feeding on

zooplankton or preying on *usipa*, and gathering in hunting packs to increase their rate of success. Similar behavior is seen in some shallow-water hunters such as *Nimbochromis polystigma* and *Placidochromis johnstoni*. During the course of evolution these different species may have optimized their behavioral camouflage by developing similar coloration.

All known species of the genus have a black and/or black-and-white male breeding coloration while females of all species have a silvery body and clear fins. The dark pigment of the male breeding color may be an adaptation to the deep and dim levels at which these species probably breed. All colors appear black at depths of more than 50 meters. To explain the many different species we can assume that either the ancestral forms have experienced genetic isolation—separate ancestral breeding grounds or non-overlapping breeding periods due to local environmental factors—or that they evolved from different ancestors. Genner *et al.* (2007a) found that differences in the monochromatic male breeding coloration pattern of four syntopic *Diplotaxodon* species were sufficient to maintain reproductive isolation, even when some of these were morphologically indistinguishable. To maintain the genetic integrity of the various species they may breed also at different localities and/or at different times, and in the case of any species that use the bottom as a spawning substrate a further distinction may be achieved by differences in the males' spawning structures.

Ncheni

The origin of *Rhamphochromis* may also be polyphyletic, but their very similar morphology suggests monophyly. All are elongate piscivores with silvery backs, and are designed to swim swiftly in pursuit of prey. They swim in the open water and usually congregate and form schools. *Rhamphochromis*, collectively called *ncheni* in the native tongue, are known throughout the lake and are frequently caught together with their prey, *usipa*. They are important food fishes around the lake and appear to be abundant in very deep water, although three species (*R. longiceps* and *R.* sp. 'chilingali' (see page 301), and *R. esox* (see page 164)) range in relatively shallow water close to shore and have already been discussed. Most others, however, are found at least a few hundred meters offshore.

Species identification in *Rhamphochromis* is extremely difficult and the type series of most of the described taxa include specimens of two or more different species (Turner, 1996). The most recent taxonomic publication on this group (Turner *et al.*, 2004) reports about 14 different species and Genner *et al.* (2007b) recognize 15 on the basis of male breeding coloration. A few of the described species are now considered junior synonyms, but Genner does not always agree with the ideas of Turner. The latter considers *Rhamphochromis brevis* a junior synonym of *Rhamphochromis woodi*, but Genner believes that two different species were identified as *R. woodi* by Turner. Since the types of *R. woodi* are juveniles and the morphology of adult specimens is difficult to extrapolate from these, Genner is of the opinion that the name *R. brevis* should be retained for the large, common species and the name *R. woodi* restricted to the species characterized by a large premaxillary pedicel (the sliding element of the upper jaw) which gives the snout a hooked upper profile. *R. brevis* is called *batala* (butter) by fishermen as it reminds them of the color of the local margarine, but in the southern part of the lake this name is applied to almost all species of *Rhamphochromis*. The species I have previously termed *R.* sp. 'ferox yellow-fin' (Konings, 2001: 336) is conspecific with *R. brevis*.

Turner *et al.* (2004) found that the two type specimens of *Rhamphochromis ferox* are not conspecific. One was regarded a specimen of *R. longiceps* and the other designated as lectotype of *R. ferox*. Genner *et al.* (2007b) have discovered a *Rhamphochromis* which, in terms of its morphology, corresponds to the lectotype of *R. ferox*, a species not yet identified in the lake, and term it *Rhamphochromis cf. ferox* pending further study.

Although females and juveniles of *Rhamphochromis longiceps* are common in the shallow vegetated areas of the lake (see page 301), adult males have been found only in the open lake. Genner *et al.* (2007b) believe that the type material of *R. macrophthalmus* probably represents adult males of *R. longiceps*. Based on the breeding coloration of males they recognize two other species closely related to *R. longiceps*: *Rhamphochromis* sp. 'longiceps grey-back' (= *R.* sp. 'slender' (Turner *et al.*, 2004)) and *Rhamphochromis* sp. 'longiceps yellow-belly'. The maximum total length of all three species of the *longiceps* group is about 25 cm.

Rhamphochromis sp. 'grey' (Turner *et al.*, 2004) is distinguished from all other *ncheni* by the relatively small mouth, the small, closely-packed teeth, and the orange suffusion in the dorsal and the lower lobe of the caudal fin. Turner *et al.* (2004) also suggest that the cichlid I have previously (Konings, 2001) termed *Pallidochromis* sp. 'chicken' is in fact this small-mouthed *Rhamphochromis*. It can attain a maximum total length of about 40 cm.

Rhamphochromis sp. 'maldeco' is a plump-looking *ncheni* from the southern part of the lake that has been termed *R.* sp. 'maldeco yellow' by Genner *et al.* (2007b). The mouth of this species is smaller and the upper jaw thinner than that of *R. brevis*, the only known species with which it could be confused. In addition, maximum total length is about 35 cm, 5 cm shorter than is usual for large adult *R. brevis*. When adult both male and female have a yellow belly and orange fins. The dorsal fin of breeding males is yellow.

Rhamphochromis sp. 'long-fin yellow' (Turner, 1996) has a much smaller adult length than the previous species and the largest specimens recorded were about 25 cm. Females and non-breeding males are silver with a slightly brownish hue (Turner *et al.*, 2004). Breeding males are characterized by long pelvic fins and by a bright yellow-orange color on the ventral part of the body and ventral fins. *R.* sp. 'long-fin yellow' has been encountered mostly in the southern part of the lake but some have been collected at Tukombo on the central western shore of the lake.

Turner *et al.* (2004) list *Rhamphochromis* sp. 'stripe' as an undescribed species with a possibly lake-wide distribution, but Genner *et al.* (2007b) believe that most of the specimens involved belong to *R. esox* (see page 164). A few specimens, however, appear to be different and these continue to be referred to *R.* sp. 'stripe'. These specimens were all collected in the southeastern arm of the lake, which thus becomes the currently known distribution of the species.

Rhamphochromis sp. 'long-snout south' is another species restricted to the southeastern arm of the lake. Its maximum total length is about 37 cm (Genner *et al.*, 2007b).

In coloration *Rhamphochromis* sp. 'long-snout north' resembles *R.* sp. 'long-fin yellow' from the southern half of the lake and has thus far been collected at Nkhata Bay (Martin Genner, pers. comm.) and at Chizumulu Island (Konings, 2001: 336, incorrectly identified as *R. ferox*). Breeding males are extremely rare but can be distinguished from those of *R.* sp. 'long-fin yellow' by the gray dorsal fin (yellow in the latter species). The male in the photo on page 391 has a total length of approximately 27 cm.

Rhamphochromis sp. 'big-tooth' (Genner *et al.*, 2007b) is another rare species which has been collected at Nkhata Bay and at Kande. Maximum total length is estimated at about 30 cm. It is characterized by very large, widely-spaced teeth.

Because several similar *Rhamphochromis* species live in mixed schools it is not unreasonable to assume that some sort of reproductive segregation takes place. Apart from the fact that males of several species can be distinguished by their breeding coloration they may have separate traditional breeding grounds; breed at different times of the year; hold territories in different biotopes—sand, rocks, or mid-water; have different depth preferences when it comes to choosing a spawning site; or any combination of these. At present, however, no data are available.

Pallidochromis tokolosh exhibits similarities to both *Rhamphochromis* and *Diplotaxodon*. The shape of the body is streamlined and similar to that of a *Rhamphochromis*, but the teeth are small and resemble those of a *Diplotaxodon*. *P. tokolosh* has been found at great depths in the southeastern arm, along the Malaŵi east coast, and at Tukombo on the central western shore.

Martin Genner

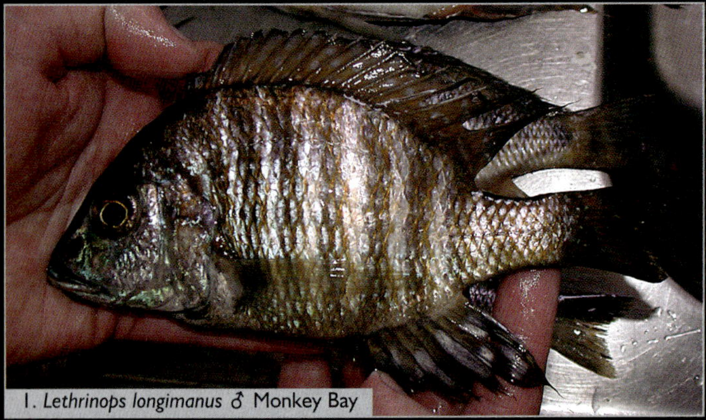

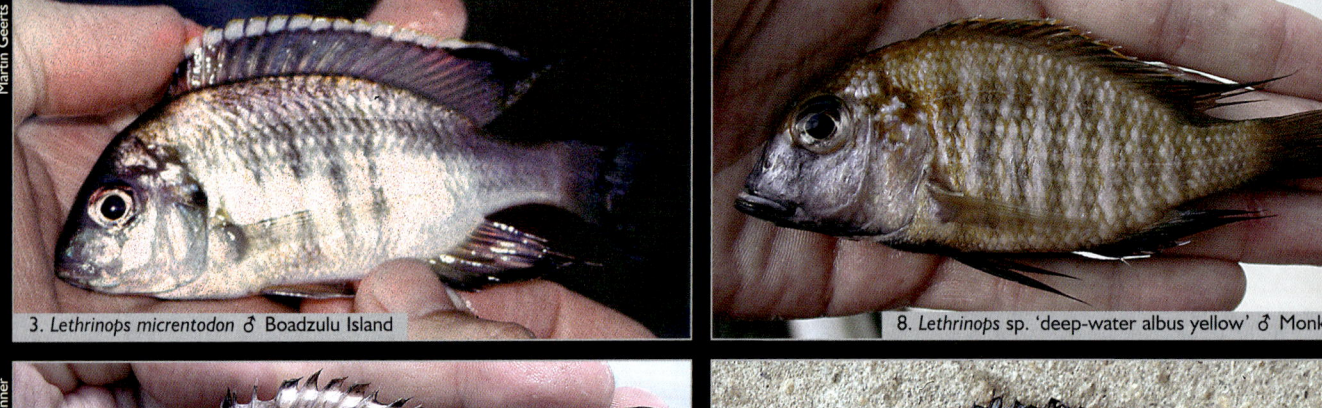

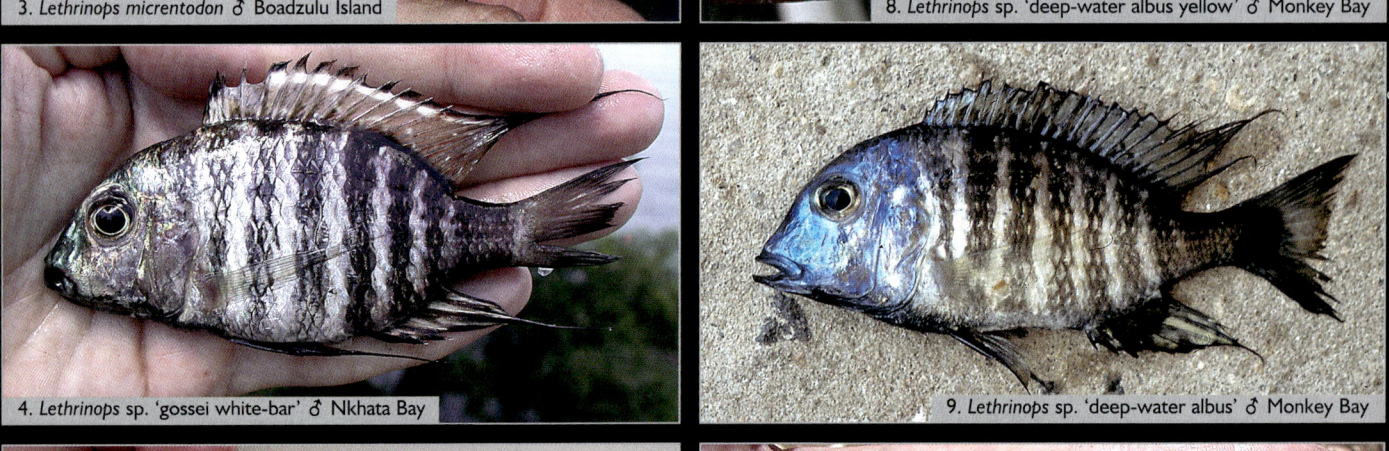

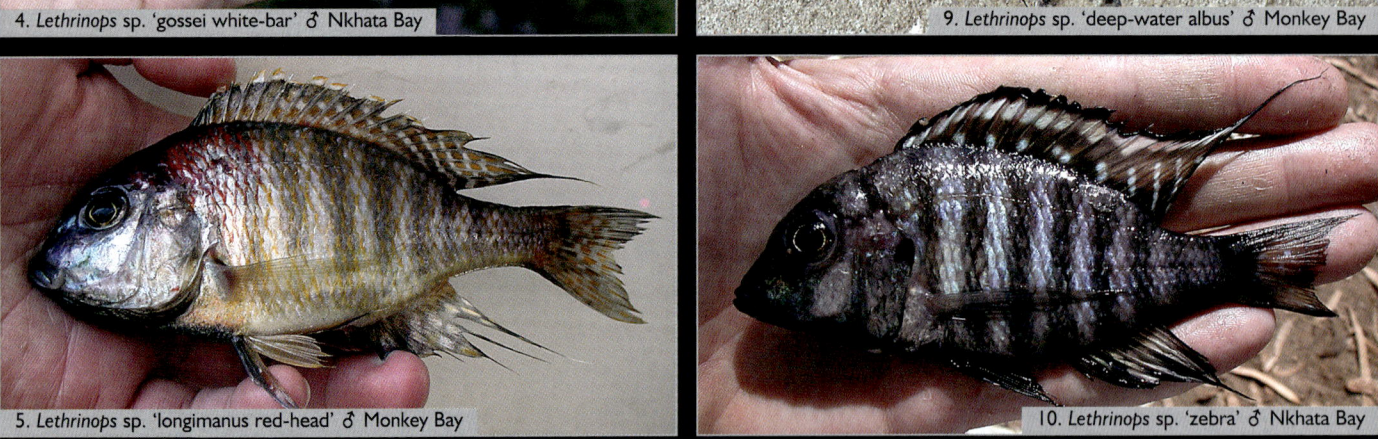

1. *Lethrinops longimanus* ♂ Monkey Bay

George Turner

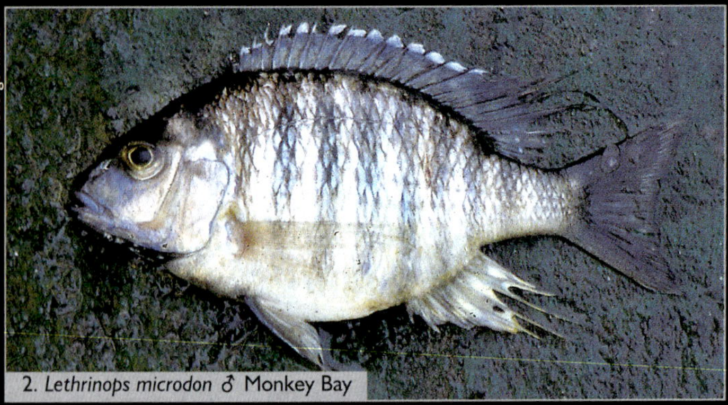

2. *Lethrinops microdon* ♂ Monkey Bay

Martin Geerts

3. *Lethrinops micrentodon* ♂ Boadzulu Island

Martin Genner

4. *Lethrinops* sp. 'gossei white-bar' ♂ Nkhata Bay

Martin Genner

5. *Lethrinops* sp. 'longimanus red-head' ♂ Monkey Bay

George Turner

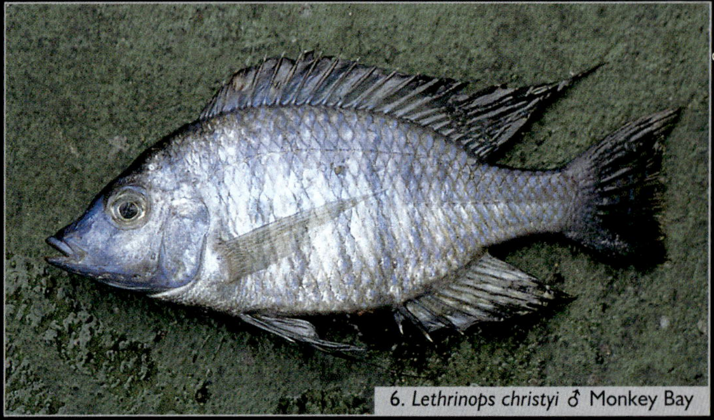

6. *Lethrinops christyi* ♂ Monkey Bay

George Turner

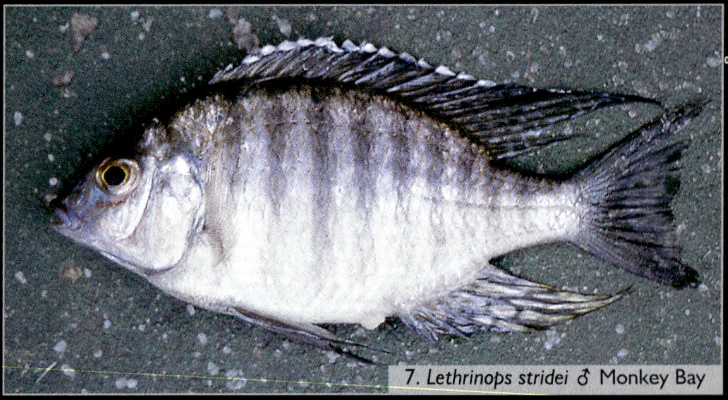

7. *Lethrinops stridei* ♂ Monkey Bay

Martin Genner

8. *Lethrinops* sp. 'deep-water albus yellow' ♂ Monkey Bay

George Turner

9. *Lethrinops* sp. 'deep-water albus' ♂ Monkey Bay

10. *Lethrinops* sp. 'zebra' ♂ Nkhata Bay

Lethrinops

The group of deep-living *Lethrinops* comprises deep-bodied cichlids that are conspicuously marked with vertical bars. The breeding coloration of males includes the intensification of these bars. Most, if not all, species of the group prefer the deeper regions of the lake. They have been recorded from depths between 20 (top of the gill net, which may not the actual depth of collection) and 100 meters and seem to be common at most locations. All males have distinct egg-spots, the function of which may be to attract females or show the females the location of the spawning site even under conditions of reduced light.

All of the following species live at deep levels and most of them can be found syntopic (but a few may be sibling species (see below) which are geographically isolated). Some (e.g. *L. christyi*) have a rather localized distribution as they congregate at particular sites where their preferred food is abundant. Some are found scattered over their foraging grounds as these offer less food per square meter.

Lethrinops mylodon is highly specialized in crushing snails and is found in deeper water over sand. The species was originally described with two subspecies, *L. mylodon mylodon* and *L. mylodon borealis*, but Snoeks & Hanssens (2004) were unable to find any clear separation between the northern and southern forms. *L. mylodon* grows to a maximum total length of about 20 cm. The head is very large as it has to accommodate the powerful muscles of the snail-crushing pharyngeal apparatus.

A sibling-species relationship of the type mentioned above may exist between *Lethrinops macracanthus* and *Lethrinops gossei*. *L. macracanthus* is known from many parts of the lake and may have a lake-wide distribution. *L. gossei* was described from Monkey Bay but is distributed over much of the southern part of the lake. It is generally found in much deeper water than *L. macracanthus* (Turner, 1996). Both species have large, molariform teeth on the pharyngeal bones, but these teeth are not as stout as those of *L. mylodon*. Stomach inventories of *L. macracanthus* revealed a lot of sand grains besides crustaceans and occasional snails (Eccles & Lewis, 1979). This indicates that it lives over pure sand.

Snoeks & Hanssens (2004) found that the cichlids previously generally regarded as *Lethrinops longipinnis* constitute a complex of four different species, probably including *Lethrinops argenteus*, which was previously known only from the four specimens described by Ahl in 1927. All members of the *L. longipinnis* complex prefer soft substrates such as mud or diatomaceous ooze. As well as *L. longipinnis* and *L. argenteus*, Snoeks & Hanssens distinguish *Lethrinops* sp. 'longipinnis deep-water' and *Lethrinops* sp. 'longipinnis white-lappets'.

Lethrinops longimanus grows to a maximum total length of about 15 cm and has a shape not unlike that of *L. auritus* (page 371). It lives over pure sandy bottoms from which it sifts out insect larvae. Its preferred habitat is at moderately deep levels (between 20 and 60 meters) and it is abundant at these depths in many parts of the lake (Turner, 1996). It is a deep-bodied cichlid with rather strong jaws and relatively thick lips. Females and non-breeding males have a pinkish hue on the flanks (Turner, 1996).

Lethrinops christyi has very fine teeth on the pharyngeal bones, which points to a diet of small or delicate foods. It may in fact feed on plankton drifting just above the bottom or it may gather its dinner by filtering the muddy sediment. It can reach a length of about 18 cm.

A large number of undescribed *Lethrinops* species have to date been collected from deep water and these are shown in photographs on the following pages. Several of these species are discussed in detail by Turner (1996).

Diatom-feeding *Lethrinops*

Three species of *Lethrinops*, *Lethrinops microdon*, *Lethrinops micrentodon*, and *Lethrinops stridei*, feed on the diatomaceous ooze which is abundant in the southern part of the lake (Eccles & Lewis, 1977). Their distribution seems to be restricted to this area.

L. stridei is the most generalized diatom-feeder of the three. It grows to a maximum total length of about 13 cm and occurs throughout much of the southern half of the lake. It is also the most abundant species. It feeds on zooplankton as well as on diatoms on the bottom. The other two species also feed in midwater on plankton when this is abundant, but are more reluctant to make the food-switch, instead moving to areas where diatoms are plentiful. This may be why *L. microdon* has such a restricted distribution in the southeastern arm of the lake, although in its preferred habitat, at a depth of about 50 meters, it is abundant (Eccles & Lewis, 1977). Its distribution may be related to the periodic deposition of large amounts of diatomaceous material occurring in this area. The layer of sediment may be as much as 20 meters thick in some places (Eccles, 1974), and is both accessible to and of nutritive value for the *L. microdon* found south of Monkey Bay. Further north the sediment lies deeper than the penetration level of the sunlight required to allow growth of diatomaceous algae, and so microbial processes break down the sediment instead. The distribution of the third species, *L. micrentodon*, is patchy, and it seems to select a specific type of bottom from which to feed, although gut contents analysis has revealed mostly diatoms as in the other two species.

These three diatom-feeding species have developed different breeding coloration and different breeding seasons in order to ensure clear genetic segregation between them. *L. stridei* has a similar shape and male breeding colors to *Placidochromis longimanus* but the latter is found in shallower water (see page 325). *L. stridei* and *P. longimanus* males have a blue breeding color with faint (in *P. longimanus*) or prominent (in *L. stridei*) vertical bars. The breeding coloration of *L. microdon* males is dark bronze with distinct barring below the dorsal. Males of *L. micrentodon* are more metallic with an electric blue head; the vertical barring is only faintly visible (Eccles & Lewis, 1977).

Alticorpus

A number of deep-living, deep-bodied, barred cichlid species are assigned to another genus, *Alticorpus*. They can be distinguished from *Lethrinops* by the presence of enlarged lat-

1. *Lethrinops* sp. 'Iowae' ♂ Monkey Bay

2. *Lethrinops* sp. 'grey' ♂ Monkey Bay

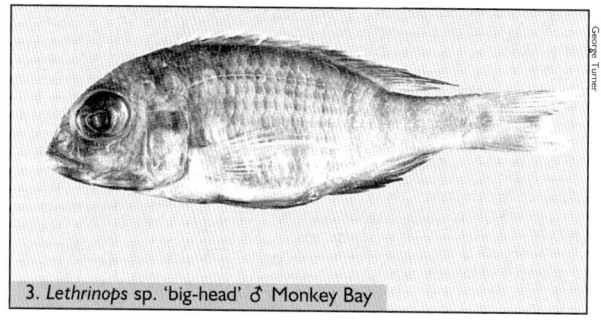

3. *Lethrinops* sp. 'big-head' ♂ Monkey Bay

eral pores on the lower part of the head. Their feeding technique is possibly analogous to that observed in *Aulonocara*—*Alticorpus* species can locate their prey in the sand by just "listening" to it. As with all species discussed in this chapter, however, the details of their lifestyle are largely a matter for surmise. None of these species has ever been observed in the lake so it is not actually known if they use their sensory capabilities for sonar detection of prey. They may hunt for specific food items rather than randomly filtering the substrate as in *Lethrinops*. This would permit them to forage in areas that are less rich in food, with sufficient food being located as they move slowly over the substrate. They may also feed in areas where light is dim or completely absent due to the turbidity of the water or its depth. On the other hand, their behavior may resemble that of *Trematocara* in Lake Tanganyika, that is, they may forage at night

George Turner

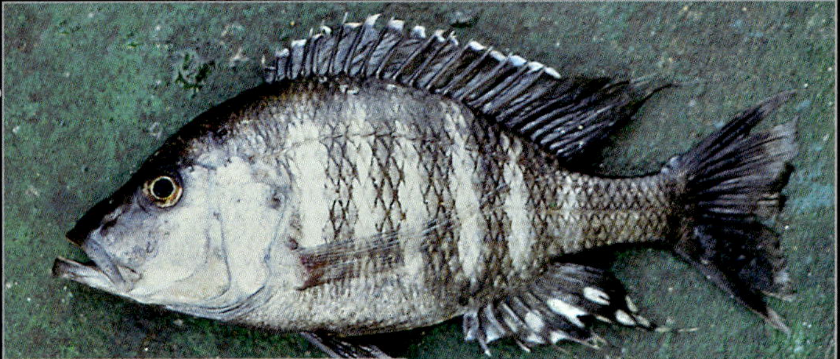

1. *Alticorpus mentale* ♂ Monkey Bay

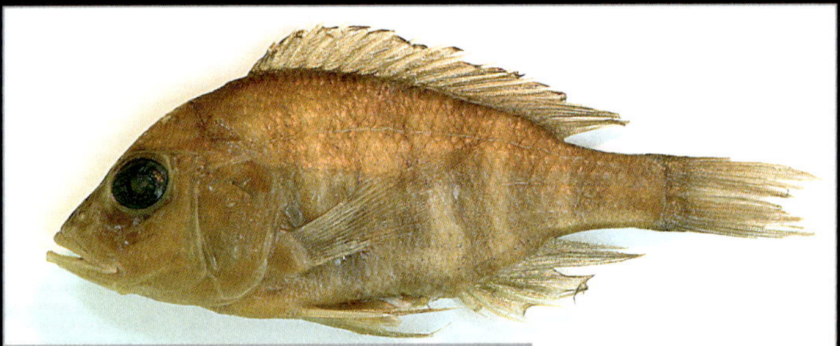

2. *Alticorpus profundicola* Nkhotakota (paratype)

Martin Genner

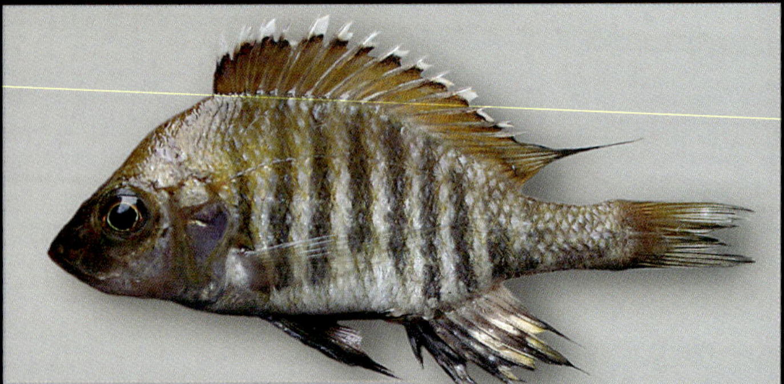

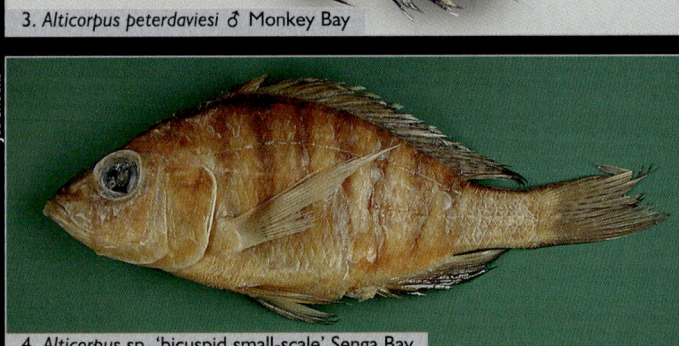

3. *Alticorpus peterdaviesi* ♂ Monkey Bay

Jos Snoeks

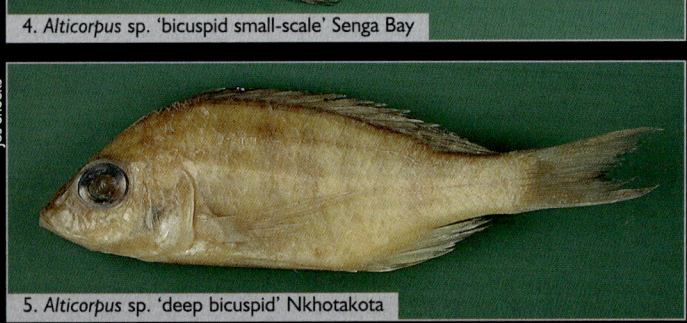

4. *Alticorpus* sp. 'bicuspid small-scale' Senga Bay

Jos Snoeks

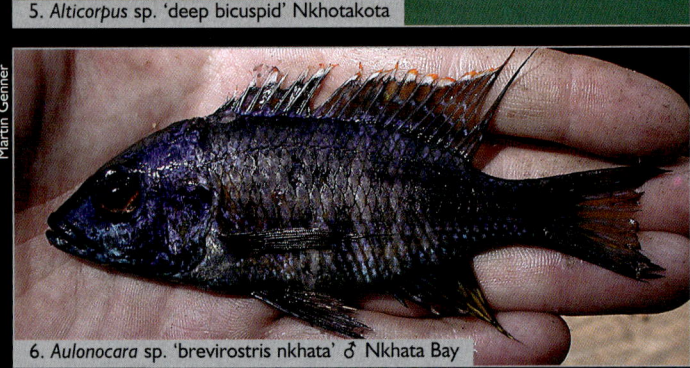

5. *Alticorpus* sp. 'deep bicuspid' Nkhotakota

Martin Genner

6. *Aulonocara* sp. 'brevirostris nkhata' ♂ Nkhata Bay

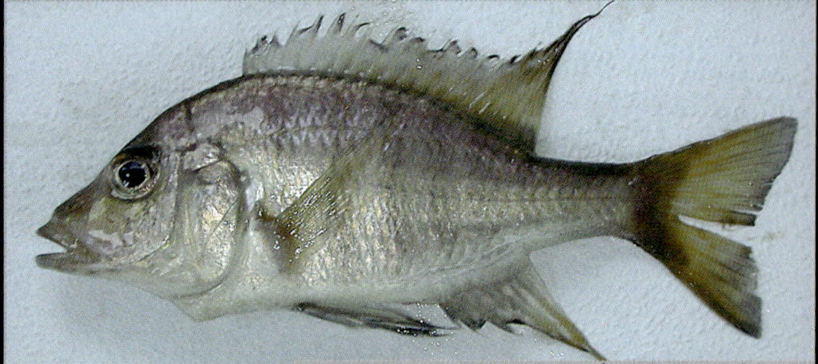

7. *Alticorpus macrocleithrum* ♂ Nakantenga Island

Martin Genner

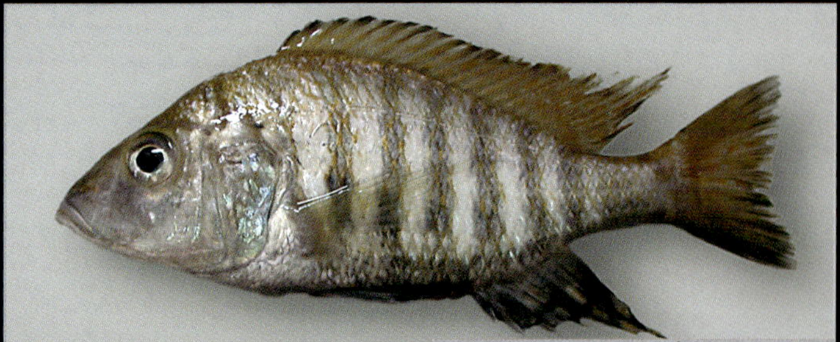

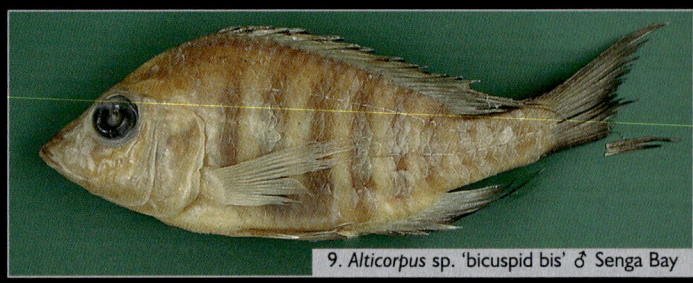

8. *Alticorpus geoffreyi* ♂ Monkey Bay

Jos Snoeks

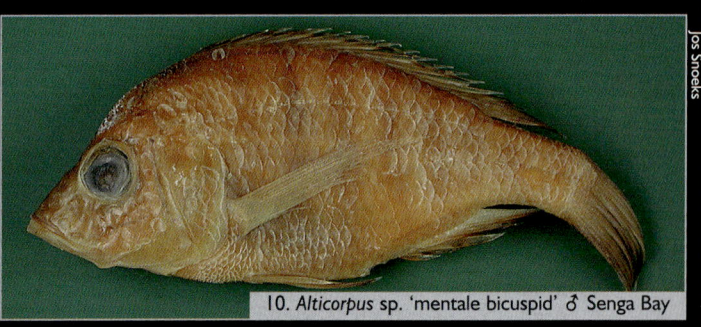

9. *Alticorpus* sp. 'bicuspid bis' ♂ Senga Bay

Jos Snoeks

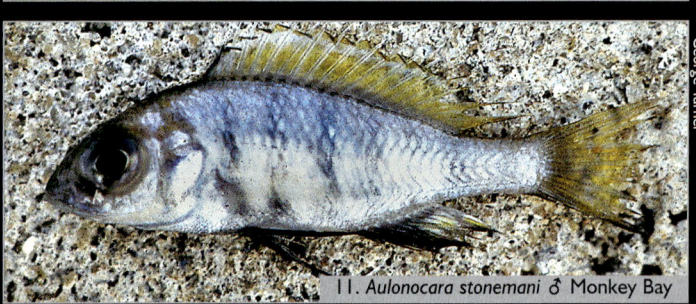

10. *Alticorpus* sp. 'mentale bicuspid' ♂ Senga Bay

George Turner

11. *Aulonocara stonemani* ♂ Monkey Bay

Martin Genner

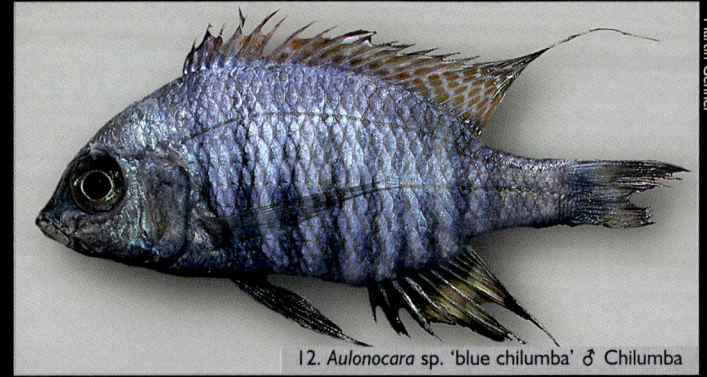

12. *Aulonocara* sp. 'blue chilumba' ♂ Chilumba

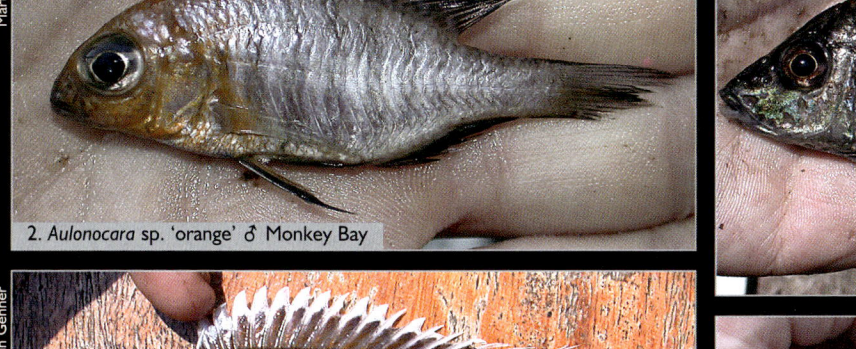

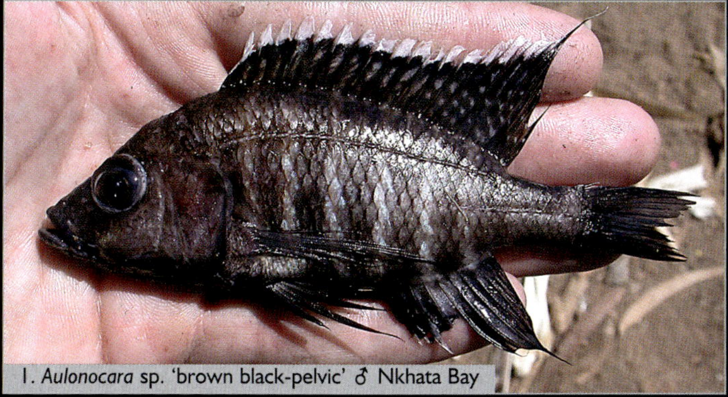
Martin Genner
1. *Aulonocara* sp. 'brown black-pelvic' ♂ Nkhata Bay

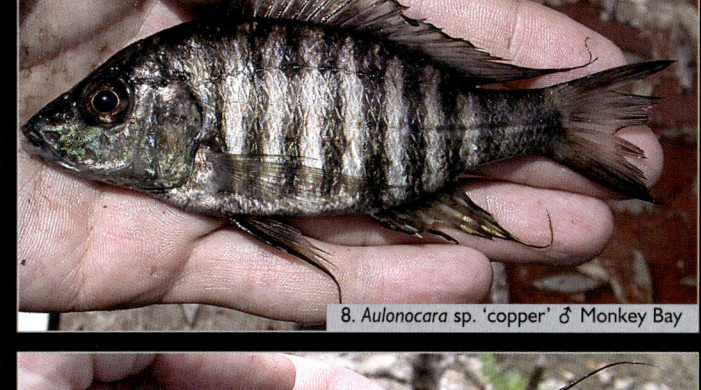

Martin Genner
2. *Aulonocara* sp. 'orange' ♂ Monkey Bay

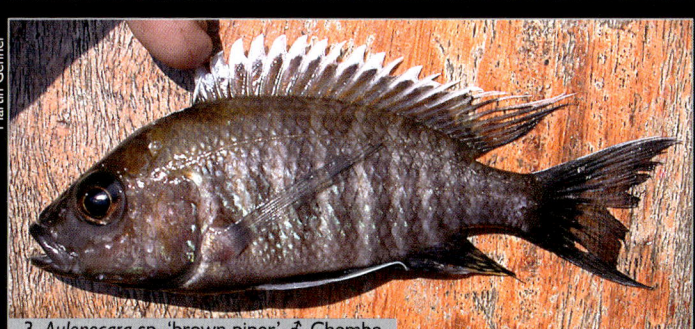

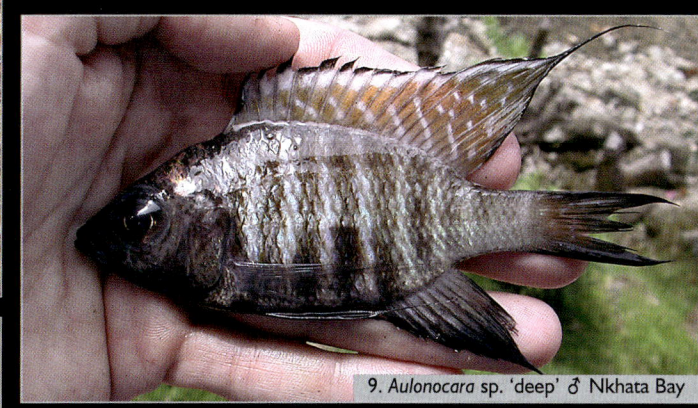

Martin Genner
3. *Aulonocara* sp. 'brown piper' ♂ Chembe

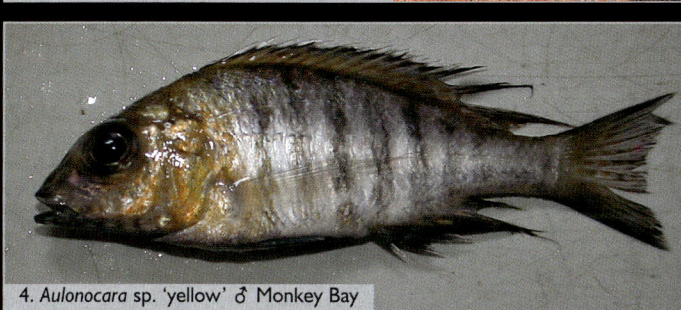

Martin Genner
4. *Aulonocara* sp. 'yellow' ♂ Monkey Bay

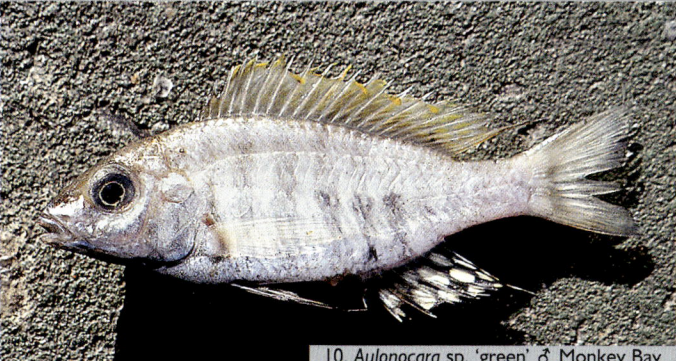

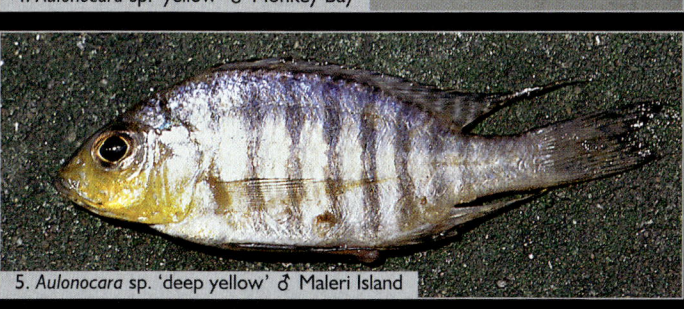

George Turner
5. *Aulonocara* sp. 'deep yellow' ♂ Maleri Island

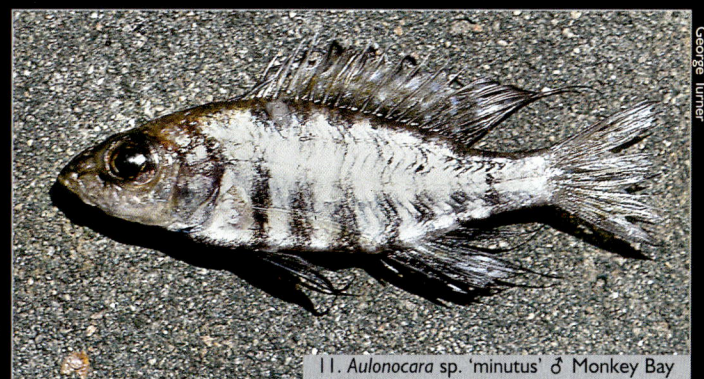

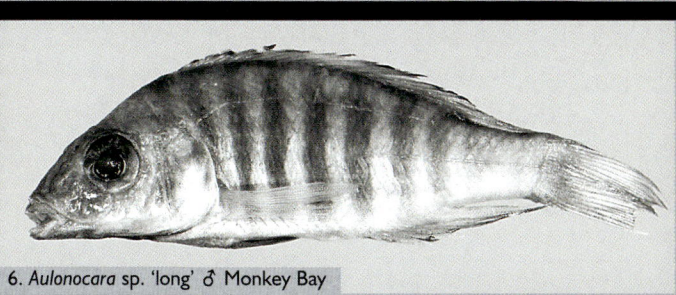

George Turner
6. *Aulonocara* sp. 'long' ♂ Monkey Bay

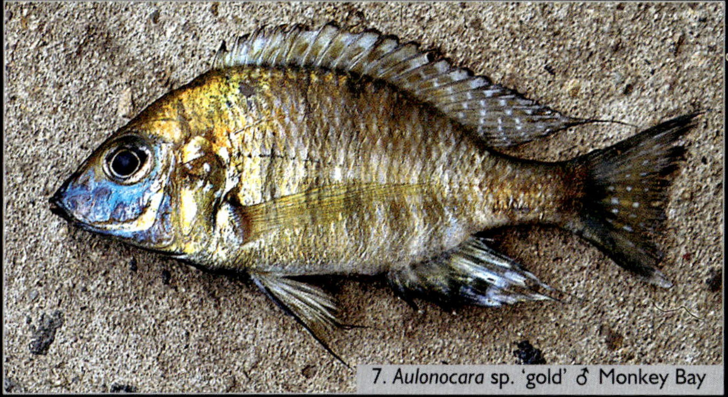
George Turner
7. *Aulonocara* sp. 'gold' ♂ Monkey Bay

Martin Genner
8. *Aulonocara* sp. 'copper' ♂ Monkey Bay

Martin Genner
9. *Aulonocara* sp. 'deep' ♂ Nkhata Bay

George Turner
10. *Aulonocara* sp. 'green' ♂ Monkey Bay

George Turner
11. *Aulonocara* sp. 'minutus' ♂ Monkey Bay

(or dusk) in the shallower regions. During the day they may live at deep levels and perhaps even breed there, but when the day is over they may ascend the slopes and forage at levels that are frequented by other species in the daytime. At present, however, there are no indications to confirm any of these possibilities.

Alticorpus mentale, the type species of the genus, has been caught at a depth of 75 meters near Monkey Bay. This cichlid has a maximum total length of about 24 cm and is the largest known member of its genus. All the other species remain smaller than 16 cm. The mouth structure and the sharp teeth on the pharyngeal bones indicate piscivorous behavior. This is rather unexpected in a so-called "bottom-grubber" which can detect prey in the sand. This species is sometimes caught on hook and line with a piece of *usipa* as bait, and this may refute the nocturnal feeding hypothesis since they are caught during the day.

Alticorpus peterdaviesi is characterized by numerous (16 to 21) gill-rakers on the first lower gill arch, which suggests a diet of plankton or other small foods. The pharyngeals, however, exhibit some enlarged teeth and it may thus feed on other larger items as well. It has been caught at the same depth and site (near Monkey Bay) as the previous species, but where *A. mentale* has a lake-wide distribution *A. peterdaviesi* is restricted to the southern part of the lake. In fact *A. peterdaviesi* is not unlike *Lethrinops macracanthus* and *L. gossei* (page 391), which also have numerous gill rakers and a similar pharyngeal dentition. *Alticorpus pectinatum* is regarded as a junior synonym of *A. peterdaviesi* (see Snoeks & Walapa (2004)).

At Nkhotakota *Alticorpus profundicola* has been caught by a trawler at an astounding depth of 159 meters. Sunlight barely penetrates to such depths. When a plankton bloom is overhead, the light may be sharply reduced and visibility drop to zero. Even under these circumstances *A. profundicola* is apparently still able to locate the crustaceans that crawl over the sand and may thus remain at these deep levels for its entire life. The only three specimens collected to date had a maximum total length of about 14 cm.

The fourth species in this genus, *Alticorpus macrocleithrum*, has a bizarre anatomical feature: it has a very large cleithrum (part of the shoulder girdle) that protrudes from the fish. This remarkable feature is assumed to have a crucial function in the feeding behavior of this fish. It has been suggested that it may prevent the cichlid from digging too deep into the bottom (Axelrod & Burgess, 1979: 80). David Eccles (pers. comm.), however, has provided a more plausible alternative explanation. He notes that the pectoral fins of this species are appreciably wider at the base than in other members of the genus, and suggests that these powerful fins may be used to push the fish out of the mud after it has dived into it to feed. To be able to operate such powerful fins its musculature would need a firm point of attachment; some of the muscles in question are attached to the cleithrum, which would thus need to be enlarged to support them. *A. macrocleithrum* has been repeatedly caught at depths below 75 meters, sometimes in huge numbers. Its maximum total length is about 16 cm.

Recently Snoeks & Walapa (2004) have described *Alticorpus geoffreyi*, which is common throughout the lake at levels deeper than 60 meters. It is characterized by a low number of gill rakers (9-13 versus 14-21) when compared to *A. peterdaviesi* and *A. profundicola* and by a shorter jaw than *A. mentale*. Snoeks & Walapa also report the discovery of five further species of *Alticorpus* which have not yet been scientifically described as insufficient specimens have so far been collected.

Deep-water *Aulonocara*

Aulonocara stonemani is a small species—maximum total length is about 6 cm—and was originally described as *Haplochromis stonemani* (Burgess & Axelrod, 1973). It was caught at a depth of 75 meters. Turner (1996) reports on various other deep-living species of *Aulonocara*, most of them small but all with enlarged sensory pores on the head. Males of some of these species have spectacular colors, e.g. *A.* sp. 'gold' and *A.* sp. 'minutus', which suggests that they breed at depths where enough sunlight penetrates for females (or competing males) to see their finery. In total a dozen undescribed species of *Aulonocara* have been collected in the deep waters of the southeastern arm of the lake. Some of these species appear to be rare, but others—for example *A.* sp. 'orange' and *A.* sp. 'yellow'—are common at depths of 30-50 meters, and *A.* sp. 'deep' and *A.* sp. 'copper' appear common at depths of 60-120 meters (Turner, 1996).

Deep-water *Placidochromis*

When Hanssens (2004) described no less than 36 new species of *Placidochromis* it became clear that Lake Malaŵi harbors an additional, previously unsuspected, species flock at great depths (deeper than 50 meters). Most of the newly described species are small and most have the habitus of a bottom-dweller. Together with almost 200 other cichlid species they make up a fish fauna that apparently lives and breeds in the subdued light of the depths as none has ever been seen in the accessible waters of the lake. The 47 deep-water species of *Placidochromis* now known resemble each other mainly in their basic melanin pattern (consisting of vertical bars); morphological characters, however, vary considerably.

Because of the multitude of species Hanssens divided these deep-living *Placidochromis* into five groups. The grouping is based on important diagnostic features such as body depth and number of gill rakers, but does not necessarily indicate a close relationship. Group 1 contains the very elongate species; group 2 is represented by a single species, *Placidochromis nkhotakotae*; group 3 comprises species with 14 to 24 gill rakers; group 4 all species with 8 to 10 gill rakers; and group 5 those with 11 to 13 gill rakers.

Group 1 contains the taxa *Placidochromis platyrhynchos*, *P. longus*, and *P. elongatus*. *P. platyrhynchos* has a wide mouth and a horizontally flattened snout. It appears to be one of the most common species and a single specimen has even been collected alive and kept in the aquarium (Patrick Tawil, pers. comm.). *P. longus* has a shorter snout than *P. elongatus* and nine vertical bars below the dorsal (6-7 in *P. elongatus*).

The single species in group 2, *P. nkhotakotae*, is characterized by 27-30 gill rakers and is probably conspecific with a species Turner (1996) named *P.* sp. 'hennydaviesae II'. It may feed in a similar way to *Ctenopharynx pictus* (page 221), as like the latter it has a very long premaxillary pedicel measuring about 35 % of head length.

Group 3 comprises *P. longirostris*, *P. macroceps*, *P. minutus*, *P.* sp. 'big mouth', *P. boops*, *P. nigribarbis*, *P. ecclesi*, *P. trewavasae*, *P. lukomae*, *P. chilolae*, *P. intermedius*, and *P. obscurus*.

P. longirostris has a longer snout than other members of this group while *P. macroceps* has a larger head than any of the others. *P. minutus* has 24 gill rakers while the others of the group have 19 or fewer. The other species of this group differ in various anatomical characters (Hanssens, 2004).

Group 4 comprises *P. hennydaviesae*, *P. macrognathus*, *P. acuticeps*, *P. nkhatae*, *P. koningsi*, *P.* sp. 'big eye', *P. domirae*, *P. communis*, *P. polli*, *P. lineatus*, *P. acutirostris*, *P. ordinarius*, *P. turneri*, *P.* sp. 'small big eye', and *P. mbunoides*.

P. hennydaviesae is distinguished by having a larger mouth than all others in this group. The lower jaw of *P. macrognathus* (maximum standard length about 13 cm) is much stronger than of any other member of the group and it gives the fish the appearance of a miniature version of *Tyrannochromis nigriventer* (and probably denotes similar piscivorous behavior). *P. acuticeps* has a pointed head (as its name suggests) and long snout. *P. nkhatae* is a heavily-built species that resembles a small *Mylochromis* except that it has no diagonal stripe. *P. acutirostris* is distinguished from the others of this group by a longer snout. The remaining species differ in anatomical features that probably reflect their feeding behavior (see Hanssens, 2004). *P. polli* was described as a member of *Lethrinops* closely resembling *L. christyi*, but Hanssens (2004) points out that it lacks the *Lethrinops*-typical dentition in the lower jaw. This yet again shows how similar some sand-dwelling species can be in order to blend in with the school.

Group 5 contains *P. argyrogaster*, *P.* sp. 'deep cheek', *P.* sp. 'deep', *P. vulgaris*, *P.* sp. 'pale elon-

1. *Sciaenochromis benthicola* ♂ Domira Bay

2. *Sciaenochromis* sp. 'deep water' ♂ Monkey Bay

3. *Sciaenochromis* sp. 'elongate' ♂ Nkhata Bay

4. *Sciaenochromis* sp. 'torpedo head' ♂ Monkey Bay

5. *Sciaenochromis* sp. 'spilostichus deep-water' Ntekete

6. *Sciaenochromis* sp. 'spilostichus makanjila' ♂ Makanjila Point

7. *Otopharynx speciosus* ♂ Boadzulu Island

8. *Otopharynx* sp. 'brooksi nkhata' ♂ Nkhata Bay

9. *Trematocranus brevirostris* ♂ Boadzulu Island

10. *Trematocranus* sp. 'brevirostris deep' ♂ Monkey Bay

11. *Trematocranus* cf. *labifer* ♂ Boadzulu Island

1. *Placidochromis longus* ♂ Monkey Bay

1. *Placidochromis nigribarbus* ♂ Chilumba

2. *Placidochromis nkhotakotae* ♂ Nkotakota

2. *Placidochromis ecclesi* ♂ Lukoma Bay

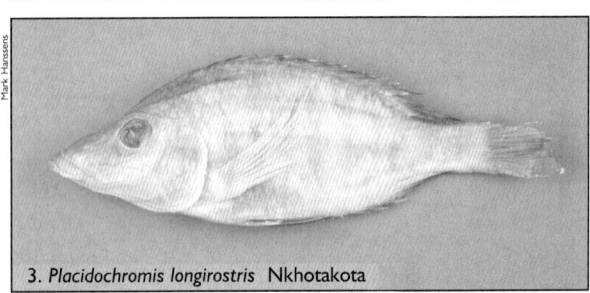

3. *Placidochromis longirostris* Nkhotakota

3. *Placidochromis trewavasae* Kadango

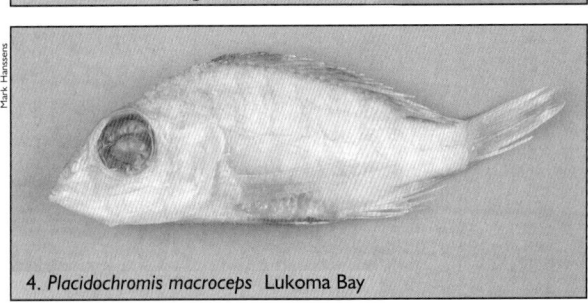

4. *Placidochromis macroceps* Lukoma Bay

4. *Placidochromis lukomae* ♂ Lukoma Bay

5. *Placidochromis minutus* Nkhotakota

5. *Placidochromis chilolae* Chilola Bay

6. *Placidochromis boops* Monkey Bay

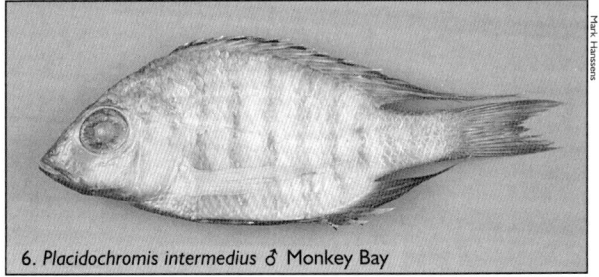

6. *Placidochromis intermedius* ♂ Monkey Bay

gate unicuspid', *P. fuscus*, *P.* sp. 'green orange deep', *P. orthognathus*, *P. pallidus*, *P. minor*, *P. rotundifrons*, *P.* sp. 'elongate thin bar', *P. borealis*, *P.* sp. 'pale elongate blunt snout', *P.* sp. 'pale elongate dull', and *P. msakae*.

P. argyrogaster, characterized by a silver belly, has a deeper snout than the other members of this group. *P. orthognathus* has strong jaws and an oblique gape reminiscent of the paedophages. I would not be surprised if one day it was found to rob broods from mouthbrooding females of the deep-water species flock. *P. minor* is possibly the smallest member of the genus with a maximum recorded standard length of 49 mm.

The deep-water flock of *Placidochromis* consists of very small species—most of them smaller than 10 cm standard length—that will never play an important role in any fishery as they live too deep for beach seines and are too small for the deep-reaching *chirimila* nets.

It is interesting to observe how various traits, described in previous chapters for a wide range of species from different genera, are here seen again in a group of species that probably all belong to a single genus.

Turner (1996) has also reported a series of undescribed deep-water species of *Placidochromis* and a number of these are included in the 36 species described by Hanssens, but a few could not reliably be matched.

Sciaenochromis and *Stigmatochromis*

Members of the genera *Sciaenochromis* and *Stigmatochromis* seem to prefer the deeper regions of the lake. Snoeks & Hanssens (2004) mention several species for each genus, although it is not always known at what depth they were caught.

Sciaenochromis benthicola, a common species from deep water (40-100 meters: Turner, 1996), has already been mentioned because some specimens have been exported alive and are kept in hobbyists' tanks. However, there appear to be several other members of the genus that are restricted to the depths of the lake. Turner (1996) discusses *Sciaenochromis* sp. 'deep water', from depths of 100-128 meters in the northern

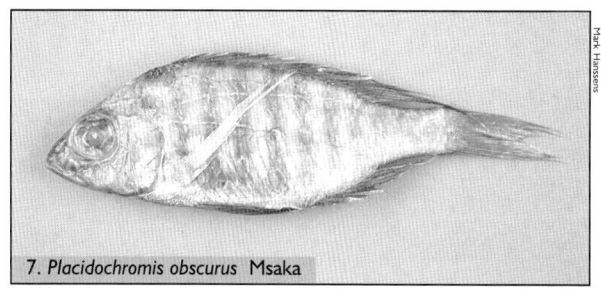
7. *Placidochromis obscurus* Msaka

8. *Placidochromis hennydaviesae* ♂ Monkey Bay

9. *Placidochromis acuticeps* ♂ Mvunguti

10. *Placidochromis nkhatae* Nkhata Bay

11. *Placidochromis koningsi* ♂ Nkhotakota

12. *Placidochromis domirae* ♂ Domira Bay

1. *Placidochromis lineatus* ♂ Lukoma Bay

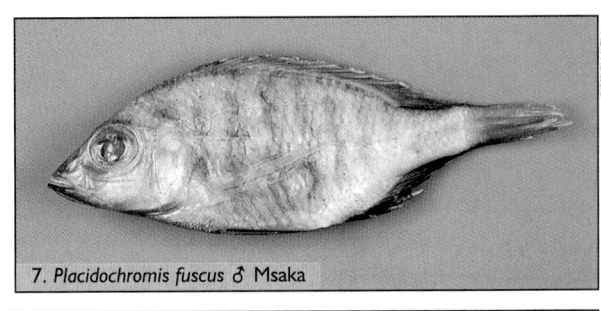
7. *Placidochromis fuscus* ♂ Msaka

2. *Placidochromis acutirostris* Wissman Bay

8. *Placidochromis orthognathus* Chilola Bay

3. *Placidochromis ordinarius* Chuanga Bay

9. *Placidochromis pallidus* Chuanga Bay

4. *Placidochromis turneri* Nkhata Bay

10. *Placidochromis minor* ♂ Msaka

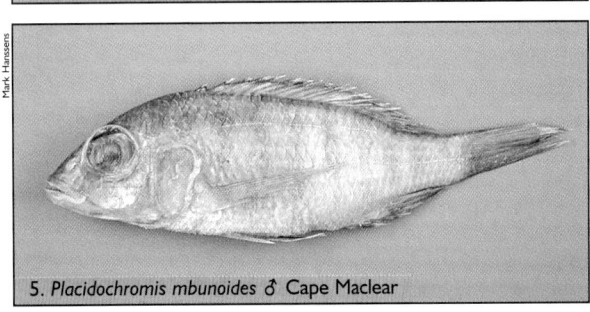
5. *Placidochromis mbunoides* ♂ Cape Maclear

11. *Placidochromis rotundifrons* ♂ Msaka

6. *Placidochromis argyrogaster* ♂ Chilola Bay

12. *Placidochromis borealis* ♂ Wissman Bay

1. *Placidochromis* sp. 'hennydaviesaeIV' ♂ Monkey Bay

2. *Placidochromis* sp. 'hennydaviesaeV' ♂ Monkey Bay

3. *Sciaenochromis* sp. 'psammophilus broad' Youngs Bay

4. *Sciaenochromis* sp. 'spot bicuspid' ♂ Chilola Bay

5. *Sciaenochromis* sp. 'small interorbital' Wissmann Bay

6. *Sciaenochromis* sp. 'deep' Youngs Bay

7. *Stigmatochromis* sp. 'big-head' Domira Bay

8. *Stigmatochromis* sp. 'big-eye' Nkhotakota

9. *Otopharynx pachycheilus* ♂ Ngara (holotype)

10. *Otopharynx* sp. 'round head' Nkhotakota

11. *Otopharynx* sp. 'flat jaw' Senga Bay

12. *Otopharynx* sp. 'high fin' ♂ Nkhotakota

part of the southeastern arm of the lake. In shape this species resembles two other deep-water species, *Sciaenochromis* sp. 'elongate' and *Sciaenochromis* sp. 'psammophilus broad', both reported by Snoeks & Hanssens (2004), but is much smaller than either. Turner reports a maximum total length of 12 cm for *S.* sp. 'deep water' while the specimens of *S.* sp. 'psammophilus broad' and *S.* sp. 'elongate' have a total length of about 17 cm.

Virtually nothing is known of *Sciaenochromis* sp. 'spilostichus deep-water' apart from the fact that the few specimens recorded were collected in deep water. It is easily distinguished from *Mylochromis spilostichus* (see page 344), with which it was previously confused (Snoeks & Hanssens (2004), by the very shallow preorbital depth (eye very close to upper lip).

Three further species are reported by Snoeks & Hanssens (2004). *Sciaenochromis* sp. 'deep', with a total length of about 17 cm, has a short but powerful mouth and a deeper body than the various other species in the genus; it is probably a piscivore. *Sciaenochromis* sp. 'spots bicuspid' is characterized by three distinct, round spots which would normally be indicative of a *Stigmatochromis* rather than a *Sciaenochromis*, but Snoeks and Hanssens find its general morphology more like *S. benthicola*. *Sciaenochromis* sp. 'small interorbital' resembles *S. psammophilus* (see page 354) but has a narrower interorbital (between the eyes) region.

Mark Smith (pers. comm.) photographed a further species of *Sciaenochromis* at Makanjila. He obtained the specimen from a fisherman who had hooked it in deep water. This species is referred to as *Sciaenochromis* sp. 'spilostichus makanjila'.

Snoeks & Hanssens (2004) also examined a large number of *Stigmatochromis* and found that the genus is characterized by backward-inclined outer teeth in the lateral series of the lower jaw in addition to the melanin pattern of three lateral spots. Two of the species they mention I have not recognized underwater: *Stigmatochromis* sp. 'big eye' and *Stigmatochromis* sp. 'big head'.

Other deep-water species

Species other than *ncheni* can sometimes be found among the catches of the hook-and-line fishermen. One of these, *Otopharynx speciosus*, is a large predator with a maximum total length of about 25 cm, and occurs at rather deep levels. It is one of the very few piscivores in the genus.

Arnegard & Snoeks (2001) described *Otopharynx pachycheilus* from deep water near Ngara (holotype) and in Domira Bay, both in Malaŵi. This species is characterized by greatly enlarged, lobed lips and resembles a *Placidochromis milomo* with spots instead of bars. It was collected at a depth of 78-135 meters over a hard bottom consisting of coarse sand or gravel and the largest specimens measured about 20 cm total length. The authors found shrimp remains in the stomach of a single specimen. An interesting finding was that the lips contained taste buds on the exposed outer surface of the lips, which would, in the view of the authors, facilitate the location of prey in deep-water environments. Taste buds are found in the lips of all cichlids and it is as yet unclear whether those in *O. pachycheilus* evolved to increase the sensory capability of the fish or simply developed simultaneously with the growth of the lips. Even with swollen lips a fish needs to secure prey between its jaws before deciding, using its taste buds, whether to eat it or let it go. I therefore think that the thick lips of *O. pachycheilus* serve mainly the same function as in the other thick-lipped species, i.e. they seal off the area from which a prey item is to be sucked.

Snoeks & Hanssens (2004) report numerous as yet undescribed species of *Otopharynx* that they found during their surveys. I have been able to match, with some confidence, some of the species they list with species I have encountered in the shallow waters of the lake and these have been referenced throughout this book, but 11 of their species were new to me.

The distribution of *Trematocranus brevirostris* seems to be restricted to the southern tip of the southeastern arm of the lake, south of Boadzulu Island (Turner, 1996). Turner found from stomach analyses of three specimens that *T. brevirostris* is a generalized benthic feeder. He found it in large numbers just south of Boadzulu Island at depths ranging between 19 and 40 meters. Maximum total length is about 10 cm.

The shape and structure of the mouth of *Trematocranus labifer* resembles that of *Otopharynx ovatus* (page 263) and *Protomelas insignis* (page 263). A specimen found in the dugout canoe of a fisherman, who had been fishing with hook and line, may have been *T. labifer* (see page 403) but it was not preserved for proper identification. Neither Turner (1996) nor Snoeks & Hanssens (2004) found this species during their surveys.

Mylochromis sp. 'melanonotus deep' has been found only in the northern part of the lake. It is probably restricted to the shores north of Chilumba.

The remainder of this chapter consists of photographs of cichlids collected either by deep-set gill nets or by trawling. Often there is no information available other than the collection site, and in some cases even the generic designation is questionable. There are simply too many species involved and each of them needs a thorough examination before a classification can be suggested. The main reason these photos are presented here is to provide the reader with a complete overview of all the species known to date from Lake Malaŵi, even though by the time you read this book more new species will have undoubtedly have been added to the constantly growing list of Malaŵi cichlids.

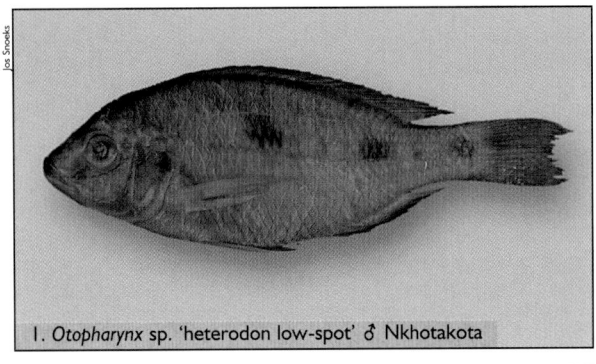

1. *Otopharynx* sp. 'heterodon low-spot' ♂ Nkhotakota

6. *Otopharynx* sp. 'red flat-jaw' ♂ Kadango

2. *Otopharynx* sp. 'blue flat-jaw' ♂ Kadango

7. *Otopharynx* sp. 'molariform striped' Senga Bay

3. *Otopharynx* sp. 'golf-head blue' ♂ Lutara

8. *Otopharynx* sp. 'high-fin low-GR' Leopard Bay

4. *Otopharynx* sp. 'elongate-spot tanzania' ♂ Lutara

9. *Mylochromis* sp. 'melanonotus deep' Kaporo

5. *Otopharynx* sp. 'circle' Nkhotakota

10. *Trematocranus labifer* ♀ Nkopola (lectotype)

1. *Potamonautes orbitospinus*

2. *Labeo cylindricus*

3. *Barbus arcislongae*

4. *Labeobarbus johnstonii*

5. *Synodontis njassae*

6. *Mastacembelus shiranus*

7. *Mastacembelus* sp. 'rosette'

8. *Mormyrops anguilloides*

9. *Anguilla bengalensis labiata*

References

AHL, E. (1927) Einige neue Fische der Familie Cichlidae aus dem Nyassa-See. *Sitz. Geselsch. Naturf. Freunde,* 1926. No 1-10: 51-62.

AMBALI, A., H. KABWAZI, L. MALEKANO, G. MWALE, D. CHIMWAZA, J. INGAINGA, N. MAKIMOTO, S. NAKAYAMA, M. YUMA, & Y. KADA (2001) Relationship between local and scientific names of fishes in Lake Malawi/Nyasa. *Afr. Study Monogr.* 22(3): 123-154.

ARNEGARD, M.E., J.A. MARKERT, P.D. DANLEY, J.R. STAUFFER JR., A.J. AMBALI, & T.D. KOCHER (1999) Population structure and colour variation of the cichlid fish *Labeotropheus fuelleborni* Ahl along a recently formed archipelago of rocky habitat patches in southern Lake Malawi. *Proc. R. Soc. Lond. B,* 266: 119-130.

ARNEGARD, M.E. & J. SNOEKS (2001) New Three-Spotted Cichlid Species with Hypertrophied Lips (Teleostei: Cichlidae) from the Deep Waters of Lake Malaŵi/Nyasa, Africa. *Copeia* 2001(3): 705-717.

AXELROD, H.R. & W.R. BURGESS (1979) *African Cichlids of Lakes Malawi and Tanganyika.* 8th Ed. TFH Publ. Neptune, New Jersey.

BAASCH, P. (1991) *Sciaenochromis gracilis. Cichlids Yearbook,* 1: 41.

BAASCH, P. (1992a) *Dimidiochromis strigatus. Cichlids Yearbook,* 2: 42.

BAASCH, P. (1992b) *Lethrinops micrentodon. Cichlids Yearbook,* 2: 50.

BAASCH, P. (1993) *Copadichromis chrysonotus.* Cichlids Yearbook, 3: 48-49.

BARNES, B.H. (1933) *Johnson of Nyasaland: a study of the life and work of William Percival Johnson,* D.D. London, Universities Mission to Central Africa.

BERTRAM, C.K., H.J.H. BORLEY & E. TREWAVAS (1942) *Report on the Fish and Fisheries of Lake Nyasa.* London, Crown Agents.

BOWERS, N.J. & J.R. STAUFFER (1997) Eight new species of rock-dwelling cichlids of the genus *Melanochromis* (Teleostei: Cichlidae) from lake Malawi, Africa. *Ichthyol. Explor. Freshwaters,* 8 (1): 49-70.

BURGESS, W.E. & H.R. AXELROD (1973) New cichlids from Lake Malawi. *TFH mag.,* Oct.:14/87-98.

BURGESS, W.E. & H.R. AXELROD (1975) *Pseudotropheus tursiops,* a new species of cichlid fish from Lake Malawi. *TFH mag.,* 24(Nov.): 86-90.

BURGESS, W.E. (1976) A new *Melanochromis* from lake Malawi, with comments on the genus. *TFH mag.* 24(Feb): 61-65.

CHISAMBO J. & J. SNOEKS (2004) Key to the deep-bodied, spotted *Copadichromis* species: 261-265. In: J. Snoeks (ed.) *The cichlid diversity of Lake Malawi/Nyasa/Niassa: identification, distribution and taxonomy.* Cichlid Press, El Paso, U.S.A.

DELANGHE, G. (1982) Ervaringen met *Haplochromis moorii. Cichlidae* (Belg. Cichl. Ass.), 8: 31-34.

DEMASON, L. (1993) Into Africa: exploring the Tanzanian coast of Lake Malawi –part 1. *Cichlid News,* 2(4): 22-23.

DORENSTOUTER, C.F. (1982) *Haplochromis fusco-taeniatus* Regan, 1921. *NVC Periodiek,* April, 43.

DRUMMOND, B. (1976) How I Keep...*Haplochromis annectens.* Buntbarsche Bulletin Dec.: 29-30.

ECCLES, D.H. (1974) An outline of the physical limnology of Lake Malaŵi (Lake Nyasa). *Limnol. Oceanogr.,* 19(5): 730-742.

ECCLES, D.H. & D.S.C. LEWIS (1976) A revision of the genus *Docimodus* Boulenger (Pisces: Cichlidae), a group of fishes with unusual feeding habits from Lake Malawi. *Zool. J. Linn. Soc.,* 58: 165-172.

ECCLES, D.H. & D.S.C. LEWIS (1977) A taxonomic study of the genus *Lethrinops* Regan (Pisces: Cichlidae) from Lake Malawi. Part 1. *Ichthyol. Bull. J.L.B. Smith Inst. Ichthyol.,* 36.

ECCLES, D.H. & D.S.C. LEWIS (1978) A taxonomic study of the genus *Lethrinops* Regan (Pisces: Cichlidae) from Lake Malawi. Part 2. *Ichthyol. Bull. J.L.B. Smith Inst. Ichthyol.* 37.

ECCLES, D.H. & D.S.C. LEWIS (1981) Midwater spawning in *Haplochromis chrysonotus* (Boulenger) (Teleostei: Cichlidae) in Lake Malawi. *Env. Biol. Fish.,* 6 (2): 201-202.

ECCLES, D.H. & E. TREWAVAS (1989) *Malawian cichlid fishes. The classification of some Haplochromine genera.* Lake Fish Movies, Herten, Germany.

FRYER, G. (1956a) New species of cichlid fishes from Lake Nyasa. *Rev. Zool. Bot. afr.,* 53: 81-91.

FRYER, G. (1956b) Biological notes on some cichlid fishes of Lake Nyasa. *Rev. Zool. Bot. afr.,* 54: 1-7.

FRYER, G. (1956c) A new species of *Labeotropheus* from Lake Nyasa, with a redescription of *Labeotropheus fuelleborni* Ahl, and some notes on the genus *Labeotropheus* (Pisces: Cichlidae). *Rev. Zool. Bot. afr.,* 54: 290-289.

FRYER, G. (1956d) A report on the parasitic Copepoda and Branchiura of the fishes of Lake Nyasa. *Proc. zool. Soc. Lond.,* 127: 293-344.

FRYER, G. (1957) A new species of Gephyrochromis (Pisces: Cichlidae) from Lake Nyasa with notes on its ecology and affinities. *Rev. Zool. Bot. afr.,* 55: 347-352.

FRYER, G. (1959) The trophic interrelationship and ecology of some littoral communities of Lake Nyasa with special reference to the fishes and a discussion of the evolution of a group of rock-frequenting cichlidae.

Proc. zool. Soc. Lond., 132(2): 153-281.

FRYER, G. & T.D. ILES (1972) *The cichlid fishes of the great lakes of Africa.* TFH Publications, Neptune, New Jersey.

GEERTS, M. (1995) Malawi cichlids: a different perspective. *Cichlids Yearbook*, 5: 92-95.

GENNER M.J., P. NICHOLS, G.R. CARVALHO, R.L. ROBINSON, P.W. SHAW, A. SMITH & G.F. TURNER (2007b) Evolution of a cichlid fish in a Lake Malawi satellite lake. *Proc. R. Soc. B*, 274: 2249-2257.

GENNER M.J., P. NICHOLS, G.R. CARVALHO, R.L. ROBINSON, P.W. SHAW, & G.F. TURNER (2007a) Reproductive isolation among deep-water cichlid fishes of Lake Malawi differing in monochromatic male breeding dress. *Mol. Ecol.*, 16: 651-662.

GENNER M.J., M.I. TAYLOR, D.F.R. CLEARY, S.J. HAWKINS, M.E. KNIGHT, & G.F. TURNER (2004) Beta diversity of rock-restricted cichlid fishes in Lake Malawi: importance of environmental and spatial factors. *Ecography*, 27: 601-610.

GENNER M.J., G.F. TURNER, S. BARKER, & S.J. HAWKINS (1999) Niche segregation among Lake Malawi cichlid fishes? Evidence from stable isotope signatures. *Ecol. Letters*, 2: 185-190.

GREENWOOD, P.H. (1959) A revision of the Lake Victoria *Haplochromis* species (Pisces, Cichlidae), Part III. *Bull. Brit. Mus. Nat. Hist. (Zool.)*, 5(7): 179-218.

GREENWOOD, P.H. (1984) What is a Species Flock? in: A.A. Echelle & I. Kornfield (eds.) *Evolution of Fish Species Flocks.* Univ. Maine at Orono Press. USA.

GREENWOOD, P.H. (1993) A review of the serranochromine cichlid fish genera *Pharyngochromis, Sargochromis, Serranochromis* and *Chetia* (Teleostei: Labroidei). *Bull. nat. Hist. Mus. (Zool.)*, 59(1): 33-44.

HANSSENS M. (2004) The deep-water *Placidochromis* species: 104-197. In: J. Snoeks (ed.) *The cichlid diversity of Lake Malawi/Nyasa/Niassa: identification, distribution and taxonomy.* Cichlid Press, El Paso, U.S.A.

HOLZBERG, S. (1978) A field and laboratory study of the behaviour and ecology of *Pseudotropheus zebra*, an endemic cichlid of Lake Malawi. *Zeit. Zool. Syst. Evol.*, 16: 171-187

ILES, T.D. (1960) A group of zooplankton feeders of the genus *Haplochromis* (Cichlidae) in Lake Nyasa. *Ann. Mag. Nat. Hist.*, 13(2): 257-280.

JACKSON, P.B.N. (1961) Check list of the fishes of Nyasaland. *Occ. Pap. Natl. Mus. S. Rhodesia.* 3: 25B.

JOHNSON, D.S. (1985) Lake Malawi's monster *Melanochromis. Today's Aquarist*, 1: 1.

KIDD M.R, C.E. KIDD, & T.D. KOCHER (2006) Axes of differentiation in the bower-building cichlids of Lake Malawi. *Mol. Ecol.*, 15: 459-478.

KNABE, P. (1994) The "Red-Fin Tropheops". *Cichlids Yearbook*, 4: 37.

KNIGHT M.E. & G.F. TURNER (2004) Laboratory mating trials indicate incipient speciation by sexual selection among populations of the cichlid fish *Pseudotropheus zebra* from Lake Malawi. *Proc. R. Soc. B,* 271: 675-680.

KOCHER, T.D. & K.R. MCKAYE (1983) Defense of heterospecific cichlids by *Cyrtocara moorii* in Lake Malawi, Africa. *Copeia* 1993(2): 544-547.

KONINGS, A. (1989) *Malawi cichlids in their natural habitat.* Verduijn Cichlids, Zevenhuizen, Netherlands.

KONINGS, A. (1990) *Book of cichlids and all the other fishes of Lake Malawi.* TFH Publ., Neptune, New Jersey.

KONINGS, A. (1991) *Copadichromis* sp. "Virginalis Gome" and *C.* sp. "Virginalis Chitande". *Cichlids Yearbook*, 1:46-47.

KONINGS, A. (1995a) A review of the sand-dwelling species of the genus *Aulonocara,* with the description of three new species. *Cichlids Yearbook*, 5: 26-36.

KONINGS, A. (1995b) *Malawi cichlids in their natural habitat.* Cichlid Press, St. Leon-Rot, Germany.

KONINGS, A. (1998) *Tanganyika cichlids in their natural habitat.* Cichlid Press, El Paso, U.S.A.

KONINGS, A. (1999) Description of six new *Copadichromis* species (Labroidei: Cichlidae) from Lake Malawi, Africa. *TFH mag.*, 47 (May): pp 62-64, 66, 68, 70, 72, 74, 76-77, 82, 84.

KONINGS, A. (2001) *Malawi cichlids in their natural habitat. 3rd edition.* Cichlid Press, El Paso, U.S.A.

KONINGS, A. (2004a) More discoveries from Lake Malawi. *Cichlid News*, 13(2): 6-13.

KONINGS, A. (2004b) Orange-Blotch polychromatism in cichlids. *TFH mag.*, (Jul).

KONINGS A. & H.W. DIECKHOFF (1992) *Tanganyika secrets.* Cichlid Press, St. Leon-Rot, Germany.

KONINGS A..F. & J.R. STAUFFER JR. (2006) Revised diagnosis of *Metriaclima* with description of a new species (Teleostei: Cichlidae) from Lake Malaŵi National Park, Africa. *Ichthyol. Explor. Freshwaters*, 17(3): 233-246.

LEWIS, D.S.C. (1980) A further examination of the taxonomic status of *Labidochromis joanjohnsonae* Johnson, 1974 with a redescription of the species. *Revue Zool. afr.*, 94: 959-971.

LEWIS, D.S.C. (1982) A revision of the genus *Labidochromis* (Teleostei: Cichlidae) from Lake Malawi. *Zool. J. Linn. Soc.*, 75: 189-265.

LIPPITSCH E. (1993) A phyletic study on lacustrine haplochromine fishes(Perciformes, Cichlidae) of East Africa, based on scale and squamation characters. *J. Fish Biol.*, 42: 903-946.

LOWE, R.H. (1953) Notes on the ecology and evolution of Nyasa fishes of the genus *Tilapia*, with a description of *T. saka* Lowe. *Proc. zool. Soc. Lond.*, 122: 1053-1041.

MARKERT, J.A., P.D. DANLEY, & M.E. ARNEGARD (2001) New markers for new species: microsatellite loci and the East African cichlids. *Trends Ecol. Evol.*, 6(2): 100-107.

MCKAYE, K.R. (1981) Field observation on death feigning: a unique hunting behavior by the predatory cichlid, *Haplochromis livingstoni*, of Lake Malawi. *Env. Biol. Fish.*, 6(3/4): 361-365.

McKaye, K.R. (1986) Trophic eggs and parental foraging for young by the catfish *Bagrus meridionalis* of Lake Malawi, Africa. *Oecologia*, 69: 367-369.

McKaye, K.R. & T. Kocher (1983) Head ramming behaviour by three paedophagous cichlids in Lake Malawi, Africa. *Anim. Behav.*, 31: 206-210.

McKaye, K.R., S.M. Louda, & J.R. Stauffer Jr. (1990) Bower size and male reproductive success in a cichlid fish lek. *Am. Naturalist*, 135(5): 597-613.

Menger, G. (1986) *Cyrtocara moorii*. *Het Aquarium*, 56(10):256-258.

Moran, P., I. Kornfield & P. Reinthal (1994) Molecular systematics and radiation of the haplochromine cichlids (Teleostei: Perciformes) of Lake Malawi. *Copeia* 1994(2): 274-288.

Ngatunga B. & J. Snoeks (2004) Key to the shallow-water species of *Lethrinops* sensu lato: 252-260. In: J. Snoeks (ed.) *The cichlid diversity of Lake Malawi/Nyasa/Niassa: identification, distribution and taxonomy*. Cichlid Press, El Paso, U.S.A.

Oliver, M.K. (1975) *Labidochromis textilis*, a new cichlid fish (Teleostei: Cichlidae) from Lake Malawi. *Proc. Biol. Soc. Washington*, 88: 319-330.

Oliver, M.K. & K.R. McKaye (1982) Floating islands: a means of fish dispersal in Lake Malawi, Africa. *Copeia*, 1982(4): 748-754.

Owen, R.B., R. Crossley, T.C. Johnson, D. Tweddle, I. Kornfield, S. Davison, D.H. Eccles & D.E. Engstrom (1990) Major low levels of Lake Malawi and their implications for speciation rates in cichlid fishes. *Proc. R. Soc. Lond. B*, 240: 519-553.

Plenderleith M., C. VanOosterhout, R.L. Robinson, & G.F. Turner (2005) Female preference for conspecific males based on olfactory cues in a Lake Malawi cichlid fish. *Biol. Letters*, 1: 411-414.

Poll, M. (1987) Un genre inédit pour une espèce nouvelle du lac Tanganyika: *Trematochromis schreyeni* gen. n., sp. n. Statut de *Tilapia trematocephala* Blgr 1901. *Cybium*, 11(2): 167-172.

Pyke, G.H., H.R. Pulliman, & E.L. Charnov (1977) Optimal foraging. *Quart. Rev. Biol.*, 52: 137-154.

Regan, C.T. (1922) The cichlid fishes of Lake Nyassa. *Proc. zool. Soc. Lond.* 1921: 675-727.

Reitz, E. (1992) *Aulonocara rostratum* Trewavas, 1935. *Cichlid Yearbook*, 2: 46-47.

Reinthal, P.N. (1990) The feeding habits of a group of herbivorous rock-dwelling cichlid fishes (Cichlidae: Perciformes) from Lake Malawi, Africa. *Env. Biol. Fish.*, 27: 215-233.

Ribbink, A.J. (1984) The feeding behaviour of a cleaner and scale, skin and fin eater from Lake Malawi (*Docimodus evelynae*; Pisces, Cichlidae). *Neth. J. Zool.*, 34(2): 182-196.

Ribbink, A.J. & D.S.C. Lewis (1982) *Melanochromis crabro* sp. nov.: a cichlid fish from Lake Malawi which feeds on ectoparasites and catfish eggs. *Neth. J. Zool.*, 32(1): 72-87.

Ribbink, A.J., B.A. Marsh, A.C. Marsh, A.C. Ribbink & B.J. Sharp (1983b) A preliminary survey of the cichlid fishes of rocky habitats in Lake Malawi. *S. Afr. J. Zool.*, 18(3): 149-309.

Ribbink, A.J., A.C. Marsh, B. Marsh & B.J. Sharp (1980) Parental behaviour and mixed broods among cichlid fish of Lake Malawi. *S. Afr. J. Zool.*, 15: 1-6.

Ribbink, A.J., A.C. Marsh, B.A. Marsh & B.J. Sharp (1983a) The zoogeography, ecology and taxonomy of the genus *Labeotropheus* Ahl, 1927, of Lake Malawi (Pisces: Cichlidae). *Zool. J. Linn. Soc.*, 79: 223-243.

Schönen, P. (1979) Verzorging en kweek van *Labeotropheus trewavasae*, Fryer, 1956. *Cichlidae* (Belg. Cichl. Ass.), 5: 37-42.

Scholz, C.A. & B.R. Rosendahl (1988) Low lake stands in Lakes Malawi and Tanganyika, East Africa, delineated with multifold seismic data. *Science*, 240: 1645-1648.

Seegers, L. (1996) The identity of *Pseudotropheus elongatus*, with the description of *P. longior* from Mbamba Bay, Tanzania, and notes on *Genyochromis mento* (Teleostei: Cichlidae). *Ichthyol. Explor. Freshwaters*, 7(2): 97-110.

Smith, P.F., A. Konings, & I. Kornfield (2003) Hybrid origin of a cichlid population in Lake Malawi: Implications for genetic variation and species diversity. *Mol. Ecol.*, 12(9): 2497-2504.

Smith, P.F., & I. Kornfield (2002) Phylogeography of Lake Malawi cichlids of the genus *Pseudotropheus*: significance of allopatric colour variation. *Proc. Roy. Soc. B, London*, 269 (1509): 2495-2502.

Snoeks, J. (1994) The haplochromines (Teleostei, Cichlidae) of Lake Kivu (East Africa). A taxonomic revision with notes on their ecology. *Ann. Sci. zool.*, 270: 1-221.

Snoeks, J (ed.) (2004) *The cichlid diversity of Lake Malawi/Nyasa/Niassa: identification, distribution and taxonomy*. Cichlid Press, El Paso, U.S.A.

Snoeks, J. & M. Hanssens (2004) Identification guidelines to other non-mbuna: 266-310. In: J. Snoeks (ed.) *The cichlid diversity of Lake Malawi/Nyasa/Niassa: identification, distribution and taxonomy*. Cichlid Press, El Paso, U.S.A.

Snoeks, J. & R. Walapa (2004) The genus *Alticorpus* Stauffer & McKaye, 1988: 27-56. In: J. Snoeks (ed.) *The cichlid diversity of Lake Malawi/Nyasa/Niassa: identification, distribution and taxonomy*. Cichlid Press, El Paso, U.S.A.

Spreinat, A. (1991) Beobachtungen an *Rhamphochromis*-Arten. *DATZ*, 43: 528-533.

Spreinat, A. (1994) *Malawisee-Cichliden aus Tansania*. Unitext Verlag, Göttingen, Germany.

Spreinat, A. (1997) *Pseudotropheus* "Ndumbi Gold" und "M12", *DATZ*, 50: 640-642.

Staeck, W. (1976) Ergebnisse einer ichthyologischen

Sammelreise zum Nordende des Nyassasees. *Das Aquarium*, 10: 486-492.

STAUFFER, J.R. (1991) Description of a facultative cleanerfish (Teleostei: Cichlidae) from Lake Malawi, Africa. *Copeia*, 1991(1): 141-147.

STAUFFER, J.R. (1993) A new species of *Protomelas* (Teleostei: Cichlidae) from Lake Malawi, Africa. *Ichthyol. Explor. Freshw.*, 4(4): 343-350.

STAUFFER, J.R. (1994) A new species of *Iodotropheus* (Teleostei: Cichlidae) from Lake Malawi, Africa. *Ichthyol. Explor. Freshw.*, 5(4): 331-344.

STAUFFER, J.R. & J.M. BOLTZ (1989) Description of a rock-dwelling cichlid (Teleostei: Cichlidae) from Lake Malawi, Africa. *Proc. Biol. Soc. Wash.*, 102 (1): 8-13.

STAUFFER, J.R., JR., N.J. BOWERS, K.A. KELLOGG, & K.R. MCKAYE (1997) A revision of the blue-black *Pseudotropheus zebra* (Teleostei: Cichlidae) complex from Lake Malawi, Africa, with a description of a new genus and ten new species. *Proc. Acad. Nat. Sci. Phil.*, 148: 189-230.

STAUFFER, J.R., JR., & A.F. KONINGS (2006) Review of *Copadichromis* (Teleostei: Cichlidae) with the description of a new genus and six new species. *Ichthyol. Explor. Freshw.*, 17(1): 9-42.

STAUFFER, J.R., T.J. LOVULLO & K. MCKAYE (1993) Three new sand-dwelling cichlids from Lake Malawi, Africa, with a discussion of the status of the genus *Copadichromis*. *Copeia*, 1993(4): 1017-1027.

STAUFFER, J.R. & K.R. MCKAYE (1986) Description of a paedophagous deep-water cichlid (Teleostei: Cichlidae) from Lake Malawi, Africa. *Proc. Biol. Soc. Wash.*, 99(1): 29-33.

STAUFFER, J.R. & K.R. MCKAYE (1988) Description of a genus and three deep water species of fishes (Teleostei: Cichlidae) from Lake Malawi, Afrika. *Copeia*, 1988(2): 441-449.

STAUFFER, J.R., JR. & E.S. VANSNIK (1996) New species of *Petrotilapia* (Teleostei: Cichlidae) from Lake Malawi, Africa. *Copeia*, 1996 (3): 695-702.

STEIN, K. (1976) Beobachtungen an *Haplochromis moorii* (Boulenger, 1902). *DCG-Info* (German Cichl. Ass.), 7(8): 149-150.

STOCK, A.D. (1976) The taxonomic status of *Labidochromis joanjohnsonae* Johnson, *Labidochromis fryeri* Oliver and *Melanochromis exasperatus* Burgess. *Buntbarsche Bull.*, 55: 14-19.

TAWIL, P. (2002a) Notes sur le genre *Melanochromis* et l'appartenance générique de *Pseudotropheus johannii* Eccles, 1973, et espèces apparentées. *L'an Cichlidé*, 2: 61-68.

TAWIL, P. (2002b) Description de *Cynotilapia pulpican* n. sp. (Pisces, Teleostei, Cichlidae), nouvelle espèce du lac Malawi, avec remarques sur les genres *Cynotilapia, Microchromis, Maylandia* et *Metriaclima*. *L'an Cichlidé*, 2: 72-82.

TREWAVAS, E. (1931) A revision of the cichlid fishes of the genus *Lethrinops*, Regan. *Ann. & Mag. Nat. Hist. Zool.*, 10(7): 133-152.

TREWAVAS, E. (1935) A synopsis of the cichlid fishes of Lake Nyasa. *Ann. & Mag. N. Hist.* 10(16): 65-118.

TREWAVAS, E. (1984) Nouvel examen des genres et sous-genres du complexe *Pseudotropheus-Melanochromis* du Lac Malawi (Pisces, Perciformes, Cichlidae). *Revue fr. Aquariol.*, 10(3): 97-106.

TREWAVAS, E. & A. KONINGS (1992) Spawning techniques in mouthbrooders. *Cichlids Yearbook*, 2: 93-97.

TURNER, G.F. (1994) Description of a commercially important pelagic species of the genus *Diplotaxodon* (Pisces: Cichlidae) from Lake Malawi, Africa. *J. Fish Biol.*, 44: 799-807.

TURNER, G.F. (1996) *Offshore cichlids of Lake Malawi*. Cichlid Press, Lauenau, Germany.

TURNER, G.F. & J.D. HOWARTH (2002) Description of two new species of *Mylochromis* (Teleostei: Cichlidae) from Lake Malawi, Africa. *Ichthyol. Explor. Freshw.*, (2001)12(3): 205-212.

TURNER, G.F. & ROBINSON, R.L. (1991) Ecology, morphology and taxonomy of the Lake Malawi *Oreochromis* (*Nyasalapia*) species flock. *Ann. Mus. Roy. Afr. Centr. Sc. Zool.*, 262: 23-28.

TURNER, G.F., R.L. ROBINSON, P.W. SHAW, & G.R. CARVALHO (2004) Identification and biology of *Diplotaxodon, Rhamphochromis* and *Pallidochromis*: 198-251. In: J. Snoeks (ed.) *The cichlid diversity of Lake Malawi/Nyasa/Niassa: identification, distribution and taxonomy.* Cichlid Press, El Paso, U.S.A.

TURNER, G.F. & J.R. STAUFFER, JR. (1998) Three new deep water cichlid fishes of the genus *Diplotaxodon* from Lake Malawi, with a redescription of *Diplotaxodon ecclesi*. *Ichthyol. Explor. Freshw.*, 8(3): 239-252.

VANDUINEN, H.H. (1978) *Pseudotropheus lanisticola*, Burgess, 1976. *NVC Periodiek*, 20(June).

VANOPPEN, M.J.H., G.F. TURNER, C. RICO, J.C. DEUTSCH, K. IBRAHIM, R.L. ROBINSON, C.M. HEWITT (1997) Unusually fine-scale genetic structuring found in rapidly speciating Malawi cichlid fishes. *Proc. R. Soc. Lond. B*, 264: 1803-1812.

YARNTON MILLS, D.S. (1911) *What we do in Nyasaland*. Universities' Mission to Central Africa, London.

WICKLER, W. (1966) Ein augenfressender Buntbarsch. *Natur. Mus. Frankf.*, 96: 311-315.

WILHELM, W. (1980) The disputed feeding behavior of a paedophagous haplochromine cichlid (Pisces) observed and discussed. *Behaviour*, 74: 310-323.

WILLEMSE, H.S. (1976) *Haplochromis livingstoni* (Günther, 1983). *NVC Periodiek* (Dutch Cichl. Ass.) Hapl. 01.01:1–4.

Index

In this index all names, formal and informal, of the Malaŵi cichlids are arranged alphabetically with the abbreviation 'sp.' disregarded in the order. Trade names are accompanied by the scientific name used in the text. Some trade names are identical to scientific names even though they may apply to different species. In order to avoid confusion all parts of a trade name begin with a capital letter. Scientific names that are thought (by the author) to be junior synonyms, and which have been discussed in the text, are here accompanied by the name thought to be more appropriate.

Alticorpus sp. 'bicuspid bis' **398**
Alticorpus sp. 'bicuspid small-scale' **398**
Alticorpus sp. 'deep bicuspid' **398**
Alticorpus geoffreyi **398**, 400
Alticorpus macrocleithrum **398**, 400
Alticorpus mentale **398**, 400
Alticorpus sp. 'mentale bicuspid' **398**
Alticorpus pectinatum = *Alticorpus peterdaviesi*
Alticorpus peterdaviesi **398**, 400
Alticorpus profundicola **398**, 400
Aristochromis christyi 125, **127**
Astatotilapia calliptera 13, 281, **283**, 284
Astatotilapia sp. 'calliptera chizumulu' **283**, 284
Aulonocara 240
Aulonocara aquilonium 360, **362**
Aulonocara auditor 356, **358**
Aulonocara baenschi **23**, 249, **250**
Aulonocara sp. 'blue chilumba' **398**
Aulonocara Blue Gold = *A. ulonocara korneliae*
Aulonocara Blue Gold Sand = *Aulonocara brevinidus*
Aulonocara Blue Neon = *A. stuartgranti*
Aulonocara brevinidus 360, **362**
Aulonocara sp. 'brevirostris nkhata' **398**
Aulonocara sp. 'brown black-pelvic' **399**
Aulonocara sp. 'brown piper' **399**
Aulonocara Chilumba = *Aulonocara stuartgranti*
Aulonocara sp. 'chitande type kande' 252, **254**
Aulonocara sp. 'chitande type masinje' 252, **254**
Aulonocara sp. 'chitande type mozambique' 249, **254**
Aulonocara sp. 'chitande type nkhomo' 252, **254**
Aulonocara sp. 'chitande type north' 249, **251**
Aulonocara Cobwe = *Aulonocara stuartgranti*
Aulonocara sp. 'copper' **399**, 401
Aulonocara sp. 'deep' **399**, 401
Aulonocara sp. 'deep yellow' **399**
Aulonocara ethelwynnae 249, **251**
Aulonocara gertrudae 357, **359**
Aulonocara sp. 'gold' **399**, 400
Aulonocara sp. 'green' **399**
Aulonocara Green Metallic = *A. saulosi*
Aulonocara guentheri 357, **359**
Aulonocara hansbaenschi = *Aulonocara stuartgranti*
Aulonocara hueseri 249, **251**
Aulonocara jacobfreibergi 241, **243**
Aulonocara sp. 'jalo' 244, **246**
Aulonocara kandeense 252, **255**, 360
Aulonocara koningsi 248, **250**
Aulonocara korneliae 249, **251**
Aulonocara sp. 'long' **399**
Aulonocara sp. 'Iwanda' 244, **246**
Aulonocara cf. *macrochir* 356, **358**
Aulonocara maylandi 252, **255**, 360
Aulonocara sp. 'minutus' **399**, 401
Aulonocara nyassae 356, **358**
Aulonocara sp. 'nyassae mumbo' 357, **358**
Aulonocara sp. 'orange' **399**, 401
Aulonocara sp. 'pyramid' 360, **362**
Aulonocara Red Dorsal = *A.* sp. 'Iwanda'
Aulonocara Red Flush = *A. stuartgranti*
Aulonocara rostratum 356, **358**
Aulonocara saulosi 252, **255**
Aulonocara Special = *A. saulosi*
Aulonocara steveni = *Aulonocara stuartgranti*
Aulonocara stonemani **398**, 400
Aulonocara stuartgranti 21, 245, **247**
Aulonocara sp. 'stuartgranti maleri' 249, **250**
Aulonocara sp. 'stuartgranti mbenji' = *Aulonocara koningsi*
Aulonocara trematocephalum 244, **246**
Aulonocara sp. 'trematocranus masinje' 244, **246**
Aulonocara Usisya = *A. stuartgranti*
Aulonocara sp. 'walteri' 244, **246**
Aulonocara White Top = *A. hueseri*
Aulonocara sp. 'yellow' **399**, 401
Aulonocara sp. 'yellow collar' 252, **255**
Aulonocara Yellow Tanzania = *A. stuartgranti*
Benga Aulonocara = *A. baenschi*
Benga Zebra = *Metriaclima cyneusmarginatus*
Black Dorsal Zebra = *Metriaclima flavifemina*
Blue Orchid Aulonocara = *Aulonocara kandeense*
Blue Regal = *Aulonocara koningsi*
Buccochromis atritaeniatus = *Buccochromis nototaenia*
Buccochromis heterotaenia 161, **166**
Buccochromis sp. 'large mouth' 349, **350**
Buccochromis lepturus 348, **350**
Buccochromis nototaenia 348, **350**

Buccochromis oculatus = *Buccochromis nototaenia*
Buccochromis rhoadesii 348, **350**
Buccochromis spectabilis 348, **350**
Caprichromis liemi 165, **167**
Caprichromis orthognathus 164, 260, 345, **347**
Champsochromis caeruleus 349, **351**
Champsochromis spilorhynchus 300, **302**
Chilotilapia euchilus 213, **215**
Chilotilapia rhoadesii 289, **291**
Chimoto Red / Yellow = *Protomelas* sp. 'taiwan'
Chitande Aulonocara = *Aulonocara ethelwynnae*
Cobalt Zebra = *Metriaclima callainos*
Copadichromis 120
Copadichromis atripinnis **18**, 232, **234**
Copadichromis azureus 229, **230**
Copadichromis sp. 'azureus jalo' 229, **231**
Copadichromis borleyi 120, **122, 123**
Copadichromis Chingata = *Copadichromis* sp. 'flavimanus lundu'
Copadichromis sp. 'chitimba' 233, **235**
Copadichromis sp. 'chizumulu blue' = *Copadichromis chizumuluensis*
Copadichromis chizumuluensis 233, **235**
Copadichromis sp. 'chizumuluensis londo' 233, **235**
Copadichromis chrysonotus 124, **126**, 156
Copadichromis cyaneus **18**, 121, **123**
Copadichromis cyanocephalus 232, **234**
Copadichromis diplostigma 233, **235**
Copadichromis sp. 'eastern three-spot' = *Copadichromis atripinnis*
Copadichromis sp. 'fire-crest mloto' 149, **150**
Copadichromis sp. 'flavimanus lundu' 240, **242**
Copadichromis geertsi 152, **154**
Copadichromis sp. 'grey' 240
Copadichromis ilesi 149, **151**
Copadichromis insularis 229, **231**
Copadichromis jacksoni 121, **123**
Copadichromis sp. 'kawanga' 21, 233, **235**
Copadichromis sp. 'kawanga no-spot' 233, **238**
Copadichromis likomae 237, **239**
Copadichromis sp. 'likomae masinje' 237, **239**
Copadichromis sp. 'likoma blue' = *Copadichromis diplostigma*
Copadichromis sp. 'lupingu blue' 236, **238**
Copadichromis sp. 'maisoni' 237, **239**

Copadichromis sp. 'makanjila' 236, **238**
Copadichromis sp. 'mbenji blue' 237, **238**
Copadichromis mbenjii 228, **230**
Copadichromis melas 232, **234**
Copadichromis sp. 'midnight mloto' = *Copadichromis melas*
Copadichromis mloto 149, 313, **315**
Copadichromis sp. 'mloto goldcrest' **315**, 316
Copadichromis sp. 'mloto likoma' = *Copadichromis trewavasae*
Copadichromis sp. 'mloto liuli' 240, **242**
Copadichromis sp. 'mloto reef' 124, **126**
Copadichromis sp. 'mloto undu' 236, **238**
Copadichromis cf. *nkatae* 153, **155**
Copadichromis parvus 232, **234**
Copadichromis sp. 'pictus maleri' 237, **239**
Copadichromis pleurostigma 237, **239**
Copadichromis pleurostigmoides 237, **242**
Copadichromis quadrimaculatus 153, **154**
Copadichromis sp. 'quadrimaculatus yellow' 153, **155**
Copadichromis sp. 'stigma' 240
Copadichromis sp. 'taiwan yellow' 124, **126**
Copadichromis trewavasae 232, **234**
Copadichromis trimaculatus 153, **154**
Copadichromis sp. 'tumbi two-spot' 240, **242**
Copadichromis verduyni 229, **231**
Copadichromis sp. 'verduyni blueface' = *Copadichromis cyanocephalus*
Copadichromis sp. 'verduyni dwarf' = *Copadichromis parvus*
Copadichromis virginalis 148, **150**, 157
Copadichromis sp. 'virginalis chitande' **151**, 152
Copadichromis sp. 'virginalis gold' **151**, 152
Copadichromis sp. 'virginalis kajose' 148, 149, **150, 151**
Copadichromis sp. 'yellow black lupingu' 152, **155**
Copadichromis sp. 'yellow jumbo' **123**, 124
Corematodus shiranus 385, **386**
Corematodus taeniatus **351**, 352
Ctenopharynx intermedius 337, **339**
Ctenopharynx nitidus 337, **339**
Ctenopharynx pictus 221, **223**
Cyathochromis obliquidens **26**, 280, **282**
Cynotilapia 24, 64, 65
Cynotilapia afra 69, **70**, 192

Cynotilapia axelrodi 192, **194**
Cynotilapia sp. 'black dorsal' = *Metriaclima* sp. 'black dorsal mbenji'
Cynotilapia sp. 'black eastern' = *Cynotilapia* sp. 'mbamba'
Cynotilapia sp. 'blue black' 133
Cynotilapia sp. 'chinyankwazi' **26**, 69, **71**
Cynotilapia sp. 'elongatus chitimba' 192, **194**
Cynotilapia sp. 'elongatus mbenji blue' **71**, 72
Cynotilapia sp. 'elongatus taiwan' **71**, 72, 92
Cynotilapia sp. 'flavus deep' 133, **135**
Cynotilapia sp. 'hara' 192, **194**
Cynotilapia sp. 'lion' 21, 181, 192, **194**
Cynotilapia sp. 'lion chinyankwazi' 133, **135**
Cynotilapia sp. 'lion ntekete' 184, 192, **194**
Cynotilapia sp. 'maleri' 133, **135**
Cynotilapia sp. 'mbamba' 69, **71**
Cynotilapia sp. 'mbweca' = *Metriaclima* sp. 'mbweca'
Cynotilapia sp. 'ndumbi' **71**, 72
Cynotilapia pulpican = *Metriaclima pulpican*
Cyrtocara sp. 'kaporo' 321, **323**
Cyrtocara moorii 16, 321, **323**
Dimidiochromis compressiceps 300, **302**
Dimidiochromis dimidiatus 301, **303**
Dimidiochromis kiwinge 349, **351**
Dimidiochromis strigatus 300, **303**
Diplotaxodon 388
Diplotaxodon aeneus 388
Diplotaxodon apogon = *Diplotaxodon ecclesi*
Diplotaxodon argenteus **387**, 388
Diplotaxodon sp. 'black argenteus' 389
Diplotaxodon sp. 'deep' 389
Diplotaxodon ecclesi **387**, 388
Diplotaxodon greenwoodi **387**, 388, 389
Diplotaxodon sp. 'holochromis' **387**, 389
Diplotaxodon sp. 'large black' 389
Diplotaxodon limnothrissa 388, **390**
Diplotaxodon sp. 'limnothrissa black-dorsal' 389, **390**
Diplotaxodon sp. 'limnothrissa black-pelvic' 389, **390**
Diplotaxodon sp. 'limnothrissa msaka' 389, **390**
Diplotaxodon macrops **387**, 388
Diplotaxodon sp. 'macrops black-dorsal' **387**, 389
Diplotaxodon sp. 'macrops ngulube' **387**, 389

Diplotaxodon sp. 'macrops north' **387**, 389
Diplotaxodon sp. 'macrostoma' = *Diplotaxodon* sp. 'holochromis'
Diplotaxodon sp. 'similis white-back north' **387**, 389
Diplotaxodon sp. 'similis white-back south' **387**, 389
Diplotaxodon sp. 'white spot' = *Diplotaxodon limnothrissa*
Docimodus evelynae 168, **170**
Docimodus johnstonii 168, **170**
Dolphin mbuna 264
Electric Blue = *Sciaenochromis fryeri*
Electric Blue Kande = *Sciaenochromis psammophilus*
Electric Yellow = *Labidochromis caeruleus*
Exochochromis anagenys **127**, 128
Fire Blue = *Protomelas taeniolatus*
Fire-Crest Mloto = *Copadichromis* sp. 'fire-crest mloto'
Flavescent Peacock = *Aulonocara stuartgranti*
Fossorochromis rostratus 320, **322**
Gaisi = *Hemitaeniochromis* spp.
Genyochromis mento 16, **19**, **26**, 112, **114**, 209
Gephyrochromis 205
Gephyrochromis lawsi 309, **311**
Gephyrochromis moorii 309, **311**
Gephyrochromis sp. 'patricki minos' 205, **207**
Gephyrochromis sp. 'sand' 205, **207**
Gephyrochromis sp. 'sand blackfin' 205, **207**
Gephyrochromis sp. 'zebroides' **26**, 205, **206**
Giant Flame Oxyrhynchus = *Mylochromis lateristriga*
Haplochromis Chrysonotus = *Copadichromis azureus*
Haplochromis Electric Blue = *Sciaenochromis fryeri*
Haplochromis Hinderi = *Protomelas taeniolatus*
Haplochromis Jack Dempsey = *Naevochromis chrysogaster*
Haplochromis Jahni = *Placidochromis electra*
Haplochromis Lobochilus = *Protomelas ornatus*
Haplochromis Margaretae = *Otopharynx* sp. 'auromarginatus margrette'
Haplochromis Mbwanae = *Champsochromis spilorhynchus*
Haplochromis Ovatus = *Protomelas spilonotus*

Haplochromis Royal Blue = *Otopharynx heterodon*
Haplochromis Steveni = *Protomelas taeniolatus*
Haplochromis Super VC 10 = *Placidochromis milomo*
Haplochromis Thola = *Champsochromis caeruleus*
Haplochromis Yellow Fin Mloto = *Otopharynx tetraspilus*
Haplochromis Yellow-Black Line = *Mylochromis melanonotus*
Hemitaeniochromis sp. 'insignis mumbo' 165, **167**
Hemitaeniochromis sp. 'paedophage' 164, 260, **263**
Hemitaeniochromis spilopterus 164, 260, 344, **346**
Hemitaeniochromis sp. 'spilopterus blue' 165, **167**
Hemitaeniochromis sp. 'spilopterus jalo' 165, **167**
Hemitaeniochromis sp. 'spilopterus kande' 344, **347**
Hemitaeniochromis sp. 'spilopterus yellow' 164, 344, **347**
Hemitaeniochromis urotaenia 344, **346**
Hemitaeniochromis sp. 'urotaenia tanzania' 260, **263**
Hemitilapia oxyrhynchus 280, 285, **287**
Imperial Tigress = *Protomelas* sp. 'steveni imperial'
Iodotropheus 40
Iodotropheus declivitas = *Iodotropheus sprengerae*
Iodotropheus sp. 'londo' 105, **106**
Iodotropheus sprengerae **26**, **103**, 104, **106**
Iodotropheus stuartgranti 273, **275**
Kaligono = *Nimbochromis livingstonii*
King-of-Cave = *Otopharynx* sp. 'cave'
Labeotropheus fuelleborni **26**, **27**, 28, **30**, **31**, 89, 93
Labeotropheus trewavasae **19**, 21, 88, **90**, 93, 273
Labeotropheus sp. 'trewavasae chiloelo' 273, **275**
Labidochromis sp. 'blue bar' 44, **46**
Labidochromis caeruleus 16, 21, **22**, 137, **139**
Labidochromis sp. 'caeruleus brown' 140, **142**
Labidochromis sp. 'caeruleus chilucha' 140, **142**
Labidochromis sp. 'caeruleus jalo' 137, **138**
Labidochromis chisumulae 137, **142**
Labidochromis sp. 'chisumulae mbweca' 137, **142**

Labidochromis Ewarti = *Labidochromis freibergi*
Labidochromis flavigulis 269, **271**
Labidochromis freibergi 41, **43**
Labidochromis gigas **26**, 101, **103**, 141
Labidochromis sp. 'gigas chidunga' **103**, 104
Labidochromis sp. 'gigas chilumba' 101, **103**
Labidochromis sp. 'gigas cobwe' 101, **103**
Labidochromis sp. 'gigas lupingu' 101, **103**
Labidochromis sp. 'gigas mara' **103**, 104
Labidochromis sp. 'gigas pombo' 101, **103**
Labidochromis heterodon **27**, 41, **43**
Labidochromis sp. 'hongi' 208, **210**
Labidochromis sp. 'hora' 272, **274**
Labidochromis ianthinus 137, 208, **210**
Labidochromis sp. 'likomae' 140, **143**
Labidochromis lividus 272, **274**
Labidochromis sp. 'lividus mozambique' 272, **274**
Labidochromis sp. 'lividus nkhungu' 272, **274**
Labidochromis sp. 'lundu blue' 272, **274**
Labidochromis maculicauda 44, **46**
Labidochromis sp. 'mara' 272, **274**
Labidochromis sp. 'mbamba' 140, **143**
Labidochromis mbenjii 44, **46**
Labidochromis mylodon 140, **143**
Labidochromis pallidus 140, **143**
Labidochromis sp. 'perlmutt' 140, **142**
Labidochromis shiranus 272, **274**
Labidochromis strigatus 41, **43**
Labidochromis textilis **271**, 272
Labidochromis sp. 'textilis blue' 41, **42**
Labidochromis sp. 'textilis cobalt' 41, **42**
Labidochromis vellicans 44, **46**
Labidochromis sp. 'zebra eastern' 208, **210**
Labidochromis zebroides **43**
Lethrinops albus 372, **375**
Lethrinops altus 376, **379**
Lethrinops argenteus 396
Lethrinops sp. 'aulonocara type' 372, **374**
Lethrinops auritus 369, **371**
Lethrinops sp. 'auritus lion' 369, **371**
Lethrinops sp. 'auritus selewa' 369, **371**
Lethrinops sp. 'big-head' **397**
Lethrinops sp. 'black chin' **395**
Lethrinops sp. 'blue-orange' **395**
Lethrinops sp. 'boadzulu' 373, **375**
Lethrinops christyi **394**, 396
Lethrinops sp. 'christyi fort maguire' **395**
Lethrinops sp. 'dark' **395**
Lethrinops sp. 'deep-water albus' **394**

Lethrinops sp. 'deep-water albus yellow' **394**
Lethrinops sp. 'deep-water altus' **395**
Lethrinops sp. 'domira blue' **395**
Lethrinops furcifer 364, **366**
Lethrinops gossei **391**, 396
Lethrinops sp. 'gossei white-bar' **394**
Lethrinops sp. 'grey' **397**
Lethrinops leptodon 376, **379**
Lethrinops lethrinus 361, **366**
Lethrinops longimanus **394**, 396
Lethrinops sp. 'longimanus likoma' 373, **375**
Lethrinops sp. 'longimanus red-head' **394**
Lethrinops longipinnis **391**, 396
Lethrinops sp. 'longipinnis deep-water' 396
Lethrinops sp. 'longipinnis ntekete' 377, **379**
Lethrinops sp. 'longipinnis white-lappets' 396
Lethrinops sp. 'lowae' **397**
Lethrinops lunaris 376, **378**
Lethrinops macracanthus **391**, 396
Lethrinops macrochir 376, **378**
Lethrinops sp. 'macrochir mumbo' 376, **378**
Lethrinops sp. 'macrochir nkhudzi' 376, **378**
Lethrinops macrophthalmus 372, **375**
Lethrinops sp. 'macrostoma' **395**
Lethrinops marginatus 373, **375**
Lethrinops sp. 'marginatus liuli' 373, **375**
Lethrinops sp. 'matumbae' **395**
Lethrinops sp. 'mbasi' 372, **375**
Lethrinops sp. 'mbenji deep' **395**
Lethrinops sp. 'mbenji roundhead' 377, **379**
Lethrinops sp. 'mdoka red' 372, **374**
Lethrinops micrentodon **394**, 396
Lethrinops sp. 'micrentodon makokola' 373, **375**
Lethrinops microdon **394**, 396
Lethrinops microstoma 361, **363**
Lethrinops sp. 'microstoma gold' = *Lethrinops parvidens*
Lethrinops mylodon **391**, 396
Lethrinops sp. 'nyassae' 369, **374**
Lethrinops oculatus = *Lethrinops marginatus*
Lethrinops sp. 'oliveri' **395**
Lethrinops parvidens 361, **363**
Lethrinops sp. 'red bar' 372, **374**
Lethrinops sp. 'red cap' 372, **374**
Lethrinops sp. 'red cap tsano' 372, **374**
Lethrinops sp. 'silver crescent' **395**
Lethrinops stridei **394**, 396
Lethrinops turneri 373, **375**
Lethrinops sp. 'yellow' **395**

Lethrinops Yellow Black Dorsal = *Lethrinops microstoma*
Lethrinops sp. 'yellow chest' 377, **379**
Lethrinops sp. 'yellow chin' **395**
Lethrinops sp. 'yellow collar' 372, **374**
Lethrinops Yellow Red Dorsal = *Lethrinops macrochir*
Lethrinops sp. 'yellow tail' **395**
Lethrinops sp. 'zebra' **394**
Lichnochromis acuticeps 157, 213, **215**
Macrophthalmus Red Cheek = *Tropheops* sp. 'red cheek'
Malawi Butterfly = *Aulonocara jacobfreibergi*
Mamelela = *Aulonocara jacobfreibergi*
Maylandia = *Metriaclima*
Mchenga 120, 312
Mchenga conophoros 312, **314**, 315
Mchenga cyclicos 312, **314**
Mchenga eucinostomus 312
Mchenga flavimanus 313, **315**
Mchenga inornata 312, **314**
Mchenga thinos 312, **314**
Melanochromis 105
Melanochromis auratus 17, 108, **110**
Melanochromis sp. 'auratus elongate' 109, **110**
Melanochromis baliodigma 105, 144, 209, **211**
Melanochromis sp. 'blotch' = *Melanochromis baliodigma*
Melanochromis brevis 37, **38**, 105
Melanochromis 'brown' = *Metriaclima* sp. 'chinyankwazi'
Melanochromis chipokae 208, **210**
Melanochromis cyaneorhabdos 109, **111**
Melanochromis dialeptos 109, **110**, 208
Melanochromis sp. 'dialeptos blue' **110**
Melanochromis heterochromis 37, 105, **107**, 108, 273
Melanochromis interruptus 109, **111**, 112
Melanochromis joanjohnsonae 40, **42**, 105
Melanochromis johannii 109, **111**
Melanochromis labrosus 20, 105, 212, **214**
Melanochromis lepidiadaptes 209, **211**
Melanochromis melanopterus **26**, 144, **147**, 149, 273
Melanochromis sp. 'northern blue' 209, **211**
Melanochromis parallelus 105, **106**, 144
Melanochromis sp. 'parallelus mbweca' **106**, 108
Melanochromis perileucos 109, 212, **214**
Melanochromis robustus 145, **146**

Melanochromis sp. 'robustus mbenji' 105, **147**, 148
Melanochromis simulans 109, 208, **211**
Melanochromis vermivorus 105, 273, **275**
Metriaclima 24, 65
Metriaclima sp. 'aggressive bars' 64, **66**, 72
Metriaclima sp. 'aggressive greyhead' 188, **190**
Metriaclima sp. 'aggressive zebra maleri' 93, 264, **266**
Metriaclima aurora 176, **178**
Metriaclima sp. 'aurora bevous' 177, **178**
Metriaclima sp. 'aurora blacktail' 180, **182**
Metriaclima sp. 'aurora blue' 177, **179**
Metriaclima sp. 'aurora chinuni' 180, **182**
Metriaclima sp. 'aurora lumbaulo' 177, **178**
Metriaclima sp. 'aurora north' 177, **178**
Metriaclima sp. 'aurora yellow' 180, **182**
Metriaclima barlowi 180, **182**
Metriaclima benetos 177, **179**
Metriaclima sp. 'black dorsal chiloelo' 173, **174**
Metriaclima sp. 'black dorsal cobalt' = *Metriaclima* sp. 'black dorsal lundo'
Metriaclima sp. 'black dorsal cobalt' = *Pseudotropheus* sp. 'sand cobalt'
Metriaclima sp. 'black dorsal lundo' 173, **175**
Metriaclima sp. 'black dorsal mbenji' 176, **178**
Metriaclima sp. 'black dorsal nkhungu' **131**, 132
Metriaclima sp. 'black dorsal nkolongwe' 173, **174**
Metriaclima sp. 'black dorsal thundu' 173, **174**
Metriaclima sp. 'blue reef' 60, 177, **179**
Metriaclima sp. 'boadzulu' 64, **66**
Metriaclima callainos 56, **58**
Metriaclima sp. 'cave manda' 133, **134**
Metriaclima sp. 'chinyankwazi' 64, **66**, 148
Metriaclima chrysomallos 60, 177, **179**, 184
Metriaclima cyneusmarginatus **62**, 64, 172
Metriaclima sp. 'daktari' 189, **191**
Metriaclima sp. 'dolphin' 65, **66**
Metriaclima sp. 'dumpy tanzania' 184, **186**
Metriaclima sp. 'dumpy' 133, 181, **186**
Metriaclima sp. 'elongatus bee' 188, **190**
Metriaclima sp. 'elongatus chailosi' 188, **190**

Metriaclima sp. 'elongatus chewere' 185, 188, **190**
Metriaclima sp. 'elongatus chidunga' 189, **191**
Metriaclima sp. 'elongatus goldbar' 189, **191**
Metriaclima sp. 'elongatus linganjala' 65, **67**
Metriaclima sp. 'elongatus mdoka' 65, **67**
Metriaclima sp. 'elongatus ngkuyo' 65, **67**
Metriaclima sp. 'elongatus usisya' 189, **191**
Metriaclima sp. 'elongatus yellow tail' 65, **67**
Metriaclima emmiltos 53, **54**
Metriaclima estherae 20, 57, **59**
Metriaclima sp. 'estherae blueface' **59**, 60
Metriaclima fainzilberi **26**, 61, **62**, **63**
Metriaclima flavifemina **171**, 173, 201
Metriaclima greshakei 53, **55**
Metriaclima hajomaylandi 180, **182**
Metriaclima sp. 'hajomaylandi pombo' 180, **182**
Metriaclima sp. 'kingsizei lupingu' 24, 181, **183**
Metriaclima sp. 'kingsizei masimbwe' 181, **183**
Metriaclima lanisticola 305, **310**
Metriaclima sp. 'lanisticola north' 308, **310**
Metriaclima sp. 'lime' 24, 189, **191**
Metriaclima sp. 'lime jalo' 189, **191**
Metriaclima sp. 'lime nkhomo' **191**
Metriaclima livingstonii = *Metriaclima lanisticola*
Metriaclima lombardoi 17, 185, **187**
Metriaclima mbenjii 53, **55**
Metriaclima sp. 'mbweca' 188, **190**
Metriaclima sp. 'membe deep' 188, **190**
Metriaclima sp. 'msobo' **175**, 176
Metriaclima sp. 'msobo heteropictus' 173, **175**
Metriaclima sp. 'patricki' 185, **187**
Metriaclima sp. 'patricki minos' = *Gephyrochromis* sp. 'patricki minos'
Metriaclima phaeos 173, **174**
Metriaclima pulpican 24, 181, **183**
Metriaclima pursus = *Metriaclima lanisticola*
Metriaclima pyrsonotos 20, 52, **54**
Metriaclima sp. 'red top gallireya' 185, **187**
Metriaclima sp. 'red top londo' **55**, 56
Metriaclima sandaracinos = *Metriaclima pyrsonotos*
Metriaclima sp. 'taiwan' 132, **134**

Metriaclima sp. 'taiwan masimbwe' 132, **134**
Metriaclima thapsinogen = *Metriaclima pyrsonotos*
Metriaclima xanstomachus **62**, 64
Metriaclima zebra **19**, 48, **50**, **51**
Metriaclima sp. 'zebra chilumba' 61, **62**
Metriaclima sp. 'zebra gold' 68, 129, **130**
Metriaclima sp. 'zebra long pelvic' 184, **186**
Metriaclima sp. 'zebra long pelvic hara' = *Metriaclima* sp. 'red top gallireya'
Metriaclima sp. 'zebra mbamba' = *Pseudotropheus* sp. 'sand cobalt'
Metriaclima sp. 'zebra mbowe' 184, **186**
Metriaclima sp. 'zebra ruarwe' 184, **186**
Metriaclima sp. 'zebra slim' **55**, 56
Metriaclima sp. 'zebra yellow tail' **131**, 132
Mloto Likoma = *Copadichromis trewavasae*
Mylochromis 216
Mylochromis anaphyrmus 328, **330**
Mylochromis balteatus 293, **294**
Mylochromis sp. 'balteatus mozambique' 293, **295**
Mylochromis chekopae 328, **330**
Mylochromis sp. 'chrysogaster line' 344, **346**
Mylochromis sp. 'deep' 328, **330**
Mylochromis ensatus 332, **334**
Mylochromis epichorialis 216, **218**
Mylochromis ericotaenia 329, **331**
Mylochromis formosus 341, **343**
Mylochromis gracilis 341, **343**
Mylochromis guentheri 293, 328, **331**
Mylochromis sp. 'guentheri mbenji' 221, **223**
Mylochromis sp. 'ikombe' 221, **223**
Mylochromis incola 291, 292
Mylochromis sp. 'incola mumbo' 221, **223**
Mylochromis sp. 'kande' 344, **346**
Mylochromis labidodon 216, **218**
Mylochromis lateristriga **18**, 292, **294**
Mylochromis sp. 'lateristriga makanjila' 217, **219**
Mylochromis sp. 'lateristriga nkhata' 217, **219**
Mylochromis sp. 'liemi small-mouth' 329, **331**
Mylochromis Mchuse = *Mylochromis* sp. 'lateristriga makanjila'
Mylochromis melanonotus 168, 332, **331**
Mylochromis sp. 'melanonotus deep' 409, **410**
Mylochromis melanotaenia 328, **330**
Mylochromis mola 292, **294**

Mylochromis mollis 217, **219**
Mylochromis sp. 'mollis chitande' 220, **222**
Mylochromis sp. 'mollis gallireya' 220, **222**
Mylochromis sp. 'mollis likoma' 217, **219**
Mylochromis sp. 'mollis north' 220, **222**
Mylochromis obtusus 261, **263**
Mylochromis plagiotaenia 292, **294**
Mylochromis sphaerodon 328, **330**
Mylochromis sp. 'sphaerodon nkhomo' 328, **330**
Mylochromis spilostichus **343**, 344
Mylochromis subocularis 277, **278**
Mylochromis sp. 'torpedo elongate' 293, **295**
Naevochromis chrysogaster 260, **262**
Ncheni 164, 301, 392
Ndunduma 388
Nimbochromis fuscotaeniatus 297, **299**
Nimbochromis linni 160, **163**
Nimbochromis livingstonii 296, **298**
Nimbochromis polystigma 288, 297, **299**, 348
Nimbochromis venustus 352, **354**
Northern Aulonocara = *Aulonocara ethelwynnae*
Nyassachromis 120, 316
Nyassachromis boadzulu 316, **318**
Nyassachromis breviceps 316, **318**
Nyassachromis sp. 'interruptus' 317, **319**
Nyassachromis leuciscus 317, **319**, 332
Nyassachromis microcephalus 317, **319**
Nyassachromis sp. 'mphanga' 317, **319**
Nyassachromis nigritaeniatus 317, **319**
Nyassachromis sp. 'otter' 320, **322**
Nyassachromis prostoma **22**, 313, 316, **318**
Nyassachromis purpurans 317, **319**
Nyassachromis serenus 317, **319**
Orange Peacock = *Aulonocara* sp. 'stuartgranti maleri'
Oreochromis karongae 304, **306**, 384
Oreochromis lidole 384, **386**
Oreochromis shiranus 304, **306**
Oreochromis squamipinnis 384, **386**
Otopharynx argyrosoma 332, **335**
Otopharynx sp. 'argyrosoma deep' **335**, 336
Otopharynx sp. 'argyrosoma red' = *Otopharynx argyrosoma*
Otopharynx auromarginatus 224, 336, **338**
Otopharynx sp. 'auromarginatus goldhead' 224, **226**
Otopharynx sp. 'auromarginatus jakuta' 336, **338**

Otopharynx sp. 'auromarginatus mara' 224, **226**
Otopharynx sp. 'auromarginatus margrette' 224, **226**
Otopharynx sp. 'auromarginatus stripe' 337, **338**
Otopharynx sp. 'blue flat-jaw' **410**
Otopharynx brooksi 161, **163**
Otopharynx sp. 'brooksi nkhata' **403**
Otopharynx sp. 'cave' 156, **158**
Otopharynx sp. 'circle' **410**
Otopharynx decorus 333, **335**
Otopharynx sp. 'decorus featherfin' **335**
Otopharynx sp. 'decorus jumbo' 333, **335**
Otopharynx sp. 'elongate-spot tanzania' **410**
Otopharynx sp. 'flat jaw' **407**
Otopharynx sp. 'golden blueface' 228, **230**
Otopharynx sp. 'golf-head blue' **410**
Otopharynx heterodon 224, **227**
Otopharynx sp. 'heterodon boadzulu' 225, **227**
Otopharynx sp. 'heterodon ikombe' 225, **226**
Otopharynx sp. 'heterodon likoma' 337, **338**
Otopharynx sp. 'heterodon longnose' 225, **227**
Otopharynx sp. 'heterodon low-spot' **410**
Otopharynx sp. 'heterodon nankumba' 224, 225, **226**
Otopharynx sp. 'high fin' **407**
Otopharynx sp. 'high-fin low-GR' **410**
Otopharynx lithobates 156, **158**
Otopharynx sp. 'molariform striped' **410**
Otopharynx ovatus 22, 261, **263**
Otopharynx sp. 'ovatus likoma' 157, **159**
Otopharynx pachycheilus **407**, 408
Otopharynx sp. 'red flat-jaw' **410**
Otopharynx sp. 'round head' **407**
Otopharynx selenurus 324, **326**
Otopharynx sp. 'silver torpedo' 332, **334**
Otopharynx speciosus **403**, 408
Otopharynx sp. 'spots' 225, **226**
Otopharynx tetraspilus 293, **295**
Otopharynx sp. 'tetraspilus molariform' 293, **295**
Otopharynx tetrastigma 293, **295**
Otopharynx sp. 'torpedo blue' 332, **334**
Otopharynx walteri = *Otopharynx lithobates*
Pallidochromis sp. 'chicken' = *Rhamphochromis* sp. 'grey'
Pallidochromis tokolosh **391**, 393

Pearl of Likoma = *Melanochromis joanjohnsonae*
Pearl Zebra = *Metriaclima callainos*
Petrotilapia 33
Petrotilapia sp. 'black flank' 76, **79**
Petrotilapia sp. 'chitande' 265, **267**
Petrotilapia sp. 'chitimba' 193, **194**
Petrotilapia chrysos 73, **75**
Petrotilapia sp. 'fuscous' 73, **74**
Petrotilapia genalutea 265, **267**
Petrotilapia sp. 'hara' 193, **194**
Petrotilapia sp. 'likoma barred' 36, **38**
Petrotilapia sp. 'likoma variable' 76, **78**
Petrotilapia microgalana 76, **78**
Petrotilapia sp. 'mumbo blue' 72, **74**
Petrotilapia sp. 'mumbo yellow' 73, **74**
Petrotilapia nigra 73, **75**
Petrotilapia sp. 'nigra tanzania' 76, **78**
Petrotilapia sp. 'nigra tumbi' **75**, 76
Petrotilapia sp. 'orange pelvic' 36, **38**
Petrotilapia sp. 'retrognathous' 72, **74**
Petrotilapia sp. 'ruarwe' 76, **78**
Petrotilapia sp. 'small blue' = *Petrotilapia microgalana*
Petrotilapia tridentiger 33, **35**
Petrotilapia sp. 'yellow chin' 265, **267**
Petrotilapia sp. 'yellow ventral' **26**, **35**, **75**, 76
Placidochromis acuticeps 401, **405**
Placidochromis acutirostris 401, **406**
Placidochromis argyrogaster 405, **406**
Placidochromis sp. 'big eye' 401
Placidochromis sp. 'big mouth' 401
Placidochromis sp. 'blue otter' 157, **159**
Placidochromis sp. 'blue-head piper' **402**
Placidochromis boops 401, **404**
Placidochromis borealis 405, **406**
Placidochromis sp. 'carnivore' **402**
Placidochromis chilolae 401, **404**
Placidochromis sp. 'chinyankwazi' 157, **159**
Placidochromis communis 401, **402**
Placidochromis sp. 'deep' 405
Placidochromis sp. 'deep cheek' 405
Placidochromis domirae 401, **405**
Placidochromis ecclesi 401, **404**
Placidochromis electra 321, **323**
Placidochromis sp. 'electra blackfin' 321, **326**
Placidochromis sp. 'electra blue' 321, **326**
Placidochromis sp. 'electra boadzulu' 324, **326**
Placidochromis sp. 'electra mozambique' 324, **326**
Placidochromis sp. 'electra type' 324, **326**
Placidochromis sp. 'elongate thin bar' 405

Placidochromis elongatus 401, **402**
Placidochromis fuscus 405, **406**
Placidochromis sp. 'green orange deep' 405
Placidochromis hennydaviesae 401, **405**
Placidochromis sp. 'hennydaviesaeIV' **407**
Placidochromis sp. 'hennydaviesaeV' **407**
Placidochromis intermedius 401, **404**
Placidochromis sp. 'jalo' 157, **159**
Placidochromis johnstoni 284, 288, **290**
Placidochromis sp. 'johnstoni solo' = *Protomelas* sp. 'johnstoni solo'
Placidochromis koningsi 401, **405**
Placidochromis lineatus 401, **406**
Placidochromis longimanus 325, **327**
Placidochromis sp. 'longimanus mumbo' 325, **327**
Placidochromis sp. 'longimanus namiasi' 325, **326**
Placidochromis sp. 'longimanus thumbi' 325, **327**
Placidochromis longirostris 401, **404**
Placidochromis longus 401, **404**
Placidochromis lukomae 401, **404**
Placidochromis macroceps 401, **404**
Placidochromis macrognathus 401, **402**
Placidochromis sp. 'mbamba' 157, **159**
Placidochromis mbunoides 401, **406**
Placidochromis milomo 27, 160, **162, 163**
Placidochromis minor 405, **406**
Placidochromis minutus 401, **404**
Placidochromis msakae **402**, 405
Placidochromis nigribarbus 401, **404**
Placidochromis nkhatae 401, **405**
Placidochromis nkhotakotae 401, **404**
Placidochromis obscurus 401, **405**
Placidochromis ordinarius 401, **406**
Placidochromis orthognathus 405, **406**
Placidochromis sp. 'pale elongate blunt snout' 405
Placidochromis sp. 'pale elongate dull' 405
Placidochromis sp. 'pale elongate unicuspid' 405
Placidochromis pallidus 405, **406**
Placidochromis phenochilus 324, **327**
Placidochromis sp. 'phenochilus gissel' 324, **327**
Placidochromis sp. 'phenochilus tanzania' 324, **327**
Placidochromis platyrhynchos 401, **402**
Placidochromis polli 401, **402**
Placidochromis rotundifrons 405, **406**
Placidochromis trewavasae 401, **404**
Placidochromis turneri 401, **406**
Placidochromis vulgaris **402**, 405

Placidochromis sp. 'white-orange dorsal' 401, **402**
Protomelas annectens 321, **323**, 325
Protomelas dejunctus = *Protomelas taeniolatus*
Protomelas fenestratus 213, **215**
Protomelas festivus = *Protomelas ornatus*
Protomelas sp. 'hertae' 117, **119**
Protomelas insignis 261, **263**
Protomelas sp. 'insignis small' = *Protomelas insignis*
Protomelas sp. 'johnstoni solo' 216, **218**
Protomelas kirkii 284, **286**
Protomelas labridens 284, **286**
Protomelas lobochilus = *Protomelas ornatus*
Protomelas macrodon **287**
Protomelas marginatus 309, **311**
Protomelas sp. 'mbenji thick-lip' 212, **214, 215**
Protomelas ornatus 125, 157, 273, **278**
Protomelas sp. 'oxyrhynchus mix' 288, **290**
Protomelas pleurotaenia 284, **286**
Protomelas similis 284, **286**
Protomelas spilonotus 45, **47**
Protomelas sp. 'spilonotus likoma' 45, **47**
Protomelas sp. 'spilonotus mozambique' 45, **47**
Protomelas sp. 'spilonotus tanzania' 45, **47**
Protomelas sp. 'steveni black belly' 117, **119**
Protomelas sp. 'steveni imperial' **23**, 116, **118**, 160
Protomelas sp. 'steveni taiwan' 116, **119**
Protomelas taeniolatus **115**, 116, 117
Protomelas triaenodon 289, **291**
Protomelas virgatus 116, 276, **278**
Protomelas sp. 'virgatus luwala' 216, **218**
Protomelas sp. 'virgatus mumbo' 285, **287**
Pseudotropheus 24, 65, 85, 89
Pseudotropheus sp. 'acei' 309, **311**
Pseudotropheus sp. 'aggressive brown' **95**, 96
Pseudotropheus sp. 'aggressive grey' 265, **267**
Pseudotropheus sp. 'aggressive yellow fin' 273, **275**
Pseudotropheus sp. 'aggressive zebra likoma' 93, **95**
Pseudotropheus sp. 'aggressive zebra mbenji' 93, **95**
Pseudotropheus sp. 'aggressive zebra' = *Metriaclima* sp. 'aggressive zebra maleri'
Pseudotropheus sp. 'aggressive zebra' = *Pseudotropheus* sp. 'aggressive zebra likoma'
Pseudotropheus sp. 'aggressive zebra' = *Pseudotropheus* sp. 'aggressive zebra mbenji'
Pseudotropheus ater **26**, 93, **95**, 113
Pseudotropheus sp. 'burrower' 204, **206**
Pseudotropheus crabro 141, **146**
Pseudotropheus sp. 'crabro blue' 144, **146**
Pseudotropheus cyaneus 93, **94**
Pseudotropheus demasoni 40, **42**
Pseudotropheus sp. 'dumpy chitimba' 201, **203**
Pseudotropheus sp. 'dwarf gold' = *Cynotilapia* sp. 'lion ntekete'
Pseudotropheus sp. 'dwarf nkhata' 136, **138**
Pseudotropheus elegans = *Pseudotropheus livingstonii*
Pseudotropheus elongatus **91**, 92
Pseudotropheus elongatus complex 85, 89, 188, 192
Pseudotropheus sp. 'elongatus aggressive' **27**, 89, 93, **95**
Pseudotropheus sp. 'elongatus brown' 93, **94**
Pseudotropheus sp. 'elongatus kirondo' 92, **94**
Pseudotropheus sp. 'elongatus makonde' 92, **94**
Pseudotropheus sp. 'elongatus masimbwe' **91**, 92
Pseudotropheus sp. 'elongatus mbenji brown' 200, **203**
Pseudotropheus sp. 'elongatus mozambique brown' 200, **202**
Pseudotropheus sp. 'elongatus mphanga' **91**, 92
Pseudotropheus sp. 'elongatus ndumbi' 89, 92, **95**
Pseudotropheus sp. 'elongatus nkhata blue' **91**, 92
Pseudotropheus sp. 'elongatus nkhata brown' 136, **138**
Pseudotropheus sp. 'elongatus ornatus' 17, **18**, 92, **94**
Pseudotropheus sp. 'elongatus ornatus tanzania' 93, **94**
Pseudotropheus sp. 'elongatus ruarwe' **91**, 92
Pseudotropheus sp. 'elongatus slab' 93, **95**
Pseudotropheus sp. 'elongatus spot' **91**, 92
Pseudotropheus sp. 'elongatus thumbi' 136, **138**
Pseudotropheus Flameback = *Metriaclima* sp. 'aurora blue'
Pseudotropheus flavus 93, **94**, 113
Pseudotropheus fuscus 264, **266**
Pseudotropheus sp. 'fuscus dwarf' 273, **275**
Pseudotropheus galanos 37, **38**
Pseudotropheus Greberi = *Metriaclima hajomaylandi*
Pseudotropheus heteropictus 25, 201, **203**
Pseudotropheus Jacksoni = *Tropheops* sp. 'lucerna blue cobalt'
Pseudotropheus sp. 'kingsizei londo' = *Metriaclima pulpican*
Pseudotropheus sp. 'kingsizei north' = *Metriaclima* sp. 'aurora north'
Pseudotropheus sp. 'kingsizei tumbi' **203**, 204
Pseudotropheus sp. 'kingsizei' = *Metriaclima pulpican*
Pseudotropheus livingstonii 25, 185, 305, **307**
Pseudotropheus longior 65, **91**, 92
Pseudotropheus minutus 96, **98**
Pseudotropheus sp. 'minutus mozambique' 97, **98**, 273
Pseudotropheus sp. 'minutus tanzania' 96, **98**, 272
Pseudotropheus sp. 'ndumbi gold' 133, **135**
Pseudotropheus perspicax 97, **99**
Pseudotropheus sp. 'perspicax hara' 97, **99**
Pseudotropheus sp. 'perspicax likoma' 136, **138**
Pseudotropheus sp. 'perspicax orange cap' **99**, 100
Pseudotropheus sp. 'perspicax tanzania' **99**, 100
Pseudotropheus sp. 'perspicax yellow breast' **99**, 100
Pseudotropheus sp. 'polit' **99**, 100, 188
Pseudotropheus sp. 'polit tumbi' **99**, 100
Pseudotropheus purpuratus 265, **267**
Pseudotropheus sp. 'sand cobalt' **207**, 208
Pseudotropheus saulosi 101, **102**
Pseudotropheus socolofi 204, **206**
Pseudotropheus sp. 'socolofi nkolongwe' 273, **275**
Pseudotropheus sp. 'thin stripe' 136, **138**
Pseudotropheus sp. 'three peaks' 136, **138**
Pseudotropheus sp. 'tiny' 97, **98**
Pseudotropheus tursiops 264, **266**
Pseudotropheus sp. 'tursiops chitande' **27**, 264, **266**

Pseudotropheus sp. 'tursiops mbenji' 264, **266**
Pseudotropheus sp. 'variable eastern' 100, **102**
Pseudotropheus sp. 'variable kande' 100, **102**
Pseudotropheus sp. 'variable mozambique' 100, **102**
Pseudotropheus williamsi 24, 36, **39**, 89
Pseudotropheus sp. 'williamsi makanjila' 36, **39**
Pseudotropheus sp. 'williamsi maleri' 37, **39**
Pseudotropheus sp. 'williamsi nkhudzi' 36, **39**
Pseudotropheus sp. 'williamsi north' 36, **39**
Red Empress = *Protomelas taeniolatus*
Red Zebra = *Metriaclima estherae*
Rhamphochromis 388
Rhamphochromis sp. 'big-tooth' **391**, 393
Rhamphochromis brevis **390**, 392
Rhamphochromis sp. 'chilingali' 301, **303**
Rhamphochromis esox 164, **166**
Rhamphochromis cf. *ferox* **390**, 392
Rhamphochromis sp. 'ferox yellow-fin' = *Rhamphochromis brevis*
Rhamphochromis sp. 'grey' **390**, 393
Rhamphochromis leptosoma = *Rhamphochromis esox*
Rhamphochromis sp. 'long-fin yellow' **391**, 393
Rhamphochromis longiceps 301, **303**, **390**, 392
Rhamphochromis sp. 'longiceps greyback' **390**, 393
Rhamphochromis sp. 'longiceps yellowbelly' **390**, 393
Rhamphochromis sp. 'long-snout north' **391**, 393
Rhamphochromis sp. 'long-snout south' **391**, 393
Rhamphochromis lucius = *Rhamphochromis esox*
Rhamphochromis macrophthalmus = *Rhamphochromis longiceps*
Rhamphochromis sp. 'maldeco' **391**, 393
Rhamphochromis sp. 'stripe' **390**, 393
Rhamphochromis woodi **390**, 392
Sciaenochromis ahli 257, **259**
Sciaenochromis benthicola 352, **354**, **403**, 405
Sciaenochromis sp. 'deep' **407**, 408
Sciaenochromis sp. 'deep water' **403**, 408
Sciaenochromis sp. 'elongate' **403**, 408
Sciaenochromis fryeri **27**, 253, **258**

Sciaenochromis sp. 'nyassae' 257, **258**
Sciaenochromis psammophilus 352, **354**
Sciaenochromis sp. 'psammophilus broad' **407**, 408
Sciaenochromis sp. 'small interorbital' **407**, 408
Sciaenochromis sp. 'spilostichus deepwater' **403**, 408
Sciaenochromis sp. 'spilostichus makanjila' **403**, 408
Sciaenochromis sp. 'spot bicuspid' **407**, 408
Sciaenochromis sp. 'stripe tanzania' 257, **258**
Sciaenochromis sp. 'torpedo head' **403**
Serranochromis robustus 13, 277, **279**
Steveni 116, 213
Steveni Eastern = *Protomelas* sp. 'steveni imperial'
Steveni Thick Bars = *Protomelas fenestratus*
Steveni Tiger = *Protomelas* sp. 'steveni imperial'
Stigmatochromis sp. 'big-eye' **407**, 408
Stigmatochromis sp. 'big-head' **407**, 408
Stigmatochromis sp. 'guttatus' 340, **343**
Stigmatochromis modestus 161, **163**
Stigmatochromis sp. 'modestus eastern' 156, **159**
Stigmatochromis sp. 'modestus makokola' = *Otopharynx brooksi*
Stigmatochromis sp. 'modestus mbenji' 260, **262**
Stigmatochromis pholidophorus 340, **342**
Stigmatochromis pleurospilus 341, **342**
Stigmatochromis sp. 'pleurospilus mdoka' 341, **343**
Stigmatochromis sp. 'spilostichus type' 340, **342**
Stigmatochromis sp. 'tolae' 340, **342**
Stigmatochromis woodi 340, **342**
Sunshine Peacock = *Aulonocara* sp. 'stuartgranti maleri'
Taeniochromis holotaenia **347**, 348
Taeniolethrinops cyrtonotus 384, **386**
Taeniolethrinops furcicauda 377, 381, **383**
Taeniolethrinops sp. 'furcicauda liuli' 381, **386**
Taeniolethrinops sp. 'furcicauda ntekete' 381, **383**
Taeniolethrinops laticeps 377, 381, **383**
Taeniolethrinops macrorhynchus 377, 380, **382**
Taeniolethrinops praeorbitalis 321, 377, **382**
Tilapia rendalli 304, **306**
Tramitichromis 296, 364
Tramitichromis brevis 221, 364, **366**

Tramitichromis sp. 'brevis magunga' 365, **367**
Tramitichromis sp. 'brevis two' 365
Tramitichromis sp. 'chembe circle' 369, **370**
Tramitichromis sp. 'chembe shallow' 369, **370**
Tramitichromis sp. 'east-coast shallow' 369, **370**
Tramitichromis sp. 'false lituris' 368, **370**
Tramitichromis intermedius 296, **298**
Tramitichromis sp. 'kande' 369, **371**
Tramitichromis lituris 365, **367**
Tramitichromis sp. 'lituris yellow' 368, **370**
Tramitichromis sp. 'maculae' 365, **367**
Tramitichromis sp. 'mvunguti' 369, **371**
Tramitichromis sp. 'red gular' 369, **371**
Tramitichromis trilineatus 365, **367**
Tramitichromis variabilis 365, **367**
Tramitichromis sp. 'variabilis likoma' 365, **367**
Trematocranus labifer **403**, 409, **410**
Trematocranus brevirostris **403**, 408
Trematocranus sp. 'brevirostris deep' **403**
Trematocranus microstoma 353, **355**
Trematocranus placodon 353, **355**
Trematocranus sp. 'thicklip bicuspid' 353, **355**
Trematocranus Walteri = *Aulonocara* sp. 'walteri'
Tropheops 24, 77
Tropheops sp. 'aurora' 81, **83**
Tropheops sp. 'band' 269, **271**
Tropheops sp. 'black' = *Tropheops gracilior*
Tropheops sp. 'black dorsal' 85, **86**
Tropheops sp. 'black hara' 80, **82**
Tropheops sp. 'boadzulu' **195**
Tropheops sp. 'broadmouth' 196, **198**, 280
Tropheops sp. 'chilumba' 84, **86**
Tropheops sp. 'chilumba type' 85, **86**
Tropheops sp. 'chinyamwezi' 79, 80
Tropheops sp. 'chinyankwazi' 79, 80, 85
Tropheops sp. 'chitimba' 269, **271**
Tropheops sp. 'dark' 80, **82**
Tropheops sp. 'deep' 197, **199**
Tropheops sp. 'elongatus boadzulu' 85, **87**
Tropheops sp. 'elongatus chisumulu' **87**, 88
Tropheops sp. 'elongatus greenback' 85, **87**
Tropheops sp. 'elongatus mbako' **87**, 88
Tropheops sp. 'elongatus metangula' **87**, 88
Tropheops sp. 'elongatus namalenje' **87**, 88

Tropheops sp. 'elongatus reef east' 88, **91**
Tropheops sp. 'elongatus reef' 88, **91**
Tropheops sp. 'gold otter' 33, **35**, 84
Tropheops sp. 'goldbreast' 32, **34**
Tropheops sp. 'gome yellow' 81, **82**
Tropheops gracilior 25, 80, **79**
Tropheops sp. 'gracilior nankumba' 193, **195**
Tropheops sp. 'higga' 84, **86**
Tropheops sp. 'lilac' 33, **35**
Tropheops lucerna 268, **270**
Tropheops sp. 'lucerna blue aggressive' = *Tropheops lucerna*
Tropheops sp. 'lucerna blue cobalt' 268, **270**
Tropheops sp. 'lucerna blue mozambique' 268, **270**
Tropheops sp. 'lucerna blue tanzania' 268, **270**
Tropheops sp. 'lucerna brown chia' 268, **271**
Tropheops sp. 'lucerna brown' 268, **270**
Tropheops sp. 'lucerna fin spot' 268, **270**
Tropheops sp. 'lucerna nkhata' 268, **270**
Tropheops sp. 'lucerna north' 197, 269, **271**
Tropheops sp. 'lumessi blue' 32, **34**
Tropheops macrophthalmus 81, **83**
Tropheops sp. 'macrophthalmus chitimba blue' 200, **202**
Tropheops sp. 'macrophthalmus chitimba' 84, 200, **202**
Tropheops sp. 'macrophthalmus gallireya' 200, **202**
Tropheops sp. 'maleri blue' 33, **35**
Tropheops sp. 'maleri yellow' **26**, 196, **198**
Tropheops sp. 'mauve yellow' 81, **83**
Tropheops sp. 'mauve' 32, 81, **83**, 269
Tropheops sp. 'mbenji blue' 32, **34**, 81
Tropheops sp. 'mbenji yellow' 32, 196, **198**
Tropheops sp. 'membe' 197, **199**
Tropheops microstoma 193, **195**
Tropheops modestus **87**, 88
Tropheops sp. 'mumbo' **195**, 196
Tropheops novemfasciatus 196, **198**, 280
Tropheops sp. 'olive' 29, **31**
Tropheops sp. 'orange head' 197, **199**
Tropheops sp. 'red cheek north' 32, **34**
Tropheops sp. 'red cheek' 32, **34**
Tropheops sp. 'red fin' 21, 197, **199**
Tropheops romandi 193, **195**
Tropheops sp. 'rust' 197, **199**
Tropheops sp. 'sand' = *Gephyrochromis* sp. 'sand'
Tropheops sp. 'sand blackfin' = *Gephyrochromis* sp. 'sand blackfin'
Tropheops sp. 'taiwan' 84, **86**
Tropheops tropheops **19**, **27**, 33, **79**, 80
Tropheops sp. 'weed' 200, 281, **283**
Tropheops sp. 'yellow chin' 80, 196, **198**
Tropheops sp. 'yellow gular' 80, **82**
Trout Cichlid = *Champsochromis caeruleus*
Tyrannochromis macrostoma 253, **259**
Tyrannochromis sp. 'macrostoma short pedicel' 253, **259**
Tyrannochromis nigriventer **18**, 125, **127**, 297
Utaka 120, 148, 229
Virginalis Blotch = *Copadichromis geertsi*
Yellow Labidochromis = *Labidochromis caeruleus*
Yellow Princess = *Otopharynx tetraspilus*